Fashion Cultures Revisited

Following on from the ground-breaking collection *Fashion Cultures*, this second anthology, *Fashion Cultures Revisited*, contains 26 newly commissioned chapters exploring fashion culture from the start of the new millennium to the present day. The book is divided into six parts, each discussing different aspects of fashion culture:

- Shopping, spaces and globalisation
- Changing imagery, changing media
- Altered landscapes, new modes of production
- Icons and their legacies
- Contestation, compliance, feminisms
- Making masculinities.

Fashion Cultures Revisited explores every facet of contemporary fashion culture and the associated spheres of photography, magazines and television, and shopping. Consequently it is an ideal companion for those interested in fashion studies, cultural studies, art, film, fashion history, sociology and gender studies.

Stella Bruzzi is Professor of Film and Television Studies, University of Warwick and Fellow of the British Academy. Her publications include: *Undressing Cinema: Clothing and Identity in the Movies* (1997), *New Documentary* (2000 and 2006), *Bringing Up Daddy: Fatherhood and Masculinity in Post-war Hollywood* (2005) and *Men's Cinema: Masculinity and Mise-en-scène in Hollywood* (2013). She is currently writing *Approximation: Documentary History and the Staging of Reality*, the culmination of a Leverhulme Major Research Fellowship, due to be published by Routledge in 2015.

Pamela Church Gibson is Reader in Cultural and Historical Studies at the London College of Fashion, University of the Arts London. She is Principal Editor of the journal *Film, Fashion and Consumption* and has published widely on film, fashion and gender. Her publications include *The Oxford Guide to Film Studies* (1998), *More Dirty Looks: Gender, Power, Pornography* (2004) and *Fashion and Celebrity Culture* (2012). In 2012 she helped to found the European Popular Culture Association and her forthcoming project will examine the history of t

Fashion Cultures Revisited

Theories, explorations and analysis

Edited by

Stella Bruzzi and
Pamela Church Gibson

Routledge
Taylor & Francis Group

LONDON AND NEW YORK

First published as 'Fashion Cultures: Theories, Explorations and Analysis' 2000

This edition published as 'Fashion Cultures Revisited' 2013
by Routledge
2 Park Square, Milton Park, Abingdon, Oxon, OX14 4RN

and by Routledge
711 Third Avenue, New York, NY 10017

Routledge is an imprint of the Taylor & Francis Group, an informa business

British Library Cataloguing in Publication Data
A catalogue record for this book is available from the British Library

Library of Congress Cataloging in Publication Data
  Fashion cultures revisited: theories, explorations and analysis/[edited by]
  Stella Bruzzi, Pamela Church Gibson. – Second edition.
  pages cm
  1. Fashion – Social aspects. 2. Mass media – Social aspects. I. Bruzzi,
  Stella, 1962– II. Gibson, Pamela Church.
  GT525.F37 2013
  391—dc23
  2013020815

ISBN: 978-0-415-68005-9 (hbk)
ISBN: 978-0-415-68006-6 (pbk)
ISBN: 978-0-203-13054-4 (ebk)

Typeset in Perpetua and Bell Gothic
by Florence Production Ltd, Stoodleigh, Devon, UK

MIX
Paper from
responsible sources
FSC   FSC® C013056
www.fsc.org

Printed and bound in Great Britain by
TJ International Ltd, Padstow, Cornwall

To our mothers
Zara Bruzzi (1935–2000)
and Josephine Church

Contents

Figures

Contributors

Christopher Breward is Professor of Cultural History at the University of Edinburgh, where he also holds the positions of Principal of Edinburgh College of Art and Vice Principal (Creative Arts). Prior to that he was Head of Research at the Victoria and Albert Museum, London. He has published widely on the history and theory of fashion and its relationship to masculinities and urban cultures, including *The Culture of Fashion* (1995), *The Hidden Consumer* (1999), *Fashion* (2003) and *Fashioning London* (2004). He has most recently co-curated the V&A's Olympic season exhibition 'British Design 1948–2012'.

Adam Briggs is head of Cultural and Historical Studies at the London College of Fashion. Briggs' career began in nursing but he then moved into radio journalism at the BBC. His academic career began as a senior lecturer in Communications at London Metropolitan University, before moving to the London College of Fashion. Briggs' research interests primarily concern the relationship between the production and consumption of fashion. Alongside Paul Cobley, he co-edited *The Media: An Introduction* and has published academic articles on a range of fashion and marketing related issues.

Stella Bruzzi is Professor of Film and Television Studies, University of Warwick and Fellow of the British Academy. Her publications include: *Undressing Cinema: Clothing and Identity in the Movies* (1997), *New Documentary* (2000 and 2006), *Bringing Up Daddy: Fatherhood and Masculinity in Post-war Hollywood* (2005) and *Men's Cinema: Masculinity and Mise-en-scène in Hollywood* (2013). She is currently writing *Approximation: Documentary History and the Staging of Reality*, the culmination of a Leverhulme Major Research Fellowship, due to be published by Routledge in 2015.

Pamela Church Gibson is Reader in Cultural and Historical Studies at the London College of Fashion, University of the Arts London. She is Principal Editor of the journal *Film, Fashion and Consumption* and has published widely on film, fashion and gender. Her publications include *The Oxford Guide to Film Studies* (1998), *More Dirty Looks: Gender, Power, Pornography* (2004) and *Fashion and Celebrity Culture* (2012). In 2012 she helped to found the European Popular Culture Association and was its first President. Her forthcoming project will examine the history of the fashion documentary.

Judith Clark is Professor of Fashion and Museology at London College of Fashion, University of the Arts London. She has curated major exhibitions at the V&A in London, ModeMuseum in Antwerp, Boijmans van Beuningen, Rotterdam and Palazzo Pitti, Florence. Recent exhibitions include 'The Concise Dictionary of Dress' (with Adam Phillips) at Blythe House, London, commissioned by Artangel; and 'Diana Vreeland after Diana Vreeland' at Palazzo Fortuny, Venice, and 'Chloe. Attitudes' (Palais de Tokyo, Paris 2012). In July 2012 she opened the first museum of handbags in Seoul, South Korea, documented in a publication *Handbags: The making of a Museum* (Yale University Press). Forthcoming with Yale University Press is *Exhibiting Fashion: Before and After 1971*, out in Autumn 2013.

Fiona Cox undertook doctoral research at the Film and Television Studies Department at the University of Warwick. She is particularly interested in work on representations of women and sexual identities from queer and feminist perspectives. Her PhD thesis looks at the costuming and styling of lesbian characters and celebrities in contemporary visual cultures and includes an audience research project that aims to analyse how such images might contribute to the politics of personal dress sense for lesbians today.

Louise Crewe is Professor of Human Geography at the University of Nottingham. Her publications include *Second Hand Cultures* (with Gregson, Oxford: Berg), and she has written numerous notable journal articles for, among others, *Society & Space*, *Media, Culture and Society*, *Cultural Sociology* and *The Journal of Consumer Culture*. Her forthcoming book *Iconic Design: 50 Stories and 50 Things* will be published in 2013 by Berg.

Armida de la Garza is Associate Professor of Film at Xi'an Jiaotong-Liverpool University, which she joined in February 2012 to set up the Communication and Media Studies department. She is editor of the book series Topics and Issues in National Cinemas (New York/London: Continuum) as well as co-editor of the *Transnational Cinema Journal* (Bristol: Intellect). Her current research projects include the exploration of synergies between screen media and fashion for aesthetic, creative and marketing purposes; cinema and the museum; and experiential learning.

Peng Ding obtained her PhD from the School of English Studies at the University of Nottingham, UK, and is currently Lecturer of Applied Linguistics at Xi'an Jiaotong-

Liverpool University. Her research interests include motivation, cross-cultural communication and HE internationalisation. She is also a recipient of funding for several research projects, including a programme from the National Social Science Fund, and a project on the motivation of designers and buyers in the fashion industry of Shanghai.

Caroline Evans is Professor of Fashion History and Theory at Central Saint Martins (University of the Arts London) and a visiting professor at the Centre for Fashion Studies at Stockholm University. She is the author of *Fashion at the Edge* (Yale 2003) and *The Mechanical Smile: Modernism and the First Fashion Shows in France and America, 1900–1929* (Yale 2013).

Lorraine Gamman is Professor of Design at Central Saint Martins College of Arts (University of the Arts London) and Design and Director of the award-winning Design Against Crime Research Centre, which she founded in 1999. She has written many articles and several books on visual culture and design. Her PhD on shoplifting completed at Middlesex in 1999 engendered a spin-off book *Gone Shopping; The Story of Shirley Pitts, Queen of Thieves* (Penguin). TV/film rights were recently acquired by Tiger Aspect (2012).

David Gilbert is Professor of Urban and Historical Geography at Royal Holloway, University of London. He is director of the department's Social and Cultural Geography Group. His publications include *Class, Community and Collective Action: Social Change in Two British Coalfields, 1850–1926* (1992), *Imperial Cities: Landscape, Display and Identity* (with Felix Driver, 1999 & 2003), *Swinging Sixties: Fashion in London and Beyond* (with Christopher Breward and Jenny Lister), and *Fashion's World Cities* (with Breward, 2006).

Sally Gray is a Visiting Scholar in Cultural History at the College of Fine Arts, at the University of New South Wales, Sydney. Her fashion and art scholarship has been published in leading scholarly journals and book chapters and she is currently completing the book resulting from her (2010–12) Australian Research Council Postdoctoral Fellowship.

Claire Jenkins is Lecturer in Film and Media Communications at Bath Spa University. Her research interests include the representation of gender and the family in popular film and television texts, with recent publications exploring *Mamma Mia!* and 'older bird' chick flicks, masculinity, the superhero family in Hollywood films and the wedding dress as a symbol of femininity in Hollywood rom-coms. She is currently completing her first monograph *Home Movies: The American Family in Contemporary Hollywood*, to be published in 2014.

Meredith Jones is a media and cultural studies scholar. Her research is based on the intersections between culture and technology, gender, popular media studies and feminist theories of the body. One of the pioneers of Cosmetic Surgery Studies,

Meredith is the author of *Skintight: An Anatomy of Cosmetic Surgery* (Oxford: Berg 2008) and *Cosmetic Surgery: A Feminist Primer* (2009, Ashgate, England and USA, with Cressida Heyes). She is currently working on a large international project about cosmetic surgery tourism. Meredith is the co-founder (with award-winning designer Suzanne Boccalatte) of the innovative Trunk book series, the first two volumes of which are *HAIR* (2009) and *BLOOD* (2012).

Vicki Karaminas is Associate Professor of Fashion Studies and Associate Head of the School of Design at the University of Technology, Sydney. Her publications include *The Men's Fashion Reader* (Berg 2009), *Fashion in Fiction: Text and Clothing in Literature, Film and Television* (Berg 2009), *Fashion and Art* (Berg 2012), *Fashion and Popular Culture. Literature, Media and Contemporary Culture* (Intellect 2013), *Shanghai Street Style* (Intellect 2013) and *Queer Style* (Berg 2013). She is the co-editor of *The Australasian Journal of Popular Culture*.

Nathalie Khan lectures in cultural and historical studies at Central Saint Martins, London College of Fashion (University of the Arts London), the Condé Nast School of Fashion and Design in London and Sotheby's Institute of Art in New York. Her work is focused on contemporary image and fashion image production and consumption. Khan is a theorist and writer on contemporary fashion media and the impact of new technology on the traditional catwalk show and fashion photography within the digital frame.

Reina Lewis is Artscom Centenary Professor of Cultural Studies at the London College of Fashion (University of the Arts London). Forthcoming is *Re-Fashioning Orientalism: New Trends in Muslim Style* (Duke University Press 2014). She is author of *Rethinking Orientalism: Women, Travel and the Ottoman Harem* (2004), and *Gendering Orientalism: Race, Femininity and Representation* (1996). She is editor *of Modest Fashion: Styling Bodies, Mediating Faith* (2013), and, with Nancy Micklewright, of *Gender, Modernity and Liberty: Middle Eastern and Western Women's Writings: A Critical Reader* (2006), with Sara Mills, of *Feminist Postcolonial Theory: A Reader* (2003), and, with Peter Horne, of *Outlooks: Lesbian and Gay Visual Cultures* (1996). Reina Lewis is also editor with Elizabeth Wilson of the book series Dress Cultures, and with Teresa Heffernan of the book series Cultures in Dialogue.

Rachel Lifter is currently a Postdoctoral Fellow in Fashion Studies at Parsons The New School for Design. She recently completed her PhD on contemporary indie – a 'mainstream' youth cultural formation in the UK – at London College of Fashion, University of the Arts London. She is currently developing scholarly articles from that project, contributing a new theoretical framework for the analysis of 'mainstream' youth cultures, an analysis of 'festival fashion' and the performance of contemporary fashionable femininities and, finally, an examination of 'alternative' forms of cultural production and mediation within the contemporary fashion industry.

Peter McNeil is Professor of Design History at the University of Technology, Sydney and Professor of Fashion Studies at Stockholm University, Sweden. He works mainly on eighteenth-century Western Europe and on twentieth-century Anglo-American topics ranging from fashion to the politics of the domestic interior. He is currently writing a book entitled *Pretty Gentlemen* to be published in 2015.

Silvano Mendes is a Paris-based journalist who graduated from the Institut Français de la Mode and broadcasts for Radio France International. He writes on fashion for the French and Brazilian press including *Veja* and *Trends* and *Living* magazines. He is an associate lecturer in Fashion Communications at ESMOD in Paris and has worked as a brand image consultant for LVMH.

Janice Miller is Senior Lecturer in Cultural and Historical Studies at London College of Fashion. Her recent research work has focused on the relationship between fashion and music and culminated in a monograph *Fashion and Music*, published in 2011. She is currently developing a new book on the culture of makeup as well as scholarly articles that consider the role of adornment in music performance.

Gary Needham is Lecturer in Film and Television Studies at Nottingham Trent University. He is the author of *Brokeback Mountain* (Edinburgh University Press 2010), from the American Indies series he also co-edits, and has co-edited *Asian Cinemas: A Reader and Guide* (Edinburgh University Press 2006), and with Glyn Davis the collections *Queer TV: Histories, Theories, Politics* (Routledge 2009) and *Warhol in Ten Takes* (British Film Institute). He is currently writing a book on the films Edie Sedgwick and Andy Warhol made together.

Alistair O'Neill is Reader in Fashion History and Theory at Central Saint Martins College of Arts and Design (University of the Arts London). He is the author of *London: After a Fashion* (Reaktion 2007) and is a curatorial consultant for Somerset House, London.

Hilary Radner is Professor of Film and Media Studies in the Department of History and Art History at the University of Otago. Her books include *Shopping Around: Feminine Culture and the Pursuit of Pleasure* (1995) and *New-Feminist Cinema: Girly Films, Chick Flicks, and Consumer Culture* (2010). She is co-editor of various anthologies including *Film Theory Goes to the Movies* (1993), *Jane Campion: Cinema, Nation, Identity* (2009) and *Feminism at the Movies* (2011). She is currently working on a monograph on romantic melodrama in Hollywood.

Nick Rees-Roberts is Lecturer in Film and Cultural Studies in the Department of French at the University of Bristol. He is the author of *French Queer Cinema* (Edinburgh University Press 2008) and co-author with Maxime Cervulle of *Homo exoticus: race, classe et critique queer* (Armand Colin 2010). He has also published articles in *Fashion Theory* and *Film, Fashion and Consumption* and is currently writing a book entitled *Fashion in Motion: Film, Art and Advertising in the Digital Age* for Bloomsbury.

Giorgio Riello is Professor of Global History and Culture at the University of Warwick. He is the author of *A Foot in the Past* (Oxford University Press 2006) and has written and edited several books on the history of textiles, dress, fashion and design in early modern Europe and Asia, including *Cotton: The Fabric that Made the Modern World* (Cambridge University Press 2013). With Peter McNeil he is currently writing a book entitled *Luxury: A Rich History* to be published by Oxford in 2015.

Agnès Rocamora is Reader in Social and Cultural Studies at the London College of Fashion (University of the Arts London). She is the author of *Fashioning the City: Paris, Fashion and the Media* (2009). Her writing on the field of fashion, on the fashion media and on fashion blogging has appeared in various journals, including *Fashion Theory, Sociology*, and the *Journal of Consumer Culture*. She is a co-editor of *The Fashion Studies Handbook* (2013) and of *Fashion Media: Past and Present* (2013). She is currently developing her work on fashion and digital media.

Elliott Smedley began his career as a fashion editor at *Dutch Magazine* in Paris. He then went on to contribute to publications such as *L'uomo Vogue*, Italian *Vogue, The Face* and *V* magazine among others. He has worked with photographers including Mario Testino, David Sims, Corrine Day and Alistair Mclellan. Since 2002 Elliott has been Creative Consultant for Burberry, working with Christopher Bailey on the creative vision for the brand. Elliott is also a guest tutor at the Royal College of Art.

Natalie Smith holds a PhD in Art History and Theory and is affiliated to the Department of History and Art History, University of Otago. Her research interests include New Zealand art and fashion industry, film and fashion and New Zealand visual culture.

Lauren Jade Thompson has recently completed a PhD in the Department of Film and Television Studies at the University of Warwick. Her research interests include interactions between masculinity and postfeminist culture, domesticity in film and television, and television and the everyday. As well as the chapter in this volume, she has published work in the edited collection *Postfeminism and Contemporary Hollywood* (Gwynne and Muller, Palgrave 2013).

Monica Titton is a sociologist and a freelance fashion writer. She is currently completing her PhD thesis about fashion and street style blogs and their impact on fashion. She was a visiting researcher at the London College of Fashion and an external lecturer in Sociology at the University of Vienna.

Clare M. Wilkinson-Weber is Assistant Professor in the Department of Anthropology, Washington State University, Vancouver. Her book *Embroidering Lives: Women's Work and Skill in the Lucknow Embroidery Industry* was published in 1999 (State University of New York Press). She has published extensively in various academic journals on Hindi cinema, film costume and design activity in South Asia. Her forthcoming book *Fashioning Bollywood: Making and Meaning in Hindi Film Costume* is due to appear in 2013.

Acknowledgements

At Routledge we are extremely grateful to our first editor, Aileen Storry, who commissioned this second edition, Natalie Foster who took on the project, Sheni Kruger and Charlotte Hiorns at Florence Production Ltd, who oversaw the production of this book so expertly. As with the first edition, we would like to thank all of our contributors, invariably working under great pressure, both personal and professional. We would particularly like to thank those who, while organising REF submissions, mounting major exhibitions and leading their departments, nevertheless managed to write the kind of essays for which we had hoped – and to those who stepped in at the last moment and so saved the day.

Images were reproduced with the invaluable help from and kind permission of Diktats Bookstore, Shaun Cole, Ben Whyman and Lucie Russell for her drawing of Adele. We are very grateful to Garance Doré for generously giving us an image from her blog. Finally, we would especially like to thank Judith Clark for providing us with our inspirational cover image and Anne-Marie Michel, student and photographer extraordinaire.

Pamela Church Gibson would like to thank Oriana Baddeley and Tony Kent at the University of the Arts for arranging a period of relief from teaching and administration to ensure the successful completion of the project, and her immediate colleagues at the London College of Fashion. Stella Bruzzi would like to thank her department, especially Karl Schoonover for his fashion knowledge as well as his subscription to US *Vogue*.

Finally, we would like to thank our families and friends.

Stella Bruzzi and Pamela Church Gibson

INTRODUCTION
The changed fashion landscape of the new millennium

IT IS NOW SOME THIRTEEN YEARS since our first anthology was published. In the intervening decade, the fashion landscape has changed almost beyond recognition. Shopping was already, by then, an established national pastime; it is now an international obsession. Bicester Village in the UK, a discount outlet for high-end fashion, is a top-priority international tourist destination. Luxury brands show a growth in profit year on year and have been made, in part, more accessible through their collaborations with the high street and their consistent presence online. Elderly couture houses such as Balenciaga and Lanvin have been rejuvenated, while the two major fashion conglomerates LVMH (Louis Vuitton Möet Hennessey) and PPR (Pinault Printemps Redoute) have extended their respective fiefdoms in various ways. Online shopping has transformed retailing; some have suggested that online fashion films are now more important than the traditional runway shows. The other area of growth is in 'fast fashion'; cheap copies of designer creations can now appear on the high street within a couple of weeks. Fast fashion is the very antithesis of sustainability. The past ten years have also seen a move towards 'eco-chic', towards a desire for long-lasting and environmentally friendly garments, as opposed to inexpensive clothes with a truncated life span. 'Eco-chic' does not have to be prohibitively expensive: Armand Basi makes garments out of bamboo, but then so too does Muji. However, there is a new worrying dependence on cheap disposable fashion, now taken for granted, certainly in the West.

Arguably the vectors of fashion diffusion have shifted. Models have been replaced as cover girls by celebrities, themselves absolutely central within fashion's changed topography; the most fashion-friendly celebrities are currently assured of a place on fashion's famous front rows, just as the most photogenic dominate the lucrative luxury-brand advertising campaigns. Fashion magazines retain their status and influence, but they also need an online presence; in cyberspace they are joined by bloggers and street photographers, whose power within the industry has increased rapidly. Another global sphere of influence is the television reality show. In the United States, the Kardashians created a thriving retail empire after the success of their televisual family saga *Keeping up with the Kardashians* (2007–). In the UK, singer Cheryl Cole's popularity reached its zenith when she was seen weekly as a judge on the *X Factor* (2004–); her outfits each week were discussed, dissected, purchased or emulated. Across the Atlantic, Jennifer Lopez saw a significant rise in her popularity after her involvement in *American Idol* (2002–). Makeover programmes have also increased in number, popularity and the radical nature of the expected transformation.

The desire for fast fashion has been exacerbated by the extraordinary influence of celebrity culture, one of the most notable features of the new millennium. Celebrities not only 'model' designer creations both on magazine covers and for their public appearances, they go further; they now apparently create their own lines and even their stylists may have a public face. Jay-Z and his wife Beyoncé are arguably as well-known a couple as Barack Obama and his wife, not only for their music and their striking appearance but also for their style and their syndicated fashion lines; fellow musician Kanye West has designed sunglasses for Louis Vuitton. Celebrity culture is of course a global phenomenon, but it moves along the traditional, well-worn path of historical imperialism from west to east. The stars of Hindi cinema, so powerful on the Indian subcontinent, are not copied worldwide. There are occasional, surprising exceptions. Korean popular music was unknown in the west until Korean rapper Psy's Gangnam Style of 2012, the most downloaded video from YouTube that year. Eton schoolboys made their own version, while British Prime Minister David Cameron told the press how he and the Mayor of London, Boris Johnson, had tried to dance 'gangnam style' in the kitchen of his official residence. In a real accolade, Madonna attempted to share in his popularity; she persuaded Psy to perform with her at Madison Square Gardens and they danced together before ecstatic crowds.

The new global obsession with celebrity and with a particular type of look has meant a rise in the statistics that chart cosmetic surgery and chemical intervention. There is a growth in the numbers of those who seek to attain Caucasian features and paler skin, while among western women, not only the spread of cosmetic surgery but also its shift to a younger demographic is another development to note. Cosmetic surgery is now as much a feature of the new fashion landscape as the cheaply made throwaway garments – and as controversial. With the proliferation of celebrity images on the Internet, women everywhere are confronted endlessly with carefully retouched images of perfection – for some, a reminder of their own perceived shortcomings.

A 'celebrity' is no longer merely an actor or performer; politicians' wives and even politicians themselves are watched and criticised for their style and self-presentation. Michelle Obama has twice featured on the cover of US *Vogue,* in March 2009 and April 2013 – one appearance for each of her husband Barack's terms in office. Avid Michelle Obama fans follow her religiously on Twitter, care of 'FLOTUS', an account run by the Office of the First Lady, and on the blog

Mrs O (mrs-o.com), which charts her every clothes move and updates her fashionable appearances almost daily. On both *Vogue* covers Mrs O is bare-armed, showing off her by now famously toned upper limbs. But whereas in the earlier image she is dressed in fuchsia pink, elbow leaning on a sofa arm, in the later Annie Liebowitz picture, she is sitting and looking out at the camera much more assertively: she owns that space. Mrs Obama is then pictured inside the April 2013 *Vogue* wearing the same blue Reed Krakoff dress in the Red Room of the White House, her flawless arms draped around her husband. Under the subheading 'American Ideal', the US's most glamorous and statuesque First Lady since Jacqueline Kennedy is pictured in a simple but striking Michael Kors ensemble of black sweater and ball skirt, standing, softly overlapping hands in front of her, framed by a sequence of White House doors and staring out of a window. The mixing of the formal (the ball skirt, the surroundings) and the casual (the fitted jumper, the easy smiles for the camera) is Mrs O's trademark; as the accompanying April 2013 article confirms: 'she has inspired a modern definition of effortless American chic' (Van Meter, 2013: 255). The First Lady goes on to say of her relationship to fashion:

> I always say that women should wear whatever makes them feel good about themselves. That's what I always try to do . . . In every interaction that I have with people, I always want to show them my authentic self.
> (quoted in Van Meter, 2013: 255)

Leaving aside the potentially problematic issue of 'authenticity', the comfortable quality that Michelle Obama conveys and her ease with people are not only the characteristics that define her particular fashion, but are also the reasons why she so swiftly acquired such an ardent following. On 'Mrs O', she is seen regularly donning J. Crew and other patriotic, accessible high street and ready-to-wear clothes alongside couture outfits, such as her Prabal Gurung 'charcoal brush painted rose silk twill gazar dress and coat from the designer's Spring 2010 collection' (mrs-o.com). We have quoted the assiduously adoring website intentionally, to demonstrate the manner in which the outfits 'Mrs O' dons for every public appearance are described so fully and so lovingly. As the link to the site suggests: 'Follow the fashion and style of the First Lady Michelle Obama'. There are links to each designer and each previous siting of a First Lady outfit to complete the fashionista's celebrity round trip.

Underpinning the media obsession with Mrs Obama is, of course, the fact that she is the wife of the first African-American President of the United States, a man who was pictured for *Vanity Fair* in March 2008, in his then senatorial office, relaxed and lying back on his chair in front of pictures of not only Abraham Lincoln but of black icon Muhammad Ali. Although the staged photographs in which Barack Obama crouches under his Oval Office desk when entertaining Caroline Kennedy consciously draw parallels with the iconic white President John F. Kennedy, he and Michelle led the first African-American family into the White House. Other politicians and politicians' wives are likewise followed for their sartorial choices and fashion impact, such as Carla Bruni, the wife of former

French President (2007–2012) Nicolas Sarkozy. Bruni, an Italian heiress, former top model and singer, accompanied her far less elegant, stumpy husband on state visits, adding glamour and chic in her John Galliano-designed Christian Dior clothes. The global press loved the meetings between the two most stylish wives, and when the Obamas were in Paris for Easter 2009, pretty much ignored German President Angela Merkel in her long dusty pink jacket and black trousers.

One female politician whose style was not ignored was former British Prime Minister, Baroness Margaret Thatcher. In the aftermath of her death in April 2013, several newspapers around the world ran articles that considered whether or not Mrs Thatcher had been a fashion icon. While Alexander Fury argued that 'Margaret Thatcher was no style icon, she just dressed well' (*The Independent*, 15 April 2013), Delhi Style Blog on Monday April 08, 2013 compared the '80's power dressing', 'helmet hairstyles' and 'restrained dressing' of Thatcher and India's first woman prime minister, Indira Gandhi. As Delhi Style Blog argued, both 'favoured local textiles and fashions', both wore 'the feminized version of the necktie – pearls for Lady Thatcher and a Rudraksha bead mala for Mrs Gandhi' and both 'led their nations through turbulent times'.[1] Thatcher's style was quint-essentially conservative but it was not inconspicuous. She married the classic business suit (single- or double-breasted) with a variety of blouses, commenting once on how 'terribly important' it was 'to have a wardrobe full of attractive blouses'.[2] In homage to Thatcher's particular predilection for the pussycat-bow blouse, Samantha Cameron wore a gold bow under a sombre black suit to the Baroness's funeral on 17 April 2013. In 2012, seven suits worn by Thatcher during her 12-year premiership were auctioned by Christie's and fetched just over £75,000 – about ten times their lower estimate. One, an old-fashioned aquamarine suit with contrasting green, brown, orange and pink striped bow and detailing, sold for £25,000. The source of the media's enduring fascination with Thatcher's fashion was that her sartorial flamboyance and femininity contrasted so deeply and unnaturally with her tough, iron lady politics. She – inexplicably to some – possessed considerable sex appeal. As François Mitterand once remarked, she had the eyes of Caligula, but the mouth of Marilyn Monroe.

Thatcher famously underwent a major makeover upon becoming Conservative Party leader: lowering her voice, fixing her teeth and discarding her previously ubiquitous hats. Prior to becoming the icon who helped launch SuperDry (but who failed to make the sarong into a 'must have' item in every gentleman's wardrobe), David Beckham was likewise 'made over', from hair to voice to strides. We reprint here the essay on football and fashion from the first anthology. In the intervening decade, Victoria, once retired singer, footballer's wife and mother, has become an acknowledged designer praised by, among others, Anna Wintour. David too has endorsed, if not designed, various fashion 'lines', and even second son Romeo, who has already featured on the *GQ* annual 'best dressed' list and modelled for Burberry, has endorsed a line of sunglasses (see Church Gibson 2011). In 2004, Sam Taylor Wood's vast video installation 'Sleeping Beckham' drew crowds at the National Portrait Gallery; in 2013, a match between his new club Paris Saint Germain and Barcelona was notable for the commentators' obsession with the thirty-eight year old Beckham, despite the presence on the pitch of Lionel Messi, supposedly the best footballer in the world.

Victoria Beckham operates as an independent designer – others are less fortunate. LMVH and PPR have spent the past ten years acquiring as many leading design houses as they can. They have also increased their power within the art world, and thus acquired for themselves both a higher public profile and coveted cultural capital (see Ryan 2011: Schieren and Sich 2012). Tom Ford left the 'Gucci Group' in 2004 after a discussion and a difference around 'overall artistic control'. However, his own power within the fashion world is unchanged, even improved; he has used it to launch his new career as a film director (see Black 2013: Church Gibson 2011).

When it comes to the cinema, conventional theatrical-release films have retained their power to influence as well as reflect fashion; the fuss in 2013 over Miuccia Prada's fairly limited involvement in the costuming of Baz Lurhmann's *The Great Gatsby* (2013) is testament to that. Prada, who had contributed a few items such as Leonardo DiCaprio's suit to Lurhmann's *Romeo + Juliet* (1996), showed in *Vogue* and other magazines the sketches for four dresses designed for Carey Mulligan as Daisy Buchanan, which manage to look authentically 1920s while retaining recent Prada signature styling. There are still three primary ways in which cinema and fashion collaborate: films that overtly showcase designers' work, as occurs in 'fashion films' such as *The Devil Wears Prada* (2006); films that are genuine collaborations between costume designers and couture houses, as exemplified by *The Great Gatsby*; vanity films, such as Ford's *A Single Man* (2009), which adopt a holistic attitude to design, décor and overall vision. *A Single Man* is an entirely different venture for the designer than, for instance, *Skyfall* (2012), in which James Bond rides atop the roofs of the Grand Bazaar in an exquisitely tailored, sharkskin-patterned Tom Ford suit, while the more traditional Gareth Mallory (Ralph Fiennes) is dressed in three-piece, blue pinstripe Timothy Everest. Joe Wright's lavishly costumed *Anna Karenina* (2012) inspired Marc Jacobs' Louis Vuitton show in which models in vintage style fantasy clothes strode alongside a royal blue steam train, but arguably cinema's instant ability to produce spin-offs or provide accessories and garments that are copied by audiences has transferred to television.

After *Sex and the City* drew to a close in 2004, it was swiftly superseded by shows such as *Ugly Betty*, another sartorially influential long-running series (2006–2010) costumed by Patricia Field. While *Ugly Betty* (2006–2010) chimed with youthful fashions, AMC's *Mad Men* (2007–) has inspired countless store windows and features in a serious number of style and fashion magazines worldwide, eager to capture Janie Bryant's block-coloured retro early 1960s look. However, the phenomenon of 'e-tailing' is exemplified by the six-season CWTV teenage show *Gossip Girl,* which ran from 2007 to 2012. *Gossip Girl,* set amidst the wealth and privilege of New York's Upper East Side, offers recent television's quintessential example of 'e-tailing', as spectators can go from seeing a garment or accessory they like on screen to buying it in minutes via links on websites such as *Celebrity Style Guide.* Click on a production still and a character's outfit is broken down into its constituent parts; decide that what you want is the Alexander Wang neoprene inverted pleat skirt; click on the 'Buy It!' button; arrive at a separate window and, if the skirt is sold out (as seems often to be the case), then you are helpfully redirected to a series of 'You May Also Like' alternatives.

But appearances on television and cinema screens are certainly not enough for the leading design houses, who now seek, too, an association with more venerable institutions. Consequently, several have now opened their own art galleries – following a trend which began in the 1990s – while continuing, as before, to fund major art exhibitions across Europe and America (Ryan 2007/ 2011). François Pinault, the head of the PPR group and a well-known collector, now has not one but two well-regarded museums in Venice, home to both permanent and temporary exhibitions (Schieren and Sich 2011). The House of Gucci, by contrast, has created a museum in Florence to show off, not the work of other artists but its very own heritage, offering up its own past designs as artefacts. There is, too, another new form of collaboration, the creating of fashion merchandise by visiting artists rather than by permanent in-house designers; since 2003, Marc Jacobs at Louis Vuitton has employed the Japanese artist Takashi Murakami to create prints, handbags and even commercials for the brand. Their liaison culminated in an exhibition at the Guggenheim Museum in Bilbao in 2009; Jacobs described their relationship as 'a monumental marriage of art and commerce, the ultimate crossover – one for both the fashion and art history books' (vogue.co.uk). Jacobs has worked with other artists, including Steven Sprouse, Richard Prince and Yayoi Kasama. Finally, he found himself forming the subject of an exhibition, in the Musée des Arts Decoratifs in Paris in 2012, *Louis Vuitton–Marc Jacobs*, which celebrated both the history of the house and Jacobs' own work there.

The 'blockbuster' fashion exhibition has become one of the most interesting phenomena of the past ten years. In 2011, the Alexander McQueen retrospective *Savage Beauty* at the Metropolitan Museum of Art in New York caused queues three-deep to form around the block. It was soon followed by the *Schiaparelli and Prada: Impossible Conversations* exhibition (MoMA, Spring/Summer 2012). If Jacobs merits a gallery presence, then so too might Miuccia Prada, indefatigable patron of the arts (see Ryan *op.cit.*); however, attendance at the show in which she featured was disappointing. Nevertheless, more major fashion exhibitions are in the pipeline. In New York, the Met opened its programme for 2013 with *Punk: Chaos to Couture* showcasing the work of Givenchy, Galliano, Chanel, Versace and Moschino as well as – predictably – Vivienne Westwood. This was intended, presumably, to bring back a wider audience after the Prada/Schiaparelli disappointment. Also in New York in the same year, the exhibition *Front Row: Chinese American Designers*, at the Museum of Chinese Art will display among others the work of Jason Wu, a favourite of Mrs Obama, while the Brooklyn Museum is to commemorate the career of Jean-Paul Gaultier in *From Sidewalk to Catwalk*-2014 will bring to the Museum at FIT in New York the exhibition *Queer Style: Gay and Lesbian Fashion*.

The well-publicised, heavily sponsored fashion exhibition has arguably become a permanent fixture of this new landscape. And the honouring of living designers is a new departure; Valentino had a London retrospective in Somerset House: *Valentino: Master of Couture* 2012–13. Elsewhere in London, the extraordinary success of *Hollywood Costume* at the V&A was trumped by its David Bowie exhibition of 2013, sold out online before the doors had opened. Fashion has successfully moved from the marketplace into the temples of high culture. And leading designers, who now see their own work displayed in museums and galleries, are sufficiently well known, in our fashion-literate new millennium, to merit the making of documentary films depicting their careers. Three alone have appeared to depict the life and work of the late Yves St Laurent,[3] another examines the work of the indefatigable Jacobs, while Valentino and Karl Lagerfeld have been the subject of the commercially successful films *Valentino: The Last Emperor* (2008) and *Lagerfeld Confidential* (2007). We might note too the commercial and critical success of two other documentaries, *The September Issue* (2009) and *Bill Cunningham: New York* (2010), both showing the internal workings of the world of fashion journalism in very different ways. Presumably, *The Devil Wears Prada* played a part in the appeal of the *Vogue* film, but the second film, partly set in the offices of the *New York Times,* would not have attracted a young, fashionable audience a decade earlier.

Thirteen years ago, we talked of fashion's still uneasy relationship with the academy. But now that fashion has marched unabashed into museums, while continuing to expand and develop its profitable century-long old relationship with the screen, its presence in the academy is surely assured and unassailable. What is perhaps more problematic are changes within the academy itself. Thirteen years ago we could write, simply, of 'feminism'. Now, as the penultimate section of this book clearly illustrates, it might be wiser to talk of 'feminisms'; there are conflicting ideas and ideals in an area where previously there was some form of consensus. The theories used to understand and interpret 'fashion cultures' may themselves be shifting and varied. But academic interest is still solid and still growing; certainly there are now endless fashion anthologies, both in print and at press. We make no apology for adding to their number; we would, however, hope that the interdisciplinary and international nature of this volume gives it strength and justifies its position on the shelf. It perhaps provides our book with what those in advertising used to call 'added value', the factor that tempts women to buy a Chanel lipstick with its unmistakable packaging and visible logo – though that may be hubris. We do, however, see interdisciplinary scholarship as essential for the future study of fashion.

Fashion has a prominence, a pre-eminence and a democratic presence within visual culture that we could not have imagined thirteen years ago. A telling illustration of its new significance and potency was the mixture of spectacle, theatre and celebrity cachet, not to mention publicity, provided by socialite Daphne Guinness. In 2011 she staged a performance in Barneys' famous windows on New York's Fifth Avenue, dressing publicly for the evening ahead and donning her McQueen gown in preparation for the 'Met Ball'. This annual gala is seen as the fashion equivalent of the Oscars and that year McQueen was to be posthumously honoured; it preceded the opening of his commemorative exhibition. Guinness had a further motive: it marked her own collaboration with the famous shop, who were staging an exhibition of clothes from her personal archive, including garments once owned by McQueen muse Isabella Blow. Blow herself had committed suicide five years earlier and McQueen had helped to stage her highly spectacular funeral. Now, if we study the many photographs taken outside McQueen's own memorial service in St Paul's Cathedral, we find something troubling and uncanny; they resemble nothing so much as a series of paparazzi shots that might have been taken outside any significant runway show during a major Fashion Week. The new hagiography has its own disturbing elements; these could generate essays for *Fashion Cultures Three* in the next decade.

Notes

1   http://www.delhistyleblog.com/2013/04/margaret-thatcher-fashion-icon-style.html.
2   http://fashion.telegraph.co.uk/Article/TMG9979381/1548/Margaret-Thatchers-fashion-and-beauty-tips.html.
3   *Yves Saint Laurent: Le temps retrouvé* (David Teboul, 2002), *5 Avenue Marceau, 75116 Paris* (David Teboul, 2002), *L'amour fou* (Pierre Thoretton, 2010).

References

Black, Prudence (2013) 'Designed to Death: Tom Ford's *A Single Man*' in *Film, Fashion and Consumption*, vol. 2 no. 1, Spring 2013.
Church Gibson, Pamela (2011) *Fashion and Celebrity Culture*, London: Berg.
Ryan, Nicky (2012) *Patronage*, in Adam Geczy and Vicki Karaminas (eds.) *Fashion and Art*, London and New York: Berg.
——— (2007) 'Prada and the Art of Patronage' in *Fashion Theory: The Journal of Dress, Body and Culture* 11/1 (March): 7–23.
Schieren, Mona and Sich, Andrea (2011) *Look at Me: Celebrity Culture at the Venice Biennale*, Verlag für modern kunst Nürnberg: Nürnberg.

PART ONE

Shopping, spaces and globalisation

Chapter 1

David Gilbert

A NEW WORLD ORDER?
Fashion and its capitals in the twenty-first century

IN JANUARY 2013, FRANCA SOZZANNI, editor-in-chief at *Vogue Italia*, visited Dubai to announce the 'Vogue Fashion Dubai Experience' at the Dubai Mall, due to take place later that year. Sozzanni took twelve local designers under her wing for a special mentoring session, and declared to the press that 'three or four of them are very good' (Al Arabiya News 2013). She added: 'it is heartening to see designers here not copying the work of others but rather displaying their creativity and tradition. They are authentic.' Sozzanni promised to help with a mission including 'some supermodels' and 'some of the top designers, like Ricardo Tsici and Karl Lagerfeld'. Outside the world of elite fashion, this kind of patronising orientalism is increasingly rare and anachronistic, but the worldview from *Vogue Italia* seems relatively untouched either by the work of Edward Said, or by a little reflection on changing world orders in the aftermath of the global economic crisis and collapse of the Italian economy. At the heart of that worldview is an enduring sense of certain places as centres of fashion, as places from that style emanates and is spread to the rest of the world. In her comments Sozzanni reached for one of the oldest and strongest expressions of that relationship between fashion and geography: 'Dubai has the potential but is not regarded as a fashion capital in the world.'

On Planet Condé Nast, there doesn't seem to be much evidence of the wider changes that have taken place within the global economy and geopolitical world order of the early twenty-first century. To be sure, there are now twenty-one national editions of *Vogue* that include editions for Russia, India, China, South Korea, Thailand and Ukraine. However, the content of these magazines (and associated new media) fits a pretty consistent pattern of a focus on local designers, shops and events, mixed with constant reference back to the established centres of fashion's world order. It's not just in *Vogue*, however, that this sense of a global geography of fashion is expressed. Each year Global Language Monitor, a media-analytics company based in Austin, Texas publishes a ranking of 'global fashion capitals', based on analysis of the internet, blogosphere, the top 250,000 print and electronic news media, as well as new social media sources including Twitter. The cities are tracked in relation to their frequency, contextual usage and appearance in global media outlets. London retained its position at the top of the list for 2012, buoyed up by references to the Olympics and Kate Middleton, but the record of the index shows the continuing primacy of London, New York, Milan and Paris (Global Language Monitor 2013).[1] Some cities move up or down the charts in a kind of urban fashion cycle, associated with short-term trends and events, while those four cities retain their place near the top. An indication of the power of cities in the imagination of fashion is also shown by the word 'London' being Global Language Monitor's top fashion buzzword for 2013, taking its place as the key trending word in fashion's discourse ahead of 'high slits', 'textures' and 'nail art' (Global Language Monitor 2013).

It's easy to suggest that something like the Global Language Monitor index is measuring little more than noise and gossip, but perhaps that's just the point. The idea of the fashion capital has long been about more than statistics for the volume of fashion production or the size of the design sector in a particular city. There's a familiar mantra of a very few city names that are regularly incanted in the advertising of high fashion, after the name of a designer or brand, or etched into the glass of a shop window. In some cases the name of the fashion capital is incorporated into a brand name itself, perhaps most famously in the case of DKNY – Donna Karan New York. The list of cities is an almost transparent sign, only noticed when disrupted. In 2004 as part of an advertising campaign to market itself as 'the Fashion Capital' for the Melbourne metropolitan area, a suburban mall covered the city's billboards, trams and buses with the slogan 'New York, Paris, London, Rome, Chadstone'. Writing recently on the hierarchy of fashion cities, sociologist Lise Skov somewhat bizarrely compares fashion's cities to the geopolitical ordering of the UN, suggesting that London, Paris, New York, Milan and perhaps Tokyo are the equivalents of the permanent members of fashion's Security Council, but that there is effectively a rotating 'sixth seat' representing what is possible for other cities and smaller nations in a 'polycentric fashion world' (Skov 2011). This chapter has its focus on what Skov terms the 'top tier' or perhaps the seemingly permanent members of fashion's security council, its world cities, but sees this ordering neither as a given, nor necessarily as a permanent fixture. The first section relates the idea of fashion capitals to the wider literature on global or world cities. The following section reiterates arguments made in the first edition of *Fashion Cultures* about the historical development of a world ordering of fashion centres, connecting these developments to wider shifts in economic, political and cultural power (Gilbert 2000; see particularly Gilbert 2006a and other essays in Breward and Gilbert 2006 for further discussion of the idea of the Fashion World City). The final section considers the changing urban hierarchy of fashion's centres in the twenty-first century, and particularly the hollowing-out of its capitals, and the potential emergence of new sites of creativity.

Fashion capitals as world cities

The notion of a fashion capital, or a 'fashion world city' seems ubiquitous, yet hard to pin down directly. If we consider the longest-running of fashion's claimed capitals, we see just what complexity is to be found in this construction. The concept of 'Paris fashion' is one of the most powerful and long-running reifications of place. The routine description of the city over the past 200 years as the 'capital' of world fashion disguises the ways in which different aspects of the city's relationship with fashion contribute to this understanding. A dominant representation of Paris has emphasised the clustering of elite designers, the structure of the couture system, and the power of the Paris fashion industry to direct fashion styles far beyond the limits of the city. However, Paris's role as fashion capital has also been related to its industrial structure, particularly to the long-term survival of a production sector of specialist workshops and individual craft workers, concentrated in the Sentier district of the city. As Nancy Green suggested in her superb comparative study of Paris and New York, both cities had 'flexible specialisation before the term was coined' (1997: 4). Elaborate contracting and subcontracting systems in the apparel industries has been a vital element in sustaining a rapid turnover and adaptation of styles. At other times, Paris has been interpreted as a world centre of fashion because of its distinctive metropolitan cultures of consumption, both in the narrow sense of shops and shopping, and in a broader sense of the practices associated with the wearing of fashionable dress in the spaces of the city. Paris has also had a long history of representation, particularly in the fashion press, as the first city in an almost free-floating symbolic order of fashion-ability (Rocamora 2006). There has been something approaching a naturalisation of Paris's relationship with fashion, often around the elevation of a certain construction of fashionable femininity to a symbol of Parisian superiority.

The idea of a fashion world city also necessarily involves the relationships between places, both between imagined or actual centres of influence and 'peripheral' places in the geography of fashion, but also tellingly between different fashion centres. We need to pay attention to what might be described as the historical geography of fashion's world cities – the processes by which some cities become identified as central sites of global significance in fashion culture, and the competition and interconnections between those cities. The focus is on the fashion capital both as a changing historical formation, and relationally as a form of urban ordering or hierarchy. Approaching fashion's world cities from a perspective that emphasises their position within wider structures of economic and political power draws us towards the tradition in urban studies that has focused on 'world cities' or 'global cities'. In 1986, John Friedmann put forward what he described as 'the world city hypothesis' (see Friedmann and Wolff 1982 for an earlier version of these ideas). Friedmann's ideas were less a formal hypothesis than an agenda for research concerning the relationship of cities to the development of the world economy. Friedmann argued that increasing economic globalisation had shifted the balance between major cities' roles as centres of territorially bounded political states and as sites for the management of global capital.

In Friedmann's analysis, the decisive variable in explaining the nature of key 'world cities' was 'the mode of their integration with the global economy' over and above 'their own historical past, national policies, and cultural influences' (1986: 69). This claim had several consequences for the analysis of cities. First, he suggested that structural changes in the economies of such world cities (and consequent changes in their physical forms, social composition and urban cultures) were dependent on the form and extent of their integration into the world economy. Second, Friedmann argued that it was necessary to understand cities as part of a world system, thus emphasising not only the significance of connections and interdependencies between major cities, but also their positions within a structured hierarchy of cities.

Friedmann paid particular attention to those cities at the very top of his hierarchy, what he described as 'primary core cities'. In the mid-1980s he suggested that these were London, Paris, New York, Chicago, Los Angeles and Tokyo. Here there is significant overlap with what Saskia Sassen later described as 'global cities' (1991; 2001). In the late twentieth and early twenty-first centuries these cities developed intense concentrations of 'advanced producer services', typically in sectors such as banking, accountancy, advertising, insurance, commercial law and management consultancy, while experiencing a parallel process of deindustrial-isation of more traditional urban activities. Sassen argues that financial deregulation and the development of new forms of telecommunications, media and informa-tion technology, far from dispersing economic activities as some predicted, created an aggressive new logic for their concentration of these activities in a few great cities. Sassen further argued that the global cities, particularly London and New York, are marked by increasing economic and social polarisation. Alongside the development of advanced producer services has been a parallel development of a low-paid service sector, often characterised by a casualised labour force with a high proportion of immigrants. In Sassen's account of the distinctive characteristics of the global city, fashion appears only in the guise of the sweatshops of the garment industry.

One response to this emphasis on 'world cities' and 'global cities' has focused on the significance of urban hierarchies, and has attempted to produce different taxonomic strategies for ordering and categorising cities. At its worst this work has descended into a fixation with league tables and debates about the best way to measure the ranking of a world city. Beyond consideration of the location of the corporate headquarters of fashion and luxury goods conglomerates such as LVMH (Louis Vuitton Moët Hennessy), fashion has rarely been factored into such urban ranking schemes. These have been dominated by analyses of advanced producer services, which have been used to measure the 'global capacity' of various cities. Following Friedmann's original arguments such advanced producer services (and financial services in particular) are seen as the primary driving forces of the global urban order.

There is clearly a significant overlap between the cities routinely described as world fashion cities, and those identified by Friedmann, Sassen and their followers as primary world cities or global cities. Given, in Friedmann's terminology, the embeddedness of a 'transnational capitalist class' whose 'ideology is consumerist' in such world cities, and given fashion's inherent elitism and consumerism, it would be very surprising if this were not the case (Friedmann 1995: 26). The emergence of New York as a world city of fashion in the early twentieth century, or Tokyo's rise as an international fashion centre in the late 1970s and 1980s were not unrelated to the position of those cities in rising economic super-powers. However, the major centres of world fashion cannot be simply read off from a list of the main world business centres. For example, within Western Europe, Frankfurt and Milan can be taken as contrasting examples. While the financial centre of Frankfurt has a range of elite designer stores, catering for an affluent, international population, it hardly registers in the wider symbolic or economic geographies of fashion. By contrast, Milan, although certainly one of the most significant business command and control centres in the European Union, has been regarded since the 1970s as one of fashion's four or five front-rank world centres (see Segre Reinach 2006). Viewed historically, there are also significant discontinuities between the development of fashion's ordering of world centres and the urban geographies of global finance, demonstrated most clearly in Paris's long history as the claimed centre of the world fashion industry, despite the vicissitudes of the French economy and catastrophic interruptions by war. The argument here is not that analysis of fashion culture's fixation with urban orderings and world centres can produce a more accurate overall metric of the global significance of certain cities. There are, however, a number of potential insights that can come from bringing the perspectives of the world cities literature together with consideration of the geographies of fashion.

The best work on world cities addresses not just the position of cities in a rank-order, but also analyses the nature of connections between cities, and the institutions and processes that work to include, exclude and position cities in the hierarchy (Taylor 2004). Recent work has involved mapping the inter-city structures of multinational corporations or the contractual networks of firms in different sectors. Clearly one task for research into the geographies of fashion is to map these kinds of connection. This work has also emphasised the way that even in a world with massive capacity for instantaneous long-distance communication and financial transfer, the relationship between cities is shaped by very basic constraints of time and space. The most common example given is the way that 24-hour trading of shares, currency and commodities has strengthened the position of primary financial markets in different time-zones. Fashion's urban world order has worked in different ways, with seasonality as an important factor. As the Australian geographer Sally Weller has noted, all of the conventional world fashion cities, Paris, New York, London, Milan and Tokyo, are situated between 35 and 52 degrees latitude in the northern hemisphere (Weller 2004: 109). This is not to suggest, like some early twentieth-century proponents of Paris's natural fashion superiority, that the fashion capitals are determined by climate. Writing in 1908, Edouard Debect argued that France's fashion success came from its perfect climatic position somewhere between the 'cold countries' and the 'blazing' (quoted in Green 1997: 108). What it does mean is that the operation of global fashion has become locked into the seasonal rhythms of the temperate northern hemisphere. The major fashion collections are constrained by this seasonality. Given the need to place collections at strategic points in the year, avoiding clashes, there is probably time for no more than three or four collections that can guarantee global media attention, and that can work as part of the travelling circus of the controlling elites of fashion culture.

If the literature on world cities can inform an understanding about fashion's urban ordering, there are also important lessons that travel in the opposite direction, deepening our ideas about urban centrality and ordering. Fashion's slippery character is key to this, stretching standard categories of analysis. Fashion works through a 'never-ceasing play between the processes of production and consumption', it involves both the sale of commodities and the exercise of the creative imagination, and it is at once highly symbolic and yet an intimate part of embodied, everyday experience (Breward 2003: 21). As such, it helps us to think about other ways that cities and the spaces within them are ordered and connected. Arjun Appadurai famously argued that globalisation needs to be understood not as a singular process but as multiple and differentiated, working through a series of overlaid '-scapes' or morphologies of flow and movement. (Appadurai 1990) Alongside a 'finanscape' shaped by the shifting global disposition of capital are other global geographies that he describes variously as ethnoscapes, mediascapes, technoscapes and ideoscapes. Commenting directly on the world city literature, Anthony King used these ideas to point to different dimensions of the ways that certain cities constitute central places of global significance. For King,

> the problem with the term 'world' or 'global city' is that it has been appropriated, perhaps hijacked, to represent and also reify not only just one part of a city's activity . . . but also has been put at the service of only one representation of 'the world' – the world economy.
>
> (King 1995: 217)

Even within the economic realm, the conventional world city literature gives precedence to one particular dimension, with activities such as consumption and tourism relegated to secondary considerations, although both are economic activities with distinctive geographies of flows and central places.

There are other kinds of urban centrality that are highlighted by King's comments. Fashion capitals have also often been heavily dependent on their positions in global networks of migration, of individual designers, of entrepreneurs in the garment trades, and of course of workers in the fashion industry. King also argues that alongside the political economy approach of the world city literature, the nature of urban power and centrality has to be understood within the historical, political and cultural framework of post-imperialism or post-colonialism. The idea of fashion authority, of certain specific urban milieu as the sources of style, has been a powerful form of cultural imperialism. While fashion's world cities have often been examined in terms of distinctive national and metropolitan cultures – in terms of the 'Frenchness' of Parisian fashions, or the edginess of a distinctively London look – they have also worked as a key element of a wider long-running discourse that divided the world into forward and backward regions. Every bit as much as imperial monuments or the great exhibitions, fashion was used as a means of expressing the superiority of certain places in the world order.

Versions of 'Parisian' fashions had an extraordinary reach in the late nineteenth century, available to elites in urban contexts as different as Meiji Tokyo, gold-rush Melbourne, and the newly prosperous and expanding South American capitals of Montevideo and Buenos Aires. In these contexts, 'Paris' fashions were understood as expressions of modernity, and their consumption as a marker of belonging and status in a world order centred in the great European capitals. This relationship extended (and indeed still extends) beyond the direct consumption of clothes with some lingering connection with Paris, or the vicarious consumption of the fashion capital in novels, film or the fashion press. Just as more official town-planning and architecture attempted to map European modernity into the urban fabric of colonial cities, so the examples of the fashion capitals provided models for the spaces of elite consumption. Shanghai's claims in the early twentieth century to be the 'Paris of the East' worked through fashions and attitudes towards consumption, but also in the design and culture of the shopping area of the Bund. In Melbourne, locals have talked of the 'Paris end of Collins Street' for over a century. Both the revived Bund and contemporary Collins Street retain this mimetic relationship with Paris, indicating its continuing force as a symbolic marker of high fashion. Clearly this kind of relationship is embedded within the geography of Appadurai's mediascape, dependent on long-running tropes promoted by the fashion press, films and elsewhere that have sustained a powerful imaginative geography of style and sophistication. But it is also possible to stretch Appadurai's concept of globally dispersed ideoscapes to encompass fashion as a particular commercialised expression of the Enlightenment 'image-idea' of progress.

Fashion and its world cities: The long-term development of an urban hierarchy

The continuing status of London, New York and Paris as major centres of fashion culture has to be understood through a long-term history that places fashion at the intersection of key cultural and economic processes that shaped the urban order. In thinking about the long-term development of the geography of fashion's world cities, it is useful to identify five main themes:

- the urban consumer revolution of the eighteenth century;
- the economic and symbolic systems of European imperialism;
- the development of rivalries between European fashion cities;
- the influence of an American engagement with European fashion;
- the development of a symbolic ordering of cities within the modern fashion media.

Discussions of the emergence of modern consumption patterns now conventionally stress the importance of an urban renaissance and 'consumer revolution' of the late seventeenth and early eighteenth centuries, rather than the later industrial revolution. Glennie and Thrift (1992) suggested that European and new North American urban contexts were central both to the learning of new consumption practices and to their pursuit. Yet not all cities were equally suited to the development of the fashion process. If, as Glennie and Thrift argued, knowledge of consumption was essentially practical, acquired not so much through instruction or advertising as through 'quasi-personal contact and observation in the urban throng', then some cities (particularly London and Paris) were more thronging than others (1992: 430). And if the rise of fashion was dependent on the prioritisation of novelty, then some cities (and again particularly London and Paris) were in positions in the networks of world trade that enhanced the supply of novel experiences, and encouraged the acceleration of the fashion cycle. Albeit in rather different ways, eighteenth- and early nineteenth-century London and Paris were both sites that combined long traditions of elite fashion (and associated specialist urban producers of fashionable goods), strongly growing 'professional-bourgeois' markets, and increasingly significant central roles in imperial structures of political control and trade.

Part of the shock-value of the extreme figure of the *Macaroni*[2] on the London streets of the 1770s came not just from the speed at which his fashions changed, but also from the seemingly wasteful and indulgent geographical reach of his clothing. As Miles Ogborn has suggested, the *Macaroni* was 'understood within the international chains of commodities that made London itself a dangerous place through the ways in which its endless varieties of consumption brought together the produce of the world' (Ogborn 1998: 139) These early developments were of vital significance for London's long-term status as a fashion centre; while fashions themselves came and went rapidly, the overall spatial ordering of fashion proved remarkably stable.

The 'consumer revolution' also shaped London's internal geography, establishing a pattern that appeared in other important fashion centres. In a sense, London's geography remained pre-industrial, with an economic structure character-ised not by factory production, but by small-scale workshops, often involved in the finishing of fashions and luxury goods. Fashion was therefore significant not only in the elite 'front regions' of the city, where it was displayed, purchased and worn, but also in 'back regions' where it was made, finished and often copied. The proximity of these front and back regions has been one of the key characteristics of the experience of fashion's world cities, producing unexpected crossings and blurrings of the boundaries between different social worlds. Modern Parisian shoppers who abandon the rue du Jour to slum for bargains among the workshops of the passage du Caire are following a journey made many times before, perhaps in late nineteenth-century Whitechapel, or the New York Garment District in the 1930s. In a beautiful essay on her childhood as the daughter of a Jewish master tailor in the London rag trade, Ruth Gershon described how her life was saturated with experiences of the latest styles and cuts: 'swaggering around Hendon Central in a copy of a 1961 Cardin suit in a brilliant blue-and-black tweed with a fur collar' (Gershon 1999: 82). Fashion's great centres have long contained over-lapping fashion cultures and spaces, in which conventional models of the fashion process – trickle-down emulation or bubble-up street innovation – prove hope-lessly inadequate as descriptions of the interlocking circuits of production and consumption, imitation and intimidation.

The growth and systemisation of European imperialism was an important phase in the development of fashion's world cities. Most obviously this worked in terms of the relationship between the great metropolises and the colonised world, especially the world of the settler colonies. London and Paris came to be understood as sites of both innovation and of fashion authority. This worked through the actual export of clothes and designs, but also through the symbolic projection of these cities as avatars of fashionable modernity. Other kinds of flow and connection between the colonies and the imperial metropolises also reinforced their status. The new department stores of London, Paris and other European capitals promoted themselves through a rhetoric and performance of world significance and centrality. Guidebooks and other promotional literature for those arriving from the colonies stressed the significance of London as a capital of style and luxury (Gilbert 1999). The spheres of influence of imperial fashion trade were of lasting significance for the major fashion cities. While the international sale and licensing of haute couture designs underpinned Paris's reputation as the predominant fashion capital, the French colonies formed an important market for its ready-made clothes from the late nineteenth century until decolonisation in the 1950s and 1960s (Green 2002: 32).

The age of Empire was marked not only by highly unequal relations between Europe and the rest of the world, but also by intense economic, political and cultural competition between the European powers. High fashion became another of the ways that European national cultures could measure themselves against each other. Berlin, Brussels, Vienna and Milan all combined significant local fashion production, distinctive design traditions and spectacular shops with the public display of fashion among the crowds in their streets, squares and arcades. However, even within Europe, such competition took place within a developing hierarchy of fashion cities, in which Paris was increasingly best able to position itself as the world capital of fashion. Anticipating the twentieth-century relationship between the French and American industries, from its origins the European fashion system was marked by an uneasy mixture of competition and synergy between its major centres. Neil McKendrick argued that the veneration of Paris was a significant dimension of the consumer revolution centred on eighteenth-century London. Fashion that was 'expensive, exclusive and Paris-based' was translated into something that was 'cheap, popular and London-based' (McKendrick 1983: 43). It was vital that the process of translation from exclusive Parisian fashion to popular London fashion was incomplete, and that a residue of Parisian origins remained on clothes that were intended for consumption outside the traditional elites.

Despite London's incontrovertible economic and political supremacy, it is Paris that is remembered, in Walter Benjamin's phrase, as the 'capital of the nineteenth century', not least because its cityscape was remade as a global object of desire and consumption (Hancock 2003: 75). The 'Haussmannisation' of Paris changed more than its street pattern and its architecture; it also altered the imagined geography of the city, locking together a strong visual trope of the material city with ideas about its cultural life, in which the consumption and public display of high fashion were key elements. London and Paris represented different sides of the modern city, with the feminised 'capital of pleasure' routinely contrasted with a more masculine city of work and business. This gendering of urban identities corresponded with a division in the dominant characterisations of the cities as fashion centres, with London associated with elite male tailoring, and Paris the dominant centre for women's fashion.

By the late nineteenth century, tourism was an increasingly significant element in fashion's urban order. European and North American cities promoted themselves as centres for luxury shopping, and magazines and tourist guides were increasingly significant in the production of international understandings of the fashion cultures of major cities. International tourism was one of the growth industries of Second Empire Paris, and by the end of the nineteenth century developments in trans-atlantic travel helped to turn the city into the hub of the European tour for thousands of upper- and middle-class Americans. More than the clothes of particular designers, the fashion object that was being consumed was the city itself, and the spectacle of high fashion in situ.

Those Americans who travelled to experience Paris were just part of the wider popular consumption of the idea of the city as an elite space. The development of the international fashion system in the early twentieth century was marked by both an unprecedented democratisation as more and more people had access to fashion clothing and fashion imagery, and also by a concentration of the control of style and design (Craik 1994: 74). Lipovetsky (1994: 50) may be guilty of polemical exaggeration in suggesting that 'with the hegemony of haute couture, a hyper-centralised fashion appeared, entirely indigenous to Paris and yet at the same time international: Parisian fashion was followed by all the "up-to-date" women in the world'. Other fashion centres did retain independent significance, and the geographies of male fashions were always more complex. Nonetheless, the insti-tutionalisation of the couture system strongly reinforced Paris's claims to be the world's capital of fashion. In the second half of the nineteenth century, Charles Frederick Worth particularly had reinvented the role of the couturier, placing it at the core of the Parisian fashion system. Worth inaugurated the cult of the designer, producing a figure that was seen as the author of new styles. This owed something to Worth's design talents, but much more to his innovations in marketing and business organisation, effectively creating the first designer brand (see De Marly 1980). The same period saw the development of strongly enforced systems of licensing and legal restrictions on copying in France, which further concentrated the industry in Paris, and enhanced the sense that fashion was something that was diffused from the city's designers.

In the early twentieth century there was a formal institutionalisation of the distinction between couturiers and other fashion professionals with the establishment of La Chambre Syndicale de la Couture Parisienne in 1910. Organised fashion shows and seasonal collections also began in this period. These developments had a number of implications for fashion's geographies. The first shows with live models and music were criticised in L'Illustration as part of a 'hideous crisis of bad taste' (quoted in Steele 1988: 228). However, what seemed likely to be a short-lived gimmick became an integral element of modern fashion promotion, turning the launch of new fashions into a focused performance. The fashion show worked to focus attention on key spaces within the city, but was also a perfect fit for the requirements of the new fashion and news media. The Paris fashion system became more structured in its annual timetable in this period. After the First World War, seasonal shows presenting the new collections of the major couture houses were organised at more or less fixed dates in the calendar. This new systematised haute couture system regularised the rhythms of fashion, with a normalisation of change brought about at fixed dates by specialised groups (Lipovetsky 1994: 58). The bi-annual collections gave precedence to foreign agents and buyers, who were able to purchase reproduction rights.

In this new formation of the international fashion system there was a strong interdependence between Parisian and American fashion. The American film industry recast the mythologies of Paris for a global audience. However, Paris – or more accurately the aura of Parisian fashion authority – was also a critical feature in the systematisation of the American fashion cycle, used to organise seasons into particular looks and colours. The sale of patterns to foreign ready-to-wear companies (illegal in France itself) underpinned the mythology of Paris as the authoritative source of fashion edicts. This system reached a high point in the postwar accommodation between the French and American fashion industries that was aggressively promoted in US *Vogue*. The period after Christian Dior's 'New Look' of 1947 was marked by an unprecedented penetration of Parisian designs and influences into the American market. At the top end these were officially licensed copies, but the rapidly expanding American middle market was dominated by copies of the season's Parisian looks, taking advantage of the USA's more liberal laws on style copyright (Green 1997: 120). As the Broadway musical *Sweet Charity* put it, what many American women wanted was a 'copy of a copy of a copy of Dior'. As the designs were copied and recopied, making their way down the social hierarchy, the patina of Parisian design became thinner and thinner, but what was important was that there was still some lingering connection to the authentic original in the Paris collections.

In the early twentieth-century New York City became established as another place which existed both as an actual site of elite fashion consumption and as an imagined space of fashion fantasy (Rantisi 2006). Since the late eighteenth century New York had been the dominant economic city of the United States, and a public culture of socially choreographed displays of fashion, taste and difference on Broadway and Fifth Avenue was well developed by the 1860s (Domosh 1998). By the late nineteenth century, the city was the match of London and Paris in both its scale and its 'intensely urban qualities' that stimulated the development of a vibrant commercial culture (Hammack 1991: 37). Like the great European capitals, it possessed a highly flexible local manufacturing sector able to respond rapidly to changes of style, at least in part due to the heterogeneity of a population in which immigrants were a majority.

A number of factors pushed New York into the front rank of fashion cities in the early twentieth century. To some extent, this was a direct reflection of the rise of American political and economic power. The development of New York's international fashion prestige depended on the development of a class of the super-rich resident in the apartments and hotels of the city. As the novels of Edith Wharton and Henry James indicate, this new elite often sought to validate and consolidate their status through connections with established European aristocratic families. High fashion formed part of the performance of this new status, but what was significant was that this performance was increasingly one with a global audience. The image of elite New York consumption was one element in an unprecedented promotion of a city as a spectacle of commercial culture. Alongside the emerging vertical city of skyscrapers, and Broadway's 'great white way', the high-fashion shops of Fifth Avenue became a familiar part of a cityscape that was celebrated in film, song, literature, and indeed in tourist literature for those now making the journey across the Atlantic from East to West (Gilbert and Hancock 2006).

In the twentieth century, the hierarchy of fashion cities was mediated particularly through the fashion press. Although fashion's metropolitan centres had long been consumed vicariously through magazines and other forms of publicity, the development of the modern fashion press reinforced the idea that a very few cities had a distinctive global importance. The *Vogue* titles were particularly important in this respect. US *Vogue* was founded in 1892, but was only dedicated to fashion from 1909. It was followed by London and Paris editions in 1916 and 1920 respectively. It was not until after the Second World War that other international editions appeared, for example in Italy in 1950, and in Australia the same year. Such magazines became desirable consumer objects in their own right, disseminating knowledge about elite design far beyond the elite customers of Paris, London and New York. However, the world represented in *Vogue* was tightly constrained. Not only were readers shown designs and collections that came almost exclusively from the main fashion centres, they were taught about the detailed shopping geographies of those cities, through columns such as British *Vogue*'s 'Shophound' (Edwards 2006). Newer fashion and lifestyle magazines, such as *Elle*, published in France from 1945, or *Cosmopolitan* (UK 1963), may have had a more democratic view of affordable fashion, but still retained a fixation with certain key sites in fashion's world order.

The postwar period saw significant shifts in fashion's ordering of cities, both in the institutional organisation of the industry, and in the symbolic promotion and understanding of fashion capitals. For some, the international success of the 'New Look' seemed to presage a lasting return to Parisian domination of the international fashion system. However, a number of changes were undermining the long-defended division between couture and ready-made copies. During the 1950s, Parisian originated fashions came under sustained competition from Italian fashions, also targeted at the lucrative American market. Italian style was well suited to the mythologisings of Hollywood and the fashion press, and an imagined Rome played an important part in its promotion (see Church Gibson 2006). The structure of the Italian industry was distinctively different, with its cutting-edge consisting not of hand-made couture, but designed ready-to-wear fashions. In the 1960s, London was the locus of a different kind of challenge to the established order that drew on a newly affluent youth market. The significance of designers like Mary Quant was that they showed that cutting-edge fashion could be very different from the Parisian model. In place of the wealthy, elite and mature couture customer, Quant promoted the Chelsea Girl, a figure defined by her youth (and her skinny body shape), her casual confidence in the city, and her willingness to experiment with a rapid succession of new looks. London fashion in the 1960s, while still in part about the work of a group of designers identified with the city, was as much about the development of a distinctive urban fashion culture, seemingly more spontaneous, and associated with the boutique, street and club (Gilbert 2006b).

The postwar period, and particularly the period from the 1960s onwards, was therefore characterised by a less concentrated and more differentiated ordering of fashion's major centres. The Parisian collections were joined by others, and the bi-annual journeys of international buyers turned into a moving road show of events. The first shows in Florence were organised in 1951, and 1958 saw the first London fashion weeks. Other cities formed organisations to protect and promote local design traditions, such as the Council of Fashion Designers of America founded in New York in 1963. However, what was taking place was not that other cities were threatening to usurp Paris's established position, but that the whole geometry of fashion's urban ordering was changing. For a time in the 1960s, particularly when viewed through developments in London or the West Coast of the USA, it looked as if this might see a transition to a new fashion order that was less controlled and hierarchical. However, what did take place between the late 1950s and the 1980s was a reconfiguration of the relationship between elite fashion and mass-market clothes that redefined the role of key cities.

Sally Weller (2004) has suggested that the crisis in the couture system brought about responses that reconfigured the global geographies of the fashion system in the second half of the twentieth century. These, she argues, marked a fundamental break in the relationship between fashion design as a form of commodified knowledge and the actual production of clothes. The first major development was the expansion of licensing and branding. There is a long association between couture houses and licensed perfumes and accessories; Ernest Beaux developed the 'No. 5' fragrance for Chanel in 1921. However, the 1950s and 1960s saw a significant extension of perfume ranges, and of the direct licensing of ready-to-wear fashions marked with designer names. Weller argues that licensing is a commodification of elite designers' reputations, and that its viability 'depends on continued public recognition of designers' names and the maintenance of designers' elite status in the public arena, through the media and through events that create media interest' (2004: 97). This development placed even greater emphasis (and clear economic value) on the constructed traditions and mythologies of the great fashion cities.

Fashion's world order was also transformed by the international restructuring of elite garment production. The rapid rise of Milan as a fashion capital in the 1970s was due to its position in this process (Segre Reinach 2006). Between 1971 and 1978, established Italian fashion designers abandoned the Florence shows to display their work in Milan. At the same time a new generation of entrepreneur designers who had trained in the industrial and commercial enterprises of Northern Italy became established in Milan. Milan's position as a fashion city drew upon its established traditions in design, and the developing 'flexible specialisation' and 'vertical integration' of the industrial regions of Northern Italy. Segre Reinach (2006) suggests that Milan's position in fashion's world order was as the central city for prêt-à-porter. However, the 1970s and early 1980s also saw a broader shift in the geographies of production of elite fashions. Italian manufacturers, particularly the giant Gruppo GFT, contracted major French designers to produce ready-to-wear fashions, alongside the emerging Italian names. While the fashion press emphasised the rivalries between Paris and Milan, this new prêt-à-porter system of internationalised production networks drew upon the design reputations and symbolic power of both cities. The creation of this new axis between Paris and Milan was part of a wider late-twentieth-century reordering of fashion's world cities, which also saw a more general shift towards ready-to-wear fashions converged with an increasing demand for a more 'American sensibility' in high-end fashion, and increased New York's significance as a centre of design (Rantisi 2004: 103).

A new world order? Fashion and its capitals in the twenty-first century

The early years of the twenty-first century have perhaps been the strongest indication of the staying power of the great capitals in fashion's symbolic geographies. Despite economic turmoil, and a continuing shift of economic and geopolitical power from west to east, there has been little sign of a fundamental re-ordering of the geography of fashion's capitals. To be sure, Tokyo seems to have slipped from its place as the 'fifth city', established in the 1970s and 1980s with the emergence of several world-ranked Japanese designers. As Kawamura has argued, Tokyo's position was always somewhat contradictory, with the career trajectories of key Japanese designers closely locked into the fashion institutions of Paris in particular (Kawamura 2006). The long economic stagnation has perhaps also seen Tokyo shaded by Hong Kong or Shanghai as the most dynamic of East Asia centres. Beyond this, at least in the kind of measurement of the symbolic urban hierarchy undertaken by the likes of Global Language Monitor, there seems to be little change – New York, Paris, London and Milan retain their significance, while other cities have their time in the fashion cycle.

Such a view over-simplifies the developments of the new century; the same city names may crop up in such lists, but there is significant change taking place in the relationship between fashion and the geography of major cities. In 2002 the geographer Allen Scott attempted to identify what would be needed to move Los Angeles to 'the front rank of world fashion centres', competing directly with 'New York, Paris, Milan and London' (2002: 1304):

- A 'flexible' manufacturing basis.
- A core cluster of specialist and skill-intensive contractors capable of high-quality work on short turnaround times.
- A dense 'groundwork' of fashion training and research institutes in the city region.
- A new infrastructure of regionally based but internationally recognised publicity and promotional vehicles, including fashion media, major fashion shows and other fashion events.
- An evolving fashion and design tradition with strong place-specific elements.
- Formal and informal connections between the fashion industry and other cultural products industries of the region (particularly Hollywood).

Scott's checklist seems closer to the ideal-type of an older formation of fashion capital – perhaps what might be described as a fashion capital of the twentieth century – than the emergent fashion city of the new century. The close inter-connections and geographical clusterings of design, craft finishing and flexible manufacturing that have been a central feature of fashion's world cities are being eroded by the direct competition of off-shore subcontracting, and particularly by the logic and logistics of 'fast fashion'. In the 1980s and 1990s the emergence of a system of rapid production of relatively high-quality clothes in quick response to new designs and trends was thought to give a benefit to established, high-skill manufacturing clusters, notably in the cities and industrial regions of Europe and

North America. However, what is emerging is the capacity and competence to manufacture such high-quality garments with flexibility and speed outside the old cores, in places such as China, India, Morocco and Turkey (Segre Reinach 2005; Tokatli 2008). Outside of the very specific example of Parisian haute couture, the kinds of intimate interconnections between a strong fashion design sector and skilled craft workers that were the mark of the older fashion city formation are being replaced by new distantiated relationships that work through digital transmission of designs and patterns and rapid global delivery systems. The next generation of digital production technologies, particularly associated with relatively cheap 3-D 'printing' are likely to strengthen this change.

What seems to be taking place is shift to a new formation of major fashion city, in which the symbolic production of fashion has become more significant than the physical production of garments. In some ways, fashion in its world cities has become hollowed out, and increasingly like just another producer service industry. Some have argued that this has seen a Parisian model of the fashion capital increasingly replaced by a New York model (see Rantisi 2004 and 2006). The fashion industry has become more locked into the concentration and centralisation of advanced capitalism. In this view, the new fashion world city has less significance as a cluster of highly skilled manufacturing centre or even a design tradition as the organisational headquarters of a global branding industry. Terry Agins described this as the 'end of fashion' and the 'death of couture' (a demise admittedly proclaimed pretty regularly over the past hundred years). This transformation, Agins argued, has seen New York usurp Paris's position as the dominant fashion centre. The development of American 'designer' sportswear and leisurewear brands in the 1980s and 1990s (such as Calvin Klein, DKNY, Tommy Hilfiger) disrupted the connection between design and skilled, locally based manufacturing.

Since the time of Charles Worth modern fashion has always been about the creation of brand identities and a complex relationship between haute couture and the industrial production of copies. But recent developments seem to mark a profound change in the balance between brands and the significance of actual garments, with most production moving to off-shore suppliers. In the new organisational order of the fashion industry most elite designers, and certainly most of those shown in the main seasonal collections, are first and foremost global brand identities, part of the portfolio of powerful conglomerates. The development of this fashion oligarchy has strengthened the connections between the networks of fashion and corporate finance. At the same time, the primary importance of branding has strengthened the importance of connections with activities like advertising, management consultancy and corporate law, heavily concentrated in certain key cities. This shift has been accompanied by a continuing squeeze on small-scale production and even design activities in the central districts of major world cities. While even as late as the 1980s some central areas of London and Manhattan contained cheaper 'interstices' of relatively inexpensive areas for smaller businesses to rent, the hyperinflation of world city property and rental prices of the past two decades has seen the exclusion of such enterprises in favour of larger corporations, and the return of upmarket residential developments. The consequence has been a narrowing of the range of economic activities, and also a loss of an immediate connection with a world beyond the major corporations. The kind of fashion revolution associated with the King's Road and Carnaby Street in 1960s London is now an economic impossibility (Breward and Gilbert 2008).

Recent times have also seen a further strengthening of the symbolic power of the major fashion centres. In her recent commentary on the development of 'second-tier' fashion cities and nations, it is telling that Lise Skov elides the category of the 'global' with the usual key cities: 'for a small nation, the international success of a few individual designers in Paris, London or New York can be of enormous importance, not only symbolically, but because they act as conducting wires between the local and the global' (Skov 2011: 152). What Skov describes as the 'success criterion' of 'global connectivity' is effectively another way of indicating the reinforced power of a highly concentrated international fashion press, and the enduring power of city-based collections. One of the features of the fashion cultures of such 'second-tier' fashion centres is the 'extreme effort put into soliciting editors of the leading fashion magazines in New York, London and Tokyo to visit second-tier fashion weeks, and ensuring easy transport from fashion show to fashion show' (Skov 2011: 152; see also Skov and Meier 2011). As Norma Rantisi has discussed, the development of Fashion Weeks in emerging fashion centres (as for example in Europe in Amsterdam, Berlin, Cork and Oslo since 2005) acts to showcase local design talent and sometimes craftwork, but also often reinforces engrained relationships between 'first-tier' and 'second-tier' centres (Rantisi 2011).

There are further changes to the relationship between fashion and its major centres. Scott's analysis of the characteristics of major fashion centres has been criticised for treating fashion consumption as a secondary activity (see Gilbert 2006a). Throughout the modern history of fashion's capitals, a key component has been the close connection between the design and production of fashion and its urban consumption. This extends beyond the practices and spaces of shopping, as important as the department store and boutique have been in the history of modern fashion, to include the ways that fashion is worn and performed on the streets of major cities. As Elizabeth Wilson has famously argued, there was a close relationship between fashion, modernity and urbanisation, and central to that were districts of experimentation and performance in dress as much as in the arts (Wilson 1991; 2000; 2003). Wilson is far from alone in bemoaning the increasing uniformity of fashion's capitals, and the wider uniformity of urban retail spaces:

> it is sometimes difficult to remember whether one is in Oxford or Oxford Street, Stafford or Stanford, California Shopping Mall, for the same chain stores are everywhere to be seen, and for that matter Nanjing Road more closely resembles Bond Street or Fifth Avenue than it resembles Shanghai in the 1930s.
>
> (Wilson 2006: 37)

It is in this geography of increasingly similar branded elite consumption spaces, not through the presence of a handful of local 'very good' designers, that Dubai can claim to be a significant fashion city, a more opulent version of something available in many other places.

In all of this there is a depressing model of fashion's new world order. Of course, as Wilson warns, we must guard against 'sentimental nostalgia' and overstating the contrasts between a 'grim or at least banal present' and 'some lost golden era of authenticity' (Wilson 2006: 36). Nonetheless, the model is of 'Potemkin cities' of fashion, with fashion's order dominated by the same old places, but now hollowed-out by the forces of advanced capitalism. These are fashion world cities that have not merely deindustrialised, but through processes of gentrification, corporatisation, and the sanitation and securitisation of public urban space have cut themselves off from the wellsprings of modern urban fashion that sustained and reinvented earlier formations. At the same time the symbolic power of these few cities has been reinforced, through the power of brands, the fashion media in old and new digital forms, and through the atrophication of the system of collections and fashion weeks, which has stabilised into a layered hierarchy of choreographed events. The final element is the increasing invisibility of production and craft in system where the geographies of design and consumption are greatly separated from the geographies of garment making.

For those who retain some faith in fashion as more than just a corporate exercise, but see it as a key element of what makes great cities great, there are some spaces of hope. In the established capitals, we can look to the margins, outside the Circle Line, over bridge or through tunnel, beyond the Peripherique, to find new kinds of fashion cultures that challenge the hegemony of the central city, and our expectations of the suburban. Elsewhere, as Skov (2011) argues, the best of the 'second-tier' fashion centres are not forever looking 'up' to Paris, London, New York and Milan, nor are they slavishly following the kind of top-down prescriptions for urban boosterism replicated in hundreds of cities across the globe that have attempted to foster a Richard Florida-style 'creative class' (Florida 2004). Instead, what we have seen in different forms at different times in cities such as Antwerp, Reykjavik, Copenhagen or Dublin have been attempts to make local formations that connect design, craft production skills, with a sense of place. At their best these 'dreams of small nations' do not simply mine the seams of established or invented authenticity, but are alive to the possibilities of remaking distinctive place-based traditions.

However, and as several of the chapters in this collection indicate (see those that follow, which discuss the 'BRICS'), those places that are most likely to disrupt fashion's current urban ordering are the cities of emerged and potentially emergent economic powers. As has been argued here, however, there is no automatic, straightforward connection between changes in economic or geopolitical power, and fashion's global geographies. Nor can we simply map the orderings of fashion cultures onto a map of the shifting geographies of garment production. We perhaps naturally look to the BRICS and beyond for the next great fashion cities for the twenty-first century. The temptation is to turn to Shanghai as the most obvious candidate, although the experience so far shows the limits of a model that works through a combination of flexible production, brand-focused consumption and heavy-handed state initiatives to organise trade fairs and collections. The Communist Party of China is not normally encouraging of the kind of urban lifestyles and experimentation that have been a feature of previous fashion capitals. Maybe we need to turn to other cities that are less controlled, more culturally open, and with stronger existing traditions of fusion. The great Brazilian cities are already established locations in fashion's imagined geographies and seem likely to continue to flourish in the coming decade; beyond that we might look to India, and even the already highly dynamic fashion cultures of some African cities. São Paulo, Mumbai, Dakar – perhaps it is in these places that the idea of the fashion city will be reinvented, not as a copy of twentieth-century Paris, London, New York, but as a distinctive new combination of urban and fashion cultures.

Note

1

Table 1   Global Language Monitor's annual ranking of top fashion capitals.

2012	2011	2010	2009
1 London	London	New York	Milan
2 New York	New York	Hong Kong	New York
3 Barcelona	Paris	London	Paris
4 Paris	Milan	Paris	Rome
5 Madrid	Los Angeles	Los Angeles	London
6 Rome	Hong Kong	Milan	Los Angeles
7 Sao Paulo	Barcelona	Sydney	Hong Kong
8 Milan	Singapore	Miami	Sao Paulo
9 Los Angeles	Tokyo	Barcelona	Sydney
10 Berlin	Berlin	Madrid	Las Vegas

Source: Global Language Monitor www.languagemonitor.com/category/fashion/fashion-capitals

2   The *Macaronis* were those young men of London in the 1770s who adopted a particularly extravagant mode of dress. The style was most notable for the towering wigs with long pigtails they all wore. They often carried canes and quizzing-glasses, and some adopted particular verbal affectations. The actual word 'macaroni' refers to the tiny tricorn hats which they wore perched atop their elaborate wigs. They were mocked in the press and in cartoons; the 'dandies' of the following century were positively restrained by comparison.

References

Agins, T. (1999) *The End of Fashion: The Mass Marketing of the Clothing Business*, New York: Diane Publishing.

Al Arabiya News (2013) 'Vogue announces its Fashion Dubai Experience', online. Available at www.alarabiya.net/articles/2013/02/05/264503.html (published 5 Feb 2013).

Appadurai, A. (1990) 'Disjuncture and difference in the global cultural economy', *Theory, Culture and Society* 7: 295–310.

Breward, C. (2003) *Fashion*, Oxford: Oxford University Press.

Breward, C. and Gilbert, D. (eds) (2006) *Fashion's World Cities*, Oxford: Berg.

Breward, C. and Gilbert, D. (2008) 'Anticipations of the new urban cultural economy: fashion and the transformation of London's West End 1955–75', in M. Hessler and C. Zimmermann (eds) *Creative Urban Milieus. Historical Perspectives on Culture, Economy and the City*, Frankfurt: Campus.

Church Gibson, P. (2006) 'New stars, new fashions and the female audience: cinema, consumption and cities 1953–1966', in C. Breward and D. Gilbert (eds) *Fashion's World Cities*, Oxford: Berg.

Craik, J. (1994) *The Face of Fashion*, London: Routledge.

De Marly, D. (1980) *The History of Haute Couture, 1850–1950*, New York: Holmes and Meier.

Domosh, M (1998) 'Those "Gorgeous Incongruities": Polite politics and public space on the streets of nineteenth-century New York City', *Annals of the Association of American Geographers* 88: 209–26.

Edwards (2006) '"We are fatally influenced by goods bought in Bond Street": London, shopping and the fashionable geographies of 1930s *Vogue*', *Fashion Theory* 10: 73–96.

Florida, R. (2004) *Cities and the Creative Class*, New York: Routledge.

Friedmann, J. (1995) 'Where we stand: a decade of world city research' in P. Knox and P. Taylor (eds) *World Cities in a World System* Cambridge: Cambridge University Press.

Friedmann, J. (1986) 'The world city hypothesis', *Development and Change*, 17: 69–83.

Friedmann, J. and Wolff, K. (1982) 'World city formation: an agenda for research and action', *International Journal of Urban and regional Research* 6: 309–44.

Gershon, R. (1999) 'A life in clothes', *Granta* 65: 77–102.

Gilbert, D. (1999) '*London in all its Glory – or how to enjoy London*: guidebook representations of Imperial London', *Journal of Historical Geography* 25: 279–97.

——— (2000) 'Urban Outfitting: the city and the spaces of fashion culture', in S. Bruzzi and P. Church Gibson (eds) *Fashion Cultures: Theories, Explorations and Analysis*, London: Routledge.

——— (2006a) 'From Paris to Shanghai: The changing geographies of fashion's world cities', in C. Breward and D. Gilbert (eds) *Fashion's World Cities*, Oxford: Berg.

——— (2006b) '"The Youngest Legend in History": Cultures of consumption and the mythologies of Swinging London' *London Journal* 31: 1–15.

Gilbert, D. and Hancock, C. (2006) 'New York City and the transatlantic imagination: French and English tourism and the spectacle of the modern metropolis, 1893–1939', *Journal of Urban History* 33: 77–107.

Glennie, P. and Thrift, N. (1992) 'Modernity, urbanism, and modern consumption', *Environment and Planning D: Society and Space* 10: 423–43.

Green, N. (1997) *Ready-to-wear and Ready-to-work: A Century of Industry and Immigrants in Paris and New York*, Durham: Duke University Press.

——— (2002) 'Paris: A historical view', in J. Rath (ed.) *Unravelling the Rag Trade. Immigrant Entrepreneurship in Seven World Cities*, Oxford: Berg.

Global Language Monitor (2013) 'London edges New York for top global fashion capital', online. Available at www.languagemonitor.com/fashion/london-edges-new-york-for-top-2012-global-fashion-capital (accessed 30 March 2013).

Hammack, D. (1991) 'Developing for commercial culture', in W. Taylor (ed.) *Inventing Times Square: Commerce and Culture at the Crossroads of the World*, Baltimore: Johns Hopkins University Press.

Hancock, C. (2003) '*Capitale du plaisir*: the remaking of imperial Paris', in F. Driver and D. Gilbert (eds) *Imperial Cities*, Manchester: Manchester University Press.

Kawamura, Y. (2006) 'Placing Tokyo on the fashion map: from catwalk to streetstyle', in C. Breward and D. Gilbert (eds) *Fashion's World Cities*, Oxford: Berg.

King, A. (1995) 'Re-presenting world cities: cultural theory/social practice', in P. Knox and P. Taylor (eds) *World Cities in a World-System*, Cambridge: Cambridge University Press.

Lipovetsky (1994) *The Empire of Fashion. Dressing Modern Democracy*, Princeton: Princeton University Press.

McKendrick, N. (1983) 'The consumer revolution of eighteenth-century England' in N. McKendrick, J. Brewer and J. Plumb (eds) *The Birth of a Consumer Society: The Commercialisation of Eighteenth-Century England*, London: Hutchinson.

Ogborn, M. (1998) *Spaces of Modernity: London's Geographies 1680–1780*, London: Guilford.

Rantisi, N. (2004) 'The Ascendance of New York Fashion', *The International Journal of Urban and Regional Affairs* 28: 86–106.

—— (2006) 'How New York stole modern fashion', in C. Breward and D. Gilbert (eds) *Fashion's World Cities*, Oxford: Berg.

—— (2011) 'The prospects and perils of creating a viable fashion identity', *Fashion Theory*, 15: 259–66.

Rocamora, A. (2006) 'Paris capitale de la mode: representing the fashion city in the media', in C. Breward and D. Gilbert (eds) *Fashion's World Cities*, Oxford: Berg.

Sassen, S. (2001) *The Global City*, 2nd edn. Princeton: Princeton University Press.

—— (1991) *The Global City: New York, London, Tokyo*, Princeton: Princeton University Press.

Scott, A. (2002) 'Competitive dynamics of Southern California's clothing industry: The widening global connection and its local ramifications', *Urban Studies*, 39: 1287–1306.

Segre Reinach, S. (2005) 'China and Italy: Fast Fashion versus *Prêt à Porter*. Towards a new culture of fashion', *Fashion Theory*, 9: 43–56.

—— (2006) 'Milan: The city of Prêt-à-Porter in a world of fast fashion', in C. Breward and D. Gilbert (eds) *Fashion's World Cities*, Oxford: Berg.

Skov, L. (2011) 'Dreams of small nations in a polycentric fashion world', *Fashion Theory* 15: 137–56.

Skov, L., and Meier, J. (2011) 'Configuring sustainability at fashion week', in Moeran, B., and Strandgaard Pedersen, J. (eds) *Negotiating Values in the Creative Industries*, Cambridge: Cambridge University Press.

Steele, V. (1988) *Paris Fashion: A Cultural History*, New York: Oxford University Press.

Tokatli, N. (2008) 'Global sourcing: insights from the global clothing industry – the case of Zara, a fast fashion retailer', *Journal of Economic Geography* 8: 21–38.

Weller, S. (2004) 'Fashion's influence on garment mass production: knowledge, commodities and the capture of value', unpublished thesis University of Melbourne.

Wilson, E. (1991) *The Sphinx in the City: Urban Life, the Control of Disorder and Women*, London: Virago.

—— (2000) *Bohemians: The Glamorous Outcasts*, London: I.B. Tauris.

—— (2003) *Adorned in Dreams: Fashion and Modernity*, London: Virago.

—— (2006) 'Urbane fashion', in C. Breward and D. Gilbert (eds) *Fashion's World Cities*, Oxford: Berg.

Chapter 2

Silvano Mendes and
Nick Rees-Roberts

BRANDING BRAZILIAN FASHION
Global visibility and intercultural perspectives

Just a few years ago, Brazil's only famous fashion exports were bikinis, Havaianas and Victoria's Secret models. Now, established brands such as Osklen, Issa, Carlos Miele, Pedro Lourenço, Alexandre Herchcovitch and Lucas Nascimento sell internationally, and at home a diverse camp of designers is proving that Brazilian fashion has grown up.
(Helen Jennings, *Guardian*, 22 November 2012)

IN OCTOBER 2012 BRAZIL'S MAIN FASHION events, the São Paulo Fashion Week and Rio FashionWeek, announced a radical calendar change. Instead of hosting events each January and June, the Autumn/Winter collections are now presented in October and November and the Spring/Summer collections in March and April, part of a broader global shift in the presentational strategy of fashion. In a sector still dominated by the four main fashion capitals – London, Milan, New York and Paris – the decision signals Brazil's national ambition to have a fashion industry befitting its status as the world's sixth economic power in 2013. Brazilian designers have traditionally taken advantage of the chronological division of the fashion calendar by editing Western designs and adapting styles shown on the runways of Europe and New York. The emergence since the 1990s of a young generation of fashion designers is part of the drive to be taken more seriously as a creative force, to move beyond the traditional imitation of European and North American labels to a position of stylistic influence. Previously, collections by Brazilian designers were on sale six months after their American and European competitors, given the time delay. The decision to bypass the official calendar shows the high financial stakes and national-political implications of the economic ascendency of Brazil, whose strategy is to position its fashion industry at the start of the design, image and production chain.

Brazil is currently the world's third largest cotton manufacturer. However, given its booming domestic market, its manufacturing competition with East Asian markets, and the ongoing difficulties linked to uncompetitive import and export tariffs, the Brazilian fashion industry is now looking for a new business model adapted to the country's current economic positioning and future aspirations. Rejecting the low-level option of following China as the latest emblem of globalised fast fashion, the Brazilian fashion sector seems intent on investing in creativity, with its inevitable added value, as the means to make its mark on the global stage. Despite having an integral production chain, the country has been more successful at exporting its image than its fashion, which in part explains the Western focus on Brazilian models rather than designers. With its important cotton and denim production, the manufacturing capacity of the textile industry is a major strength. Brazilian fashion has yet to emerge as a global player due to government-imposed barriers such as taxes on manufacturing, overpriced labour costs and poor trans-portation infrastructure. The domestic market is a priority for Brazilian designers given the commercial potential of a population of over 200 million, half of which is an affluent middle class. Given the size of this market and the country's wealth of natural resources and its industrial capacity, the question is why Brazil has not actively promoted its own fashion design more successfully to compete with the local presence and market dominance of the global fashion brands.

Global fashion

It may be that the emergence of new circuits of production, distribution and exhibition that see the current balance of power shift to the emerging economies of the BRICs will mark a dramatic change in the industrial practices of clothing production. The move away from the model of global convergence (multinational conglomerates housing super-brands reliant on delocalised labour practices) to a more self-contained model in which global brands produce locally – in Brazil *for* Brazil for example – would involve exploiting the growth of an affluent middle class and relying on local design talent and creative industries. This shift in the location and production of global fashion would have the potential to feed back into the overall branding strategy of the label, thereby varying its geographical focus and displacing the current top-down focus of the super-brands whose design creativity and corporate implementation strategies are driven almost entirely from the Western fashion capitals.

This potential recalibration of the global assembly line would short-circuit some of the current geographical disadvantages of de-territorialised production, namely distance, complex delivery schedules, quality control, labour exploitation, and the risk of devaluation in the case of the high-end fashion and luxury goods that superficially bear a heritage stamp of approval. In fact they are often in part outsourced to any number of interchangeable contractors and anonymous subcontractors on the fringes of Europe (Romania, Morocco and Turkey), or in China, Mexico and Bangladesh. Since the shift towards a globalised network economy in the early 1980s the main preoccupations of Western fashion cultures have been more obviously focused on advertising imagery, brand identity and patterns of consumption rather than the less visibly attractive modes and circuits of production (Rabine 2010: 372). Such shifts in the material organisation of the global fashion industry signal more problematic tensions between the promotion of local specificity and individual creativity; between the specifically local and the broader cosmopolitan appeal of fashion design; in short, between the promotion of a discrete *national* identity and a specific *design* identity.

For Brazilian designers the difficulty is how to find a language that can speak to the domestic market and translate to the sensibilities of global consumers, a productive tension paralleled by the global super-brands whose own aspirations are similarly founded on the contrived promotion of their national provenance – Louis Vuitton's elaborate articulation of a specifically French design heritage of luxury travel, for example. In their discussion of the relationship between fashion, identity and globalisation, Eugenia Paulicelli and Hazel Clark explain how locally specific designs are both formative of a national fabric while also circulating widely within a global market (Paulicelli and Clark 2009: 2). The branding of Brazilian fashion involves not only the circulation of consumables domestically and internationally, but also the exportation of a Brazilian design identity channelled through the iconographic branding of the nation. In her historical assessment of Brazilian fashion in terms of its stylistic influences blending the exotic, the urban and the marginal, Valéria Brandini raises the issue of cultural identity in the definition of a specific Brazilian design heritage, one including the imposed and assumed exotic stereotypes of Latin physicality and the more varied cosmology of local street culture. Brandini asks 'whether fashion expropriates cultural meanings for commercial ends, or whether it elevates them, turning their aesthetic content into clothes that exalt cultural richness' (Brandini 2009: 167), thereby differentiating between the two ends of the spectrum, from the textile industry's mass production of apparel to the individual creative strategies of contemporary Brazilian designers working through questions of cultural specificity and ethnic diversity.

The polarising image of contemporary Brazilian fashion as framed by the dominance of mass-produced clothing complemented by a limited number of designers – from established names Alexandre Herchcovitch and Carlos Miele to the emerging talents Pedro Lourenço and Lucas Nascimento – reflects broader tensions relating to the integrative processes of globalisation. The view of globalisation as the import and export of culture shows how it operates as a portmanteau term for a number of competing economic, political and socio-cultural shifts in connectivity, or else 'a communicational concept, which alternately masks and transmits cultural or economic meanings' (Jameson 1998: 55). It is axiomatic in understandings of globalisation to assume that the process does not only reproduce the homogenising effect of Western imperialism but also signals the more complex commercial engagement in intercultural exchange between the 'peripheries' and the 'centre'. By tracking the global flows of capital, commodities, ideas, images and people, anthropologists Jonathan Xavier Inda and Renato Rosaldo build on the preoccupation with the shrinking globe – the speeding-up and shortening of time that geographer David Harvey earlier theorised as the fundamental compression of space and time in postmodernity (Harvey 1989). Inda and Rosaldo accept the basic spatial-temporal parameters of globalisation as the combination of 'speeding up, intensification, and stretching' (Inda and Rosaldo 2008: 11), but they also emphasise the complex two-way traffic between the global and the local in any conceptual grasp of the de-territorialising processes at work in the production and distribution of consumables across the globe. This follows Arjun Appadurai's critique of a simplistic model of homogenisation emphasising in its place the uneven and local-ising processes of globalisation (Appadurai 1996: 17). Appadurai argued that the creative models transposed from Western metropolises are indigenised through fusion with local artistic practices. The Brazilian *Tropicália* movement of the 1960s, for example, witnessed the creative overlap between the social politics of contestation and a broad spectrum of cultural expression from across the arts – in visual art, fashion, design, cinema and music – that mirrored concurrent political upheavals elsewhere in the West. Against the imposition of the super-narratives of economic modernisation channelled through Western media, Appadurai argued that disjuncture better epitomised the flows of contemporary culture beyond a centrifugal model of dissemination from the Western centres of power to a number of multiple peripheries.

One of the difficulties in writing on fashion from a global perspective is the tendency to position the consumers of the 'Global South' as passively in thrall to Western designer brands, which leaves very little room for coverage of local fashion per se, or for analysis of the more complex negotiations of local practices and design aesthetics that work both through and against the templates of Western fashion history. Giorgio Riello and Peter McNeil point to the challenges faced by scholars today in

> redefining the meaning of fashion to include fashion consumers, producers and mediators well beyond the geographical boundaries of Western Europe, North America and perhaps those outposts frequently forgotten in the northern hemisphere, of South Africa, Australia, and parts of South America, the latter two being in the post-war period significant markets for French couture.
>
> (Riello and McNeil 2010: 4)

The history of trade between Brazil and the West positions Brazilian fashion on the cusp – at once in creative dialogue and commercial exchange with the West, yet also stylistically and culturally distinct from it. Riello and McNeil point to the history of exchange between French couture and the metropolitan centres of South America, as well as their instrumental position in the change of perspective from a Eurocentric appreciation of fashion to its global recalibration in terms of industrial production, consumer base and cultural specificity. However, this global perspective should not simply equate to fashion history rewritten from an integrative vantage point (Riello and McNeil: 5). Against this image of convergence, we argue that the emerging Brazilian fashion industry, while eager for European recognition of its creative innovations, is more preoccupied with the consumer demands of its own affluent middle class. The key to understanding the recent global strategy of Brazilian fashion is to be found closer to home.

Intercultural fashion history

The international promotion of Brazilian design predates the country's economic emergence over the last decade. It is worth noting that the domestic fashion industry itself did not miraculously emerge out of post-1980s globalisation. From attempts to professionalise the sector, Brazil has attempted to export its national image through its clothing industry. Paris has consistently figured as the critical arbiter of stylistic trends, the vector through which Brazilian industry could display its textiles and designs to the world. This relationship predates the more recent manifestation of Brazilian fashion designers on the Parisian stage such as Pedro Lourenço, who has been part of the ready-to-wear calendar since 2010. Lourenço made his debut at the age of twelve at the São Paulo Fashion Week, and has since garnered impressive reviews from editors for his early collections, which displayed a creative manipulation of fabric through futuristic geometric shapes. Lourenço's first Paris show in 2010 at the age of nineteen attracted the attention of a number of key fashion editors: in attendance were Carine Roitfeld, Anna Dello Russo, Virginie Mouzat, Jefferson Hack and Hamish Bowles. Against the neo-tropical imagery so skilfully blended with digital technology by Carlos Miele for international appeal, the more modernist forms of Lourenço's Spring/Summer 2013 collection referenced the saturated colours used by surrealist photographer Richard Mosse, known for his artificially modulated landscapes. Lourenço is an example of a Brazilian designer using the Parisian stage for reasons of prestige, recognition and visibility. Beyond the obvious impact on international sales, it is worth questioning who constitutes the target consumers for such collections. Is the target for an emerging Brazilian designer not more realistically the domestic consumer, access to whom is assured through the cosmopolitan cachet of Parisian recognition?

The manipulation of an archetypal French modernity for aspirational Brazilian consumers draws on a history of intercultural influence, itself part of the more generalised imagery of France circulating within Brazilian culture during the twentieth century. Paris has played a pivotal role in the international circulation of Brazilian fashion imagery. Despite its history of Portuguese colonisation Brazil has always maintained a special relationship with France, investing in the mythical importance of the capital city. France had as much indirect cultural influence on the formation of Brazilian national identity as Portugal, the coloniser whose own sixteenth-century court was itself heavily Francophile and consequently influenced by French art, language and thought in shaping its own moral codes and cultural values (Skidmore 1994: 36).

Mario Carelli has traced the history of cultural interchange between Brazil and France, emphasising the former's primitivism and exotic allure and the latter's civilisation and intellectual heritage, a problematic form of reciprocal admiration founded on a dissymmetrical power structure and a bedrock of casual stereotypes, aptly described as a sort of 'ready-to-wear of the mind' (Carelli 1993: 21). The Brazilian elites of the late nineteenth and early twentieth centuries were willing receptacles for the assimilation of a European modernity channelled through an ethnocentric gaze and the universalising tendencies of French civilisation. The transposition of metropolitan fashions was part of this larger process of cultural modernisation and national identity-formation. For example, the silhouette of the

Parisienne was imported wholesale to mid-nineteenth century Brazil including the linguistic borrowing of vernacular terms for evening jacket, corset and petticoat, used to label garments cut from imported fabrics with certain morphological adjustments made to emphasise chest and waist, despite the reluctance to tailor according to a tropical climate. This preference for French style was accentuated at the start of the twentieth century by the economic modernisation that followed the coffee boom. Economic expansion financed the launch of a Brazilian garment industry eager to edit European styles and to imitate consumer practices. An example of this was the importation of the department store, a concept that had originated in England and France in the 1830s, transposed to the expanding metropolises of South America by the chain Mappin (Andrade 2005: 181). The chain drew inspiration from the original Parisian model conceived by Aristide Boucicaut, the founder of the prototypical ladies' paradise, Le Bon Marché, in 1838. From the mid-1920s onwards the São Paulo store hosted its very own fashion shows, establishing the main metropolitan stage to display the collections of many of the influential Parisian designers of the day such as Drécoll and Patou, and in so doing served as a permanent conduit for the transmission of a European stylistic heritage.

The textile industry began a concurrent initiative, expanding the number of cotton-producing factories (Braga and Prado 2011: 116). While Europe rebuilt itself following the devastation of the First World War, a publicly bankrolled Brazilian business culture began to emerge in response to the commercial needs of an expanding domestic market. The international visibility of this emerging textile industry only developed later in the 1950s through a promotional initiative of Brazilian industrialists, who hosted extravagant private parties in France and Italy to show off their cotton production displayed on dresses worn by live models. In 1952 the textile manufacturer Companhia Progresso Industrial do Brasil (Bangu) began to host events in Brazil and abroad to generate international publicity, which is how Bangu encountered the mid-century French couturier Jacques Fath, known for his costume designs for Powell and Pressburger's film *The Red Shoes* (1948) and for his clientèle of major Hollywood stars of the postwar era. Fath agreed to host an extravagant Brazilian-themed ball at the Château de Corbeville in 1952 aimed at exhibiting cotton production displayed on the dresses worn by the guests. There was no fashion design as such on show; instead the clothing was simply perceived as a means to an end. The incentive was to publicise Brazilian fabrics through journalistic coverage of the sophisticated lifestyles of the Parisian elites, mediated through reports in newspapers belonging to the local Diários Associados press group, owned by the controversial media mogul Assis Chateaubriand – nicknamed the Brazilian Citizen Kane – whose sphere of influence spanned the clothing industry (Braga and Prado 2011: 207). The star-studded event – guests included Orson Welles and Ginger Rogers – attracted two whole convoys of artists, models and denizens of Brazilian high society. Beyond the event's inclusion in the history of postwar Parisian glamour – the star turn was Elsa Schiaparelli's spectacular arrival on horseback – the extensive press coverage in Brazil ensured a return on investment for the industrialists. The event successfully promoted tropical fibres not to the Europeans but to the Brazilian elites, who thought it demeaning to wear locally produced garments.

The stylistic sensibilities of the elites, however, were still orientated towards the traditional models of French haute couture. Dener, the prestigious imitator of haute couture, aspired to reproduce the aura of the star couturier for the Brazilian elites, editing French designs for his sophisticated public. He claimed to direct consumer tastes towards the dominant styles of haute couture in order to reflect back a specifically Brazilian image, thereby removing the stigma attached to wearing locally designed and manufactured garments. The cultural shift marked by the fashionable pop styles of the 1960s was also reflected in changes to the relationship between the Brazilian clothing industry and its French design templates. Trade between the two countries took off in the 1960s following the expansion of the French chemical company Rhodia to Brazil. Rhodia organised trade fairs and introduced synthetic fibres, publicising their advantages to receptive local consumers preoccupied with modernisation and efficiency. Rhodia essentially used these collections to communicate, touring Europe with Brazilian-themed fashion shows such as the 'Coffee Collection' presented in Paris at an exclusive function in 1960. This was followed by collections promoting 'Brazilian Nature' in 1962 and 'Brazilian Style' in 1964, both manipulating cultural identity not to sell the designs themselves but to showcase the country's manufacturing. The designs worked as pastiche copies of Parisian haute couture transposed to local fabrics, including explicit homages to Dior's New Look graphically adapted to tropical prints. These commercial operations were not primarily concerned with promoting Brazilian design to a European audience, but had the inadvertent knock-on effect of creating a national design identity based on the skilful packaging of tropical exoticism. These operations began with the presentations in Europe and were adapted to Brazil following international attention. A few select presentations in France and Italy would be rolled out months later in cities across Brazil. The story of European approval was spun as a narrative for the domestic market, thereby laying the foundations for the clothing industry to create in embryonic form a national design tradition.

Emerging designers, celebrity models and foreign ambassadors

The international promotion of the Brazilian national brand over the first decade of the 2000s follows the country's emergence as a global economic power, and its strategic visibility in the current decade ensures continuing investment in the country's infrastructure and lucrative partnerships with the local creative industries. The promotion of São Paulo Fashion Week from the late 1990s as a design platform has been crucial to this latest phase of national-global visibility, garnering intense international press interest. In 2000 Guy Trebay in *The New York Times* noted a tilt in the global fashion axis, welcoming the new wave of models and designers (Trebay 2000). In the 1990s a young generation of designers had emerged as the creative focus for the commercial fashion circuit, including labels such as Alexandre Herchcovitch and Fause Haten, both taking inspiration from street styles and urban subcultures, complemented by Lino Villaventura and Ronaldo Fraga, both drawing on traditional craftsmanship and national folklore. Fraga's idiosyncratic designs are

Figure 2.1   Fraga's runway look here combines, in one image, the myth of the forest and of football with the bamboo frame, constructed across the catwalk. From Summer 2014 collection. Copyright Ronaldo Fraga. Reproduced by courtesy of Fotosite.

rooted in a creative dialogue between the world of contemporary consumer fashion and the local socio-political realities of those artisans who craft it, his various projects aiming to generate egalitarian labour practices within the garment industry. Carlos Miele is similarly committed to fair-trade practices and collaboration with Brazil's *favelas* and indigenous communities. His eponymous label, launched in 2002, has consistently sought to blend technological innovation with traditional Brazilian handicrafts including elements of indigenous folklore transposed to the stylistic exigencies of an urban brand, which now has boutiques in New York and Paris. Surfacing in the early 1990s, Herchcovitch has also shown at the London, New York and Paris fashion weeks. His design aesthetic, however, while incorporating eclectic prints, broke radically with the more traditional cultural template of Brazilian fashion by channelling the codes of gay club culture and the urban street trends of 1990s São Paulo into a conceptual style subverting Brazilian ideals of beauty and physicality (Brandini 2009: 172–4).

Beyond the critical recognition of these individual designers, the 2000s also witnessed the visibility and celebrity of a number of high-profile catwalk models, as instrumental in promoting Brazilian fashion culture at a global level as the creative designers, industrialists and intermediaries. Coming of age following a period that popularised a 'heroin chic' norm for the shape of the fashion model, and in the midst of mass-media fixation about anorexia in the industry, Shirley Mallmann, Ana Claudia Michels, Fernanda Tavares, Jeísa Chiminazzo, Mariana Weickert and Raquel Zimmermann – who was included in *Vogue* Paris's top 30 models of the 2000s – all gained attention due to their healthy shapes and cultivated sexiness. But no Brazilian model has had the individual appeal, media coverage and commercial success of Gisele Bündchen, the most lucrative player in Brazilian global fashion, worth an estimated 250 million dollars in 2012. A German-Brazilian in origin, discovered as a teenager in the mid-1990s, Gisele is seen as the heir to the late twentieth-century prenominal super-models and was known at the height of her fame for her contract with Victoria's Secret, which raided the bank of Latin clichés, reuniting mixed ethnicity, tropical 'exoticism' and curvaceous sexiness. Early in her career *Vogue* used a black-and-white photo of Gisele to illustrate an editorial called 'The Return of the Curve' for its July 1999 issue, allegedly photo-shopping the image to augment the model's cleavage. Gisele went on to appear on a further three *Vogue* covers in 2000 alone, and in so doing launched a trend for Brazilian models.

Beyond this focus on the international profiles of celebrity models, the Brazilian clothing industry also began to brand its fashion culture more persuasively. Foreign journalists were invited to catwalk shows, to lecture and to visit boutiques on all-expenses-paid tours. An example of this common practice of industry lobbying was the late, iconic fashion editor for the *Sunday Times*, Isabella Blow, who was invited to Brazil in January 2000 to attend the São Paulo Fashion Week, at the time called *Morumbi Fashion* (Roberts 2012). With Blow allegedly cashing a cheque for 15,000 dollars for her services (Marthe 2000), the operation was deemed successful and six months later Blow was invited back along with eighteen foreign journalists to participate in a round table discussion on the international image of Brazilian fashion. Blow's function was to lend an aura of personal glamour and critical credibility to Brazilian fashion through her status as a nomadic ambassador, whose presence at such events led to increased foreign press attention.

The emergence of a new model for Brazilian fashion

Founded in the early 1960s the Brazilian Textile and Apparel Industry Association (ABIT) is the main sponsor of Brazilian designers and clothing companies, supporting the sustainable development of Brazilian textiles and essential crafts. The association plays a central role in professionalising the sector, including the launch of trend forecasting agencies, fashion education and international PR initiatives. The huge scale of the domestic market explains the rationale behind such international promotion. According to ABIT/Texbrasil, the fashion industry constituted 5.5 percent of Brazilian GDP in 2012. The domestic market could therefore be self-sufficient without fashion labels needing to sell abroad at all. Brazilian fashion brands still operate, however, according to the same commercial logic as Rhodia a half-century ago: Western recognition is not intended to lift global sales. Rather the cultural prestige of a strategically positioned boutique in London, New York or Paris implies recognition, a value that supposedly legitimises the label in the eyes of domestic consumers. Local labels now face stiff competition from the luxury global fashion brands that are investing massively in Brazil and from the arrival of design-savvy European high street brands such as Topshop or Zara, which are positioning themselves as selective mid-range brands in the Brazilian market.

The economic reason for the relatively modest exportation of Brazilian fashion is that the production costs are prohibitively high, making the final product excessively expensive for international consumers. Herchcovitch can be as expensive as Prada or Gucci, minus the global brand appeal, therefore out-pricing the local designer from the international market. Prohibitively high import-export taxes represent a further obstacle for the long-term global sustainability of Brazilian trade. Take, for example, the urban sports label Osklen, whose fashion-forward profile has been hyped in recent years. The label's founder, Oskar Metsavaht, began in 1989 with leisure and sportswear collections, before turning to beachwear in the 1990s and luxury ready-to-wear in 2003 with the launch of the Osklen Collection, an urban style with touches of surf culture channelled through an ecological lens. The local fashion media mention Osklen as if he were widely celebrated in Europe and the USA. His collections are found in a handful of department stores and luxury multi-brand boutiques and the label does own stores

Figure 2.2   Osklen's outfit blends the straw top (typical Brazilian natural material) with the Brazilian cultural cliché of the beach print on the skirt. From Summer 2013 collection. Copyright Osklen.

in Italy, Japan and the USA; but in sales terms this is relatively marginal. Being visible at L'Eclaireur in Paris is only a minimal entry into the global luxury market considering that Osklen's overall international sales account for a mere 5 percent of the label's total turnover (Viturino 2011).

Brazilian fashion designers and brands are torn between the power of the cultural legacy, heritage and craftsmanship of the European tradition – with its haute couture model of apprenticeship and succession – and the 'American' mythology of the self-taught designer breaking free from the constraints of European tradition. Working outside the apprentice model whereby a designer would gain experience by working for an illustrious fashion house, 'the new Brazilian fashion is not established in the couture tradition, with its references to high art, but derives its aesthetic from local culture and ethnicity' (Brandini 2009: 165). True, but the value of international approval, measured through geographical positioning and press visibility, nonetheless locks the Brazilian consumer mentality into a neo-imperial relationship of cultural dependency with its global partners.

Since the start of the global economic recession in 2008, there has been some hope that the emerging economies of the BRICS would decouple and continue to expand despite the downturn experienced elsewhere – a hope undermined by the reported slowdown of both the Brazilian and Chinese economies in 2012. Global luxury brands are nevertheless prioritising the BRICS as key expanding markets to underwrite and revitalise the Western design houses. To achieve this goal the luxury conglomerates are investing massively in the consumer potential of Brazil. Despite the barrier of fiscal protectionism, the big-name fashion brands are moving in en masse. The luxury shopping malls of Cidade Jardim or JK Iguatemi in São Paulo host the majority of the recognisable super-brands, illustrating the decision to plug the luxury gap before the full emergence of local design. Brazil has understood the shift in global power and is staking out a more strategic position on the fashion map – not simply as a consumer of global brands or as a manufacturer of textiles but as a creative force in itself. The challenge is how to define a stylistic grammar adapted to the 'new' economic order while responding to the demands of the expanding domestic market.

Design, the creative backbone of the industry, now constitutes the main focus of attention in Brazilian fashion culture. Designer brands are torn between the model of cross-cultural exchange with European heritage and the 'American' model of fashion empires. Although the new Brazilian fashion is embedded in local forms of popular culture and ethnic specificity, the commercial value of cross-cultural interaction and European recognition is not to be underestimated in the domestic positioning and promotion of Brazilian fashion. External approval is still seen as necessary for the domestic market, conceived in the terms of marketing discourse as immature – however problematic the use of this linguistic imperialism to qualify emerging markets. Nevertheless, the ideal of a creative and dynamic Brazil shared by millions of Brazilians – an image the nation seeks actively to export – still requires a global stamp of approval for national consumers to believe in the economic miracle, the term used in the past to denote periods of growth such as the 1970s, a period of parallel European economic 'stagflation'. Ultimately, Europe is used strategically as an adoring mirror for Brazilian fashion to reflect back its own self-promotional ideal to domestic consumers.

References

Amado, Gilberto (1954) *Mocidade no Rio e primeira viagem à Europa*, Rio de Janerio: José Olympio.

Andrade, Rita (2005) 'Mappin Stores: adding an English Touch to the São Paulo Fashion Scene', in Regina A. Root (ed.), *The Latin American Fashion Reader*, Oxford: Berg, pp. 176–87.

Appadurai, Arjun (1996) *Modernity at Large: Cultural Dimensions of Globalization*, Minneapolis: The University of Minnesota Press.

Braga, João and Prado, André Luis do (2011) *História da Moda no Brasil – das Influências às Autorreferências*, São Paulo: Disal Edita/Pyxis Editorial.

Brandini, Valéria (2009) 'Fashion Brazil: South American Style, Culture and Industry', in Eugenia Paulicelli and Hazel Clark (eds), *The Fabric of Cultures: Fashion, Identity and Globalization*, Abingdon and New York: Routledge, pp. 164–76.

Carelli, Mario (1993) *Cultures croisées: histoire des échanges culturels entre la France et le Brésil de la découverte aux temps modernes*, Paris: Nathan.

Harvey, David (1989) *The Condition of Postmodernity: An Enquiry into the Origins of Cultural Change*, Oxford: Blackwell.

Inda, Jonathan Xavier and Rosaldo, Renato (2008) 'Tracking Global Flows', in Jonathan Xavier Inda and Renato Rosaldo (eds), *The Anthropology of Globalization: A Reader* (second edition), Oxford: Blackwell, pp. 3–46.

Jameson, Fredric (1998) 'Notes on Globalization as a Philosophical Issue', in Fredric Jameson and Masao Miyoshi (eds), *The Cultures of Globalization*, Durham and London: Duke University Press, pp. 54–77.

Marthe, Marcelo (2000) 'A lobista da moda', *Veja Magazine*, 15 November.

Paulicelli, Eugenia and Clark, Hazel (2009) 'Introduction', in Eugenia Paulicelli and Hazel Clark (eds), *The Fabric of Cultures: Fashion, Identity, and Globalization*, Abingdon and New York: Routledge, pp. 1–11.

Rabine, Leslie W. (2010) 'Globalization', in Valerie Steele (ed.), *The Berg Companion to Fashion*, London: Berg, pp. 372–4.

Riello, Giorgio and McNeil, Peter (eds) (2010) *The Fashion History Reader: Global Perspectives*, Abingdon and New York: Routledge.

Roberts, Michael (2012) 'Brazilian Blow Out', *The Wall Street Journal*, 15 June.

Skidmore, Thomas E. (1994) *O Brasil visto de fora*, Rio de Janeiro: Paz e Terra.

Trebay, Guy (2000), 'Big Models, Big Brands: The Year in Fashion; The Noise from Brazil', *The New York Times*, 26 December.

Viturino, Robson (2011) 'A nova multinacional brasileira', *Época Negócios*, 31 January.

Chapter 3

Clare M. Wilkinson-Weber

INDIA AND FASHION'S NEW GEOGRAPHY

THE PROFUSION OF DESIGNER COLLECTIONS, brand-label
outlets, red-carpet gowns and celebrity endorsements in Indian print and
virtual media create the impression of a well-rooted, self-confident fashion industry.
Strikingly, many of these phenomena had their beginnings in a commercial environment that emerged as recently as the late 1980s and early 1990s, when the Indian
government set India on a new development course by embracing so-called
'liberalisation' (Deshpande 2003; Mazumdar 2007: xxi; Vedwan 2007: 665; Virdi
2003: 201). Relaxing import restraints and removing obstacles to the growth of
private enterprise led to seismic changes in production, marketing and retailing.
An energetic fashion industry sprang up amidst innovations in telecommunications,
media and finance, nurturing as well as being nurtured by advertising and marketing
that tap into the same global flows and currents that swirl around other parts
of the world. Among middle- and upper-class consumers, there are clear signs of
the impact of new styles and conventions of dress, particularly in metropolitan
centres.

However, the contrary assumption, that fashion is a new intrusion of external
forces and trends into the subcontinent, is equally mistaken. Fashion — whether
we are referring to the making and dissemination of novel styles of dress and
appearance, or the varieties of self-making that have become part and parcel of
modernity, 'fashionable' or otherwise — has been part of Indian life for decades.
Indigenous and foreign styles alike have participated in this world of sartorial devices
and distinctions, the indigenous clothes drawing on associations and meanings that
have their own discrete history. As elsewhere, dress in the subcontinent continues
to be a powerful signifier concerning gender, region and status — and in the particular case of Indian Hindus — caste. Additionally, cloth is a transactional medium
par excellence, a necessary component of major moments of social exchange (such

as marriage), and a vector for the movement of power and influence between individuals (Bayly 1986; Cohn 1989).

The current scene is indelibly marked by the experience of colonialism. Early seventeenth-century British traders encountered a set of sartorial regimes that included numerous styles of stitched clothing introduced from Southwest and Central Asia, many reproduced in portraits of nobility in and around the Mughal Empire's territories. Some early colonial officers enthusiastically adopted the dress of their hosts, literally fashioning themselves in the dress of the Indian notables they sought to emulate. At the same time, the cloth, clothes and accessories they imported were being adapted to indigenous exchange circuits. As the British grip on power strengthened, the imperative to set the rulers apart from the ruled in, among other things, dress, abolished the earlier ecumenism. To this day, a line is drawn between what is Western and what is Indian. Fashion, conceived in these terms, has been a crucial element in debates before and after Indian Independence in 1947 about the tastes and outward appearance of the 'authentic Indian'.

In the realm of production, however, a more complicated picture emerges. Makers of 'traditional' fabrics and forms of dress have struggled in trying circumstances, despite moral support from champions of clothing that is 'genuinely' Indian. Meanwhile other producers – factory workers, independent tailors, embroiderers, weavers, dyers – have been making Western as well as Indian clothing for some time, specialising in one or the other perhaps, but largely eschewing the moral arguments that crop up around them. In a supreme irony, a new lifeline thrown to India's handicrafts is now coming from an eclectic fashion world that embodies much of what nationalist philosophy spurned in the run-up to and aftermath of Independence.

Conundrums of dress and identity

The impact of colonialism ideologically and economically upon textiles was tremendous, as was its influence on standards of dress. By the end of the nineteenth century, the most educated and well-off Indian men had adopted suits, ties and so forth for public activities, and over succeeding decades Western dress established itself as an 'aspirational category' for men across a range of regions and social positions. A contrary swing towards rejecting and devaluing the clothes and commodities of the British took hold with the rise of the Independence movement. M. K. Gandhi propelled the message of *swadeshi* (home industry / self-determination) forward, taking up hand spinning, and settling upon a short *dhoti* (a wrapped and draped garment for the lower half of the body, worn by men) and simple shawl as a form of Indian dress that persuasively captured the layered meanings of the nationalist struggle (Bean 1989; Tarlo 1996). Nehru and others settled on a compromise of *kurta pajama* or *churidar* (a long shirt with loose or tight trousers), with a *sherwani* (a tailored coat that reached to the knees or below) or waistcoat, which kept all the component parts of a suit only using an Indian silhouette and *khadi* or homespun cloth for fabric (Tarlo 1996).

Most Indian women, no matter their social position or religion, stuck to familiar garments, such as *saris* (a single piece of cloth, wrapped and draped around the body, with or without a blouse or *choli*), variations on the basic theme of blouse (*kameez*) and pants (*salwar*) or *gharara* (voluminous trousers) accompanied by a scarf (*dupatta*), and *lehengas*, *ghagharas* (varieties of long skirt) with *odhnis* (scarf-like material used to cover the head and upper body). Unlike men's clothes, women's clothes have always carried the distinct burden of signalling moral and marital status, and thus resist change: in the twenty-first century, the vast majority of Indian women in cities, towns and villages continue to wear clothes marked as 'Indian'. The sari, in particular, acquired heightened status among anti-colonialists as the exemplary dress of uncorrupted (and Hinduised) India, with the Indian woman transformed into the guardian of hearth, home and traditional values. A certain standardisation of the sari, prompted in part by artist Raja Ravi Varma's paintings of women and goddesses, culminated in the *nivi* sari, at first regarded as the height of fashion, now so ubiquitous in its uses as middle-of-the-road style and corporate uniform as to be almost banal (Banerjee and Miller 2003).

The thrust of nationalist ideology with respect to material consumption was towards constraint and self-discipline. However, the handicraft sector was one avenue through which enjoyment of clothing could be legitimately expressed. For several decades, central and state governments played a key role in small-scale textile and embroidery industries, channelling goods into emporia aimed at tourists and middle-class shoppers. Side by side with the government, NGOs (non-governmental organisations) meshed a social agenda of empowerment with the production of craft objects whose appeal rested on their embodiment of Indian 'tradition' (Greenough 1995; Wilkinson-Weber 2004).

In spite of a distrust of 'fashion' as ephemeral and inauthentic, officially endorsed policies of craft preservation and a devotion to native textiles ultimately produced their own fashion market, sutured to an ideology of nationalism by the compelling theme of craft revival and preservation (Tarlo 1996; Wilkinson-Weber 2004). Such objects were marketed as touchstones of Indian heritage and authenticity, and incidentally provided the escape valve for a fashion sensibility by rendering it morally acceptable. The example par excellence is arguably 'ethnic chic', a design sensibility that came to the fore in the 1980s and has reached its commercial apogee in the present-day Fab India chain. It comprises Indian-style clothing in a distinctly 'peasant' vein, typically intensely dyed cottons, along with chunky accessories. The designers that presided over ethnic chic and orchestrated its production and marketing appear, with hindsight, to be the forerunners of the far more numerous and diversified fashion designers of the present day (Tarlo 1996). But to find the most powerful source of novel clothes, fabrics and styles in modern India, we must turn to film.

The contrariness of film

Popular film has existed in India almost as long as anywhere else in the world. There are several centres of the film industry throughout the country, of which the two largest are Chennai (formerly Madras) and Mumbai (Bombay) (Dickey and Dudrah 2011; Rajadhyaksha and Willemen 1999). While Hindi-language films made in Mumbai have the greatest reach within India and beyond, it is important to realise that film across the subcontinent influences the dress and behaviours of its audiences.

The leaders of the Independence movement dismissed film in part because of its frivolity and in part because of its uncomfortably close relationship to a foreign-tinged modernity. It did not, in short, participate in a version of 'tradition' that anti-colonial and post-Independence authority was inclined to accept. The film industry was, however, without doubt one of the main conduits for forms of modernity to reach a vast cross-section of the Indian public. The costuming of its early stars was extravagant and diverse: saris mixed with evening dresses, 'Oriental' styles, and almost always suits for men (Bhaumik 2005; Ramamurthy 2008). Decade after decade, film remained the most popular and widely accessed source of all that was new in dress, from assorted Western styles to reinterpretations of Indian ones.

Filmmakers were hardly indifferent to the nationalist cause; in fact, support for Independence was very strong in the film community. The portrayal of women in films shifted during the 1930s in large part to coincide with nationalist values, with female characters split into virtuous, sari-clad women (the normative heroine) and modern, audacious 'vamps' in Western clothing who materialised their distance from the heroine through allusion to open sexuality and contempt for authority (Bhaumik 2005; Dwyer 2000; Ramamurthy 2008). Heroes, on the other hand, were habitually dressed in Western styles and took on the task of mediating modernity for audiences via their ability to embody all the moral expectations of virtuous masculinity while wearing foreign clothes. A series of heroes – Dev Anand, Shammi Kapoor, Raaj Kumar, Rishi Kapoor and Rajesh Khanna to name a few – premiered several distinct styles for Indian audiences: smartly cut suits, tuxedo jackets, drainpipe trousers and polo shirts, sweaters and collarless shirts. In contrast, the villain had to speak to the deepest anxieties about non-Indian influence by pushing the boundaries of acceptable style to its limits. By the 1960s, villains were unambiguous devotees of Western clothes, with the best-cut suits in sometimes striking colours.

As clear as the division between hero and villain and heroine and vamp appears and indeed is still believed to be, in fact the tensions and transactions between misbehaviour and virtue have often been extremely complex. As the vehicle for these interpretive currents which both support and occasionally offer a counterpoint to the dominant narrative, fashion is at its most effective. Western clothes betoken visual and sensual pleasure, a willingness to embrace a light-hearted and youthful modernity – if animated by appropriately pliant and obedient bodies. If those bodies are, instead, unruly, then the clothes by extension become disruptive and destabilising. The shameless and often ruthless hedonism embodied by the villain and vamp are easily recognisable as the kind of enchantment with Westernisation that has until recently run counter to dominant narratives of the nation. In contrast, the fashionably dressed hero and heroine exist in the borderlands where morality and decadence meet. The hero must demonstrate the stability of authentic values by overcoming the villain, a feat that is occasionally but not always marked in a shift in dress toward more Indian forms. In contrast, the heroine staked her position on a reorientation of youthful indulgence towards a more demure and conventional familial and social position, marked by assuming Indian clothes at the end of the film – typically a sari. I should note that this is by no means a universal eventuality; it is, though, so thoroughly understood by filmmakers and audiences that it might as well be.

For heroines, a further complication issues from the fact that even Indian clothes tend towards the spectacular in Hindi films. The stereotype of the older, respectable matron in a sombre sari is well known. Heroines, however, may wear saris in unusual fabrics with offbeat designs. They model – in every sense – innovative styles of choli (sleeveless, backless and so on) and play up the unmistakably erotic associations of the sari via manipulation of its drape and fall. The tight, body-hugging choli, customised to produce the deepest cleavage and largest swelling of the breasts, is the starting point (the expert tailor who can create the most tight-fighting and amply padded cholis is much in demand in the industry). The sari then may be wrapped and draped to offer the maximal view of the torso, chest and arms. A similar set of operations goes on with respect to ghaghara cholis, popular in dance scenes. Many so-called 'item numbers' in which specialist dancers or stars in cameo performances are at the centre of spectacular song and dance pieces, employ such costumes. The 'filmi' (neologism meaning glitzy, or overdone, as would be expected of a costume in a film) sari, or the 'filmi' ghaghara choli, which simultaneously expose the heroine's flesh while sculpting the portions that are concealed, dovetails perfectly with dances in which the heroine's body is set into delirious motion.

The relaxation of dress codes among the wealthiest and most worldly Indians has led to a freer adoption of edgy film styles – be these daring saris and ghaghara cholis, or cocktail dresses and evening gowns from designer collections that would have been almost unthinkable a few decades ago. Wearing jeans, tee-shirts, tank-tops, skirts and so forth goes almost without note in contemporary films, while comparably dressed individuals are more apparent than ever in certain metropolitan areas. But conservatism is very much alive and well among the vast majority of Indian women, and one can rarely go wrong in referencing the indecency of Western clothes. The star who makes a public announcement about refusing to wear a bikini will rarely be heard to complain about a skimpy sari (see recent stories in BBC India FM 2008; bollywoodlife.com 2013; Indo-Asian News Service 2012). In another example of conservatism, larger numbers of Muslim women and men have been re-adopting and modifying various forms of 'Islamic dress', replacing the Indian styles of burqas, prayer caps and sherwanis with styles prevalent in the Gulf States, and increasingly fashionable among Muslims worldwide (Tarlo 2010).

Glamour and grit

Films of the 1960s and 1970s delighted in showing the 'modern' settings in which fashion and vice were uniquely commingled: hotels, nightclubs, luxury flats (Mazumdar 2007). But cinema has not shied away from showing villages and crowded *bastis* (urban tenements) or the nondescript homes of civil servants when needed. The seamier underbelly of modernity – corruption, smuggling, violence and entrenched poverty – came to the surface of films in the 1970s, illustrated by clothes that appealed to a more demotic aesthetic: denim jeans and jackets, unbuttoned, wide-lapel shirts (Dwyer 2000). Heroes from this point on were more likely to be dressed in casual clothes, presaging a shift towards more youthful protagonists (or at least, to actors pretending to be youthful). Menswear stores and local tailors were still the first port of call for stitching shirts, fitted trousers and jackets, but several items were bought off the rack, in India perhaps, but stars frequently got ready-mades abroad.

Heroines underwent a rather different transition. Far from the pugnacious, anti-hero, it was the 'college girl' that began to take shape – usually a privileged, sometimes pampered, young woman with a broad-minded view of fashion. Zeenat Aman and Parveen Babi, two stars credited with shifting the moral fulcrum upon which heroines' clothing and lifestyle choices rested, had careers as fashion models before entering film. Modelling entailed a different working orientation to the body and bodily display than was the norm among female actors. Already both heroes and heroines had graced the pages of film fan magazines such as *Stardust* or *Filmfare* in film stills or specially staged photo spreads for decades. These images brought daring and novel clothes to the sustained gaze and contemplation of audiences; for instance, photographs from 1980s magazines show 'big hair', loose, thigh-length tops, and peg pants that bear at least a passing resemblance to the contemporary fashions in Europe and the USA. However, a professional background in the fashion business was an entirely different affair. By the 1980s and 1990s, a path from modelling or beauty pageants to film was more or less well trodden, with stars such as Aishwarya Rai, Sushmita Sen and Priyanka Chopra making their names this way.[1]

Figure 3.1   Film star Aishwarya Rai is featured on a billboard advertising the luxury watch brand Longines. Film stars have considerable cachet as the 'faces' of new brands on the Indian retail scene. Photograph taken by Aseem Chandaver.

Fashion unbound

After the Indian government effectively welcomed consumer capitalism in the 1990s, the country began to replace the old ideals of patriotic self-restraint with ones of (equally) patriotic expenditure (Deshpande 2003; Mazzarella 2003). With respect to fashion, the biggest shock was a flood of brand-label clothing, accessories and beauty products and services. Over time these extended to high-end brands that of late have been finding their way into films – for example, Christian Dior, Hermès and Salvatore Ferragamo (entertainment.oneindia 2013; *The Telegraph* 2013). Film narratives meanwhile underwent a shift towards portraying the lives of affluent and Westernised Indian youth as global citizens well versed in the ways of the world. Many scholars and critics have noted sardonically that mere decades after the apogee of the debauched albeit well-dressed villain, the hero had appropriated his dissolute consumerism – heroism and villainy have converged in a 'good life' that un-ironically fuses commodity capitalism with regressive social conformity (e.g. Kaarsholm and Bisvasa 2002; Mazumdar 2007; Dwyer and Patel 2002).

Adjustments in how film costume design was accomplished, and by whom, facilitated a seamless and mutually reinforcing relationship between film and a rapidly growing fashion world. Stars hiring their own personal designers, as opposed to having one designer for the entire film, had been a given in film since the mid-twentieth century. Essentially subordinating the design demands of the film to the demands of the actor, this arrangement enabled the fine-tuning of star identities around certain styles, but rarely translated into a distinct fashion career for the designer him- or herself. This changed in the 1990s when a clutch of designers with a deeper immersion in fashion retailing and design entered the scene. Anna Singh, Manish Malhotra, Rocky S., Surily Goel and others sustained parallel film and fashion careers, and saw their key contribution as the introduction of a more refined and globally aware fashion sense to the movie industry.

The demand for show-stopping outfits remained, but added to it now was 'styling' – the name given in Bollywood to the practice of composing a costume out of off-the-rack components. The much-vaunted professional ideal of using costume to construct convincing characters could thus be aligned with acknowledgement and use of the flourishing retail market. Until more brands, in greater quantity, entered India, designers were forced to launch shopping expeditions to Dubai, Bangkok, London and New York, to make the most of richer retail environments. Nevertheless, a template was now established for future costuming practice.

Designers then capitalised on the power of stardom and reach of film to build awareness of their own brands. Their names appeared in the film magazine photo spreads as stylists or designers, and they could get their heroes and heroines to model their fashion collections on the runway or in advertisements. At the same time, stars augmented their own value as both assets and commodities by taking on product endorsements. This was not a new phenomenon: the silent movie star Devika Rani advertised Palmolive (Ramamurthy 2008); generation upon generation of heroines pitched for Lux soap. These activities, though, pale in comparison to the product portfolios of contemporary stars, including Kareena Kapoor, who was estimated to be earning 50 crore (approximately nine million dollars at time of writing) from product endorsements in 2013 alone.

If in the 1990s it was expected that a model would try acting, so now actors turn models at the drop of a hat, not just in the familiar environs of a magazine or newspaper, but as a 'show-stopper' – the final act of a runway show, or as a 'red carpet' clotheshorse. Stars in effect are the binding 'agent' of multiple marketing strategies – global brands promoted via product placement and endorsements; and local designers via photo spreads and special event wear. Unlike North America and Europe, where the ecology of celebrity is more diverse, film stars in India have few competitors. To date, the possibility of the star over-whelming the brand has yet to outweigh the huge benefits that come with their recruitment. Since apparel endorsements showcase and popularise brands that were almost entirely absent from the retail scene a few decades ago, stars play a critical role in ushering the public into particular paths of consumption.

Justification for these marketing strategies comes from clear evidence for the copying of screen costumes: popular print media accounts, as well as personal testimony by both tailors and film viewers attest to the eagerness with which customers have sought to model their own sartorial choices on those they have seen on screen. Men could pick and choose from collar styles, colours and cuts of shirts and suits. Women meanwhile stuck mostly to Indian styles. Sadhana and Sharmila Tagore's churidar kurtas in the 1965 film *Waqt* were such a sensation that women paid for their tailors to see the film, the better to make a copy (Athaiya 2010). In other instances, a particular colour or design in a sari would sweep the shops and shrewd tailors learned to copy an outfit worn by a star in a new release in anticipation of demand. The newest alternative, with more time and attention going into pre-production and marketing, includes collections designed by the costume designer him or herself, or put together by a brand name outfitter, and offered within selected retail settings.

Fashion in place

In India's major cities and towns, new retail spaces have shot up side-by-side with the mainstays of India's world of apparel – sari shops, roadside stalls and tailoring businesses. More and more global brand-label stores are seen in metropolitan streets and marketplaces – Levis, Wrangler, Mango, Benetton, Lacoste and Guess, among many others. Alongside them can be found revitalised brands such as Provogue, Flying Machine and Reliance Trends, which belong to large Indian conglomerates. Inevitably, the marketplace is also host to a plethora of fakes – some of them extremely crude, others indistinguishable from the 'real' thing. Evidence of various industrial synergies are also apparent in the launch of *Vogue* India, *GQ*, *Elle* and several other high-profile magazines, as well as internet news and gossip sites featuring fashion images and stories.

One should not assume, though, that the intense and spectacular retail and production spheres in India's metropolises are all there is to fashion in the subcontinent. Assumptions about the fundamental conservatism of India's villagers in matters of dress persist among urbanites, but in reality rural styles have changed markedly in the past several decades (Tarlo 1996). True, one will not find some of the most outré fashions of the city in the village, even among the wealthiest

Figure 3.2   An open air market in suburban Mumbai. All manner of cheap shoes, Indian apparel, and accessories can be bought here. Note the sport shoes and shirts on men, and the preference for Indian clothing of most women in this photograph, as well as hybrid styles in which leggings and skinny jeans can be paired with long *kamiz*, or Indian-style 'tunics'. Photograph taken by Clare M. Wilkinson-Weber.

families, and transformation in rural dress may not necessarily concern the style and silhouette of clothing. More often it entails choices of fabric, the occasions at which certain kinds of outfits can be worn, and the proportion of ready-mades and urban-sourced garments compared to those that originate in the village itself.

Outright copying of film costume or of urban styles glimpsed on trips to the city has not always been possible, owing to the greater constraints on what is considered appropriate in the village, as well as villagers' limited means. Wadley (2008), for example, notes that it is only the more privileged members of rural society who can buy several choices of outfit, reminding us that fashion as 'self-making' depends critically on having enough clothes so that one can actually discern and anticipate various constitutive possibilities. The same problem of course besets the urban poor, who remain beyond the reach, and thus beyond the interest of the fashion industry.

Fashioning India

The commercial and cultural ramifications of a vibrant fashion industry are many. As more designers take the opportunity to create seasonal collections and film ensembles, so they provide more items for shop-owners to reproduce and sell to middle-class buyers. Complex questions of intellectual property, ownership of brand names and so on are pushed to the fore as more designers and entrepreneurs at all levels enter the fashion industry. No longer is it a straightforward matter to copy a dress seen in a designer's collection and put it on an actor; conversely, the unhindered reproduction of favourite film costumes – once tolerated, even celebrated – is beginning to seem like a lost commercial opportunity (Wilkinson-Weber 2010).

A crop of filmmakers in the 2000s have set store by bringing to the screen characters whose clothes allude more to an observed reality 'out there' than in years past. 'Ordinary' characters often bear a more than passing resemblance to designers themselves, or their assistants, meaning that the quotidian experience of urban consumption can be fruitfully invoked to craft 'realistic' costumes. Designers such as Niharika Khan, Mandira Shukla, Manoshi Nath and Rishi Sharma, Shahnaz Vahanvaty, and perhaps the most well-known, Arjun Bhasin, tend to use the new wealth of costume resources to dress characters that do not so much pioneer new looks as animate them more intensively.

In the twenty-first century, most dynamic fashion designers now draw inspiration from fashion innovations in Europe, the Americas and Asia, as well as the very same handcrafted textiles and crafts celebrated by adherents of the older, Gandhian model of policy and development. Designers have co-opted some of this same rhetoric, professing their commitment to 'reviving' crafts that, at a conservative estimate, have been targets of 'revival' every generation for over 100 years.[2] A market for expensive original designs has inspired some breathtaking collaborations between designers and artisans. With the quality of goods for the tourist market pitched at a consistently passable but not outstanding level, the remaining outlets for bravura craftsmanship are personal patronage of the well-off, top-drawer couture and prêt lines, and expensive film costumes – far from what the nationalist boosters of handicrafts imagined.[3] The majority of designers like to devote a portion of their work to interpretations of Indian costume, specifically for trousseaux costing in the millions of rupees. There are also designers such as Sabyasachi Mukherjee who have built their reputation imparting intensified fashion allusions to 'traditional' items such as saris and even using archaic silhouettes from India's dress history.

As for film, the burden of showcasing the new is shifting from the screen to the red carpet, much as observers have noted in America and Europe (Church Gibson 2011). Television, with its preference for striking but fundamentally conservative styles, is now cited as a more potent contemporary dictator of fashion, at least among older women who are among the most devoted TV watchers. It is, though, rare for TV programmes to attract the kind of budget and design talent that films still command, and for this reason film retains its privileged position as the ultimate arbiter of what should be worn, how it is to be worn, and what the entailments of such embodiments are likely to be. As the middle and upper classes become more familiar with these materials, and confident with the practices and forms of knowledge essential to being a competent 'fashioner' of the self, it remains to be seen if and how film can retain its significance as the fashion 'interpreter' for the Indian public.

Notes

1   Men may also parlay modelling into acting – two examples are John Abraham and Arjun Rampal.
2   Craft industries are historically and organisationally far more diverse than much literature lets on. Craft industries such as leather-working, textile weaving, jewellery-making and so on changed markedly in the latter half of the nineteenth century and early twentieth century and never conformed to an ideal of dedicated artisans making finest quality products (Roy 1999).
3   Outside India, designers in diasporic communities inject South Asian sensibilities into fashion markets around them (e.g. Bhachu 2004).

References

Athaiya, Bhanu Rajodadhye. 2010. *The Art of Costume Design*. HarperCollins.

Banerjee, Mukulika, and Daniel Miller. 2003. *The Sari*. Oxford: New York.

Bayly, C. A. 1986. 'The Origins of Swadeshi (Home Industry): Cloth and Indian Society, 1700–1930', in A. Appadurai (ed.) *The Social Life of Things: Commodities in Cultural Perspective*, New York: Cambridge University Press, pp. 285–322.

BBC IndiaFM. 2008. 'Ayesha Takia Won't Wear a Bikini for Hollywood.' www.entertainment.oneindia.in/bollywood/gupshup/2008/ayesha-takia-no-bikini-080108.html.

Bean, Susan S. 1989. 'Gandhi and Khadi, the Fabric of Independence,' in *Cloth and Human Experience*, Annette B. Weiner and Jane Schneider (eds), Washington, DC: Smithsonian Institution Press, pp. 355–76.

Bhachu, P. 2004. *Dangerous Designs: Asian Women Fashion, the Diaspora Economies*. New York: Routledge.

Bhaumik, K. 2005. 'Sulochana: Clothes, Stardom and Gender in Early Indian Cinema,' in *Fashioning Film Stars: Dress, Culture, Identity*. New York: Routledge, pp. 87–97.

bollywoodlife.com. 2013. 'Diana Penty: I'll Never Wear a Bikini on Screen! – Bollywood News & Gossip, Movie Reviews, Trailers & Videos at Bollywoodlife.com.' Accessed 16 September 2013. www.bollywoodlife.com/news-gossip/diana-penty-ill-never-wear-a-bikini-on-screen/.

Church Gibson, Pamela. 2011. *Fashion and Celebrity Culture*. Berg Publishers.

Cohn, Bernard S. 1989. 'Cloth, clothes, and Colonialism: India in the Nineteenth Century,' in *Cloth and Human Experience*, Annette B. Weiner and Jane Schneider (eds), Washington, DC: Smithsonian Institution Press, pp. 303–54.

Deshpande, Satish. 2003. *Contemporary India: A Sociological View*. Viking.

Dickey, Sara, and Rajinder Dudrah (eds) 2011. *South Asian Cinemas: Widening the Lens*. Routledge.

Dwyer, Rachel. 2000. 'Bombay Ishtyle', in *Fashion Cultures*, S. Bruzzi and P. Church Gibson (eds), New York: Routledge, pp. 178–90.

Dwyer, Rachel and Divya, Patel. 2002. *Cinema India: the Visual Culture of Hindi Film*. New Brunswick, New Jersey: Rutgers University Press.

entertainment.oneindia. 2013. 'International Brands Tie up with Aisha.' Entertainment.oneindia.in. Accessed 27 March. www.entertainment.oneindia.in/bollywood/news/2010/international-brand-aisha-200710.html.

Greenough, Paul. 1995. 'Nation, Economy, and Tradition Displayed: The Indian Crafts Museum, New Delhi', in Carol A. Breckenridge (ed.) *Consuming Modernity: Public Culture in a South Asian World*. Minneapolis: University of Minnesota Press, pp. 216–48.

Indo-Asian News Service. 2012. 'Sonakshi Sinha Says No to Bikini', *The Times Of India*, May 23 edition. www.articles.timesofindia.indiatimes.com/2012–05–23/news-interviews/31813932_1_sonakshi-sinha-bikini-vidya-balan.

Kaarsholm, P. and Bisvasa, M. 2002. *City Flicks: Cinema, Urban Worlds and Modernities in India and Beyond*. Roskilde, Denmark: Graduate School, International Development Studies, Roskilde University.

Maskiell, Michelle. 1999. 'Embroidering the Past: Phulkari Textiles and Gendered Work as "Tradition" and "Heritage" in Colonial and Contemporary Punjab', *The Journal of Asian Studies* 58 (2) (May): 361.

Mazumdar, Ranjani. 2007. *Bombay Cinema: An Archive of the City*. 1st edn. University of Minnesota Press.

Mazzarella, W. 2003. *Shoveling Smoke: Advertising and Globalization in Contemporary India*. Durham: Duke University Press.

Rajadhyaksha, A. and Willemen, P. 1999. *Encyclopaedia of Indian Cinema*. Vol. New rev. London: British Film Institute.

Ramamurthy, Priti. 2008. 'All-Consuming Nationalism: The Indian Modern Girl in the 1920s and 30s', in *The Modern Girl Around the World*. Durham, NC: Duke University Press.

Roy, Tirthankar. 1999. *Traditional Industry in the Economy of Colonial India*. Cambridge University Press.

Tarlo, E. 1996. *Clothing Matters: Dress and Identity in India*. Chicago, IL: University of Chicago Press.

—— 2010. *Visibly Muslim: Fashion, Politics, Faith*. First Edition. Bloomsbury Academic.

The Telegraph. 2013. 'Five Fashionable Things from Zindagi Na Milegi Dobara', accessed 27 March. www.telegraphindia.com/1110723/jsp/entertainment/story_14275325.jsp.

Vedwan, N. 2007. 'Pesticides in Coca-Cola and Pepsi: Consumerism, Brand Image, and Public Interest in a Globalizing India', *Cultural Anthropology* 22 (4): 659–84.

Virdi, J. 2003. *The Cinematic Imagination: Indian Popular Films as Social History*. New Brunswick, NJ: London: Rutgers University Press.

Wadley, Susan S. 2008. 'Clothing the Female Body: Education, Social Change and Fashion in Rural India', in *Wife, Mother, Widow: Exploring Women's Lives in Northern India*.

Wilkinson-Weber, C. M. 2004. 'Women, Work and the Imagination of Craft in South Asia', *Contemporary South Asia* 13 (3): 287–306.

—— 2010. 'From Commodity to Costume: Productive Consumption in the Production of Bollywood Film "Looks"', *Journal of Material Culture* 15 (1): 1–28.

Chapter 4

Armida de la Garza and
Peng Ding

A NEW FASHION CAPITAL
Shanghai

I S SHANGHAI A FUTURE FASHION CAPITAL? In 2006, David
Gilbert answered this question with a tentative 'no'. He cited as the main reasons
the decline of world fashion capitals in general, which he traced to 'the precise
geopolitical circumstances of the times' – fewer American buyers and the rise of a
'fortress Europe' with less access to the required cheap labour, entrepreneurship
and ideas from abroad; gentrification processes in urban centres such as London,
Paris and Milan that had pushed the real 'laboratories of style' away, if not dispensed
with them altogether; and in general, the growing corporatisation of consumer culture (Gilbert 2006: 30–31). Therefore, he concluded, 'for all the efforts that its
planners and politicians are taking to make Shanghai fit the mould of the fashion
world city, this is the place where that mould is most likely to be broken' (Gilbert
2006: 32). In a similar vein, Elizabeth Wilson adds Shanghai to the list of cities that
have lost authenticity and edge due to the homogenisation that accompanies globalisation, arguing that 'Nanjing Road more closely resembles Bond Street or Fifth
Avenue than it resembles Shanghai in the 1930s' (Wilson 2006: 37).[1]

We ask, though, if there are other ways in which the concept of a world
fashion capital can be reworked for a new context. Central to this concept is the
idea that the city in question be the centre of a design tradition, a site where the
headquarters of key brands worldwide are located, and, too, that it features a
cluster of highly skilled manufacturing, relevant to the technology and business
practices of the day. Is it true that such cities are no more? We argue that while
a new geopolitical order is already in place, this spells the transformation, rather
than the end, of world fashion capitals. Perhaps alongside São Paulo, Moscow or
Dakar, Shanghai is certainly a future capital of world fashion.

It may not be immediately obvious that this is so. Fashion has long been, and
remains, a thoroughly Western-dominated area of culture. Indeed, as Gilbert

readily acknowledges, 'the idea of fashion authority, of certain specific urban milieux as the sources of style, has been a powerful form of cultural imperialism . . . a key element of a wider long-running discourse that divided the world into forward and backward regions' (Gilbert 2006: 14–15). So effectively was this discourse spread over the 'backward' regions that, for one of the most successful Chinese designers, Zhang Da, 'some of the Chinese would think fashion *is an understanding of Western lifestyle*' (Leung, our emphasis). In China, exporting a national brand for it to gain credibility abroad and then re-importing it has reportedly been proposed as a strategy to succeed domestically (Dodd 2005). What Pierre Bourdieu would call the 'consecrating' power of the West, in the cultural field of global fashion is still all-pervasive (Bourdieu 1993). Moreover, Shanghai, like the rest of China, has only recently begun to re-connect with its own culture, much of which was fragmented, if not obliterated, during the Cultural Revolution (Jiang 2010: 232). These days Chinese designers are often trained abroad, and if in the past their view was that 'the more national, the more international' (Wu 2009: 153) the opposite seems to have become the norm among more confident designers: they no longer feel they have to become, as it were, 'professional Chinese' (Sullivan 1997: 195), drawing from the imperial tailoring motifs and techniques, to succeed. Just what exactly 'a design tradition' might mean in this context is debatable.

However, we believe the characterisation of Shanghai as future world city, global fashion capital, is accurate. First, there is the city's obsession with the future as *a concept*, its futuristic architecture and design styles, also evident in much of its avant-garde fashion production, where the same close connection between fashion and architecture as in other world fashion cities can be found (Wigley 1995). Second, there is Shanghai's traditional role as site of encounters between East and West, a port of entry of Western culture and ideas, fostering innovation through cultural hybridity. Lastly, because the birth of Shanghai's fashion industry coincides with the rise of eco-fashion and 'green practices', a concern over a sustainable future for the industry as a whole, Shanghai may eventually become synonymous with the future of fashion in this sense. Below we discuss these three arguments.

Shanghai fashion and the idea of the future

Arguing that history can be understood in ways other than a linear succession of events, for instance as discrete points in time connected by similarities in kind, Walter Benjamin wrote:

> History is the subject of a structure whose site is not homogenous, empty time, but time filled by the presence of the now. Thus, to Robespierre ancient Rome was a past charged with the time of the now which he blasted out of the continuum of history. The French Revolution viewed itself as Rome incarnate. It evoked ancient Rome the way fashion evokes costumes of the past. Fashion has a flair for the topical, no matter where it stirs in the thickets of long ago; it is a tiger's leap into the past.
>
> (Benjamin 2003: 395)

So, to Benjamin, despite the years that had elapsed, there was continuity between the Romans and the French Revolution, and fashion, despite its being driven by a search for the new, is already cast in the past – it can only innovate on the basis of the already known, often working in cycles. Building on this understanding of history, the historical parallelism that springs to mind is the one between modern Shanghai and the cities in Europe that gave rise to the avant-gardes. Indeed, 'Shang Xia', Hermès' brand for the Chinese market – with a flagship store in Shanghai and a second one in Paris – features a ready-to-wear Autumn/Winter 2013 collection that strongly recalls the kind of surrealism that made Elsa Schiaparelli famous in the 1930s, probably designed by the above-mentioned Zhang Da. Instead of Schiaparelli's famous ribbons painted on sweaters, however, this time it is the cheongsam's collars, lapels and knotted buttons that have been outlined in red on dark woollen dresses.

Together with surrealism, it is futurism, which spread across Europe in the first half of the twentieth century, that is evoked in much of Shanghai's fashion design field today. In Europe and the USA, the series of sweeping changes in technology and culture at that time created the distinctive new modes of thinking about and experiencing space expressed in futurism. Changes in modes of transport, from steam-powered ships and trains to aeroplanes, and the development of wireless telegraphy are often credited, as are photography and cinema, with bringing a 'new experience of the instantaneous and the simultaneous that gripped many artists' (Humphreys 2006: 16). Futurism emphasised and glorified themes related to technology, speed, youth and the industrial city.

In 2011, the Shanghai Expo glorified the very same themes. Indeed, the phase of capitalism that David Harvey has famously termed 'flexible accumulation of capital' (Harvey 1991), to which China as a country and fashion as an industry have both been instrumental, is closely related to speed, to the rapid flows of information from points of sale to suppliers that have enabled 'just-in-time' production – based on forecasting, on the anticipation of customers' expectations, and on the constant innovation of products as a means to remain competitive. Amidst the massive economic and social change brought by the digitisation of media and culture, Shanghai is today at the forefront of similarly radical transformations, 'globalisation' of the kind that Saskia Sassen has argued gave rise to the concept of the global city itself (Sassen 2001). Shanghai's Magnetic levitation train, running from PuDong international airport to the city centre in seven minutes at 430 km per hour, is already the fastest in the world. And just as futurist artists once tried to convey the constant movement of the perceived world, representing lines and forms in motion, so do some fashion designers working in Shanghai today. It is surely no coincidence that 'futuristic' is a word consistently employed to describe some of the best known, most influential designers.

Yirantian Guo's designs displayed construction, abstraction and modernism, through an array of unusual shapes and experimental outfits, inspired by Cubism and broken objects. Qiu Hao, named as one of the twenty-five most influential individuals in the Chinese fashion industry, designs 'fluid draping, lean silhouettes and delicate knots', while Chi Zang is 'a master of futuristic avant-garde', his collections infused with cutting-edge designs and experimental garments.

And it is not only the designs themselves that are often futuristic, in the ways described above. By and large, fashion in Shanghai is invariably consumed with an orientation towards the future that now seems different in kind from the consumption of the fashion capitals of the twentieth century. For, while shopping in general is a future-oriented activity, large personal debt levels, recession and unemployment have contributed to produce a climate of anxiety in the consumption of fashion in Europe and North America. Anxiety, to quote Kierkegaard, 'entails an impatient expectation of a future whose signifiers are still floating freely' (Kaiser and Ketchun 2005: 134). But over the past twenty-five years per capita income, based on purchasing power parity, has grown by over 1,500 percent in China, and with the world economy recovery led mostly by countries in Asia, this trend will most likely continue. Impatient expectation of a future is thus here not fraught, but eagerly anticipated and acted upon: there is anticipation and hope, rather than fear and dread. From the luxury fashion houses to the fast-fashion boutiques, fashion consumers in the city purchase clothing items for the shaping of their individual and collective identities, for the crafting of their own bricolage with colours, bits and pieces, to express both who they hope to become, and who they are already 'becoming'.

Innovation in Shanghai fashion

A second vital reason why Shanghai is a future capital of world fashion is its role as a centre of innovation on the basis of interaction and exchange with Western cultures. British, American and French concessions were established in the city between 1842 and 1946, following the Treaty of Nanking, which ended the Opium War and gave Western powers substantial extraterritorial rights. The evolution of the cheongsam, known in the Chinese mainland as *Qipao* and recognised today as unmistakably Chinese, is in fact a good example of this sort of innovation, traced back to the cultural exchange with the West that took place in the Concessions.

As has been documented in the relevant literature, the cheongsam adapted the Manchu traditional loose dress or 'long robe' – worn, initially, by men – to the form-fitting style of Western dress (Clark 2000), resulting in the garment that is today regarded as the epitome of both elegance and femininity in Chinese clothing. It was the university students of Shanghai (Clark 1999: 158), followed by women from the emerging middle class, 'the female face of a progressive China' to quote Steele and Major (1999: 48), who adopted it and made it popular. Paradoxically, the encounter with Western construction techniques that gave rise to the cheongsam 'feminised' an initially perceived trend towards androgyny, with women donning male dress – thereby constraining, rather than enhancing, their freedom of movement. Nonetheless, the cheongsam has continued to be the site where modernity is represented in Chinese dress through its further modification over the late twentieth century, when it started to be worn again. First, this was done through *quotation*, with geometrical and abstract shapes in synthetic fibres preferred to the original traditional floral and patterned designs in silk. Designs from computer graphics and videogames are also displayed these days in the windows of some of the shops along Changle Lu, in the former French concession.

But most important, the cheongsam is also a site of negotiating modernity through its use; it has recently been adopted by sub-cultural groups including, briefly, the lesbian community (Wu 2009: 117).

If the popularity of the cheongsam in the West was initially 'a product of colonisation', as it 'became a vehicle for the identification of Chinese women as a whole' (Clark 1999: 158), and its rebirth in the 1990s, following Hong Kong's return to China, is often interpreted as a re-enactment of Orientalism, in today's Shanghai, the issues of agency in the cultural processes that re-inscribe hybridity are less clear-cut. To one of the most successful designers in the younger generation, Lu Kun, the change in attitudes has been deep and very rapid, taking place within the past few years. In his words:

> As a fashion designer I always wear this . . . kind of crown . . . on my head, being Chinese. But while when I started attending the shows in New York and Milan people would say, dismissively, 'Oh, so you are from China', and stop paying attention, they now say it quite attentively, and want to know more about my designs.
>
> (Lu 2013)

While the first cheongsams sold abroad might have been aimed at Western consumers, either as chinoiserie or simply as embodying the Other, the exotic, reinterpretations of the cheongsam are today made in the West, for Chinese consumers. What John Corbett said of Chinese composers might well be said of the cheongsams that John Galliano, Yves Saint Laurent and Christian Lacroix crafted throughout the 1980s and 1990s:

> an Asian composer in the West uses techniques devised by a Western composer inspired by Asian philosophy; the work is played for an Asian audience which hears it as an artifact of the bizarre West. Orientalism is reflected back and forth like a music-cultural *mise-en-abyme*.
>
> (Corbett 2000: 180)

But will the modes of transference and syncretism that have worked so well with the cheongsam, back and forth with Western fashion, become a feature of Chinese design? Some designers believe that the most important form of innovation is yet to happen, and will 'push the boundaries' of what today counts as fashion design. In the words of another designer, what first happened when Japanese fashion was included in the canon will now happen with Chinese design:

> I like Japanese design because of its great achievements. In the beginning, Japanese clothing wasn't included in discussions of design theory. *So when Japanese fashion first went international there was no basis for judging it.* This really shook up the fashion industry. Rei Kawakubo and Yōhji Yamamoto's first guerrilla shows in Paris scandalized the French public, because their collections rendered traditional design concepts totally irrelevant.
>
> (Leung; emphasis ours)

And what exactly constitutes 'Chinese design'? Lu Kun explains that many in his generation now see it as related to the principles of Confucianism and Tao, which Chinese designers learn at school (Lu 2013). It is about the inscribing of a whole worldview, an anti-dialectic world order where opposites do not clash, or cancel each other, but co-exist in the designs. Zhang Da also put the issue in very similar terms, arguing that he draws inspiration from Oriental philosophy, literature, garden design and sartorial culture, adding: 'You are done if you follow what they [the West] understand as Chinese' (Wu 2009: 151). For his own brand, 'Boundless', with a store at the heart of the Bund area in Shanghai, he designed 2D, flat garments that look entirely different when on the body, harking back to the draping techniques of the twentieth-century avant-garde movements. But where Madeleine Vionnet and Alix Grès were inspired by Greek and Roman tunics, Lu Kun and his contemporaries find inspiration in the principles of Zen. Fashion journalist Honora Shea described his work thus: 'The aesthetic he has introduced forces a new perspective on the way we see materials and wear our clothes. For some, this gives fashion a new dimension' (Shea 2012).

A sustainable future for fashion: The view from Shanghai

We have quoted Walter Benjamin's characterisation of fashion as a tiger's leap into the past. This phrase could be changed into a 'frog-leap into the future', to refer to the way technological development is taking place in emerging countries, skipping, as it were, stages – such as the mobile phone network now available in Africa where there are nonetheless very few landlines, or the Brazilian digital cinemas that have sprawled across various cities despite the fact there were relatively few traditional film theatres. Is Shanghai's twenty-five-year-old fashion industry going to leap-frog into sustainable fashion?

There is some evidence that it might. One important initiative has been the use of eco-friendly materials and working methods. Fashion brand La Vie stresses its locally sourced fibres made from bamboo, while the above-mentioned Shang-Xia highlights the green credentials of all its products, and lines such as Urban Tribe stress their use of natural fabrics such as cotton, linen, hemp and wool, and ancient production techniques, including the 3,000-year-old traditional Chinese dyeing method, which uses brown from tea leaves, red from logwood and blue from indigo. Shokay, a brand which advertises itself as having been born out of a concern for socially responsible industrial practices in fashion, uses yarn made from yaks in the West of China for its collections, sold in Shanghai. Central to all these brands are their minimalist designs, and the values of heritage, craftsmanship and community building. Urban Tribe has also benefited from its location in Tianzi Fang, one of the creativity clusters sponsored by the Shanghai city government, the kind of laboratory for experimentation that has become increasingly difficult to find in earlier world fashion capitals.

Tangy, a brand with shops in Shanghai, uses silk dyed with yam nectar, a procedure recently awarded UNESCO's special recognition for protecting the world's natural culture inheritance. In the words of Liang Zi, brand founder and design director, 'a bolt of silk is processed into gambiered Canton gauze through bleaching and dying up to thirty times, and a five to seven day exposure to the sun' (De Muynck and Carriço 2012: 49). The resulting cloth features different colours on each side, thus described by the designer: 'The dark side looks like black pottery, while the coffee-coloured side with the irregular texture looks like the remains of bones or tortoise shells unearthed from the Shang dynasty' (De Muynck and Carriço 2012: 49). It may be worth noting that all these designers see their use of such materials and techniques as an added contribution that Chinese fashion is bringing to the global fashion system.

Another strand of the growing trend towards eco-fashion in Shanghai is the appeal of vintage and other recycling initiatives. The Eco-chic Shanghai show, held in 2008, featured the work of forty local and international designers and showed vintage and second-hand clothing; sustainable ready-to-wear labels, and sustainable couture. Related media events included information on the environmental waste caused by the fashion industry, working to disseminate this information. In 2012, the Eco-chic Design Award was officially launched at Shanghai Fashion Week. Also worth singling out is Zhang Da's 'Reuse' initiative, which, although small in scale, has the potential to become significant if it were to be replicated across China. The designer called upon members of the local community to bring old, no longer wanted clothing and textile items, and promised that they would get a specially made work of art made from them in return.

Conclusion

During the first half of the twentieth century, the system of fashion depended on haute couture, which represented high-bourgeois taste, and after the Second World War on ready-to-wear, which arguably represented the democratisation of fashion. Today, motivated as ever by changes in the production, marketing and retailing of fashion, as well as a drastically changed geopolitical context, fashion seems to have become either the proliferation of luxury brands or so-called 'fast-fashion', both areas where China is taking the lead. But rather than understanding this as simply the end of fashion, we regard it as a new stage in fashion's development. The broadening of the boundaries of fashion as art, industry and cultural product, continues – becoming for the first time a truly global, rather than a Western endeavour.

The fashion system is not going to end because of the relative decline of earlier fashion capitals, and the changing socio-economic context within which these evolved. Rather, new fashion cities are emerging, and they require an engagement with the earlier capitals in order to thrive. Fashion was, and continues to be, a mainly urban phenomenon: as a centre of design tradition, a location of the headquarters of the main fashion brands, and as a cluster of highly skilled manufacturing, relevant to the technology and business practices of the day, Shanghai is without doubt a future world fashion city, a new capital. Elizabeth Wilson concluded her essay on the relation between modernity and fashion with the words: 'We should be looking at the cities of the Pacific Rim for a view of the future, and the future of fashion' (Wilson 2006: 38). We concur. Driven and inspired by visions of the future, with both a *sustainable* future for the industry and innovation through cultural exchange at heart, Shanghai could not be better placed to take up this role.

Acknowledgements

We are grateful to the University of Xian Jiaotong-Liverpool for the research grant that allowed us to conduct the fieldwork in Shanghai that was required to complete this chapter.

Note

1   Not only do we take issue with this characterisation of Nanjing Road, which is an avenue expanding for several miles and, at the time of writing (2013) is totally different on the East side, but we also fail to understand why Shanghai in 2006, the date of Wilson's piece, should have resembled Shanghai in the 1930s to seem 'authentic'.

References

Benjamin, Walter. *Selected Writings 1938–1940,* edited by Howard Eiland and Michael W. Jennings. Vol. 4. Cambridge: Harvard University Press, 2003.

Bourdieu, Pierre. *The Field of Cultural Production.* Cambridge: Polity, 1993.

Clark, Hazel. *The Cheongsam.* Oxford: Oxford University Press, 2000.

—— 'The Cheung Sam: Issues of Fashion and Cultural Identity.' In *China Chic: East Meets West*, edited by Valerie Steele and John S. Major. New Haven: Yale University Press, 1999, pp. 155–65.

Corbett, John. 'New Music and Other Others.' In *Western Music and its Others*, edited by Georgina Born and David Hesmondhalgh. Berkeley: University of California Press, 2000, pp. 163–86.

De Muynck, Bert, and Monica Carriço. *Fashion in China Mapping.* Commissioned Report, Shanghai: Moving Cities, 2012.

Dodd, Philip. 'China Chic, Not China Cheap.' *The Observer*, 12, 2005.

Gilbert, David. 'From Paris to Shanghai.' In *Fashion's World Cities*, edited by Christopher Breward and David Gilbert. Oxford: Berg, 2006, pp. 3–32.

Harvey, David. *The Condition of Postmodernity.* Oxford: Blackwell, 1991.

Humphreys, Richard. *Futurism.* London: Tate, 2006.

Jiang, Yuqiu. 'Zhongshan to Pierre Cardin: 30 Years of Chinese Fashion.' In *Contemporary Chinese Visual Culture: Tradition, Modernity and Globalization*, edited by Christopher Crouch. Amherst: Cambria Press, 2010, pp. 225–38

Kaiser, Susan B., and Karyl Ketchun. 'Consuming Fashion as Flexibility: Metaphor, Cultural Mood and Materiality.' In *Inside Consumption: Consumers Motives, Goals and Desires*, edited by S. Ratneshwar and David Glen Mick. London: Routledge, 2005, pp. 122–43.

Leung, Karchun. *Satellite Voices.* www.dazeddigital.com/satellitevoices/shanghai/fashion/2166/zhang-da (accessed 16 July 2013).

Lu, Kun, interview by Armida de la Garza and Peng Ding. *What is Chinese Design?* (25 January 2013).

Sassen, Saskia. *The Global City: New York, London, Tokyo.* Princeton: Princeton University Press, 2001.

Steele, Valerie, and John S. Major. *China Chic: East Meets West*. New Haven and London: Yale University Press, 1999.

Sullivan, Michael. *The Meeting of Eastern and Western Art*. Berkeley: University of California Press, 1997.

Tsui, Christine. *China Fashion: Conversations with Designers*. Oxford and New York: Berg, 2010.

Wigley, Mark. *White Walls, Designer Dresses: The Fashioning of Modern Architecture*. Cambridge: MIT, 1995.

Wilson, Elizabeth. 'Urbane Fashion.' In *Fashion's World Cities*, edited by Christopher Breward and David Gilbert, Oxford: Berg, 2006, pp. 33–9.

Wu, Juan Juan. *Chinese Fashion From Mao to Now*. Oxford: Berg, 2009.

Chapter 5

Sally Gray

'SYDNEY STYLE'
Camping it up in the Emerald City[1]

THROUGHOUT THE 1970S AND 1980S, Sydney attracted gays and lesbians from around Australia, the Asia-Pacific region, North America and elsewhere. By the early 1980s, this Pacific-rim city of three million people had become Australia's diasporic queer city.[2] This was especially so following the inauguration of the culturally influential style of the Sydney Gay Mardi Gras street parades and dance parties, with artist Peter Tully the inaugural artistic director from 1982 to 1986. The presence of a public gay subculture in the inner suburbs of Sydney and the prominent annual Mardi Gras events – attracting local and international crowds of up to 700,000 – endorsed a confident colourful approach to 'Sydney' style.[3] In this chapter, rather than trace the kinds of identificatory clothing worn by gays and lesbians, which in any case were very similar in the large gay cities of the Western world,[4] I investigate the camp sensibility, which, during the 1970s and 1980s, inflected Sydney style.

In the early to mid-1970s, four young creatives arrived in Sydney. They were Linda Jackson, Jenny Kee, Peter Tully and David McDiarmid; all were in their twenties, and all became influential in developing a certain 'Sydney' sartorial style. Jackson moved from Melbourne in 1973 with her then girlfriend, publicist and photographer Fran Moore; they decided on the move so that Jackson could design clothes for Jenny Kee's iconic new 'frock shop' Flamingo Park, opened that year in Sydney's Strand Arcade. Melbourne-trained, Jackson had worked in Paris with the Mia and Vicki label and her years of travel in South East Asia, the Pacific, Turkey and Europe gave her an eclectic visual sensibility which would inform her fashion design. Sydney-born Chinese-Australian, Jenny Kee returned to her hometown in 1972, after several years in London. She had worked for the Australian antique clothing dealer, Vern Lambert, at the influential Emmerton and Lambert stall at Chelsea Antique Market. Kee, who credits Lambert and his close friend and collaborator Anna Piaggi with educating her fashion sensibility,[5] describes her sense of a new optimism on her return in December 1972:

> Sydney was brash, bright, clean: harsh light; everyone and everything vibrant and open; bare brown bodies; thongs [flip-flops] and shorts; easy-going, friendly. I felt like a stranger from another world. With the changing of the guard in federal politics there was already a feeling that a new era had begun. [6]

Together, Kee and Jackson would become famous for adopting Australiana motifs in their clothing designs, expressing their affectionate, yet ironic enthusiasm for the visual motifs of their postwar suburban childhoods, and for Sydney itself – its beaches, sun-drenched colour, popular culture icons, irreverent humour and distinctive flora and fauna.

Peter Tully was also known for his kitsch Australian iconography – kookaburras, kangaroos, outline maps of Australia, surfboards, boomerangs, Vegemite jars – and his innovative use of plastics and vinyls. His jewellery and sculptural wearables teem with camp cultural allusions and amiable ironic humour. Tully moved to Sydney in early 1975 after travelling for several years in South East Asia, Europe and Africa.[7] He arrived with his ex-boyfriend David McDiarmid who, the following year, became the first Australian artist to exhibit overtly political gay art. McDiarmid had previously lived in Sydney, when he moved temporarily from Melbourne to help establish Sydney Gay Liberation. He wrote for and illustrated its first publications in 1972. Tully made jewellery for Flamingo Park and McDiarmid hand-painted fabrics for Linda Jackson's fashion designs. The four were friends, cultural fellow-travellers, and collaborators.

A desire to view sartorial aesthetics in an oblique, humorous, questioning and parodic manner was expressed in the fashionable dress designed and worn by the artistic circle surrounding Flamingo Park. This group of creative friends had, in turn, a disproportionate influence on what came to be seen as a 'Sydney' style of dress – involving high key colour, bold allusive graphics, visual excess, a self-conscious embrace of 'Australianness' and campily quotational approach to gender and sexuality. The ability, and the desire, to read cultural and social norms from the outside, and potentially to de-naturalise them, is most often found in those of outsider status. Queer scholar David Halperin sees camp as 'a form of cultural resistance . . . inescapably situated within a powerful system of social and sexual meanings'.[8] He sees camp strategies, such as parody, exaggeration and literalisation, as making transparent the kinds of power relations that normally never have to be 'explicitly articulated',[9] such as masculinity and femininity. Far from camp being a strategy exclusively available to people identified as gay, Halperin sees it as a form of positionality *vis-à-vis* the normative.[10] In this case, camp is a feminist strategy as well as a queer one. As feminist scholar Pamela Robertson writes: 'For feminists, camp's appeal resides in its potential to function as a form of gender parody'.[11]

In the 1970s, fashion and dress became engaging topics in Sydney feminist circles, as ideas of the 'feminine' came under scrutiny. At the time, the visual excess of Flamingo Park fashion, with its camp localism and sense of fun, was a countervailing force to contemporaneous politically correct neo-puritanism. Australian cultural theorist Meaghan Morris described this as a cultural and political 'surveillance system' which was 'absolute' in its policing of the visual semiotics of everyday life.[12] In strong contrast to this politically correct forestalling of the visual, the camp fashion of the Flamingo Park collaborators established a domain in which various forms of visual pleasure and sexual play could be implicated in a humorous and ironic approach to female dress. Gender norms were up for discursive play in an atmosphere of sexual and gender liberation. Feminism, dress and adornment coalesced, if uneasily, in the idea that independence and a self-fashioned life could be expressed through personal style.

By the mid-twentieth century Sydney was Australia's nightlife centre, and by the 1960s its sophisticated mid-century nightclub scene had given way to less class-conscious and more gay-oriented venues, where drag shows became a marked characteristic of the city's nightlife.[13] Historically, Sydney had long been the more rakish Australian city.[14] Historian Garry Wotherspoon notes in his study of the city's homosexual past that Sydney was no exception to the rule that the cultural and social diversity of large cities acts as a magnet for all forms of social complexity and divergent sexual tastes.[15] The movement for gay civil rights in Sydney was as much cultural as political, with radical performance groups such as Sylvia and Synthetics[16] and the Gay Mardi Gras giving the city's nightlife, and its gay politics, a particular flavour. Mardi Gras, inaugurated in June 1978 as a political protest demanding gay rights, became a galvanising force for the eventual decriminalisation of male homosexuality in 1984, and an influential cultural movement in its own right, through its compelling visual stylistics. Around this time, David McDiarmid, who like Tully became a Mardi Gras artistic director, had his first solo gallery exhibition in December 1976. His drawings and collages explored with clever ironic humour the secret and public codes of the gay city's cruising spots, beats, bath-houses, clubs and bars, simultaneously proposing gay rights and a camp aesthetic. He brought his queer politics into the sartorial realm, designing and making lamb-suede clothing for the huge gay dance parties, which became a distinctive feature of Sydney nightlife in the 1980s. Linda Jackson's glamorous couture and casual beachwear performed rather than naturalised tropes of the feminine, re-enacting 1920s Shanghai vamps and 1950s Miami beach queens. McDiarmid's hand-painted fabrics, which he designed for Jackson's dresses, appropriated Australian popular culture and tourist icons such as the Sydney Opera House, Aboriginal designs and native flora.

The art critic for *The Australian* newspaper, Sandra McGrath, stated in 1978 that 'Sydney it occurs to me must be the centre of camp art'.[17] McGrath was responding to a joint exhibition of Peter Tully jewellery and wearables and David McDiarmid interior installations. They both employed ironic humour, visual excess and parodic exaggeration to advance their consciously non-normative agenda – strategies Susan Sontag attributes to camp.[18] Tully's creative practice had been refined out of his gender-bending outfits for arts balls in Melbourne in the 1960s. For the 1982 Gay Mardi Gras parade, he outfitted himself in his self-invented, hand-made 'Tojo Tunic', one of his rampantly camp cross-cultural appropriations. Complete with a non-PC title, referring to the wartime Japanese Prime Minister, the vinyl and plastic outfit was inspired by Akira Kurasawa's 1980 film *Kagemusha* ('Impersonator').[19]

Figure 5.1
Peter Tully wears his 'Tojo Tunic',
Sydney Gay Mardi Gras 1982.
Photography: William Yang (1982).
Photograph reproduced with permission.

Tully and McDiarmid were engaged in the invention of a queered approach to style within the temporal space between Stonewall (1969) and the politics of the AIDS epidemic in the 1980s.[20] Their respective Art Director roles in the Sydney Gay Mardi Gras street parades and parties, their prominent gay liberationist art and design and their respective work in the fashion world were in stark contrast to the dress typologies of the homo-normative commercial Sydney bar scene.[21] Here they were designated 'the art and fashion queens' or sometimes 'fluoro queens', by virtue of their divergent personal dress, their use of accelerated colour and their 'attitude'. The Flamingo Park group positioned itself against the grain of the fashion and art mainstream and the homo-normative gay scene, assuming a detached vantage point on established taste regimes. Their appropriative obsessions included early twentieth-century decorative arts, retro kitsch, tribal arts, visual tropes from popular culture, Australian flora and fauna and East Asian visual culture. The group's quotational sensibility resonates, not just with postmodern appropriation, but also with Sontag's view that 'so many of the objects prized by Camp taste are old-fashioned out-of-date, démodé'.[22] As Sontag writes, 'Camp art is often decorative art, emphasising texture, sensuous surface, and style at the expense of content'.[23] Jenny Kee describes the consciously démodé aesthetic she adopted for her 'romantic, exotic and kitsch'[24] shop Flamingo Park thus:

> I would call it a frock salon not a boutique, because boutiques were so sixties 'modern'. 'Salon' had connotations of the fine arts and of Chanel's salon in the thirties. Salons were retro and that's just what I wanted.[25]

Kee and Jackson inaugurated a new Australian, camply performative, style of fashion presentation with their 'Flamingo Follies' fashion parades. These were highly staged events with contemporary music, wittily retro printed programmes, and ironic titles for the outfits. The first Follies was held in December 1974, at the Hingara Chinese restaurant in Sydney's Chinatown. The choice of venue itself, with its postwar chinoiserie of yellow, pink and aqua laminated walls, established a glamorous retro-kitsch aesthetic. Dim sum was served signifying that this was Sydney, a city in the Asia-Pacific region, not an emulation of Paris. The first outfit to appear was Linda Jackson's 'Opera House' suit, in blue linen with white satin 'sail' designs, referencing the roof structure of the recently opened, Jørn Utzon-designed, Sydney Opera House. The catalogue of garments for the first Flamingo Follies was inflected with ironic humour – the campily named 'Polly Pleat', 'Dilly Dirndl', 'John Dory' (a local fish) and 'True Blue', slang meaning 'real Aussie'. A decade later, queer scholar Michael Bronski wrote that 'Camp is re-imagining the material world into ways and forms which transform and comment on the original. It changes the "natural" and "normal" into style and artifice'.[26]

McDiarmid and Tully were in Sydney in time to participate in the next Flamingo Follies parade held in 1975 at the Bondi Bathers Pavilion, another site of iconic resonance. Kee's koala jumpers and Jackson's silk taffeta evening dresses with Australian floral motifs and visual quotations from art history, hand-painted by McDiarmid, established critical and popular enthusiasm for a repositioned ironic Australianness.[27] Tully created plastic 'artist palette' jewellery to go with outfits entitled 'Artiste', 'Matisse' and 'Cocteau'. In his own outfit worn to the show, David McDiarmid adopted the camp trope of 'artiste'. His sartorial invention consisted of a sleeveless, black satin chemise on which he hand-painted a replica of the KY sexual lubricant tube – a trope that would reappear in his first exhibition the following year. The painted KY tube 'squirted' its contents, like artist's paint, over the wearer's shoulder onto the back of the garment where it met the painted outline of a palette. McDiarmid's consciously camp gesture established him as, simultaneously, 'artist', 'fashion queen' and gay sexual radical.

The 'Sydney style' deployed within this group in the 1970s and 1980s worked against an established cultural embarrassment about being Australian – part of the national 'cultural cringe'.[28] Refusing to adhere to a 'cringing' disdain for Australian vernacular taste, the Flamingo Park group embraced it, in an ironic and humorous way, confusing those for whom international modernism was the enlightened direction for progressive Australian culture. Their witty embrace of the vernacular, makes transparent the 'cultural cringe' involved in seeing Australian popular taste, and provincial visual tropes, as 'less than' metropolitan modernist taste. Christopher Breward, writing on how camp sensibility is implicated in what we now see as the 'postmodern turn', notes that Sontag was in effect articulating this cultural turn, before the fact, when she claimed camp as a 'revolutionary' aesthetic with the capacity to move beyond accepted standards.[29] 'Camp taste turns its back on the good–bad axis of ordinary aesthetic judgement', Sontag says, 'Camp doesn't reverse things. It doesn't argue that good is bad or bad is good. What it does is to offer art (and life) a different – and supplementary – set of standards'.[30]

The camp appearance politics of the Sydney scene in the 1970s and 1980s was part of the postmodern turn in Australia, unsettling received ideas of what was what in fashion and art and introducing a popular kitsch sensibility as a creative modality for 'Sydney style'. Breward notes that Sontag in effect created a 'lexicon of style against which the avant-garde offerings of the first generation of postmodernists, and the languid rhetoric of the 1970s and early 80s high glamour, might be read', making camp 'a clarion call for those who positioned their work and attitude beyond the more reductive tenets of modernism'.[31]

The continuing influence of the camp Sydney style of the 1970s and 1980s is evident in the creative vision of twenty-first century Sydney designers, Anna Plunkett and Luke Sales, of the fashion label Romance Was Born. Both claim to have been 'obsessed with'[32] Jackson, Kee and Flamingo Park since they were students. At Australian Fashion Week 2009, Romance Was Born presented the quaintly ironic 'Iced Vo Vo' dress, in what became one of the week's 'most talked about and acclaimed collections'.[33] 'Iced Vo Vo' used red and pink cotton pom-poms to imitate the shape, form and colour of the familiar Australian tea biscuit of the same name, registered by Arnotts biscuit company in 1906. It was described by the company as 'a lovely biscuit topped with two strips of pink fondant and a strip of strawberry jam, all sprinkled with coconut – a symphony in pink'.[34] The 'Iced Vo-Vo' dress of 2009, with its distinctly Tully-esque quotational gesture, reinstated the camp vernacular deployed by Jackson, Kee, Tully and McDiarmid, to whose creative output and sensibility Romance Was Born's designers are indebted.

Since Romance Was Born's first collection, 'Cat Alley', in 2005, the label has established a creative trajectory that relies on independence from international trends and fashion industry predictions. Instead they have adopted a quirky 'localness', including their claim to be 'obsessively' influenced by the earlier Flamingo Park generation.[35] Sales and Plunkett met while studying at the Fashion Design Studio of Sydney Institute of Technology. After graduation they were selected to attend The Fourth International Talent Support Awards in Italy where they turned down an invitation to intern with John Galliano at Dior in order to pursue their own vision in Australia.[36] Their presence on the Sydney scene has created a distinct rupture in the endeavour by the Australian fashion industry as a whole, especially since the 1990s, to see itself as 'classic' and 'international' rather than local or 'embarrassingly Australian'.[37] Plunkett and Sales met their long-admired fashion idols, Jackson and Kee, at *Vogue Australia*'s 50th anniversary party in 2009, and soon afterwards were accompanied by the latter through the Jackson and Kee archive at Sydney's Powerhouse Museum. 'We were freaking out', says Plunkett, 'It was amazing and pretty emotional because it was all the things you see and read about'.[38]

By 2009 Romance Was Born – with a confident lack of concern about whether their output might be seen as provincial, crafty or kitsch – had established a set of design tropes that included ironic cultural appropriation, Australian vernacular motifs, camp humour, gender confusion, rampant visual excess, use of cheap materials such as fun-fur and redundant crafts such as granny-style crochet. Their label opened Mercedes-Benz Fashion Week, Australia for 2012, presenting bold comic-book graphics, in high-key colour, derived from vintage Marvel Comics.[39] At the same 2012 Fashion Week Jenny Kee presented her first solo fashion show in over thirty years – which had been styled by Plunkett and Sales – a collection of silk scarves, based on her paintings.[40] Through direct influence and the kind of 'morphic resonance', which makes something more possible and acceptable once it has been done before, Romance was Born has reinstated a camp way of seeing into Sydney fashion.[41]

Notes

1   David Williamson's 1987 play, *Emerald City*, focused on the perceived glitzy vulgarity of Sydney experienced by newcomers from the more conservative southern city, Melbourne. The title references Sydney's sparkling 'emerald' harbour; its fixation on glamour and excess and ultimately derives from the magical city in the Frank Baum books which inspired the 1939 Hollywood film *The Wizard of Oz*.

2   The terms 'gay', 'queer' and 'camp' have specific historical and more general usage. In this essay I use them as follows. 'Gay' is used in the post-Stonewall sense to allude to homosexual men and lesbians who self-identify as such. My use of 'queer' follows the post-1980s reappropriation into radical sexual discourse of the former term of abuse. In particular, I favour Eve Kosofsky Sedgwick's formulation of 'queer' as an unsettling of normative conceptions of sexual subjectivity. She locates 'queer' between and across categories, rather than as a label for a fixed sexual category (Eve Kosofsky Sedgwick (1993). *Tendencies*. Durham, Duke University Press). 'Camp' is used in this essay, following Susan Sontag, and others, to refer to a visual and cultural sensibility (Sontag (1966 [1964]).

3   Sydney Gay Mardi Gras (which was renamed Sydney Gay and Lesbian Mardi Gras in 1988, and Sydney Mardi Gras in 2011) was founded subsequent to a 1978 gay rights protest. It was in the years of Tully's formative inaugural artistic directorship (1983–6) that it assumed the aesthetic sensibility which helped define Sydney as 'queer city'. Tully's approach to Mardi Gras' visuality was continued under the art direction of Ron Smith (1987–8) and David McDiarmid (1988–90).

4   See Cole 1997; Gray 2010.

5   Jenny Kee interview with the author, February 2011.

6   Kee 2006: 131. Her reference to 'federal politics' is the December 1972 election of the socially progressive Whitlam Labor government after 23 years of conservative national government. This event triggered a new cultural optimism and the return of numerous creative Australian expatriates to their homeland.

7   Tully's performative costumes were precursors to those of Australian Leigh Bowery in London and African American Nick Cave, see Bowery et al. 2003 and Eilertsen 2009.

8   Halperin 1995: 29.

9   Ibid.

10   Halperin 1995: 62.

11   Robertson 1996, p. 10.

12   Morris 1988: 178.

13   Fashion historian Alexander Joel describes Sydney's mid-century nightclubs as, 'perfect place[s] for young society beauties to while away the time in glamorous surroundings' in her (1998) *Parade: The Story of Fashion in Australia*, Sydney, HarperCollins, 114–15.

14   This derives in part from Sydney's colonial past, see Birmingham 2000; Wotherspoon 1991.

15   Wotherspoon 1991: 70.

16   Sylvia and the Synthetics' unsettling gender antics exceeded the more conventional gender parody of drag. The group modelled a Zandra Rhodes range for a fashion feature for *POL* magazine, shot by Rhodes's then boyfriend, Sydney photographer Grant Mudford, see Neville 1973: 47–50.

17   McGrath 1978: 6.

18   Sontag 1966 [1964]: 277–9.

19   This reference to wartime Japan had ironic resonance in the context of Sydney, which had come under Japanese attack as part of the Asia-Pacific conflict in the Second World War. Young Australians of Tully's generation, many of whose fathers had fought in the Asia-Pacific conflict, advocated more open Australia–Japan relations.

20   The riots at the Stonewall Inn in lower Manhattan in June 1969 are credited with being the symbolic beginning of the Gay Liberation Movement and of the notion of Gay Pride. The period between Stonewall and awareness of the seriousness of the AIDS crisis, in the early 1980s, is widely regarded by gay male cultural figures, certainly by McDiarmid and Tully, as a period of utopian political and sexual freedom; e.g. White 2005. Tully died of AIDS-related conditions in 1992, McDiarmid in 1995.

21   Gray 2010.

22   Sontag 1966 [1964]: 285.

23   Ibid: 278.

24   Kee 2006: 133.

25   Ibid.

26   Bronski 1984: 138.

27   Images of Kee's koala jumpers were disseminated globally when a pregnant Princess Diana was photographed wearing one in May 1982. The Australiana of Jackson and Kee was enthusiastically taken up by Anna Piaggi in Italian *Vogue*, December 1977, while Karl Lagerfeld used Jenny Kee's silk opal prints for sixty-three garments in his first prêt-à-porter collection, Spring/Summer 1983, for Chanel in October 1982.

28   The term 'cultural cringe' was coined in an influential 1950 essay by Australian critic, *A. A. Phillips*, to describe an Australian sense of provincial inferiority in the face of northern hemisphere metropolitan cultures. It is now used more broadly in post-colonial studies.

29   Breward 2011: 168.

30   quoted in Breward 2011: 167.

31   Ibid.

32   Evans 2010.

33   Ibid.

34   www.arnotts.com.au/about-us/arnotts-heritage.aspx (23 July 2012).

35   Ibid.

36   Evans 2010.

37   Riley 1997: 43–5 and Peers 2005: 133–53.

38   Leek 2012: 62.

39   Safe 2012: 5.

40   Leek 2012: 62.

41   The term 'morphic resonance', coined by British biologist Rupert Sheldrake, provides a poetic way in which to imagine how cultural tropes reoccur in different times and settings. Sheldrake writes: 'Human societies have memories that are transmitted through the culture of the group, and are most explicitly communicated through the ritual re-enactment of a founding story or myth . . . through which the past become present through a kind of resonance with those who have performed the same rituals before', see: www.sheldrake.org/Articles&Papers/papers/morphic/morphic_intro.html (4 June 2012).

References

Books and journals

Birmingham, J. (2000) *Leviathan: The Unauthorised History of Sydney*, Sydney, Random House.

Bowery, N. B. *et al.* (2003) *Take a Bowery: The Art and (larger than) Life of Leigh Bowery*, Sydney, Museum of Contemporary Art.

Breward, C. (2011) 'The Uses of "Notes on Camp"', in Glenn Adamson and Jane Pavitt (eds) *Postmodernism Style and Subversion 1970–1990*, London, V&A Publications.

Bronski, M. (1984) 'Culture Clash the Making of a Gay Sensibility', quoted in Cagle, Van, M. (2000) 'Trudging Through the Glitter Trenches', in Shelton Waldrep (ed.) (2000) *The Seventies: The Age of Glitter in Popular Culture*, New York and London, Routledge.

Cole, S. (1997) 'Macho Man: Clones and the Development of a Masculine Stereotype', *Fashion Theory* (3): 125–40.

Eilertsen, K. (2009) *Nick Cave: Meet me at the Centre of the Earth*, San Francisco, Yerba Bueno Centre for the Arts.

Gray, S. (2010) 'Crafting Hip and Cool: David McDiarmid's Handcrafted Lamb Suede Dance-floor Outfits, 1980–1989', *The Journal of Modern Craft* (3:1) March 2010: 37–54.

Halperin, D. (1995) *Saint=Foucault: Towards a Gay Hagiography*, New York and Oxford, Oxford University Press.

Joel, A. (1984) *Best Dressed: 200 Years of Fashion in Australia*, Sydney, William Collins.

Kee, J. (2006) *A Big Life*, Sydney, Lantern Books.

Leek, G. (2012) 'True Colours', *Vogue* Australia June 2012: 62.

McGrath, S. (1978) 'Rings Strings and Things', *The Weekend Australian* Magazine, 18–19 November 1978: 6.

Morris, M. (1988) *The Pirate's Fiancée: Feminism, Reading, Postmodernism*, London, Verso.

Neville, R. (1973) (guest editor), *POL* magazine Vol. 5, No. 7.

Peers, J. (2005) 'Paris or Melbourne? Garments as Ambassadors of Australian Fashion Cultures', in S. Anna and E. Gronbach (eds), *Generation Mode*, Dusseldorf, Hatje Cantz and Stadtmuseum Landeshauptstadt.

Riley, M. (1997) 'From the Bush to the Street: A Change in Direction for Australian Fashion', in *Artlink*, Vol. 17, No. 1, Autumn 1997: 43–5.

Robertson, P. (1996) *Guilty Pleasures: Feminist Camp from Mae West to Madonna*, Durham and London, Duke University Press.

Safe, G. (2012) 'Pow! Shimmering superheroes pack a powerful punch', *The Sydney Morning Herald*, 1 May 2012: 5.

Sedgwick, E. K. (1993). *Tendencies*, Durham, Duke University Press.

Sontag, S. (1966 [1964]) 'Notes on Camp' in *Against Interpretation*, New York, Delta.

White, E. (2005) *My Lives*, London, Bloomsbury.

Wotherspoon, G. (1991) *City of the Plain: History of a Gay Subculture*, Sydney, Hale & Iremonger.

Internet

Evans, R. (March 2010) 'Iced Vo Vo Dress designed by Romance Was Born' www.powerhousemuseum.com/collection/database/?irn=405571#ixzz1zKkAKQZz (23 July 2012)

Sheldrake, R. (1998) www.sheldrake.org/Articles&Papers/papers/morphic/morphic_intro.html. (June 4 2012)

www.arnotts.com.au/about-us/arnotts-heritage.aspx (July 23 2012)

PART TWO

Changing imagery, changing media

Chapter 6

Caroline Evans

YESTERDAY'S EMBLEMS AND TOMORROW'S COMMODITIES

The return of the repressed in fashion imagery today

(Second printing with new Foreword)

Foreword

THE LUSH DESCRIPTIONS IN THIS ARTICLE make 1990s fashion seem as remote as the gilded Edwardian age. Revisiting those glory days through the designs of John Galliano, Alexander McQueen and Martin Margiela is like a kind of time travel. If the article has a sort of period charm, in that respect alone it is perhaps worth reprinting, if only to remind us just exactly how fast fashion time moves. Yet, in another respect the article has come into sharper focus since it was written thirteen years ago. I suggested then that in the late 1990s the fashion garment functioned in a new way as part of 'a network of relations: as image, as cultural capital, as consumer goods, as fetish, art exhibition, item of breakfast television, show invitation or collectable magazine'.[1] All this pointed to the ubiquity of fashion as image in the consumer culture of the late twentieth century, and its proliferation via television, video, internet websites, galleries and new types of fashion magazine. But when I suggested that fashion had become image as much as object as a result of new networks and new communications, I had no idea how much more radically things were just about to change. Digital and web-based fashion coverage exploded from 2000, the year the article was published. The intervening thirteen years have seen the development of fashion film, fashion blogging and online fashion publishing. These new forms of fashion communication have both engendered new practices and generated a vast quantity of information and images that dwarf the scale of the designer bricolage and cultural rag-picking that I described in my article.

All this has happened very fast. I was not wrong to argue that contemporary fashion was part of a 'society of the spectacle' in the process of rapid transformation; I just didn't know quite how rapid it was going to be. When I suggested, on the cusp of the new century, that the previous ten years had seen a new digital culture of fashion that was changing its nature, I had in mind two enterprises: Firstview (founded 1996), a subscriptions-based website showing the current season's collections which made its archive of previous collections open-access to the public; and the subscription-only web coverage of fashion shows by the fashion forecasting company WGSN that started in 1999. But these were nothing compared to what was to follow. In 2000 Condé Nast launched style.com, a public access fashion website which for the first time brought the closed world of fashion shows to a mass audience. Roger Tredre, MA fashion journalism tutor at Central Saint Martins and founder of WGSN, recalled that 'Anna Wintour [the editor of US *Vogue*] sent letters and forms to all the designers, probably in early 2000, requesting their permission to photograph entire shows and put the images online. Unlike WGSN, which was a trade-only password-protected website, *Vogue* – through *style.com* – was of course publishing the images online to anyone for free access. So it was a breakthrough moment in the transition of the fashion show from trade event to public spectacle. Some designers initially consented only grudgingly, but everyone quickly realised that the fashion show would never be quite the same again and they had to go with the flow'.[2]

In the way they have developed since then, style.com and similar websites have had a ground-changing impact on fashion journalism. The intensification of image culture, and the capacity to connect at speed, have produced a new experience for the 'reader', so-called. On style.com, there are options to look at fashion shows as a series of still images that can be slowly scrutinised, or to click the 'move it' feature on each look to see a short clip of the model walking. Sally Loxley, an assistant stylist working during London Fashion Week, commented:

> It seems to me to highlight how editors and spectators feel the need for a moving image. It is often useful at work when we are choosing looks as you can get a sense of the fabrics a bit better. Style.com is our bible – by the end of the season you feel like you know every show inside out. When communicating with PRs the look numbers are always taken from style. com, it's taken for granted now that the industry uses it. It's such an important resource for us, I'm not sure how I'd do my job without it.[3]

Unlike the industry websites from the late 1990s, however, style.com is accessible to all, not only to people in the fashion industry. It allows users to navigate between fashion shows, parties, designer profiles, 'fashion moments' and 'after hours', bringing a layered experience of the world of fashion to a public audience. When a website operates visually on so many levels at once, then the relationship between word and image is transformed. Such visual layering and collaging makes the written word seem curiously one-dimensional and underscores the linearity of traditional fashion journalism. Furthermore, online fashion journalism imitates the forms and manners of social media. Fly-on-the-wall camerawork shows us parties and people; it takes us backstage before the show, and between shows it steers us through the streets of London, Paris, Milan or New York, pausing for vox pop interviews with journalists who tell us what they are wearing. All the while, its shaky handheld camera mimics the style of home movies, as if we were really there.

Another major innovation in 2000 was the launch of the website SHOWstudio by the photographer Nick Knight. Though not a commercial site, it became influential in pioneering the emerging genre of fashion film, which is examined elsewhere in this anthology by Gary Needham. From SHOWstudio's inception, Knight and his first editor Penny Martin understood the creative potential of moving image for fashion. The website gave an international audience instant access to the previously closed world of high fashion, very much as traditional print fashion magazines had always done. Rather than simply reporting, however, the website set up its own projects with emerging designers, photographers and models. Its projects were frequently interactive, and it encouraged its audience to respond and contribute creatively to its projects, documenting, communicating and evaluating the results. Its collaborations extended beyond fashion into the worlds of music, art, architecture and performance, but always with an eye on the possibilities of digital moving image for fashion, and it worked with fashion designers, image-makers and artists including Alexander McQueen, Gareth Pugh, Elaine Constantine, Sølve Sundsbø, Juergen Teller, Ruth Hogben, Inez & Vinoodh, Bernhard Willhelm, Bjork, and many others. All these moving image pieces are archived today on the SHOWstudio website where they can still be viewed. It currently bills itself as the 'home of fashion film'.[4]

SHOWstudio was closely watched by the industry for the first ten years of its life, and it was the subject of a major gallery exhibition at Somerset House in London in 2009. From approximately 2010 international fashion brands increasingly began to produce digital, moving and screen-based publicity. And when luxury brands with global markets such as Yves Saint Laurent, Chloé, Prada, Dior and Chanel no longer sit on the sidelines to watch but themselves produced fashion film, then we know these new forms of fashion film have entered the mainstream. When a company such as Lanvin shows it understands the value of a fashion viral, and even uses it to make jokes, in the form of a cameo performance by Lanvin's artistic director Alber Elbaz dancing at end of the Fall 2011 campaign movie, then we know that the global luxury industry has taken the form to its heart.[5]

Fashion blogging, another area of digital culture which grew fast in the first ten years of the century, was, by contrast, at the opposite end of the spectrum to the high production values of the luxury brands. Explored in this volume by Agnès Rocamora and Monica Titton, it is currently the subject of burgeoning academic interest.[6] 'High end' blogs such as *The Sartorialist* and *Bryanboy* attract much critical attention, and often turn their authors into minor media stars, like the juvenile Tavi Gevinson who started her fashion blog, *Style Rookie*, at the age of eleven and within five years was an unofficial spokeswoman for teenage girls, having given a TED talk (www.ted.com) and starred in a public service announcement in the 2012 American election supporting women's and girls' rights. The journalist Susie Lau, an ex-editor at the online magazine *Dazed Digital*, posts as Susie Bubble on her blog *Style Bubble*. Yet blogging also gives non-experts a voice and there are a great many fashion blogs by so-called 'ordinary people', as opposed to industry insiders. Blogging is potentially democratic in that it gives outsider voices a new platform, but has occasionally provoked debates about whether such 'amateurs' are entitled to speak as experts.

The third area of new digital activity since 2000, and straddling these two, is digital fashion publishing in the form of online fashion magazines that are faster, cheaper and more immediate than their print versions, such as *AnOther Magazine*, which launched online in 2009, eleven years after its print counterpart. Not only are the digital editions of such magazines free, as opposed to the expensive printed versions, but also they offer more content and immediacy. *Dazed Digital*, for example, has up to five daily updates. Nor are they always small independents. *Nowness.com* is owned by LVMH (Louis Vuitton Moët Hennessy) and while that makes it more mainstream it also proves how the once conservative and cautious world of Paris fashion is gradually embracing the new technology and realising the importance of digital platforms. Indeed, it is often the faster-moving digital versions of print magazines that are more integral to the industry.

All these changes highlight how new communications are restructuring the industry, and recalibrating the relationship between the virtual and the real. In some ways, however, they are a continuation of older forms, particularly of fashion magazines, which have existed almost as long as there has been a fashion industry. The first ready-to-wear clothes were made in the seventeenth century and this in turn gave rise to the first fashion magazines, to publicise fashion to the novice. And fashion magazines have always gone beyond merely describing clothes, to manufacturing dreams. In the early twentieth century, Baron Adolphe de Meyer's Paris column in *Harpers Bazar* took the reader into the exclusive backstage world of the couture house where the journalist conversed loftily with 'Mlle Chanel' and 'M. Worth'. The sense of taking the reader into an exclusive world where in real life they have no entrée is nothing new, and digital fashion publishing simply continues this tradition. What has changed, however, due to the internet and social media, and was already changing when I wrote my article, is the status of the image, which has become as real a 'product' as the object. As Elizabeth Wilson wrote in 2003, in her revised edition of *Adorned in Dreams*:

> Today newspapers, fashion magazines, television programmes and the internet bombard us with information and advice on dress and appearance. We are saturated with images of fashion. 'Fashion' is a rack of garments we can touch and feel in the department store or the high street boutique, but it is equally a virtual spectacle, a regime of images, celebrating a continual carnival of change.[7]

The very rapidity with which this communications landscape has changed suggests that digital publishing, fashion film and fashion blogs are the 'present' through which we have to re-view the past. In my article I cited Foucault's argument that the present throws up the themes to be studied historically, so that every shift in the present demands a re-evaluation of the past. There are many histories to be written of the same period, and many ways of writing them. In *The Archaeology of Knowledge*, Foucault itemises histories of ideas, science, philosophy and literature. Within those, he goes on to say, there are many models of periodisation and change: from continuity to rupture, from 'vast unities' such as historical periods to particularities, and from microscopic to macroscopic scales of history.

> *Recurrent redistributions* reveal several pasts, several forms of connexion [sic], several hierarchies of importance, several networks of determination, several teleologies, for one and the same science, as its present undergoes change: thus historical descriptions are necessarily ordered by the present state of knowledge.'[8]

If there are several pasts, as Foucault asserts, this is no less true of the recent past than of the deep past. What are the histories, waiting to be written, of these new websites, blogs and fashion films? Are they testaments of everyday life and sensibilities; documents of industry and commerce; monuments to technology; or critiques of the politics of information? In some way, and in whatever form, we will write these histories as histories of ourselves, and of our historical moment. For as Foucault argues at the end of *The Order of Things*, we constitute ourselves as subjects precisely by writing ourselves into history: 'the history of living beings, the history of things, the history of words' and (although Foucault is generally silent on this topic) the history of images.[9]

Important as it is to review our past, as I argued in the article, the distinction between past and present is not so clear in fashion where each is already imbricated with the other. This seems paradoxical, but written into fashion's fascination with the new is an addiction to its own history. With nothing to turn its back on, fashion would be stuck in a perpetual present: fashion's past propels it into its future. In the same way, the images of the old media are written into the new media, as writers on remediation have observed.[10] History, too, is a kind of technology and therefore a form of remediation of older histories, and this also has to be borne in mind when revising the histories of fashion, media and spectacle.

So perhaps less has changed than appeared at first sight. For my article was not just about how fashion had become image, a digital shift from material object to immaterial idea. It was also, indeed primarily, about the temporal relays of contemporary fashion and the 'tiger's leap' it made into the past. Concerned less with the determining effects of the new technologies, and more with the ways in which models of time can become sedimented in images and artefacts, it looked at how history and image were imbricated in the new digital culture of the late twentieth century. This principle still holds, it seems to me, even if fashion imagery and design have changed out of all recognition since the 1990s, for if the new technology offers anything it is simply larger and more rational ways of organising and rearranging information.

The historians Jacques Le Goff and Pierre Nora have both discussed the computer as a new form of modern memory that functions like the traditional archive in its capacity to contain, order, classify and structure information, and hence knowledge. They write about how new technologies shape modern memory, and Le Goff in particular has shown how the advent of technologies such as photography and computing have structured not only what, but also how, we remember.[11] Le Goff described the late-twentieth-century practice of oral history as a form of social memory, as well as a kind of archive, and Nora argued that the vast data banks being created in the 1980s were part of a modern obsession with archiving that amounted to a form of 'terrorism of historicised memory'.[12] As the historian Carolyn Steedman points out, however, there is a flaw in the argument that the archive is a form of memory because the structure of the archive is quite unlike the structure of the human mind.[13] Indeed, if one were looking for a metaphor for memory, then the internet — with its ad hoc development and sprawling reach — might be a better one. A vast repository of modern sensibilities, memories and practices, the internet, although messier and less ordered than an archive, has the capacity to function as a kind of unclassified archive, an unedited and uncatalogued collection of modern mores.

As such, its contents are up for grabs. As a disorganised archive of the cultural imaginary, the internet gives increased scope for remixing and reappropriation of ideas and images about fashion — far more than the 1990s fashion that I argued scrambled time, such as Galliano's luxury revision of the nineteenth century, or Margiela's poetic evocations of time through dereliction and decay. Indeed, if anything, the new media allow people increasing fluency and access to the facility of 'thinking in terms of images', a concept I quoted from Italo Calvino. And in this respect, my use of Benjamin's concepts 'wish-images' and 'dialectical images', and of Stefan George's *Denkbilder*, or 'thought-images', might have even more currency nowadays, when the internet gives ragpicking fashion designers more opportunities than ever to scavenge images and ideas from the world around them. For ultimately my discussion of dialectical images and of Benjamin's writing on the trace, as well as of cultural ragpicking, was simply a way to think about fashion design creativity, and how that creativity moves in new circuits as image and idea. If, as I wrote in 2000, 'images are a cultural archive which can be raided to make sense of the present', and the ragpicking designer is akin to the historian,[14] the digital realm provides a vastly magnified archive in which to scavenge and bricolage, so as to construct the 'cultural poetics' of the day.

Today, tomorrow, yesterday

IN 1991, WHEN THE FILMMAKER DEREK JARMAN, already fatally ill, was canonised as Saint Derek of the Celluloid Knights by the Sisters of Perpetual Indulgence, an order of gay nuns, he wore a woollen hat by Joe Gordon embroidered with the words 'today, tomorrow, yesterday'. He also wore a six-foot long necklace set with gilded spring bulbs and porno pictures, made for him by the jeweller Simon Fraser. The necklace was to be planted in Jarman's garden in Dungeness. Although he was not expected to survive the winter, unexpectedly he did live and, when the bulbs came up in spring, took issue with the planting scheme, dug up some of the bulbs and replanted them, much to Simon Fraser's amused exasperation.

On his death, Jarman was buried in the hat; before then, the necklace had been buried in his garden but the artist cheated time and restructured the *memento mori*, leaving only traces of gilt from the original planting in the soil. This chapter is concerned with similarly unexpected reversals of, and loops in, time which characterised fashion from the 1990s, scrambling and re-ordering its chronology like the inscription 'today, tomorrow, yesterday'. The chapter maps out the way in which the past spools back into the present and reverberates into the future in contemporary fashion.[1] That this temporal scrambling could occur with particular intensity from the 1990s onwards was due, in part, to the pre-eminence of the image in contemporary culture. This chapter looks at the way in which fashion mutated in the digital culture of the late twentieth century and, in particular, how history and image were imbricated in its new formations.

The conceptual Dutch designers Viktor & Rolf assert that 'fashion doesn't have to be something people wear, fashion is also an image',[2] and their work reminds us that designers are also semiotic tacticians. Like all the designers discussed below, I have privileged visual over verbal communication in my references to fashion images as, variously, emblems, 'thought-images', hieroglyphs, and, citing Walter Benjamin, 'dialectical images'. The exploration of fashion as a 'dialectical image' is the central crux of my argument, for it is intended to serve not only as an interpretative tool but also to offer a meta-narrative of the operations of fashion today through the process of historically referencing it. The way in which the fashion object mutated into image in the last ten years of the twentieth century gives us an insight into how the industry works, and the focus on image does not occlude 'the real' so much as recontextualise what 'the real' is in digital culture. Although I do not discuss them in depth, the industrial base of fashion and its relation to 'the real' underpin my analysis of the form and 'content' of contemporary design. As Lorraine Gamman and Merja Makinen have pointed out, the nature of commodity fetishism has shifted since Karl Marx described the mystification of the object itself in the nineteenth century to a late-twentieth-century form of fetishised representation of the object. They identify the way that, in Jean Baudrillard's writing, commodity fetishism is 'about more than just the disavowal of production . . . commodity fetishism occurs at the level of the sign' in post-industrial society. They also point out that Baudrillard's formulation, in its disavowal of 'real production of real commodities by real people in the real world', represents an epistemological break with Marx.[3] While acknowledging the recent past as having been characterised by just such an epistemological break, resulting from the proliferation of new technologies of the image and their impact upon commerce and culture, this chapter attempts to treat the commodity as 'sign' without simultaneously disavowing 'the real'.

Arguing that yesterday's emblems have become tomorrow's commodities, it uses 'dialectical images' to explain how contemporary fashion is part of a 'society of the spectacle' in the process of transformation. Of spectacle in general, Hal Foster argued in the 1990s that 'we become locked in its logic because spectacle both effects the loss of the real and provides us with the fetishistic images necessary to assuage or deny this loss'.[4] Yet, I would argue that 'the real' is not irretrievably lost in such representations, only repressed. As such, it returns in contemporary fashion design when designers intuitively reinterpret past images of instability in the present. Kevin Robins has argued that the contemporary proliferation of images via new media signals a drive to disembodiment and a retreat from experience, and 'provides the means to distance and detach ourselves from what is fear-provoking in the world and in ourselves'.[5] Yet, in the 1990s the perfect body of mainstream fashion was progressively challenged by the abject, fissured and traumatised body of more cutting-edge fashion, another form of the return of the repressed, suggesting fashion as an important arena for articulating the complexities and contradictions of embodiment in the present day. And because all fashion is corporeal, the body, its pleasures, and its anxieties are rarely completely obliterated, even in the new digital culture. For even, perhaps especially, when fashion is at its most pictorial, it plays with images of two- and three-dimensionality, layering traces of bodies on fabrics, and vice versa. Olivier Theyskens clothed the body in a second skin like an anatomical drawing, appliquéd with arteries and a red lace heart. Two of Walter Van Bierendonck's menswear collections featured cutaway panels at the chest and crotch, under which the models wore thin body suits printed with *trompe l'œil* body parts.[6]

Spectacle

'In societies where modern conditions of production prevail, all of life presents itself as an immense accumulation of *spectacles*. Everything that was directly lived has moved away into a representation.' With these words, Guy Debord opened his *Société du spectacle* of 1967.[7] Debord characterised modern life as a world colonised by false desires and illusions, epitomised by the ubiquity of the commodity form. Although he demonised not vision but the way it operated in Western society, it is hard not to see a mistrust of the image itself in his writing.[8] Sometimes his writing suggests the puritanism of an author who is himself incapable of being ravished by the visible world. The spectacle is deathly for him because it is capital become an image; it is the other side of money:[9] it is death, or, rather, 'it is the visible *negation* of life'.[10] Debord wrote that 'the spectacle in general, as the concrete inversion of life, is the autonomous movement of the non-living'.[11]

However, at other times his gloomy prescriptions also read as descriptions, anticipating the deathly and spectacular effects of some 1990s fashion shows. The spectacle of the undead was made palpable in Antonio Berardi's 'Voodoo' collection, shown in London in September 1997, when models with dishevelled hair and dirty faces danced round a fire to the accompaniment of techno music and live African drumming. One in particular acted 'spooked': nervy but trance-like. The show was accessorised with celestial candle-holders with burning candles shaped into a crown, worn on the head, with shells and feathers plaited into long braids. A more Utopian spectacle of the 'undead' was exemplified by Jean-Paul Gaultier's cyber-collections of the mid-1990s, which mixed traditional elements from Asian and African dress with references to the European past and then added in elements of computer technology and club and festival culture. The visual reference to nomadic travellers who move in real space and time was transmogrified into an idea of cyberspace travellers who left spectral traces of their presence behind.

In these examples the fashion show could be construed as the paradigm of the modern spectacle which seduces us with the 'hyper-reality' of ravishing and perfect images. These fashion shows suggest that 'the society of the spectacle' that Debord identified in 1967 has merely intensified its effects, harnessing the new technologies of the image to do what it always did so well: visual seduction through fetishising the commodity form, succinctly demonstrated by the fashion photographer Richard Avedon's statement in 1984 that he saw his role at *Vogue* as 'selling dreams, not clothes'.[12] As Rosalind Williams describes in her book on nineteenth-century consumption, *Dream Worlds*, the seduction of the commodity form lies precisely in its ability to veil the real, commercial nature of the transaction with seductive 'dream worlds' in which the consumer loses him or herself in fantasy and reverie.[13] On the face of it, the contemporary fashion show, as one example of late-twentieth-century spectacle, seems to be a very precise evocation of this principle, the starriest of star commodities: 'when culture becomes nothing more than a commodity, it must also become the star commodity of the spectacular society'.[14] Debord predicted that by the end of the century culture would become the driving force in the development of the economy, as the car was at the beginning of the century, or the railway in the second half of the last. Indeed, we do now refer to the 'culture industries', suggesting that culture is the new motor that drives the economy of our information society, just as coal and iron powered the economy of an earlier, industrial society. Yet, despite his prescience, Debord failed to imagine the developments in information technology which so transformed the late twentieth century from the 1960s when he was writing.

Although Debord located the origins of the society of the spectacle in the 1920s, his analysis has proved a fruitful model for understanding a number of other periods, from the origins of modernity in the Paris of the Impressionists, to the commodity culture of nineteenth-century London, and the image of woman as spectacle in relation to modernity.[15] Clearly it had a pressing relevance to the anticonsumerist left politics of the 1960s and 1970s. Yet today, for all its interesting academic applications, its sour denunciations of the image seem curiously redundant in relation to contemporary culture. I suggest this is because the nature of the commodity has changed since Debord was writing, so that his descriptions no longer chime with the world of spectacle we inhabit, a spectacle in perpetual transformation. Whereas Debord's descriptions of the commodity were rooted in Marxist critiques of the form as economic object, the overarching transformations of the 1990s (globalisation, new technology and communications) have radically altered its form. Indeed, Thomas Richards suggests that the days of spectacle are numbered, and that 'it may turn out that the semiotics of spectacle played a transitional role in capitalist mythology'.[16]

Current fashion participates in an economic system that is developing very differently from its nineteenth-century origins, which pioneered the techniques of retail and advertising to promote the garment. Now the fashioned garment circulates in a contemporary economy as part of a network of signs, of which the actual garment is but one. From its existence primarily as an object, the fashion commodity has evolved into a mutant form with the capacity to insert itself into a wider network of signs, operating simultaneously in many registers. Whereas it used to exist as, for example, a dress, which preceded its single representation in the form of an advertisement or fashion photograph, it is now frequently disembodied and deterritorialised. As such, it can proliferate in many more forms, within a larger network of relations: as image, as cultural capital, as consumer goods, as fetish, art exhibition, item on breakfast television, show invitation, or collectable magazine.

It is because the commodity form is evolving that we can talk about fashion signifying in a new way, as part of the circulation of signs and meanings in a global economy unchecked, since the fall of the Berlin Wall, by any alternative economic system. The development of the commodity is paralleled by many other kinds of social organisation. For example, Richard Sennett has described how management pyramids in the workplace are being replaced by 'flexible networks' and he differentiates this 'flexible bureaucracy' from 'Balzac-ian capitalism'.[17] In the same way, modern fashion is part of a network of themes, ideas and motifs that spread, viruslike, by contact with and colonisation of their subjects. Gilles Lipovetsky has argued that the development of business practices in nineteenth-century Parisian couture houses played a significant part in the bureaucratisation of the nineteenth century;[18] similarly today fashion, that most spectacular sign, is at the vanguard of a new model of social and commercial organisation, the network.

Thus, in the technological and information revolution of the late twentieth century, the role of image in fashion shifted. No longer mere representation, the image frequently became the commodity itself, in the form of exclusive fashion shows, internet websites, television programmes and a new kind of fashion magazine, such as *Tank*, *Purple* and *Visionaire*. New media and increased fashion coverage made previously elite fashion accessible to a mass audience, but only as image, never as object. Throughout the 1990s the fashion show as a genre became increasingly spectacular, sometimes seeming to have evolved into pure performance in the extravagant shows of designers such as Alexander McQueen and John Galliano, evoking Susan Sontag's claim that 'a society becomes "modern" when one of its chief activities is producing and consuming images'.[19] For the public, it became possible to acquire a high degree of familiarity with such contemporary fashions, even a kind of 'ownership' of them, through the power of the image. Alison Gill suggests that contemporary fashion is

> worn first by 'star' bodies on runways, in a continuing flow of new commodifiable themes, gestures and styles . . . Yet we must also acknowledge the immaterial domain that has arrived with the material forms of fashion and extends its effects beyond clothing; fashion both designs and is designed by an empire of signs that propel and commutate at an ever-increasing speed, a domain into which we are all interpellated as 'fashioned people' whether we like it or not . . . Within this empire . . . our bodies . . . are repetitively styled and styling across lived domains both spectacular and mundane.[20]

Gill's references to 'star' bodies in the first line, and to 'spectacular domains' in the last, clearly evoke Debord's identification of culture as a star commodity in the society of the spectacle. She suggests, however, that the spectacle, far from simply seducing us visually, has become a regime, or practice, through which we are 'fashioned' as modern subjects. Similarly, Foucault reminds us that

> Our society is not one of spectacle, but of surveillance; under the surface of images, one invests bodies in depth . . . the play of signs defines the anchorages of power; it is not that the beautiful totality of the individual is amputated, repressed, altered by our social order, it is rather that the individual is carefully fabricated in it, according to a whole technique of forces and bodies.[21]

To Foucault, the spectacle was simply another technique of surveillance or, more subtly, as is suggested in this quotation, one of the forms of the 'the care of the self'.[22] The passage expresses the germ of an idea which Foucault was later to explore in his study of ancient Greek and Roman etiquette and other pre-Christian practices which, he argued, revealed the origins of the modern idea of existence as being dominated by self-preoccupation. Anthony Giddens has termed this modern self 'reflexive'[23] and identified it as particular to modernity because specific anxieties and risks are attached to it. Foucault, too, when he writes about dietary regimes and sexual activity as producing a 'modelled self',[24] draws a parallel between the pre-Christian world he writes about and the modern period. He argues that both are periods of transition in which, with the collapse of conventional morality, people have to create new and appropriate codes of behaviour and ethics.[25]

Yet while the image plays a role in 'the care of the self' it also, simultaneously, functions as 'sign' commercially. In the 1990s such images were not free-floating signifiers but part of a network of signs which constituted an expanded 'society of the spectacle' promoted and disseminated through the media. John Galliano was described by the British fashion journalist Sally Brampton as 'the greatest 3-D image-maker alive'. Brampton argued that he was partly responsible for the greatly increased attendance at the Paris shows, which she described as 'a media feeding frenzy as newspapers and television stations around the world give increasing prominence to fashion'.[26] For these designers the spectacle of the fashion show, simultaneously enticement and advertisement, was 'the theatre through which capitalism acts'.[27] Stéphane Wagner, professor and lecturer in communications at the Institut Français de la Mode, said in 1997: 'If we accept that much of haute couture is about squeezing out maximum media coverage – good or bad – then the more spectacular the presentation and collection, the better.'[28] It follows that if the garment as commodity mutated into new and hybrid forms, so too did the fashion show in the 1990s. A Prada menswear show took the form of a theatre play, with actors and dialogue. Helmut Lang put his show out on the internet. Hussein Chalayan's shows were designed like art installations by an architect, and featured male voice choirs or avant-garde music. John Galliano's were based on theatrical fantasy and excess. Alexander McQueen drenched his models in 'golden showers' or surrounded them with fake snowstorms. By contrast to the theatrics of many London designers, the Belgian Martin Margiela pioneered the use of derelict urban spaces for his shows; on one occasion the show invitations so closely resembled a cheap publicity flyer that rumour had it that fashion editors threw them away without recognising what they were. While, on the one hand, Margiela's undoubtedly innovative show designs could be said to function as Situationist-style stratagems to evade the ubiquitous 'society of the spectacle', it could equally be argued that Margiela simply traded on a particularly exclusive kind of 'distinction' which required insider knowledge of new fashion signs.

Perhaps it is because of the fashioned object's evolving status as 'sign' that so much was made in the 1990s of the affinities of art and fashion, an affinity charted by significant exhibitions,[29] coverage of fashion in art magazines,[30] academic discussion of the relationship of art to fashion,[31] and the evolution of a more 'conceptual' type of fashion designer[32] and design outlets.[33] One could also point to the establishment in Britain of the Jerwood prize for fashion, following the precedent set by the Jerwood prize for painting; the establishment in the USA and UK of *Fashion Theory*, the first academic journal devoted exclusively to that topic; and to the more general expansion of fashion studies in publishing and academia. Writing in *Fashion Theory*, the academic John Styles related the changing significance of fashion studies to:

> the postmodern turn in the human sciences – a downplaying of long historical trajectories and deep causes, a focus on surface phenomena and on diversity, a concern with the personal, the subjective and with identity. These postmodern priorities have worked to move the history of dress from the wings to the centre stage . . . Questions of meaning and interpretation now dominate the intellectual agenda . . . The broader intellectual developments that have propelled the history of dress to its new respectability have brought with them new ways of conceptualising that history.[34]

History

Ironically, however, the 'downplaying of long historical trajectories' in the human sciences was paralleled, in fashion design, by a renewed interest in historical citation. Just at the moment that the fashion commodity became image, it also became more referential, more historically or conceptually 'themed', perhaps to adapt to its additional role as bearer of ideas as well as socially constructed object. John Galliano evoked the seductive and vampish women of the beginning of the last century, mixing *belle époque* opulence with tribal imagery. Alexander McQueen's designs revealed a dark, sometimes cruel sexuality which was also historically nuanced, particularly in its play on the dark side of Victoriana, a theme also strikingly developed in the work of Belgian designers Olivier Theyskens and Veronique Branquinho. Vivienne Westwood recycled the sixteenth to the eighteenth centuries, particularly in her 'Britain must go Pagan' collections of the late 1980s to early 1990s.

How did these images of the past resonate in the visual economy of the late twentieth century? In the 1930s, Walter Benjamin wrote that 'every image of the past that is not recognized by the present as one of its own concerns threatens to disappear irretrievably'.[35] Later in the century, critics of postmodernism argued that in the 1980s and 1990s history was plundered to make a postmodern carnival, and that the incessant return to the past was itself a kind of deathly recycling of history which emptied it out of meaning, rendering it bankrupt, good only for costume drama and fantasy.[36] I would argue to the contrary, that contemporary fashion has an unerring eye for the topical in its choice of historical imagery, be it that of the sixteenth-century anatomist or the twentieth-century showgirl. Walter Benjamin wrote:

> [To the French Revolution] ancient Rome was a past charged with the time of the now . . . blasted out of the continuum of history.

> The French Revolution evoked ancient Rome the way fashion evokes
> costumes of the past. Fashion has a flair for the topical, no matter where
> it stirs in the thickets of long ago; it is a tiger's leap into the past.[37]

When John Galliano summoned up the luxurious dream worlds of nineteenth-
century Paris for Christian Dior, despite the nostalgia of his designs, his flair was
for the topical as it stirred 'in the thickets of long ago'. His designs evoked the
link between modernity, spectacle and consumption in the nineteenth-century city,
a link that was exemplified in the ambiguous figure of the *femme fatale* in which
desire was tinged with dread. But rather than literal re-creation, Galliano's 'tiger's
leap into the past', fusing cultures and histories, reconfigured the past in the light
of the present, 'a past charged with the time of the now . . . blasted out of the
continuum of history' to echo current concerns.

Benjamin's text implicitly recognises the pictorial and, particularly, emblematic
nature of fashion. If the fetishised commodity became image in the late twentieth
century, it began to function more like a Renaissance emblem than a commodity
per se, as the image became flooded with meaning. Like Renaissance and Baroque
emblem books, modern fashion gives us a collection of dislocated images in which
many narratives, histories and images are condensed. Fashion images, like emblems
or metaphors, are by their very nature densely packed with meanings which may
be both complex and contradictory. Their interpretation is inevitably marked
by the author's subjectivity. Yet because they also function in the modern period
as a 'semiotic consolidation of capitalism',[38] one can begin to trace connections,
re-seeing the past through the filter of present concerns, allowing fragments from
the past to illuminate the present.

Just before his death in 1985 the Italian writer Italo Calvino planned a series
of lectures on the future of literature in the new millennium. Making an eloquent
plea for the power of the image, he included visibility as a value to be saved in
the future in order to preserve the faculty of '*thinking* in terms of images'.[39] He
discussed the potentially debased value of the image in an image-saturated society
but also stressed the connection between image and the imaginary. As a child of
the 'civilisation of images', he had grown up 'daydreaming *within* the pictures'
of children's cartoons. Reading pictures without words was, for him, 'a schooling
in fable-making, in stylisation, in the composition of the image'.[40] As in Calvino's
writing, so in a certain school of 1990s European fashion design. The spectacular
fashion shows of the 1990s were characterised by these three things: fable-making,
stylisation, and highly mannered, elaborately composed images. Like writers, these
fashion designers were fabulists, for their work was profoundly narrative, structured
around stories and fables to produce what the German writer Stefan George, in
a discussion of Mallarmé, called the *Denkbild*, or thought-image, a way of writing
with hieroglyphic clarity in which found objects are 'steeped in traces and energies,
electric with significance'.[41] Calvino described the idea for a story coming to him
as an image that was 'charged with meaning', even though he could not formulate
it in discursive or conceptual terms. As it clarified in his mind, he set about making
it into a story: 'Around each image others come into being, forming a field of
analogies, symmetries, confrontations.'[42] Only then does the writer start to give

concrete form to these images. This concept of the image has something of the quality of the emblem. For the designer it permits the image to remain charged, forever potential rather than fixed, so that its meanings are always immanent, 'electric with significance'.

Via the fashion show, the single collection is further distilled, through press and magazine coverage, into a few pixilated emblems for the twenty-first century. One such example is encapsulated by Vivienne Westwood's persistent fascination with royalty, particularly with styling herself as the British queen. Her Autumn/Winter 1997–8 collection featured a black model as Queen Elizabeth I, and Westwood wore the same dress herself as Elizabeth I for a publicity photograph by Gian Paolo Barbieri. Jonathan Sawday interprets the lavish dress and bare chests of Elizabeth I and all her court ladies prior to marriage, in which each displayed her stomach and breasts, as a kind of female blazon; and he argues that where the queen teasingly revealed and then concealed her body before her courtiers, 'she appeared to control her own self-blazoning'.[43] A blazon was an erotic poem to a woman's body parts. The sixteenth-century blazon was a self-perpetuating poetic form; blazons produced counter-blazons and counter-counter-blazons in which male poets traded the images of their mistresses' body parts, turning erotic hymn into rivalry and, in the process, piling up images of body parts like contemporary anatomists. Sawday argues that the English blazon was produced in a forum that was more erotically charged than the French court, because of the sex of the ruling monarch, Elizabeth I, the 'virgin queen'.[44] To the image of Westwood as Elizabeth I, one could add another: the image of Westwood insouciantly blazoning herself outside Buckingham Palace, the home of the second Queen Elizabeth. As Westwood posed for the press outside Buckingham Palace where she had just received an OBE, her skirt blew up to reveal that she wore no knickers under her tights. The image of Westwood with her skirt blowing up also evokes the famous scene in *The Seven Year Itch* when Marilyn Monroe's skirt is blown up by a gust from a vent but with the difference that Westwood was in her fifties, amply at ease with her own body and, unlike the tragic Monroe, in charge of her own destiny.

In other respects, too, the sixteenth and seventeenth centuries were evoked in contemporary design. The shows of the London designers Alexander McQueen, Andrew Groves and Tristan Webber, evidenced a fascination with Baroque theatricality, artifice and the staging of perversion in the violence and drama of their stagecraft. Even where their themes were contemporary, such as the troubles in Northern Ireland or J.G. Ballard's *Cocaine Nights*, these were tinged with Jacobean cruelty and sexuality. For Walter Benjamin the fragmented nature of the German Baroque mourning play (a play about loss, ruination and transience) mourns the off-stage transition to capitalist modernity. As such, it helps us to understand the fragmented nature of modernity in the nineteenth century when, he writes, 'the emblems return as commodities.'[45] Something of this idea was caught in Alexander McQueen's second couture collection for Givenchy, 'Eclect Dissect', shown in Paris in July 1997, which was based on the story of a fictional *fin de siècle* surgeon and collector who travelled the world collecting exotic objects, textiles and women which he subsequently cut up and reassembled in his laboratory. The 'scenario' of the catwalk show staged the return of these gruesomely murdered women who came back to haunt the living. It was shown in a Paris medical school, swathed with blood-red velvet curtains and decorated with medical specimens.

'Eclect Dissect' fused seventeenth-century anatomical drawings and late-Victorian dress references with the entirely modern theme of the serial killer. For Benjamin, there was a link between nineteenth-century consumption and the rise of mercantile capitalism in the seventeenth century. The culture of the Reformation was a culture in the early stages of capitalist transition; the culture of the nineteenth century one in which capitalist production was consolidated, expanded and modified through the processes of industrialisation and urbanisation. Both were cultures of transition, in which all fixed points seem to have been removed. Our own period of globalisation and fast-changing technology shares this characteristic, which may account for some writers' fascination with the themes of abjection, trauma and anxiety in the present.[46] In moments of rapidly changing fashion, mutability itself becomes charged with meaning because it can enact, or speak, anxiety through the process of change. Fashion 'acts out' transition in periods which feel, to their participants, unstable. Thus its 'tiger's leap' into what can seem over-the-top historical pastiche frequently reveals the same aesthetic and cultural concerns as the period which is seized on in the present, and can be construed as a kind of 'acting out' of current concerns as they are revealed through past images.

Dialectical images

Whereas fashion's transience guaranteed it a marginal role in historical accounts of more stable social periods, the emphasis on change, fluidity and risk in contemporary society[47] makes it an avatar of modern sensibilities. As such, fashion is a paradigm of a mutated commodity form in a society of the spectacle in transition. The new, and still evolving, visual economy in which fashion operates feeds on instability and alteration, always the defining characteristics of fashion. Now, however, those characteristics typify the modern world, not just fashion, so that it becomes an emblem of modernity itself. In this it functions as what Walter Benjamin called a dialectical image. In his unfinished *Arcades Project*[48] Benjamin fastened on certain images of the nineteenth century which he felt resonated in his own period, the 1930s: the figure of the prostitute, the city of Paris, its early nineteenth-century arcades and late nineteenth-century shop windows, urban consumption on the one hand and, on the other, urban dereliction and detritus in the form of the ruin, dust, and the ragpicker. These 'dialectical images' were not based on simple comparisons between past and present; rather, they created a more complex historical relay of themes. For Benjamin, the relationship between images of the past and the present worked like the montage technique of cinema.[49] The principle of montage is that a third meaning is created by the juxtaposition of two images, rather than any immutable meaning inhering in each image. Benjamin conceived of this relationship as a dialectical one: the motifs of the past and the present functioned as thesis and antithesis. The flash of recognition of the historical object within a charged forcefield of past and present was the dialectical image that transformed both.[50]

Onto the idea of *Denkbilder*, or 'thought-images', one could graft Benjamin's description of 'wish images' in which 'the old and new interpenetrate'.[51] One such example is 'passing fashions', which display both a desire to rid oneself of the unsatisfactory present, especially the recent past, and a utopian desire for newness.[52] As a dialectical image, fashion anticipates technological change by creating its effects through other means, which prefigure the technology of the future. Benjamin argues that fashion's mutability is a kind of semaphore of secret signals of the future: 'Whoever understands how to read these semaphors would know in advance not only about new currents in the arts but also about new legal codes, wars and revolutions.'[53]

Yet, at the same time that it looks forwards, fashion also looks backwards. For Benjamin, 'the true dialectical theatre of fashion' is due to its ability to refabricate the very old as the most up to the minute.[54] Ulrich Lehmann draws on Proust's and Benjamin's formulation of true memory as 'involuntary' to argue that 'in fashion, quotation is sartorial remembrance', and that fashion activates the past in the present by rewriting its own themes and motifs through historical quotation.[55] In Proust's '*mémoire involontaire*', chance encounters with objects bring back experiences that would otherwise have remained dormant or forgotten.[56] Lehmann discusses how the turn-of-the-century designs of Jeanne Paquin evoked the revolutionary period of a hundred years earlier. Today Paquin's period furnishes the imagery for John Galliano's vamps, sirens and seductresses.[57] Yet the historicism of Galliano's evocations of the image of woman as 'commodity and seller in one', as Benjamin described the prostitute,[58] does not simply recreate the past nostalgically, but also brings it into the present by picturing the relationship between fashion, women, spectacle, and commodification today.[59] Esther Leslie argues that Benjamin jolts Proust's method into modernity by imagining memories as 'involuntarily summonised strips of montaged images' which flash past in rapid sequence, to provide 'an unexpected, shocking link between an experience in the present and one in the past. It disrupts linearity, confounds temporality.'[60]

For Benjamin, some historical images only 'developed' in the future:

> If one wishes to view history as a text, then it is valid to suggest what a recent author has said about literary ones: the past has deposited such images in them as can be compared with those that are caught on a light-sensitive plate. 'Only the future has at its disposal a developer strong enough to let the image appear in all its details.'[61]

The imagery of fashion today can be construed as the 'developer' of earlier moments of capitalist production and transition, be they the sixteenth, seventeenth or nineteenth centuries. Current fashion imagery is the means of developing the image in the 'light' (that is, the darkroom) of the present, whether those images are historical ones, such as Galliano's opulent *fin de siècle* evocations, or images of the passage of time itself, such as Margiela's use of decay and dereliction, discussed in the next section. And the afterlife of today's imagery will perhaps develop again, in ways we cannot imagine, in the future.

Jolted out of the context of the past, the dialectical image can be read in the present as a 'truth'. But for Benjamin it was not an absolute truth, rather a truth that was fleeting and temporal, existing only at the moment of perception, characterised by 'shock' or vivid recognition: 'the true picture of the past flits by. The past can be seized only as an image which flashes up at the instant when it can be recognised and is never seen again.'[62] It was not that the past simply illuminated the present, or that the present illuminated the past; rather, the two images came together in a 'critical constellation', tracing a previously concealed connection.[63] Fashion was one of the key tropes of nineteenth-century Paris identified by Benjamin as a 'dialectical image' precisely because of its capacity to reverberate in time, to obscure the linearity of history in favour of what Jean Baudrillard calls the 'cyclical time' with which fashion replaces linear time.[64] Citing the French historian Michelet's epigram that 'each epoch dreams the one that follows', Benjamin wrote that 'every epoch, in fact, not only dreams the one to follow but, in dreaming, precipitates its awakening'.[65] And he argued that dialectical thinking was the organ of historical awakening.

Benjamin believed that conventional historical writing promulgated fictions which concealed the truth; indeed, he regarded such history-writing as having been 'the strongest narcotic of the [nineteenth] century',[66] a phrase that recalls Marx's categorisation of religion as the opium of the people. The role of the dialectical image was to rescue the historical object by ripping it out of the narratives of law, religion and art. Crucially, for Benjamin, his 'truth' was to be revealed through visual rather than linear logic. 'As in a flashing image, in the now of recognition, the past is to be held fast', wrote Benjamin.[67] His ideas offer art and design historians a complex and sophisticated model of how visual seduction works, because his ideas are predicated on an understanding of how visual similes function in an image-driven society, something which other historians have not privileged. Benjamin gives us a methodology particularly appropriate to fashion, and also particularly appropriate to the present moment, because of the way visual culture has developed in recent decades. His method allows us to perceive similarities across periods apparently separated by rupture and discontinuity, and to plot historical time not as something that flows smoothly from past to present but as a more complex relay of turns and returns, in which the past is activated by injecting the present into it.[68] Thus, for example, in the designs of John Galliano, we can 'activate' the excess and opulence of nineteenth-century Parisian consumer culture by 'injecting' it with the excess and opulence of Galliano's contemporary designs, to understand both in terms of 'modernity' and how it can resonate in the present.

Dereliction

Even where a designer does not explicitly use historical references, nevertheless the passage of time can be conjured up by the lustre, sheen or patina of a garment. Grant McCracken has argued that patina and fashion are inimical: in his analysis patina was a signifier of social status until the eighteenth century, when it was eclipsed by the consumer revolution that formed the bedrock of the modern fashion system in which status is marked by novelty rather than by the signs of longevity and age.[69] Thus, he states, fashion is the 'terrible rival' of patina. Yet at the end of the twentieth century, just as one group of designers began to play with historical citation in the most up-to-the-minute clothes, so too did another group begin to introduce the theme of patina into their more avant-garde designs. The signs of ageing, and the idea of a history, were replicated in the work of a number of designers whose work was not overtly historically themed but which, instead, drew on motifs of refuse, detritus, remnants from the past which were transformed in the present. Martin Margiela re-used second-hand clothing, which he described as giving it a new life, as did the New York designer Susan Cianciolo and the British-based Jessica Ogden whose clothes were patterned with biography. Made from second-hand fabrics, they bore the trace of the past in their stains, darns and hand-sewn seams. Where Ogden used new cloth she often stained it first, not to 'antique' it but to imbue it with feeling. She described her garments as if they were sentient, capable of bearing memory traces. Robert Cary-Williams too created a stage setting for the history and the life of a garment:

> My kimono dress is tattered so it will leave pieces behind everywhere it is worn until there is only a little bit left at the top, then it has had its life . . . Some pieces will be at a party and others will be at someone's house, like some of the spirit of the garment is left everywhere.[70]

Viktor & Rolf's second collection in 1994 consisted of twenty versions of the same white dress in early nineteenth-century style on which they had carried out various experiments: slamming it in a door, cutting it, burning it, and embroidered stains on it. Themes of death and disaster permeated some other collections: Robert Cary-Williams' Autumn/Winter 1999 collection was called 'Victorian Car Crash':

> the inspiration for this collection was a woman from the Victorian era who somehow ends up in the present day . . . She's run over by a car. She survives, but the clothes get damaged.[71]

Latex and leather jackets, dresses and full skirts were cut away so they fell from the body, leaving only an armature of seams and zips to trace the ghostly presence of the former garment in space. In the same period, the design team Boudicca produced shattered tailoring, inspired by genetically misshapen clothing forms, grafting jacket parts on to coats and dresses. Their Autumn/Winter 1999–2000 'Distress Dress', in high-visibility orange nylon, was based on the black box after a plane crash: 'In fact it is orange. We thought it was interesting because it contains the pilot's last words.'[72] These designs were predicated on the conceit that the supposedly inanimate garment assumed an uncanny life of its own, not unlike Max Klinger's series of etchings *The Glove* from the 1880s, which depict the proto-Surrealist adventures of the glove in episodes of abduction, seduction and abandonment.

For other designers, the theme of decay evoked the passage of time. As Marx wrote, 'in history as in nature, decay is the laboratory of life'.[73] Hussein Chalayan's 1993 graduate collection featured fabrics which had been buried with iron filings for several weeks before being dug up to reveal a veneer of rust. In 1997 Martin Margiela produced an entire exhibition where moulds and bacteria were 'grown' on his clothes. The London-based designer Shelley Fox gave her textiles a patina of decay and age; wool was felted and scorched, laser-cut and bubbled, or burnt with a blow torch. Her wrecked textiles, like Margiela's tracery of mould and decay, summoned up another of Benjamin's figures, the nineteenth-century ragpicker who scavenged cloth for recycling, recuperating cultural detritus cast aside by capitalist societies.

Although Margiela and Fox used the techniques of the avant-garde, their practice was rooted firmly in commerce. As 'dialectical images', their patinated textiles illuminated the parallels which underwrite the free-market economy of fashion, both past and present: between elite fashion and ragpicking, luxury and poverty, excess and deprivation. All the examples of late twentieth-century fashion design cited in this article are framed, symbolically, by two nineteenth-century emblems of the capitalist process: the woman of fashion on the one hand, and the ragpicker on the other. Though they seem diametrically opposite to each other, and the status of one was as exalted as that of the other was debased, yet both were part of the same economic process, equally locked into the fashion system by nineteenth-century *laissez-faire* policies. Fox and Margiela's images of melancholy dereliction are the flipside of capitalist excess, just as the nineteenth-century ragpicker formed an eloquent counterpoint to the woman of fashion. These are the twin ghosts of the past that today's designers call up: John Galliano, in his evocations of *fin de siècle* luxury and excess; Martin Margiela in the mouldy tatters of his more experimental practice. Margiela's mannequins and mouldy clothes draw our attention to the darker side of capitalist modernity, a darkness that also surfaces when earlier centuries of capitalist transformation are drawn on in contemporary design such as Alexander McQueen's 'Eclect Dissect' collection for Givenchy. As I have suggested, this is due in part to the sense of instability produced in a period of rapid change that leads it to track back to comparable images of instability in the past. However, this historical relay is an index not merely of sensibilities but also, and equally, of how such sensibilities are anchored in specific moments of capitalist production and consumption, and of technological change.

Trace

The haunting of contemporary fashion design by images from the past is a kind of return of the repressed, in which shards of history work their way to the surface in new formations and are put to work as contemporary emblems. The fragmented and episodic traces of the past that surface in contemporary designs are traces of instability and transience. These traces come back as fragments under the weight of some cultural trauma, which has been expressed by historians of modernity as 'shock' and 'neurasthenia',[74] and by writers about contemporary culture as 'trauma' or 'wound culture'.[75] In particular, contemporary fashion has fastened on the themes of instability and alteration, selecting past images of mutability which resonate in the present. Fashion imagery, itself semiotically unstable, thus fixes images of instability and change, but in ways that destabilise conventional history, and run counter to the idea of coherent narrative. They demand, rather, a re-evaluation of the imagery of the past in the light of the present – something that characterises the work of Michel Foucault as well as that of Walter Benjamin.

For Foucault, the breaks, ruptures, and discontinuities of history serve to unravel the straightforward relationship of causes and effects over time. All history is written about from the perspective of the present, in the sense that the present throws up the themes to be studied historically. Because the present is always in a state of transformation, the past must constantly be re-evaluated; and the past takes on new meanings in the light of new events in the present. This is 'genealogy': history written in the light of current concerns.[76] It is also something very like the actual process of fashion design. John Galliano and Alexander McQueen's work reveals complex historical relays between past and present. In one collection McQueen explored the relationship between the nineteenth-century Arts and Crafts movement and what he called 'the hard edge of the technology of textiles'. Segueing between pre-industrial craft imagery and post-industrial urban alienation, the collection combined moulded leather body corsets with frothy white lace, punched wooden fan skirts and regency striped silk. The show was opened by the athlete and model Aimee Mullins in a pair of hand-carved prosthetic legs designed by McQueen (the model was born without shin bones and had her legs amputated below the knee at the age of one), and was closed by the model Shalom Harlow, who revolved like a music box doll on a turntable as her white dress was sprayed acid green and black by two menacing industrial paint sprays which suddenly came to life on the catwalk.

Juxtaposing the organic with the inorganic (a model that mimicked a doll, a paint spray that mimicked human motions, and an artificial leg that enhanced human performance), the collection skewed the relation of object and subject to evoke Marx's nineteenth-century commodity exchange in which 'people and things traded semblances: social relations take on the character of object relations and commodities assume the active agency of people.'[77] In the figures of these two young women the ghosts of Marx seemed to flutter up and live again at the end of the twentieth century, as the embodied forms of alienation, reification and commodity fetishism.

In such collections, fragments and traces from the past reverberate in the present. Reversing Foucault's idea of 'genealogy'; that is, of history written in the light of current concerns, one might use the idea of the historical fragment to uncover traces from the past and to read the present through them. All the traces, or fragments, of history that surface in fashion design do so as images. This is how the connections made between past and present are tracked, by finding traces of the past in the present, articulated through visual means. Raphael Samuel's *Theatre of Memory* uses the idea that objects are emotion holders, traces of the past, and carriers of discourse from other times into the present.[78] The artist Joseph Beuys believed that materials, such as the felt and fat which he used, carried traces of the past with them.[79] In a similar way contemporary fashion images are bearers of meaning and, as such, stretch simultaneously back to the past and forward into the future. Not just documents or records but fertile primary sources, they can generate new ideas and meanings and themselves carry discourse into the future, so that they take their place in a chain of meaning, or a relay of signifiers, rather than being an end product of linear history.

In other words, images are a cultural archive which can be raided to make sense of the present. However, for an understanding of how visual similes work, we must turn back to Walter Benjamin because, as I have argued, only his analysis engages with the singular and complex nature of images themselves. In this context, his concept of the 'trace', from his Arcades project, could be used in a new kind of cultural analysis, more fragmented and less coherent than the historian's, in which the fashion historian and the designer alike are scavengers, moving through cultural history like the figure of the ragpicker sifting rubbish in the nineteenth-century city.[80] The historical fragment, or trace, can illuminate the present. Benjamin uses the term 'trace' to describe the mark left by the fossil (that is, the commodity) on the plush of bourgeois interiors or on the velvet linings of their cases.[81] Here, history turns into detective story, with the historical trace as a clue. The figures of the collector, the ragpicker and the detective wander through Benjamin's landscape. Thus the historian/designer's method is akin to that of the ragpicker who moves through the city gathering scraps for recycling. Irving Wohlfarth argues that the ragpicker, as a collector of 'the refuse of history', is the incognito of the author: 'the historian as *chiffonier* unceremoniously transports these leftovers of the nineteenth century across the threshold of the twentieth.'[82]

I have assumed an equivalence here between the historian and the designer. Perhaps, however, the designer makes a better cultural *chiffonier* than the historian. Stephen Greenblatt has articulated the notion of a historical method of 'talking to the dead' and the dead themselves leaving textual traces.[83] Howard Felperin has taken him to task for his tendency to 'cultural poetics' rather than 'cultural material-ism', and Graham Holderness has suggested that Greenblatt's approach tells us more about our own concerns in the present than about the period studied.[84] While such criticisms may legitimately be made of the historian, designers can take liberties and poeticise; Leila Zenderland talks about how the past can be put to use by non-his-torians, suborning ghosts to speak to contemporary concerns.[85] Citing the popular-ity in the 1970s, among both black and white Americans, of Alex Haley's book and television drama *Roots*, she talks about 'myth-symbol scholarship' where history becomes myth in the course of its redeployment. As such, it allows us to scan traces of the past for their mythic meanings, rather than their historical truths.

My descriptions of 'dialectical images' in contemporary fashion are not properly cultural materialism at all, but, rather, examples of how the traces of the past can be woven into the fabric of a new story to illuminate the present. Yet Benjamin's concept of 'dialectical images' serves as something more than a hermeneutic tool to interpret the work of a few designers. Rather, it unlocks the way in which the work of these designers – fragmented, episodic and emblematic – helps us to make sense of contemporary culture and its concerns. The designers I have discussed all practise a form of 'cultural poetics', evoked through visions of either capitalist excess or melancholy dereliction, the two opposing poles of nineteenth-century *laissez-faire* economic policies, both locked equally into the fashion system. I have suggested that this is due in part to the sense of instability produced in a period of rapid change that leads it to track back to comparable images of instability in the past. Perhaps this is connected too with the nihilism that characterises the present moment. Whereas modernism thought it could produce a brave new world, the postmodern period has been marked, rather, by the sense of an ending;[86] this shift is reflected in the 'cultural poetics' of today's designers, whose evocations of history and time suggest a sense of crisis or trauma in the present.

Acknowledgement

Thanks to the Arts and Humanities Research Board of Great Britain whose funding of the 'Fashion and Modernity' research group at Central Saint Martin's College of Art and Design, London, 1999–2000, facilitated the writing of this chapter.

Notes to the Foreword

1   p. 85, this edition.
2   Roger Tredre, interview with the author, 3 March 2013.
3   Sally Loxley, assistant stylist and PhD candidate at Central Saint Martins (University of the Arts London), interview with the author 1 April 2013. I am indebted to her postgraduate research in constructing the brief chronology of the developments in digital and moving fashion images since 2000 contained in this article.
4   'Fashion film' would be more accurately termed 'fashion moving image' but the former term has become current usage and for that reason I adopt it here. For SHOWstudio, see www.showstudio.com. On fashion film, see: Nathalie Khan, 'Cutting the Fashion Body: Why the Fashion Image is No Longer Still', 16 (2), *Fashion Theory* (June 2012, pp. 235–49); Marketa Uhlirova, '100 Years of the Fashion Film: Frameworks and Histories', 17 (2), *Fashion Theory* (April 2013, pp. 137–58); Marketa Uhlirova, 'The Fashion-Film Effect', in Djurdja Bartlett, Shaun Cole and Agnes Rocamora (eds.) *Fashion Media: Interrogating Words and Images,* (Oxford: Berg, 2013).
5   www.youtube.com/watch?v=S3N8QZTsZic. The film attracted over 150,000 viewers on You Tube in the first few days.
6   See too Agnès Rocamora, 'Remediation and Hypertextuality in the Fashion Media: The Case of Fashion Blogs', *Journalism Practice,* 6 (1), 2012, pp. 92–106.
7   Elizabeth Wilson, *Adorned in Dreams: Fashion and Modernity*. (London and New York: I.B. Tauris, revised and updated version, 2003), p. 248.
8   Michel Foucault, *The Archaeology of Knowledge*. [1969] Trans. A.M. Sheridan Smith. (London: Routledge, 1997), p. 5.
9   Michel Foucault, *The Order of Things: An Archaeology of the Human Sciences*. [1966] Trans. from the French. (London: Routledge, 1997), p. 369.
10 On remediation, see Lev Manovich, *The Language of New Media*. (Cambridge, Mass and London UK: MIT Press, 2001).
11 Jacques Le Goff, *History and Memory*. Trans. Steven Rendell and Elizabeth Claman. (New York: Columbia University Press, 2002), pp. xvii and 89–92.
12 Le Goff, *History and Memory,* p. 96. Pierre Nora, 'Between Memory and History: *Les Lieux de Mémoire*'. *Representations*, 26, Spring 1989, pp. 7–25. The Nora quotation is from p. 14.
13 Carolyn Steedman, *Dust*. (Manchester: Manchester University Press, 2001), p. 68.
14 pp. 96–7, this edition.

Notes

1   I have used this opportunity to draw extensively on theory; this has precluded my giving as much space to contemporary fashion design as I would have liked. The fashion examples given are brief illustrations.
2   Stephen Gan, *Visionaire's Fashion 2001: Designers of the New Avant-Garde*, edited by Alix Browne, London, Laurence King, 1999.

3   Lorraine Gamman and Merja Makinen, *Female Fetishism: A New Look*, London, Lawrence & Wishart, 1994, 32–5.

4   Hal Foster, *The Return of the Real: the Avant-Garde at the End of the Century*, Cambridge, MA and London, MIT Press, 1996, 83.

5   Kevin Robins, *Into the Image: Culture and Politics in the Field of Vision*, London and New York, Routledge, 1996, 12.

6   Olivier Theyskens, Autumn–Winter 1998–9. W. & L.T., Autumn–Winter 1996–7 and Autumn–Winter 1997–8. Illustrated in: Luc Deryke and Sandra Van de Veire (eds), *Belgian Fashion Design*, Ghent and Amsterdam, The Netherlands, Ludion, 1999, 202–3.

7   Guy Debord, *Société du spectacle*, Paris, Buchet/Chastel, 1967. English edn: *The Society of the Spectacle*, London, Zone Books, 1994, para. 1.

8   Martin Jay, *Downcast Eyes: The Denigration of Vision in Twentieth-Century French Thought*, Berkeley and London, University of California Press, 1993, 427. Debord, op. cit., para. 4.

9   Debord, op. cit., para. 49.

10 Debord, op. cit., para. 10.

11 Debord, op. cit., para. 2.

12 Martin Harrison, *Shots of Style: Great Fashion Photographs Chosen by David Bailey*, London, Victoria & Albert Museum Publications, 1985, 13.

13 Rosalind H. Williams, *Dream Worlds: Mass Consumption in Late Nineteenth-Century France*, Berkeley, Los Angeles and Oxford, England, University of California Press, 1982.

14 Debord, op. cit., para. 193.

15 T.J. Clark, *The Painting of Modern Life: Paris in the Art of Manet and his Followers*, Princeton, Princeton University Press, and London, Thames & Hudson, 1984. Thomas Richards, *The Commodity Culture of Victorian England: Advertising and Spectacle, 1851–1914*, London and New York, Verso, 1991. Heather McPhearson 'Sarah Bernhardt: portrait of the actress as spectacle', *Nineteenth-Century Contexts*, 1999, 20 (4): 409–54. Thanks to Carol Tulloch for bringing this invaluable article to my attention.

16 Richards, op. cit., 258.

17 Richard Sennett, *Welfare after the Welfare State*, lecture at Bishopsgate Institute, London, 20 May 1999.

18 Gilles Lipovetsky, *The Empire of Fashion: Dressing Modern Democracy*, trans. Catherine Porter, Princeton, Princeton University Press, 1994.

19 Susan Sontag, *On Photography*, Harmondsworth, Penguin, 1979, 153.

20 Alison Gill, 'Deconstructing Fashion: The Making of Unfinished, Decomposing and Re-assembled Clothes', *Fashion Theory: The Journal of Dress, Body and Culture*, March 1998, 2 (1): 25–49, 27.

21 Michel Foucault, *Discipline and Punish; The Birth of the Prison*, trans. Alan Sheridan, Harmondsworth, Penguin, 1977, 217.

22 Michel Foucault, *The History of Sexuality, Volume 3: The Care of the Self*, trans. Robert Hurley, Harmondsworth, Penguin, 1984.

23 Anthony Giddens, *Modernity and Self-Identity*, Cambridge, Polity Press, 1991.

24 Michel Foucault, *The History of Sexuality, Volume 2: The Use of Pleasure*, trans. Robert Hurley, New York, Viking, Pantheon, 1985.

25 For a discussion of Foucault in relation to contemporary postmodernism and fashion see Elizabeth Wilson, 'Fashion and the postmodern body' in Juliet Ash and Elizabeth Wilson (eds), *Chic Thrills: A Fashion Reader*, London, Pandora Press, 1992, 3–16.

26 *Guardian*, 14 October 1998.

27   Richards, op. cit., 251.

28   Quoted in Stephen Todd, 'The Importance of Being English', *Blueprint*, March 1997, 42.

29   In 1983 the Costume Institute of the Metropolitan Museum of Art in New York showed a 25-year retrospective exhibition of Yves Saint Laurent, after which other museums gradually also began to mount fashion exhibitions, not always on the topic of single designers. These included: *Fashion and Surrealism* at the FIT Gallery in New York in 1987 and the Victoria and Albert Museum in London in 1988; *Infra-Apparel* at the Costume Institute of the Metropolitan Museum of Art in 1991; *Street Style* at the Victoria and Albert Museum, London, 1994. In the 1990s, three internationally reviewed exhibitions explicitly linked art and fashion thematically: *Mode et Art*, Brussels and Montreal, 1993; *Il tempo e le mode* (Looking at Fashion), Florence Biennale, 1996, which was further developed as *Art/Fashion*, Guggenheim Museum, Soho, New York, 1997; and *Addressing the Century: A Hundred Years of Art and Fashion*, Hayward Gallery, London, 1998, and Kunstmuseum, Wolfsburg, 1989. In the same period there were also a range of smaller, innovative exhibitions linking art and fashion in Europe and New York.

30   The March 1982 issue of the New York magazine *Artforum* featured an Issey Miyake collaboration on its cover. Throughout the 1980s and 1990s art magazines such as *Artforum*, *Art in America*, *Flash Art* and *Frieze* began to give editorial coverage to more 'avant-garde' designers such as Comme des Garçons and Martin Margiela and, subsequently, to feature advertisements from fashion companies like Helmut Lang and Prada. There is a list of some of this editorial coverage tabulated in: Sung Bok Kim, 'Is fashion art?', *Fashion Theory*, March 1998, 60–61. See, too, Michael Boodroo, 'Art and fashion', *Artnews*, September 1990, 120–27.

31   For example, Robert Radford, 'Dangerous liaisons: art, fashion and individualism', *Fashion Theory*, June 1998, 151–64.

32   Following on from the first wave of Japanese designers in the 1970s–80s, namely Issey Miyake, Comme des Garçons and Yohji Yamamoto, in the 1990s one could cite graduates of the Antwerp Academy of Design and London's Central St Martins College of Art and Design, such as Martin Margiela and Hussein Chalayan. In New York in the late 1990s Susan Cianciolo was a rare American practitioner of a more conceptual trend in fashion design.

33   Such as The Pineal Eye in London and Colette in Paris. While not a retail space, the Judith Clark Costume Gallery in London was also influential in promoting critical attitudes to fashion.

34   John Styles, 'Dress in history: reflections on a contested terrain', *Fashion Theory*, December 1998, 387.

35   Walter Benjamin, 'Theses on the philosophy of history', *Illuminations*, trans. Harry Zohn, London, Fontana/Collins, 1973, 257.

36   Fredric Jameson, *Postmodernism, or the Cultural Logic of Late Capitalism*, London and New York, Verso, 1991.

37   Walter Benjamin, op. cit., 263.

38   Richards, op. cit., from the acknowledgements, unpaginated.

39   Italo Calvino, *Six Memos for the Next Millennium*, trans. Patrick Creagh, London, Jonathan Cape, 1992, 92.

40   Ibid, 94.

41   Esther Leslie, 'Souvenirs and forgetting: Walter Benjamin's memory-work' in Marius Kwint, Christopher Breward and Jeremy Aynsley (eds), *Material Memories: Design and Evocation*, Oxford and New York, Berg, 1999, 112.

42   Calvino, op. cit., 89.

43   Jonathan Sawday, *The Body Emblazoned: Dissection and the Human Body in Renaissance Culture*, London and New York, Routledge, 1995, 198. Sawday quotes the words of the French ambassador in 1597 who described the queen as wearing: 'black tafetta, bound with gold lace . . . a petticoat of white damask, girdled, and open in front, as was also her chemise, in such a manner that she often opened this dress, and one could see all her belly, and even to her navel . . . she has a trick of putting both her hands on her gown and opening it insomuch that all her belly can be seen.'

44   Sawday, op. cit., 197.

45   Susan Buck-Morss, *The Dialectics of Seeing: Walter Benjamin and the Arcades Project*, Cambridge, MA and London, MIT Press, 1989, 181.

46   See Hal Foster, *The Return of the Real*, op. cit., for a discussion of 'trauma' culture by an art historian; Peggy Phelan, *Mourning Sex: Performing Public Memories*, London and New York, Routledge, 1997; Paul Aritze and Michael Lambek (eds), *Tense Past: Cultural Essays in Trauma and Memory*, London and New York, Routledge, 1996; and, for a characterisation of 'wound culture', Mark Seltzer, *Serial Killers: Death and Life in America's Wound Culture*, New York and London, Routledge, 1998, which discusses anxiety, change, fear and trauma in relation to contemporary culture. A number of cultural critics since the 1990s have adapted pathological terms such as trauma and anxiety to discuss wider formations of cultural anxiety and trauma. Frank Füredi, *Mythical Past, Elusive Future: History and Society in an Anxious Age*, London, Pluto Press, 1992, characterises contemporary nostalgia as a form of anxiety about the future. See, too, Sarah Dunant and Roy Porter (eds), *The Age of Anxiety*, London, Virago, 1996 and Jeffrey Weeks, *Inventing Moralities: Sexual Values in an Age of Uncertainty*, New York, Columbia University Press, 1995.

47   Anthony Giddens, *The Consequences of Modernity*, California, Stanford University Press, 1990 and Cambridge, Polity Press, 1991. Ulrich Beck, *Risk Society: Towards a New Modernity*, trans. M. Ritter, London, Sage Publications, 1992.

48   Walter Benjamin, *The Arcades Project*, trans. Howard Eiland and Kevin McLaughlin, Cambridge, MA and London, The Belknap Press of Harvard University Press, 1999.

49   Buck-Morss, op. cit., 250.

50   Buck-Morss, op. cit., 250, 219.

51   Benjamin, 1999, op. cit., 4.

52   Benjamin, 1999, op. cit., 4–5.

53   Benjamin, 1999, op. cit., 64. As a marginal note Adorno wrote, 'I would think, counterrevolutions.'

54   Benjamin, op. cit., 64.

55   Ulrich Lehmann, '*Tigersprung*: fashioning history', *Fashion Theory*, September 1999, 308.

56   See Esther Leslie, op. cit., 116–17.

57   Colin McDowell, *Galliano*, London, Weidenfeld & Nicolson, 1997.

58   Buck-Morss, op. cit., 184.

59   Caroline Evans, 'John Galliano: spectacle and modernity', in Ian Griffiths and Nicola White (eds) *The Fashion Business: Theory, Practice, Image*, Oxford, Berg Publishers, 2000 discusses the relationship between nineteenth-century consumption, modernity and the 1990s fashion designs of Galliano.

60   Leslie, op. cit., 117.

61   Benjamin, cited in Leslie, op. cit., 109.

62   Benjamin, 1973, op. cit., 257.

63   Buck-Morss, op. cit.,185, 221, 250, 290.

64   Jean Baudrillard, *Symbolic Exchange and Death*, trans. Iain Hamilton, London, Sage Publications, 1993.

65   Benjamin, 1999, op. cit., 13.

66   Benjamin, 1999, op. cit., 218.

67   Benjamin, 1999, op. cit., 219.

68   For a discussion of fashion and Benjamin's historical method, see Ulrich Lehmann, '*Tigersprung*: fashioning history', *Fashion Theory*, September 1999, 297–322. Hal Foster, *The Return of the Real: The Avant Garde at the End of the Century*, Cambridge, MA and London, MIT Press, 1996, is similarly concerned with the temporality of twentieth-century avant-gardes, and with what Foster calls 'the co-ordination of diachronic (or historical) and synchronic (or social) axes in art and history' (p. xii).

69   Grant McCracken, *Culture and Consumption: New Approaches to the Symbolic Character of Consumer Goods and Activities*, Bloomington, Indiana University Press, 1990, 31–43.

70   Robert Cary-Williams interviewed by Lou Winwood, *Sleazenation*, 7 Nov. 1998.

71   Stephen Gan, op. cit.

72   Quoted in Susannah Frankel, 'We want to be', *Independent Magazine*, 8 May 1999, 30.

73   Cited in Georges Bataille, *Visions of Excess: Selected Writings, 1927–1939*, ed. and trans. Allan Stoekl, Minneapolis, University of Minnesota Press, 1985, 32.

74   Walter Benjamin's concept of 'shock' and Georg Simmel's notion of 'neurasthenia' are summarised and discussed in Mike Featherstone, *Consumer Culture and Postmodernism*, London, Sage Publications, New Delhi, Thousand Oaks, 1991; Bryan S. Turner (ed.), *Theories of Modernity and Postmodernity*, London, Sage Publications, New Delhi, Newbury Park, 1990.

75   See Foster, op. cit., and Seltzer, op. cit.

76   Michel Foucault, *The Order of Things: An Archaeology of the Human Sciences*, trans. A. M. Sheridan-Smith, New York, Vintage, 1973; Michel Foucault, *The Archaeology of Knowledge*, trans. A. M. Sheridan-Smith, London, Tavistock, 1974.

77   Hal Foster, 'The art of fetishism', *The Princeton Architectural Journal*, vol. titled 'Fetish', 1992 (4): 7.

78   Raphael Samuel, *Theatres of Memory: Past and Present in Contemporary Culture*, London, Verso, 1994.

79   Caroline Tisdall, *Joseph Beuys*, Soloman R. Guggenheim Foundation, 1979, 7.

80   For an account of the historian as ragpicker, see Irving Wohlfarth, 'Et cetera? The historian as chiffonier', *New German Critique*, 39, Fall 1986: 142–68.

81   Buck-Morss, op. cit., 211.

82   Irving Wohlfarth, op. cit., 146.

83   Stephen Greenblatt, *Renaissance Self-Fashioning: from More to Shakespeare*, Chicago, University of Chicago Press, 1980.

84   See essays by Howard Felperin and Graham Holderness in Francis Barker, Peter Hulme and Margaret Iverson (eds), *Uses of History*, Manchester, Manchester University Press, 1991.

85   Leila Zenderland (ed.) *Recycling the Past: Popular Uses of American History*, Philadelphia, University of Pennsylvania Press, 1978, viii.

86   Francis Fukuyama, *The End of History and the Last Man*, London, Hamilton, 1992. Jean Baudrillard, *The Illusion of the End*, trans. Chris Turner, Cambridge, Polity Press, 1994.

Chapter 7

Gary Needham

THE DIGITAL FASHION FILM

Fashion 2.0

SINCE THE FIRST EDITION of *Fashion Cultures* in 2000, coincidentally the same year in which net-a-porter went live, the most obvious and immediate developments to have taken place are the ascendancy of new media forms that for many have become an extension of their very being. We are now in an era in which *Vogue* describes itself as a 'consumer interface in high fashion media' and style.com claims to 'blur the lines between an industry publication and consumer media' (Industrie 2011: 20). The last decade of fashion culture has seen it engage with a plethora of technological and communication advances and, while the subject of this chapter is fashion film and media, these changes can also be seen at the level of production – for example, the centrality of the computer-generated digital print in British fashion exemplified by Alexander McQueen, Mary Katrantzou and Christopher Kane. It would appear that fashion in all its guises is now wholly integrated and synergistic with aspects of information technology, thus affecting the ways in which we access and participate in fashion culture as digital citizens and consumers. But we are also producers of information about fashion – in the sense that we are now more active in the meaning-making of fashion culture in ways that were previously unthinkable. From desktop computers to mobile devices, the screen has become a key point of contact for the experience of fashion culture, often presenting us with digital content packaged in the rhetoric of democratisation. This is most keenly felt in online fashion journalism and the widening access to luxury. There is a sense in which fashion and the digital screen have become so mutually entangled that there is an over saturation and proliferation of digital fashion culture. The extent of this situation is apparent when the primary means through which Gucci celebrates the sixtieth anniversary of its horsebit loafer is to present an untitled two-minute fashion film (2013) that extensively quotes *The Shining* (1980). Furthermore, fashion technocrats frequently prophesise the death of off-line, conventional, analogue, and material experiences of fashion.

The hyperbole in this overly deterministic position praises the yoking together of what was once distinct; for example, the link between editorial content and point of purchase which has created the neologism 'advertorial', whereby e-stores present clothing in an editorial context so that they look less like shops and more like digital versions of print magazines. There is definitely a distinct amalgamation of editorial content and commerce to create a new, hybrid, fashion culture that closes the gap between journalism and shopping. This is an era dominated by search engine culture, inhabited by the 'netizen' with their increasing fluency in digital convergences, where successful online retailers and teenage bloggers collude unabashed; formerly 'old guard' couture houses are no longer staid, but themselves at the forefront of pioneering media technologies with new media-savvy hipsters in the role of 'creative directors' – even Hermès has a Tumblr page these days! Here are a few other examples: the online version of *Vogue Italia* records 1.6 million hits per month in 2011; former *Esquire* editor Jeremy Langmead moves from print to online when he takes on the role of 'multiplatform content director' for e-tailer Mr Porter; Burberry Prorsum streams catwalk shows live and offers customers the ability to buy the clothes and accessories *immediately*, thus challenging the temporal organisation of the fashion season. Is this really Fashion 2.0 or simply the emperor's new clothes?

One of the most keenly felt transformations within this new media fashion landscape has been the emergence, rise and proliferation of the digital fashion film as a discrete and identifiable generic form. These fashion films are not to be confused with 'fashion in film' – although they are not entirely unrelated, given that the screen is the means through which fashion is being mediated. Before the digital screen and the new media fashion film, both cinema and television in their 'old media' role have operated in creative tension with fashion and how to represent it. There has always been a distinction between what looks good on screen against what actually works in reality; 'screen costume' is not equivalent to 'wearable fashion' and a good deal of the work done at the juncture of film studies and fashion studies is keen to address this in detail (Gaines and Herzog 1990; Bruzzi 1997; Jeffers-McDonald 2010; Munich 2011). It is worth reminding readers that clothes are chosen for the screen because they *film* well rather than wear well and that this also extends to the computer screen – where fashion images exist as electronic information, files, and coding. The way clothes look, and how certain fabrics and colours will appear on the digital screen, are now taken into consideration at the level of design and production. These are some of the problems that underscore recent fashion–screen relations – but they are hardly new. There is a forgotten Hollywood film, *Made in Paris* (1966) starring Ann-Margret, who plays a US department store buyer attending the Paris couture shows. *Made in Paris* problematises 'looking' at fashion on screen through the tenets of spectatorship as identification and point of view where the translation from one context (a Paris couture show) to another (a Hollywood movie) suggests different ways of looking at fashion. There is a central fashion show number in *Made in Paris*, an ersatz couture presentation designed by Hollywood costumier Helen Rose, that is viewed

Figure 7.1   *Made in Paris* (1966). The film here restages the *Rear Window* perspective on the fashion world.

not from a front row point-of-view shot perspective – like an audience shot from a Hollywood backstage musical – but instead from a hidden elevated vantage point of voyeurism above the catwalk, reflexively framed as a window onto the fashion world. In other words, both spectators and protagonist access the world of fashion at once removed and in secret, as pure *spectacle*, not as a front-row customer or buyer but rather as mediation through the framework of spectatorship, which the film reinforces in its near-identical recreation of the set-up from *Rear Window* (1954). The reason for citing this example of Hollywood cinema, and an older concept of the 'fashion film', is to reinforce the idea that once fashion is mediated by a screen, whether classical Hollywood cinema or the iPad, then its frameworks may be fundamentally altered in ways more conducive to the apparatus which mediates it – in this case screen culture or digital culture rather than simply just fashion culture. It is this tension that also haunts the digital and the viral fashion films when the conventions of the new – the computer screen and digital media culture – brush up against the old: the historical and cultural conventions of fashion.

The new fashion film

These digital fashion films are not to be confused with popular films about fashion such as *Made in Paris*, filmed catwalk shows or their background visuals. These digital fashion films instead cover a range of digital moving image features that include promotional videos for seasonal collections, substitutes for conventional catwalk display, electronic look-books, experimental films used to advertise brands (clothing, accessories, and perfume), 'promos' for the digital platform versions of print magazines, e-stores, and brand-funded artists' videos. Most of the films are between one and ten minutes long. Despite some initial reservations regarding their online presence, especially widening access to luxury through e-stores, nearly all brands, digital platforms and hosts produce these 'fashion films' – to the extent that they now constitute a very recognisable media trend in contemporary fashion culture. Nathalie Khan (2012a; 2012b), among others (Berra 2012), has identified the fashion film as a new media genre. Khan makes a useful distinction in the fashion film between the large-scale budgeted films for brands such as Dior and Chanel, directed by David Lynch and Martin Scorsese respectively, that employ widely accepted classical Hollywood conventions, versus the more unconventional and 'edgy' experimental fashion films that eschew these Hollywood norms. One of the key changes in the new fashion film that Khan recognises is the introduction of narrative and a 'shift from the viewer as consumer to the viewer as spectator' (2012a: 237). The idea here is that fashion advertising's transformation from a still image, and a position of consumption, to a moving image and a position of spectatorship is brought about through the import of cinematic conventions of editing and narration, which render the once still fashion image as *moving*. There is an echo of Barthes here implicit in these shifts and mergers – especially as Barthes writes in *S/Z* that 'the goal of the literary work [or literature as work] [. . .] is to make the reader no longer a consumer, but a producer of the text' (Barthes 1974: 4). Now that it is moving, the fashion image apparently offers a Barthesian writerly position or a consciously active position of 'seeing fashion' that in Khan's argument derives from an imported model of film spectatorship. However, I would argue that this is less a shift or a displacement from one of consumption-based looking to one of spectatorial engagement; I would instead propose a situation whereby there is a merging of the two – something occurs that collapses consumption and some kind of film spectatorship into one another. To map film spectatorship on to the digital fashion films needs a careful avoidance of a monolithic conception; the context of the fashion film as an experience of the digital screen bears no relationship to the social and psychic conditions of the cinematic apparatus foundational in theories of film spectatorship.[1] Like watching television on YouTube, in which surfing or browsing dovetails with television viewing, from which the awkward term 'viewsing' is derived, the fashion film as a digital moving image produces hybrid modes of engagement in which old and new media, and activity and passivity, productively merge.

It is worth dispelling any claims that fashion is being overtaken by new forms of screen media – a suggestion often made by designers themselves, or suggesting that some of fashion's principal experiences have become overwhelmingly screen-based. This is merely another chapter in fashion's ongoing relationship with the screen, which has existed from its earliest incarnations: in the use of flowing gownage to first demonstrate the moving image as attraction in Edison's *Annabelle Serpentine Dance* (1895); and the early cinema fashion shows identified by Caroline Evans (2011); through *Made in Paris*, mentioned above and, more recently, a digital fashion film like the Argentinean art-house director Lucrecia Martel's film *Muta* (2011) for Miu Miu, with its twitchy ghost motifs seemingly borrowed from Japanese horror.

The digital fashion film presents itself as the most recent tension in which the screen is in a creative tussle with the culture it appears to represent; it continues to pose those ubiquitous questions of how to see, how to evaluate, how to display, and how to experience fashion on screen. 'Fashion' as actual clothes, their touch and texture, and the forms and pleasures of shopping in store, trying on, seeing a collection on the rack, and the buzz of the catwalk itself are all being reified through screen alternatives; but one should be cautious in claiming any wholesale displacement of the more 'live' and material experiences of fashion culture. In order to explore some of these concerns and issues, whether they involve a real change to aspects of fashion culture or are just simply faddish and supplementary, and how the different aspects of fashion culture converge with screen media, I offer an analysis of one particular kind of digital fashion film that I am calling 'the boutique film'. There are a number of other types or sub-genres of fashion films that can be identified as distinct categories within this fashion film. In addition to the boutique film associated with e-stores, one can identify 'the designer's film' associated with the creative individual or brand, 'the authored film' created by a known film director, and 'the artist's film' which is a brand-funded feature created by an established artist. Nor are these mutually exclusive. In brief, the second category of 'the designer's film' is best exemplified by Gareth Pugh, who has spoken at length on the function of the fashion film and the distinctions between his catwalk and film presentations (Business of Fashion, 2011). Pugh works in collaboration with the filmmaker Ruth Hogben and they have created a distinct niche and visual signature that is often imitated. The third category of 'director's films' are the ones that tend to get the most press and exposure as they are created by established filmmakers and may be extravagantly budgeted. Many of these are created for the perfume-wing of a brand (with authored films dating back much further than this recent phenomenon), such as Wes Anderson and Roman Coppola's direction of a feature for Prada's perfume flanker 'Candy L'eau' (2013) – executed as an irritating homage to the French Nouvelle Vague. A list of brand–auteur collaborations would be exhaustive, but some of the more notable commissions include legendary underground filmmaker Kenneth Anger's film for Missoni (2011), indie antagonist Harmony Korine for Proenza Schouler (2010), and Roman Polanski *A Therapy* for Prada (2012) featuring Ben Kingsley and Helena Bonham-Carter. The fourth category is the 'artist's film', which are fewer in number and more exclusive, yet they serve the same advertising function as the others; however, through associations with Art and patronage they attempt to elevate themselves above all other categories. Both Prada and LVMH lead this pack with their investment in the contemporary art world, including their galleries and support for artists, leading the *London Evening Standard* to ask at one point: 'is Miuccia Prada the next Peggy Guggenheim?' (Field 2009). Prada sponsored Damien Hirst's Venice Biennale exhibition back in 1996 and more recently in the fashion film milieu, commissioned Chinese video artist Yang Fudong to create a film, *First Spring* (2010), that featured the S/S 2010 collection and brought the art world and the fashion film further into creative dialogue.

The boutique film in focus

The boutique film describes the digital fashion features that are created for e-stores and whose function is primarily to advertise the brands and clothes that can be purchased in the online store. These boutique films often represent an individual designer; for example, one that is exclusive to the e-store, or perhaps the arrival

Figure 7.2   Exercise, Director Malcolm Pate, 2011.

of a seasonal collection – perhaps the collaboration on a capsule collection between e-store and brand. A good example of this is the fashion film *Exercise* (dr. Malcolm Pate) that appeared online from February to March 2011 to promote a capsule collection by Damir Doma, exclusively available at the Italian e-store The Corner. The landing page where the film was imbedded included some framing commentary on the film, describing the three-minute *Exercise* as 'a new geometric silhouette in tension between lightness and drama' and 'soft fabrics and fiery saffron hues against the dark background of a harsh industrial reality'. The text is both pretentious and meaningless – but it points towards a particular function of the digital fashion film, one other than simply advertising products, and this is how to substitute the touch and feel of fabric so often central to the shopping experience. How can I be sold clothes in the absence of touch, in the absence of a physical shopping space, and any other experiences of material presence associated with shopping? This is where the boutique films become quite canny in their use of experimental film techniques, extreme close-ups, jump cuts, and slow motion, which I would suggest are premised on being substitutions for the experience of touch and the buzz of an exciting retail space. In *Exercise* the actor/model stands at first in a medium-long-shot in a studio surrounded by smoke and industrial detritus. He moves awkwardly (a common mode of performance in these films and here also suggesting the avant-garde ethos of the brand); we then see a repeated motif of extreme close-up shots of his eyes, fingers and ears (wearing these clothes is an experience of the senses), while the camera flirts with being in and out of focus (are the clothes so wonderful as to be intoxicating?). We then see close-ups of saffron-coloured fabric, texture, and movement and the fragments of the jacket and top are intercut with plastic industrial material, black sand (to emphasise texture), and more close-ups of fingers (to emphasise touch) and eyelashes (which appear thread-like). *Exercise* more or less continues in this fashion with the model eventually on the ground, in the sand, dragging his fingers through the grains in a Zen-like fashion. There are more repeated close-ups of fabric, and the film ends with the model in a state of near-ecstasy with his skin and clothes covered in black sand and industrial sludge.

Exercise is an advertisement for an online store's capsule collection but more than that, especially if one is asked to part with £875 for the featured jacket, the film compensates for a number of absences which are principally connected to the experience and centrality of touch and trying on clothes which would take place in physical retail spaces. If clothes don't feel as good as they look, then we are likely to be dissuaded – which is why the luxury market is so dependent on the feel of quality and rarity. The simplicity of a fairly plain Hermès crew neck jumper belies the exquisite, almost transcendent feel that their cashmere induces upon touching skin. It is that tangible quality that the boutique film attempts to capture and this also extends to some of the online graphic features of e-store digital still images, which can be magnified in ways that allow us to see detail and fabric as texture. This is why the close-up and the extreme close-up, especially in tandem with slow motion, are common formal tropes in the boutique film: they function as a substitution for touch through their meaning as both optic and haptic experiences. Laura U. Marks proposes the concept of haptic visuality as an alternative to optic visuality in her book *The Skin of the Film* (2000). She suggests that 'haptic looking tends to move over the surface of its object rather than to plunge into illusionistic depth, not to distinguish form so much as to discern texture' (Marks 2000: 162). Haptic visualities are like acts of touching through visual perception, drawing the viewer into an intimate relationship with the clothing on screen, rendering the fabric as materially present through repeated close-up shots that evoke a sense of touch. In other words, the formal and aesthetic closeness to the clothes in the boutique film is an attempt to substitute a closeness we are denied since the clothes are physically absent. Therefore, the boutique film's close-ups do not serve the conventional cinematic use where such shots, in the Hollywood system at least, are highly motivated and indicate within a narrative system something significant that we need to see up close; for example, a gun in a desk drawer. Yet the cinematic meaning is not entirely lost in the boutique film if we follow Mary Ann Doane's work on the cinematic close-up, in which she suggests that it 'transforms whatever it films into a quasi-tangible thing, producing an intense phenomenological experience of presence' (2003: 94). What the boutique film's formal techniques of repeated close-ups present is a phenomenological substitution of feeling and touching as emotional process and physical act. These films work hard to counter the many absences opened up by screen-based fashion experiences where, for example, the absence of a physical retail space is most obvious. However, there is one advantage in the boutique film that cannot be expressed so precisely by retail spaces or the tactile encounter with fashion and thus may be considered an advantage. In *Exercise* the range of experimental formal and aesthetic devices, the model's styling and performance, and the electronic soundtrack render the avant-garde associations with the brand and the garments meaningful in ways that retail spaces and clothes on the hanger often struggle to achieve – they are, after all, shops. What the boutique film loses in terms of touch it gains in terms of conveying an avant-garde sensibility, if we consider avant-garde fashion to be an attack on more mainstream forms of fashion and the breakdown of barriers between fashion, film and shopping. *Exercise* and many other boutique films conform to avant-garde definitions in suggesting a new relationship to fashion through the possibilities of digital screen media to the extent that one might enthusiastically claim that our relationship to fashion is being restructured.

A final thought

The last sentence perhaps suggests more of a revolution than what has actually taken place. It is worth a cautionary reminder; media and cultural synergies in all their new guises, and the marriage of fashion culture and information technology, are typical of how capitalism has developed during the digital era. What is also being transformed is our relationship to consumption, in the sense that we see the fashion film not as an advertisement or digital look-book but as art, creative experimentation, as something that often circulates seemingly autonomous from the business. The fashion film may be having its moment in creating new ways of looking at fashion and consuming fashion because, as the cliché goes, fashion thrives on the new. Immanuel Kant recognised this as far back as 1798 when he wrote that it is 'novelty that makes fashion popular' (2006: 142), and the fashion film would seem to be our novelty of the moment.

Note

1   For those unfamiliar with this concept in film theory the cinematic apparatus, as proposed by Jean Louis-Braudy, describes an institutional and technological arrangement in the cinema (darkened theatre, comfy seating, the hidden projector) that produces both a social and psychic effect as a consequence of how technology and ideology disguise the construction of reality.

References

Barthes, Roland (1974) *S/Z*, R. Miller (trans.), New York: Hill and Wang.

Berra, John (2012) '*Lady Blue Shanghai*: the strange case of David Lynch', *Film, Fashion, and Consumption*, Vol. 1, No. 3: 233–50.

Bruzzi, Stella (1997) *Undressing Cinema*, London: Routledge.

Business of Fashion 2011, www.businessoffashion.com/2011/03/quotable-gareth-pugh-on-fashion-films-versus-fashion-shows.html (accessed 28 March 2013).

Doane, Mary Ann (2003) 'The close-up: scale and detail in the cinema', *Differences* Vol. 14, No. 3: 89–111.

Evans, Caroline (2011) 'The walkies: early French fashion shows as a cinema of attraction', in A. Munich (ed.) *Fashion in Film*, Bloomington: Indiana University Press, 100–134.

Field, Marcus (2009) 'Is Miuccia Prada the next Peggy Guggenheim?' www.standard.co.uk/lifestyle/is-miuccia-prada-the-next-peggy-guggenheim-6743044.html (accessed 28 March 2013)

Herzog, C. and Gaines, J. (eds) (1990), *Fabrications: Costume and the Female Body*, London and New York: Routledge.

Industrie (2011), 'The Fashion Media A-List', *Industrie*, No. 4.

Jeffers-McDonald, Tamar (2010), *Hollywood Catwalk*, London: I.B. Tauris.

Kant, Immanuel (2006) *Anthropology from a Pragmatic Point of View*, trans. Robert B. Louden, Cambridge: Cambridge University Press.

Khan, Nathalie (2012a) 'Cutting the fashion body: why the fashion image is no longer still', *Fashion Theory*, Vol. 16. No. 2: 235–50.

——(2012b) 'Stealing the moment: the non-narrative fashion films of Ruth Hogben and Gareth Pugh', *Film, Fashion, and Consumption*, Vol. 1, No. 3: 251–62.

Marks, Laura U. (2000) *The Skin of the Film: Intercultural Cinema, Embodiment, and the Senses*, Durham: Duke University Press.

Munich, A. (ed.) (2011) *Fashion in Film*, Bloomington: Indiana University Press.

Chapter 8

Agnès Rocamora

PERSONAL FASHION BLOGS
Screens and mirrors in digital self-portraits*

Introduction

THE SEPTEMBER 2009 ISSUE of the British magazine *Elle* features a photographic report on some of the fashion celebrities who attended a recent edition of the collections. Among them is Susie Lau, also known as Susie Bubble, from the eponymous blog. Her presence at the shows, and *Elle*'s decision to report it, showing her picture alongside that of the famous Jade Jagger, Natalia Vodianova, Rachel Zoe, and other stars of the field of fashion, is witness to the growing significance, in this field, of a new genre of actors: bloggers. They are the focus of this chapter.

The term 'blog' comes from the contraction of the words 'web' and 'log'. Blogs are internet sites on which individuals regularly publish their thoughts on a particular subject. The texts – called posts – appear anti-chronologically and are usually accompanied by images, and, sometimes, videos and music. Blogs date back to the mid-1990s. However, until the end of the decade blogging was not a very common practice (Lovink 2008: x). In 1999 there were about fifty blogs, but by 2005 the number reached eight million (Kaye 2007: 128). At the time 'about 27% (32 million) of all Internet users accessed blogs and 12% had posted comments or links on these sites'[1] (Ibid). In 2008, the blogosphere – the internet space comprising all blogs – counted 184 million blogs and 346 million readers (Technorati 2008).

If the launch around the mid-1990s of platforms such as Blogger.com and Blogspot.com, which provide internet users with ready-to-use blog templates, allowed for their multiplication, the 9/11 attack on the World Trade Centre is often identified as having heralded their rapid proliferation (Bruns 2005: 175; Tremayne 2007b: xii). Indeed, blogs' ability to quickly report on an event and update readers on its evolution on a frequent basis lends itself particularly well to the constant desire for new information that key events generate, while the presence of a 'commentary' section that allows readers to join in a discussion constitutes an important platform for dialogue and communion around such events.

Blogs do not deal with key historical moments and other public events only. Rather, recent studies have shown that they are chiefly devoted to their authors' everyday life, to the ordinary practices and moments it is made of. A survey conducted by AOL, for instance, reveals that in 2005 50 percent of American bloggers used blogs as a therapeutic tool, against 7.5 percent only who were interested in politics (Sundar *et al.* 2007: 87). A 2006 national telephone survey carried by the Pew Internet Project also shows that:

> most are focused on describing their personal experiences to a relatively small audience of readers and that only a small proportion focus their coverage on politics, media, government, or technology. Blogs, the survey finds, are as individual as the people who keep them. However, most bloggers are primarily interested in creative, personal expression – documenting individual experiences, sharing practical knowledge, or just keeping in touch with friends and family.
>
> (Pewinternet 2006, cited in Lovink 2008: 260)

In spite of this, the few academics who have looked into blogs (see, for instance, Bruns 2005; Carlson 2007; Tremayne 2007a) have tended to privilege sites devoted to topics such as politics and current affairs (see also Sundar *et al.* 2007: 87); that is, topics which in the hierarchy of social and cultural practices are often perceived as 'noble', in contrast with other fields, such as fashion, seen as trivial and unworthy of academic inquiry (but see Rocamora and Bartlett 2009 for a general discussion of fashion blogs).

However, with more than two million bloggers listed, in July 2010, by Blogger.com as being 'with an industry of fashion' (Blogger 2010), and following the launch in 2003 of the first fashion blog – *nogoodforme* – the fashion blogosphere has asserted itself as a key space for the production and the circulation of fashion discourse.

Although it encompasses a wide variety of sites, it can be split into two main categories: independent blogs and corporate blogs. The former include a broad range of genres. Examples are blogs that focus on street fashion (e.g. *facehunter*; *thesartorialist*), on celebrities (e.g. *cocostea-party*; *redcarpet-fashionawards*), or on a particular type of commodity (shoes, for instance, with *seaofshoes*; *shoeblog*). They are usually run by one individual only, as opposed to corporate blogs, which are the voice of a fashion institution whether it be a magazine (see, for instance, vogue. co.uk/blog; wmagazine.com/w/blogs/editorsblog), a brand (see, for instance, paulsmith.co.uk/paul-smith-blog; americanapparel.net/presscenter/dailyupdate) or a store (see, for instance, blogs.colette.fr/colette; topshop.com/webapp/wcs).

This article is devoted to independent blogs, and more specifically to a sub-genre sometimes referred to as 'personal fashion blogs' or 'personal style blogs' in reference to those blogs whose authors post pictures of themselves to document their outfit on a regular basis. Although some are run by and for men (see, for instance, *stylesalvage*; *dennysworld*; *fashionbitsandbobs*), the following pages focus on blogs created by women. *Stylebubble*, *karlascloset*, *tavi-thenewgirlintown*, *veckorevyn*, *thecherryblossomgirl*, *jestemkasia*, *theblondesalad*, *kertiii* are only a few of the numerous personal fashion blogs to have emerged on the World Wide Web in recent years. Their authors display their new acquisitions, their rediscovery of an old piece of clothing, or their new way of mixing things together on their body. The bloggers are usually featured in their bedroom, their living room, or their back garden. The setting is often unadorned, the props minimal.

In the first part of this chapter I argue that by bringing together new and old technologies of the self – screen and blog on the one hand, photography and fashion on the other – personal fashion blogs assert themselves as a privileged space of identity construction. I then develop this argument further in the light of gender. Exploring the idea of computer screens as mirrors, and the presence of mirrors in the self-portraits posted on personal fashion blogs, I discuss such blogs as a space for the articulation of a panoptic gaze that reproduces women's position as specular objects, but also as a space of empowerment through the control it grants bloggers over their own image, as well as through the alternative visions of femininity it allows them to circulate.

Fashion blogs: New technologies of the self

With identity seen as a process, a 'becoming' rather than a 'being', various bodily 'regimes' (Giddens 1991: 62), various 'techniques' or 'technologies' of the self – to borrow the concepts Michel Foucault (1984: 18; 1988) uses in reference to the principles and rules developed, throughout time, for the conduct of the self – can be appropriated to facilitate 'the ongoing "story" about the self' (Giddens 1991: 54). Among them are fashion and dress, as many authors have shown.[2] Personal fashion blogs document this process of identity construction through clothes. Blogger Annie Spandex's 21 June 2010 post, for instance, draws attention to their role in the construction of oneself – here a gendered self prone to a nostalgia for girlhood – when she writes:

> Sometimes I feel like a little kid dressing myself. I look at this outfit now and think maybe I went too far. I mean, I look like a damned Lisa Frank trapper keeper! Just slap some holographic dolphin stickers on me and I've got a costume ready for next Halloween . . . Did you have any Lisa Frank stuff when you were a kid? I'll never forget my fuchsia lunch box with anthropomorphic koalas living in a psychedelic world. Lisa Frank is very all about the id. It's a celebration of excess: vivid, optically stimulating imagery without apology or restraint. Kind of like my outfit. If you loved Lisa Frank, you should check out Iron Fist Clothing. It's like Lisa Frank for grownup girls. Just look at my shoes!
> (*anniespandex*)

On 12 May 2010, Arabel, of *fashionpirates*, notes:

> I hate clogs. I hate them, I don't care if Chanel does them (then again, when do I care about Chanel anyway? . . . man it must seem like I hate Chanel . . . I don't! I swear. Karl is Kaiser.), they are just ugly gardening shoes to me. Give me a break ok. I am really into the clean lines that 90's postmodern offers, and I have a big soft spot for CK and Margiela and all that jazz but I just feel incomplete without shiny or colors in my outfits. Wearing all monochrome or nuetral shades just makes me feel lame.[3]

Colour helps Arabel feel whole. It is one of the fashion tools she uses to articulate her self. Fashion, she also writes on 25 May 2010, 'is also what got me into feminism in the first place, because it's a form of self-expression. And as a feminist I do think every woman has a right to express themselves in whatever medium they so desire, including fashion.'

Through their engagement with dress bloggers partake in processes of identity construction, as they do through the very act of keeping a blog. Indeed, researchers have shown the role of new media for the construction of identity and the creative processes it entails (Lister *et al*. 2009: 267). Thanks to 'the bricolage of interest, images and links' that they allow, personal home pages, for instance, are spaces wherein a sense of self is articulated (Lister *et al*. 2009: 268). So too are personal blogs, for which individual websites paved the way (Lister *et al*. 2009: 268). With blogs this process of self-expression and construction is encouraged by the constantly renewed communication that the blog technology allows (Lister *et al*. 2009: 268), and indeed the genre requires, as well as by the authoring, not only of the written texts, but also of the images and videos that bloggers, including personal fashion bloggers, partake in. With blogs, 'identity performance' is 'ongoing' (Lister *et al*. 2009: 268–9), a performance which, with personal fashion blogs, is supported by dress's performative quality.

Moreover, the ongoing communication that blogs allow has seen them likened to diaries, a genre that various authors have argued is instrumental to the processes of identity construction (see, for instance, Serfaty 2004). Of diaries and autobiographies, Giddens (1991: 76), for instance, notes that they are 'at the core of self-identity in modern social life. Like any other formalised narrative, [they are] something that has to be worked at, and call . . . for creative input as a matter of course.' A type of hypermodern diary,[4] public rather than private – French author Sébastien Rouquette (2009) talks of '*journal* [diary] *extime*',[5] a conflation of the French word '*intime*' [intimate] and the prefix 'ex-,' which stands for 'out' – personal blogs allow their authors to construct this 'ongoing "story" about the self' (Giddens 1991: 54) that is at the heart of contemporary identity formation. Thus, Geert Lovink (2008: 6), who notes the parallel between blog and private diary, mobilises the Foucauldian concept of 'technology of the self' to underline their function as identity tools. Because they enable self-reflection, blogs facilitate identity construction (Sundar *et al*. 2007: 90) through creative processes of articulation of the self, a creativity that bloggers often lay claim to. The Pew Internet Project Survey on American life mentioned earlier, for instance, found that 'Three in four bloggers (77%) told us that expressing themselves creatively was a reason that they blog' (Pewinternet 2006).

Thus, the self that bloggers display on their pages is not a visual self only, but one whose external rendering is intertwined with autobiographical details. Indeed, following a personal fashion blog means not only discovering the sartorial style of its author, but also regularly finding out a bit more information about her life, the moments and events that punctuate it. Personal stories are narrated, supporting the practice of fashion as a technique of the self. In one of her posts Géraldine Grisey (also known as Punky B, of *punky-b.com*), for instance, talks about her adolescent past, here also mobilising memory and self-history, two devices at the heart of processes of identity confirmation (Lury 1998: 8). She writes:

> I am going to bore you again with one of the relics from my college love stories . . . You can guess that if I was called 'the squaw' in my teens, it had to come from somewhere. The love of tasseled outfits was already deeply rooted on my grungette tastes. (24 February 2009)

On 23 November 2009, Betty (*leblogdebetty*) publishes the pictures of a brunch she shared with her boyfriend in Paris's Hotel Amour, thereby revealing some information about her private life while also including a visual and written account of the outfits they were wearing. On 19 December 2008, Annie Spandex writes:

> I can't upload my digital camera photos until I get back home so I've taken some pics with my cell phone to share with you. They're not the best quality, but they're better than nothing for now. We . . . made it to Denver last night, but had to change our path and head south to avoid a snowstorm . . . After that we'll spend a day fossil hunting in the desert (per Mister's request), then head to Sedona to meet up with my parents for Christmas . . . I'd go on but it's late and I'm exhausted! I've been sending out Twitter texts along the way, though. ☺ Thank you for all your kind comments, everyone!

As one navigates through personal fashion blogs and their many entries a portrait of their authors emerges, creating a feeling of intimacy. Thus, although posts constitute independent entries, they are related by the thread which is the life of the blogger as revealed through time. Continuity, and therefore fidelity to the blog, is created, which bloggers also support through the use of various technologies and narrative tools. The 'archive' section, for instance, allows readers to read ulterior texts; when an entry refers to an old post readers can access it by clicking on the word or the sentence that refers to it, highlighted in bold or in colour. To link the posts together, bloggers also regularly mobilise phrases that invite their readers to return to the site in the near future, constituting a kind of 'to follow' of personal fashion blogs: 'we'll talk about it again very soon, I promise', writes Punky B on 30 November 2009. 'I don't have the time to explain what's really happening', Betty announces on 5 September 2008, 'but I'm still leaving a quick note to tell you that in a few hours I'm flying to New York! . . . I'll tell you everything from there!! See you later duckies!' (*leblogdebetty*). Games and competitions are organised, future posts are announced, to attract the attention of readers and prompt them to visit the blog again at a later date. On 23 December 2008, for instance, Punky B writes:

Come around here tomorrow because, as I'd told you last week, a real cool competition will start on the 24th . . . but don't panic, first come won't necessarily be first served, we're on holiday (or rather almost) and we take our time! So I say see you tomorrow and I wish you a lovely evening!:).

On 12 November 2009 Alix Bancourt, the author of *thecherryblossomgirl*, declares: 'Yes, yet again some leopard print worn with denim shorts. I can't do anything about it, I really love that at the moment! Have a good weekend. I'll be back as a preppy girl on Monday.' Weekends are breaks after which bloggers and readers meet again. The narrative thread, that of the written self, and that of the story read by the readers, is thereby tightened, reinforcing the link between bloggers and their audiences.

The self that personal fashion blogs narrate is articulated through writing but also through the images the bloggers post of and by themselves. By appearing on their site, they have appropriated a third technique of the self which fuses with the other two, fashion and blogging, to support their identity construction: photography. Indeed, as Patricia Holland (2009: 123) suggests, 'Personal photography . . . has developed as a medium through which individuals confirm and explore their identity, that sense of selfhood which is an indispensable feature of a modern sensibility.'

The photographic portrait in particular has been key to the articulation and documentation of identity (Lury 1998), and photographic self-portraits, more specifically, have asserted themselves as a privileged mode of articulation of the self (Jones 2006). However, once the preserve of a social minority, artists such as Claude Cahun, Lee Miller or Cindy Sherman, for instance, they have become, like photography more generally and thanks to technological inventions such as Kodak's Instamatic camera in the 1960s, and digital cameras in the late 1990s, an ordinary practice. Personal fashion blogs are testament to this 'banalisation' of photographic self-portraiture as a means of self-expression.

Fashion, blogging and photography as technologies of the self come together through a fourth technology of the self, a contemporary space of individual expression: the computer screen. In *The Language of New Media*, Lev Manovich (2001) traces a genealogy of this particular genre of screen. He makes a distinction between three types of screens: the 'classical screen', a flat rectangular surface that frames a fixed image destined to be seen frontally (2001: 95); the 'dynamic screen', which allows for the showing of images from the past – cinema screen, TV screen, video screen – (2001: 96); the 'screen of real time' – the computer screen for instance – sub-genre of the dynamic screen which allows one not only to see many images simultaneously but also to control their flow and see them unfold in real time (2001: 97–9). This type of screen that 'shows the present' (2001: 103) dominates contemporary cultural life (2001: 99). They are the now-banal objects of everyday life in the developed world, omnipresent elements of a society of the spectacle turned 'society of the screen' (2001: 94).

Thus, computers have become so central to our day-to-day existence that the self is no longer played out only in the three-dimensional space our bodies move in, real space – IRL (In Real Life) as it is also known – but on the actual screen of our computers, as fashion blogs also illustrate. Sherry Turkle (1995) talks about *Life on the Screen*. In the eponymous book she describes computer screens as a space for identity production, arguing that 'it is computer screens [and not cinema screens] where we project ourselves into our own dramas, dramas in which we are producer, director, and star. Some of these dramas are private, but increasingly we are able to draw in other people' (Turkle 1995: 26).

At the time Turkle was writing her book fashion blogs did not exist, but new technological tools were emerging – digital cameras for instance, photo editing software such as Photoshop – which were already facilitating and popularising the featuring of oneself on computer screens. The early 2000s also saw the creation on the web of various social network sites – Myspace (2003), Flickr (2004), Facebook (2004), for instance – that participated in the banalisation of this process of self-construction Turkle discusses. As she also notes: 'The Internet has become a significant social laboratory for experimenting with the constructions and reconstructions of self that characterize postmodern life. In its virtual reality, we self-fashion and self-create' (1995: 180). This is an idea Bolter and Grusin (2000: 232) share when they observe that:

> we employ media as vehicles for defining both personal and cultural identity. As these media become simultaneously technical analogs and social expressions of our identity, we become simultaneously both the subject and object of contemporary media. We are that which the film or television camera is trained on, and at the same time we are the camera itself . . . New media offer new opportunities for self-definition.

Computer screens: The mirrors of hyper-modernity

However, Bolter and Grusin's idea that in today's computer-mediated society one's position in the construction of images is that of both subject and object should be seen in the context of gender. Indeed, one's relation to images is structured by power relations between men and women. In Western visual culture the former have generally been in command of the production of images, thereby creating a visual field wherein the latter have been positioned as objects of the masculine gaze. The product of a patriarchal society, this objectification has been internalised by women as a way of relating to themselves. As John Berger famously argued: 'men act and women appear. Men look at women. Women watch themselves being looked at . . . the surveyor of woman in herself is male: the surveyed female' (1972: 47). Women's identity is lodged in the surface of the body, in the visuality of its materiality.

Makeup and dress become tools for their self-accomplishment, mirrors instruments for the satisfactory completion of their femininity. As Diana Tietjens Meyers (2002: 115) writes: 'Women are supposed to depend on their mirrors to know who they are . . . For women, to know oneself is to know one's appearance and the worth of that appearance in the parallel economy of heterosexual partnership.' And the author adds: 'How apt that the French call a woman's boudoir mirror her *psyché*!' (2002: 115). For women, mirrors are not just a device in a stage only towards the formation of the I (see Lacan 1966 on 'The mirror stage as formative of the function of the I') but an ever-present prompt for its affirmation. In her seminal *Le Deuxième Sexe*, Simone de Beauvoir also underscores the importance of gender in one's relation to mirrors when she notes that:

> Male beauty is an indicator of transcendence, that of woman has the passivity of immanence: only the latter is made to arrest the gaze and can therefore be caught in the immobile trap of the reflective surface, the man who feels and wants himself activity, subjectivity, does not recognise himself in his fixed image; it has no attraction for him since man's body does not appear to him as an object of desire; whereas woman, knowing, making herself, object, truly believes she is seeing herself in the mirror . . . The whole future is condensed in this blanket of light whose frame makes a universe; outside of its narrow limits, things are but a disorganised chaos.
>
> (Beauvoir 1976 [1949]: 527–8)

Through the recurring depictions of mirrors in representations of women, art has played a key role in illustrating and sustaining the importance of appearance in the make-up of femininity (Tietjens Meyers 2002). Indeed, in the field of art, images of women contemplating themselves abound. Tietjens Meyers gives the example of Titian's, Rubens's, and Velazquez's Venuses (respectively, *Venus with a Mirror*, 1555; *Venus at a Mirror*, 1616; *Venus at her Mirror*, 1647–51), to which could be added the work of Manet (*Nana*, 1877), Degas (*Woman Combing her Hair*, 1883), or Picasso (*Girl before a Mirror*, 1932), to mention only a few of the many representations of women with mirror.

Cinema also abounds in such images. In Agnès Varda's *Cléo de 5 à 7*, for instance, Cléo, who is anxiously awaiting the results of a medical test that might announce an early death, finds in a mirror the comforting reassurance that she is alive. Contemplating her image she says: 'to be ugly, that's what death is, as long as I am beautiful I am alive' (Varda 2000[1962]). As Tietjens Meyers also observes, 'women are positioned to believe that they will perish if the image in the glass disappears' (2002: 123).

In *Pretty Woman*'s (Marshall 1990) famous shopping scene, where Julia Roberts tries on various outfits in front of the mirror of a fitting room, the character finds an opportunity to assert her beauty, and the financial and romantic success it will grant her. The spectator contemplates her contemplating herself as a loveable women; a potential object of love and covetousness, as her status as a prostitute also incarnates, but whose image is changed by the male gaze that reveals her to herself by modifying her appearance.

Like mirrors, and thanks to the transfer of images onto computers that new technologies have enabled, digital screens allow one to look at oneself. With personal fashion blogs in particular, the logic of self-projection onto a reflective surface in which a woman can look at and evaluate herself, and thereby confirm her identity, is reproduced. Indeed, the commentaries that readers leave on blogs are evocative of a famous fictional scene involving a mirror; one bloggers are probably familiar with: the recurring moments when in the Brothers Grimm's *Snow*

White the queen asks her mirror who the most beautiful woman is. With fashion blogs the comforting voice is that of the many readers who have left a commentary in the eponymous section. Although criticisms exist they are rare. By moderating their blog bloggers can of course choose never to publish unflattering remarks, thereby choosing to represent themselves in a favourable light, but the blogs abound in praise for the beauty or style of the blogger. One reader tells Susie Lau, for instance: 'Susie, sometimes it just doesn't work for me, but today is not one of those times. These looks are magical, especially the first . . . And I have to say that you look really gorgeous in the first photo' (c, 26 January 2010). When on 10 November 2009, Punky B reveals her new boots, also admitting that 'I hate my legs so much', one reader reassures her: 'You're legs are perfect miss' (Victimdelamode R). Another one declares: 'You're legs R very nice you are slim. But us girls and our complexes!:D' (Mélina). On 27 November 2009, Christelle writes of Betty:

> Waowww this dress is top notch and the pictures R so beautiful!!! really it's a pleasure to come see your blog! However, @ June, I don't think that betty looks like Lea (the actress Lea Seydoux) . . . Betty is prettier I think,has a much more thin face and more harmonious than Lea Seydoux . . . xx Betty! carry on!

While in the Brothers Grimm's tale the magic mirror breaks the reassuring echo when one day it tells the queen that it is now Snow White who is the most beautiful woman, on fashion blogs the voice of the other is gracious and friendly, the mirror admiring. As one reader tells Alix Bancourt (*thecherryblossomgirl*): 'You are amazing in this dress and the fairest of them all in this mirror! More, more;)' (Anne, 23 January 2010).

The relation between mirrors and computer screens has been exploited in various ways, such as for the production of online amateur makeup tutorials, as can be found on beauty blogs and YouTube; for instance with Lauren Luke, one of the most high-profile figures. As a video tutorial unfolds users watch the amateur makeup artist put on her makeup facing the screen as if she were in front of a mirror. Indeed, connected to a computer a webcam turns a monitor into a reflective surface that bloggers and other makeup fans can see themselves in. The viewer is simultaneously placed in the position of the one doing the looking, and, through identification, the one being looked at. This process of identification is supported by the gaze often adopted by beauty bloggers and YouTubers as well as personal fashion bloggers: a full frontal gaze. Of such a gaze, Burgin notes: 'a posture almost invariably adopted before the camera by those who are not professional models, [it] is a gaze commonly received when we look at ourselves in a mirror, we are invited to return it in a gaze invested with narcissistic identification' (1982: 148). The screen/mirror shows an idealised self the viewer can identify with and therefore appropriate to work on her own identity construction, while also indulging in the pleasure of voyeurism her status as a spectator grants her.

Leblogdebetty's mast-head also draws on the parallel between screens and mirrors by showing Betty's name written across the page as if with lipstick. This feature is evocative of a visual trope of both photographic and cinematic images: the writing of a message across a mirror with a red lipstick. Beneath the name is a shoulder-length image of Betty, again as if reflected on a mirror, which hints at the possible perception, by the blogger, of her computer screen as a mirror. Indeed, computer monitors look more and more like mirrors: I am writing this article on an iMac, whose screen when switched off allows me to see myself. Propped on my desk, with its flat shiny surface standing on a base, its resemblance to the mirror of a dressing table is striking.

Personal fashion blogs are flattering and comforting but they are also spaces of surveillance, by oneself and by others, and this also pertains to the character-istic of computer screens as mirrors. Indeed, the screen as appropriated by fashion blogs can be perceived as yet one more instrument imposing on woman the panoptic control which mirrors and the masculine gaze subject them to; one more surface onto which women can, or rather must, reflect themselves to think themselves, on which they must survey themselves to assert themselves. Like mirrors, computer screens are omnipresent. Like them they have become instruments of control and regulation that allow women to comply with their role as an object whose duty is to look at herself. As Manovich (2001: 98) notes, computer screens were developed for military purposes, thereby reminding us that they were first con-ceived as tools for surveillance rather than entertainment. With personal fashion blogs surveillance by and of women is legitimated, its presence and its role in daily life is further banalised. Kelli Fuery's (2009: 142) comment that self-surveillance techniques are now acknowledged as belonging to our everday life, thereby turning panopticism into a more subtle apparatus, is here particularly resonant: computer self-control is the more pernicious in that it is inscribed in a playful, banalised, and voluntary logic.

Celia Lury (1998: 41–5) also reminds us of the ambivalent role of photographic portraits as sites both for the articulation of self-identity but also classification, instrumental to control and surveillance. In that respect too, the photographic portraits bloggers post on their sites can be seen as part of a panoptic system aimed at ordering and containing individuals, and women in particular.

However, if 'for women images are first and foremost tyrannic', as Michelle Perrot (1998: 378) observes, 'images are also a source of delight: pleasure of being featured, celebrated, embellished, a Virgin above the door of a cathedral, a lady on the frescos of a castle' (1998: 380), and, one can now add, fashionable woman on a computer screen, a pleasure presumably heightened by the feeling of control that comes with representing herself. 'The awareness of the self-image', Perrot writes, 'creates the desire to manage it, and even to produce it' (1998: 380). If until recently this desire has been restrained by men's ownership of the tools of artistic production such as the brush or the camera as well as of the spaces of display such as galleries and museums, it has been freed by some of the new technologies born in a society wherein gender relations are becoming more balanced. Among such technologies, then, are those on which the blog rests; a tool for potential self-representation that many women have appropriated, thereby appropriating the power of representation that has often eluded them. Personal fashion bloggers sometimes request the help of a friend to take a picture of themselves but at other times cameras, fixed on a tripod for instance, are set on a timer or used through remote control, giving bloggers operational power in their own portraiture and the full independence, creativity and control this power enables.

Thus, although the bloggers often represent themselves in banal everyday spaces – their bedroom, the street, their garden – some have stretched the power of representation to staging themselves in fantasy backgrounds. The author of *thecherryblossomgirl*, for instance, works both on the decor she photographs herself in as well as on the pictures themselves, which she often edits using software to create 'a sweet vintage effect' as she puts it in the 'FAQ' section of her blog, where readers can also find out, as they often can on personal fashion blogs, the particular make of camera she uses. In the early days of her blog, Susie Lau often represented herself with fashion images as a backdrop to her poses. She turned into a model whose colourful outfits contrasted with the black and white images she superimposed herself on, the large scale of her self-portraits also a vivid contrast with the frail silhouettes of the glossy models she placed herself next to.

If remote control and self-timers are often used to allow the bloggers to capture their own image, so also are mirrors. Indeed, a particular genre of photographs recurs in personal fashion blogs; that which shows the blogger reflecting herself in a mirror. The camera is often held in front of the blogger's face, sometimes to grant her a desired anonymity, but also simply the better to fully display an outfit. However, in appropriating mirrors as a tool for their own practice, fashion bloggers have also produced images that are strangely disruptive of the gaze and visions of women as specular objects; with the camera covering her face, the blogger is shown as the eye, the camera itself, as Bolter and Grusin's words suggest earlier, hence the subject.

Artists have often used mirrors as a tool to facilitate the realisation of their self-portrait, with the mirrors sometimes shown in the resulting artwork. But where their presence in paintings of women has generally been used 'to make the woman connive in treating herself as, first and foremost, a sight' (Berger 1972: 51), feminist artists have subverted it to emphasise subjectivity (see, for instance, Doy 2005; Jones 2006) and thereby challenge dominant visions of women with mirror. As Gen Doy (2005: 52–3) notes:

> the conscious activity of the woman artist works against . . . objectifica-
> tion, since she is also the creative subject and agent who constructs her
> own image, rather than reflecting outward appearances, as the mirror
> does. The mirror becomes a tool for the woman artist, like a brush or
> a camera. The mirror in itself is neither objectifying nor subjectifying.
> It is the human social and cultural relations in which it functions that
> are of prime importance.

Shown in the context of personal fashion blogs, mirrors remind the viewers that, to play on Laura Mulvey's (1989: 15) words, women are not only the bearers of meaning but its makers too,[6] that they can be in control of their own image and take over processes of representation. In a field – fashion – where those in charge of taking photographs have been predominantly men, and those photographed women, visuals showing the latter behind the camera actively engaged in an act of self-representation contrast with doxic views of men as photographing subject and women as photographed object. Personal fashion blogs are also spaces where male domination is challenged in that they support women's representation in a field – new technologies and digital media – which is still often associated with masculinity: witness the very masculinist bias of one of the leading titles on the subject: *Wired*.

Moreover, although the female subject may well be a vector of the male gaze through internalisation, a vehicle for patriarchal domination, as Berger (1972) and Mulvey (1989) have famously argued, the outfits shown on personal fashion blogs are often removed from a traditional feminine ideal. The bloggers often break with sartorial rules that can be perceived as part of the apparatus of submission of women to men. The very popular *stylebubble* in particular is the vector of an aesthetic situated outside of established canons of femininity (Rocamora and Bartlett 2009: 110). On 14 June 2010, for instance, Lau (aka Style Bubble) is wearing a Peter Jansen denim top. The replica of the upper part of a skirt, zipper, top-button, belt hoops, and side pockets included, it is see-through in the back. 'it needs to be counteracted with a few layers or two just to tone down the err . . . "sexy back" . . .', she writes, hence the addition of 'a fluffy bum bag', and of a Cooperative Designs necklace whose 'mix of wood grains and metal hardware really enhances the often Bauhaus-inspired lines of Cooperative's stuff. In my case', Lau adds, 'I'm just adding a handsome bit of jangling distraction from zee back . . .' To go with the top is a white skirt patterned with drawings of pencils and chains layered over a pair of brown rolled-up trousers. Brown leather tasselled wedges round up her outfit. Unexpected juxtapositions, colour clashes, holes and asymmetrical cuts are regulars, perverting stereotypical definitions of sartorial femininity. On 11 January 2010, Punky B shows her new pair of shoes: 'comfort of the plateau + semi-wedged bevelled heel = they are stable and comfortable as sleepers, no joke! The style is particular, I think they attract as much as they make one vomit.' On 4 July 2009, Annie Spandex is wearing a pair of leggings with black and white stripes cut below the knee under a purple flowery dress, a large grey sleeveless waistcoat, and flat low boots. On her blog, as on many personal fashion blogs, room is made for a female gaze, a gaze informed by the pleasures found in disrupting conventional visions of femininity, in experimenting with alternative aesthetics, in dialoguing with ever shifting and unstable fashion rules.

It is a gaze structured by women's perception of and judgement on fashion in a space created and nourished by women for an audience imagined as female; witness the expression 'girls', which authors such as Punky B often address their audience with.

Finally, personal fashion blogs have also enabled women traditionally excluded from the realm of fashion imageries to enter its visual scape. Although some bloggers are often praised by their readers for their model-like appearance, which has earned some a contract with a fashion brand,[7] the physical traits many bloggers display do not conform to the beauty criteria the fashion press conventionally promotes. The popular Karla of *karlascloset*, for instance, has a body whose fullness contrasts with the emaciated limbs that are the currency on the catwalk and in the pages of glossy magazines. Some fashion blogs have even established their success on their author's desire to display a different bodily aesthetic, one where fashion-ability is not associated with extreme slenderness only. As blogger J. puts it in her 'About me' section: 'I think you can be fat/plus size and fashionable – hence my blog name': *fatshionable.blog*. On 10 May 2010, she writes, referring to her outfit of the day: 'Years ago I would have been afraid to even try on a short skirt due to my fear of showing cellulite but I say to hell with fearing cellulite! Wear what you love and be happy. Thanks for visiting the blog!' On 9 June 2010, Christina, of *musingoffat-fashionista*, also invites larger women not to shy away from wearing what they want:

> Partly inspired by the recent post on Beth Ditto and also my June 2010 moodboard, I decided today would be the perfect day to debut my new crop top . . . Now some may shy away from the exposed stomach but I've always wanted to destroy any pre-conceived notions about what a fat girl should or should not wear. If there's something I want to wear, I just figure out how to make it work for me, simple as that. It may not work but at least I tried it, right? If I've learned anything from Beth, its to never let anyone else dictate how I should dress my body.

A black woman, Christina's skin colour also contrasts with that, predominantly white, of models in the traditional media – a field, notwithstanding token gestures such as *Vogue Italia*'s July 2008 black issue, that shows little ability to depart from normative visions of beauty.

Conclusion

Personal fashion blogs constitute an ambivalent space, a space that echoes the position of women in contemporary society (Heinich 2003). While it reproduces the mirror's panoptic logic and the related duty that weighs on them to work on their appearance in order not to be denied their female identity, it is also a possible space of articulation of a female voice on appearance, by and for women; a space for the expression of other images of the fashionable. Fuery notes that 'The newness of new media is not necessarily its technical inventions, it is the transformation of vision that affects how we make sense of, and even actually make, the world and its social orders' (2009: 21). So it is with personal fashion blogs: more important perhaps than the technological innovation of which they are the outcome is the new outlook on the field of fashion they allow, a fashion that is not centred on a producing elite and ruled by the male gaze only but a fashion open to appropriation and interpretation, including that of women's visions of themselves and by themselves.

Notes

1   A link (also called a hyperlink) allows internet users to move from one site to another by clicking on the related signifier, usually displayed in a different colour, font or style.

2   See, for instance, on masculinity Edwards (1997) and Nixon (1997); on femininity Evans and Thornton (1989), Guy *et al.* (2001), and Woodward (2007); on class Jefferson (1976) and Partington (1992); on ethnicity Eicher (1995) and Rabine (2002); and on age Bennett (2005) and Hebdige (1979).

3   I have left unchanged all grammatical and spelling mistakes as well as typos. With quotes translated from the French, equivalent English errors are given. In both languages, stylistic choices (abbreviations, capitalisation, spacing, etc.) and emoticons are left unchanged.

4   With 'hyper-modernity', while nodding to the historical time that Gilles Lipovetsky (2005) refers to, I am not seeking to engage with his definition of the term (which refers to a 'consummate modernity' (2005: 32), marked by extreme individualism, consumerism and anxiety, coupled with a resurgent humanism). Rather I am using this term in reference to the type of textual platform blogs belong to, one made of hyperlinks (see note 1) and hypertexts; that is, texts linked in a non-linear, non-hierarchical fashion, or, to borrow a Deleuzian concept (see Deleuze and Guattari 1980), in a rhizomatic manner.

5   He is also drawing on the title of French writer Michel Tournier's book: *Journal Extime*.

6   Mulvey discusses the place of woman 'as bearer, not maker, of meaning' (1989: 15).

7   Gala Gonzales, for instance, of *am-lul.blogspot.com*, landed a contract with Spanish company Loewe for their 2010 'leather icons' advertising campaign.

Acknowledgements

* © Agnès Rocamora, 2011, *Fashion Theory: The Journal of Dress, Body and Culture*, Volume 15, Issue 4, pp. 407–24, Berg, an imprint of Bloomsbury Publishing.

References

Beauvoir, S. de. 1976[1949]. *Le Deuxième Sexe. II*. Paris: Gallimard.

Bennett, A. 2005. 'Fashion.' In A. Bennett (ed.) *Culture and Everyday Life*. London: Sage, pp. 95–116.

Berger, J. 1972. *Ways of Seeing*. London: Penguin.

Blogger. 2010. www.blogger.com/profile-find.g?t=j&ind=FASHION. (accessed 9 July 2010).

Bolter, J. D. and R. Grusin. 2000. *Remediation: Understanding New Media*. Boston, MA: MIT Press.

Bruns, A. 2005. *Gatewawatching*. New York: Peter Lang.

Burgin, V. 1982. 'Looking at Photographs.' In V. Burgin (ed.) *Thinking Photography*. New York: Palgrave, pp. 142–53.

Carlson, M. 2007. 'Blogs and Journalistic Authority: The Role of Blogs in US Election Day 2004 Coverage.' *Journalism Studies* 8(2): 264–79.

Deleuze, G. and F. Guattari. 1980. *Mille Plateaux: Capitalisme et Schizophrénie 2*. Paris: Minuit.

Doy, G. 2005. *Picturing the Self: Changing Views of the Subject in Visual Culture*. London: I.B. Tauris.

Edwards, T. 1997. *Men in the Mirror*. London: Cassell.

Eicher, J. B. (ed.) 1995. *Dress and Ethnicity*. Oxford: Berg.

Evans, C. and M. Thornton. 1989. *Women and Fashion*. London: Quartet Books.

Foucault, M. 1984. *Histoire de la Sexualité II*. Paris: Gallimard.

—— 1988. 'Technologies of the Self.' In M. Foucault (ed.) *Technologies of the Self: Seminar with Michel Foucault*. London: Tavistock, pp. 16–49.

Fuery, K. 2009. *New Media: Culture and Image*. New York: Palgrave.

Giddens, A. 1991. *Modernity and Self-Identity*. Cambridge: Polity.

Guy, A., E. Green, and M. Banim. 2001. *Through the Wardrobe*. Oxford: Berg.

Hebdige, D. 1979. *Subculture and the Meaning of Style*. London: Routledge.

Heinich, N. 2003. *Les Ambivalences de l'Emancipation Féminine*. Paris: Albin Michel.

Holland, P. 2009. '"Sweet it is to scan . . .": Personal photographs and popular Photography.' In L. Wells (ed.) *Photography: A Critical Introduction*. London: Routledge, pp. 115–58.

Jefferson, T. 1976. 'Cultural Responses of the Teds.' In S. Hall and T. Jefferson (eds) *Resistance through Rituals*. London: Routledge, pp. 81–6.

Jones, A. 2006. *Self/Image: Technology, Representation and the Contemporary Subject*. New York: Routledge.

Kaye, B. 2007. 'Blog Use Motivations: An Exploratory Study.' in M. Tremayne (ed.) *Blogging, Citizenship, and the Future of the Media*. New York: Routledge, pp. 27–148.

Lacan, J. 1966. 'Le stade du miroir comme formateur de la fonction du Je.' In J. Lacan (ed.) *Ecrits I*, Paris: Seuil, pp. 89–97.

Lipovetsky, G. 2005. *Hypermodern Times*. Cambridge: Polity.

Lister, M., J. Dovey, S. Giddings, I. Grant and K. Kelly. 2009. *New Media: A Critical Introduction*. New York: Routledge.

Lovink, G. 2008. *Zero Comments: Blogging and Critical Internet Culture*. London: Routledge.

Lury, C. 1998. *Prosthetic Culture: Photography, Memory and Identity*. New York: Routledge.

Manovich, L. 2001. *The Language of New Media*. Boston, MA: MIT Press.

Marshall, G. 1990. *Pretty Woman*. DVD. Touchstone Home Entertainment.

Mulvey, L. 1989. 'Visual Pleasure and Narrative Cinema.' In L. Mulvey (ed.) *Visual and Other Pleasures*. London: Macmillan, pp. 14–26.

Nixon, S. 1997. 'Exhibiting Masculinity.' In S. Hall (ed.) *Representation*. London: Open University, pp. 291–330.

Partington, A. 1992. 'Popular Fashion and Working Class Affluence.' In J. Ash and E. Wilson (eds) *Chic Thrills*. London: HarperCollins, pp. 145–61.

Perrot, M. 1998. *Les Femmes ou les Silences de l'Histoire*. Paris: Flammarion.

Pewinternet. 2006. http://pewinternet.org/Reports/2006/Bloggers.aspx (accessed 12 July 2010).

Rabine, L. 2002. *The Global Circulation of African Fashion*. Oxford: Berg.

Rocamora, A. and D. Bartlett. 2009. 'Blogs de mode: Les nouveaux espaces du discours de mode.' *Sociétés* no 104(2): 105–14.

Rouquette, S. 2009. *L'Analyse des sites internet*. Bruxelles: De boeck.

Serfaty, V. 2004. *The Mirror and the Veil: An Overview of American Online Diaries and Blogs*. Amsterdam: Rodopi.

Sundar, S., H. Hatfield Edwards, H. Yifeng Hu and C. Stavrositu 2007. 'Blogging for better Health: Putting the "Public" back in Public Health.' In M. Tremayne (ed.) *Blogging, Citizenship, and the Future of the Media*. New York: Routledge, pp. 83–97.

Technorati. 2008. www.technocrati.com/blogging/state-of-the-blogo sphere (accessed 27 October 2008).

Tietjens Meyers, D. 2002. *Gender in the Mirror*. Oxford: Oxford University Press.

Tremayne, M. (ed.) 2007a. *Blogging, Citizenship, and the Future of the Media*. New York: Routledge.

Tremayne, M. 2007b. 'Introduction: Examining the Blog–Media Relationship.' In M. Tremayne (ed.) *Blogging, Citizenship, and the Future of the Media*, pp. x–xvi. New York: Routledge.

Turkle, S. 1995. *Life on the Screen: Identity in the Age of the Internet*. New York: Simon and Schuster.

Varda, A. 2000[1962]. *Cléo from 5 to 7*. The Criterion Collection.

Woodward, S. 2007. *Why Women Wear What They Wear*. Oxford: Berg.

Chapter 9

Monica Titton

STYLING THE STREET – FASHION PERFORMANCE, STARDOM AND NEO-DANDYISM IN STREET STYLE BLOGS

IN SEPTEMBER 2009 THE ITALIAN FASHION HOUSE Dolce & Gabbana invited four fashion bloggers (Garance Doré, Bryan Grey Yambao,[1] Tommy Ton and Scott Schuman) to attend the runway show for their ready-to-wear spring collection. The bloggers were not only accommodated in the front row (traditionally reserved for the most 'important' guests), but each of them was also provided with a computer, mounted on a small desk in front of them, as if to demonstrate clearly their place within the staging of the fashion show (*Women's Wear Daily* 2009). The carefully orchestrated event caused a calculated media sensation and initiated a fervent debate about the legitimisation of bloggers as equal partners of editors and journalists. A few seasons later, a few particularly ambitious and persistent street style bloggers are still invited to major runway shows, showing their successful positioning within the social hierarchy of fashion media. Today there are few fashion magazines (in print or online) that do not feature their own 'street style' sections, while dozens of bloggers have created a career out of a hobby by working as professional photographers. The enormous popularity of the format of street style blogs relates to the centrality of the city as both scene and real space for the photographic staging of fashion throughout the twentieth century, as I shall argue. I then discuss street style blogs as sites of a form of public fashionable performance that goes back to the practices of the dandies, and show how street style blogs contributed to the constitution of a new category of cyber-celebrities.

A brief account of street fashion photography

Photography was invented at a time when the pulsating, thriving and hectic modern metropolis was at the heart of many artistic and literary observations. Decades before the city entered the artificial world of fashion imagery, pioneers of street photography Eugene Atget, Alfred Stieglitz, Jaques Henri Lartigue and August Sander documented urban phenomena in cities such as Paris, Berlin and New York City (Westerbeck and Meyerowitz 1994: 39–44; Scott 2007: 68). Unlike fashion photographers, who made of the city a symbolic location where artificial experiences of a fictional person (the fashion model) took place (Barthes 1990: 258), street photographers like Sander, and later Brassaï, Henri Cartier-Bresson, Walker Evans, Leon Levinstein, and Diane Arbus (to mention only a few) documented city life with a realistic and documentary intention (see Meyerowitz and Westerbeck 1994).

From the 1930s onwards, urban landmarks such as the Eiffel Tower were used as background for fashion models, just as anonymous scenes of deserted street corners or busy roads, have become part of the standard settings in fashion photo shoots (Rocamora and O'Neill 2008: 187). At about that time, fashion photographers started to take pictures in 'natural' settings outside their studios (Monneyron 2010: 135; Holschbach 2008: 176) and the city emerged as one of the most popular locations for photo shoots. In the 1950s and 1960s, luminaries of modern fashion photography such as Irving Penn, Richard Avedon and William Klein set up shoots for fashion magazines in urban landscapes. The city functioned as the perfect backdrop to create images of fashion as the epitome of modernity, as a site that would evoke a belief in progress and emancipation, but also a place that could express uncertainty and alienation (Vettel-Becker 2005: 83; see William Klein, 'Mirrors and Roofs', 1961). In the late 1970s and early 1980s, the approximation of fashion photography with urban documentary photography and street photography began, which would eventually lead to the emergence of street style photography as a genre in its own right. It is arguable that two approximately contemporaneous creative developments in photography led to the formation of the genre and its most recent renaissance within street style blogs.

On the one hand, there is the work of photo-reporter and society photographer Bill Cunningham, who started work as a fashion journalist in 1963 (see Gross 1990). His actual career as a photo-reporter began in 1978, the year his first pictures of fashionable people on the streets of New York were published (see Cunningham 2002). Cunningham's weekly photographic column 'On the Street' has appeared in the *New York Times'* Sunday edition since 1993. He assembles around thirty to forty pictures in a collage, thus documenting a different trend or fad each week, always spotted on the streets of New York (Press 2010). It is the assemblage of many small photographs into one big picture that distinguishes his column from other street style photographers. Every photo-collage is accompanied by a deft description of its contents; the function and the details of an ensemble are depicted with admiration and understatement.[2] Cunningham's column is one of the first street style documentations published regularly in a newspaper and therefore he can be seen as the forerunner of contemporary bloggers.

The influence of Cunningham can clearly be identified in the work of one of the most famous bloggers, Scott Schuman of *The Sartorialist*. The unpretentious style of Schuman's photographs and the tone in his short texts are reminiscent of Cunningham's playful writing.

The second photographic tradition that had a visible influence on the aesthetic formation of many street style bloggers is 'street fashion' photography. 'Street style' as fashion category was introduced in August 1980, in the first edition of the British *i-D* (Rocamora and O'Neill 2008: 186). The magazine's 'straight-up' section showed images of punks and new wave kids, discovered by photographers on the streets of London. These semi-documentary images – full-length figures, shot in natural light, against a simple backdrop of walls or house fronts – were in stark contrast to the conventional studio photography of the glossy magazines (Breward 2003: 128; Rocamora and O'Neill 2008: 190; Titton 2010: 134).

In 1980, too, American photographer Amy Arbus started to publish a monthly street fashion column (also entitled 'On the Street') in the New York alternative newspaper *The Village Voice* (see Arbus 2006). Whether in a remarkable case of serendipity or because the photographers were mutually inspired, either by each other or by the work of Amy's mother Diane Arbus, her pictures bear a considerable resemblance to those featured in *i-D*; she snapped 'scenesters' and stylish kids in her neighbourhood, the East Village.

In the course of the last twenty years, gradual commercialisation has meant the loss of street style photography's subversive, anti-high-fashion attitude, and it has gained popularity as a genre within mainstream fashion journalism (Rocamora and O'Neill 2008: 190; Breward 2003: 129). When the first street style blogs were founded in the mid-2000s, street style photography was already established as a genre in niche style magazines and mainstream fashion media alike, but it had preserved its 'contemporariness' and authenticity (Rocamora and O'Neill 2008: 189).

From backstage to front page – the birth of a fashion icon

Armed with a DSLR camera and a good eye for catchy outfits, street style bloggers collect pictures of everyday people encountered on the streets and publish them on their blogs, followed by thousands of readers (see Berry 2010). The success of their blogs could in part be attributed to the fact that the format fits well with the iconoclastic, fast-paced consumption patterns of digital media. It takes only a minute to look at the latest entry on a blog. Street style bloggers like Garance Doré, Tommy Ton, Scott Schuman and Yvan Rodic started to initiate their first commercial collaborations with 'gatekeepers' in the field of fashion media in 2009,[3] and soon after that were given commissions as photographers for advertising campaigns, by brand managers hoping that the bloggers would rejuvenate their brand's image by conferring on it some sought-after street style credit.

During this process of commercialisation and professionalisation, the attention of many street style bloggers[4] focused on those who adapted the latest fashion trends faster and more consistently than others: namely, those in the fashion industry who travel to runway shows in Paris, Milan, London, New York and Florence. Thanks to their professional involvement with magazines, many street style bloggers are also able to travel to these shows, where they wait in front of the venues for the fashion editors to show up (Rosser 2010: 160; Amed 2011). Women like Anna Dello Russo, Kate Lanphear, Giovanna Battaglia, Taylor Tomasi Hill and Joanna Hillman have become the 'stars of street style'. The documentation of street style during fashion week has grown into a theme of its own within the overall narrative of street style, conveying the street aesthetic with the styling of fashion spreads and the atmosphere of celebrity magazines, suggested by the impression of staged yet surreptitious acts. Fashion editors, stylists and other fashion industry insiders are often photographed while walking, objects in their hands showing that they are at work (mobile phones, documents, tablet computers) and therefore caught in their daily routine. Thus the pictures evoke those images in celebrity magazines where women are snapped by paparazzi in urban settings and so shown as similar to 'normal' people.

Due to their strategic positions near the fashion venues and their increasing number, street style bloggers have been compared to paparazzi and criticised for their questionable behaviour (Amed 2011). Not only are photographers taken to task, but those who have their picture taken are accused of opportunism and lack of authenticity. Voices have been raised to denounce the strategic practices of those who try to promote themselves via street style blogs (Odell 2011; Menkes 2013). The fashion editors, stylists and other industry insiders who are photographed for these blogs are very conscious of the fact that this will happen. That is why the outfits of the women on street style blogs are too perfectly styled, the looks on their faces too self-aware for true snapshots. From a sociological point of view, the myth of street style photography as the expression of an unmediated reality, sustained carefully by the photographers themselves and also to a great extent by the media, should not be taken at face value (Titton 2010: 136).

The formation of celebrity-like admiration for a handful of fashion editors and stylists is the result of both their initial willingness to get photographed and the bloggers' persistency in posting their pictures. This led subsequently to the fashion editors' heightened awareness of their status as possible role models and encouraged them to engage in their own presentation on street style blogs, whose authors then take yet more pictures of them, so boosting their status as 'cyber heroines'.

The autopoietical dynamic of 'celebrification' that turns a handful of well-dressed fashion editors into venerated fashion icons follows the same rules as the 'celebrification' of not particularly talented actresses (Church Gibson 2010: 127). Perhaps it was only a matter of time before the focus of fashion's obsession with celebrities from the film and music industry (see Church Gibson 2012) would shift to fashion editors, to those who were responsible for its visual and symbolic production. The appeal of fashion editors, stylists and other 'fashion insiders' as fashionable subjects might be quite simply that they are famous for their style alone. Their private life is rarely made the subject of discussion, and they seem able to keep a high level of privacy. Thus, on street style blogs, a visual narrative is constructed that is not based on the 'accidental personification' (Holschbach 2008: 175) of fashion models, of their anonymity, but on the 'authenticity' of the women depicted, the connection between body and identity. Their status as fashion celebrities results from the oscillation between their actual position as professionals in the fashion industry and their place in fashion's collective narrative. Moreover, they recall the portrayal of fashion editors in popular culture, from Robert Altman's *Prêt-à-Porter* (1994) and the television series *Absolutely Fabulous* to *The Devil Wears Prada* (2006).

Dandyism redux – the fashion practices and style politics of street style stars

The attention of street style bloggers is presumably not to everybody's taste, but for some people it is a pleasurable opportunity for self-promotion vital in the fashion industry's competitive environment (Wazlawik 2010: 132). The Italian fashion editor Anna Dello Russo has become famous through her presence on these blogs and able to profit substantially from her status as 'Queen of Street Style'.[5] In a report for French television network 'Paris Premier', Dello Russo goes to the Tuileries with a journalist and camera crew. When she descends from the taxi, she comments on her imminent walk across the Gardens: 'This is the fashion moment. Walking in the sun. Since I started it's a religious moment for me' ('La Mode La Mode La Mode', April 2010). Dello Russo's pleasure at being the centre of attention is evident. She clearly enjoys the fame and adoration of bloggers and makes no secret of it. Dello Russo's fashionable performance for the bloggers appears to be a ritual of self-affirmation, similar to press events in show business where actresses pose in sumptuous evening gowns in front of a crowd of photographers.

Dello Russo's ostentatious devotion to fashion and her own narcissism are reminiscent of the description of dandies by nineteenth-century writer Thomas Carlyle. His ironic characterisation of dandies and their existential obsession with clothing, taken from his book *Sartor Resartus* (1833), could be a description of street style stars like Dello Russo:

> A Dandy is a Clotheswearing Man, a Man whose trade, office, and existence consists in the wearing of Clothes. Every faculty of his soul, spirit, purse, and person is heroically consecrated to this one object, the wearing of Clothes wisely and well: so that as others dress to live, he lives to dress.
>
> (Carlyle 2008: 207)

Dello Russo's strategic sartorial *mise-en-scène* can be considered a hyperbolic aggrandisement of the fashion practices employed by dandies.[6] There are further commonalities between dandy fashion practices and those of street style stars; the most apparent is the use of the city as performance space for fashionable self-representation. Christopher Breward underlines the importance of London as an arena for dandies: 'Without the tools and props, the roles and opportunities which the "World City" provided, the dandy's trade would be of little use to these self-obsessed men in their short rise to celebrity and longer notoriety as ciphers for the triumph of style over substance' (Breward 2004: 22). Similarly on these blogs, the city as symbolic space for fashion performance plays a key role. The fashion-ability of female street style stars is enhanced by their presence in cities known to be 'fashion capitals': Paris, Milan, London and New York (Rosser 2010: 161).

Another similarity between dandies and 'street style stars' can be identified in the meticulous care for details. Beau Brummel was obsessed with perfect tailoring and preferred an understated, elegant style, which had an enormous impact on English fashion for men (North 2011: 55). Elizabeth Wilson stresses the importance

Figure 9.1 Anna dello Russo photographed by Garance Doré in Paris, September 2010. Copyright Garance Doré.

of self-display for dandies: 'The role of the dandy implied an intense preoccupation with self and self presentation; image was everything' (Wilson 2005: 180). 'Street style stars' are always dressed impeccably – they obviously curate their public appearances during fashion week with the same savoir-faire as they prepare a fashion spread in a magazine. Lastly, the narcissism that is a necessary precondition for accepting this level of attention links those 'street style stars' to dandies – as Elizabeth Wilson writes, '[T]he dandy was a narcissist' (Wilson 2005: 180).

Whereas the dandy's public display of his fashionability took up the aesthetic philosophy of *l'art pour l'art* and was characterised by the absence of any social purpose other than to please and be noticed (Breward 2004: 22), the element of narcissism in modern street style stars moves beyond the purpose of validating their self-consciousness. A dynamic of mutual dependency has developed between street style bloggers and the women they photograph. Without the work of these bloggers, formerly unknown editors and stylists would not have attracted the attention of fashion brands; as a result, they were subsequently hired as walking testimonials in lucrative advertising campaigns. Neither would their journalist colleagues have produced profiles and articles centred on the sartorial vicissitudes of these 'street style stars'.

Thus, in addition to the financial gains from advertising campaigns and other commercial collaborations, street style celebrities accumulate symbolic prestige within the fashion industry due to their fame on these blogs. On the other hand, without the cooperation of some fashion professionals in their photographic endeavour, street style bloggers would not have become so successful. By posing for them, the various fashion editors, stylists and buyers also implicitly acknow-ledged the legitimacy of these blogs as media formats in fashion journalism. As a result, the bloggers were able successfully to pursue their careers as freelance photographers or as staff photographers in fashion magazines (Watzlawik 2010: 132).

Conclusion – the idiosyncrasy of fashion media

What is really new about street style blogs, besides their global reach through their presence on the internet, is the fact that they have created a visual space within fashion's collective narrative for the representation of those who them-selves work in the image-making industry. With the advent of these blogs and their interest in fashionable people, formerly anonymous fashion editors, stylists and buyers, whose names, faces and figures were familiar only to their colleagues and in their work environment, have become part of fashion media imagery. To understand this dynamic, it is crucial to note that fashion editors, stylists and journalists occupy the position of gatekeepers in the field of fashion (Mears 2010: 24). That status does not only entail the privilege of attending runway shows and other fashion events centred on the presentation of novelty; it also confers upon them advantage in their everyday fashion practice through their professional immersion in the fashion industry. Using Bourdieu's concept of the 'habitus', defined as 'a disposition that generates meaningful practices and meaning-giving perceptions' (Bourdieu 1984: 170), it can be argued that the 'habitus' of fashion editors is characterised by their professional *and* personal dedication to fashion. Hence these 'street style icons' incorporate the newest fashion trends into their wardrobes according to the same aesthetic rules governing their presentation in the fashion media – because they themselves are involved in or responsible for the very production of this type of fashion imagery. Even if the phenomenon of street style blogs is often described as one of the key factors that allegedly drove the 'democratisation' of fashion in the 2000s by transforming everyday people into style models (see Berry 2010), I would argue that many bloggers simply re-introduced the body image, racial stereotypes and sartorial style of mainstream fashion into a new media format and an old photographic genre (Titton 2010: 135). Only those who did so succeeded in making their career in the fashion industry. The fact that fashion editors, of all people, dominate this potentially 'democratising' medium results in an idiosyncratic form of self-reference of fashion media, which is intensified by the fact that some of these fashion editors – such as Giovanna Battaglia and Hanneli Mustaparta – are themselves *former* fashion models. The establishment of street style blogs was only possible through the intense cooperation with fashion industry insiders and resulted in the reinforcement of prevailing power structures and visual narratives.

Notes

1 Better known under his *nom de plume* BryanBoy.
2 Cunningham publishes a second photo column in Sunday's *New York Times* edition beside 'On the Street': 'Evening Hours' is a society photo column, showing pictures of the society events in New York. While he omits the names of the people portrayed for 'On the Street', the names of those portrayed for 'Evening Hours' are listed in the caption – sometimes, the faces in the pictures are the same, partly dissolving the anonymity of the people in 'On the Street'.
3 Garance Doré was hired to create a photographic column for *Vogue* Paris, Scott Schuman started to work as a street style photographer for American *GQ* and Yvan Rodic started by working as a photographer for fashion magazines like *Elle*, *Cosmopolitan* and *Vogue*.
4 Given the thousands of street style bloggers all around the world still struggling to gain more attention from or power within the fashion industry, together with those who prefer to stay in their digital niche and wish to set themselves apart from 'mainstream' street style blogs, it is necessary to specify that this text deals explicitly with those street style bloggers who have at least once collaborated with an internationally known fashion publication or an internationally known fashion brand and who regularly visit the ready-to-wear or haute couture shows in New York, Milan, London or Paris.
5 She launched her own perfume in November 2010 and collaborated with fast-fashion brand H&M on the design of a 'limited edition' of accessories in October 2012.
6 I thank Professor Caroline Evans for suggesting the kinship between people photographed on street style blogs and dandies at the Conference 'Fashionable Queens – Body Power Gender' in December 2010 in Vienna.

References

Amed, I. (2011) *Autumn/Winter 2011 – the Season That Was*, The Business of Fashion, www.businessoffashion.com/2011/03/autumnwinter-2011-the-season-that-was (accessed 26 March 2013).

Arbus, A. (2006) *On the Street*, New York: Welcome Books.

Barthes, R. (1990) *The Fashion System*, Berkeley and Los Angeles, California/London: University of California Press.

Berry, J. (2010) *Flâneurs of Fashion 2.0.* Scan: Journal of Media Arts Culture, 8: 1–20.

Bourdieu, P. (1984) *Distinction: A Social Critique of the Judgement of Taste*, London: Routledge & Kegan Paul.

Breward, C. (2003) *Fashion: Oxford History of Art*, Oxford: Oxford University Press

—— (2004) *Fashioning London: Clothing and the Modern Metropolis*, Oxford/New York: Berg.

Carlyle, T. (2008) *Sartor Resartus*, Oxford: Oxford University Press.

Cunningham, B. (2002) 'Bill on Bill.' *The New York Times*, 27 October 2002.

Church Gibson, P. (2010) 'Celebrities.' in V. Steele (ed.) *The Berg Companion to Fashion*, Oxford/New York: Berg.

—— (2012) *Fashion and Celebrity Culture*, Oxford/New York: Berg.

Gross, M. (1990) 'I Am a Camera. Reclusive Bill Cunningham Is the Indefatigable Proust of Fashion and the Beau Monde.' *New York Magazine*, 24–31 December.

Holschbach, S. (2008) 'The Pose: Its Troubles and Pleasures.' in Eskildsen, U. (ed.) *Street & Studio. An Urban History of Photography*, London: Tate Publishing.

'La Mode La Mode La Mode.' *Paris Premier*, Paris 13 April 2010. Television, www.annadellorusso.com/2010/04/la-mode-la-mode-la-mode.html (accessed 9 February 2013).

Mears, A. (2010) 'Size Zero High-End Ethnic: Cultural Production and the Reproduction of Culture in Fashion Modeling', *Poetics*, 38: 21–46.

Menkes, Suzy (2013) 'The Circus of Fashion.' *The New York Times Style Magazine*, 17 February 2013, 91–4.

Meyerowitz, J. and Westerbeck, C. (1994) *Bystander. A History of Street Photography*, Boston: Bulfinch Press.

Monneyron, F. (2010) *La Photographie De Mode. Un Art Souverain*, Paris: Presses Universitaires de France.

North, S. (2011) 'From Neoclassicism to the Industrial Revolution: 1790–1860.' in Lillethun, L. and Welters, A. (eds) *The Fashion Reader*, Oxford/New York: Berg.

Odell, A. (2011) 'Sally Singer on Her First Year at T, the "Comic Mess" of Fashion Week Street Style, and More.' Nymag.com The Cut, viewed on 9 February 2013, http://nymag.com/daily/fashion/2011/12/sally-singer-on-the-comic-mess-of-street-style.html.

Press, R. (2010) *Bill Cunningham New York*, Zeitgeist Films.

Rocamora, A. and O'Neill, A. (2008) 'Fashioning the Street: Images of the Street in the Fashion Media' in Shinkle, E. (ed.) *Fashion as Photograph: Viewing and Reviewing Images of Fashion*, London/New York: I.B. Tauris, 2008.

Rosser, E. (2010) 'Photographing Fashion: A Critical Look at the Sartorialist.' *Image & Narrative*, 11(4): 158–70.

Scott, C. (2007) *Street Photography. From Atget to Cartier-Bresson*, London/New York: I.B. Tauris.

Titton, M. (2010) 'Fashion in the City. Street Style Blogs and the Limits of Fashion's Democratization', *Texte zur Kunst*, 20 (78): 133–8.

Vettel-Becker, P. (2005) *Shooting from the Hip. Photography, Masculinity, and Postwar America*, Minneapolis/London: University of Minnesota Press.

Watzlawik, J. C. (2010) 'Straßen. Stile. Sensationen – Die Präsenz des Streetstyles in Weblogs.' Mentges, G.; König, G. (eds), *Medien Der Mode*, Berlin: Edition Ebersbach.

Wilson, E. (2005) *Adorned in Dreams. Fashion and Modernity*, revised and updated edition, London: I.B. Tauris.

Women's Wear Daily (2009) 'Bricks versus Clicks: Front Row at D&G', *Women's Wear Daily*, www.wwd.com/fashion-news/fashion-scoops/bricks-versus-clicks-front-row-at-dg-2311802 (accessed 26 March 2013).

Chapter 10

Christopher Breward and Judith Clark

EXHIBITION-MAKING
A conversation

T HIS REFLECTIVE CONVERSATION was commissioned to follow on from Fiona Anderson's important contribution to the first edition of *Fashion Cultures* (2000, 37–89), entitled 'Museums as Fashion Media'.

In her chapter Anderson looked at three museum and gallery case studies 'selected in order to compare and contrast the approaches taken by a leading national museum (the Victoria and Albert Museum); a small independent gallery (Judith Clark Costume Gallery), and a designer who co-curated an exhibition of his own work (Hussein Chalayan's 'Echo Form' exhibition held at the Atlantis Gallery in 1999).'

Anderson's piece was in part a response to the changing position of fashion within the museum during the 1990s, both in terms of its use as part of a marketing strategy and in relation to an increasing interest in fashion as an academic research subject in the social sciences and humanities. It was also the result of the growing media interest in fashion and expansion of the locations in which it was discussed.

Over the past thirteen years, museums and galleries have continued to enjoy an unprecedented success in terms of the content and interpretation of their fashion-related programmes. Two consecutive special issues of the academic journal *Fashion Theory* (12:1 March 2008: 'Exhibitionism' and 12:2 June 2008: 'Fashion Curation') have explored in some detail the various curatorial methods and approaches involved in gallery practice and the resulting controversies that have accompanied new approaches to the collecting, display, sponsorship and marketing of fashion curation in the museum sector.

This candid conversation reflects on progress within the field, particularly in relation to Judith Clark's work, in the intervening period.

Figure 10.1   Simon Thorogood's 'C4i' exhibition at the Judith Clark Gallery, 1998. Photograph taken by Judith Clark.

Christopher Breward: Judith, in simple terms describe the context and mission of the Judith Clark Gallery, both at the moment of Fiona's review and in the subsequent two years until its closure.

Judith Clark: When Fiona Anderson interviewed me for her second case study on the small gallery that I had only run for two years, I had staged around ten exhibitions. The gallery's brief at that time was to illustrate the breadth of curatorial possibilities associated with dress and if possible – and I did not of course know for how long I would have the gallery – each exhibition would be informed by a distinct curatorial question. The gallery was privately funded and so operated outside the pressure to attract large visitor figures, prompted, as Anderson noted, 'by reductions in government or local authority grants'. The gallery did receive donations, though these were largely from private patrons who were not expecting a commercial return.

By 2000, I had curated 'Pampilion' (head pieces by Dai Rees, accompanied by commissioned photographs by Mat Collishaw); 'Details from a Private Collection' (three couture dresses from Baroness Fiona Thyssen-Bornemisza's wardrobe; Balenciaga, Givenchy and Grès); C4I; Simon Thorogood (Futurist dress and soundscape); 'Parure de Plumes' (an 1850s 'Peacock Dress, in a tableau dedicated to Whistler'); 'Cape Chic' (an exhibition of capes inspired by their reappearance on the catwalk earlier that year); 'Garden' (themed to a decorative motif); Sergei Paradjanov (the film director's costume collages); 'Semen of the Gods' (designer Arkadius's graduation collection); 'Be-hind, Be-fore, Be-yond' (jeweller Naomi Filmer's ice jewellery); and 'Pre-Inca Feather Dress' (tunics from 300–600 AD on loan from Paul Hughes Fine Art).

The average duration of each exhibition was six to eight weeks, though some were shorter. After 2000 the gallery hosted more exhibitions (*note list) and closed in 2002, when I was appointed London College of Fashion/Victoria and Albert Museum Research Fellow in Fashion, hosted within the Victoria and Albert Museum Research Department and funded by London College of Fashion, University of the Arts London.

CB: How did the fellowship shift the nature and context of your practice?

JC: Even though in many ways my practice has grown in scale it is not a progressive story but one of changing contexts. I feel as though what I have been doing has remained largely the same in intention but I am now possibly better equipped to articulate it. The luxury of having had a research position for over ten years is fundamental to this, and the timing of it – coinciding with a moment of profound change in relation to the curation of fashion exhibitions in the UK and beyond.

The fellowship meant that I had to engage with some of the realities as described by Fiona Anderson from a position of relative naivety. Anna Piaggi once told me that she had always 'squatted' within the format of Italian *Vogue* – she was given a certain amount of space, a certain number of pages and that is what she would fill and importantly 'push against'. She said she pushed against the other material in the magazine. I felt as though I was squatting at the V&A. I was always an outsider and the fact that I was funded externally by London College of Fashion legitimated that. When I interviewed for the post, at the moment when Andrew Bolton, the first incumbent of the position, was leaving to join Harold Koda at the Costume Institute at the Metropolitan Museum of Art, New York, I had already been asked by Linda Loppa to curate an exhibition at MoMu in Antwerp which I was determined to do. It was unclear to me at the time whether I was appointed on the back of the exhibitions that I had curated at the Judith Clark Gallery, which showed commitment but were not exactly widely documented, or whether the College and the Museum wanted a stronger association with the avant-garde scene in Antwerp.

CB: That's an interesting insight, given that I was on the interview panel for the post. My sense was that your approach to curation at the Judith Clark Gallery made an impact far in excess of the scale and physical and resource constraints of the Gallery itself, and was quickly noted in academic and museum contexts. In a period that had seen the publication of the journal *Fashion Theory*, the growth of international networks of scholars and curators interested in innovation in fashion curation and critique and the introduction of new postgraduate courses, your work made a welcome intervention. You had of course, also collaborated with the London College of Fashion on the project 'The Englishness of English Dress' and, as noted, were in mid-curation of the project with MoMu. Describe the challenges that the translation of that project to the V&A raised.

JC: At the outset I was asked to translate the MoMu exhibition title 'Malign Muses: When Fashion Turns Back' to 'Spectres: When Fashion Turns Back' as the V&A marketing department felt the word 'Malign' was too negative for their audiences. This alerted me to the power of marketing departments in large, brand-conscious national institutions. In Antwerp I had been given virtual carte blanche, as for them experimentation and risk was the point. I think they were at some level wondering what the museological equivalent of their fashion scene might be and the fact that they were so closely entwined with the fashion school (the Antwerp Academy) also made a huge difference. They didn't care that I had no museum experience. Linda just asked me to do for her what I was already doing at the Gallery. Perhaps this reflects the fluidity of roles and disciplines in Antwerp. For example, in 2001 Walter van Bierendonck was designing his own collections and curating the Biennale of Fashion in Antwerp, and he is now head of the Academy. This sense of flux and inter-disciplinarity was more difficult to achieve in a large organisation with an acute sense of its internal and external boundaries.

CB: 'Malign Muses' was a deeply historiographical show that seemed to play with questions around the theorisation of fashion, memory, archives and the relationship between present and past. How did that manifest itself in the research process and installation of the exhibition?

JC: I was preoccupied with fashion theory – and the sudden proliferation of so many more fashion texts – and its evocative motifs, and how a complex idea could be translated into three dimensions. What I didn't articulate at the time was my debt to exhibition histories. There is much more literature to draw on now about this than there was then. I wasn't saying then 'my debt is to Harald Szeeman', I was saying, 'Well, I want these materials to look a bit like those installation art photos, the ones where I always wish I could do something in a space like that. . .' So a lot of thought is now retrospective. I do know it is about creating a resonance between objects that are not only those explicitly on display, but also those that may have existed before.

CB: Your method sounds quite art historical, or at least informed by paradigms from contemporary art practice. Is that fair comment?

JC: I have never thought that fashion is art and I believe I will never be convinced of this. I know for sure that I am more interested in art history than dress history. But when I do read art history I am constantly translating what I am reading for the purpose of exhibiting dress. For example, I recently curated an exhibition titled 'The Judgment of Paris'. I looked at many different representations of the known tale: Niklaus Manuel Deutsch, Cranach the Elder, Rubens, Watteau, August Renoir and Manet. I read Hubert Damisch's wonderful book on the retelling of the myth. But the meaning of the exhibition was reduced to one vivid proposition: How do we tell one mannequin or protagonist from another in an exhibition tableau? The exhibition was made up of three cabinets (given the importance of three characters in the story), each divided into three: three heads (heads are very important in exhibitions of dress as they often show the aesthetic hand of the curator; in the Judgment of Paris the often-naked Goddesses are given their most telling identifying clues through variations in headdress); three torsos (each orientated differently – back, front and side; we are told by Damisch that Venus is depicted in profile as it is the most flattering aspect); and the last cabinet carried three props (the shield, the peacock and cupid; it questioned when and if we need props in exhibitions).

CB: That's a complex re-telling. Does the term 'curation' adequately describe the intellectual and physical labour that under-pinned its production?

JC: I am very keen to use the description of 'exhibition-maker' as it better describes working in the round. All but a very few of the exhibitions I have curated have been designed by me as well, as it is so integral to the process. I enjoy the fact that this resonates with a period of 'exhibition activism' and so associates it with positive change.

I certainly still have a loyalty to my original intention to use different curatorial criteria for each exhibition I have worked on. This comes from the material, however. I won't go into an archive with a pre-conditioned idea of what I want to do. The exception to that was 'The Concise Dictionary of Dress', where the project was generated to 'fit' the criteria and collaborative aspirations of the commissioning organisation (Artangel).

CB: Can you define those aspects of your work as 'exhibition-maker' that represent the development of a unique practice over the past decades?

JC: The continuities have happened at different levels, so for example I put on an exhibition at the Gallery called 'Captions' where I displayed a dramatic Alexander McQueen silhouette and invited visitors to write their own associative captions; so at one end of the spectrum I had little girls writing stories about the princess, and at the other art historians listing materials. 'Spectres' was the first time that the V&A had not put captions on the exhibits (we did have a leaflet that you could pick up at the entrance if you wanted to which had the captions on it). I felt that the traditional list of date, designer, and so on was not the information I wanted to privilege. I instead wanted to highlight the resonance between the objects as staged. I did not want to hide that information. It was used against me by some dress historians, of course, as though this was proof of a disregard for the object. But it drew attention to the caption by omitting it. It was my intention for people to wonder about it. In 'The Concise Dictionary of Dress' the caption was replaced by a definition written by Adam Phillips, of a word associated with the installation as a whole (sometimes one dress, sometimes more). This created a fury in some viewers. I remember hearing someone on the radio review it, I think it was Esther Freud, saying 'I would have preferred a caption saying "Private Collection. Date unknown". I loved that.'

The innovative and sometimes risky use of mannequins has been another consistent obsession. In Fiona Anderson's essay of 2000, I am quoted saying that in the Gallery I could afford to 'get it wrong'. I was referring largely to an investment in individual mannequins (of which I only needed a few per exhibition as the space was so small). Within museums mannequins often represent a lasting investment and commitment – looking at images of exhibitions you can often place and more or less date them according to the mannequin that was associated with that institution at that time.

They present individual histories of fashionability in themselves: the invisible Armani mannequins, D.V.'s dramatic Schlappi poses, followed by an era of headless politically correct caution. In the Gallery I made Perspex mannequins that revealed the interior structure of couture pieces and wooden mannequins to follow the lines of Simon Thorogood's toiles, which re-imagined the body as angular geometries. I commissioned Naomi Filmer's prosthetics for Spectres as both an illustration of the double role of representing the body bolted onto a conservation mannequin, remembering the museum's role in the care of historical dress, but also adding details. In one instance I divorced it from the mannequin totally and turned it into a prop – a ballet pump/foot with the harlequin theme (the most associated part of the body of a harlequin is the pointed toe). Recently I have collaborated with Angelo Seminara a lot on wigs, something I would not have dared to do without the budgets that have supported our work. It has often been around mannequins that I have repeated collaborative relationships – again underpinning a sense not that we are trying to get it right, but that we want to keep trying to do something else.

CB: The willingness to take risks and follow the path least taken would seem to characterise a career that has clearly 'upped the ante' in relation to the presentation of fashion in a gallery or museum context, and the success that has come with that has inspired further innovation: the virtuous cycle of research and development.

JC: Larger budgets have meant that I have been working with a fabrication company. I used to bend the Perspex in the Gallery with a lighter. Now the projects that I work on justify a building budget and so I have been looking at props – which were once considered so unfashionable! The idea of placing a big banana in a scene would have just been unthinkable in the last decade or so. I don't like the word 'purity'. I don't like the idea that seemed to be prevalent that a dress with a spotlight is 'right', rather than just being one way to do it. I was in the Chloe archive and there were all these dresses on hangers, mainly day dresses. And they were talking about drama, and I was thinking – how? The dresses needed wigs, they needed props, they needed attitude. These were not sculptural dresses, they were playful and witty. Not all exhibitions are about ball gowns. Some are about commissioning a banana copied from an invitation in the archive and placing it in the scene. It says as much about Chloe as the dress.

I have always resisted catwalk footage. One can believe – and I understand it – in the avant-garde sense that the first appearance of a work of art is its truest. And I am sure it has something of the intention of the designer. But I think that is then, and an exhibition has different rules. I am not frustrated by the fact that mannequins can't walk.

Exhibitions included at the Judith Clark Costume Gallery

2002: 'Adelle Lutz: View: Re:View: Costume Design, 1986–2002'.

2001: 'Paris Fashion on Paper, 1920–1930'; 'Pablo and Delia: The London Years, 1970–1975'; 'Madeleine Vionnet: 15 Dresses from the Collection of Martin Kamer'.

2000: Captions – Museology study: Captions to one dress, Alexander McQueen A/W 2000/1; Fascia: Garments and Constructions Simon Thorogood Spring/

Summer 2001; Play Hussein Chalayan Remote Control Dress S/S 2000; The Englishness of English Dress: Frills and Flounces; Orientalism: Léon Bakst Costume for Le Dieu Bleu 1912.

1999: Pre-Inca Feather Dress, 500-1200 AD; Be-hind, Be-fore and Be-yond: Naomi Filmer; Material Evidence: La Femme 100 Tetes, Martin Grant and Julia Morrison; Semen of the Gods: Graduation Collection by Arkadius; Sergei Paradjanov: Costumes and Sketches from the Paradjanov Museum, Armenia; Garden; Cape Chic.

1998: Parures des Plumes: Peacock motif 1858-1998; C4i: Simon Thorogood Spring/Summer 1999 couture; Details From a Private Collection: Baroness Fiona Thyssen-Bornemisza 1950s Couture; Pampilion: Dai Rees Autumn/Winter Couture Collection 1998.

PART THREE

Altered landscapes, new modes of production

Chapter 11

Alistair O'Neill

FASHION PHOTOGRAPHY
Communication, criticism and curation
from 1975

A N INTERROGATION OF HOW FASHION photography might contribute to a broad-based visual culture, functioning beyond its commercial remit, was first established in the mid-1970s. However, as photographic historian Val Williams has noted, 'The presence of fashion photography within the new photographic arena of the 1970s and early 1980s was an awkward one' (Williams 2008: 208). This chapter aims to unpack the conditions of this fertile period. The viability of examining fashion photography was informed by critical writing about the nature of photographs as representations, by the development of collections of photography both public and private, through an emerging culture of reviews and commentaries on temporary exhibitions and magazine editorials, and in the saturation of colour photo reproduction distributed in print media and the urban environment.

In academic and critical terms, this was facilitated by new ways of thinking about a culture of photography as a system of representation. Not only did it expand the kinds of photographs that could be considered – documentary, advertising, amateur, scientific – but also the different kinds of critical methodologies that could be employed to unpack them. It was an era marked by what Rosalind E. Krauss identifies as 'photography's emergence as a theoretical object' (Krauss 1999: 290), infused by the percolation of Walter Benjamin's two key essays on photography written in the 1930s, but translated into English in 1969 (Benjamin 1969).

In 1975 the art department of Wellesley College, Massachusetts, staged a series of symposia called *Photography within the Humanities*, published as a source book in 1977. Ten speakers were invited to talk about their critical attention to the medium and select ten photographs for a group show: they included the Director of the Department of Photography at the Museum of Modern Art, New York, John Szarkowski; cultural critic Susan Sontag; photographer Robert Frank; Picture Editor of the *New York Times*, John Morris; filmmaker Frederick Wiseman; and fashion photographer Irving Penn.

They argued for the rejection of realism, abandoning its view of the photograph as an unmediated document of reality: 'photographs "masquerade as it-ness"', to quote an apt formulation. They carry information clothed in a curious visual organisation' (Parry and McNeil 1977: 7). They reasoned that meaning lay in analysing the processes involved in the production of photography as much as in its reception; bringing attention to the different contexts –political, economic, technological and cultural – which harness meaning from an engagement with photography, claiming it as socially produced.

In turn, this was answered by theories that coalesced around the idea of photography as a language. Jacques Lacan's theorisation of the unconscious as structured by language was also applied to representation, suggesting that images mobilise desire and therefore structure visual pleasure (Lacan 1977; Mulvey 1989). Roland Barthes' work on the semiotics of photographic representations found in advertising studied the symbolism employed in composing images and in reading them as visual statements (Barthes 1957; 1977). The citation of fashion photography in this new landscape of enquiry was often seen through a Marxist critique of consumer advertising as promoting false consciousness (Williamson 1978), or found within a feminist analysis of the role of ideology in representations of women (Pollock 1977).

It is also in this period that photographic collections in museums are formalised, paralleled by the rise in collecting photography by private collectors and public institutions. Much of this newfound enthusiasm was in reclassifying photography as a medium of representation in its own right, meriting its own collection or department as separate from pre-existing classifications. This was mirrored by the secondary art market, which established auction-house departments devoted to photography servicing both the collectors and fine art markets. The identification of photography as an autonomous medium was later defined by the critic Douglas Crimp, following the exhibition staged in 1977 by Julia van Haaften, a reference librarian at the New York Public Library; this drew its material from the vast uncredited collection of photographic works, often included as illustration plates in books, housed across the library's departments. Crimp described this project as indicative of the changing classification and status of photography in museums and the auction market at this time:

> And thus the list goes on, as urban poverty becomes Jacob Riis and Lewis Hine; portraits of Delacroix and Manet become portraits by Nadar and Carjat; Dior's New Look becomes Irving Penn . . . for if photography was invented in 1839, it was only discovered in the 1960s and 1970s – photography, that is, as an essence, photography itself.
>
> (Crimp 1989: 218)

Aligned to this newfound sense of discovery was a need to define some of the lesser-regarded areas of photographic practice as histories in themselves. Many of these investigations were staged as temporary exhibitions, including the first attempt to create a pictorial history of fashion photography.

Fashion photography exhibited

In 1975, Robert R. Littman, Director of the Emily Lowe Gallery at Hofstra University, Long Island, curated the exhibition 'Fashion Photography: Six Decades', which displayed over 300 works by 25 photographers.[1] The exhibition was reviewed by *The New York Times*, which claimed it as the first survey of this form of photojournalism. The review was honest in its appraisal of contemporary examples, drawing attention to the sense of disturbance they raised within a broader visual development based on prevailing definitions of aesthetic beauty, forcing a different reading of what the survey actually charted beyond successive authors and styles:

> But perhaps overriding all the show's other intrinsic themes is the sociological and psychological development that it, however unwittingly, reflects. From swooning prima donnas to tough women in mink coats giving the clenched fist salute . . . (the exhibition) presents the changing attitudes towards women and the changing attitudes of women towards themselves.
>
> (Funke 1975)

Thus one of the earliest reviews of the first fashion photography exhibition stresses that its images are socially produced; they are not just the constructed intentions of those who produce fashion images of women, but also a reflection of how women perceive themselves, through a culture of looking at and consuming these images as an aspect of urban experience.

The exhibition transferred to the Kornblee Gallery, a commercial art gallery in Manhattan, before moving on to the Baltimore Museum of Art and the Museum of Contemporary Art, Chicago. The exhibition was clearly popular in New York, as it received a second review in *The New York Times*, this time by its principal art critic Hilton Kramer: 'It will draw sizeable crowds of curiosity seekers as well as aficionados of fashion, photography and whatever it is that passes for the latest artistic sensation.' Kramer was dismissive of 'the "conversion" of such work into an object of artistic interest'; he regarded fashion photography not as a genre, but as a 'somewhat special branch of photojournalism' aligned to advertising (Kramer 1975). The critic was unwavering in his view that fashion photography was undeserving of the kind of critical engagement offered by a gallery.

Debate about the contribution of the exhibition to an understanding of photography was furthered by *Print: America's Graphic Design Magazine*, which published a special issue on fashion photography and illustration in July 1976.[2] It offered an overview of twentieth-century fashion photography, delineating a shift whereby 'the loosening restrictions of technology and society have drastically altered the face of photography'. But Rose de Neve also noted a quality of anxiety in the work of some contemporary photographers:

> But something else is happening in fashion photography, too, most noticeably in the photographs of Deborah Turbeville, Helmut Newton, and Guy Bourdin. . . . It's the underlying tensions of the models – the actors, if you will – that one finds so deeply disturbing. . . . These

people totter on the brink of some unfathomable abyss; their poses are intimately linked with psychosis and despair.

(de Neve 1976: 26)

Similar to Funke's approach in his review of the 'Six Decades' exhibition, de Neve was keying into the psychological aspects of the works as expressive of a new kind of fashion photography, at odds with the usually accepted definition of its imagery as being either aspirational, desirable or frivolous. According to art critic Rosetta Brooks, it was in the mid-1970s that 'fashion photography converted this utopia into dystopia' (Brooks 2003: 127). The work of these three photographers was regularly raised as expressing this new condition in commentaries and reviews of the time. In order to examine this, it is worth returning to the sites of their first publications – precisely the kind of context (that was) lost in the first stagings of fashion photography in exhibition terms, where invariably they were presented as exhibition prints, shorn of the original framework of art direction, editorial copy, caption and credit.

Vogue (US) and (Paris) 1975

While the work of Newton and Bourdin had been published in European fashion titles since the 1960s, it was the May 1975 issue of US *Vogue* that introduced Newton and the lesser-known Turbeville to a US readership. According to *The New York Times*,

> The photographs by Helmut Newton in the May issue created something of a stir because they showed a number of sexual vignettes such as a man taking off (or putting on) a woman's bra with front snaps, and a woman sitting with spread legs and a knowing look, eyeing a bare-chested man.

(Morgan 1975)

This was additionally underlined by the publication of *Time Life's Photography Year* of 1976/77, which examined the photographs as 'more like sophisticated movie stills or excerpts from interpretive news features than the photographic versions of dress-shop windows usually seen in fashion publications' (*Photography Year* 1976/77: 24).

The issue published Helmut Newton's 'The Story of Ohhh' across fourteen pages, and Deborah Turbeville's ten-page spread 'There's More to a Bathing Suit'. Both editorials proposed scenarios that were provocative in content, problematising the offer of aspiration usually provided by fashion images. The disparity between these two editorials and the rest of the imagery published in the issue is noticeable, as is the closer affinity to some of the written articles published alongside them. The issue included an essay on ways to cope with today's anxiety written by Dr Arnold A. Hutschnecker, famed as Richard M. Nixon's psychotherapist and another, on beauty, by cultural critic Susan Sontag. Hutschnecker called into question 'a strong and effective-looking façade based on impressive outer values and an imposing make-believe lifestyle' (Hutschnecker 1975: 114), as if indicting the very magazine in which his article appeared for contributing to this modern psychological affliction. Sontag's essay debunked classical notions of beauty by exploring the current play with its lack of fixity, which she saw as underpinned by the logic of the fashion magazine: 'Expensively produced magazines that articulate and promote fashion contribute, inadvertently, to the demolition of the reactionary idea of beauty as much as do such sharp-eyed critics of the fashion industry' (Sontag 1975: 174).

Clearly, the articulation of what might represent fashionable preoccupations of interest is raised as being as complicated and contested as the photographic contributions of Turbeville and Newton. This issue of US *Vogue* unpacks the purchase of fashion in magazine format, as page after page of probing self-reflection. It presents any entry to the offer of its world as disquieting and disorientating, as a far from simple form of acquisition. *Print* magazine's special issue (op. cit) also considered the citation of fashion photography in specialist sex magazines, such as *Viva*, published in New York by Bob Collacello and the US edition of *Oui* published by Playboy Enterprises (Opat 1976: 53). The article was illustrated with editorials by Newton and Turbeville, published in *Oui* and *Viva* respectively, which are clearly connected to the concerns of their work for *Vogue* in May 1975, be it the themes of exploitation and domination between men and women for Newton, or the

Figure 11.1   Deborah Turbeville, 'The Fashion Plate: From Cool to Kinky and How It Got There'. *Print: America's Graphic Design Magazine*, July 1976, 32–3 (Central Saint Martins Library Special Collections).

setting of a bathhouse for a sexually charged but disconnected grouping of women by Turbeville.

In the July 1975 issue of *Vogue* Paris, another preoccupation is documented: the contextualisation of current fashion photography within a wider tradition of image making. For its beauty pages, it begins with a short feature of summer photographs taken by Jacques Henri Lartigue in the 1920s and 1930s, before contrasting them with swimwear photographs by Newton and Bourdin. Here, the poise and serenity of Lartigue's subjects is contrasted by their modern counterparts. Newton had his swimwear model contemplate a kitchen refrigerator of caught fish (the eye of the fish in the model's hand captures Newton's flash ring) while Bourdin's swimsuit model, wearing the latest style of high wedge espadrille, tumbles twice across the spread, as if somersaulting in water or more likely falling over her own encumbered feet. While Lartigue was never a fashion photographer, his work had recently been reappraised due to Richard Avedon, who had long been an admirer of Lartigue's effortless style of motion capture.[3] It is from this principle of comparing contemporary fashion photography to its history of past images that a new departure for the genre emerges.

The fashion photography archive

In the same year, the notion of the fashion photography archive emerged in tandem with a realisation of its material history arising out of vintage prints circulating at auction; unpacked not just as exhibitions, but also offered as commodified style statements for the secondary art market.

The increased visibility of *Vogue* photographers contributing to an international agenda for commercial imagery celebrated in print and in exhibitions did not go unnoticed by Condé Nast. In 1975, Robert Caille, publisher of the French edition demanded that a number of photographers surrender their negatives for the magazine's archive. Condé Nast maintained that the copyright of any image taken by a photographer under contract remained with the publisher first.

Helmut Newton's response was to surrender his negatives, but only after cherry-picking them first. This meant that while *Vogue* might have the published shot, likely to have been chosen by the art director or fashion editor, Newton took the frame he actually preferred. This selection informed the works printed for Newton's first one-man show at Gallerie Nikon, Paris, in 1975. Thus, Newton's first commercial exhibition as a fashion photographer is predicated on his reaction to the notion of archiving his work. Newton confirmed this in 2003:

> So, I got busy with scissors and started cutting up my rolls of film, surrendering what I felt I had to, to keep 'them' quiet and saving the best negatives for themselves. . .
>
> Years later, a woman who had the job as archivist of French *Vogue* decided that all this was too much trouble and threw all the negatives into the trash outside the door of no. 4 Place du Palais Bourbon.
>
> (Newton 2003: 184–5)

The other photographer likely to have been given this directive from *Vogue* Paris is Guy Bourdin, who at this point was producing as much editorial for the title as Newton, although there is no record of his response. However, since Bourdin's death in 1991, a view of how he regarded his own work has emerged (Gingeras 2011). It indicates that Bourdin did not believe in an afterlife for his photographs once they were published. Hence Bourdin did not take great care of his own archive of photographic materials; after his death, many of the original negatives retrieved by his estate were found to be in poor condition due to inadequate storage. It is not possible to establish if Bourdin's viewpoint was hardened by Caille's demand, but thinking about the relationship between photography and the archive was certainly in evidence in the period.

In May 1975, the University of Arizona established its Centre for Creative Photography, introducing 'a radical concept for acquiring archival material' (*Photography Year 1976/77*: 234). The curators purchased five archives of living American photographers including Ansel Adams and Aaron Siskind, buying ultimate rights to negatives, selected prints and written documentation. The contracts allowed the photographers full use of their materials with ongoing commissions for the Centre.

In the very same month, Irving Penn staged two exhibitions: first his photographs of enlarged cigarette butts as commanding platinum prints at the Museum of Modern Art, New York; and second a mixed show of platinum prints based on existing magazine work staged in Turin, which also travelled to London for October 1975.[4]

Penn was motivated to work with platinum printing as he had retained little control over how his negatives had been printed for magazine publishing over the span of his commercial career. While the 'cigarette butt' pictures represented new work, the exhibition in Italy and the UK showed commercial work, including fashion, reprinted for consideration as exhibition prints. Penn was aware of the fact that his archival exercise could be construed not just as a technical exercise in printmaking, but a means of producing highly gilded reproductions for both exhibition and sale: 'While the platinum versions are very beautiful, they are sort of bastard pictures, and I have very mixed feelings about them. . . . There's something somewhat uncontemporary about them' (Parry and MacNeil 1977: 137).

Penn's doubtful self-appraisal of his commercial photography and the place it might occupy was echoed in a letter he wrote to Cecil Beaton, thanking him for including his work in *The Magic Eye*, a survey of the history of photography co-authored by Gail Buckland, a former curator of the Royal Photographic Society Collection, published in June 1975. Penn declared himself grateful 'for the incredible piece of work the book is as contemporary history' (Vickers 1985: 576). The survey consisted of commentaries of the great names of photography, but significantly included an appendix of essays dealing with commercial photographers from the 1860s to the 1930s and the specialist work of architectural, fashion, press, theatre and ballet photographers.

It was the first to suggest an early history of fashion photography, documenting the role of late nineteenth-century Paris photography studios such as Reutlinger. It qualified photographic styles, drawing connections between photographers of different eras, so Baron Adolphe de Meyer's 'silver world of grace and poetry' of the 1920s could be related to Richard Avedon's stark white 'lighting-flash onto an "oblivion" background' of the 1960s. And it created lineages, so that the lesser-known work of Peter Rose Pulham from the 1930s 'led the way to Guy Bourdin and so many followers today' (Beaton and Buckland 1975: 277).

The publication also afforded an understanding of where Beaton's work might be placed, underscored by the preparation of the sale of Beaton's archive, arranged by Philippe Garner at Sotheby's across three auctions, agreed in February 1976. The auction was intended to secure an income and the cost of care for Beaton, in recovery from a stroke that had partially paralysed him. It included the sale of all negatives and prints by Beaton (excluding Royal subjects) as well as his scrapbooks and the works of other photographers.[5]

The history of fashion photography

In 1977, the first museum exhibition of fashion photography was staged. 'The History of Fashion Photography' was curated by Nancy Hall-Duncan at the International Museum of Photography at George Eastman House in Rochester, New York – the oldest museum dedicated to photography, established in 1949 by the photography firm Kodak. Hall-Duncan openly acknowledged the swiftly built cultural framework that her large-scale exhibition and catalogue was entering into, describing it as 'the creation of gallery and public interest in the fashion print and an increased critical reaction to the fashion idiom' (Hall-Duncan 1979: 221).

Hall-Duncan's exhibition started with the origins of studio portraiture in the 1860s, before tracing the earliest evidence of photographic reproductions in late nineteenth-century mass-produced periodicals and illustrated magazines, and then embarking on a twentieth-century account. Reviewing the exhibition when it travelled to the Brooklyn Museum at the end of 1977, Gene Thornton of *The New York Times* noted:

> By bearing down on a frankly commercial art with all the scholarly apparatus of the modern art historian, this exhibition demonstrates the close ties that do exist between the art of the media and the art of the museum, and casts into doubt any definition of art that does not include both types.
>
> (Thornton 1977)

Thornton pointed to a confluence between high and low forms of visual culture, citing the museum as an appropriate space for critically engaging with the intersections between creative expression and commercial design. He praised Hall-Duncan for her ability to raise a comprehensive history of the genre, albeit through a linear articulation of authorship and successive styles.

Hall-Duncan's curatorial position was informed by debates around the nature and function of commercial imagery, still aligned to the polarities of high and low culture and the principle of denigrating work commissioned by a market-driven model of production. Even in the world of advertising, fashion imagery still suffered from the perception of being insubstantial or not being taken seriously by advertising and publishing professionals.

However, Hall-Duncan's project did argue that this view was changing in the light of critical responses to a new culture of fashion photography. She identified a difference in publishing markets: the American model responding much more to consumer taste and having a heavy ratio of advertising to editorial, the European model more intellectual in its editorial position and often trying to lead readership tastes – consequently circulation there was smaller and there was a reduced ratio of advertising. Hall-Duncan also noted that the sexually provocative and deviant imagery produced from France in the 1970s was a response to the sexually emancipated work that came out of the USA in the late 1960s as a point of difference and distortion.

In her entry for fashion photography for the *Berg Companion to Fashion*, Hall-Duncan confirmed that 'French *Vogue* took the creative lead in fashion photography in this decade and offered their two leading photographers, Helmut Newton and Guy Bourdin, complete creative autonomy' (Hall-Duncan 2010: 302). The influence of these editorials extended beyond the intended readership. Philippe Garner, who was appointed head of photographs and twentieth-century decorative arts at Sotheby's auction house in London in 1971, recalls being in thrall to reading *Vogue* Paris:

> Thinking of those pages of French *Vogue* in the seventies, to which I was kind of addicted – I would buy every month with a fascination to see how this competition was going between Bourdin principally, and Newton. In the pages of the magazine they were pushing the limits of what could be published.
>
> (BBCTV 1996)

Garner's admission demonstrates the interconnected nature between 'the art of the media', the secondary art market, and, in turn, the museum in this elemental period. It also provides evidence that the work of these two photographers was appreciated beyond the specialism of the genre. More often than not, it was the citation of fashion imagery in the real world, beyond the covers of a magazine and visually distributed within the urban environment, which was another feature of its graphic ubiquity in this period.

Bloomingdale's, 1976

In terms of the new fashion photography in question, it is arguable that the American department store, typified by the design-led marketing strategies of Bloomingdale's, adopted a number of initiatives that led this new kind of promotional imagery to enter into a wider form of visual distribution.[6] In 1976, Bloomingdale's secured two significant campaigns that led to national news stories. First, for spring they issued 500,000 shopping bags printed with a photograph of fashion model Yasmin Sokal; the image was misattributed to Princess Yasmin Khan, daughter of Rita Hayworth, who sued for misrepresentation. For Christmas, Arthur Cohen, the store's vice-president of marketing, commissioned Guy Bourdin to produce a lingerie catalogue that would be sent to the 650,000 charge customers and further distributed to potential customers, supplied within Sunday newspapers. Titled *Sighs and Whispers*, the catalogue featured noticeably young models who Bourdin

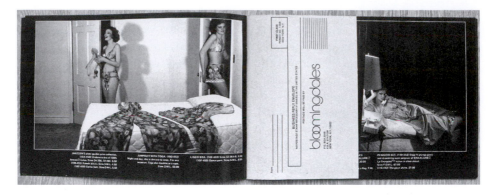

Figure 11.2   Guy Bourdin, *Sighs and Whispers*, Bloomingdale's Lingerie
Catalogue, 1976. (Private Collection).

had street-cast, arranged in a series of New York apartment interiors wearing
fashionable lingerie and sport-inspired casualwear.

> Bourdin paraded these sloe-eyed Lolitas through a series of scenes
> showing the young women doing what young women do in the privacy
> of a house: sitting, three abreast on a sofa, dressed in nothing but sheer
> bras, panties (in two out of three cases), high-heeled gold shoes, and
> that come-hither makeup; . . . gazing restlessly out the curtainless
> window into the city that holds the keys to excitement.
>
> (Brady 1980: 187)

Reactions to the catalogue were mixed – 'while some customers considered it
brilliant, others threatened to burn their charge plates' (Hartman 1980: 129), but
surviving copies quickly became a collector's item, selling for $20 at specialist
bookshops.

The legacy of the catalogue as a document of fashion photography in the period
lies in an essay written by the critic Rosetta Brooks in 1980, first published in
Camerawork. Since then, it has been reprinted in a number of different contexts,
most notably in *ZG* magazine in 1981 – which at the time was also edited by
Brooks – and in the catalogue to the Victoria and Albert Museum's retrospective
of Guy Bourdin staged in 2003.

The essay established that in the mid-1970s 'the nature of the relationship
between product-image and product (form and content) changed' (Brooks 1981:
n.p). By this, Brooks identified the fact that the conveyance of the product image and
its authorship eclipsed the communicative potential and function of the product. In
her analysis of Bourdin's catalogue, Brooks noted the double-page spreads and
the flow of images they unpack as a series of spatial devices, so that the 'New York
apartment' where the story is set offers 'not a real space of erotic encounter, but a
space between images – between the wallpaper pattern and its reversal in space and
between shots in time'. Thus, Bourdin's photographs serve to arrest the viewer's gaze
through their constructed nature as images, veiling their commercial function.

The appearance of the essay in issue 5 of *ZG* magazine, dedicated to New York, contextualised Bourdin's catalogue as a feature of the city's crosscurrents of cultural activity. The issue argued for a terrain of enquiry that considered 'the institutional thinness and arbitrariness of the divide between activities which "belong" to the galleries or the museum and those that belong to the street or the club' (Brooks 1981: n.p). In these terms, Bourdin's work appeared not just as commercial fashion imagery, but as a visible and covetable indicator of a metropolitan image culture operating across the polarities of high and low. In essence, Brooks' citation of her essay and of the Bloomingdale's catalogue within the special issue of *ZG* marked how the parameters that had been raised when commercial fashion photography of this kind was first discussed in the new photographic arena of the mid-1970s, were now less clearly signposted.

Reflecting on the essay again in 1996, Brooks suggested that the fashion photography of the mid-1970s, typified by Bourdin, Newton and Turbeville, 'proved that advertising need not be an invitation to a cosy-other world of the imagination: it can be a challenge' (Brooks 1996: 205). Her view remained unchanged when her essay was updated for the Victoria and Albert Museum's Bourdin exhibition catalogue in 2003, even though she acknowledged that the realm of fashion photography had altered greatly since 1976:

> Sadly, the excitement and exhilaration in the air back then has given way to a gloomy re-entrenchment, a movement back to a conservative attitude towards making and experiencing the image.
>
> (Brooks 2003: 133)

While this is certainly true, it is arguable that this re-entrenchment is a side effect of the greater appreciation of fashion photography and its assimilation into a broad-based visual culture whereby it may emerge in the form of commercial imagery, within a digital image bank, a creative website, blog summary, temporary exhibition or picture library – or as museum object, archive item, auction lot, or part of a private collection.

With the collapse of the distinction between mass and elite culture, museums, galleries and publishers have mined the popular appeal of fashion photography as a 'way in' to other concerns. For example, a thematic collection display at Tate Modern in 2002, titled 'Nude/Action/Body' contained a gallery of fashion photography loaned from the Victoria and Albert Museum. However, some of fashion photography's most obvious features such as its commercial imperative, the contextual framework within which it is produced and consumed, its interconnectedness to practices and to further forms of collaboration, are often the first to be mislaid in the attempts to re-present fashion photography beyond its primary articulation.

There has been a small but consistent voice of dissent from cultural commentators about this predicament.[7] By far the most potent was Abigail Solomon-Godeau's critical review of the Museum of Modern Art's first large-scale fashion photography exhibition, 'Fashioning Fictions', in 2004. It argued that a lack of committed interrogation into the formal and conceptual functions of fashion photography is not solely attributable to fashion photographers, but also to those employed in curating and interpreting their images. As Solomon-Godeau asserted, 'regardless of the individual intention of artists and photographers, there is a difference between art and fashion, documentary and advertising, however fragile or provisional it is' (Solomon-Godeau 2004: 192).

It is notable that the recognition of fashion photography in contemporary visual culture, even after what is nearing thirty years of awareness, remains tentative and provisional. As Williams has rightly concluded, 'the ever-deeper delving by curators and scholars into the history, power, and presence of the fashion photograph, is one important route to uncovering its many, and complex, meanings' (Williams 2008: 217).

Notes

1   It included 34 studies by Georges Hoyningen-Heune, as well as works by Cecil Beaton, Man Ray, Irving Penn, Richard Avedon, Toni Frissell, Deborah Turbeville, Helmut Newton, and Guy Bourdin.

2   The fashion photographs reproduced were based on the selection in Litman's 1975 exhibition.

3   Avedon worked on Lartigue's 'Diary of a Century' from 1968. The monograph was published in 1970.

4   Irving Penn: Recent Works, Photographs of Cigarettes, Museum of Modern Art, New York, 23 May–3 August 1975. I Platini di Irving Penn: 25 Anni di Fotografia, Galleria Civica d'Arte Moderna, Turin, June 1975. Irving Penn: Platinum Plates, The Photographer's Gallery, London, 1–31 October 1975.

5   It was the first photo auction to stipulate that the negatives of vintage prints sold were retained by the seller. Sotheby's remain the copyright holder of Beaton's work today.

6   In 1975, Saks ran a widespread print campaign featuring works by Deborah Turbeville and Arthur Elgort.

7   e.g. Michael Bracewell's *A Fine Romance*, published in issue 5 of *Frieze* magazine in 1991 regarding the Aperture publication, *The Idealised Image*, and the V&A fashion photography exhibition of the same year, *Appearances*.

References

Journal articles

Brooks, R. 1981. 'Sighs and Whispers in Bloomingdales.' *ZG*, issue 5, n.p.

Krauss, R. 1999. 'Reinventing the Medium.' *Critical Inquiry*, Vol. 25, No. 2, Winter: 289–305.

Naudet, J. J. 1975. 'Helmut Newton interview.' *PHOTO*, No. 92, May.

Pollock, G. 1977. 'What's Wrong with "Images of Women".' *Screen Education*, No. 24: 25–33.

Solomon-Godeau, A. 2004. 'Modern Style: Dressing Down.' *Artforum*, issue 429, May: 192–6.

Williams, V. 2008. 'A Heady Relationship: Fashion Photography and the Museum: 1979 to the present.' *Fashion Theory*, Vol. 12, No. 2, 197–218.

Single author publications

Barthes, R. 1957. *Mythologies*. Paris: Seuil.

—— 1977. *Image, Music, Text*. London: Fontana.

Brady, M. 1980. *Bloomingdale's*. New York: The Authors' Group.

Gingeras, A. 2011. *Guy Bourdin*. London: Phaidon.

Hall-Duncan, N. 1979. *The History of Fashion Photography*. New York: Abrahams.

Hartman, R. 1980. *Birds of Paradise*. New York: Delta.

Lacan, J. 1977. 'The Mirror Stage as Formative of the Function of the I as revealed in psychoanalytic Experience.' In *Écrits: a Selection*. London: Tavistock.

Mulvey, L. 1989. 'Visual Pleasure and Narrative Cinema.' in *Visual and Other Pleasures*, Basingstoke: Macmillan.

Newton, H. 2003. *Autobiography*. London: Duckworth.

Townsend, C. 2002. *Rapture: Art's Seduction by Fashion since 1970*. London: Thames & Hudson.

Vickers, H. 1985. *Cecil Beaton: The Authorised Biography*. London: Weidenfeld and Nicolson.

Williamson, J. 1978. *Decoding Advertisements – Ideology and Meaning in Advertising*. London: Marion Boyars.

Edited anthologies

Beaton, C. and Buckland, G. 1975. *The Magic Eye: The Genius of Photography from 1839 to the Present Day*. London: Weidenfeld and Nicolson.

Benjamin, W. 1969. 'The Work of Art in the Age of Mechanical Reproduction' and 'A Small History on Photography.' In Arendt, H. (ed.), *Illuminations*. London: Cape.

Brooks, R. 1996. 'Fashion: Double-Page Spread.' In *The Camerawork Essays: Context and Meaning in Photography*. London: Rivers Oram Press.

—— 2003. 'Sighs and Whispers.' in Cotton, C (ed.) *Guy Bourdin*. London: V&A Publishing.

Crimp, D. 1989. 'The Museum's Old/The Library's New Subject.' In *The Contest of Meaning: Critical Histories of Photography*. Bolton, R (ed.) Cambridge, MA: MIT Press.

Hall-Duncan, N. 2010. 'Fashion Photography.' In *The Berg Companion to Fashion*, Oxford: Berg.

Parry, E and MacNeil, W (eds) 1977. *Photography within the Humanities*. Danbury, NH: Addison House.

'The Turn of Fashion.' in *Photography Year 1976/77*. Edition by the Editors of Time Life Books, Nederland: Time-Life International.

Journalism

Bellison, L. 1978. 'Future Events in the Spirit of Easter', *The New York Times*, 19 March.

Edwards, O. 1976. 'Fashion Photography is Good to Look At, But Not Always Good', *The Village Voice*, January 12.

Funke, P. 1975. 'Art of Photography in Fashion Shown', *The New York Times*, 9 November.

Hutschnecker, A. 1975. 'Is Fear Contagious?', *Vogue* (US), May: 144–5, 173.

Morgan, T. 1975, 'I'm the biggest model, period', *The New York Times*, 17 August.

de Neve, R. 1976. 'The Fashion Plate: From Cool to Kinky and How It Got There.' *Print: America's Graphic Design Magazine*, XXX: IV July: 24–33.

Opat, E.J. 1976. 'Stalking the Wild Fashion Photography', *Print: America's Graphic Design Magazine*, July: 53–9.

Sontag, S. 1975. 'Beauty: How Will it Change Next?', *Vogue* (US), May: 116–17, 174.

Thornton, G. 1977. 'Fashion Pictures Taken Seriously', *The New York Times*, 11 December.

—— 1978. 'Who Took the Fashion Model Outdoors?', *The New York Times*, 2 April.

Television programme

'Dreamgirls: the photographs of Guy Bourdin'. BBC TV 1996

Chapter 12

Elliott Smedley

ESCAPING TO REALITY
Fashion photography in the 1990s

Foreword
By Pamela Church Gibson

WE HAVE ELECTED TO REPRINT Elliott Smedley's essay of 2000 for a number of reasons. It captures as eloquently as any photograph the decade that was closing as he wrote, which had seen 'grunge' and 'heroin chic' enter the international vocabulary. His essay, read today, enables us to follow the process of 'action and reaction' not only in the decade he describes and which is here vividly recreated for us, but in that which followed when the 'realist fashion imagery' which he analysed was, as he predicted, 'inevitably . . . superseded'.

The new century has, of course, brought with it an extraordinary technical innovation in the form of digital manipulation. This is the most radical change within fashion photography, but interestingly there is no single dominant aesthetic. Instead, there is now a bewildering diversity of images, ranging from the high-gloss colour-saturated photographs of Mert and Marcus to more romantic pictures, like some of the fashion spreads created by David Sims with Grace Coddington at US *Vogue*. The other change to affect fashion photography is the new power and prominence of the luxury brands; there is a seamless sweep of photographs across and through magazines, between the fashion editorials and the endless pages of advertising that preface and follow them, so funding many of these publications. There are some constant elements within the overall picture; many of the photographers whose work has been most prominent in magazine journalism across the last decade have now been working continuously for twenty years or more — Mario Testino, Peter Lindbergh and Steven Meisel, for example.

Juergen Teller, whose earlier work is described in the essay that follows, is still taking fashion photographs; perhaps the changes in his work perfectly illustrate the power of the brands and the lure of advertising. His best-known work during the last decade was probably his collaboration with Marc Jacobs and the celebrities whom Jacobs tempted into one particular advertising campaign. Victoria Beckham, in the fallow years before her reincarnation as designer, was shown struggling inside an enormous carrier bag while Winona Ryder, at that time in the public eye after her arrest for shoplifting, was depicted lying across a bed surrounded by endless, possibly pilfered, paper bags containing designer merchandise. The campaign was notable for its pallid, carefully chic colour palette. In contrast to Teller, Nan Goldin has not abandoned her original aesthetic. She has continued to work within fashion and in 2010 created a series of advertising images for luxury brand Bottega Veneta. But this particular campaign quite deliberately evoked the photographs taken for her book of 1986, *The Ballad of Sexual Dependency*. She has continued with her documentary work, while her images have made the transition from printed page to gallery wall. The current work of other contemporary photographers may not follow quite the same trajectory.

Reference

Goldin, Nan (1986) *The Ballad of Sexual Dependency*, New York: Aperture.

Escaping to reality: fashion photography in the 1990s

> I want to make photographs of very elegant women taking grit out of their eyes, or blowing their noses, or taking the lipstick off their teeth. Behaving like human beings in other words . . . It would be gorgeous, instead of illustrating a woman in a sports suit in a studio, to take the same woman in the same suit in a motor accident, with gore all over everything and bits of the car here and there. But naturally this would be forbidden.
>
> (Cecil Beaton cited in Hall 1979: 202)

IN THE 1990S, THE DESIRES of that seemingly conservative fashion photographer, Cecil Beaton, are no longer 'forbidden'. Clothing manufacturer Diesel has produced advertising that imitates motor crashes, while models taking grit out of their eyes or lipstick from their teeth are perfectly normal – as in David Sims' pictures of supermodel Linda Evangelista, fingers in mouth, for a Jil Sander campaign in 1993. Behaving like 'human beings' and documenting 'realistic' activities became a prominent feature of contemporary fashion photography in the early 1990s, and dominated the decade. The role of fashion photography as a commercial instrument, although still intrinsic to its purpose, seemingly became superseded in this decade by the need to reflect wider concerns, rather than just endorsing product placement. This became manifest in a gritty 'warts and all' realistic style that eclipsed the glossy, groomed fashion spreads of the past, which had served to convey a seemingly unattainable ideal of beauty. Such a shift may seem unsurprising, given the socio-economic conditions of the time and the perceived ability of fashion photography to 'capture the spirit of an era' (Craik 1994: 101). Yet the concerns that this style introduced and conveyed in the 1990s have implications both for, and beyond, fashion photography.

It is important to establish and understand the motivation for the prevalence of this style in the 1990s, since a 'recourse to the documentary and vernacular image is not entirely a contemporary phenomenon' (Williams 1998: 104). Periodically, there is an attempt by the fashion world to shed what it perceives as an overly commercial image – and its search for something new often results in a flirtation, even a courtship, between fashion and the art world. In this case, the 'art' concerned is documentary photography, a strand of photographic practice now accepted as a legitimate art form. This courtship is crucial to the realist aesthetic of the 1990s, with practitioners in both arenas crossing the boundaries – and thus blurring them. The concerns of documentary photography – 'the perfect tool for the representation of the human plight and experience' (Mack 1996: 232) – presented fashion photography with the chance to challenge its own role. While this role has traditionally been to create fantasy, fusing this notion with that of documentary has led to some misinterpretation.

Paving the way: historical precedents

Fashion photography emerged within and grew to dominate the commercial arena during the 1920s and 1930s, largely as a reaction against fashion illustration – or what Condé Nast, the publisher of *Vogue*, called 'wilful, wild, willowy, wonderful drawings'. *Vogue* readers, he exclaimed, 'were so literally interested in fashion that they wanted to see the mode thoroughly and faithfully reported – rather than rendered as a form of decorative art' (Seebohm 1982: 178–9). Photography was at first seen as a form of representation that possessed the ability to depict clothes realistically, without any artistic distortion.

However, rather than just providing an exact likeness of fashionable garments, in practice it constructed other forms of representation that held wider connotations. These were the same as those of the fashion illustration: the impression of a fashion ideal or chic – 'a far more tantalising and marketable idea than a precisely detailed photograph' (Maynard, quoted in Craik 1994: 98). In effect, early fashion photography was a continuation of this ideal, creating a visual fantasy to which women could aspire, and a standard that conventional fashion photography still pursues. The practice of using aristocrats or socialites further endorsed such a concept and it was not until art movements – surrealism, realism and modernism – surfaced within fashion and its photographic representations that such notions were challenged.

Certain fashion photographers borrowed from the different movements, creating a plurality of photographic styles. Modernism gave to fashion photography a graphic and geometric influence; surrealism inspired dream-like images. Realism, on the other hand, inspired a less formal approach: sometimes models were depicted (as never before) in action and in movement. Such a look came from 'the realist imagery of sports fashion photography which offered the modern woman a look she could apply to her own life' (Hall-Duncan 1979: 77). Static poses began to disappear, to be replaced by moments of narrative, fleeting impressions and relaxed actions. Elitist fashion imagery, which owed much to illustration, was superseded by more commercial pictures. While clearly shaped by the fashions of the day, such as the influence of sportswear, the impact of Hollywood was central to the construction of this new ideal. 'Films threw up the new role models, images of a consumer society, visually based fantasies and narratives, and new codes of representation' (Craik 1994: 101). These representations were plundered by fashion photography, most notably in the way models became 'blemish free' and 'uniformly youthful' while their potential as commodity increased (Craik 1994: 101).

While early fashion photography became less restricted, its capacity to reflect women realistically was not fully realised until the 1940s, and specifically during the Second World War. This furthered the transition to a realistic approach to photographing fashion, since magazines discouraged displays of excess and frivolity while fashion itself became more austere due to the rationing of fabrics. Lee Miller, the one-time partner of Man Ray, emerged as a key fashion photographer of this period, mainly working for British *Vogue*. Her photographs were as much a social documentary as a recording of fashion, showing women in wartime Britain in everyday situations. Condé Nast complimented her on one series for *Vogue* in 1942, asserting that:

> The photographs are much more alive now, the backgrounds more interesting, the lighting and posing more dramatic and real. You managed to handle some of the deadliest studio situations in the manner of a spontaneous outdoor snapshot.
>
> (Seebohm 1982: 244)

This emerging realist aesthetic was also felt in America; the art director at *Vogue*, Alexander Liberman, realised that 'the immediacy of the unopposed news photograph could be grafted onto fashion photographs to give them a wider appeal, greater realism' (Harrison 1991: 42). In the 1950s, Liberman commissioned photographers who used the techniques of social documentary, specifically Richard Avedon and Irving Penn, whose images contained a contrived spontaneity. Avedon captured the looks, mannerisms and gestures of 'human beings', while Penn emphasised the anthropological and sociological elements of fashion (Hall-Duncan 1979: 140–54).

In Britain a similar style to that of the 'spontaneous snapshot' became a hall-mark of certain photographers during the 1950s. While this trend contained an element of 'reality', signified by the use of locations rather than the studio, its limitations were seen in the continuing construction of an aspirational feminine ideal. In effect, many of these photographs contained a fiction of reality; idealised moments that enabled 'women to imagine what they would look like, to men, in this situation or outfit, without having to commit themselves in any way to that situation or that outfit' (Barnard 1996: 120). While this notion may hold true of much conventional fashion photography, consumed as it is primarily by women, it is not the aim of this chapter to challenge any notion of the 'female gaze' – although in the 1990s, it raises problems around fashion imagery.

In the 1960s, a shift in social attitudes and new directions in publishing – particularly the influence of the magazine *Nova* – traversed the boundaries customarily placed around the editorial fashion story in a defiant yet controlled way. These conventions extended the role of fashion photography into a larger debate that encompassed discussions of race, sexuality and class within fashion and style (see Williams 1998). The emphasis on sexuality in fashion photography was promoted by the self-styled 'Terrible Three' – David Bailey, Terence Donovan and Brian Duffy – working-class Londoners with an irreverent attitude to the world of fashion and the pretensions of its protagonists. Theirs was a vision that developed a theme of women's independence, yet also placed value on beauty, sexuality and success. In summing up their style, Brian Duffy stressed the fact that the three of them were 'violently heterosexual butch boys . . . We emphasised the fact that there were women inside the clothes. They started to look real' (Craik 1994: 96). This was evident in a look, a gesture, a way of wearing clothes – and in documentary observations taken from their East End roots. Models such as Jean Shrimpton and Twiggy typified this new ideal; indeed, Shrimpton attributed her success to 'ordinariness' (Craik 1994: 105).

They were also identifiable role models for a newer, younger audience who were more attuned to the rising success of the new designers and smaller boutiques that emerged as the dominance of couture waned. The liberated new woman, who was as much a *Nova* construction as a reflection of the time, was reinforced within fashion imagery by the influence of metropolitan youth culture. While much 1960s fashion imagery was resolutely positive in its construction and depiction of the 'liberated woman', Bob Richardson reflected another side of her personality that had rarely been seen in fashion photography. He incorporated images of despair, melancholy and anxiety, using images that clearly resembled snapshots, often within a wealthy or glamorous setting – such as the famous narrative sequence set on a Mediterranean beach. However, Richardson invariably used clearly constructed tableaux to portray these wider concerns; despite the fact that he developed realistic themes within his narratives, they cannot properly be described as 'realistic'.

In the 1970s some of these themes were taken up by photographers such as Helmut Newton and Guy Bourdin, whose style Jennifer Craik (1994: 108) calls 'brutal realism'. However, the glamorous fashions of the period and the highly stylised images in which they were portrayed could hardly be seen as documentary. But the issues they developed, mainly the eroticism of the women, involved wider cultural debates. They could be seen as reflecting the underlying tensions about the fantasies, myths and images of sexuality – and in many ways, therefore, there is a questioning of the dominant orthodoxy of the 'liberated woman' that was the creation and legacy of the 1960s. Their photographs were extraordinarily explicit; it has been suggested that 'it was difficult to imagine the spectator, whether male or female, identifying with anyone in the photograph' (Harrison 1991: 52). They therefore encountered charges of misogyny and sexism; the photographers were accused of being exploitative and regressive. Here, fashion photography encountered critical discourse – and entered the public consciousness – through feminist debate.

Yet a new strand of documentary photography was emerging, that recorded the street styles of the time, specifically the subculture of punk. This genre had originated in the 1960s, when photojournalists captured the upsurge in youth cultures for the newspapers and supplements of the time. Its purpose was not to record styles of dress but to document this new social phenomenon. Fashion photography had never even attempted this; it had merely tried to reflect and respond to the youthful spirit of the age and its attendant subcultural styles, while never fully abandoning its preoccupation with conventional ideals of beauty and with aspirational images of women. The powerful, growing influence of subcultures – and of increasingly subversive forms of self-presentation – was largely ignored by high-profile magazines such as *Vogue*, until in 1978 its then art director, Terry Jones, produced a volume entitled *Not Another Punk Book*; this featured portraits of punks on London's Kings Road (Williams 1998: 11).

In 1980 this work became the basis for the magazine *i-D* which he founded. Its fashion editorials, known as the 'straight up', owed much to these portraits. The 'straight up' pages of photographs – featuring people spotted on the streets rather than using professional models – functioned both as portraiture and as social documentation. Yet, because of the use of credits informing the reader where the subjects had purchased their clothes, they were also within the domain of fashion photography. These images took as their point of reference and basis of style the notion of the 'ordinary person'. However, they still worked to create an ideal of the 'fashionable' self. This style, which *i-D* and its competitor, *The Face*, made into the visual currency of the early 1980s, reinforced the credo that fashion was 'lifestyle'. This notion, which has continued within their fashion editorials, has acted as a formative influence on many of the most directional photographers of the last two decades – and other publications have followed where the 'style magazines' led.

While maverick tendencies within fashion photography and publishing were pioneering the idea that a fashionable lifestyle was accessible to many, rather than the prerogative of a favoured few, their traditional glossy counterparts continued to depict an upwardly mobile lifestyle based on the glamorous heritage of fashion photography. This was seen in the construction of an inaccessible ideal that perfectly reflected the excess associated with the 1980s, exemplified in fashion pages by the repeated use of certain models possessed of almost super-human physical qualities. Later, these particular women were to be nicknamed 'supermodels' and they would become staple journalistic fare. It was the chasm between this unattainable ideal of beauty and the very different notion of the fashionable self previously created by *i-D* and *The Face* that created a space, even a vacuum, within which the new realism in fashion photography could operate, and which it proceeded to fill. This was a realism never witnessed before within fashion photography. By breaking completely with tradition, it exceeded the confines that the unspoken politics of fashion had placed upon photography in the past, and thus called into question its role not only in the portrayal of the fashionable, but in a far wider social context.

Harsh reality: fashion photography in the 1990s

> Decisive moments and turning points in fashion photography have been identified as successive styles reflecting new moods. Fashion photography has constituted both techniques of representation and techniques of self formation. It has served as an index of changing ideas about fashion and gender and about body habitus relations.
>
> (Craik 1994: 93)

As the history of fashion photography shows, it has developed the ability to reflect the spirit of its time rather than merely to showcase the preferred modes of the day. However, a number of photographers – often subversives within their field – have tried to reflect this mood as realistically as possible. Such endeavours, while still servicing the needs of fashion, have questioned preconceived ideals in a way that their conventional counterparts have not. These successive attempts paved the way for a photographic practice within the fashion arena that captures the reality of everyday life in a defiant and deliberate 'anti-glamour'. This style, which has been labelled the 'school of London' (Muir 1997: 14), has stripped bare the fantasies and the superficial ideals that the fashion industry had formerly felt compelled to portray and disseminate. Iwona Blazwick (1998: 7) describes this 1990s style of realism: 'Constructed tableaux are rejected for a truth located in the artless, the unstaged, the semiconscious, the sexually indeterminate and the pubescent – the slippages between socially prescribed roles.'

The photographers who worked in this way, although not strictly London-based, had surfaced from within the innovative style magazines currently centred there. Among the most prolific were Corinne Day, David Sims, Juergen Teller and Nigel Shafran. While they each had their distinctive individual style, they all shared a similar aesthetic based around notions of realism. Their style had its roots in the insecure political climate of post-Thatcherism and global recession; there was a perceived platform for change. Fashion had reacted to this mood – designers presented expensive versions of the street style that the press quickly designated 'grunge'. In fashion photography, such a change was not just made manifest in its depiction of a particular reality, but also in its rejection of the precise photographic techniques that had helped to construct the ideal images of perfection of the past. Corinne Day, an ex-model turned photographer, was one of the first to define this change. She encompassed the mood of the new decade with a seemingly 'unprofessional' technique – exemplified by a series of photographs of Kate Moss (not then a 'supermodel') that appeared in *The Face* in 1990.

On a denotative level, the series shows a young, free-spirited girl, happily playing on a beach, in simple relaxed clothes or in a state of near-nudity. Her semi-nakedness signifies not an eroticism but a natural quality that is also denoted by her surroundings, her lack of grooming and the daisy chain that she wears in one particular shot within the series. Her laughing expression, her squinting eyes and playful gestures hold connotations of innocence, immaturity and a teen spirit that is further signified by her under-developed body. In some ways Moss's 'ordinariness' and waifish appearance parallels that of models such as Twiggy in the 1960s. Where they differ is that, although the 1960s images reflected the new, 'liberated' woman of that era, who owed much to the sexual revolution, the photographs themselves were taken by male photographers, invariably the 'Terrible Three', who infused the images with their own sexual desire. In contrast, Day's images neither empower nor undermine Moss's sexuality, which remains passive; this is an image of a woman taken by a woman. The intimacy that is apparent within them, and the natural surroundings within the image, deflect any erotic interpretation and resemble more a private, unstaged moment being acted out before the camera – like a snapshot in a family photo album. That Corinne Day was at this time a close friend of Kate Moss adds credence to this feeling, as does a photographic technique that clearly eschews the technical perfection of conventional fashion photography. Day explained, 'She was like my little sister; we'd go off, have a laugh, take some pictures' (Roux 1996: 12). In essence, this is what Day captures, combining a realistic documentation and a fashion photograph, thereby negating the strictures of a precise photographic technique and the false ideals of 'femininity' previously created within fashion imagery.

However, the title of Day's series, 'The Third Summer of Love' is of course a direct reference to the 1960s and the original 'Summer of Love' of 1967. The evocation of the hippie ethos of 'peace and love', and an alternative lifestyle that was a reaction against consumerism, in some ways reinforces the connotations of Day's images. Where it differs is in the impetus behind the second Summer of Love: the second time this term was used, in 1988, it was to describe the emergence of acid house and rave culture. Although vaguely similar in its ideals to its 1960s counterpart, it was rooted firmly in drug culture and hedonism, particularly in the use of Ecstasy, rather than in the counter-cultural philosophical concerns of the original hippies (Polhemus 1994: 64). While Day's images in this series do not directly draw on such references, apart from that implicit in its title, her realist style later explored the surrounding culture and therefore lost much of its optimism.

These pessimistic signs, which in some ways reflect Bob Richardson's style of the 1960s, can be seen in a series of photographs for *Vogue* in 1993 entitled 'Under Exposure'. Here Day's style switches from a sense of the abandonment embodied by her youthful models into one that evokes a feeling of loneliness and urban alienation. This is signified by Kate Moss alone, in her cold, starkly furnished flat, again in a state of undress. That it is cold is signified by Kate sitting on a radiator, in a dishevelled quilt that connotes poverty; so too does her pale thin body and the sparse surroundings. The sense of urban alienation is indicated by Kate looking out of her window on to the world outside, with a television and telephone as her only means of communication. Her expression is mainly blank as she stares out of the shot, or window, suggesting boredom; this is further connoted by her nonchalant poses, which may indicate a reference to drug culture, as could the Lou Reed cassette seen in one image.

The narrative of this series seems to suggest an awkwardness and uncertainty that are integral to youth; its grim reality likens it to a series of snapshots, further enhancing this feeling. But there is an ambiguity about these images. Writing in the *New Yorker*, Hilton Als remarked:

> The pictures in question were in some ways Day's apotheosis as a photographer. Besides being intensely moving – Day had managed to catch

on film Moss's transition from young chum to commodity – they are a first testimony to the fashion industry's now pervasive flirtation with death. The naked bruised look in Moss's eyes was an apt expression of the brutality that Day was beginning to experience in the fashion world.

(Als, quoted in Williams 1998: 114)

While Als notes that the photos are a form of documentation in the sense of Moss's career trajectory, like many other media commentators he saw them primarily as holding wider connotations – for him, these spoke of death and mortality. Such a message was conveyed by elements of despair within the narrative of this series – but that these images held such extreme connotations is largely due to their context in a glossy fashion magazine, and specifically within the pages of *Vogue*. Als's understanding of these images seems to be based on the perception of traditional fashion photographs, which is that they are designed to create an unattainable ideal and a fantasy, in other words to function as fiction. However, Day seems to challenge the notion of how fashion photography should be perceived by breaking with the previously accepted practices that created these impossible ideals. Robin Muir, picture editor of *Vogue* at the time, describes them as 'eerie stills from a gritty documentary or freeze frames from someone's home movie. Whatever they were, they weren't fashion photographs' (Muir 1997: 14). As Als and Muir both note, Day challenges what a fashion photograph should be by incorporating elements of documentary. She seems to back this up in her description of the pictures and of Moss herself:

> we were poking fun at fashion. Halfway through the shoot, I realised it wasn't fun for her and that she was no longer my best friend but had become a model. She hadn't realised how beautiful she was and when she did, I found I didn't think her beautiful anymore.
>
> (Day quoted in Muir 1997: 14)

Therefore these images are as much, if not more, about making a documentary of her friend, in her own flat, evolving into a model and consequently into a commodity, as they are a narrative of a typical teenage girl. Indeed, the fact that the photographs were shot in Moss's own flat further links them with documentary photographs. However, as this fact is not usually known to the spectator, they can only be understood within the context of traditional fashion photography. They are therefore seen to create not a realistic ideal but a narrative of misfortune. In doing this, Day pokes fun not only at fashion conventions – showing tights-over-knickers as never before seen in *Vogue* – but at the industry as a whole. Whatever the ambiguous function and possible readings of these images, whether they are seen as documentary or as realistically stylised tableaux, there is an element of discomfort about the possibly voyeuristic nature of viewing such intimacy that has led to misinterpretation. Their context, then, can be seen to confuse their meaning; indeed, if they had been placed within *The Face* or on a gallery wall, it is likely that they would not have caused any offence.

Testament to this assumption is the social documentary work of photographic artist Nan Goldin. Cited as a major influence for fashion photographers of the

1990s, Goldin has created a compelling photographic diary of her life that explores the depths and heights of human existence, recording the deaths of many of her friends and fellow-travellers from drugs and AIDS-related illnesses. Michael Bracewell, writing in *Frieze*, notes that 'she records photographically, that portion of society that is divorced from the usual restraints and support systems that service and control contemporary urban life' (Bracewell 1993: 34). However, the apparent intimacy between Goldin and her friends in her photographs deflects the sense of voyeurism, while the snapshot aesthetic further averts such a feeling. It is as if we were invited to join and view her world with all of its highs and lows – above all because it is hung on a gallery wall, or seen within a book, and thus validated by the critical value that the art world places upon it.

In contrast, Day's images could – wrongly – be seen as exploiting her intimacy with Moss due to their primary use within a fashion magazine. It was never the job of fashion photography and fashion magazines to invite us into a private world; theirs has never been a domain of truth but rather one where the prevailing function is that of commerce. It therefore seems that the context in which photographic realism is seen confounds its meaning; seemingly 'art photography' and 'realist' fashion photography have ostensibly different roles. In fashion's case, this role is seen as promoting a destructive ideal, rather than the fantasy which it is normally expected to purvey; within an art context it is seen as making visible the situation and the needs of the less fortunate. As Scott William (1986: 9) writes, 'social documentary encourages social improvement . . . It works through the emotions of the members of its audience to shape their attitude toward certain public facts . . . It is that maligned thing, propaganda.'

With the blurring of these boundaries, both art and fashion photography are imbued with different meanings; fashion appropriates the richness of art, while art – in this case Nan Goldin – can fall prey to the fictitious values of fashion. Thus, when Goldin works in the fashion arena, the validity of her personal work has been questioned. Collier Schorr in *Frieze* comments that 'as much as we count on fashion to lie, perhaps we have begun to rely rather too heavily on art to be sincere' (Schorr 1997: 93). But while some question Goldin's work in fashion, her intention is clearly that of the documentary photographer – to work on the viewer's emotions, to shape attitudes. In Goldin's fashion work, for Matsuda and Helmut Lang, she affronts her audience into questioning the preconceived ideals that fashion holds. In one advertising image for Matsuda, two fully clothed women are seen lying in a form of embrace on a bed. One of the women is wearing revealing, sheer clothing, while both have sweaty complexions. The photograph is entitled 'Sharon and Kathleen embracing, Bowery, NYC, 1996', furthering the ambiguous connotations; the Bowery in New York is synonymous with social deprivation. These women could be prostitutes, lesbian partners or friends comforting each other, sharing an intimate moment. Their grimy complexions and setting also reference a drug-induced setting. Goldin's previous work, including her book *The Ballad of Sexual Dependency* (1989), lend credence to such connotations, although its implications are apparent even for a spectator completely unaware of her other work.

The fact that this work is actually fashion advertising confuses the issue further since the role of fashion advertising (even more than that of the fashion editorial spread) has traditionally been to sell an ideal and a lifestyle. Therefore Goldin's images could be seen as an attempt to promote an ideal of deprivation. However, the idea that fashion photography could play an active role in influencing social habits and lifestyles is not wholly convincing, despite a plethora of media claims during the last decade. Indeed, such claims have never been substantiated – Goldin was not trying to promote prostitution or drug abuse; Corinne Day was not advocating anorexia. Such images can work as a conventional marketing tool when used in a context where their audience will understand the dominant conventions, especially in fashion advertising, where they can promote a completely different lifestyle to that actually depicted. The prospective clients are not buying into a world of deprivation but into the usual 'ideal that anybody can be fashionable',[1] however disenfranchised from society that person is. However the book *Fashion Photography of the Nineties* (Nickerson and Wakefield 1996) seems to suggest that such images do have a deeper meaning, other reverberations. Containing images culled from the fashion world, both traditional celebrations and their 'wilder counterparts', and using both 'art' and documentary photography, the book confuses fiction with reality by placing these various images within the context of a single volume. The very brief text claims that:

> in these photographs the body and its gestures report on the defining characteristics of a decade . . . The ambiguity of gender and beauty lays bare our secret desires, dissolving the boundaries between what is worn and the way we wear it . . . Out of the collision between style and the subconscious emerges a portrait of our time.
>
> (Nickerson and Wakefield 1996)

That it 'lays bare our secret desires' is an ambitious claim, but one image by Juergen Teller reproduced within the previous edition, 2000, of this book consolidates many of the issues surrounding the realist fashion imagery of this decade. First published in the German broadsheet supplement *Suddeutsche Zeitung Magazin*, the image is taken from a series entitled 'Morals and Fashion'. In the series the model Kristen McMenamy is seen naked but for the word 'Versace' written in lipstick in a heart shape on her breasts and buttocks. In part of the series the poses replicate that of contrived fashion photography, in others she is walking around a stark room like a model preparing for a fashion show. In what is clearly a constructed tableau, although formally resembling a series of snapshots, Teller sends up the fashion ideals denoted by the use of the word 'Versace', whose clothing is generally considered to connote glamour and sex. McMenamy's skin is mottled, scarred and bruised, while a tampon string is clearly visible. Teller is surely questioning the value of Versace's sexy ideals by showing very different images of women within this tableau. In a sense, considering McMenamy's bruised body, Teller seems to go as far as suggesting that women are exploited by the fashion industry. That McMenamy appeared flawless in a glamorous high-profile advertising campaign for Versace, shot by Richard Avedon, in some ways substantiates this suggestion. Of the images, Teller said,

> I chose Kristen because I am fed up with the glorification of the model.
> You see her in so many magazines looking glamorous and polished, but

she's not like that. She's wild and funny and more like an actress. I
agree that the bruising is quite grotesque, but that shows the fragility
of the body. And that fragility is more beautiful to me than any amount
of retouching.

(Roux 1996: 42)

However, the result of these images is almost a parody of his own work and of
the realist fashion photographs of the decade. By mixing the realist snapshot
aesthetic with contrived tableaux to make clear his own feelings about the fashion
industry, Teller renders the images' likeness to reality inauthentic, since they are
clearly as constructed as those criticised for conveying ideals of perfection. This
questions the authenticity of other 'realist' images, and in doing so suggests that
this style has possibly lost its primary impact – the ability to shock. However,
realism in fashion photography, although less prevalent now than in the early 1990s,
has refused to go away and its proliferation in the 1990s raises certain questions.

Can we agree that out of the 'subconscious emerges a portrait of our time'
(Nickerson and Wakefield 1996)? Can we consider this style, then, as a collective
movement? Roland Barthes has said of documentary photography that it is an
'explosion of the private into public, or rather into the creation of a new social
value, which is the publicity of the private' (Barthes 1981: 98). Surely realist
fashion photography possesses this capacity and, in the 1990s, this rendering of
the private into the public acted as a subconscious attempt to affirm what has been
lost through increasing virtual reality, through the process by which technology
and media take the place of society or community. This implication can be seen
in Corinne Day's series 'Under Exposure' for *Vogue*, where a sense of urban
isolation, physical loneliness and social alienation are forcefully conveyed through
these particular images of Kate Moss in her sparse flat, where her television set
connotes her only visible bond with the outside world. Yet while images such as
these may be seen as disquieting and uncomfortable (as indicated by the hostile
media reaction), the sight of these fundamental actions and private moments are
'reassuring in their familiarity' (Muir 1998: 105). In effect, they seem to reinforce
the bonds of human community by 'reclaiming lost areas of compassion and
humanity' (Bracewell 1993: 37).

Perhaps realist fashion photography has been successful in pointing to this
aspect of our culture where photojournalism has, seemingly, failed. As Michael
Mack writes:

In an era dominated by the technological intrusion of the spectacular,
the lament rings wide that such is our over-exposure to scenes of
individual suffering and mass disaster that we are encompassed by a
malaise and a hedonism that preclude their continuing significance.

(Mack 1996: 232)

It therefore seems that realist fashion photography in the 1990s has that function
that photojournalism has lost, perhaps through its sheer volume. Furthermore,
realist fashion photography can reach a wider audience than social documentary or
art photography could ever hope to achieve. Indeed, when President Clinton of

the United States of America refers to fashion photography's ability to influence social behaviour, as in his attack on 'heroin chic' (CNN 1997), then clearly it has a deeper impact, even if it does not or cannot activate any radical social change. By complicating its formerly established role, and in its evident capacity to evoke both literal reality and the collective unconscious, fashion photography now has much more to say to us than is credited or acknowledged.

In its inherent search for the new, fashion stumbled upon this particular photographic practice, which, while rooted in the avant-garde, went on to penetrate the mainstream. Perhaps the images that proliferated did more than present a challenge to conventional ideals, suggesting that fashion was now more democratic and that anybody could be fashionable. Nan Goldin, among others, chose to document and depict 'real' people wearing fashionable clothes.

One cavil, however – realist fashion imagery did not, and does not, go as far as it might. The exclusion here as elsewhere of the non-slim, the non-young and those who are not able-bodied must have certain implications. The collaboration between Alexander McQueen and Nick Knight on the 'Fashion-Able' shoot for *Dazed and Confused* (October 1998) is notable within fashion photography precisely because it is without precedent and – so far – without parallel.

But this is not to detract, hopefully, from the implications and potential of 1990s realism. Yet, through the sheer velocity of the mechanics that constitute the fashion industry, this style will at some point be superseded. But its impact, its ability to cause controversy where photojournalism has lost that power, is undeniable. It can confront problematic issues, force us to ask questions and to address wider concerns. Susan Sontag's axiom makes a fitting conclusion: 'Great fashion photography is more than the photography of fashion' (Sontag 1978: 104).

Note

1   Interview with Charlotte Cotton, assistant curator of photography, Victoria and Albert Museum, 20 December 1998.

References

Ash, Juliet, and Wilson, Elizabeth (eds) (1992) *Chic Thrills: A Fashion Reader*, London: Pandora.

Barnard, Malcolm (1996) *Fashion as Communication*, London and New York: Routledge.

Barthes, Roland (1977) *Image-Music-Text*, London: Fontana.

—— (1981) *Camera Lucida*, London: Jonathan Cape.

Blackwell, Lewis (1997) 'Man of the moment', *Creative Review*, April.

Blazwick, Iwona (1998) 'Feel no pain', *Art Monthly*, November: 7.

Bracewell, Michael (1992) 'A fine romance', *Frieze*, 3.

—— (1993) 'Making up is hard to do', *Frieze*, October.

Burgoyne, Patrick (1996) 'Beyond the supermodel', *Creative Review*, May.

CNN (1997) 'Clinton urges pop culture to stop glamorising drugs', posted 11 Oct. (www.druguse.com./news.html)

Cooke, Rachel (1997) 'Curse of the catwalk', *Sunday Times*, Style section, 4 May.

Craik, Jennifer (1994) *The Face of Fashion*, London and New York: Routledge.

Devlin, Polly and Garner, Philippe (1994) *Essays from 'A Positive View'*. V&A Publications: London.

Evans, Caroline and Thornton, Minna (1989) *Women and Fashion: A New Look*, London: Quartet Books.

Farrelly, Liz (1996) 'Fashion, art and rock'n'roll', *The Face*, October.

Goldin, Nan (1989) *The Ballad of Sexual Dependency*, London: Secker & Warburg.

Hall-Duncan, N. (1979) *The History of Fashion Photography*, New York: Alpine Book Co. Inc.

Harrison, M. (1991) *Appearances: Fashion Photography since 1945*, London: Jonathan Cape.

—— (1998) *Young Meteors, British Photojournalism: 1957–1965*, London: Jonathan Cape.

Howell, Georgina (1991) *In Vogue, 75 Years of Style*, New York: Random Century.

Januszczak, Waldemar (1998) 'The poor relation no more', *Sunday Times*, Culture supplement, 5 April.

Mack, Michael (ed.) (1996) *Surface: Contemporary Photographic Practice*, London: Booth-Clibborn.

McRobbie, Angela (1998) *British Fashion Design: Rag Trade or Image Industry?*, London and New York: Routledge.

Muir, Robin (1997) 'What Katy did', *Independent Magazine*, 22 February.

—— (1998) *Subverting the Genre, Addressing the Century: 100 Years of Art and Fashion*, London: Hayward Gallery Publishing.

Nickerson, Camilla and Wakefield, Neville (1996) *Fashion Photography of the Nineties*, New York: Scalo.

Polhemus, Ted (1994) *Street Style*, London: Thames & Hudson.

Rombough, Howard (1987) 'Fashioning reality', *Creative Review*, November.

Roux, Caroline (1996) 'Reality bites', *Guardian*, 2 November.

Schorr, Collier, (1997) 'A pose is a pose is a pose', *Frieze*, April: 63.

Scott, William (1986) *Documentary Expression and Thirties America*, Chicago: University of Chicago Press.

Seebohm, C. (1982) *The Man Who Was Vogue*, London: Weidenfeld & Nicolson.

Sontag, Susan (1978) 'The Avedon eye', *Vogue*, Dec.

—— (1979) *On Photography*, Harmondsworth: Penguin.

Stout, Lindy (1998) 'Breaking style', *Creative Review*, November.

Stungo, Naomi (1998) 'Representing fashion', *Blueprint*, May.

Wargnier, Stéphane (1993) 'Le style Anglais', *Vogue Homme International*, Autumn/Winter: 137.

Williams, Val (1998) *Look at Me: Fashion Photography in Britain 1960 to the Present*, London: The British Council.

Windlin, Cornel (1996) *Juergen Teller*, Cologne and London: Taschen.

Chapter 13

Rachel Lifter

FASHIONING INDIE
The consecration of a subculture and the emergence of 'stylish' femininity

THE TERM 'INDIE' is an abbreviation of the word 'independent'. Originally, it was coined to refer to the independent music scene that emerged in the wake of punk in the United Kingdom during the late 1970s and early 1980s (Reynolds 2005). This scene was understood not only to be punk's *chronological* successor, but also its *heir* (Hesmondhalgh 1999). That is, uncontrolled by the music industry, the small labels and musicians working in the independent scene were to carry on the legacy of punk by revolting against – *resisting* – 'mainstream' pop music. Simon Reynolds' (1989) reading of the indie look of the 1980s explores this idea of 'resistance'. In an article that appeared in Angela McRobbie's (1989) edited volume *Zoot Suits and Secondhand Dresses*, Reynolds subjects the indie look of the 1980s to semiotic analysis. In a discussion that implicitly references Hebdige's (1979) definition of subcultural style as a 'Refusal', he describes the indie look as a rejection of the celebration of sexual maturity promoted by popular fashion culture of the 1980s. He continues: 'this 'dream of purity' is made manifest in a sartorial obsession with the 1960s and childhood – two pre-sexual periods' (1989: 250). Reynolds' analysis is extremely interesting, not least because he provides a detailed description of the garments and styles commonly associated with the indie look of the 1980s: for example, 'cardigans, overcoats, slacks, short jackets, caps, headscarves, quaint jewellery, short-back-and-sides (absolutely *no* long hair or perms)' (1989: 250–51; emphasis in original). However, his analysis needs to be updated to account for changes in indie and the indie look since the late 1980s.

Over the past twenty years, indie has expanded and diversified. At various points in its history, indie music has become widely visible in the UK and also internationally. In the mid-1990s, for example, indie bands such as Suede, Elastica, Blur and Pulp emerged onto the centre stage of popular music as part of the indie sub-genre known as Britpop. In the early 2000s, indie music experienced a second explosion when bands like The Strokes, The Libertines, Bloc Party and The Arctic Monkeys became widely popular throughout the UK. Indie's growth has to do not only with music, moreover, but also fashion. My own introduction to indie came in the summer of 2005, when images of supermodel Kate Moss and her then-boyfriend Libertines frontman Pete Doherty at the Glastonbury summer music festival were ubiquitous throughout the popular fashion media. Such images served as my introduction to indie and its defining look of skinny jeans; however, they also drew attention to a blurriness of the boundaries around indie. By 2005, Moss was established as an internationally recognised supermodel, and outside of her relationship with Doherty she had few ties to indie. In the images of the two, she is representative of contemporary fashionable ideals and, specifically, British fashion. It is the goal of this chapter to problematise these interconnections between indie and popular fashion in the UK: how these connections were forged over the last twenty years and how they persist today.

Drawing on Pierre Bourdieu's (1993a; 1993b) concepts of 'consecration' and 'field', the chapter begins by examining indie's evolution, focusing on the way in which its figures and styles were consecrated within the field of popular fashion in the UK: first by the style press and later by the high-fashion media and broadsheet press. This story sheds light not only on developments within indie, but also on changes in the value system and organisation of the field of popular fashion. Specifically, it reveals a proliferation of discourses on 'style' across a range of print media genres. It is this pervasive discourse on 'style' that stands at the centre of analysis in the second part of the chapter. Drawing on Michel Foucault's (2002) concept 'discourse', the chapter analyses contemporary representations of indie – specifically, a sub-set of indie representations having to do with 'festival fashion' – to explore how this discourse on 'style' creates a space for feminine identities to form. 'Stylish' femininity is not unproblematic, however. As the chapter shows, within contemporary culture 'style' is constituted through notions of both democratisation *and* exclusivity. The goal of the chapter is thus to provide an integrated account of indie and the wider field of popular fashion, into which it has become embedded. It is the contention of the chapter that such an exploration of the two sides together reveals new information about both.

Consecrating indie

As has already been noted, Reynolds (1989) contends that the indie look of the 1980s did not cohere aesthetically with contemporaneous popular fashion trends. This point can be explored not only in relation to the material garments used to construct the indie look, but also in relation to the representation – or rather, lack of representation – of the indie look within the popular fashion media. For example, across the years 1986 and 1987 – important years for the establishment of indie as a space for musical production – the youth style magazine *i-D*'s coverage of indie consisted of *one* article by William Leith that read,

> What it comes down to is that today's 'Indie Scene' . . . are not 'anti-style'. They're just not stylish. For the most part, they don't wear

anoraks and national health specs as some kind of showbiz rejection number. They wear them because they can't afford anything else [. . .] They can't be bothered with all the fashion sophistication and they're wondering whether it's possible to just . . . opt out

(*i-D* October 1986: 76–7).

Unlike Reynolds, Leith refuses to draw on the subcultural definition of style and thus identify indie as anti-fashion, aligning it with the spectacular subcultures that preceded it. Instead, his words reveal a precise vocabulary of 'style' – one that is specific to *i-D* magazine.

The origins of *i-D* as one of three youth cultural publications (alongside *The Face* and *Blitz*) consciously establishing themselves in opposition to high-fashion magazines in 1980 is well documented within existing literature from fashion studies. Agnès Rocamora (2009: 61) suggests that style magazines emerged as a distinct genre 'perhaps to reassure readers by keeping at bay the negative connotation attached to the femininity that the word "fashion" still evokes'. Indeed, the style magazines were aimed at young people and made by young people, whatever their gender (Lynge-Jorlén 2010). Paul Jobling (1999: 35) writes that these magazines attempted 'to tap both the imagination and the wherewithal of young adults who had grown up in the shadow of punk'. Using Bourdieu's (1993a: 58) phrasing, *i-D* and the other youth style publications acted as 'newcomers' to the field of popular fashion, 'assert[ing] their difference [. . .] by endeavouring to impose new modes of thought and expression, out of key with the prevailing modes of thought and expression' – the latter of which were constructed within the pages of high-fashion magazine titles, such as *Vogue* (see also Lynge-Jorlén 2010 on the establishment of the style press within the field of fashion media). Indeed, 'style' was this 'new mode of thought or expression' and it emerged forcefully in *i-D*'s 'straight-up' images.

The 'straight-up' was a photograph taken of a person, randomly stopped on the street and wearing his/her own clothes. Elliot Smedley (2000: 147) describes the 'straight-up' 'as portraiture and as social documentation', as the goal of the 'straight-up' is not to photograph fashionable display, but rather to document 'real' styles and 'real' identities. Val Williams (1998: 112) identifies the ensembles featured in the 'straight-up' photographs as mix'n'match assemblages of clothes, 'ranging from expensive to high street to secondhand'. Rocamora and Alistair O'Neill (2008) suggest that these ensembles were understood as being 'combined in apparent disregard of dominant fashion codes' (186), and, as a result, the 'ordinary individuals' featured in the photographs were understood to be 'creators in their own right' (190). Thus, Caroline Evans (2004: 143) describes street-style as a 'catwalk identity parade', in which identities are promenaded on the street as fashion designs are on the catwalk. However, referencing Sarah Thornton's (1995) work, McRobbie (1998: 154) argues that the 'identities' shown in *i-D*'s 'straight-up' images were only those of the young and hip, and 'style' was constituted specifically as the visual manifestation of young people's 'subcultural capital'. In sum, these 'straight-up' images worked to produce the notion of 'style' as a version of fashionable display that emerged from an individual's creativity as opposed to from influence by designers' runways and the pages of fashion magazines such as *Vogue*.

It is with this context in mind that we can return to the issue of *i-D*'s representation of indie in 1986. When Leith calls indie 'just not stylish', he is drawing on a definition of 'style' that, to an extent, can be equated with the term 'fashionable'. That is, having 'style' is a marker of a certain level of 'savviness' or 'sophistication' with clothing, and, according to *i-D*, in 1986 the members of the indie scene did not demonstrate this savviness. By the mid-1990s, however, due to both the influence grunge had on the fashion industry in the early 1990s and the international popularity of the indie sub-genre known as Britpop, *i-D* would change its opinion of indie. For example, in an article in the December 1993 issue of *i-D*, Tony Marcus described Pulp as 'the ultimate Oxfam band'. The article continued, '"Pulp keep using everybody's cast-offs, the things other people have rejected," says Jarvis [Cocker, the lead singer of Pulp]. He's wearing an old LCD wristwatch, the kind that tells the time in flashing electric red when you press the button' (*i-D* December 1993: 18). Whereas Leith's description of the indie look is scathing, Marcus seems to admire and to take pleasure in Jarvis Cocker's dress practices, as this sartorial ragpicking is key to *i-D*'s version of fashionability. Thus, within these contrasting articles on indie from 1986 and 1993, *i-D* promotes its own ideals. This point is significant because, as will hopefully become clear within the remainder of this chapter, representations of 'style' – understood as a mix-and-match assemblage of garments to create an individual look in opposition to the directives of the contemporary fashion industry – have proliferated throughout the fashion media over the past 20 years, altering the nature of 'style' and creating a space for the emergence and performance of new fashionable feminine subjectivities.

Although the style press worked to consecrate indie figures and the indie look in the 1990s, indie continued to be ignored by the high-fashion press of the decade. This would change in 2001, however, when a New York-based five-piece band called The Strokes stormed the UK and placed the indie look at the centre of popular fashion. In the November 2001 issue of *Vogue*, journalist Bethan Cole described the new hot look for young people in London as 'jumbled-together smart and casual [. . .] the latest version of the knowing mix of distressed and smart'. She continued, 'The smart-casual trend has made off-runway appearances in New York, where groovers like rock band The Strokes . . . have been sporting combinations such as tweed jackets with white shirts and jeans for many months' (*Vogue* November 2001: 111, 113). Again, the content of this discourse is worth analysing in greater detail. Here, *Vogue* celebrates this pieced-together, mix-and-match aesthetic that is linked to the notion of 'style'. Thus, not only are these indie rockers celebrated by *Vogue* for effectively perfecting this 'mix and match' look, but such celebration signifies a shifting of the value systems of the field of popular fashion. That is, *Vogue* is arguably an 'established' player within the field with a high level of symbolic capital. Yet its celebration of this youthful style should be seen, not as an attempt by the 'established' magazine to produce what Bourdieu calls 'the defensive discourse of orthodoxy' (Bourdieu 1993b: 73), but rather as an attempt to adjust itself to and to take into consideration the increasing significance of this notion of 'style' within the broader popular fashion environment. Consecrating indie was one of the means through which this adjustment took place.

2005 was also an important year for the integration of indie into the field of fashion, as it was marked by a ubiquity of images of indie-rocker Pete Doherty and his then-girlfriend – supermodel Kate Moss – traipsing around Glastonbury summer music festival, he wearing dangerously skinny jeans and she in an impossibly short gold mini-dress coupled with wellies. As noted, these images were pervasive throughout the popular fashion media; that is, indie was not simply consecrated by the style press and high-fashion media, but rather it was celebrated throughout the field of popular fashion. It is worth considering in greater detail *why* these images were so abundant, *why* indie became so extremely visible. From 2003, Doherty had been gaining attention within the field of fashion, as it was at that point that Hedi Slimane, who was then creative director of Dior Homme, redesigned the masculine silhouette based on Doherty's boyish indie figure – a design innovation that continues to shape the construction and representation of the high-fashion male body. And yet Doherty's fame (and infamy due to his seemingly out-of-control rock'n'roll lifestyle) was arguably marginal in comparison to that of his then-girlfriend. Since her emergence onto the international fashion scene in the 1990s, Kate Moss has been celebrated not only for her physical beauty, but also for what has been understood to be her particular version of mix'n'match fashionability, combining high-fashion garments with second-hand clothing. In short, Moss personifies the discourse on 'style', and it is precisely for this reason that the images of her and Doherty going around Glastonbury were so ubiquitous. As the chapter has attempted to show, the notion of 'style' had been gaining

Figure 13.1   Dressing up has become a key mode of participating in summer music festivals. Wellies, checked shirts, leggings and denim shorts are all part of the 'festival fashion' wardrobe. Reading Festival, 30 August 2009. Photograph Rachel Lifter.

Figure 13.2   Magazine editors, 'street style' bloggers and festival-goers
document the looks they see at festivals. Here, a still from
a video made and posted to YouTube by 'SuperBeautyNerd'
(www.youtube.com/watch?v=umUmaATSWWU). Uploaded
to YouTube on 29 August 2012; accessed 22 April 2013.

prominence within the field of fashion since the 1980s, and in 2005 Kate Moss
served as the vehicle for its widespread acceptance.

Today, 'style' – defined as an individually crafted, mix'n'match assemblage of
garments – pervades throughout contemporary popular fashion discourse: within
fashion editorials like 'The Mega-Mix' from *Grazia*, which suggested to readers,
'Mix up your knits, jeans and basic tees with glamorous "look at me" accessories'
(10 August 2009: 56); in advertising material like that for Topshop, which displayed
garments through visual mix'n'match equations (Autumn/Winter Style Guide
2009: 6–7 in insert); in personal style blogs and street style blogs that follow the
'straight-up' formula of showcasing individually constructed ensembles; and, finally,
within 'festival fashion' images. Indeed, the images of Moss and Doherty at
Glastonbury in 2005 were the first of many 'festival fashion' images that have
appeared and continue to appear throughout the popular fashion press. It is worth
examining these representations further in an attempt both to explore the contemporary indie look and to reveal the contradictions through which the notion of
'style' is constituted within contemporary popular fashion culture.

'Stylish' femininities

At the start of the summer, 'festival fashion' segments appear within the popular
fashion press for women. Such images work to represent and produce knowledge

about contemporary indie; however, in so doing they draw on this wider discourse on 'style', discussed above. That is, those people who are featured in 'festival fashion' segments are often represented as constructing their own unique ensembles in contrast to dictates from the fashion industry. As a result, these images largely follow the 'street style' format, the only difference being that the setting for the images is always a summer music festival.

Representations of 'festival fashion' are rife with ambivalences, however (see also Rocamora and O'Neill 2008 and Woodward 2009 in relation to ambivalences of contemporary 'street style' images more generally). For example, in a small article from *Vogue* that features a page on what young celebrities (models, musicians and 'it' girls) wore to Glastonbury (*Vogue* September 2009: 140), the women are each wearing their own 'unique' assortment of garments, incorporating denim shorts, trilbies, tartan shirts, babydoll dresses, Wayfarers and wellies, among other garments, into varying combinations. Their images are organised by category, however. Specifically, the distinction presented to readers is, 'Trends: hotpants versus minidresses'. Sophie Woodward argues that, although the 'myth of street style' identifies it as 'innovative', the people featured in contemporary repre-sentations of 'street style' are, in fact, wearing 'whatever the current trend is' (2009: 88). Indeed, in this example, those people selected for their 'unique' ensembles are those that are wearing garments that can be categorised under the two (extremely childlike) trends of the late noughties.

Further, the festival season now occupies a specific place within the fashion calendar. Numerous articles from the contemporary popular media have the function of preparing readers for the festival season through suggestions concerning which garments to buy and how to mix them together. For example, an article from *London Lite* by Rebecca Boyce was identified through the tagline, 'Join the festival fashion parade: gear up for the Glasto catwalk'. Boyce writes that 'with the UK's largest festival, Glastonbury, kicking off on Thursday, if you haven't already considered your all-important wardrobe you'd better stock up on those style essentials sharpish' (*London Lite* 22 June 2009: 20). The way magazine readers are advised to prepare for festivals resembles to an extent the way they are advised to prepare for the summer. Whereas the latter entails working out to get a beach-ready body, the former entails purchasing a range of festival-appropriate garments. The article continues by providing a list of suggestions for appropriate festival gear that one can pick up on the high street, including wellies, hotpants and a variety of embroidered tops. Thus, it is difficult to conceive of the ensembles displayed in 'festival fashion' segments as having been constructed in opposition to current trends and the established fashion system. Speaking more generally about street style segments (and not merely about festival fashion ones), Woodward (2009: 88–9) concludes, there is a disjunction between the way in which 'street style' is produced through its own mythologies, on the one hand, and the way in which it appears in the contemporary media, on the other. She argues, 'The mediated version of street style, present in fashion magazines [such as *Grazia* and *Elle*], has mutated: the subversive has become the ordinary' (Woodward 2009: 88–9).

Perhaps a different conclusion can be drawn about this material, however. Perhaps the issue is not that there is a disjuncture between the 'myth of street style' and contemporary 'street style' representations, but rather that 'style' is constituted within these representations across the contemporary fashion media as something that a wider range of people, who may or may not be in possession of 'subcultural capital', may demonstrate. In other words, a subject position has been created from which a wide range of people can, in some way or another, align themselves with a dress practice that is defined as an individual practice of mix-and-match creation. Thus, one way to understand the proliferation of discourses on 'style' is to consider the way in which contemporary popular fashion media representations work to promote a more democratised definition of 'style'. As a '[mode] of thought and expression' (Bourdieu 1993a: 58), 'style' is not merely a concept that is consecrated by the 'style' publications and demonstrated by those people in possession of 'subcultural capital'. Instead, according to contemporary discourse, a variety of institutions and people, located at a wide range of positions within the contemporary field of popular fashion, can access and practise 'style' and thus demonstrate their own 'individuality'.

Although 'style' is largely constituted within contemporary 'festival fashion' images as being more democratic than it once was, there are other representations that constitute 'style' through codes of exclusivity. In their analysis of 'street style' images, for example, Rocamora and O'Neill (2008) argue that, although identifying the people represented as 'creators in their own right' (2008: 190), 'street style' features simultaneously work to re-affirm the position of journalists and fashion editors within the field of fashion. They explain,

> through the documentation of street styles not only do journalists offer selective definitions of the fashionable city subject, but they simultaneously construct and define their own roles. Although concessions are made to the creative style and the authorship of the people, readers are reminded that true expertise remains the attribute of fashion journalists
>
> (Rocamora and O'Neill 2008: 194).

Quoting from Bourdieu, they continue later, 'What is fashionable is what journalists *say* is fashionable. [. . .] The ultimate fashion expertise lies in the power to attribute fashion expertise, in "the power to consecrate producers or products"' (Rocamora and O'Neill 2008: 195). In that fashion experts retain the right to speak about 'style', 'style' remains in the possession of those people who are already established within the field of fashion, as opposed to the 'ordinary' people represented in the images. Moreover, frequently representations of 'style' do not actually feature 'ordinary' people, but rather young celebrities or other people known for their work in the music and fashion industries (see the *Vogue* example above, for example). Within these representations of 'style', the young celebrities, cultural producers and 'cultural intermediaries' (Bourdieu 1993a) that are featured are often represented as having, in a sense, 'superhuman' abilities for practising style.

A feature on 'festival fashion' from *The Sunday Times Style Magazine* serves as example of this form of representation. The tagline to the feature proclaimed that it was 'Time to Shine', followed by the suggestion, 'Take your fashion cue from the poster girls of summer' (*The Sunday Times Style Magazine* 24 May 2009: 26). The feature consists of four sections, each based around a different poster girl: TV presenter Alexa Chung, musician Natasha Khan (also known as Bat for Lashes), aspiring journalist Peaches Geldof and TV presenter Cat Deeley. Photographs of the four women, taken at various summer music festivals, show the women wearing ensembles put together seemingly of their own choosing, and the magazine's fashion editors make suggestions for readers as to how they could attempt to recreate the women's looks through pieces found on the high street. For example, a leather jacket from British Home Stores (BHS) and denim shorts from Topshop are suggested to recreate Chung's 'boho biker' look. The message put forward through this feature is that these women have their own 'style', and the reader can attempt to follow it as well.

This form of representing young women with a 'superhuman' sense of 'style' is worth considering further outside of the confines of 'festival fashion' representations. That is, it is worth exploring how young women who are linked to the indie scene are not only identified as having 'superhuman' skills at self-styling, but also are celebrated more widely across the contemporary fashion industry for such skills. For example, Alexa Chung (discussed above) is represented throughout many fashion features and segments as someone who is skilled at styling herself. In an interview about her MTV talk show with the American youth fashion and lifestyle magazine *Nylon*, Chung says about herself, 'I don't think MTV has had a VJ or a presenter who wants to style themselves before' (*Nylon* September 2009: 119). The author, Stephanie Trong, adds, 'Chung is quickly becoming a style icon, with a page on MTV's website that showcases what she wears each day, a lot of which is culled from her own wardrobe' (*Nylon* September 2009: 119). As a TV presenter, Chung's professional identity is tightly linked to her personal and visual identity. Moreover, both are represented as being the result of active choices she makes about the way in which she appears. For example, Chung was featured in *Vogue*'s 'Today I'm Wearing' segment from February 2010 (www.vogue.co.uk). Each month a young woman – often those who are linked in some way or another to the indie scene – is asked to document in pictures and written descriptions what she wears everyday. Over the course of her month, Chung reveals a combination of vintage garments, items she has made (such as necklaces), high street garments (mostly from Topshop) and designer pieces. She wears Margaret Howell shoes, Chanel boots, a Miu Miu coat and an Opening Ceremony dress, for example. Further, she carries a limited edition Sofia Coppola for Louis Vuitton bag one day and the Mulberry 'Alexa' bag another day, drawing attention to the fact that she has had a high-fashion bag named after her. The 'What I'm Wearing' segment relies upon a construction of Chung as extremely skilled in the art of styling herself. However, the images reveal that she is also someone who is fully immersed in the field of fashion, in that she uses garments that are inaccessible to most people in order to construct her look. Thus, although many contemporary representations of 'style' (such as 'festival fashion' representations) work to constitute it as a practice in which a wide range of people can engage, these other representations of 'style' work to constitute it through codes of exclusivity, identifying it as the practice of an elite few.

Conclusion

This chapter has attempted to produce an original analysis of indie: how it became and continues to be embedded within the wider formation of popular fashion in the UK. In order to explore this evolution, it was necessary to look beyond indie and to examine the shifts and changes in the field of popular fashion. As a result, this chapter also charted the proliferation of a discourse on 'style' throughout the field of popular fashion in the UK – a discourse that originated in the style publications of the 1980s, was taken up by the high-fashion media at the turn of the twenty-first century and now stands as a central marker of fashionability throughout contemporary popular fashion culture. The proliferation of this discourse created a space for an increasing interest in indie, as it seems that at certain points over the last twenty years indie figures personified 'style', thus bringing indie and the indie look to popular attention. Contemporary indie continues to be represented through the notion of 'style' – a point that is evidenced within contemporary 'festival fashion' images. As a result, an analysis of these images can be used to problematise this notion of 'style' as it circulates within contemporary popular fashion culture. As a historically specific construct, contemporary 'style' differs from that of the 1980s. Perhaps it is a 'bad' thing that 'style' no longer seems to be innovative, but rather is a reproduction of the current trend of mixing'n'matching; perhaps it is a 'good' thing that 'style' has become seemingly more democratic and accessible to a wider range of people; but perhaps it is a 'bad' thing that 'style' has become incorporated into the established hierarchies of the fashion industry, reflecting a person's connections to the fashion industry more than his/her innovative and original clothing choices. It will be important for future research to continue to explore the historically specific reconfigurations of 'style', as the notion informs the way in which fashionable subjectivities are constructed and performed. Moreover, it will be interesting to see whether indie will continue to be interwoven into this narrative of 'style'. Indeed, this evolving discourse on 'style' has created a space for indie to continue to live on after its original moment of inception in the 1980s, and questions remain of whether and in what ways indie will continue to evolve in the future.

References

Bourdieu, P. (1993a) *The Field of Cultural Production: Essays on Art and Literature*. London: Polity.

——(1993b) *Sociology in Question*. London; Thousand Oaks, CA; New Delhi: Sage.

Breward, C., E. Ehrman and C. Evans (2004) *The London Look: Fashion from Street to Catwalk*. New Haven; London: Yale University Press in association with the Museum of London.

Bruzzi, S. and P. Church Gibson (eds) (2000) *Fashion Cultures: Theories, Explorations and Analysis*. London; New York: Routledge.

Evans, C. (2004) 'Cultural Capital: 1976–2000'. In C. Breward, E. Ehrman and C. Evans *The London Look: Fashion from Street to Catwalk*. New Haven; London: Yale University Press in association with the Museum of London, pp. 139–59.

Foucault, M. (2002) *Archaeology of Knowledge*. A. M. Sheridan Smith (trans). London; New York: Routledge Classics.

Hebdige, D. (1979) *Subculture: The Meaning of Style*. London; New York: Routledge.

Hesmondhalgh, D. (1999) 'Indie: The institutional politics and aesthetics of a popular music genre'. *Cultural Studies*: 13(1), 34–61.

Jobling, P. (1999) *Fashion Spreads: Word and Image in Fashion Photography Since 1980*. Oxford; New York: Berg.

Lynge-Jorlen, A. (2010) *Between Edge and Elite: Niche Fashion Magazines, Producers and Readers*. London College of Fashion: PhD Thesis.

McRobbie, A. (1998) *British Fashion Design: Rag Trade or Image Industry?* London; New York: Routledge.

McRobbie, A. (ed.) (1989) *Zoot Suits and Second-Hand Dresses: An Anthology of Fashion and Music*. Basingstoke: Macmillan.

Reynolds, Simon. (1989) 'Against Health and Efficiency: Independent Music in the 1980s'. in A. McRobbie (ed.) *Zoot Suits and Second-Hand Dresses: An Anthology of Fashion and Music*. Basingstoke: Macmillan, pp. 245–55.

Reynolds, S. (2005) *Rip It Up and Start Again: Post-Punk 1978–84*. London: Faber.

Rocamora, A. (2009) *Fashioning the City: Paris, Fashion and the Media*. London; New York: I.B. Tauris.

Rocamora, A. and A. O'Neill (2008) 'Fashioning the Street: Images of the Street in the Fashion Media'. In E. Shinkle (ed.) *Fashion as Photograph: Viewing and Reviewing Images of Fashion*. New York: I.B. Tauris, pp. 185–99.

Shinkle, E. (ed.) (2008) *Fashion as Photograph: Viewing and Reviewing Images of Fashion*. New York: I.B. Tauris.

Smedley, E. (2000) 'Escaping to Reality: Fashion Photography in the 1990s'. In S. Bruzzi and P. Church Gibson (eds) *Fashion Cultures: Theories, Explorations and Analysis*. London; New York: Routledge, pp. 143–56.

Thornton, S. (1995) *Club Cultures: Music, Media and Subcultural Capital*. Cambridge; Oxford: Polity.

Today I'm Wearing: Alexa Chung. (2010) [Internet]. Available from: www.vogue.co.uk/photo-blogs/alexa-chung/alexa-chung-day-3. (Accessed 13 January 2012)

Williams, V. (1998) *Look at Me: Fashion and Photography in Britain 1960 to the Present: A touring exhibition curated by Brett Rogers and Val Williams*. London: The British Council.

Woodward, S. (2009) 'The Myth of Street Style'. *Fashion Theory*: 13(1), 83–101.

Chapter 14

Adam Briggs

'CAPITALISM'S FAVOURITE CHILD'
The production of fashion

> Fashion is the favourite child of capitalism: fashion arose from its inner essence and expresses its character as do few other phenomena of our contemporary social life.
>
> (Sombart 1902: 316)

THE FIRST YEARS OF THE TWENTY-FIRST century saw the development of 'fast fashion', the latest chapter in a narrative of commodified clothing that stretches back to at least the eighteenth century. This specific model of production is differentiated by an accentuation of mutual plagiarism in design, and an increase in the rate of the obsolescence of fashionable garments, rather than by any development of the means by which they are made. This has significant implications for both the environment and the workers who assemble garments in what remains in some respects a craft industry. This article explores the historical routes to the present mode of fashion production and highlights the way in which the seemingly wilful ignorance of fashion production, and its consequences, on the part of consumers, is reflected in academic debate.

Fashion can be seen as the political economy of the performative self – but the study of it tends to emphasise the latter over the former. Historically the study of fashion has been the subject of a 'wilful academic blindness' (Lemire 2010:15); however, recently, the study of fashion has moved from the margins of academic inquiry and fashion is now a legitimate subject within the study of popular culture. This newfound academic gaze remains, however, myopic in its focus, with an emphasis on the consumption rather than the production of fashion. The actual material object and the manner and consequences of its making are rarely foregrounded in academic studies. Prominence has been given to fashion as text and discourse, and as a key prop in the performance of subjectivity, with an emphasis on agency; moreover, the fields of fashion that draw the greatest attention are often the 'high end' and the transgressive rather than the everyday and normative.

The handful of scholars who have focused on fashion production note 'the limited knowledge we have of this industry' (Aspers and Skov 2006: 803) and its 'poorly recorded industrial development' (Godley 1997a: 3), and some speculate as to the reasons for this. Godley (1997b) Styles (1998) and Edwards (2011) emphasise the challenges arising from the complex and fragmented nature of the industry and the small scale of most producers, noting that this militates against generalisation and often serves as a troublesome exception to dominant 'grand narratives of industrialisation' (Styles 1998: 384). Edwards points to the difficulty of obtaining access to contemporary firms for reasons of commercial confidentiality and a reluctance on the part of producers to allow scrutiny of the 'often grossly exploitative working conditions that surround the cutting, sewing and finishing of garments' (Edwards 2011: 120). He suggests a reluctance to undermine the 'transformative magic' of fashion by examining the 'nauseatingly unattractive' process of its production (Edwards 2011: 20). This repugnance stems from the conditions in which, all too often, actual physical garments are made, rather than, for example, the seemingly glamorous professional lives of, say, fashion buyers (Entwistle 2009). Buyers are also active agents in producing fashion; this poses questions about how to conceptualise fashion production.

A model used by some fashion scholars who do consider fashion production (Entwistle 2009; 2000; Edwards 2011) is the 'Systems of Provision' approach developed by Fine and Leopold (1993). Their work, which advances a general argument through a detailed comparative analysis of the specificities of the historical development of the fashion and food industries, questions both liberal accounts of sovereign consumers driving the marketplace, and ways of understanding that see consumer behaviour as a direct outcome of the activities of producers. Their critique correctly emphasises the way in which the study of production and consumption in general is separated in academic literature with an emphasis on either one or the other, the critical relationship between the two unexamined; this, they argue, ignores the interconnectedness of both and leads to the implication that either one or the other is the primary determining agent. For Fine and Leopold production and consumption are not discrete entities that operate independently of each other but exist in a dialectical relationship that will vary between commodity types.

This approach, which sees 'culture' and 'economy' as 'mutually constitutive' (du Gay 1997: 2), offers a rich means of conceptualising the specificity of fashion and expands the conception of production beyond the manufacture of material objects to also include the crucial role of 'cultural intermediaries' such as buyers and merchandisers, journalists, bloggers, photographers, marketers, supply chain managers and contractors who form the 'connective tissue' between supply and demand (Fine and Leopold 1993: 96). Moreover, this approach, by highlighting the length and complexity of the chain of interconnected activities involved in the movement from the production of fashion to its consumption, draws attention to the textile industry as the origins of the material stuff of fashionable clothes and extends the frame of fashion analysis beyond their consumption to their disposal as they become outmoded.

Emphasising the notable absence of fashion production in the academic literature risks obscuring the extent that, for those prepared to cross disciplinary boundaries and dig in the academic journals, a solid foundation for further study does exist, albeit in a dispersed and fragmented form, providing an analysis of the production of ready-to-wear fashion from its earliest beginnings through to the emergence of large-scale production and the subsequent evolution of fast fashion. Within this literature on fashion production it is notable that the emphasis is primarily on processes rather than people: the culture of consumers is now a well established object of study, but the culture of production remains largely unexamined.

If, as Wilson writes, 'Fashion is dress in which the key feature is rapid and continual changing of styles' (Wilson 2003: 3),the economic advantages of this rapid tempo of change in the clothes considered desirable and appropriate were recognised as early as the seventeenth century. Brabon noted that 'Fashion or the alteration of dress, is a great Promoter of Trade, because it occasions the Expense of Cloaths, before the old ones are worn out: It is the Spirit and Life of Trade' (Brabon 1690, in Breward 1995: 128).

What Green describes as the 'specific production problem of hyper-innovation' (Green 1997: 20) was a structuring agent for the material production of fashion long before the advent of mass markets and large-scale production and has continued to be so through to the ever-increasing temporal rhythms of contemporary 'fast fashion'. Ephemerality brings production, marginalised within the study of fashion, squarely into the analytical frame by requiring attention to how this highly unstable demand is produced and the implications that this volatility has for manufacturing, garment workers and the planetary ecosystem.

The later part of the twentieth century saw fashion become increasingly pluralised, with multiple styles simultaneously in fashion. In the twenty-first century the rate of style turnover has increased considerably, with new styles being introduced within the previously stable temporal boundaries of bi-annual seasons. By 2004, Zara, for example, was introducing twenty new seasons a year (Barnes and Lea-Greenwood 2006: 261), with twice-weekly deliveries of new items to stores (Tokatli 2008: 30). This has resulted in what has been described a 'seminal change in the culture of fashion, from ready to wear to fast fashion' (Tokatli and Kizilgün 2009: 147), the spread of which, in the first decade of the century, coincided with a drop in clothing prices of 14 percent and an increase in the consumption of garments by 37 percent over a period of just four years (Allwood et al. 2006: 11–12).

While the term 'fast fashion', and the precise specifics of its supply chain innovations, date to the early years of the twenty-first century, the roots of its practice date back to the 1980s and the pioneering adoption, by Benetton, of electronic point of sale systems linked to 'just in time' production as a means of rapidly and accurately linking styles and colours produced to localised sales variances (Beluss 1987; Braham 1997; Zeitlin 1998; Taplin 1996a). Fast fashion, however, as Tokatli and Kizilgün (2009: 150) note, took 'the 1980s quick response revolution to an entirely new scale' by switching emphasis from the rapid replenishment of best selling lines to 'no, or low replenishment . . . retailers now purposefully create a climate of scarcity, the message to the consumer being that "if you do not buy it now, you will lose your opportunity"' (Tokatli and Kizilgün 2009: 148) Cheap clothing and the routine enticement of new styles make fashionable garments ever more disposable commodities. As Joy *et al.* (2012: 276) argue, 'fashion, more than any other industry in the world, embraces obsolescence as a primary goal; fast fashion simply raises the stakes'. Fast fashion products are 'non durables with sell by periods of four weeks' (Crofton and Dopico 2007: 43) and a life cycle benchmarked against the expectation of a lifespan of ten washes (Joy *et al.* 2012: 283).

The rapid introduction of a multiple succession of new short-lived styles, combined with low prices, increases sales. The rapid response facilitated by electronic point of sale data and computer-aided design and cutting allows information-driven replenishment of fast selling lines (Taplin 1996a: 204) and the near-instant translation of styles created by wholesale designer brands and retail competitors into garments for the high street (Tokatli 2008: 29). This demand-driven supply chain requires minimal pre-season ordering, low inventory levels and short production runs and sees production capacity being booked with subcontracted manufacturers but not the specification of the actual designs to be produced (Barnes and Lea-Greenwood 2006: 263). A Turkish clothing manufacturer interviewed by Tokatli and Kizilgün (2009: 157) reports, 'we used to have 6–7 months to manufacture an order. Now we only have 2–4 weeks, and Zara wants to talk about hours'. The 'just in time' aspect of the fast fashion supply chain puts considerable pressure on independent suppliers operating in a highly competitive, minimally regulated sector of the fashion industry and results in work intensification and unpaid overtime for garment workers. It further enshrines the instability of product specification that prevents further automation of garment production and ensures the continued existence of sweatshops.

The increase in the speed of turnover of styles has a concomitant effect on the environmental impact of clothing manufacture. Increased production output increases the considerable energy and toxic chemical inputs and outputs required to manufacture the textiles from which garments are made (Fletcher 2008; Allwood 2006), and their short lifespan has led to a situation in which Britain now produces 2.35 million tonnes of textile waste each year (Allwood *et al.* 2006: 16), of which only 25 percent is reclaimed in any form, the rest going to landfill (Fletcher 2008: 98).

Despite significant change in terms of the geographical dispersal of the division of labour, technological transformations in the process by which the specifics of supply and demand are brought together, and the ever-increasing speed of obsolescence, the historical narrative of ready-to-wear is one of startling continuity which reveals fashion production 'as a cottage industry that developed into a post-Fordist economy without ever truly benefiting from mass production or industrialisation' (Edwards 2011: 130).

Prior to the eighteenth century clothes would usually be made bespoke, either at home from purchased materials, or by dressmakers and tailors. There is a long and uneven journey to the present system of provision and supply of 'off the peg' ready-to-wear clothing. McKendrick argues that 'a revolutionary commitment to fashion' (McKendrick 1982: 40) occurred in the eighteenth century that saw a widespread social dispersal of the previously elite practice of fashion in clothing. This revolution, occurring in a broader context of the growth of a market society with cash wages, rising real incomes and newfound possibilities for social mobility, created a rapid acceleration in fashion change that saw 'the commercial manipulation of fashion' (McKendrick 1982: 41) by entrepreneurs 'trying deliberately to induce fashion change' (Ibid: 43). His evidence suggests that this 'manipulation' was primarily carried out by retailers who used advertising, alongside fashion dolls and fashion prints, not only to disseminate details of the latest style but also their ability to supply it; he also provides evidence suggesting that by the end of the eighteenth century fashion changes in 'colour, shape, material and style' were annual and socially uniform (McKendrick 1982: 43; see also Lemire 1991).

Despite the consensus regarding the 'heightened fashion consciousness' (Lemire 1984: 21) that developed in the eighteenth century, McKendrick has rightly been criticised for implying that the newly fashion influenced clothes were mass produced (Fine and Leopold 1993; Styles 1993). Lemire finds that fashions were often 'kept up with' by the alteration of existing garments and the use of accessories as means of conforming to 'the current mode' (Lemire 1984: 22) and argues that the 'small but impressive trade in ready made clothes' (Lemire 1984: 41) was supplied by seamstresses working in their own homes and 'small workshop manufacture overseen by sub-contractors' (Lemire 1997: 56). Subcontracting by 'putting out' garment construction, to be made to 'the master makers specification' (Styles 1993: 532) long preceded the invention and adoption of the sewing machine and the band knife.

The nineteenth century saw the gradual consolidation of ready-to-wear, if not its industrialisation. Clothing prices fell as rapid increases in cotton production after the industrial revolution led to a reduction in the raw material cost of fashionable clothing, thus allowing consumers to replace outmoded clothes as fashions changed. Chapman (1993) provides an overview of the development of widespread production of ready-to-wear fashionable clothing in the nineteenth century and highlights the central role of, among others, 'innovating entre-preneurs', wholesalers and 'mercers and drapers evolving into department stores', both of whom, rather than vertically integrating into manufacturing themselves became 'manufacturers without factories' by specifying design while subcontracting the actual making to external 'cut, make up and trim' (CMT) contractors. The commercial advantages for large retailers and wholesalers of subcontracting to a network of small workshops or individual workers, either directly or through jobbing intermediaries, stemmed from the power arising from the volume and regularity of orders and the avoidance of capital investment in the fixed costs of production facilities and has subsequently remained the dominant mode of organisation for clothing manufacture. These arrangements, which saw the rise to prominence of buyers and merchandisers, allowed large retailers and wholesalers significant control over suppliers and the ability to demand a low cost, flexible, quick response to changing trends. These demands were met by a profusion of small-scale CMT firms where 'work came cheaply, paid according to piece work at sweating rates' (Miller 1981: 57). Subcontracting also allowed the out-sourcing of responsibility for regulations over pay and conditions. Here, then, are the historical origins of contemporary sweatshops, in that the move to large-scale mass production, seen in most industries, did not occur in clothing manufacture. Why not?

The first sewing machines, which greatly increased the speed of stitching, were patented 'in the late 1840s and early 1850s',with widespread commercial adoption through the latter part of the century. (Godley 1996b: 60) The band knife, first introduced in 1860 (Green 1997: 38), similarly compressed production time by allowing multiple layers of cloth to be cut simultaneously. Technology allowed the lowering of garment prices by reducing the labour costs per garment, and, as with the mechanisation of cotton production, allowed more consumers to dance to the temporal rhythms of fashion. By the end of the century fashion seasons were 'bi-annual' (Miller 1981: 187). Unlike in textile manufacturing, however, technology did not lead to the mass production of fashion.

Such literature as there is on the historical emergence of ready-to-wear stresses that 'the clothing industry has never been a classic site for mass production' (Zeitlin 1988: 212). One of the explanations for this lies in the 'continued dependence on the individually operated sewing machine' (Fine and Leopold 1993: 102); another lies in the nature of clothing's raw material. Godley notes that 'cloth is limp and tailored, shapes complex, and there has been and remains no machinery that is able to replicate the dexterity of the human hand in manoeuvring cloth through a sewing machine . . . thus capital investment in the clothing industry has been limited to the sewing machine and not much more' (Godley 1997a: 7) Garment manufacturing is labour intensive; clothes are still hand made if not hand stitched. The distinctive nature of the material aspects of fashion production is, as Fine and Leopold argue, that 'the manufacturing of clothing was based on the mechanisation of tailoring practices rather than on the wholesale transfer of the production process to machinery . . . mechanisation in this case served to reinforce rather than undermine the craft basis of production' (Fine and Leopold 1993: 102–3). The sewing machine was not the harbinger of mass production but, rather, 'the tool of flexible specialisation par excellence' (Ibid:102).

Sewing machines are cheap; the material production of ready-to-wear has been characterised by a 'large number of small factories or workshops'. (Wray, 1957: 28). Subcontracting saw the development of division of labour, that became consolidated in clothing manufacturing over the course of the nineteenth century. In this dissaggregation of the individual stages of garment making and distribution sewing became separated from 'design, cutting and sales' (Green 1997: 145), was devalued in status and accordingly deemed to be suitable work for women and immigrants. The low capital overheads here also meant, then as now, that this sector became particularly attractive to, and viable for, cash-strapped immigrant entrepreneurs who were 'themselves often excluded from opportunities in the primary labour market (and who) are able to exploit kinship ties and more extensive forms of gender subordination, employing women from the same or other ethnic minorities who form part of the underclass or secondary labour market' (Winterton and Winterton 1997: 31).

Then, as now, subcontracting produced a hierarchically ordered vertically disintegrated – but highly organised – network where core firms retain design, marketing and logistics and outsource the actual labour-intensive making of garments to small subordinate peripheral firms. This arrangement provides the core firms with the flexibility required by the specificity of the fashion product; moreover, given the large number of these firms, and the willingness of core firms to switch suppliers (Tokatli and Kizilgün 2009) intense competition ensures low prices for finished garments. These economies were, and are, achieved by low wages, no job protection, unpaid overtime, poor work conditions, oppressive management and a lack of union representation (see labourbehindthelabel.org and other activist websites).

Godley argues that for ready-to-wear 'the innovation that prompted its development was not new machinery, but the development of standard sizes' (Godley 1997a: 4). One of the barriers to the widespread uptake of ready-to-wear was its poor fit (Styles 1994), and the development of standard sizing developed, alongside the gradual consolidation of ready-to-wear, as the norm in the first half of the twentieth century. Sizing is also central to understanding the flexibility impera- tives that contraindicate standardised mass production; the variety of the human body demands multiple variants of a single design. Alongside sizing, the continued centrality of the sewing machine and the highly competitive and flexible multiplicity of contractors, another barrier to standardised mass production in fashion is the very thing that defines it – obsolescence. Constant flux, considered desirable and appropriate, prevents the standardised high-volume production of a limited product range using dedicated machine tools, required for automated mass production. The individually operated and labour-intensive sewing machine, which does not need retooling as product specification changes, remains the industry standard technology for producing the short runs of garments demanded by fast fashion.

Large-scale production with mass production tendencies developed in the twentieth century, initially in menswear, where slower rates of obsolescence and less design differentiation produced a more stable product specification (Belfer 1954; Honeyman 2000; Goodley 1996a). This entailed the development of section work in a process of 'dividing and conquering the garment' (Green 1997: 33) that saw the breaking down of garment assembly to its individual constituent processes in 'progressive bundle' or, less successfully, 'synchro flow' systems (Odih 2007; Abernathy 1999; Taplin and Winterton 1995). Despite the continued centrality of the single operative sewing machine this led to a model of larger firms adopting a Taylorist mass production tendency: they achieved the required production flexibility lacking in large-scale sectionalised production by further subcontracting to smaller firms that gain competitive advantage by 'making through' garments and *not* adopting mass production techniques – they, in turn, will often further subcontract to other contractors and home workers (Phizacklea 1990; Odih 2007).

After wartime restrictions in design, planned obsolescence in dress returned in the postwar period – feasible due to the rapid growth of retail multiples and department store chains. In Britain these retailers accounted for 70 percent of all clothing sales by 1977 (Zeitlin 1988: 212) and competed primarily on the price and quality of that season's style. This retail concentration produced sufficiently stable aggregate demand *within a season* to justify the higher capital investment required on the part of subcontracted manufacturers to produce the economies of scale of larger scale clothing manufacturing (Talpin and Winterton 1995; Zeitlin 1988; Phizacklea 1990).

The evolution of boutiques through the 1960s (Fogg 2003), offering alternatives to the Paris-derived style of the season stocked by the retail multiples and department stores, was symptomatic of change. The sourcing approaches of the dominant retailers were geared towards achieving the economies of scale realisable by the large-scale manufacturers, but were insufficiently flexible to supply the fragmented demand brought about by the pluralisation of styles that developed from youth and subcultural fashion. This fragmentation of demand increasingly became the norm from the 1970s onwards, as the relatively stable consumption patterns arising from categories of gender, class and age were supplemented by the multiple, nebulous, mobile and transient identifications of 'lifestyle', with a parallel shift from mass to niche marketing (Braham 1997; Taplin 1996a; Taplin and Winterton 1995; Zeitlin 1988). This pluralisation of style greatly increased risk, in that, unlike a fashion market characterised by the relatively orderly succession of one style by another, customers now choose between styles within a season, thereby opening up the very real possibility of terminal stock being left on the shelf as fashions change. The management of this risk demanded an increased emphasis on design, smaller production runs and shorter lead times and consequently 'eroded the advantages of long run garment manufacture' (Zeitlin and Totterdill 1989: 162). Unsurprisingly this was synchronous with 'a rebirth of sweatshops' (Taplin and Winterton 1995: 628).

By the 1980s clothing manufacturing was seen as a 'sunset industry' in Britain (Zeitlin 1988) and the USA (Abernathy 1999); it has subsequently shifted to newly industrialising nations – with the exception of those small-scale contractors that 'replicate Third World labour market conditions with what amounts to a third world labour force' (Taplin and Winterton 1995: 629) among immigrant populations in 'informal enclaves' (Odih 2007: 176) of the industrialised world. Such firms gain competitive advantage not only through the familiar litany of sweatshop employment practices but also due to the flexible quick response capacity that derives from their closeness to the marketplace. Newly industrialising nations, faced with rapid marketisation and urbanisation, a desperate need for foreign earnings and large unskilled workforces in need of employment, and enticed by the low start-up costs and labour intensiveness of 'cut make and trim', have engaged in a 'race to the bottom' in competing to provide the lowest labour costs and the least regulation of working practices (Odih 2007; Scott 2006; Zeitlin 1988).

The final barriers to core firms overseas sourcing were overcome by a combination of developments in information technology and the deregulation of global trade. As Odih (2007: 57) maintains, 'revolutionary advances in IT have dramatically effaced the formidable time and space barriers, which separated national markets'. The use of electronic point of sale (EPOS) technology to enable real time collection and transmission of sales data enabled enhanced inventory control and risk management and allow global manufacturers far removed from local markets to rapidly match the specifics of supply to the specifics of demand, thereby minimising the risk of terminal stock that arises from the 'flexibility imperatives' (Taplin and Winterton 1995: 615) of a fragmented and unruly marketplace. Computer-controlled design and cutting, which was once, along with EPOS, seen as the potential saviour of manufacturing in the industrialised world (Zeitlin 1988; Taplin 1996) enabled cost-effective market-driven design and, in manufacturing, quick response to volatile demand in a globally dispersed division of labour

– and the deskilling of specialist graders and cutters (Taplin 1996; Taplin and Winterton 1995).

The potential of technological developments to globalise fashion production finally occurred with the neoliberal erosion of protectionism. Tariffs and quotas long used to protect Western clothing industries from import penetration from low labour cost nations ended with the eventual phasing out of the Multiple Fibre Agreement in 2005 (Pickles 2006). This globalised 'quick response revolution' and the subsequent shift in emphasis from the replenishment of popular styles to the eternally recurring new demands of fast fashion has had little impact, however, on the actual manufacturing of garments. As Taplin and Winterton (1995: 616) argue, contemporary fashion production is 'an amalgam of new technology merged with old practices . . . not . . . new production paradigms . . . but merely recon-figurations of old ones'.

While the focus here has been on the material making of the physical object, fast fashion requires the issue of symbolic production to be part of any consideration of fashion production. The implication of this is that any analysis of fashion production also needs to consider the role of branding and 'cultural intermediaries' such as those journalists, photographers, bloggers and marketers who work in the symbolic domain of fashion representation, alongside the buyers and merchandisers, supply chain managers and contractors who form the 'connective tissue' between supply and demand in the realm of the actual object. It also suggests the need to reflect on exactly how problematic 'production' is as an idea as well as a practice.

The ability to put designer-originated fashion rapidly on to high street rails, and the success of online retailers such as ASOS, add to our need to understand the semiotic basis by which consumers differentiate between multiple iterations of near-identical styles. In contemporary fashion, as Taylor (2000: 138) argues, 'the brand logo holds the magic of style'. Thus it could be expected that branding would be central in the study of fashion. This is not, however, the case; while cultural intermediation is now foregrounded, branding remains something about which 'the academic world of fashion . . . has little to say' (Edwards 2011: 143). This is a significant lacuna within any critical study of the production of fashion. Not only is the creation of brand identity central to the process of making garments uniquely desirable to consumers, but 'the product as sign' also ensures that the actual making of physical garments, and the conditions within which this occurs, along with the associated environmental impact, remain out of sight, unconsidered.

Machinists and cutters make clothes, but do they make fashion? Barthes (1983: 51) invites us to 'think for a moment of the magazine as a machine that makes fashion'; fast fashion intensifies the need to focus on the idea of fashion as a discourse that sells fashion as *system*, rather than selling individual products, through naturalising the ever-accelerating rate of stylistic obsolescence. Despite the counter-discourses of 'ethical fashion' Gibson and Stanes (2011: 172) are correct in main-taining that

> whether mass deception or means to self identification, the idea of buying new clothes at every season in now widely accepted, regardless of need. In the West, very few people own just enough clothes to get by – over consumption of clothing has become normalised.

The reference to fashion as a process of 'self identification' points to the limitations of an exclusive emphasis on the economics and supply side of fashion, in that this does not explain why consumers choose one style over another or why we accede to the ecologically deleterious 'over consumption' of fashion. The singular focus on the systemic drivers of style change, and its consequences, rather than the pleasures and anxieties from which they emerge, offers, at best, a partial analysis of fashion production. Fashion is all too often made in sweatshops, it is the inverse of sustainable, and is invariably marketed by creating dissatisfaction. But in order fully to understand fashion production, we also need to consider consumers as more than passive victims. De Certeau draws attention to:

> *another* (form of) production, called 'consumption'. The latter is devious, it is dispersed, but it insinuates itself everywhere, silently and almost invisibly, because it does not manifest itself through its own products, but rather through its *ways of using* the products imposed by a dominant social order.
>
> (De Certeau 1984: xii)

Ultimately it is consumers, not producers, who 'produce' fashion. Baudrillard (1975: 19) asserts that 'it is no longer a question of "being" oneself, but of "producing" oneself'. This effectively expands the idea of fashion production from the making of objects, and the articulation of meaning onto these in the name of competitive advantage, to fashion as an everyday ontological project on the part of consumers.

An exclusive emphasis on material production or a limited focus on the discourse of fashion as an 'ideological manifestation of a capitalist economy interested in increasing demand for its commodities' (Purdy 2004: 14) obscures the performative potential of fashion to disrupt and challenge dominant conceptions of selfhood and social structure. Moreover, it obscures the crucial economic implications of these activities. Shopping is an economic activity: it is also a cultural process through which consumers actively differentiate themselves from each other, so driving processes of diffusion that both add and subtract value from particular styles and brands. Production and consumption, economics and culture, when considered through this kaleidoscopic lens, cease to be separate entities existing in symbiotic antithesis; they become inherently unstable categories overlapping each other. The infinite cycle of 'consumption' as economic exchange and the production, by consumers, of meaning, semiotic redundancy and identity is matched by the instability of 'production' and 'consumption' in processes traditionally conceived of as 'production'. In the fragmented and dispersed fashion supply chain, producers consume – for 'production' requires the 'consumption' of raw materials and labour. We need an analysis not of production *or* consumption, but of both, with an emphasis on how they are held in a dialectical and mutually constitutive relationship. The study of production, as typically conceived, is not sufficient in itself to understand the role of fashion in our lives. However, any understanding of fashion that does not include production is not only incomplete, it is also misleading.

References

Abernathy, F. H., Dunlop, J. T., Hammond, J. H. and Weill, D. 1999. *A Stitch in Time: Lean Retailing and the Transformation of Manufacturing – Lessons from the Apparel and Textile Industries.* New York: Oxford University Press.

Allwood, Julian M., Laursen, Søren Ellebaek and Nancy, N. P. 2006. *Well Dressed? The Present and Future Sustainability of Clothing and Textiles in the United Kingdom.* Cambridge: University of Cambridge Institute for Manufacturing.

Aspers, P. and Skov, L. 2006. 'Encounters in the Global Fashion Business: Afterword', *Current Sociology*, Vol. 54, No. 5.

Barnes, L. and Lea-Greenwood, G. 2006. 'Fast Fashioning the Supply Chain: Shaping the Research Agenda', *Journal of Fashion Marketing and Management*, Vol. 10, No. 3.

Barthes, R. 1983. *The Fashion System*. Berkeley: University of California Press.

Baudrillard, J. 1975. *The Mirror of Production*. St Louis: Telos Press.

Belfer, N. 1954. 'Section Work in the Women's Garment Industry', *Southern Economic Journal*, Vol. 21, No. 2.

Belussi, F. 1987. *Benetton: Information Technology in Production and Distribution: a Case Study of the Innovative Potential of Traditional Sectors.* Occasional Papers No. 25, Science Policy Research Unit, University of Sussex.

Blaszczyk, R. L. (ed.) 2008. *Producing Fashion: Commerce, Culture and Consumers.* Philadelphia: University of Pennsylvania Press.

Braham, P. 1997. 'Fashion: Unpacking a Cultural Production', in P. du Gay (ed.) *Production of Culture, Cultures of Production.* London: Sage.

Breward, C. 1995. *The Culture of Fashion*. Manchester: Manchester University Press.

Chapman, S. 1993. 'The Innovating Entrepreneurs in the British Ready Made Clothing Industry', *Textile History* Vol. 24, No. 1.

Claudio, L. 2007, 'Waste Couture: Environmental Impact of the Clothing Industry', *Environmental Health Perspectives*, Vol. 115, No. 9.

Collins, J. L. 2003. *Threads: Gender, Labor, and Power in the Global Apparel Industry.* Chicago: University of Chicago Press.

Crewe, L. 1996. 'Material Culture: Embedded Firms, Organisational Networks and the Local Economic Development of a Fashion Quarter', *Regional Studies*, Vol. 30, No. 3.

Crewe, L. and Davenport, E. 1992. 'The Puppet Show: Changing Buyer–Supplier Relationships within Clothing Retailing', *Transactions of the Institute of British Geographers,* Vol. 17, 183–97.

Crofton, C. O. and Dopico, L. G. 2007. 'Zara-Inditex and the Growth of Fast Fashion', *Essays in Economic and Business History,* Vol XXV.

Donaghu, M. and Barff, R. 1990. 'Nike Just Did It: International Subcontracting and Flexibility in Athletic Footwear Production', *Regional Studies*, Vol. 24, 537–52.

De Certeau, M. 1984. *The Practice of Everyday Life*. Berkeley: University of California Press.

du Gay, P. and Pryke, M. 2002. *Cultural Economy: Cultural Analysis and Commercial Life.* London: Sage.

du Gay, P. (ed.) 1997. *Production of Culture, Cultures of Production.* London: Sage.

Edwards, T. 2011. *Fashion in Focus: Concepts, Practices and Politics.* London: Routledge.

Entwistle, J. 2009. *The Aesthetic Economy of Fashion: Markets and Values in Clothing and Modelling.* Oxford: Berg.

—— 2000. *The Fashioned Body: Fashion, Dress and Modern Social Theory*. Cambridge: Polity.

Fine, B. and Leopold, E. 1993. *The World of Consumption*. London: Routledge.

Fletcher, K. 2008. *Sustainable Fashion and Textiles: Design Journeys*. London: Earthscan.

Fogg, M. 2003. *Boutiques: A 60s Cultural Phenomenon*. London: Mitchell Beazley.

Gibbs, D. 1988. 'Restructuring in the Manchester Clothing Industry: Technical Change and the Interrelationships between Manufacturers and Retailers', *Environment and Planning A*, Vol. 20, 1219–33.

Gibson, C. and Stanes, E. 2011. 'Is Green the New Black? Exploring Ethical Fashion Consumption', in T. Lewis and E. Potter (eds) *Ethical Consumption: A Reader*. London: Routledge.

Godley, A. 1997(a) 'The Development of the Clothing Industry: Technology and Fashion', *Textile History*, Vol. 28, No. 1.

—— 1997(b) 'Comparative Labour Productivity in the British and American Clothing Industries, 1850–1950', *Textile History*, Vol. 28, No. 1.

Godley, A. (ed.) 1997(c) Special issue on the history of the ready-made clothing industry. *Textile History*, Vol. 28, No. 1.

Godley, A. 1996a, 'The Emergence of Mass Production in the UK Clothing Industry', in I. M. Taplin and J. Winterton (eds) *Restructuring Within a Labour Intensive Industry: The UK Clothing Industry in Transition*. Aldershot: Avebury.

—— 1996b. 'Singer in Britain: The Diffusion of Sewing Machine Technology and its Impact on the Clothing Industry in the United Kingdom 1860–1905)', *Textile History*, Vol. 27, No. 1.

—— 1995. 'The Development of the UK Clothing Industry, 1850–1950: Output and Productivity Growth', *Business History*, Vol. 37, No. 4.

Green, N. 1997. *Ready to Wear and Ready to Work: A Century of Industry and Immigrants in Paris and New York*. London: Duke University Press.

Harte, N. B. (ed.)1991. *Fabrics and Fashion: Studies in the Economic and Social History of Dress*. Special issue of *Textile History*, Vol. 22, No. 2.

Hethorn, J. and Ulasewicz, C. (eds) 2008. *Sustainable Fashion: Why Now? A Conversation about Issues, Practices, and Possibilities*. New York: Fairchild Books.

Honeyman, K. 2000. *Well Suited: A History of the Leeds Clothing Industry 1850–1990*. Oxford: Oxford University Press.

Joy, A., Sherry, Jr, J. F., Venkatesh, A., Wang. J. and Chan, R. 2012, 'Fast Fashion, Sustainability, and the Ethical Appeal of Luxury Brands', *Fashion Theory*, Vol. 16, No. 3.

Kaiser, S. B. 2012. *Fashion and Cultural Studies*. London: Berg.

Kershen, A. J. 1995. *Uniting the Tailors: Trade Unionism Amongst the Tailors of London and Leeds, 1870–1939*. Ilford: Cass.

Lemire, B. 2010. 'Fashion and the Practice of History: A Political Legacy', in B. Lemire (ed.) *The Force of Fashion in Politics and Society: Global Perspectives from Early Modern to Contemporary Times*. Farnham: Ashgate.

—— 1997. *Dress, Culture and Commerce: The English Clothing Trade before the Factory, 1660–1800*. London: Macmillan.

——1991. *Fashion's Favourite: The Cotton trade and the Consumer in Britain, 1660–1880*. Oxford: Oxford University Press.

—— 1984, 'Developing Consumerism and the Ready Made Clothing Trade in Britain, 1750–1800', *Textile History*, Vol. 15, No. 1.

McKendrick, N. Brewer and J. Plumb, J. H. 1983. *The Birth of a Consumer Society: The Commercialisation of the Eighteenth Century*. London: Hutchinson.

Miller, M. 1981. *The Bon Marché: Bourgeois Culture and the Department Store*. Princeton: Princeton University Press.

Morris, J. 1986. *Women Workers and the Sweated Trades*. Aldershot: Gower.

Odih, P. 2007. *Gender and Work in Capitalist Economies*. Maidenhead: Open University Press.

Phizacklea, A. 1990. *Unpacking the Fashion Industry: Gender, Racism and Class in Production*. London: Routledge.

Pickles, J. 2006. 'Trade Liberalization, Industrial Upgrading, and Regionalisation in the Global Clothing Industry', in, *Environment and Planning* A 38 pp. 2201–2206.

Purdy, D. (ed.) (2004) *The Rise of Fashion: A Reader*. Minneapolis, MN: University of Minnesota Press.

Rath, J. (ed.) 2002. *Unravelling the Rag Trade: Immigrant Entrepreneurship in Seven World Cities*. Oxford: Berg.

Ross, A. (ed.) 1997. *No Sweat: Fashion, Free Trade and the Rights of Garment Workers*. London: Verso.

Scott, A. J. 2006. 'The Changing Global Geography of Low Technology, Labor Intensive Industry: Clothing, Footwear and Furniture', *World Development*, Vol. 34, No. 9.

Scheffer, M. 2009. 'Fashion Design and Technologies', in Paulicelli, E. and Clark, H. (eds) *The Fabric of Cultures: Fashion, Identity and Globalization*. London: Routledge.

Schmiechen, J. A. 1984. *Sweated Labour and Sweated Industries: The London Clothing Trades 1860–1914*. London: Croom Helm.

Sombart, W. 1902. 'Economy and Fashion: A Theoretical Contribution on the Formation of Modern Consumer Demand', in Purdy, D. L. (ed.) 2004. *The Rise of Fashion: A Reader*. Minneapolis, University of Minnesota Press.

Styles, J. 1994. 'Clothing the North: The Supply of Non Elite Clothing in the Eighteenth Century North of England', *Textile History*, Vol. 25, No. 2.

—— 1993. 'Manufacturing, consumption and design in eighteenth century England', in J. Brewer and R. Porter (eds) *Consumption and the World of Goods*. London: Routledge.

Styles, J. 1998. 'Dress in History: Reflections on a Contested Terrain', *Fashion Theory*, Vol. 2 No. 4.

Sull and Turconi, 2008. 'Fast Fashion Lessons', *Business Strategy Review*, Summer.

Taplin, I. M. 1996a. 'Rethinking Flexibility: The Case of the Apparel Industry', *Review of Social Economy*, Vol. LIV, No. 2.

—— 1996b. 'Introduction', in I. M. Taplin and J. Winterton (eds) *Restructuring Within a Labour Intensive Industry*. Aldershot: Avebury.

Taplin, I. M. and Winterton, J. (eds) 1997. *Rethinking Global Production: A Comparative Analysis of Restructuring in the Clothing Industry*. Ashgate: Aldershot.

Taplin, I. M. and Winterton, J. (eds) 1996. *Restructuring Within a Labour Intensive Industry: The UK Clothing Industry in Transition*. Aldershot: Ashgate.

Taplin, I. M. and Winterton, J. 1995. 'New Clothes from Old Techniques: Restructuring and Flexibility in the US and UK Clothing Industries', *Industrial and Corporate Change*, Vol. 4, No. 3.

Tarrant, N. 1994. *The Development of Costume*. London: Routledge.

Taylor, L. 2000. 'The Hilfiger Factor and the Flexible Commercial World of Couture', in White, N. and Griffiths, I. (eds) *The Fashion Business: Theory, Practice, Image*. Oxford: Berg.

Tokatli, N. 2008. 'Global Sourcing: Insights from the global clothing industry – the case of Zara, a fast fashion retailer', *Journal of Economic Geography*, Vol. 8, No. 1.

Tokatli, N. and Kizilgűn, O. 2009. 'From Manufacturing Garments for Ready-to-Wear to Designing Collections for Fast Fashion: Evidence from Turkey', *Environment and Planning A*, No. 41, 146–62.

Tokatli, N. Wrigley, N. and Kizilgün, Ö. 2008. 'Shifting Global Supply Networks and Fast Fashion: Made in Turkey for Marks & Spencer', *Global Networks*, Vol. 8, No. 3.

Wadlinger, R. D. 1986. *Through the Eye of the Needle: Immigrants and Enterprise in New York's Garment Trades*. New York: New York University Press.

Williams, A. 2011. 'Fashionable Dilemmas', *Critical Studies in Fashion and Beauty*, Vol. 2, No. 1/2.

Wilson, E. 2003. *Adorned in Dreams: Fashion and Modernity*. London: I.B. Tauris.

Winterton, J. and Winterton, R. 1997. 'De-regulation, Division and Decline: The UK Clothing Industry in Decline', in Taplin, I. M. and Winterton, J. (eds) *Rethinking Global Production: A Comparative Analysis of Restructuring in the Clothing Industry*, Ashgate: Aldershot.

Wray, M. 1957. *The Women's Outerwear Industry*. London: Duckworth.

Zeitlin, J. 1988. 'The Clothing Industry in Transition: International Trends and British Response', *Textile History*. Vol. 19, No. 2.

Zeitlin, J. and Torrerdill, P. 1989. 'Markets, Technology and Local Intervention: The Case of Clothing', in P. Hirst and J. Zeitlin (eds) *Reversing Industrial Decline? Industry Structure and Policy in Britain and Her Competitors*. Oxford: Berg.

Chapter 15

Louise Crewe

TAILORING AND TWEED
Mapping the spaces of 'slow fashion'

Introduction

> Modern clothes have all the disposability of fast food and a trip to a
> chain store could be as instantly fulfilling as a Big Mac. And the thrill
> will last about as long.
>
> (Shulman, in O'Dwyer 2009)

THIS CHAPTER FOCUSES on the temporalities and spaces of fashion,
looking specifically at models of slow luxury fashion, craft, quality and
knowledge. The conceptual basis for the discussion lies in recent debates about
the geographies of fashion that suggest an ongoing descent into an industry founded
on a lowering of quality, and a future based on fast, cheap, throwaway fashion
produced under distant, exploitative work conditions (Crewe 2008; Siegle 2011).
Although fast fashion has been a key strategy in the industry's attempt to maintain
competitive advantage, it is also widely acknowledged to be economically, socially
and environmentally unsustainable (Brown 2010; Fletcher and Grose 2012; Minney
et al. 2011; Siegle 2011). While the global supply of cheap, fashionable clothes
may have been a perfect competitive strategy for fashion retailers, it brings with
it a set of social, economic and environmental conditions that are altogether more
troubling. And while the fashion industry has been remarkably adept at heading
off environmental and social censure, it has also enabled the creation of both
dirty, ugly business practices and giddily accelerated cycles of consumption with
long and often invisible production footprints and short (and equally invisible)
consumption lifetimes. The volume of clothing purchases has increased by over a
third in the past decade, largely because of the growth in cheap, fast fashion.
As a result waste volumes are high and rising (Allwood in Lean 2007: 16).

Consumers are buying more than they need and cheap prices are fanning hasty, thoughtless and, at times, needless consumption. The faster fashion moves, the more toxic its effects, and globalised production systems are threatening a range of geographical spaces, from cotton fields to sweatshops, high streets to landfill sites: not only are our homes becoming filled with barely worn garments, but a volume of clothing and textiles equivalent to approximately three-quarters of purchases is buried in landfill in the UK each year.

The longer-term implications of these tendencies are of note both economically and theoretically. Cost, value and the worth of objects have become confused. Why do we buy what we buy? How do we begin to understand object value? Do we care any longer about our clothes? What now informs our consumption practices? How aware are we that the life cycle of garments in terms of production, consumption and use is being rapidly accelerated, that clothes are shoddily and hastily constructed, their post-purchase lifetime intentionally truncated? Disposable fashion is unsettling, objects become expendable, things feel impermanent and consumers become restless awaiting the next quick fix, a fix that ultimately rarely satisfies. We are left hungry, wanting, desiring the next purchase. And as long as consumers continue to be seduced by cheap, fast clothing, mass market retailers will continue to tread the path of least resistance and churn out catwalk copy designs made by the world's poor, for sale on a high street near you within weeks of their runway launch.

In reaction to the increasing unease generating by fast fashion and its outcomes, two dominant responses are identifiable in both theory and practice. First, there has been a growing intellectual and industry-driven focus on sustainable or eco-fashion (Brown 2010; Fletcher and Grose 2012; Minney *et al.* 2011; Siegle 2011). Second, there has been a more politically and socially driven focus on fashion production through recycling, re-use, crafting, mending, knitting, repair. Knitting, for instance, has been argued to be an effective means to critique capitalism and its exploitative supply chains and labour practices, and forge alternative identities, communities and ways of living (Greer 2008; Buszek 2011).

The social and economic relevance of the craft renaissance is 'far more complex than the cliché of the middle-class mummy hooked on crochet' and 'speaks to a more visceral and socially urgent need to reconfigure the nature of work' (Brooks 2009). In the following discussion I offer a third alternative vision of future fashion based on a rather different set of reflections as to how fashion production and consumption might redress and counter the more deleterious aspects of cheap fast fashion. On first reading, this alternative vision that centres on slow fashion might appear to many to be every bit as as contentious and unsettling as the fast fashion model at a time of global recession, austerity economics and very real economic hardship. On a number of levels (personal, political, economic, intellectual) it is a difficult challenge to mobilise an argument in favour of luxury production and a return to quality consumption in an age of austerity and it brings with it some degree of unease. But as the narrative below unfolds, the argument for durable, crafted fashion becomes persuasive and engages us, as do the fabric and clothes of which I speak. The argument gains added validity as it has, at its heart, a commitment to a return to skilled production, using quality materials to fabricate products that are 'Made in England'. On social, environmental and employment grounds this alternative fashion future based around a return of production to the UK begins to gain credence. Additionally, the argument offers a new conceptual insight into what fashion value is, where it might lie and how it might be created and maintained.

Given that fashion has for so long been seen as trivial, excessive, hedonistic and egocentric, it may at first sight appear to be an easy target for critique during critically difficult global economic times. If fashion is seen as an unnecessary luxury, consumers should surely regulate and monitor their consumption, become frugal, discipline their consuming bodies: stop shopping? That is, of course, one possibility. But here I want to argue for a return to a different relationship between fashion and consumption in which we see our clothes as long-term investment pieces that speak of durability, love, attachment, quality and craft. Under this theorisation we shift the locus of fashion value away from notions of 'value for money' and towards an understanding of the ecology and material culture of our garments that so often accrue value because of our own personal investments in them, our connections to them, their histories, geographies and our memories of their wearing. Fashion need not be fast, cheap and disposable and a more sustainable fashion future is possible if we buy fewer, but higher quality pieces that will endure; garments that we will adore, cherish, will wear for many years and keep for many more.

This vision of future fashion is based around slow pace, craft, quality, reputational capital, knowledge and longevity. Significantly in terms of geographical debate, the arguments forwarded here work with a very different set of spatialities and temporalities to those characterising the fast fashion production model. In the fashion model proposed below, production systems are locally embedded rather than globally footloose and mobile; they are slow rather than fast; materials are traditionally crafted and garments have intentionally long consumption lifetimes rather than being 'disposable' quick fashion fixes. These 'new-old' ways of doing fashion are both competitive but also underscore the role of durability, craft and the management of sustainable and design-led supply chains. The proposed 'slow luxury' model argues that modes of production can act as levers of the imagination: just as the ugly conditions that – usually young, usually female – sweatshop workers labour under in cheap cost locations weigh heavily on consumer's minds, so too can more equitable and durable visions of production inspire us, connect us to garment creators, makers and designers. Here I argue for the inestimable value of cultural specificity, history, craft and skill that globalisation and fast fashion will not and cannot erode. Two examples are drawn on to explore the spaces and times that slow fashion inhabits, both with long and fascinating historical and geographical stories to tell: the tailoring cluster of Savile Row, London and the production of Harris Tweed on the Hebridean Islands of Scotland. Together they reveal how the place of production can be a space of engagement, a space where the mythical alchemy of the product takes place. Good products are worth the wait, they develop slowly and last, weaving together reputation and history, valorised through their cultural, historical and geographical roots. This, I suggest, offers the potential at least for a reworking of fashion's times and spaces. It reveals how locally embedded production systems offer a counter to globalised fast-fashion systems and explores the significance of place, time, skill, embeddedness and agglomeration in the generation and survival of successful fashion spaces. The chapter raises a set of broader conceptual questions about how the competitive qualities of tradition, craft and locality can endure and adapt to a rapidly changing international environment.

Hand made, hand touched: The evocative geographies of luxury fashion

> A product has the less soul, the more people participate in its manufacture.
>
> (Simmel 1957)

Slow luxury fashion reveals a very different way of understanding the customer and managing a business based on decreasing the physical and social distance between fashion producers and consumers. It enables a greater awareness of the real cost – and value – of clothes. The consumption of crafted garments places crucial importance on the precise materials from which they are made, their social, economic and historic reasons for being, and the way that we interact with them through our senses (Aynsley et al. 1999). Crafted, quality systems of supply offer both creative and economic power and acknowledge that much of the value of the garment is linked to territory, history, cultural specificity and the places of its production. While the UK may have lost the global battle for cheap clothing supply, we have demonstrated that 'we can win the battle of quality, credibility, and ideas' (Hieatt 2013: 12). Rather than cutting costs by outsourcing production and severing the ties between producer and consumer, slow fashion actively pursues non-exploitative and sustainable supply chains that re-connect the consumer with the places where their clothes originate and enrol the consumer in both the production process and the knowledge systems that underpin it.

Clothes that are beautifully made with care, sensitivity and skill are special, precious, valuable. Special garments have a soul, a meaning and an authenticity. They generate deep desire based on knowledge and aesthetics rather than price, saturation and duplication. Fashion value originates in part from our knowledge about the hands that crafted it and the memories ingrained within it from use, wear, love and emotional attachment (Crewe 2011). In turn, evocative objects have the potential to invert the economics of value and price, supply and demand by decoupling a growth in profit from increased material flow. Extending the life of clothing builds symbolic worth into systems of value determination. An increased emphasis and active promotion of durable style and design classics encourages consumers to consider moving towards the purchase of fewer, higher quality, seasonless pieces that are crafted to last: 'Slow burners work harder for your money than frivolous fashion and allow for a more conscientious kind of consumption' (Fletcher in Britten 2008: 16). Fashion-conscious consumers are increasingly aware that their purchasing decisions can have a dramatic impact on employment, industry and economy in the UK and are prepared to pay higher price points for garments that are crafted to last, using short, transparent supply chains and locally sourced materials, designed and produced domestically by some of the most skilled craftspeople in the world. Further, through such considered consumption, they are actively supporting domestic garment production and world-class training provision that the UK offers for designers and makers that will help to ensure the reproduction and transmission of this vital skills base. Such consumption practices empower consumers and provide them with a real sense of agency to effect change through what they buy and from where, on the basis of their knowledge about supply, production, use and value. In short, slow fashion offers the potential at least for the formulation of radical new perspectives on the production and consumption of fashion. It reveals that fashion can and is being done differently. 'If fashion is about ingenuity and innovation, this is a good time for the industry to draw on these qualities and return to measuring fashion in terms of something other than quantity' (Siegle 2008). The quality, frequency of wear and length of use thus transforms both the economics and value of clothing. The close relationship between fabric, creation, crafter and customer is central to the generation of quality clothing. Crafted garments are non-anonymous, they are authenticated and reveal the value of slow clock-times and long lifespans. In this context luxury can be redefined and seen less in terms of excess and the needless and more in terms of thoughtful, quality consumption. Luxury can be 'refinement not ostentation, communication not proclamation' (Kapferer and Bastien 2009). The connection of craft to time is one of its essential elements. Slow garments are both of the moment and design classics – timely and timeless, carefully crafted through painstaking design, beautiful materials and personal connection. Evocative garments are worth the wait and reveal above all that the material pleasure and symbolic expression of identity through fashion can be compatible with a more politicised, socially conscious consumption ethos (Pietrykowski 2004: 309).

Appreciative consumption: The spaces and times of crafted clothing on Savile Row

> From Savile Row to Shoreditch, from Bond Street to Brick Lane, British menswear has never been more dynamic or indeed more successful.
>
> (Jones 2013)

London's Savile Row is a short street in Mayfair with a long history of bespoke tailoring and quality craft. While Savile Row has been the subject of journalistic and historical attention ('Savile Row' BBC 4, 2009), there has been little critical geographical research to date on this iconic centre of British tailoring (although see Breward 2003). Savile Row has faced a number of challenges in recent decades that chime perfectly with the broader trajectory that the global fashion industry, discussed in the introduction, has followed. At various points in time it appeared that this industrial quarter had almost disappeared from view and vocabulary. The specific threats to this mode of production include the rise of the ready-to-wear casual market in the 1970s, a relaxing of formal dress codes in the corporate workplace through the 1980s, and most particularly in the fashion-forward creative industries, the emergence of looser tailoring pioneered by Italian companies such as Armani, and more recently the global recession and falling consumer spending. The sustainability of their market has also been called into question as both the

Figure 15.1
Recent window display on the corner of Savile Row. Photography: Anne-Marie Michel/Catchlight-Media.com.

traditional customer base and the skilled workforce of Savile Row are ageing. The Row faces difficulties recruiting and retaining apprentices to maintain and continue its bespoke tailoring skills base and has struggled to compete for young workers who – at least until the latest recessionary crisis – favoured the City over the clothing industry as a career option. In addition, Savile Row is facing a number of broader global threats and several of the firms have been taken over by large multinational investment businesses that bring very different modes of knowledge and sets of expectations about fashion futures and their spatial depth and reach. Finally, the space of Savile Row is also being challenged by a range of new entrants including ready-to-wear suit retailers, 'celebrity tailors' such as Ozwald Boateng and the highly contentious arrival of the American casual youth-wear brand Abercrombie & Fitch in 2008, all of whom may shift or dilute the profile and longstanding reputation of the Row.

And yet in spite of these very real threats and pressures, Savile Row continues to be a centre for crafted, high-quality garment production and customisation. The endurance of the fashion model that characterises Savile Row, in spite of the seemingly insurmountable economic, cultural and social pressures that it faces, suggests that quality, luxury consumption and high value added-competition continue to be important components in certain spaces for particular groups of consumers. This section of the chapter explores how this locally embedded production system is responding to the broader socio-economic threats outlined above and evaluates the key factors that begin to explain the enduring – and increasing – appeal and success of a fashion agglomeration that is committed to an economy of regard that places slow production, domestic sourcing policies, consumer relationships and the life of clothes at its heart. It is argued that the development and survival of competitive fashion spaces may be explained, at least in part, through an appreciation of the importance of place, time, identity, skill, reputational capital, agglomeration and particular sets of knowledge-based consumption practice. The particular example of Savile Row raises broader conceptual insights into how the competitive qualities of the 'Made in England' brand, with its long and credible history of skilled, high-quality production of crafted garments, rich in symbolic value and with global consumption appeal, can offer a very real alternative to the outsourced production of cheap, disposable fast fashion garments.

After many years of falling employment, margins, prices and sales in the British fashion industry, there are emergent signs that 'Made in Britain' may be regaining the kudos and respect it endured for much of the early postwar period. Long associated with a certain kind of quality, design and luxury, British fashion is estimated to employ almost 70,000 people (British Fashion Council, *The Future of Fashion* 2012). London fashion and design in particular has a long history, from the 'swinging sixties', punk and Cool Britannia through to its renewed status as the leading international centre for the global fashion industry. London is a world centre of creativity and design talent and has some of the most renowned fashion educational institutions in the world with unrivalled reputations. There is a renewed interest from industry, governments, policy-makers and publics to manufacture high-quality garments in the UK and a clear vision that the future for British fashion production must be to compete on quality, design and specialisation rather than price. This is the UK's comparative, competitive and long-established advantage. London Fashion Week is one route through which emerging British fashion talent is taken to market. It attracts in excess of £100 million of media coverage and showcases some of the most forward-facing, design-led talent that has emerged, and continues to do so, from UK Fashion Schools and educational establishments. The London Collections: Men in 2013 included the highly respected and widely reported Savile Row collective that showed in Spencer House and confirmed both the iconic status of Savile Row and the key role that London plays in incubating and developing new fashion skill and talent. More overtly, perhaps, the re-introduction of the Wool Awards and Wool Week at London Fashion Week brought the crofters and weavers of the Scottish Hebrides, the tailors of Savile Row, consumers and the global media together in a live spectacle during which Savile Row was grassed over so that flocks could safely graze – a literal juxtaposition and clear spatial manifestation of the transparency of supply chains at work.

London has arguably always been the spiritual home of the sartorial man: its menswear has been seen as both innovative and timeless; it is both understated and yet unrivalled in its attention to detail. In recent years London has enjoyed renewed levels of international success and is very much setting the pace in terms of emerging talent that is both design-led and commercial, producing garments that are ageless and work well on men of all ages. A Savile Row suit has retained a traditional understanding about quintessential fabrics and cuts that are read as a distinctively British version of style that really works:

> The suit is the default wardrobe setting; the most successful garment
> in the history of fashion and is wholly and indivisibly a British invention

. . . A suit says authority, learning, expertise, manners, probity, efficiency, trust and a certain formality; all attributes traditionally thought
of as British.

(Schofield 2011)

The Savile Row suit has successfully maintained a powerful grip on definitions of
Britishness in the postwar era. Tailors on the Row work with a clearly identifiable
aesthetic, beautiful fabrics and with domestic sourcing policies and short supply
chains. Savile Row is gaining in vision and visibility, its tailors are supremely
competent in construction and with a new confidence and directional sense of
design. In a global marketplace, a Savile Row suit can be Englishness personified.
The new generation of designers are revealing a convergence between the long-
held quirky, fashion-forward, edgy London style and the more Savile Row-
establishment sartorial reading of fashion. London has a classiness and a quality but
with none of the bland corporate styling that typifies Italy, for example, with suits
that could have rolled off a machine (Grant 2013).

There is a depth and maturity to London menswear that can only come through
time:

> The point about Savile Row tailoring is that it takes a long time and
> you build on it and you develop your skills over years and years and
> years and you don't jump from one season to the next. That's why
> people like McQueen are so fabulous because he trained on Savile Row.
> And then went to Givenchy. It's those sorts of journeys that produced
> the sort of magic that they did. And John Galliano similarly. That's the
> pleasure of London as a city in that side-by-side we have that tradition
> of tailoring and we have that bright street style too.
>
> (Grant 2013)

That many of the UK's most successful designers began their careers on Savile
Row is testament to the key role of the apprenticeship schemes and training
associations in attracting new entrants into the fashion sector and developing their
skills bases. After seeing an advertisement on television highlighting the shortage
of apprentices in the tailoring business, Alexander McQueen told how he walked
into Anderson and Sheppard on Savile Row and was hired on the spot (Knox 2010:
7). His natural talent with chalk and scissors allowed him to quickly conquer classic
cuts and shapes and develop his personal style, eventually moving further down
Savile Row to work at Gieves and Hawkes.

The micro-geographies of the tailoring houses along Savile Row also hint at
reasons for their longevity and ongoing patronage. They are at the same time retail
spaces, design studios, training sites and micro-factories. The exterior architecture
of the tailors along the Row is grand, imposing and hints at its patriarchal and
colonial history of privilege and secrecy. The uses of the Row are protected by
restrictive covenants that have ensured a long history of conservatism, discretion
and mystery. A quiet rumpus followed the introduction of the first see-through
shop windows on the Row in the 1970s and in the 1990s the introduction of an
elegant flower box outside the store caused a scandal. It wasn't until 1992 that

Saturday opening was first introduced by Richard James, revealing how the street, its appearance and covert regulations formed part of the tailors' identity. Beneath this external architectural façade of conservatism and respectability lie complex geographies of craft, design and fabrication. Given that the cheapest space on the Row is on the lower floors, it is not surprising that the pressers, steamers, cutters, finishers and tailors are going underground, living a below-stairs existence. The warren-like spaces below street-level are hives of activity comprising workrooms and studios whose tools remain the same as they have done for decades: scissors, needles, chalk, shears, fingers. The teaching of tailoring is intimate and organic, a craft passed on without books or manuals, almost by osmosis, although the investment required to sustain the apprenticeship system is considerable: it requires a minimum of five years for a junior tailor to acquire the basic skills of the trade, and many more to reach the exacting standards required by the slow and precise rhythms of work and the meticulous co-ordination of hand and fibre. Other hidden spaces include rooms of archived fabrics, bespoke samples and the marked-up patterns of Savile Row's customers over many decades: Fred Astaire, Cary Grant, Jude Law, Daniel Craig, David Beckham and Michael Gambon, the labels identifying their individual identities carefully hidden from public view. The Row reveals a long and rich tradition of quiet under-statement and self-effacement that belies exquisite materials, faultless craft and flawless finishing. A Savile Row suit is assembled using thousands of hand stitches that join cloth to linen and cotton interlinings and linings, with edges and buttonholes all finished by hand too.

It is hardly surprising, then, that a Savile Row suit is in every respect a slow garment. Once the body has been measured and the customer has selected a bolt of cloth, the pattern is 'bespoken' for and the fabric theirs. Aware of the value of provenance, customers can select a suit made with 'record bale' wool whereby they know who owns the individual sheep that provided the wool for the suit. Each suit requires between 35 and 40 individual body measurements before the pattern is drawn up to make a blueprint of the customer's body that is uniquely theirs. A suit is made specifically for an individual and is cut and stitched by hand. The tailor–client relationship is built up over time and is based on trust, discretion and confidentiality – customers develop personal relationships with their tailors. The suit will take up to three months to create and will require at least half a dozen fittings. There is certainly no instant gratification involved, but the quality and craft of the suit is worth waiting for. In a world so dominated by faceless mass production, the tailors of Savile Row recognise that handmade, craft, tradition and individualisation can be powerful counters to cheap disposable imports. These are garments that will be loved, cherished and will last many lifetimes: 'It is your labour inside a suit. It's in your heart' (Everest 2008). A Savile Row suit is created slowly and without damage to the planet, it weaves social relations through time and space and through the generations: 'When Henry Stanley finally tracked down Livingstone in the heart of Africa, the good doctor was still wearing the tweed trousers he set off in from London some four years before' (Norton & Sons). One suspects that these clothes will never be landfill. As Patrick Grant of Norton & Sons argues 'We just make beautiful, simple men's clothing that lasts for years. I'm fed up of disposable clothing. People buy too many clothes – we should buy fewer things, but better things . . . there are easy ways to buy cloth but no easy ways to produce beautiful and unique cloth' (Grant 2010). Grant insists on using only the best British materials and craftspeople and personally sources his fabrics, including Harris Tweed, on his frequent sourcing trips to Scotland. Savile Row tailoring is fashion as both product and process, a blending of time, skill, precision and place. It uses highly specific techniques of salesmanship and selling, careful and understated forms of visual display and product design that avoid overt marketing, labelling or advertising policies. This is a fashion system where you won't find discount deals, logos or sales; it is careful, considered local production for extensive and discerning global markets built on repute and reputation. It is in such spaces that the 'mythical overlap of styles forged new and challenging identities' (Breward 2002: 580).

Capturing land and life in cloth: crofting, craft and the making of Harris Tweed

> There is probably no other British cloth with as rich a fashion history as tweed, and Harris Tweed sits at the pinnacle of this heritage.
>
> (Hills 2011)

Harris Tweed is like no other fabric on earth. It is born of its environment, is organic, handcrafted and defined by time. Tweed is a place, an imaginary as much as a fabric. It is also undeniably British:

> Tweed is a parable. A stereotype of Britishness. We are tweedy. Tweed is taciturn and hardworking, sturdy, dependable, loyal. Tweed doesn't get soppy or go limp . . . I have a bit of a thing for tweed. I love its feel and its smell. I love that it's rough but homely, that it has the ability to deflect the elements with a jaunty nonchalance. Tweed is like a game terrier; always pleased to see you, always wants to go out, always optimistic . . . It is the perfect balance of utility and panache, and it is my secret vice.
>
> (A. A. Gill in Schofield 2011)

Tweed is also the only fabric that has its own legislation. Eight thousand patterns are patented and protected by the Harris Tweed Act of Parliament. The Act allows the authority to promote and maintain the authenticity, standard and reputation of Harris Tweed and includes final quality inspectors who check that the cloth is perfect with no snags, uneven surfaces or wool discolouration. Each piece of cloth is labelled with the trademark Orb logo and a series number and each meterage of fabric has uniquely identifying 'passport information' on it (Platman 2011) that encodes who has woven the cloth, the pattern used and the date it was produced. Harris Tweed cloth can only be produced by weavers who live on the Hebridean Islands, and as consumers increasingly want to know who made their fabrics and garments, where, how, and under what conditions, the Tweed provides no finer confirmation of the virtues of local production for global markets. Unlike a number of other 'luxury' products that are increasingly made under brutal working conditions paying poverty wages,[1] Harris Tweed retains its entirely local production base and the island crofters here are quite literally weaving the fabric of emotional connection: 'The long, barren archipelago on the far north west tip of Europe is home to every dyer, blender, carder, spinner, warper, weaver, finisher and inspector of Harris Tweed' (Harris Tweed Authority 2012). The Harris Tweed archive dates back well over 100 years and is a timely reminder that, in spite of increasingly long, distant and unknown supply chains across much of the fashion industry, Harris Tweed retains its strong sense of provenance and bears the personality of the weaver and the croft in which it was fabricated, acting as a powerful repository of information for tailors and customers alike who are increasingly concerned about the origins of the garments they buy. Like the skills base that remains along Savile Row, the fabrication of Harris Tweed is a skill that takes many years, if not generations, to hone: the grading and sorting of wool into different quality levels is a highly skilled activity that is still done by hand and eye; shearing is still a bodily encounter between farmer and animal.

Like Savile Row, Harris Tweed has a long and rich history. In its earliest days it was dyed using lichen and woven by hand. It was adopted during the reign of Queen Victoria for its seeming indestructibility in the wild (Brown 2009: 15) and became a staple fabric for the production of robust and hard-wearing jackets for many years. 'Britain's story, its image, is wrapped and warped in wool. Wool can be woven into a gallimaufry of cloths . . . but the greatest of all, for which the grandest sheep can aspire to give the coat off its back, is tweed' (Schofield 2011). Harris Tweed has successfully steered a long symbolic history that speaks of both the establishment and its alter ego: anti-fashion. One of the earliest pioneers to subvert the traditional, class-bound and patriarchal associations of Harris Tweed was Vivienne Westwood, who spearheaded the use of the cloth by the punk movement in the 1970s. Westwood dressed the Sex Pistols in Harris Tweed, has used it across a number of collections including the Autumn/Winter 2010/11 Prince Charming range and adopted a motif very similar to the Harris Tweed orb as her corporate logo. A number of iconic British designers have worked with the fabric as a central component in their tailored collections. Margaret Howell recently argued that 'weaving on hand looms creates a depth and complexity of texture that can't be imitated by a mechanical process. Its very nature – the resilient wool, the flecks and herringbones in earthy colours – reflects the landscape, climate and skills of the people that produce it. I've always been attracted by its authenticity and chose Harris Tweed when designing my first winter jacket and overcoat. I've used it ever since' (Howell in Platman 2011: 124). Harris Tweed is, argues the Savile Row tailor Timothy Everest, 'an amazing institution' (2009: 14); 'No-one can match it anywhere in the world' (Wylie 2009: 14). The re-launching of the Woolmark prize, originally awarded to Karl Lagerfeld and Yves Saint Laurent in the 1950s, is testament to the industrial, policy and design status again afforded to wool, and mill production increased by 12 percent in 2011 (Fisher 2012).

Although the industry was in a precarious position during the 1980s and 1990s, due to a lack of investment, a shortage of skilled workers who wanted to enter the industry and shifts in fashion and taste, the hand-woven fabric is currently enjoying a surge in production and sales and is now the Western Isles' largest private sector employer and generates approximately £10 million for the local economy per year (Carrell 2012). In part this resurgence has been the result of an initiative headed by a former Labour energy minister, Brian Wilson, who explains:

> The objective was to create a new generation interested in it. The great thing is you're selling something that is truly genuine. It's not like spinning a story around something that doesn't exist. It's completely genuine: the distinguishing features of Harris Tweed are both quality and heritage.
>
> (Wilson 2012)

One of the greatest successes in recent years has been the transformation of the image of the brand Harris Tweed into a young fabric that appeals to a new generation of consumers. Harris Tweed's client list now includes 'just about every serious designer. Every fashionable designer is now working with Harris Tweed' (Wilson 2012). Jaggy Nettle, for example, have produced a range of hi-top trainers in Harris Tweed that are stocked alongside Prada and Louis Vuitton in boutiques in New York, Tokyo and Milan: 'I chose Harris Tweed because their clothes are not designed for one season or one trend, but to last' (Lee in Carrell 2012).

Like Savile Row, the production system that underpins the creation of Harris Tweed has a long and revered history, one that is again rooted in the specificity of place and the skills of particular individuals. The isolated crofting communities who produce Harris Tweed are embedded in the islands, and see themselves as 'all one family, all working as a team, everyone helping each other' (Mary Ann Macleod in Platman 2011). The crofting communities that tend sheep and weave are an integral part of this landscape that provides much of the inspiration for the colour and texture of the cloth. The purple and lavender hues of heather on moors and braes, the purple and green moss in springtime, the clear blue northern skies and bright blue seas and lochs forms the very basis of the fabric: cloth and land woven together. The colours and qualities of Harris Tweed are unparalleled by any other fabric through a combination of the inspirational landscape in which it

Figure 15.2
Colour, texture and pattern incorporated into traditional tailoring. Photography: Anne-Marie Michel/Catchlight-Media.com.

is crafted, the ability of the wool to adopt a dazzling array of dyes and the blending, spinning and juxtaposition of yarns during the weaving process (Hills 2011: 123). The designs woven on the islands are carefully blended to the changing needs of fashion and style direction in terms of colour, density and weight but the colours of the landscape are always intertwined, an ever-present constant motif. This is a fabric that has gained its legitimacy through quality production nurtured from heritage, skill and craft. Harris Tweed speaks of landscape, place and origins, the cloth evokes heather-coloured heaths and glens, mountains, rocks, sky, water, shoreline, pebbles, moors. Its colours and textures speak of its place of fabrication, not in laboratories or dyeing factories but in crofts and farms and rural mills. It looks and smells like the land. It captures land and life in a fabric.

Conclusions

This chapter has revealed that fashion can and is being done differently. Buying without regard makes little sense and the model of cheap, fast production via the off-shoring of production and the race to the bottom of the market is becoming less convincing economically, environmentally and socially. The fashion system outlined here is based on appreciative consumption and embedded, active networks of supply and production. It offers a counter to the dominant narratives that suggest the inevitability of a low-cost global fast-fashion industry and offers, too, the potential at least for the formulation of radical new perspectives on the production and consumption of fashion. By focusing on time, place, skill and quality, the examples drawn on here reveal the very real possibility of growing a slow, design-led, domestic fashion system that has global reach and highly visible and transparent supply relations. Most significantly, the arguments forwarded here have important implications for existing debates about designing for durability in which, to date, product longevity has been considered solely in terms of an object's physical endurance. The concept of slow fashion developed in this chapter extends the notion of durability beyond its conventional interpretation to a consideration of fashion value as created through history and place, skill and craft, object quality, memory and attachment. Our clothes 'speak' to us through the memories that we associate with them. Instead of viewing the meaning of particular designs as fixed and given, by looking at the process of evocation we find an open and continuing dialogue between things, their makers and their consumers.

This approach argues for a revaluing of materials and materiality in the determination of quality and for appreciative consumption of products that we love, that engage our hearts and minds as well as our bodies and flesh. The importance of the materiality, surface, depth, construction tactility and fit of garments has been very much ignored. This chapter foregrounds these affective qualities of clothes and directly engages with the clothes that are the material subject of study. In short, durability and the long biographies of garments is just as much about our connections to our things, to desire, love, attachment and memories woven into the very fibre and fabric of our clothes as it is about their physical durability.

Note

1   See, for example, the documentary *Schiavi de Lusso* (Luxury Slaves) about the 2,500 predominantly Chinese fashion workers in the Tuscan town of Prato, Italy.

References

Andrews, M. (1997) *The Acceptable Face of Feminism. The Women's Institute as a Social Movement*. London: Lawrence & Wishart.

Atkinson, P. (2006) 'Do It Yourself: Democracy and Design', *Journal of Design History*, 19 (1): 1–10.

Aynsley, J. Breward, C. and Kwint, M. (1999) *Material Memories: Design and Evocation*. Oxford: Berg.

Bell, Q. (1976) *On Human Finery*. Hogarth Press.

Britten, F. (2008) 'Future proof your look', *Sunday Times*, 24 August, p. 16.

Breward, C. (2003) *Fashion*, Oxford: Oxford History of Art.

Brown, A. (2009) 'Are we being spun a yarn?', *Sunday Times*, 12 April.

Brown, S. (2010) *Eco Fashion*. London: Laurence King.

Black, A. and Burisch, N. (2010) 'Craft Hard, Die Free: Radical Curatorial Strategies for Craftivism', in 'Unruly Contexts' in Adamson, G. (ed.) *The Craft Reader*, Oxford and New York: Berg.

Black, S. (2011) *Eco-Chic: The Fashion Paradox*. London: Black Dog Publishing.

Bratich, J. and Brush. H. (2011) 'Fabricating Activism: Craft-Work, Popular Culture, Gender', *Utopian Studies*, 22 (2): 233–60.

Brooks, L. (2009) 'Amid the economic rubble, a revolution is being knitted,' *The Guardian*, 9 July.

Buszek, M. (2011) *Extra/Ordinary: Craft and Contemporary Art*. Duke University Press: Durham, NC.

Carrell, S. (2012) 'Harris tweed returns to global boutiques after island's renaissance', *The Guardian*, 9 November.

Chadha, R. and Husband, P. (2006) *The Cult of the Luxury Brand: Inside Asia's love affair with luxury*. Nicholas Brealey International.

Chapman, J. and Gant, N. (2007) *Designers, Visionaries and Other Stories*. London: Earthscan.

Chevalier, M. and Mazzalovo, G. (2008) *Luxury Brand Management: A World of Privilege*. Oxford. John Wiley.

Crewe, L. (2008) 'Ugly Beautiful: Counting the Cost of the Global Fashion Industry', *Geography*, 93 (1) Spring: 25–33.

Crewe, L. (2011) 'Life itemized: Lists, loss, unexpected significance and the impossibilities of erasure', *Environment and Planning*, A29(1) 27–46.

Danziger, P. (2005) *Let them Eat Cake: Marketing Luxury to the Masses*. Kaplan Business.

Design Council, Creative and Cultural Skills Sector Skills Council and the Design Skills Advisory Panel (2007) *High-level Skills for Higher Value*.

DeSilvey, C. (2012) 'Making sense of transience: an anticipatory history', *Cultural Geographies*, 19 (1): 30–53.

Edensor, T., Leslie, D., Millington, S. and Rantisi, N. (eds). (2010) *Spaces of Vernacular Creativity: Rethinking the Cultural Economy*. London: Routledge.

Everest, T. (2008) BBC2 'British Style Genius', October.

Fisher, A. (2012) 'Fashion World Warms Again to Wool', *The Observer*, 2 September.

Fletcher, K. (2008) *Sustainable Fashion and Textiles: Design Journeys*. Earthscan.

Fletcher, K. and Grose, L. (2012) *Fashion and Sustainability: Design for Change*. London: Laurence King.

Fox, I. and Chilvers, S. (2010) 'Slow fashion: forever yours', *The Guardian*, 7 July.

Gauntlett, D. (2011) *Making is Connecting: The Social Meaning of Creativity, from DIY and Knitting to YouTube and Web 2.0*. Cambridge: Polity Press.

Gieson, B. (2008) *Ethical Clothing*. Saarbrucken. VDM Verlag.

Grant, P. (2010) 'Football fashions suited me perfectly', in Salmond, C. *Edinburgh Evening News*, 19 February, p. 22.

Greer, M. (2008) *Knitting for Good*. Trumpeter Books: Boston, Mass.

Hethorn, J. and Vlasewicz, C. (2008) *Sustainable Fashion: Why Now? A Conversation Exploring Issues, Practices and Possibilities*. New York. Fairchild.

Hieatt, D. (2013) 'The best of British', in Rickey, M. *The Guardian Style*, pp. 12–13.

Hills, G. (2011) 'Fashion: Dashing Tweeds', in Platman, L. *Harris Tweed: From Land to Street*, p. 123.

Kapferer, J. N. and Bastien, V. (2009) *The Luxury Strategy*. London. Kogan Page.

Knox, K. (2010) *Alexander McQueen: Genius of a Generation*. London: A&C Black Publishing.

Lean, G. (2007) 'Chic and cheerful but not so great for the environment', *Independent on Sunday*, 28 January, p. 16.

Minahan, S. and Cox, J. (2007) 'Stitch 'n' Bitch: Cyberfeminism, a Third Place and the New Materiality', *Journal of Material Culture*, 12 (1): 5–21.

Minney, S. Watson, E., Westwood, V. and Krely, O. (2011) *Naked Fashion*. Oxford: New Internationalist.

Norton, K. (2006) 'Savile Row never goes out of style', *Business Week*, 31 October.

O'Dwyer (2009) 'Style without a use-by date', *Sydney Morning Herald*, 14 May, p. 6.

Okonkwo, U. (2007) *Luxury Fashion Branding*. Palgrave.

—— (2009) *Luxury Online: Styles, Strategies, Systems*. Palgrave Macmillan.

Pietrykowski, B. (2004) 'You are what you eat: The social economy of the slow food movement', *Review of Social Economy*, LX11 (3) 307–21.

Platman, L. (2011) *Harris Tweed: From Land to Street*. Francis Lincoln Publishers: London.

Schofield, S. (2011) 'A Man of the Cloth: A. A. Gill', *Sunday Times*, 13 March.

Siegle, L. (2008) 'Why it's time to end our love-affair with cheap fashion', *The Observer*, 24 August.

Simmel, G. (1957) 'Fashion', *American Journal of Sociology*, 62(6).

Wells, R. (2009) 'McFashion junked in the flight to sustainability', *Sunday Age*, 15 March, p. 7.

Whife, (2002) 'Modern Tailor', in Breward 2003.

Wilson, B. (2012) 'Harris Tweed Returns to Global Boutiques after Island's renaissance', *The Guardian*, 9 November.

Wood, Z. (2008) 'Slow fashion is a must have . . . and not just for this season', *The Observer*, 3 August.

Wylie, A. (2009) 'Tweed goes to Tokyo', *The Scotsman*, 16 March, p. 14.

PART 4

Icons and their legacies

Chapter 16

Peter McNeil and Giorgio Riello

THE 'FASHION ARTS'
Jean Michel Frank, Elsa Schiaparelli and the interwar aesthetic project[1]

> Even though poverty-stricken I wouldn't take a fortune for my Picasso.
> (Elsa Schiaparelli, *Shocking Life*, New York,
> E. P. Dutton, 1954, opposite frontispiece)

THE RELATIONSHIP BETWEEN ART and fashion has a long and complicated history. Their commercial potential, their reliance on creativity and the *mondaine* lives of their protagonists, have made of art and fashion an established pairing at least since the rise of couture and impressionist art in 1860s France. The same can be said for fashion and design, though theirs is a more recent affair. In the early twentieth century the couturier Paul Poiret played with the idea of design, but it was only in the postwar period that the alliance between design and fashion became strong, in particular with the rise of *prêt-à-porter*, the made-in-Italy and American casualwear and lifestyles. The danger is of constructing histories in which fashion remains a distinct unit of analysis that only interacts with other realms of material creation – as if fashion were separate from either art or design.

This essay takes a different approach to the relationship and emphasises the imbrication of interior design and fashion. Elizabeth Wilson's concept of the 'fashion arts' might be usefully employed here (Wilson 2004: 377). She argues that the interwar period saw designers' practices widen and encompass a whole range of the visual arts. The *ensemble*, whether dress or room, was more than the sum of its parts, and several famous designers extended their interests across materials, genres and professional labels. Collaborations were common as was the creation of aesthetic projects through conversations between designers, couturiers and artists. We should consider here also the view of Rita Felski (2011: 231) that the 'uncoupling of modernity' from 'aesthetic modernism' permits an eclectic yet coherent range of approaches to emerge in the 'cultures of femininity' in modern fashion. That is, a more complex range of approaches to modernism might be possible than the architecture of Le Corbusier and the Purism of Amédée Ozenfant.

Our focus is on an 'improbable' couple: the French interior designer Jean-Michel Frank and the Italian-born couturiere Elsa Schiaparelli. Frank is little known today outside the orbit of interior design specialists and his relationship with the wider fashion world is only starting to be explored. Yet in the last two decades Frank has been heralded as one of the most talented designers of the first half of the twentieth century; similarly Schiaparelli is now seen as one of the most important figures in the French fashion of the interwar period, on a par with the more famous Mme Madeleine Vionnet and Gabrielle 'Coco' Chanel. It might not be a surprise that the two – both well known 'artists' in 1930s Paris and *bon viveurs* of type – knew each other and frequented the same circles of friends. What is more surprising, however, is the extent to which Frank and Schiaparelli interacted in their aesthetic projects. This essay focuses specifically on the shaping of Elsa Schiaparelli's residences in Paris, first her flat in Boulevard Saint Germain and later two larger dwellings in Rue Barbet-de Jouy and Rue de Berri.

We use an anthropologically inspired 'thick description' methodology to reconstruct interiors that are no longer extant. The aim is to break down the barrier between the designer and the client, but also between interior decoration and dress. Fashion assumes here new connotations: first the lens moves from the boutique, the dress, and the business of fashion to the domestic space of a fashion creator. Fashion becomes a project that transcends the boundaries between public and domestic, professional and private, encapsulate all aspects of Schiaparelli's life. As a consequence, fashion should not be read as a separate chapter: Schiaparelli's playful engagement with shapes and surprising creations ranged from dresses to couches, from brooches to decorative vases. Several collaborations with Frank created a peculiar aesthetic result that we claim was as influential at the time as it was inspirational for the subsequent alliance between fashion and interior design.

Jean-Michel Frank

In an era of écru and blonde-textured minimalism for retail, domestic and hotel interiors, it is an irony that there is little general popular recognition of the role of interior and furniture designer Jean-Michel Frank (1895–1941). Frank's disciplined and elegantly severe design of interiors and furniture for transatlantic elites of the 1930s navigated between the poles of post-Bauhaus austerity and neo-Baroque opulence. Unlike art deco schemes by Émile-Jacques Ruhlmann (1879–1933) and the other *ensembliers* of the era, Frank's work redefined ideas of style and luxury. His use of modest materials – straw, leather (albeit super-fine and by Hermès), parchment, rope, plaster – made into objects and trans-formed into exclusive acts of style, suggested that the ideas and concepts of the designer and the choices of the client were more important than older notions of luxury and exclusivity.[2] Perhaps because he was not associated uniquely with one

Figure 16.1
'The interior of l'hotel des Noailles in Paris by J. M. Frank', *Art et Industrie, revue générale des industries de luxe et des arts appliqués à la maison*, Paris, Art et Industrie, 1926 et 1927; part 2, 1927. From a limited now rare edition of 200 numbered copies. It shows the interior decoration of the 'hotel des Noailles' by Jean-Michel Frank. The room featured parchment walls, rose quartz, ivory plaques, ivory Moroccan leather and the luxury of solid bronze doors. (Courtesy of Diktats bookstore)

style or medium, and due also to his untimely death in 1941, Frank is not well known within the English-speaking world outside the specialist interested in the history of interior decoration.

Frank was possibly 'le plus chic' designer of the first half of the twentieth century. He was also a tragic figure: homosexual, escaping Nazi persecution (his cousin was the equally 'famous' Anne Frank), before killing himself at a very early age. Frank had a global reach, executing schemes in South and North America, and supplied many North American interior decorators as well as designing the highly significant Rockefeller apartment in New York. Despite appearing in almost all memoirs and portraits of the style elites of the interwar years, Frank was, until recently, the subject of just one small monograph in English, that is primarily pictorial (Sanchez 1980, 1997; Baudot 1998). More recently, Pierre-Emmanuel Martin-Vivier (2008), an expert in the applied arts, published a substantial study, that focuses on the French commissions. The attention rightly paid by recent Anglo-American design history to the significant interwar designers such as Elsie de Wolfe and Nancy Lancaster has only recently been replicated for Frank.[3] This has happily been rectified with a superb study by Amelia Teitelbaum of Frank's clients and commissions in South America (Teitelbaum 2010).

The Anglophone emphasis of much design history has contributed to this situation. Frank is always present in studies of interior design history and his conceptual model of decorating drove a great deal of other works. Frank's own work managed a tension between a modernist focus on unimpeded volume, while underscoring French modernism's relationship to neo-classicism and Enlightenment ideas of purity, with gestures of baroque excess: the ornamental incursions, the *trompe l'oeil* play of materials and scale. Frank also worked in collaboration with some of the great thinkers, writers and artists of his era: Christian Bérard (1902–49), Jean Cocteau (1889–1963), Alberto and Diego Giacometti (1902–85), Elsa Schiaparelli (1890–1973), Serge Roche (1898–1988) and Emilio Terry (1890–1969). These circles were interrelated and symbiotic at a time when the relationship between art and design was actively being reformulated in French culture. Frank designed on one occasion a set of garden furniture for the villa La Armonia to be upholstered in a fabric of multi-coloured lozenge shapes, in the same proportion and tones as Picasso's series of harlequins, saying to the wealthy patroness: 'I want my lovely seats, when seen from far across the lawns of La Armonia, to look like Picasso's harlequins reclining' (Teitelbaum 2010: 134).

Elizabeth Wilson (2004: 377) notes that this was a period in which display was transformed, as was advertising: 'a new and more sophisticated and knowing environment was created for the "fashion arts"', as artists 'forged such a close relationship between fashion, popular media and commerce'. Frank's set-like designs for retail interiors underscored his relationship to contemporary ideas ranging from surrealist art and film to Hollywood design. Although Frank's work was for an exclusive elite, his aesthetic was much more widespread and had portability into upper middle-class taste, particularly through the styling industries and retailing. Elements of his style and also that of Elsa Schiaparelli's extreme fashions appear in the kitsch and hilarious George Cukor-directed film *The Women* (1939). Frank's work was disseminated more widely with the use of his sparse aesthetic and object-design (frequently collaborations with artists) in the work of prominent decorators Elsie de Wolfe, Syrie Maugham, Eleanor Brown and Frances Elkins (the latter his agent in the USA).

Frank also exemplifies the period's ability to co-opt the 'chic of poverty', that had already been suggested in the interior design of Eugenia Errazuriz (Beaton called her the 'Beau Brummel' of design) or in the deceptively simple clothing designed by Coco Chanel. As Beaton (1954: 176) noted in his 1954 book *The Glass of Fashion*, Frank 'invented new surfaces and fabrics, tables made of parchment, banquettes upholstered in sackcloth, and walls covered with great squares of raw leather . . . even encouraging people to sit on leather floor cushions'. Frank's development of objects such as lamp-bases, shades and vases with a particular handcrafted and calcified aesthetic had a cross-over to wider middle-class taste, as for instance in Constance Spry's floral arranging using dried or wild flowers and simple vessels, which promoted such ideas to the English-speaking world. His ability to leave an object such as a basket or hook in clear view, intensified through the 'naked' design of a room overall, had an enormous impact on middle-class taste to the present day. It is interesting to speculate how such gestures may have developed from modernist photography as, for example, Le Corbusier's styling his architectural interiors for publicity.[4] Unlike Cecil Beaton, Rex Whistler and Oliver Messel, Frank's theatricality never became saccharine nor was it especially camp. The discipline and restraint in his work avoided that charge. It was perhaps for that reason that Frank was able to design major schemes of interior decoration for figures such as Nelson Rockefeller.

Elsa Schiaparelli

Let us now consider the symbiotic relationship between Frank and Elsa Schiaparelli. Schiaparelli was among the greatest celebrity couturiers, and her personal style was as assured as her bold fashion design. She was a household name on both sides of the Atlantic from the late 1920s until the early 1950s, then, in terms of public memory, suffered from the closure of her 'maison' designing clothes. Italian-born, Schiaparelli was the great-niece of an astronomer, which might explain parts of her adventurous and celestial vision. As Coco Chanel (1883–1971) had done in the 1910s, Schiaparelli began her fashion business in the 1920s within the area of women's separates and sportswear, and also established a successful range of accessories and perfumes. Schiaparelli's fashion designs of the 1920s and 1930s were forged through her interest and collaboration with artists, decorative painters and interior designers. She is best known for her hand-knitted art deco *trompe l'oeil* sweaters featuring huge bows and maritime devices, and for her surrealist-inflected creations featuring everything from monkey-fur shoes to a powder compact shaped like a telephone dial. Schiaparelli dressed some of the most famous women of the interwar years – Daisy Fellowes, the Duchess of Windsor, Lady Louis Mountbatten; even Mae West and Zsa Zsa Gabor for select cinema roles.[5]

Cecil Beaton (1904–80) rather unkindly described Schiaparelli by saying that 'She injected a healthy note into the thirties, inventing her own particular form of ugliness and salubriously shocking a great many people. With colours that were aggressive and even up-setting . . . Schiaparelli began her revolution' (Beaton 1954: 184). What Beaton means can be understood by considering her installation at the 'Pavillon de l'Elegance' at the 1937 Exposition internationale des arts et techniques in Paris. The dresses were displayed next to naked Siegel mannequins created by Robert Couturier. The hand of Alberto Giacometti is evident in the stark modern plasterwork. The tableau demonstrates the strange intersections of woman and nature that intrigued Schiaparelli and features one of her typical bold floral prints and a strange spikey floral throw or wrap that is decidedly artificial. It is far from a 'pretty' fashion picture. It is bold and modern.

These well-known perverse inventions tend to mask the majority of Schiaparelli's commercial output, which consisted of dramatic sculptural dresses whose forms were derived from non-western European dress including Indian, North African, Tyrolean, Peruvian, Mexican, Russian and Central European. She proposed new ways of dressing for women including smart trouser skirts and chic dinner suits, a taste for comfort combined with glamour that Schiaparelli extended to her personal home life.[6] These were superbly cut and their embroidered and other decoration was extremely tightly controlled, never kitsch, as it sometimes appears in photography when taken out of context.

Both her fashion design and her private residences combined the themes of practicality, drama and eclectic grandeur. Schiaparelli's ability as a fashion designer to create whimsy and goddess-like stasis was also present in her self-image, which was a part of her self-promotion. This self-image was created through a range of devices, which included portrait photography by the greats such as George Hoyningen-Huene (1900–68), Man Ray and Cecil Beaton. Furthermore, Schiaparelli's appearance in the social scene of the 1920s and 1930s, which she herself helped mould through her parties and fashion design, contributed to this reputation.

The domestic interiors of Schiaparelli's private homes played a major role in the creation of this image: interiors that this couturier orchestrated in distinctive ways. Her London and Paris homes were remarkable for their unconventional and polished interior design that brought together different strands of high-style

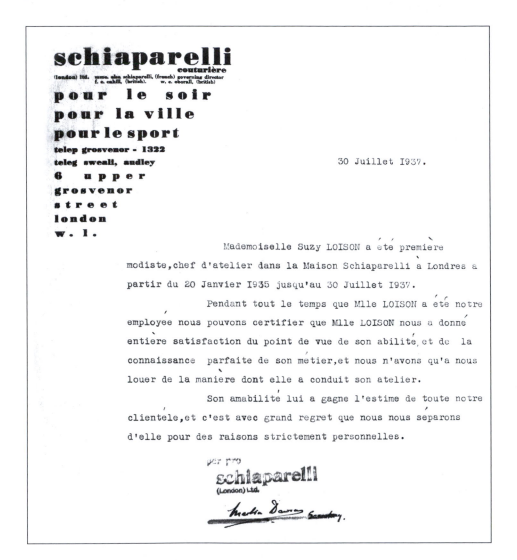

Figure 16.2   'Schiaparelli London' letterhead, July 1937. A positive reference for an employee, Suzy Loisin, 'premier modiste', and head of the workshop in the London store, 1935–1937. The stationery states that Schiaparelli designs 'for the evening, for the town, for sport'. The London boutique was at 6 Upper Grosvenor street. Note the modern gesture of the art-deco typeface and lack of capitalisation. (Courtesy Diktats bookstore.)

Figure 16.3   Schiaparelli fashion displayed at the 'Pavillon de l'Elegance' at the
Exposition internationale des arts et techniques, Paris, 1937
(vintage postcard signed on the verso by Oto Wolls). The dresses
were displayed next to naked Siegel mannequins created by Robert
Couturier. The hand of Alberto Giacometti is evident in the
modern plasterwork. The tableau demonstrates the strange
intersections of woman and nature that intrigued Schiaparelli and
features one of her typical bold floral prints that were generally
printed for her by Ducharne in Lyon. The model appears to sit
upon a three-dimensional bed of spikey flowers. (Courtesy of
Diktats bookstore)

decoration. Nonetheless, they could only have been crafted in the period before
the Second World War, a watershed that destroyed the type of theatrical and
carefree aesthetics that interwar design had celebrated. Nor are they completely
distinctive, as many of their aspects relate to other famous contemporary schemes
designed by firms such as Jansen for clients including the Duchess of Windsor
(1896–1986) (Abbott 2006: 112–17). Scholars have noted Schiaparelli's interest
in ornament, fashion as 'costume' and masquerade, and the 'culturally bizarre or
anthropologically curious aspects of adornment': themes that also recur in her
particular mode of decorating the home (Evans and Thornton 1989: 136).

Schiaparelli worked on her interior design and furniture schemes with two of
the most famous *ensembliers* of the interwar years, Frank and Stéphane Boudin of
Jansen, as well as the important illustrators and decorative painters Etienne Drian
(1885–1961) and Christian Bérard. Her work was widely known during the period,
magazines such as *Vogue* reporting on her decorative innovations. Designing a home
was central to the way Schiaparelli constructed her autobiography *Shocking Life*
(1954), an interior scheme being the site in that she dramatised even the famous

feud between herself and Coco Chanel (Charles-Roux 2005: 326–9). The spaces in which they showed the high fashions were also diametrically opposed. The drawing room of Schiaparelli's couture house on Place Vendôme, designed by Frank, included an over-size plaster shell lamp and base by Alberto Giacometti (1901–66) and a stair covered in a highly dramatic and stylised fringed and swagged curtain, that suggested the lifting of the curtain at a theatre, an invitation to view Schiaparelli's designs (Baudot 1998: 38). Chanel's famous salon de boutique, built in 1928, is generally photographed with the mirrored stairs, creating an impression of great luxury. A more 'accurate' view of the whole space reveals that the total effect was in fact industrial rather than ancien-régime, with simple basin-like chandeliers, wooden chairs and simple structural columns (Charles Roux 2005: 213). Yet Chanel always played games: her parades in the 1930s were staged with the models within a Baroque fantastical *trompe-l'oeil* frame, like a theatre fly, suggesting there might be more similarities between the two women than is sometimes supposed (British *Vogue* 1938).

Schiaparelli and Frank: Boulevard Saint Germain

Schiaparelli's first apartment on the Boulevard Saint Germain, illustrated in the *Studio Yearbook* (1931), reflected the fashion designer's close and personal collaboration with Frank. Schiaparelli shared her first 'personalised' apartment with her friend Countess 'Gab' de Robilant, a space in which Schiaparelli was able to decorate her own bedroom, drawing room, sitting room and dining corner. Schiaparelli achieved a dramatic modernist effect making use of white walls, a subdued chromatic colour scheme and Jean-Michel Frank's minimal furniture. The room included an over-sized couch in orange leather and two low armchairs in green rubber.[7] Curtains and other chair covers, Schiaparelli (1954: x) notes, 'were made of a white rubber substance that was stiff and gleaming'.[8] Schiaparelli (1954: 53) also noted wryly that the white rubber on the modernist chairs came off on the women's dresses in the heat: 'They looked like strange caricatures of the sweaters that had paid for their meal!'

This love of novel and anti-elitist materials extended to Schiaparelli's fashion design, such as her use of synthetics and Bakelite, and the room also included small lacquered black bridge tables with glass tops, which Schiaparelli used for dining. A painting by the fashionable artist Pavel Tchelitchew (1898–1957) hung over the dark marble mantel, that was decorated with a simple Frank lamp and a potted plant. White Tunisian rugs covered the floor. 'There was really nothing to it', Schiaparelli (1954: 53) later wrote, 'but the whole thing was so new and un-expected that it had charm . . . Mlle Chanel came, and at the sight of this modern furniture and black plates she shuddered as if she were passing a cemetery'. This retort to that great modernist who made little black dresses that lifted women's breasts and flattened their stomachs was designed to suggest that Chanel did not understand the avant-garde. Chanel, from a completely different social background, always surrounded herself with ancien-régime furniture and *grande luxe*.

Schiaparelli's public image was disseminated through a range of devices, and she frequently permitted the publication of photographs and drawings of herself posing in her own interiors. These images are quite different from many other contemporary photographs of highly refined sitters in their own residences, who often perch stiffly for the camera. Schiaparelli is frequently shown reclining, lying, leaning, occupying her own stylish spaces and clothes in very idiosyncratic ways. This was the case with her 1930s London apartment at 36 Upper Grosvenor Square – also decorated in the manner of Frank, if not entirely by him. A Man Ray (1890–1976) photograph of the young designer sitting curled up in a quilted-satin club chair emphasises a chaste but luxurious space in which nothing could be added or taken away. The straight-falling curtains set a modern air at a time when such window treatments were not standard for the middle and upper classes. Decorations include an over-sized spherical glass vase and dried twigs (Schiaparelli 1954: 66).

Schiaparelli and Frank again: Rue Barbet-de Jouy and Rue de Berri

Frank designed for Schiaparelli on the rue Barbet-de Jouy a spectacularly chic Paris apartment that displayed both the innovation of her own fashion design and his expert moulding of interior architecture. Schiaparelli continued with her use of novel synthetics, some of which she named herself. Such fabrics must have been truly experimental: Diana Vreeland (1903–89) is claimed to have had once had a Schiaparelli dress dissolve at the drycleaner (Beaton 1954: 185). In Schiaparelli's bedroom, the drapes, chair cover and bedspread used a blistered rayon lavender-blue fabric. Frank's rectilinear but elegant furniture and a white bear skin added a sense of luxury. Schiaparelli's love of China was indicated in the Tang-dynasty female courtier figure in a glass box on the bureau. While the arrangements were not yet 'tablescapes' in the sense of David Hicks (1928–98) and the 1960s, the way in which the couturier dispersed ornaments indicates a rigour and an interest in dissimilar forms and objects that was very modern.

The living room combined Frank's and Schiaparelli's understanding of texture and form. Leopard skin rugs and Tunisian carpets lay on the parquet floor. A wall-to-ceiling bookcase was inserted into the corner of the room and left part empty; an assertion of the minimal architectural detailing of the room. The bookcase was abutted by one of Frank's rectilinear blonde-wood secretaires, with the lamp from the previous apartment surmounting it. The real innovation was the introduction into this almost blank interior space devoid of any historical reference, of quilted-satin armchairs in the blocky form characteristic of the 1930s. Satin quilting was the height of chic in the 1930s.[9] The effect of the quilting introduced an air of luxurious informality and set off the other textures such as an azalea in a mossy terracotta pot, the type of touch not normally seen in a room of this period. A painting entitled *Bazar de l'Ocean* (1920) by surrealist artist Pierre Roy (1880–1950) rested on the mantel, underlining the air of dynamism that marks a Frank room. The inclusion of a Victorian cornucopia vase underlines the importance of this period to the style elites of England and France in the 1930s, who were rediscovering this maligned period. Indeed, Victorian devices such as mourning brooches and clasped hands as paper-weights appealed to both surrealist artists and Schiaparelli, who designed bottles for her perfumes such as Snuff – a pipe – in this mode. The decorative emphasis of the vase provided a foil to the extreme modernism of the shell of the room, in which the cornice was completely eliminated.

Schiaparelli's next dwelling was larger, grander, and set a different tone. On the rue de Berri, in a court near the Belgian Embassy, was an elegant and well-proportioned Paris townhouse, which Schiaparelli turned into a spectacular but comfortable and unpretentious space. The residence had belonged to Princesse Mathilde (1820–1904), niece of Napoleon Bonaparte and first cousin to Napoleon III, to whom Schiaparelli claimed to be related. Finding it 'a blending of Balzac, Zola, Marcel Proust, and Flaubert, the great friend of Princess Mathilde', she decided on a different approach to its interior design (Schiaparelli 1954: 101). Her autobiography notes that Boudin and Frank assisted her, and she brought the potential of their different aesthetics into a distinctive harmony. Reflecting Frank's emphasis on the chic of modest materials, the couturier noted: 'I acquired nothing merely because of its value either in money or age. Therefore the house sings with a feeling of abandon, throws its arms around you, hugs you, and whoever comes to it as a guest never wants to leave it' (Schiaparelli 1954: 101). This is a rather guileless statement, as Schiaparelli had moved away from rubber seats and stylish twigs, to embrace luxurious eighteenth- and nineteenth-century decorative objects that conferred on her the aristocratic aura to which she felt entitled.

Schiaparelli makes it very clear in her memoirs that she orchestrated the interior, casting the designers as willing collaborators: 'Jean Franck [sic] and Jansen were generous enough to help Schiap [sic] with it, though they were sometimes bewildered at the unorthodox setting of her home. As decorators they found their principles seriously disturbed' (Schiaparelli 1954: 101). Schiaparelli's use of the term 'Jansen' to describe Stéphane Boudin, President of the famous decorating firm Jansen, indicates how interchangeable the names were at this time. Cecil Beaton, who is one of the most significant popular writers and also diarist to chronicle this period (1954: 185), unkindly once again, called her 'an excellent editor of ideas'. In the absence of drawings it is difficult to assess the relative contributions.

The entrance hall marked out Schiaparelli's sense of theatricality, housing 'Mr. and Mrs. Satan', Venetian silvered nineteenth-century devil figures. She seems to have enjoyed the charge of their bodies, with the female Satan having 'a high bosom' and 'he with a pointed beard and horns' (Schiaparelli 1954: 103). They also relate to her taste for the ludic, also played out in her fashion collections such as the 'Commedia dell'Arte' (1939) and the 'Circus Collection'. Such ironic devices, which were selected to underscore an understanding of the more perverse aspects of Victorian decorative arts, were quite common among the stylist community of England and France. They are the types of objects preferred by eccentric aesthetes such as Stephen Tennant (1906–87), whose Wilsford Manor in Wiltshire, decorated with Syrie Maugham (1879–1955) from the mid-1930s, was a shrine to perversity, incorporating both fine and deliberately tacky effects and layered decoration; and Beaton, who slept at Ashcombe House, the Wiltshire Georgian property that he rented until the end of the Second World War in a painted 'circus' bed amidst what Stephen Calloway defined as 'comic Baroque' (see Calloway 1988: 280–81 on Tennant, 282 on Beaton). For her dress designs

Schiaparelli made extensive use of printed silk textiles by Ducharne, Lyon, with motifs including clasped hands and pierced arrows, sheaves of wheat and kissing doves, clearly derived from mid- to late nineteenth-century designs.[10]

Schiaparelli's library went through several incarnations and is spectacular for its tightly controlled drama, use of over-scale objects and reference to the French neo-classical tradition. Its arrangement of furniture in sparse and elegant groupings recalls the work of Jansen for the Duchess of Windsor around the same time.[11] Chinoiserie tapestry designed by the eighteenth-century artist François Boucher surrounded the mantel, and it is claimed that Schiaparelli had them cut to fit the space. The subject of this tapestry, Chinese courtiers listening to music in a tented outdoor space, echoed the genuine Tang figures that sat next to the textile, and must also have augmented the merriment of the room. Exoticism was underlined in the inclusion of a mounted elephant tusk, mannerist wood-turned and ivory spheres, silver-mounted coconuts, silver guinea fowl, and a Victorian automaton bird-cage.[12] The confluence of social class, collecting, home-decorating and design choice is understudied. Daniel J. Sherman (2004: 770) proposes that the proposition of 'home' can 'through either the actual or the vicarious arrangement of objects' point to themes such as 'authenticity, adventure, or liberation'. He points here to the concept of 'association' that developed around the strategies of the decorator Andree Putman in the French publication *L'Oeil* circa 1960. It seems that Schiaparelli (2004: 777) prefigures some of these approaches of *ratissage*, or 'combing' through goods, a colloquial term linked to anthropology and collecting.

The library included an eccentric divan that Schiaparelli described as shaped like a piano, 'upholstered in red, and two people can lie on it facing each other with a tray in between' (Blum 2003: 102). It was like an enormous low bed covered sometimes in a simple fur, sometimes leopard, and was a decidedly erotic introduction to the room. Schiaparelli's use of fur also related to trends in surrealist art practice, which valued the tactile and sensual charge of animal skins. At home, Schiaparelli did not embrace the more extreme effects of surrealist-derived furniture design, some of which were responses to her fashion design. The famous 'Mae West Lips' sofa, designed by Salvador Dali (1904–89) in several versions in 1938 and based on the artist's *The Birth of Paranoiac Furniture* 1934–5, was covered in Schiaparelli's trademark 'shocking pink' satin or felt.[13] Versions of the sofa were retailed with Frank, and Schiaparelli placed an order for a pair. For some reason the order was not delivered to her, but this is not altogether surprising, as none of her homes made use of markedly eccentric furniture.

Schiaparelli's first version of the drawing room was spare and elegant. There was none of the clutter of Chanel's apartment at the rue Cambon. By the hearth were two large tin-glazed leopards rampant. Schiaparelli posed for a photograph with Etienne Drian lying on the floor next to the leopards, which appear to paw her shoulder in a 1950s picture with Drian. The artful composition of this photograph aligns the head of the leopard with 'Schiap', Drian, and the figures in a screen.[14] This screen was a famous feature of the room and depicted melancholy subjects painted by Christian Bérard in the romantic surrealist mode that he also employed in retail design, advertising, scarf and textile design.[15] An Empire mantel with massive acanthus console supports anchored the room, and was surmounted by a handsome garniture of Paris or Berlin ceramics of the 1820s and a glass dome in the taste of the 1830s. The inclusion of this dome, the type that contained wax flowers in Restoration France, is significant, as it is this form that Schiaparelli adopted for her famous fragrance 'Shocking', introduced in 1937, in a bottle designed by the surrealist Léonor Fini (1907–96) and based on the mannequin of Mae West that Schiaparelli was using to design the actress's costumes for *Every Day's a Holiday* (1937).[16] The perfume bottle consisted of a dressmaker's dummy, a tape measure around the waist fastened with a button marked as 'S'. The stopper was surrounded by porcelain flowers. The bottle was then sat in a dome, very mid-Victorian in effect.

Drian's painting of Schiaparelli lounging at home allow us to get a sense of the vivid colours that she used in both this interior and her fashion design. A bergère covered in yellow cloth abuts a group of pink Chinese ceramics; a counterpoint to the ice-green armchair on the other side of the mantle. The late nineteenth-century gilded double-divan or tête-à-tête sings with a scarlet cushion, and suggests intimate conversations with Schiaparelli. The Victorian form of this divan was popularised in *Every Day's a Holiday*, and Jansen also made up such a piece for the Duchess of Windsor's elegant ice-blue bedroom at 4 route du Champs d'Entraînement. The point to be made here is that what might appear today to be conventional decoration might have had ludic associations at the time. Chinese or Persian bronze deer nudge from one corner, rather similar to the sculpted animals that Chanel also deployed in her famous salon on rue Cambon.

The later incarnation of Schiaparelli's drawing room is fleshed out with a denser arrangement of decorative objects, including the favoured object, a Tang statuette of a courtly lady. The room also included a Louis XVI fall-front secrétaire, a practical Anglo-Indian caned armchair and a Swedish or Russian neo-classical chandelier. Schiaparelli also later filled the room with paintings such as her earlier favourite *Bazar de l'Ocean* (1920) by Pierre Roy and candy-coloured portraits of herself in carnival costume by Marcel Vertès (1895–1961) propped on her elegant pastel chairs. Plaster shells by Giacometti, which delighted viewers for their subterfuge in appearing like a real bleached object from the ocean, appear in numerous images of these rooms over the years. Marisa Berenson (born 1946) recalled seeing her grandmother 'sitting on that sofa . . . dressed in her Chinese kimonos in amazing colors and wonderful jewelry' (Menkes 1994: 255).

Subverting bourgeois convention once again, Schiaparelli (1954: 102) described her bedroom at rue de Berri as 'small and quite plain', but provided herself with a bathroom that was 'enormous and very comfortable'. Once again this thoughtful designer prioritised the pleasures of modern life – relaxing, bathing, making up the body.

Schiaparelli held dinner parties in all rooms of her house, but formal parties were staged in the dining room. The dining room referred to the French decorative arts of the 1860s, the voluptuous and fabulously wealthy Third Empire period. It included chintz curtains in the Louis XV-revival style of this period, probably a new document print on a light ground that made it appear more contemporary. The enormous curtains, which filled a large bay window, were garnished with a thick bullion fringe picked up on the opposite wall in enormous *passementerie* tassels surmounting a painting of a canal in Venice. Gilded Louis-XV or rococo-revival balloon-back chairs surrounded a simple directoire mahogany circular table in the

English taste. The most striking aspect of the room was two enormous *lampadaires*, enormous free-standing lustres lit by candlelight as well as electricity.

Conclusion

Schiaparelli's decorative enterprises show how the work of Frank and Jansen was a flexible spatial envelope for modern living, as patrons could scale up the decoration to suit their lifestyle and collecting habits. The distinguished historian of interior design, John Cornforth (1987: 120–21), has noted that although in the future Boudin 'will appear as significant even as that of his clients' for his gift of being able 'to give expression and form' to the way in which his clients wanted to live, the taste of the international transatlantic rich was driven by patrons who wanted an eighteenth-century French background 'tempered by a 20th-century desire for lightness and ease as well as an insistence on American comfort'.

Many of these patrons might have not had any pre-established aesthetic vision. Yet, a small but important number had strong views. Among them were a number of artists and fashion designers such as Schiaparelli. The rigid boundaries between design and fashion, between innovative dress materials and similarly innovative fabric for upholstery, between composition on a mannequin and composition of spaces and objects in interiors are here atomised. The 'fashion arts' acted as one unit and also a *unicum* with collaborations across media. Schiaparelli made of her life and personal space a tangible proof of an integrated aesthetic project, yet she has been so far remembered only for her contribution to dressmaking. However, in a passage reminiscent of Elsie de Wolfe (1865?–1950), Schiaparelli (1954: 102) informed her readers that 'extravagance consists principally in the colours and the unexpected setting', and she related her use of yellow and pink tablecloths embroidered in gold from Tunisia for dining. Schiaparelli's work captured both a love of the exotic shell and a much higher artistic reference to the surrealist fascination in openings and closings.[17]

Schiaparelli's fashion did not survive wartime change, and in 1954 the fashion house was declared bankrupt and shifted some of its operations to North America. Yet her aesthetic project did not finish. She continued with a more private set of concerns. Schiaparelli re-worked her famous white and gold library in the 1950s, engaging the colour effects popularised by a designer of the 1960s generation, David Hicks. In a photograph from *House & Garden*, August 1951, the room now held jewel-like plum satin sofas strewn with leopard skin, probably the same ones that had once adorned the floor in her 1930s apartment, a Baltic fringed chandelier, and gilded pennons and sheaves of wheat above the bookshelves (Calloway 1988: 319).

While Schiaparelli's dresses and couture creations have been carefully preserved for the enjoyment of posterity, her Paris townhouse and garden have been gutted. While her fashion creations are now proudly part of history of fashion and shown in exhibitions about surrealist and haute couture design, her wider intellectual, visual and 'life' project has been neglected. As for many other creators of fashion, these links have been frequently severed, and posthumous biographies have been narrowly focused on the business of fashion. Schiaparelli's glamour lives on in the figure of her granddaughter, the fashion model and Hollywood actress Marisa Berenson. In the

Figure 16.4   Boutique de Schiaparelli, place Vendôme, Paris, showing the over-
sized gilded faux-metal bamboo cage by Alberto Giacometti for
Jean-Michel Frank, its interior designer (photograph signed André
Ostier, circa 1950). Perfume was displayed in the cage amidst fake
birds as well as live models and wax mannequins wearing fashions.
(Courtesy of Diktats bookstore)

1970s Berenson, her sister Berinthia (Beri) (1948–2001) and her friend shoe designer Manolo Blahnik (born 1942) dreamed of re-opening the famous Place Vendôme boutique of Schiaparelli with its giant gilded cage designed by Frank, but the plan could not be realised (McNeil 2007). Perhaps the project belonged to the past rather than the 1970s, from a period of particular artistic interchange and optimistic whimsy that was lost with the horror of the Second World War.

Acknowledgements

With thanks to Martin Kamer, Switzerland; the gentlemen at Diktats Bookstore, and our indefatigable research assistant, Dr Masafumi Monden.

Notes

1 Aspects of this essay have appeared in Peter McNeil, 'Fashion Houses', in Peter McNeil and Louise Wallenberg (eds), *Nordic Fashion Studies*, Stockholm, Axl Books, 2012, pp. 245–70. *See also* McNeil's review essay of '*The Stylemakers: Minimalism and Classic-Modernism 1915–45*, Mo Amelia Teitelbaum', Philip Wilson Publishers, 2011, *Journal of Design History*, vol. 26(2) 222–224.

2 Similar experimentation with 'poor' materials also took place in fashion in the 1930s, as in the case of shoe-designer Salvatore Ferragamo's use of straw and candy wrappers in response to a lack of precious materials.

3 On Elsie de Wolfe and Nancy Lancaster, see: Nina Campbell and Caroline Seebohm, *Elsie de Wolfe. A Decorative Life* (London: Aurum Press, 1993); Penny Sparke, *Elsie De Wolfe: The Birth of Modern Interior Decoration* (New York: Acanthus Press, 2005); Robert Becker, *Nancy Lancaster: Her Life, her Work, her Art* (New York: Alfred A. Knopf, 1996); Martin Wood, *Nancy Lancaster: English Country House* (London: Frances Lincoln, 2005).

4 Well known is the photo of Frank's private office in which an ashtray of butts stands in for the absent designer. See Stephen Calloway, *Twentieth-Century Decoration* (London: Thames & Hudson, 1988), p. 272.

5 Works on Elsa Schiaparelli include: *Hommage à Elsa Schiaparelli*, exh. cat. (Paris: Musée de la mode et du Costume, 1984); Palmer White, *Elsa Schiaparelli: Empress of Fashion* (London: Aurum Press, 1985); Dilys E. Blum, *Shocking! The Art and Fashion of Elsa Schiaparelli* (Philadelphia: Philadelphia Museum of Art, 2003); François Baudot, Elsa *Schiaparelli* (London: Thames & Hudson, 1997); *Surreal Things: Surrealism and Design*, exh. cat. (London: Victoria and Albert Museum, 2007).

6 For an accessible range of these images see Baudot, *Elsa Schiaparelli*, pp. 16 ff.

7 Dilys Blum notes that the same colour scheme of white, orange, yellow, green and black was used by Frank to decorate Schiaparelli's next apartment at the rue Barbet-de-Jouy. Blum, *Shocking!*, p. 36

8 The book has been more recently re-published as *Shocking life: The Autobiography of Elsa Schiaparelli* (London: V&A, 2007).

9 It was used by patrons as diverse as Henry Francis du Pont at Winterthur in Delaware, and by Jansen for the Duke and Duchess of Windsor's residence at 24 boulevard Suchet, Paris, in 1938. James Archer Abbott, *Jansen* (New York: Acanthus

Press, 2006), p. 112. Bianchini made quilted satin especially for Schiaparelli's couture collection, and George Hoyningen-Huene photographed her wearing such an ensemble for *Vogue*, November 1933. Blum, *Shocking!*, p. 65.

10   Ducharne folios for Schiaparelli, late 1930s-1940, private collection, Switzerland

11   The *salon* at boulevard Suchet is illustrated in Abbott, *Jansen*, p. 115.

12   The theme of the bird-cage appealed to her: it appeared in the Boutique in Paris and another larger one stood in her private dining room.

13   Several versions of these were made: a pair is owned by the Trustees of the Edward James Foundation (UK), but covered in red felt; another version in pink satin was made by Green & Abbott, London, with a wood carcass, now on loan to the Victoria and Albert Museum in London; another is in two tones of pink felt (Brighton Museum and Art Gallery). Frank included one in the Screening Room of the residence of Baron de l'Espée, La Muette. See Calloway, *Twentieth-Century Decoration*, p. 275; and Nicola Coleby (ed.) *A Surreal Life: Edward James, 1907–1984* (London: Philip Wilson Publishers, 1998), p. 50.

14   A similar screen by Bérard hung in her boutique, in which figures including the *saltimbanque* peer out from and seem to lift a fringed red curtain that surrounds objects by Giacometti.

15   Frank and Bérard regularly collaborated in schemes, such as the Guerlain Institute, Paris (1939), which included a spectacular *trompe l'oeil boiserie* and ceiling *trumeau* made of elegantly torn ribbons in black on a yellow ground, the ribbons masquerading as the type of sketch-like paint used in interwar illustration and scenography. Such an effect can be related to Schiaparelli's iconic dress design for a torn and shredded dress, inspired by Salvador Dali, in which both real flayed fabric and printed effects confuse the viewer about what is fictive and real, what is inside and outside. 'Violence and eroticism are simultaneously displayed and made to disappear'. See Evans and Thornton, *Women and Fashion*, p. 139.

16   Blum, *Shocking!*, p. 115.

17   *Vogue* illustrated and described the dining room thus: 'he has so many houses and apartments that one can't keep up with them. I hope she has kept that giant clam-shell table. . ., a fantastic affair made of a giant Philippine shell mounted on a gilt-bronze base. She fills the shell with ice and champagne bottles when she entertains'. 'Conversation about Decoration', *Vogue* (USA), 15 October 1939, pp. 56–7.

References

Abbott, J. A. (2006) *Jansen*, New York: Acanthus Press.

Baudot, F. (1997) Elsa *Schiaparelli*, London: Thames & Hudson.

——(1998) *Jean-Michel Frank*, Paris: Assouline.

Beaton, C. (1954) *The Glass of Fashion*, London: Cassell.

Becker, R. (1996) *Nancy Lancaster: Her Life, her Work, her Art*, New York: Alfred A. Knopf.

Blum, D. E. (2003) *Shocking! The Art and Fashion of Elsa Schiaparelli*, Philadelphia: Philadelphia Museum of Art.

Calloway, S. (1988) *Twentieth-Century Decoration*, London: Thames & Hudson.

Campbell, N. and Seebohm, C. (1993) *Elsie de Wolfe. A Decorative Life*, London: Aurum Press.

Charles-Roux, E. (2005) *Chanel and Her World*, New York: Vendome Press.

Coleby, N. (ed.) (1998) *A Surreal Life: Edward James, 1907–1984*, London: Philip Wilson Publishers.

Cornforth, J. (1987) 'The Duke and Duchess of Windsor's House in Paris', *Country Life*, 25 June: 120–25.

Evans, C. and Thornton, M. (1989) *Women and Fashion: A New Look*, London: Quartet.

Felski, R. (2011) 'Afterword', in I. Parkins and E. M. Sheehan (eds), *Cultures of Femininity in Modern Fashion*, Durham: University of New Hampshire Press: 231–8.

McNeil, P. (2007) 'Posture. Manolo Blahnik, Shoe designer. Interview.', ACNE Papers, Stockholm: ACNE Creative, 44–5.

——(2012) 'Fashion Houses', in P. McNeil and L. Wallenberg (eds), *Nordic Fashion Studies*, Stockholm, Axl Books: pp. 245–70.

Martin-Vivier, P. (2008) *Jean-Michel Frank: The Strange and Subtle Luxury of the Parisian Haute-Monde in the Art Deco Period*, New York: Rizzoli.

Menkes, S. (1994) 'Fashion Legends: Elsa Schiaparelli. Shocking Life on the rue de Berri in Paris', *Architectural Digest*, October: 252–7.

Musée de la mode et du Costume (1984) *Hommage à Elsa Schiaparelli* exh. cat. Paris.

Sanchez, L. D. (1997 [1980]) *Jean-Michel Frank. Adolphe Chanaux*, trans. J. D. Edwards, Paris: Éditions du Regard, 2nd edn.

Schiaparelli, E. (1954) *Shocking Life*, London: J. M. Dent & Sons.

——(2007) *Shocking life: The Autobiography of Elsa Schiaparelli*, London: V&A.

Sherman, D. J. (2004) 'Post-Colonial Chic: Fantasies of the French Interior 1957–62', *Art History*, 27: 5, November, pp. 770–805.

Sparke, P. (2005) *Elsie De Wolfe: The Birth of Modern Interior Decoration*, New York: Acanthus Press.

Teitelbaum, M. A. (2010) *The Stylemakers: Minimalism and Classic-Modernism, 1915–45*, London: Philip Wilson.

Victoria and Albert Museum, (2007) *Surreal Things: Surrealism and Design*, exh. cat. London.

White, P. (1985) *Elsa Schiaparelli: Empress of Fashion*, London: Aurum Press.

Wilson, E. (2004) 'Magic Fashion', *Fashion Theory*, 8, 4: 375–86.

Wood, M. (2005) *Nancy Lancaster: English Country House*, London: Frances Lincoln.

Vogue (UK) (1938) 'Scene at the Collections', March 1938, n.p.

Vogue (USA) (1939) 'Conversation about Decoration', 15 October 1939, pp. 56–7.

Chapter 17

Stella Bruzzi

THE PINK SUIT

O N THE MORNING OF 22 NOVEMBER 1963 Jacqueline Kennedy, First Lady to the 35th President of the United States, was prevaricating over what to wear for an impending visit to Dallas, Texas while her husband quipped in front of a breakfast crowd at the Chamber of Commerce, Fort Worth:

> Two years ago I introduced myself in Paris by saying that I was the man who accompanied Mrs Kennedy to Paris. I am getting somewhat that same sensation as I travel around Texas. Why is it that nobody wonders what Lyndon and I will be wearing?
>
> (Kelley 1978: 200)

Minutes later, the President's wife emerged in the Chez Ninon pink wool suit she would then wear for the fatal open-topped motorcade ride through Dallas. The image on the cover of the November 1963 commemorative issue of *Life* Magazine carries a close-up photograph in 'vibrant colour' (Lubin 2003: 115) of Jack and Jackie Kennedy prior to the president's assassination, arriving at Dallas' Love Field airfield:

> The Kennedys look tall and vibrant. They come so close to the photographic plane that they seem within our reach, giants among us . . . the photograph has the formal density of a carefully constructed painting. It is filled with intriguing visual symmetries and repetitions.
>
> (Lubin 2003: 115, 117)

For all the wrong reasons, Jackie's elegant pink wool suit rapidly became universally recognisable, the quintessential, blood-spattered relic of the assassination, withheld from public view in the National Archives.

This is an essay about authenticity, re-enactment and the afterlife of an object that, while it has been endlessly copied and reproduced, exists more as a fantasy object, a nostalgic trigger to memories of trauma and collective loss. Jackie Kennedy's iconic pink suit was itself a copy – albeit, according to recent versions of the story, an authorised New York-made copy – of a Chanel original. Whether or not the emblematic pink suit originated in France or the US is important because of Mrs Kennedy's politically unhelpful attachment to Parisian couture. When, in 1959, her Senator husband declared himself a candidate for the presidency, and especially once he had been elected president the following year, Jackie's personal style became a focus of national interest. Her preference for French fashion drew some unwelcome media attention, although she became wise to the political importance of dressing down while campaigning. In September 1960, editor of *Women's Wear Daily* John Fairchild received a cable concerning Kennedy purchases of Paris couture and, 'after checking every Paris couture house', found that Jackie Kennedy and her mother-in-law Rose were important private customers of, among others, Chanel, Dior, Lanvin, Cardin, Givenchy and Balenciaga (Fairchild quoted in Picardie 2011: 300). These and other reports caused Pat Nixon, wife of Kennedy's Republican opponent in 1960 to publicly defend US designers and shed doubt on Mrs Kennedy's patriotism. These pressures ultimately led Jacqueline Kennedy, once she had become First Lady, to entrust French-born but US-based designer, Oleg Cassini, with coordinating much of her 'official' wardrobe, starting with the long ivory satin gown she wore to her husband's inauguration.

During her White House years of 1960–63, Mrs Kennedy's predilection for Paris couture was carefully stage-managed; largely suppressed for US functions but allowed to resurface, for instance, when she accompanied her husband on a state visit to Paris in 1961. Among the many couture clothes she took to France for this visit was the elegant ivory silk evening dress designed by Hubert de Givenchy, embroidered by Hurel with silk floss, silk ribbon and seed pearls that she wore to the official dinner at the Palace at Versailles, hosted by President and Mdm. De Gaulle. The benefits of being accompanied to Paris by his couture-obsessed wife were not lost on President Kennedy who joked at a press luncheon in Paris in June 1961 (and as referenced in Fort Worth two years later): 'I do not think it entirely inappropriate to introduce myself to this audience. I am the man who accompanied Jacqueline Kennedy to Paris, and I have enjoyed it.'[1] Criticisms of her extravagances, however, meant that, on other occasions, Jackie felt compelled to mask her patronage of Parisian fashion houses (much as she also successfully hid her chain-smoking from public view) by openly championing their stateside imitators: the Manhattan boutique A La Carte, or Chez Ninon, established by Nona Park and Sophie Shonnard in the late 1920s. As the catalogue accompanying the 2001–2 John F. Kennedy museum exhibition *Jacqueline Kennedy: The White House Years* noted: 'Through Chez Ninon Jacqueline Kennedy acquired clothing that was legitimately made in America, although designed in Paris' (Bowles 2001: 31). Jacqueline Kennedy was no stranger, therefore, to the art of copying.

Exemplified by the series of multi-image portraits of Jackie Andy Warhol produced in the immediate aftermath of the assassination is the notion that there was never only one Jackie, but several. Like all icons, Jacqueline Kennedy was public property; but even after she became Jackie Onassis, even in death, her public image was shot through with nostalgia for the White House years, forever associated with JFK, 'Camelot' and the gruesome finale in Dallas 1963. After her death in 1994, much of the press coverage leap-frogged the more recent past and was accompanied (see, for example the cover of *Life* Magazine) by images of her when married to Jack Kennedy. This formal Jackie image of the 1960 to 1963 era, however, often looked as if it was such a strain to maintain: the awkwardness of being the couture-adorned wife was frequently palpable, epitomised by the disconcertingly asymmetrical bouffant hairstyle and the primly unadventurous red Chez Ninon suit she donned for *A Tour of the White House with Mrs John F. Kennedy*. This much fetishised televised tour of the newly decorated presidential residence was broadcast by CBS and NBC on St Valentine's Day, 14 February 1962 (and repeated the following night) and was reputedly watched by three out of four US television viewers. As here, Jackie Kennedy's White House years were characterised by formal glamour and conservative chic. Although she was an influential fashion leader, in the many images of her performing official duties her clothes become barriers shielding her from onlookers, particularly the stiffly structured, sculpted designs of her Oleg Cassini gowns. Rather than follow the contours of her body, her formal clothes (for all her love of couture) sit seemingly in conflict with them: the official clothes wear her, not vice versa. In his extraordinary gushing tribute *Jackie Under My Skin: Interpreting an Icon*, life-long fan Wayne Koestenbaum argues that

> We called Jackie an icon because her image was frequently and influentially reproduced, and because, even when she was alive, she seemed more mythic than real.
>
> (Koestenbaum 1995: 10)

However hard it is to imagine the average early 1960s US housewife 'reproducing' one of Jackie's Chanel knock-offs, an essential component of Jackie's iconic aloofness and unknowableness was her armoury of gleaming formal clothes.

The relationship between Jackie Kennedy and her clothes altered irreversibly on 22 November 1963. The pink wool Chez Ninon suit she wore on that day – though seldom featured in articles and books about her style and fashion – is the outfit for that she is best remembered. A tasteless and/or naive exception to this rule is the book of 'John F. Kennedy and his Family' cut out dolls, available for purchase at, among other places, the Sixth Floor Museum in Dallas, dedicated to the assassination. Here, a pristine and unbloodied pink suit – offset by the bouquet of red roses presented to her at Dallas Love Field – is included as Mrs Kennedy's final paper outfit (Tierney 1990: Plate 15). The First Lady had worn the pink suit several times between 1961 and 1963, and it was reputedly at her husband's request that she then wore the outfit for the visit to Texas. The suit is still central to how the assassination is remembered, despite – or maybe because of – the way in which its vibrant colour jars with the day's tragic violence. This collision between bright and gloom is crystallised in the 8 mm home movie footage of the assassination: local dressmaker Abraham Zapruder's flickering 26.6 seconds of colour Kodachrome film that accidentally captured the moment Kennedy was shot. The mere mention of 'the Zapruder film', art historian John Beck suggests, 'is enough to call up an entire range of pictorial and cultural connotations' including the First Lady's

> pink outfit clashing with the luminous flat green in the background, the fierce black and chrome of the limousines flashing in the Dallas sun, the shock of red from the President's head.
>
> (Beck 2005: 183)

Alongside the anomalous vividness of the Zapruder film sits the complex history of the suit itself. The colour of the suit and how it chimed with the redness of the roses presented to Mrs Kennedy on her arrival at Love Field featured in many news reports from 22 November. In *Report* (1963–67), Bruce Conner's experimental collage junk film focused on the assassination, the cheery voices of the local news reporters recounting Mrs Kennedy's radiance as she arrived at Love Field overlays both archive images of that arrival and images from later in the day, after the president has been killed. The juxtaposition between the blandness of the live news reports describing the bouquet with an image, for example, of the same bouquet abandoned, a short time later, on the back seat of the presidential limousine, adds complexity and intellectual distance to the more straightforward poignancy of the film's repeated images of Jackie Kennedy leaving Parkland Hospital with her husband's coffined body. The pink suit remains one of the most consistent signifiers of that day, though its meaning altered irrevocably in the few seconds it took to kill JFK.

The First Lady notoriously refused to take off her blood-soaked suit, standing beside Lyndon Baines Johnson in it, as he is sworn in aboard Air Force One, and emerging, still unchanged, from the aircraft in Washington hours later. Jackie's secretary Mary Gallagher, who was also in charge of her wardrobe, recalls how, outside the operating theatre in Parkland Hospital, Jackie stood waiting 'for word of her husband, whose blood had just been shed into her lap, staining her suit, legs and shoes' (Gallagher 1969: 289), refusing to change in order to 'let them see what they've done'.[2] The blood is clearly visible in photographs and newsreel, and Lady Bird Johnson recalls:

> I looked at her. Mrs Kennedy's dress was stained with blood . . . and her right glove was caked, it was caked with blood – her husband's blood. Somehow that was one of the most poignant sights – that immaculate woman, exquisitely dressed, and caked in blood.
>
> (cited in Lubin 2003: 196)

When, upon her return to the White House shortly before 5 a.m. on 23 November, Mrs Kennedy did finally take off the pink suit, her maid Provi placed it in a box, which was then passed to Jackie's mother, who inscribed 'November 22, 1963' on its lid before storing it in the attic of her Georgetown home, beside her daughter's ivory silk taffeta wedding dress. The suit was subsequently bequeathed by Caroline Kennedy to the National Archives (that also has the jacket, shirt and tie JFK was wearing when he was shot) and now resides in a vault in Maryland, uncleaned and preserved at a temperature between 65°F and 68°F and 40 percent humidity, shielded from light and to be kept from public view – at Caroline's request – until 2103.

Jackie's attire for the trip to Dallas remains a site of symbolic conflict, the place where the clash between the gentility of the House of Chanel, the suit's vibrant colour and the violence and gore of the assassination collide. As Justine Picardie argues, 'Whatever else died with Kennedy's assassination, the Chanel suit survived, a shred of visible evidence from a split second when history was made, even as it appeared to fall apart' (Picardie 2011: 306). The dried blood clearly visible when Jackie disembarked from Air Force One in Washington ensured that the dreadful stains would not be forgotten. It is often said that on that day in Dallas 'time stood still', that 'innocence died that day', that this was 'the end of Camelot'. The death of Kennedy – alongside all its attendant artefacts, including the pink suit – represents a moment of transition, loss and closure; it also offers up a momentous redefinition of the real. As Steve Seid, in an essay about Ant Farm and T.R. Uthco's video art film about the assassination, *The Eternal Frame* (1976), wrote:

> What could be considered our nation's first official snuff film, the Zapruder footage, in a mere handful of frames, encapsulated the loss of the real. Of course, this was loss was itself real – a visualized tragedy, demanding that you avert your gaze from both the death and the unknowability of death.
>
> (Seid, 2004: 32)

In *The Eternal Frame*, Doug Hall (a member of T.R. Uthco, a group of San Francisco artists) plays the 'Artist-President' – a performative, ironic rendition of President Kennedy, who (in the mid-1970s) is still alive but, as he explains during a televised address at the start of the video:

> Like all other presidents in recent years, I am, in reality, only another face on your screens. I am, in reality, only another link in that chain of pictures, that makes up the sum total of information accessible to us all as Americans.

This speech continues over the image of Hall in front of a mirror making himself up to be JFK, stating that 'the content of the image I present is no different from the image itself' and that since him/JFK 'no president can ever be more than an image, and no image can ever be in the past, or could ever be in the future, anything but dead'. In *The Eternal Frame*, Kennedy's 'image-death' as Hall refers to it also causes the demise of any naive belief in the real.

Discussing the later impact of Nixon and Watergate on 'the impossibility of rediscovering an absolute level of the real' (1994: 19), Jean Baudrillard in *Simulacra and Simulation*, returns to the day Kennedy was shot, arguing:

> All previous presidents pay for and continue to pay for Kennedy's murder as if they were the ones who have suppressed it – which is true phantasmatically, if not in fact. They must efface this defect and

> this complicity with their simulated murder. Because, now it can only
> be simulated . . . The Kennedys died because they incarnated some-
> thing: the political, political substance, whereas the new presidents are
> nothing but caricatures and fake film – curiously, Johnson, Nixon, Ford
> all have the simian mug, the monkeys of power.
>
> (Baudrillard 1994: 23–4)

Baudrillard likewise dates the death of the real to the events in Dallas on 22
November 1963, suggesting (in contradistinction to *The Eternal Frame*) that the
Kennedys (i.e. Jack and later Bobby) were substantial, whereas politicians who
followed were mere simulations. Baudrillard, like many others, over-idealises the
'long gone' pre-JFK era when 'those who died' (such as 'James Dean, Marilyn
Monroe, and the Kennedys'), 'really died simply because they had a mythic dimension that implies death' (Baudrillard 2004: 24), going on to maintain that history
became 'our lost referential' as we felt the 'death pangs of the real' and entered,
post-Second World War and Cold War, 'an age of simulation' (Ibid: 43).

There exist numerous paradoxes and contradictions when it comes to discussing
and defining the impact on representation and history of John Kennedy and the
early 1960s more generally, all of which impinge on the possible conceptualisation
of the symbolic importance of Mrs Kennedy's pink suit. One such contradiction
is that, while many commentators argue for the assassination of 1963 as the moment
when reality died and falsity or performativity took over, others associate the death
of the real with Kennedy's rise, not with his death. JFK was, from the start of
his career, all about image: his privileged childhood was immortalised in hours of
home movie footage; he was the first television era US president, whose charismatic
appearances in the televised debates against Richard Nixon are widely credited
with having helped him grind out a narrow victory in 1960; he comprehended the
value of image and participated willingly in two key direct cinema documentaries:
Primary and *Crisis: Behind a Presidential Commitment*. Writing presciently before
Kennedy's death, Norman Mailer, for example, said of Kennedy that:

> He is not a father, nor a god, not a god-figure, nor an institution, nor
> a symbol. He is in fact – permit the literary conceit – a metaphor
> . . . Jack Kennedy is somewhat more and considerably less after all than
> a hero or a villain – he is also an empty vessel, a man of many natures,
> not all of them necessarily rooted in granite.
>
> (Mailer 1967: 168, 169)

Jack Kennedy's 'genius' according to Mailer, was to recognise the immense cultural
importance of the movies (Ibid: 169), while Mailer's genius was to view Kennedy
as a palimpsest, an empty slate onto which we could inscribe our fantasies and
whose 'magnetism is that he offers us a mirror of ourselves' (Ibid: 170).

A crucial element in this discussion of the pink suit and the disintegration
of 'the real' around the time of Kennedy's assassination is Jackie's survival.
Warhol produced multiple images of Jackie (sourced largely from issues of *Life*
from around the time of the assassination) in response to the media blitz that
followed John Kennedy's death and 'the way the television and radio were

programming everybody to feel so sad'.[3] Warhol's series of Jackie silk screens functioned as metaphors for how the media successfully reached an unparalleled number of people in the immediate aftermath of the assassination; the series also highlighted the fact of Jackie's survival, and that her continued presence would inevitably inflect future re-enactments of the assassination. To re-enact a person or an event entails both acknowledging that the gap between past and present is unbridgeable, while simultaneously bringing the dead past 'back to life'. A re-enactment's ambivalence is crucial, as is maintaining and signalling the distinction between re-enactment and its original iteration.[4] It seems fundamental to all re-enactments of the Kennedy assassination that the performative copy never becomes interchangeable with the 'real' object of study, for as Bill Nichols implies, if the difference goes unrecognised, 'the question of deceit arises' (Nichols 2008: 73) – although I am more concerned with ignorance or lack of knowledge than with downright 'deceit'.

The gap between iteration and reiteration, enactment and re-enactment is a significant void, and one that I term 'approximation'.[5] The JFK assassination has spawned multiple re-enactments, from the FBI and Secret Service visit to Dallas on 24 May 1964 at the behest of the Warren Commission 'to determine as precisely as possible what happened' and 'to simulate the conditions that existed at the assassination scene on November 22'.[6] Dramatic simulations almost invariably involve the pink suit and someone taking the part of Jacqueline Kennedy, as she sat beside her husband during the fatal motorcade ride. All such versions of the pink suit, however, are inherently approximate. In spite of the importance of detachment and gaps to re-enactment, 'approximation' as a term encapsulates both distance and proximity: that an event and its re-enactments or echoes cannot be collapsed into each other, even if they help us in getting closer to the truth or to gather evidence. If something is 'approximate', even in the most ventriloquist examples, it can be mistaken for or similar to but never precisely be the same as the object it resembles. While approximation ultimately questions the very notion of originality or authenticity, Nichols posits that the re-enactment 'forfeits its indexical bond to the original event' and 'draws its fantasmatic power from this very fact' as it will never cease to be an uncanny 'repetition of what remains historically unique. A spectre haunts the text' (Nichols 2008: 74). He goes on to make the crucial observation that re-enactment is enjoyable, as 'pleasure flows from an act of imaginary engagement in which the subject knows that this act stands for a prior act, or event, with which it is not one' (Ibid: 76). Approximations or re-enactments are both propelled by the *frisson* of recognition: of knowing a film's or a drama's point of reference, while also being able to recognise that the reconstruction and its point of reference are not equivalents. It is into this gap that we insert our desires, convictions and opinions.

The pink suit has been imitated, Jackie Kennedy approximated and the assassination re-enacted many times. There are waxwork models of the ex-First Lady in pallid renditions of her Chanel knock-off, Jackie Barbie dolls and individuals, male and female, who dress up in versions of what she wore on 22 November 1963, as in the film *The House of Yes* (Mark Waters, 1997) in which Parker Posey plays an unbalanced woman who thinks she is 'Jackie O'. As I write, if you type 'Jackie Kennedy Onassis Costume – 60s Pink Suit' into your Internet search box, you can buy yourself a decent-looking 'Deluxe "Jackie in Dallas"' copy for $189.99, albeit one that uses black as opposed to blue trim and is still erroneously described as having been designed by Elsa Schiaparelli. The pink suit remains the subject of countless blogs and fashion websites, some of which trace the influence of Jackie's pink suit but most of which simply recount its by now over-familiar history. Repetition, and the repetition of information in particular, is key to understanding the enduring symbolic impact of the pink suit. One blog, for example, over a picture of Michelle Obama in a darker pink tweed suit, declares that the later First Lady 'is obviously fond of her predecessors (sic) vintage style as she was a sure fire doppelganger in the Maria Pinto pink tween suit'; and immediately underneath Obama is an image of the late Princess Diana in a Gianni Versace rendition of the ensemble: a coral pink short-sleeved spring suit with matching pillbox hat.[7]

The original pink suit – the one that in couture terms was an inauthentic, if legitimised knock-off – is perpetually recalled through these copies, these layers of approximation that on the one hand bring that original back, but on the other affirm that they will always remain differentiated, separate from it. Although still fetishised and repeated with such abandon, the pink suit will forever bring back to our collective consciousness the 'unspeakable' events that defined the 1960s (Merton 1966: 4, *passim*). I will now turn to three approximations of the pink suit in three different dramatic settings: *The Eternal Frame*, which casts Doug Michels as Jacqueline Kennedy in drag; the 1983 US mini-series *Kennedy*, in which Blair Brown plays Jackie (and Martin Sheen JFK); and the notorious, widely panned 2011 History Channel mini-series *The Kennedys*, with Katie Holmes as Jackie, dressed in a Giorgio Armani-designed replica pink suit.

The Eternal Frame centres on multiple re-enactments of the Dallas assassination, concluding with a series of vox-pops from people who have just attended a screening of the final edited piece. The starting point for all the film's re-enactments is the Abraham Zapruder footage (a bootlegged copy of which is played just after the titles), although, unlike their authentic source material, the varied reconstructions were meticulously planned. As Chip Lord of Ant Farm states:

> This was a complicated production, and we knew there had to be the Zapruder camera, there had to be the Orville Nix camera on the other side of the street, and we thought we should have color video, and black-and-white video, and super-8 film. Super-8 film would be the most authentic to the original Zapruder. So there were a number of camera positions, and then we needed still photographers.
>
> (Phillips 2007: 4)

Having said this, as Lord goes on to observe, 'it wasn't a very authentic remake' inasmuch as the filmmakers only used the one car, but 'it was enough for people to look right back in their memory to that moment and shed a tear' (Phillips 2007: 5). Jackie is the focal point of these repeated re-enactments, which typically conclude (after Zapruder, of course) with her clambering over the boot of the car, before being pushed back down into her seat by a secret service agent as the motorcade speeds away under the Stemmons Freeway. Michels' drag rendition of Jackie is the element of the performance furthest removed from the original source material and arguably the video's most irreverent and sacrilegious feature, as here the usually demure First Lady, upon successfully completing a studio rehearsal of the drive through Dallas, is seen winking at the camera, or striding across the gravel from hotel lobby to minibus on her way to Dealey Plaza brandishing her bouquet of red roses as if wielding a cudgel.

The performers are here relocating to downtown Dallas in order to perform their full site-specific re-stagings of the assassination, about which Michels says:

> there have been other reenactments . . . At the same time, the Kennedy assassination was still very sacrosanct, and I don't think anyone had really violated it as art, or interpreted it as art . . . nobody had done bloody close-ups like we did. That's for sure.
>
> (quoted in Lewallen 2004: 76)

Woven into the structuring fabric of *The Eternal Frame* is a complex ongoing dialogue about performativity and the potential collapsing of the division between the real and re-enactment. Michels is a key component in this; one of the video's enduring paradoxes, for instance, is that the pink suit he wears is a more accurate, albeit less boxy, replication of the Chez Ninon/Chanel original than many others. In addition, when the performers get to Dallas, acknowledgement of the inauthenticity of Michels' rendition of Jackie is repressed by the bystanders watching the re-enactments, one of whom explains to his grandchildren that the actor 'is dressed just like her', while another calls it 'a beautiful enactment'. The serial re-enactments are interrupted briefly by a paparazzi-style photo-shoot, as Michels and Doug Halls (as the fatally wounded president) pose in lurid colour for close-ups in the back of the president's limo. Amidst the frenzied whirring and clicking of camera shutters, Halls is slumped, his face splattered with blood with Michels rising up above him, mouth open in horror and his white gloves also caked in blood. The faithful re-enactments of the Zapruder film that, as an onlooker says, feel 'like the real thing', do not confront us with the same ethical issues as this inserted photo-shoot, which somehow crosses over into assassination forbidden territory. The Zapruder film or subsequent re-stagings of the assassination from alternative locations on Dealey Plaza preserve a safe distance between reality and fantasy through maintaining their authenticity by never giving us the close-ups of Jackie's horror at the moment her husband's head was blown off. *The Eternal Frame*'s transgression is to bring too close and in luminous colour the moment when the pink suit's elegance was violated by the president's fresh blood, violating in turn the event's mystique and fantasy to an even greater extent than when magnifying the Zapruder frames showing the impact of the third bullet on Kennedy's head, which, in the digitally enhanced versions of the home movie now freely available, remain all too graphic.

Ironically, the impact of the third and fatal bullet is handled in a comparably sacrilegious manner in the otherwise turgid and bland 1980s mini-series, *Kennedy*, in which Blair Brown and her pink suit are hosed with JFK's blood as if in some low-budget splatter movie. In contradistinction to the series' otherwise dubiously reverential dramatisation of JFK's life, the pink suit, although perhaps less elegantly fitted, is, down to the trim, the blue ring on the gold buttons, the short white

Figure 17.1   Blair Brown's pink suit before the assassination in the 1980s mini-
series *Kennedy*.

Figure 17.2   Blair Brown's pink suit after the assassination in the 1980s mini-
series *Kennedy*.

gloves and the fussy undershirt, very close to the Chez Ninon original. The suit is first glimpsed in the last episode of *Kennedy* over breakfast in Fort Worth and is swathed in pathos and poignancy, for not only are we already anticipating its imminent defilement, but also the Kennedys have, following the death of their infant second son Patrick, entered a new and happier phase in their marriage. Following a short sequence of black and white archive of Air Force One arriving at Love Field, Blair Brown as Jackie emerges in the pink suit, holding the familiar red roses to greet the people who have come to welcome her and Jack to Dallas. Here, close-ups enable us to appreciate the weight of the wool and the accuracy of the suit's colours. As the motorcade proceeds downtown, the feeling of encroaching doom, like the strain of an over-wound coil prior to being released, encircles the close-ups of Jackie smiling and waving to the assembled throngs. Suddenly, the sound becomes muffled as, in close-up from inside the car, Martin Sheen as Kennedy clutches his throat and looks over at his wife as the first bullet strikes; she bends down so they are almost touching, before a shot sounds and Jackie's face, in extreme close-up, is covered in blood. Pandemonium breaks out, the limousine screeches off and we just see the First Lady crawling along the boot before being urged back into her seat by the secret service agent, as in the authentic archive.

Upon arrival at Parkland Hospital, Jackie is cradling her husband's head, everything 'caked', as Lady Bird put it, in blood. This scene, like the suit, sticks close to the fact and is lifted pretty much verbatim from Kitty Kelley's unauthorised biography *Jackie Oh!* (which, in turn, embellished but mimicked more authoritative accounts such as Mary Gallagher's *My Life With Jacqueline Kennedy*). In Kelley's book – as in the mini-series – secret service agent Clint Hill realises what was paralysing Jackie:

> He immediately ripped off his suit coat and laid it on her lap so she could cover the President's head. The sight of his spilling brains and tissues was too unbearable for others to see. Caked with blood, Jackie stumbled into the hospital, never letting go of the coat covering her husband's head.
>
> (Kelley 1978: 203–4)

The symbolic conjunction of the First Lady, the pink suit and the blood concludes *Kennedy*, which ends on a close-up of Jackie's bloodied face looking over at her husband's corpse.

In the much later History Channel series *The Kennedys*, the contextualisation of the presidential trip to Dallas is more convoluted, as it includes, for instance, JFK's alleged affair with Marilyn Monroe in 1962, the political tensions in Texas prior to the visit, the mutual distrust between Robert Kennedy and LBJ and father Joseph Kennedy's stroke. Unlike most other accounts, the re-enactment of the assassination also shows the other side of the narrative, namely Lee Harvey Oswald's last minute preparations on the sixth floor of the Texas School Book Depository. In addition, this version, more as Oliver Stone does in *JFK* (1991) makes greater use of genuine black and white archival material (of the motorcade's stately progression through Dallas) and faked archive (of the TSBD, for example). The relevance of the black and white, I think, is twofold: first, that the series is seeking to confirm its authenticity and second, that only two artefacts of the assassination are consistently associated with colour – the Zapruder film and the pink suit.

Perplexing, therefore, is the series' relative *inauthenticity* when it comes to the suit. In this approximation, remarkably little presidential blood reaches Jackie, so little in fact that neither her face nor her jacket end up besmirched. By virtue of having been designed by Giorgio Armani, this rendition of the suit was granted a couture identity independent of the Chez Ninon original and the tragedy that engulfed it. The suit that adorns Katie Holmes in *The Kennedys* is thereby leant a symbolic existence semi-independent of the assassination. This Armani reincarnation deviates from the original in small but crucial respects: it is made from a lighter, less textured wool and in a paler fabric; the trim is black as opposed to dark blue; its buttons are gold, without the darker inner ring; its cut is slightly different and less 1960s; and, most significantly, the bowed shirt Jackie Kennedy wore underneath it has been replaced by a plain, round-collared undershirt. Armani, who, in 2006, had designed Katie Holmes' wedding outfits, was engaged, reputedly at the behest of Holmes herself, to make two outfits for *The Kennedys*: the pink suit and the imitation inauguration gown (after an original designed by Ethel Franken at Bergdorf Goodman). Reproducing such an iconic outfit as the original Chanel copy, synonymous with both a momentous historical event and another couturier's signature style, is an unexpected choice for a colleague of Armani's stature, although as series costume designer Christopher Hargadon explains, Holmes and Tom Cruise had 'a relationship with Armani, and when they found out she was doing the project, they asked to make her clothes' (Odell 2011).

More overtly than other approximations of the pink suit, the Armani version for Katie Holmes, by virtue of its small differences as well as who designed it, is uncanny. We recognise it immediately as being a replica of the assassination-day suit, but it nevertheless remains distinct from it. In his essay 'The Uncanny' (1919), Freud defines the uncanny as 'that class of the frightening which leads back to what is known of old and long familiar' (Freud 1919: 340) and offers various definitions of *Heimlich* (homely) and *Unheimlich*, positing that these are not clear opposites – that the unfamiliar or unhomely is not necessarily frightening and vice versa. He continues: 'Heimlich is a word the meaning of which develops in the direction of ambivalence, until it finally coincides with the opposite, unheimlich' (Ibid: 341).

The uncanny can be related to trauma, and indeed the convergence of the familiar and beautiful (Jackie and the suit) with the violent and brutal (the assassination) will remain forever uncomfortably uncanny. In one essential way, however, the uncanny as applied to the multiple performances of Jackie's pink suit differs sharply from Freud's when he envisages that an uncanny effect is often produced 'when the distinction between imagination and reality is effaced, as when something that we have hitherto regarded as imaginary appears before us in reality' (Freud 1919: 367).

While it is not the case that the distinction between the imagination and reality is 'effaced' when the suit is copied, it is the case that the reincarnations of the dress bring into reality and consciousness something that previously resided in the imaginary, or more accurately, in this instance, in the memory. As Freud goes on, 'the uncanny is something that is secretly familiar, which has undergone repression and then returned from it' (Ibid).

One vital aspect of the repeated re-enactment of the pink suit is that every new approximation invites us to re-enter the pleasurable fantasy that the trauma in which it became a central player – Kennedy's assassination – did not happen. Because all the dramas and reproductions of the pink suit necessarily include the outfit in its pre-assassination unsullied form, it also encapsulates the fantasy that the trauma could, this time, be averted. This uncanny dramatic irony is integrated into the drama of *The Eternal Frame*, as one of the 'reporters' in Dealey Plaza engages in a dialogue with one of the 'secret service agents':

> *Agent*: Unfortunately, we fucked up on this one.
> *Reporter*: What do you mean?
> *Agent*: Well, he got killed.
> *Reporter*: How do you know that? Did you kill the president?
> *Agent*: No. I saw it though. I saw his head come off.
> *Reporter*: Let's do it as if it hasn't happened yet.
> *Agent*: As if he's still alive? . . . It's a beautiful day.
> *Reporter*: You don't expect anything to happen, do you?
> *Agent*: Well, we're always worried about Dallas. It's a tough city. It's
> a gun city, and there's a lot of kooks here'.

So the agent rejoins the motorcade as if able to protect the Artist-President and his wife, played by a man in drag, from fatal bullets fired 12 years earlier. The uncanny layers of such impersonations of the assassination, Jackie and her pink suit bring back into consciousness not only a repressed memory of 22 November 1963 but also how nearly it could have been averted. The pink suit, as one of the day's most evocative symbols, will always be a site of rupture as well as nostalgic recollection.

Conclusion

To end with a different variety of approximation: the blog *Jezebel* asked in 2008 – that is, just after Barack Obama was elected to the office of US president – 'Michelle and Jackie O: twins separated at birth?',[8] before critiquing a series of photographs that show the two First Ladies in vaguely similar outfits: two red suits and two yellow suits. 'Long before Ted Kennedy endorsed him for president', Jennifer's page starts, 'I've been telling anyone who'll listen that I think that Barack Obama and his wife, Michelle, are the contemporary version of Camelot . . . at least sartorially: Michelle is Jackie 2.0'. Running parallel to these discussions of the similarities between the two First Ladies, there exist both the oblique and signposted overlaps between Barack Obama and Jack Kennedy, which Obama and his press office have readily endorsed with encounters such as Caroline Kennedy's visit to the Oval Office on 3 March 2009 to mark Obama's first 100 days in office, during which Obama crouches under the famous Resolute Desk, much as Caroline's baby brother John had done in 1963. The echoes between Jackie Kennedy and Michelle Obama are likewise uncanny, not because the two women look like each other, but that a sense of uncanniness is assumed and thereby imposed on Michelle Obama, which has its roots in a rather strange sentiment: she possesses a sense of style and is a First Lady, thereby assuring the similarities between her and Jackie Kennedy.

There have been numerous imitations of Jackie Kennedy for the screen, primarily on television: Francesca Annis in *Onassis, the Richest Man in the World* (1988), Michelle Gellar in *A Woman Named Jackie* (1991), Joanne Whalley in *Jackie Bouvier Kennedy Onassis* (2000), Jill Hennessy in *Jackie, Ethel, Joan: The Women of Camelot* (2001), Jacqueline Bisset in *America's Prince: The JFK Jr Story* (2003) or Jeanne Tripplehorn in *Grey Gardens* (2009). It is intriguing how many of the actresses who have played Jackie have been British. Another English actress, Rachel Weisz, pulled out of playing Jackie Kennedy in a film project *Jackie*, which dramatises the immediate aftermath of the JFK assassination, to be replaced, it is rumoured, by Natalie Portman. Perhaps so many British actresses have been cast in the role because of her peculiarly stilted speaking voice, or perhaps because it is still forbidden to render Jackie too closely. Jackie Kennedy has been much copied, but as with approximations of the pink suit, the difference between reality and representation, between original and re-enactment is consistently maintained. The pink suit will always be a defining signifier for the events in Dallas of 22 November 1963, and so, to an extent, will continue to exist independently of the person it adorned, Jackie Kennedy. Just as the suit itself is preserved under lock and key in the National Archives, Maryland, so, as a result of this absence and repression, its meaning will never be unlocked. It will be remembered only through rapidly fading memories, archival images and copies. The idea of future generations being able to finally see the authentic and bloodstained suit is a disturbing idea, but also a salutary reminder that probably the majority of people in 2103 will not care about what the suit signifies, but will view it with the interested but dispassionate detachment visitors to Ford's Theatre might now look at the frock coat, waistcoat and trousers Abraham Lincoln was wearing when *he* was assassinated in 1865. The pink suit, by virtue of its multiple inferences and subsequent re-enactments, continues to haunt us: a palimpsest or ghostly signifier as well as the ultimate fetish object of the JFK assassination.

Notes

1   This oft-cited comment is available from many sources, including YouTube, as the speech was televised, and c/o the John F. Kennedy Presidential Library and Museum in Boston (see www.jfklibrary.org/JFK/JFK-in-History/Jacqueline-Kennedy-in-the-White-House.aspx?p=4).

2   Variously attributed to Jackie, to JFK aide Kenny O'Donnell and others, a version of 'let them see what they've done' appears in most accounts of the aftermath of the assassination. Gallagher's version, attributed to O'Donnell, is: 'it'll show the world what's been done to Jack' (Gallagher 1970: 293).

3   Cf. www.artsconnected.org/resource/91183/sixteen-jackies.

4   Cf. Bill Nichols 'Documentary Reenactment and the Fantasmatic Subject', *Critical Inquiry*, 35 (Autumn 2008), 72–89.

5   This refers to my current Leverhulme Major Research Fellowship and the following book (to be published by Routledge): *Approximation: Documentary, History and the Staging of Reality*.

6   'Chapter 3: The Shots from the Texas School Book Depository – The Trajectory (Films and Tests)', *Report of the President's Commission on the Assassination of President Kennedy*, www.archives.gov/research/jfk/warren-commission-report/chapter-3.html#films.

7   'Retro Threadz: Where Fashion is Rediscovered', www.retrothreadz.blogspot.co.uk/2011/08/mod-monday-jackie-kennedy.html.

8   www.jezebel.com/351264/michelle-and-jackie-o-twins-separated-at-birth#ixzz16tmXozXq).

References

Baudrillard, Jean (1994) *Simulacra and Simulation*, transl. Sheila Faria Glaser, Ann Arbor: University of Michigan Press.

Beck, John (2005) 'Visual Violence in History and Art: Zapruder, Warhol and the Accident of Images', in Holloway, David and Beck, John (eds) (2005) *American Visual Cultures*, London and New York: Continuum, 183–9.

Bowles, Hamish (2001) *Jacqueline Kennedy: The White House Years—Selections from the John F. Kennedy Library Museum*, New York: Metropolitan Museum of Art.

Freud, Sigmund (1919) 'The Uncanny', in Angela Richards (ed.) *Art and Literature*, Penguin Freud Library Volume 14, London: Penguin, 1990, 335–76.

Gallagher, Mary Barelli (1969) *My Life with Jacqueline Kennedy*, London: Michael Joseph, 1970.

Kelley, Kitty (1978) *Jackie Oh! An Intimate Biography*, London and New York: Granada Publishing.

Koestenbaum, Wayne (1995) *Jackie Under My Skin: Intepreting an Icon*, Thorndike Press: Thorndike, Maine.

Lewallen, Constance (2004) 'Interview with Ant Farm: Constance M. Lewallen in conversation with Chip Lord, Doug Michels and Curtis Schreier', in Lewallen, Constance M. and Seid, Steve *Ant Farm: 1968–1978*, Berkeley and Los Angeles: University of California Press, 38–87.

Lubin, David M. (2003) *Shooting Kennedy: JFK and the Culture of Images*, Berkeley and Los Angeles: University of California Press.

Mailer, Norman (1967) 'The Leading Man: A Review of *JFK: The Man and the Myth*', in *Cannibals and Christians*, London: Andre Deutsch, 165–71.

Merton, Thomas (1966) *Raids on the Unspeakable*, New York: New Directions.

Nichols, Bill (2008) 'Documentary Reenactment and the Fantasmatic Subject', *Critical Inquiry*, 35 (Autumn), 72–89.

Odell, Amy (2011) 'Giorgio Armani Would Like to Make Katie Holmes's Chanel Costume, Please', 4.1.11, http://nymag.com/thecut/2011/04/giorgio_armani_would_like_to_m.html.

Phillips, Glenn (2007) 'Interview with Doug Hall (representing T.R. Uthco) and Chip Lord (representing Ant Farm) for the catalogue for *California Video*, at the J. Paul Getty Museum, Los Angeles', pp. 1–8. www.doughallstudio.com/storage/Hall_Lord%20Interview_Getty.pdf. Accessed 4 March 2013.

Picardie, Justine (2011) *Coco Chanel: The Legend and the Life*, London: HarperCollins.

Seid, Steve (2004) 'Tunneling through the wasteland: Ant Farm video', in Lewallen, Constance M. and Seid, Steve *Ant Farm: 1968–1978*, Berkeley and Los Angeles: University of California Press, 22–37.

Tierney, Tom (1990) *John F. Kennedy and His Family: Paper Dolls in Full Color*, Dover Publications.

Chapter 18

Fiona Cox

FAB LESBIANISM AND FAMILY VALUES

Costuming of lesbian identities in
The L Word and *The Kids Are All Right*

A S JANE GAINES OUTLINED in her highly influential article on costume in Hollywood cinema, onscreen clothes have traditionally reinforced narrative and revealed aspects of character – in particular female character – so that, typically, 'Dress Tells the Woman's Story' (Gaines 1990). Characters tend to be 'costumed *with* rather than against . . . personality', and onscreen outfits are expected to indicate elements of identity such as 'gender, age, nationality . . . social class' and so on (Gaines 1990: 184, 186). But what happens when a character's traits include lesbian identity?

Historically, lesbian and gay male representation in film and on television has been fraught, with such characters – where visible at all – typically depicted via negative stereotypes (Russo 1981: Tropiano 2002). Richard Dyer's foundational work on gay and lesbian representation explains stereotypes as forged by dominant cultures to 'other' groups of people, with lesbian and gay stereotypes reinforcing that such individuals 'fall short of the "ideal" of heterosexuality' and therefore belong outside of society (1977: 31). As a result, stereotypes are considered 'bad'. As recently as 2010, out lesbian comedian Sue Perkins responded in the *Guardian* newspaper to a media report on the representation of gay, lesbian and bisexual people on television with the following: 'the same issues keep arising. For gay men, it's the predominance of the camp cliché. For lesbians, despair at the outdated butch-femme stereotypes.' To replace these, Perkins called for more 'real' depictions of gay people; for example, 'just sitting around paying bills like Average Jos' (Perkins 2010).

Problematically for designers, critics like Andrea Weiss point out that avoiding typing in representations of lesbian and gay characters 'denies cultural difference' so that portraying people who do not inhabit gay types but simply '"happen to be gay" . . . become[s] another form of invisibility' (1992: 63). Offering a possible solution, Dyer differentiates between stereotypes and arguably beneficial member types, with the latter 'linked to historically and culturally specific and determined social groups', allowing for a sense of community and understanding of the factors that shape gayness without suggesting an inherent difference from the majority (1977: 37). However, gay people have historically fashioned aspects of stereotypes into lived reality so that stereotypes and member types often overlap (Dyer 2002). For example, late nineteenth- and early twentieth-century theories about homo-sexuality as congenital inversion were accompanied by connotations of perversion and degeneracy, leading to stereotypes of the sick and sinister mannish lesbian (Faderman 1992). Considering the history of such imagery, designers of lesbian costuming who wish to avoid negative associations might therefore steer clear of 'masculinity'.[1] Yet 'masculine' elements of presentation have historically been and continue to be utilised by gay women to project their sexuality; Judith Halberstam writes about 'the ongoing construction of the modern lesbian identity from the . . . role of the masculine woman' (1998: 96). Avoiding butch stereotypes in the media in favour of, for example, the 'lipstick lesbian' – as has been common since the 1990s – ignores a significant lesbian type, and notably one that poses a visible challenge to heterosexism so that its erasure has conservative implications (Ciasullo 2001).

The removal of visible signs of lesbianism from gay female characters also contradicts basic costume theory; Dyer details how the depiction of recognisable gay types through visual means is a useful way to '[condense] a wealth of social knowledge into a few striking and vivid signs' that quickly convey a character's gayness for viewers (2002: 48). Cindy Patton notes

> To simply hunt down stereotypes and attempt to replace them fails to understand that narrative film works precisely by loading up characters with signs which refer to something larger than the description of the character who wears them.
>
> (Patton 1995: 23)

This essay is an exploration of how two designers have undertaken the task of using dress to 'tell the story' of lesbianism in the arguably increasingly accepting atmosphere of twenty-first century Western culture. It makes use of in-person interviews with Cynthia Summers, costume designer for US television show *The L Word*, and Mary Claire Hannan, costume designer for independent US feature film *The Kids Are All Right*, exploring the intentions behind the onscreen styles in two relatively mainstream contexts, analysing how the costuming of lesbian identities functions within each text, and considering the effects of each strategy.[2]

The L Word

The L Word was the first television programme to place a community of gay women at the centre of its narrative. No secret was made of the lesbian content, with promotional material for the first series carrying the tagline 'Same Sex. Different City.' Janet McCabe and Kim Akass have pointed out the deliberate parallels this suggests with HBO's glamorous, fashion-centric *Sex and the City*, remarking that 'Like our girls from Manhattan, all the women are beautiful . . . and all have impeccable sartorial style' (2006: xxv). Also like *Sex and the City*, the beauty and style featured in *The L Word* has a distinctly 'feminine' appearance. Featured lesbian characters include singletons Alice (Leisha Hailey), Dana (Erin Daniels) and Shane (Katherine Moennig), long-term off-and-on-again couple Bette (Jennifer Beals) and Tina (Laurel Holloman), and Jenny (Mia Kirshner), who begins the series as the apparently heterosexual fiancée of Bette and Tina's neighbour before embracing lesbianism as the narrative progresses. Most of the central lesbian characters present in a manner that suggests modern heterosexual 'femininity', with long hair and makeup styled to present them as conventionally attractive. High heels – the opposite of stereotypically lesbian 'sensible shoes' – predominate.

Shane, the exception to this adherence to visual signifiers of 'femininity', was the only slightly butch character in the show's central cast when *The L Word* first aired. Shane always wears trousers, never dons a bra, sports a lot of leather, and never willingly puts on heels. However, the character arguably remains within the scope of attractive contemporary 'femininity', using makeup and wearing her hair longer than most traditionally 'masculine'-inspired styles. Candace Moore and Kristen Schilt have written about the character's questionable status as a butch, noting Shane's 'female visibility' which jars with the way she is sometimes mistaken for a man within the series (2006: 160).[3] They argue that 'Shane does not register explicitly butch signifiers but rather is 'implied as contextually butch when positioned alongside the other characters' femme gender displays' (Ibid: 161).

As could be reasonably expected, the favouring of traditionally 'feminine' appearances in *The L Word* was immediately noted by critics and considered to be highly problematic (Lo 2004; McCroy 2003; Vanasco 2006). However, as even critical voices accepted, this elision of butch identity in early episodes was part of a shrewd attempt to maximise ratings. While more butch characters were added later, that the core group remained as a femmes-plus-Shane ensemble no doubt played a part in securing the six seasons that *The L Word* enjoyed on air (Warn 2006). When I spoke with Summers, she explained that types were partly avoided for the benefit of non-lesbian viewers, making characters 'more accessible for the mainstream public to understand . . . because look, they're not *that* different' (Summers 2010).

Both stereotypes and types were rejected in *The L Word* in a deliberate effort to align the lesbian characters with dominant Western culture. However, homosexuality is not rendered invisible within the series, in fact giving rise to very particular stories including coming out, remaining in the closet at work and with family, and considerations surrounding gay parenting. The point is that lesbianism itself is not the overwhelming story of *The L Word*, particularly as Jenny becomes integrated into life as a gay woman in a predominantly lesbian community. Often, gay female sexuality is positioned as incidental context: an important aspect of identity but not one that dictates it.

Significantly, Dyer argues that while 'types keep the fact of a character's gayness clearly present before us throughout the text', the disadvantage of this continued visual presence is that 'it tends to reduce everything about that character to his/her sexuality' (2002: 24). *The L Word*, by presenting its gay women as 'not *that* different', was attempting the opposite project. Gaines' basic tenet of costume theory – that dress tells the woman's story – clashes and intersects with both *The L Word*'s attempt to reposition lesbianism as existing *outside* the realm of story and the lesbian-ensemble nature of the series, with a profound effect on costuming.

Specifically, Summers was tasked with costuming a group whose identities included the element 'lesbian' but who were otherwise richly diverse. A significant part of the social knowledge that is condensed into the image of the butch woman (the 'knowledge' that 'masculine' women are lesbians) means that speaking lesbianism through butch costume and style runs the risk of overshadowing other aspects of identity being telegraphed through dress. Using garments that are free of the meaning 'lesbian' potentially offers more possibilities for character differentiation. The result was a focus on costuming the women as different to each other rather than to heterosexual women. Costumes in *The L Word* draw on codes and types not necessarily related to sexuality, telegraphing personalities and pastimes and conveying shifts in character and narrative from scene to scene, with the communication of lesbianism left to dialogue and action.

Alice, for example, is quirky and enjoys attention, so wears a lot of bright colours; she is also playful and dresses for occasions, as in 'Listen Up' (#1.8), when she changes out of ripped jeans, a white tank top and green bandana to attend a conservative women's group luncheon. Claiming 'I can look Republican', she arrives at the event in a pink, short-sleeved, sheer blouse worn over a slip, with two strings of pearls around her neck and a white sweater tied around her shoulder: the ultimate WASP look, undermined only by the armband tattoo on her bicep. Alternately, Bette is costumed to communicate her high status at work as well as her assertive personality. The character's well-tailored look and preference for trouser suits and sharp-collared shirts telegraphs authority. As Summers described, Bette is 'a power dyke. . .; a woman to be reckoned with' (Summers 2010).

Figure 18.1   Leisha Hailey (left), not looking Republican, as Alice in *The L Word*.

Figure 18.2   Jennifer Beals power dressing as Bette in *The L Word*.

Although the designer uses the word 'dyke', the emphasis in Beals' costumes seems to be on power, not sexuality. While Summers spoke of putting Bette in 'a lot of cuff-linked shirts in the beginning' and mentioned that her outfits were 'all kind of men's. . .; mostly pantsuit inspired' (Summers 2010), the reason for using 'masculine'-influenced silhouettes and styles does not seem to be to convey any gender inversion or to make Bette look more recognisably lesbian: this is definitely not communicated by the character's long hair and flawless makeup. Instead, influences from male tailoring are used to suggest the status and power typically associated with 'masculinity'. This is highlighted by the fact that, when Bette does not wear trousers, the particular type of skirts she wears also signals her authority. As Summers articulated: 'Bette didn't wear skirts that were A-line . . .: she wore more of a pencil skirt, which has a little more oomph and is a little more powerful' (Summers 2010).When Bette loses her job in Season Three, she wears noticeably casual clothes that infer a lower status, for example seen in pyjamas, a shapeless brown cardigan and Ugg boots in front of strangers at a Buddhist retreat in 'Lead, Follow, or Get Out of the Way' (#3.9).

These are just two examples of costumes in *The L Word* functioning to tell aspects of stories about lesbians that exist outside of lesbianism itself. I am not arguing that elements like playfulness and authority or indeed other aspects cannot be indicated in conjunction with conveying recognisable lesbian types through style – indeed they can, as the next section will attest – but rather that using gay typing in the costuming of an ensemble lesbian cast might dominate the stories told by dress so that lesbianism would be endlessly foregrounded. Using images that don't 'other' the women from mainstream society aids with the project of lesbianism providing context and not remaining as story in *The L Word*.

Summers' alignment of lesbian costuming with mainstream 'femininity' might suggest that the series, while depicting gay women, is guilty of something akin to what Katherine Wirthlin has condemned as 'fad lesbianism'(2009: 111). Wirthlin focuses on images that are titillating to heterosexual men and 'non-threatening . . . to dominant ideologies of . . . heterosexuality and femininity', echoing Summer's self-professed strategy of sticking to mainstream ideals for the benefit of straight audiences. Yet it is important to remember that while the costumes on *The L Word* might not display recognisable images of gay women, lesbianism is ever present in the narrative. Onscreen sex renders lesbian sexuality graphically visible, and dialogue referencing lesbian clichés and the depiction of sub-cultural events like all-lesbian Olivia Cruises in 'Land Ahoy' (#2.10) and lesbian-filled Dinah Shore parties in 'Looking Back' (#1.11) allows for further specificity. The series also raises several issues of political and social significance for lesbians such as gay marriage, homophobia and even, rather self-consciously, lesbian representation in the media.[4] As M. Catherine Jonet and Laura Anh Williams put it, in focusing on multiple lesbian characters *The L Word* 'repudiate[s] the heterosexual matrix of power by decentering its privileging of itself in discourse' (2008: 155).

The L Word gives us what we might call not fad but *fab* lesbianism; images that appear mainstream enough in some ways to trouble dominant ideology in others. As Stephanie Theobald argues, 'Pushing lesbianism to the mainstream is all about Trojan horses . . . Make the chicks in The L Word shave their legs and . . . you can get yourself a second series', in which to continue representing an under-represented minority (24 September 2004). Similarly, Erin Douglas has argued that instead of perpetuating 'femme invisibility' as some have insinuated, *The L Word* undertakes a project of '*queering* femininity' precisely because, in the series, 'femininity does not signify normativity' (2008: 196). While narrative and action in *The L Word* depict lesbianism without qualm, subtle codes of dress and style are freed up to signal any number of personality quirks, vocations and vicissitudes of narrative, mainstreaming lesbian identities in order to both trouble mainstream ideologies and promote lesbianism as a valid part of society.

The Kids Are All Right

2010 saw the release of *The Kids Are All Right* (Lisa Cholodenko), starring Annette Bening and Julianne Moore as Nic and Jules, a long-term couple raising a family. The film tells the story of what happens when their teenaged children seek out their previously anonymous sperm donor, Paul (Mark Ruffalo), who disrupts the family members' lives by having an affair with Jules. The liaison is brief and does not cause Jules to question her lesbian identity and, when it is discovered, first Jules and then Nic fight to protect their family unit against Paul's interloping presence. The film ends on a symbolic gesture of intimacy as the couple hold hands, signalling the rekindling of their relationship.

Never before had major Hollywood stars portrayed lesbian characters in such a widely distributed film, in a text where lesbianism formed, like *The L Word*, pre-established context for the central characters without being the subject of the narrative. In interviews and articles, the central lesbian relationship was an understandable focus. However, the overwhelming message coming from those involved with the production was that the film is not about lesbians but instead the importance of family. Interviews and promotional materials repeatedly assured potential viewers that the context was not what the story was 'about' and framed lesbian parents as unremarkable, with any differences from other families patched over by emphasising the similarities. The dismissal of the importance of lesbianism within the film demonstrates anxiety over how audiences might respond to films seen to be 'about' gay women. Is *The Kids Are All Right* really not 'about' lesbians?

Freud classified disavowal as the rejection of a belief that results in that same belief being simultaneously retained and not retained: that which is disavowed is always present (Freud 1927). This phenomenon becomes evident through a reading of the media positioning of *The Kids Are All Right* when compared with the film itself. The emphasis in the marketing materials on family, marriage, and lesbians being just like everyone else disguises that the non-sensationalising of the lesbian relationship at the heart of the narrative is a structuring insignificance. In particular, the politically unstable time in which the film was produced affects its meaning: laws governing same-sex marriage were in a volatile condition in 2010 in California, where the film is set and where November 2008 saw the quickly appealed passing of anti gay-marriage bill Proposition 8. The legitimacy of gay families was a topical and highly contentious issue upon the film's release. The ostensibly apolitical tone of *The Kids Are All Right*, positioning it as a family movie just like any other, is in fact its most political aspect. *The Kids Are All Right* is not just a film about family and marriage, it is a film that attempts to expand what those terms are allowed to mean in a hostile environment, aggressively legitimising the lesbian family unit and defending Nic and Jules' union against the threat of outside intrusion.

The disavowal of the importance of lesbianism in *The Kids Are All Right* is also belied by the lesbian specificity that the film does exhibit. These are no 'happen to be gay' characters in Weiss's damaging, invisible sense: there are discussions in the screenplay that directly reference lesbian sexuality, such as a punchline (about Jules' tongue 'working' at the end of the couple's tale of how they met) that hinges on conceptions of oral sex as the primary lesbian sex act. However, such moments of specificity do not prevent the story itself from being universal, as many people can relate to notions of love and family, as well as long-term relationships, children growing up and acting independently of their parents, and infidelity. The film's costuming strategy is symptomatic of this dual project of specificity and universality, with Bening and Moore costumed to convey both lesbian identity and individual character traits that have nothing to do with sexuality. The result is that lesbianism forms an important part of the women's identities without the suggestion that it determines personality.

When I interviewed Hannan about her work on the film, it became clear that a significant part of the costuming strategy was designed to 'speak' lesbian identity. The designer acknowledged that 'because [Nic and Jules] are lesbian women, they might not look completely like straight women' (Hannan 2010). However, while the costumes were kept within the realm of readable lesbian style, care was taken not to overspill into either overt typing or stereotyping. Hannan explained that the 'subtleties' of the costumes were very important to her, and that she concentrated on asking 'what would a lesbian woman wear?' while at the same time favouring items that would not look out of place on heterosexual women. The designer described, for example, initially suggesting a different kind of sleepwear to the soft, casual clothes the women wore as pyjamas in the film, bringing in 'tougher looking T-shirts . . . that have a thick neck on them, and thick fabric' as an option (Hannan 2010). However, these were felt to be too butch, to 'speak' too much lesbianism, which was judged to encroach upon the message of the film as being about family rather than about lesbians. As a consequence, Hannan said:

> we decided . . . to keep it soft, keep it pretty . . . [Lisa] was trying to make a statement about family, and this just happened to be two women instead of a man and a woman. So . . . when it started to identify itself too much as lesbian, we pulled it back.
>
> (Hannan 2010)

This perceived incompatibility of 'too much' lesbianism with the universalising message of the film demonstrates how recognisable lesbian looks (here, obviously male clothing on women) that overlap too much with stereotypes (that of the mannish lesbian) are felt to tell the story of lesbianism but little else. *The Kids Are All Right* instead aims to telegraph lesbian identity alongside other aspects of character. For example, some lesbian typing is visible in the looks on display: aspects of Bening's costumes hint at 'masculinity', and Hannan mentioned that she used men's clothing for Nic such as navy and dark grey dress shirts from J Crew and a man's waistcoat from Urban Outfitters, although these items were integrated into outfits that were not overtly butch but perhaps more androgynous. In addition, neither Nic nor Jules wears significant makeup, hinting at the rejection of beauty culture associated with lesbian-feminism (Stein 1995). We get a little subcultural coding with the use of Birkenstock and Converse shoes, both brands somewhat jokingly but also reasonably associated with gay women. Hannan also used Free City clothing, a brand with lesbian credentials, designed as it is by Nina Garduno, former partner of *The L Word* actress Leisha Hailey (Summers 2010).

Further aspects of typing in *The Kids Are All Right* were inspired by real-life lesbian style; taking a cue from Bening's cropped hair, Hannan settled on Ellen DeGeneres as an inspiration for many of Nic's outfits. DeGeneres' attractive, androgynous, verging on the casual yet also slightly professional style matched Hannan's vision of Nic's character and the costume strategy for the film, adhering as it does to the ideal of being realistic yet not overly and singularly lesbian identified. '[Ellen's] very tailored', Hannan explained, 'and she doesn't necessarily look like "Oh, is that a gay woman?" but it's . . . man-tailored on a girl and it's very pretty' (Hannan 2010). DeGeneres' look matched another real-life inspiration for both Nic and Jules: the film's out lesbian director Lisa Cholodenko. Hannan noted that the casual 'hip' styles of Cholodenko and her partner, Wendy Melvoin, were neither butch nor femme but androgynous. She felt this was 'indicative of probably what . . . a lesbian woman would wear, but also a non-lesbian', choosing it for its 'neutral territory', and taking this direction for both Moore and Bening's costumes (Hannan 2010). Hannan even mined Cholodenko's and Melvoin's personal wardrobes: the director brought in several of her T-shirts for Moore to wear, and a necklace worn by Jules belonged to the couple (Cholodenko 2010).

Despite the lesbian typing visible in the costumes, there are elements of Nic and Jules' styles that have nothing to do with sexuality. Hannan revealed an adherence to Gaines' theories, explaining that, for her, what is important is not making actors look beautiful but, instead, revealing character through clothing: 'I really like to honour character and . . . different idiosyncrasies in people' she explained (Hannan 2010). The designer saw Jules, a homemaker with slight New Age tendencies and aspirations to set up an environmentally conscious landscape design business, as the 'softer' of the two main characters, 'a dreamer' (Hannan 2010). To show this, she put Moore in 'ethereal looking blouses': 'India blouses' from authentic Indian clothing stores in downtown Los Angeles (Hannan 2010). Jules' necklace displaying the word LOVE also speaks to this slightly softer, not completely practical aspect of her characterisation. Hannan felt that the character, often seen in a relaxed domestic setting, lacked a certain kind of professional responsibility. As a consequence, the designer dressed Moore quite casually, putting her in T-shirts featuring graphics that had connotations of 'fun' and leisure, like the one in the opening scene with a picture of Elvis Costello's face printed across the front (Hannan 2010).

Similarly, Nic's costumes speak more than simply her sexual orientation. Hannan saw Nic as a professional, sensible woman, particularly in comparison with Jules. Nic is a doctor, so during scenes when the character is heading to or from work Hannan put Bening in medical scrubs or items she termed 'practical clothing', like 'tailored shirts' (Hannan 2010). Here, an item that can be read as communicating lesbian sexuality – the tailored shirt speaks 'masculinity' – also conveys an entirely separate aspect of personality, showing how Hannan balanced the two aims within outfits and even within single garments. Nic also displays little touches in her costumes that speak responsibility, like her wristwatch (Jules does not wear one), and the pager clipped to the strap of her bag that indicates she never quite leaves her job behind. These non-lesbian-related elements blend in with the subtle depiction of member types, so that Nic and Jules' costumes speak both their sexuality and their personalities yet never conflate the two. By differentiating between the women while making use of recognisable lesbian styles, Hannan represented lesbian specificity without reducing the characters to their sexual identity.

Conclusion

Both *The L Word* and *The Kids Are All Right* avoid strongly differentiating lesbianism from mainstream culture. In the case of the former, this primarily takes place through image. The pre-established lesbian context and ensemble nature of *The L Word* assist in the removal of lesbianism from the level of plot. Accordingly, 'lesbian' does not dominate the sartorial story. Conversely, although the publicity campaign for *The Kids Are All Right* denied the film's lesbian specificity, costume allows for elements of such specificity to shine through. Making use of realistic social types, Hannan allowed for lesbianism to feature in the costuming while sidestepping stereotypes and heavy indications of member types, as with *The L Word*, in order to avoid alienating non-lesbian audiences. Lesbianism, while an important element of character as conveyed through costume in the film, is not the defining feature. If dress tells the woman's story, lesbianism in *The Kids Are All Right* is only a chapter. What the texts examined in this essay share is a need to differentiate between gay female characters, encouraging both Summers and Hannan to expand their use of dress beyond telling the story 'lesbian'.

Notes

1   Taking into account Judith Butler's work on gender as performative (1990), repeatedly reinforced so as to naturalise the dichotomised conflation of sex and gender, I enclose both 'masculinity' and 'femininity' (and similar) in quote marks throughout this text. This is an attempt to recognise that both concepts are cultural constructs and neither inherent nor gender-dependent traits.

2   I am not suggesting that there is, or ever will be, a 'correct' way to represent lesbian characters and although more ethnic diversity would be nice, as would a greater age range and more representations of characters with disabilities and other underrepresented groups, these areas for improvement are by no means limited to lesbian representation and have little to do with costume directly. Due to limitations of space, they are not discussed here.

3   See 'Lawfully', (#1.5).

4   See Carmen and Shane's near-nuptials in 'Left Hand of the Goddess' (#3.12); Bette's televised debate with Fay Buckley (Helen Shaver) in 'Liberally' (#1.10), in which Buckley suggests Bette and Tina's lesbianism has incurred God's wrath and caused Tina's miscarriage, and the studio-altered, heterosexual ending of Jenny's film *Lez Girls* in 'Least Likely' (#6.2).

References

Akass, K. and McCabe, J. (eds) (2006) *Reading* The L Word*: Outing Contemporary Television*, New York: I.B. Tauris.

Butler, J. (1990) *Gender Trouble: Feminism and the Subversion of Identity*, New York and London: Routledge.

Cholodenko, L. (2010) audio commentary on *The Kids Are All Right* (2010). Canada: Alliance [DVD].

Ciasullo, A.M. (2001) 'Making Her (In)Visible: Cultural Representations of Lesbianism and the Lesbian Body in the 1990s', *Feminist Studies* 27:3 (Autumn): 577–608, online. Available at www.jstor.org/stable/pdfplus/3178806.pdf (accessed 11 Feb 2010).

Douglas, E. (2008) 'Pink Heels, Dildos, and Erotic Play: The (Re)Making of Fem(me)inity on Showtime's *The L Word*', in R. Bierne (ed.) *Televising Queer Women: A Reader*, New York: Palgrave Macmillan.

Dyer, R. (1977) 'Stereotyping', in R. Dyer (ed.) *Gays and Film*, London: BFI.

——(2002) *The Matter of Images: Essays on Representation*, 2nd edn, London: Routledge.

Faderman, L. (1992) *Odd Girls and Twilight Lovers: A History of Lesbian Life in Twentieth Century America*, New York: Penguin.

Freud, S. (1927), 'Fetishism'; trans. James Strachey (1991) *On Sexuality*, Penguin Freud Library, Vol. 7, London: Penguin Books.

Gaines, J. (1990) 'Costume and Narrative: How Dress Tells the Woman's Story', in J. Gaines and C. Herzog (eds) *Fabrications: Costume and the Female Body*, New York and London: Routledge.

Halberstam, J. (1998) *Female Masculinity*, Durham, North Carolina: Duke University Press.

Hannan, M.C. (8 December 2010) Personal interview.

Jonet, M. C. and Williams, L.A. (2008) '"Everything Else Is the Same": Configurations of *The L Word*', in R. Bierne (ed.) *Televising Queer Women: A Reader*, New York: Palgrave Macmillan.

Lo, M. (2004) 'It's All About the Hair: Butch Identity and Drag on *The L Word*', online. Available at www.afterellen.com/archive/ellen/TV/thelword/butch. html (accessed 28 September 2011).

McCroy, W. (2003) 'L is for Invisible' (31 October) Online. www.thelwordonline. com/L_is_for.shtml (accessed 1 August 2012).

Moore, C. and Schilt, K. (2006) 'Is she man enough? Female masculinities on *The L Word*', in K. Akass and J. McCabe (eds) *Reading* The L Word: *Outing Contemporary Television*, New York: I.B. Tauris.

Patton, C. (1995) 'What is a nice lesbian like you doing in a film like this?', in T. Wilton (ed.) *immortal, invisible: Lesbians and the Moving Image*, London and New York: Routledge.

Perkins, S. (5 October 2010) 'Gay roles on television need to be real'. Online www.guardian.co.uk/tv-and-radio/2010/oct/05/gay-roles-television-real?INTCMP=ILCNETTXT3487 (accessed 30 May 2011).

Russo, V. (1981) *The Celluloid Closet: Homosexuality in the Movies*, New York: Harper and Row.

Stein, A. (1995) 'All Dressed Up, But No Place to Go? Style Wars and the New Lesbianism', in C. K. Creekmur and A. Doty (eds), *Out In Culture: Gay, Lesbian and Queer Essays on Popular Culture*, London: Cassel.

Summers, C. (3 December 2010), Personal interview.

Theobald, S. (24 September 2004) 'From Ikon to Dykon'. Online www.guardian. co.uk/media/2004/sep/04/tvandradio.theguide (accessed 4 October 2011).

Tropiano, S. (2002) *The Prime Time Closet: A History of Gays and Lesbians on TV*, New York: Applause.

Vanasco, J. (2006) 'The glamour factor and the Fiji effect', in K. Akass and J. McCabe (eds) *Reading* The L Word: *Outing Contemporary Television*, New York: I.B. Tauris.

Warn, S. (2006) 'Introduction' in K. Akass and J. McCabe (eds) *Reading* The L Word: *Outing Contemporary Television*, New York: I.B. Tauris.

Weiss, A. (1992) *Vampires and Violets: Lesbians in Film*, New York: Penguin Books.

Wirthlin, K. (2009), 'Fad lesbianism: Exposing media's posing', *Journal of Lesbian Studies* 13: 107–14. Online. www.tandfonline.com/doi/pdf/10.1080/073805 60802314243 (accessed 25 July 2012).

Filmography/teleography

Film 2010 (2010), London, BBC1, 22 October.

Sex and the City (1998–2004) US, HBO.

The Journey to Forming a Family, (2010), Prod. by Universal, special feature on *The Kids Are All Right* (2010) Canada: Alliance [DVD].

The Kids Are All Right (2010), Dir. by Lisa Cholodenko, US, Focus Features.

The L Word (2004–2009) US, Showtime.

The Making of The Kids Are All Right (2010), Prod. by Universal, special feature on *The Kids Are All* Right (2010) Canada: Alliance [DVD].

Chapter 19

Nathalie Khan

FASHION AS MYTHOLOGY
Considering the legacy of Alexander McQueen

'THERE IS NO MORE' were the words whispered at the end of Alexander McQueen's catwalk show on 9 March 2010 in Paris. The final design, which had entered the day-lit space, was a high-collared jacket, crafted with gold angel-like feathers and worn above a white, floating tulle skirt. The model, whose hair was covered by a skin-toned cap, had faced the select audience in silence. Traditionally a grand finale marks the end of each catwalk show, where lighting, sound and choreographed performance culminate in a climactic parade. McQueen's final show did not offer any such spectacle; instead, the model moved off slowly and the show flittered out like a light; an abrupt and silent end.

Autumn 2010/11, titled 'Angels and Demons', was the last collection McQueen designed for the Gucci Group, which had acquired the brand in 2000. The sixteen pieces, which were shown to a select group of fashion editors and journalists, were hailed by the press as a demonstration of McQueen's skill as a craftsman and designer, but also a testament to his emotional distress at the time of his suicide four weeks prior to the event.[1] Finality is seldom seen in fashion. The fashion cycle relies on constant change and renewal. But in the case of McQueen's show, the audience witnessed something that could be defined as an ending. 'Angels and Demons' was charged with emotion. Rarely is an industry so rooted in transience, confronted with matters of such permanence and reality.

This essay will examine 'Angels and Demons' and the purpose of the catwalk as momentous event. For McQueen fame, controversy and public interest were a central part of his image. His fashion shows relied on the live moment to provoke and challenge the industry. But his final show had a different effect. The myths surrounding his suicide broke with the conventional purpose of public image, aura and persona. By being present and absent at the same time, he had created, what Jean Baudrillard (2005) describes in his discussion of art and mythology, as an 'aura of derision'.

The symbolic production of fashion relies on visual representation. McQueen's role as a designer, and the use of technology, were central aspects of his work. In order to make sense of the shift from the material version to the distant digital image, one needs to explore the transition from live event to permanent image projection. This involves a close look at the role of time and place, compared to temporality and permanent image projection of catwalk shows streamed online. Lev Manovich's (2001; 2006) concept of 'permanent presence' will form a way in which both the temporal as well as the permanent image can be understood.

Richard Sennett (1977; 2006; 2008) and Frederic Jameson (2006) offer ways in which to explore the relationship between the catwalk show as live event and the living as well as virtual designer. Those who witnessed 'Angels and Demons' experienced how inherent trauma was transformed into what might be described as 'dream world'. Both Roland Barthes and Jean Baudrillard (2006; 2001; 1991) comment on the idea of aura in relation to cultural production that generates mythology.

Fashion discourse and the performing body

From early on in his career McQueen's designs as well as his presentations were intrinsically linked. Each show was a radical display of fashion and dramatic performance (Steele 2001; Khan 2000; Evans 2001; Wilcox 2001). Not without controversy, they have been described in the press as 'theatres of cruelty' (*Independent* 1993), or a 'wild rollercoaster of imagination and showmanship' (*New York Times* 2010). But it is this insistence on McQueen as a public figure and the central role of indulgent displays that play a part in his lasting legacy. McQueen rose to fame on the crest of the wave of the boom years of the 1990s and early 2000s. His death so soon after the 2008 economic meltdown marks not only an end of elaborate display and excess, it also signifies a point in which personal expression, subjectivity and emotionally charged performance are no longer central to the way fashion establishes meaning.

The catwalk show is a central part of visual culture and fashion media discourse. As such it plays an important part in the symbolic production of fashion. Agnès Rocamora (2009) and Joanne Entwistle (2012; 2001) refer to Foucault's notion of discourse when linking symbolic production and contemporary fashion. Rocamora (2009) argues that 'discourses of symbolic production are not simply concerned with commodities or texts', but also create meaning around 'individual agents such as designers and celebrities', as well as 'brands or cities' (Rocamora 2009: 55). The symbolic production of fashion is informed by the way discourse is created and Entwistle (2011; 2001) takes a more critical approach to Foucault's notion of discourse in relation to fashion when she insists on the link between the individual and the social. In the case of McQueen we can say that his shows create links between the designer and the social world. Each fashion season, the live event of the catwalk show marks the beginning of the fashion cycle. McQueen's elaborate shows played an important part in manifesting the status of the catwalk show as a moment in time and place, but have also informed discourse around the role of the designer as producer. McQueen, as well as other designers of his generation, such as John Galliano or Hussein Chalayan, have been an intrinsic part of fashion discourse.

The designer on display

When asked about the role of the catwalk show in his last interview with *Love Magazine*, McQueen expressed quite clearly why his shows were an important element of his work: 'It comes down to the fact that I don't advertise, so shows are really just self-promotion' (Isaac Lock 2010: 324).

Press and fashion media played little part in the way McQueen produced meaning around his collections. McQueen was known to embrace digital technology. In 2010 he streamed 'Plato's Atlantis' (2010) live on the internet, which at the time was still seen as unusual. He also incorporated fashion film and digital image projection as part of his catwalk shows, such as the use of the Kate Moss hologram in 'Widows of Culloden' for Autumn/Winter 2006/07.[2] Of central importance were his close collaborations with Nick Knight and SHOWstudio, which enabled him to reach a much larger audience within the digital frame. When asked about the role of the 'middle man' (that is, fashion editors and press) McQueen's answer offers an insightful perspective:

> I want this to be a company that lives way beyond me, and I believe that customers are more important in making this happen than press. When I'm dead, hopefully this house will still be going. On a spaceship. Hopping up and down above earth.
>
> (Isaac Lock 2010: 324)

Such a statement implies refusal to comply with expectations of a designer as public figure and can be seen as a provocation. Central to the emergence of digital media is the way technology has altered the way we perceive fashion. 'The media's delineation of the real offers distortion of vision, abstraction of time and a montage of images' (Khan 2012: 252). The comparison between the brand and a spaceship points to McQueen's commitment to technological advancement and the idea of fashion and image production within a digital framework.

Over the seasons that followed McQueen's posthumous show, we have witnessed an even more pronounced shift from the live event to permanent image projection. One might argue that McQueen's 'Angels and Demons' collection marked the end of the catwalk show as a momentous occasion. Central to the discussion on the impact of fashion within the digital frame are ideas around matter and materiality within the field of visual culture and media theory.

Caroline Evans (2007; 2008) speaks of fashion as image when she describes the particular spectacle of the fashion shows of Galliano and McQueen during the late 1990s. But since the death of McQueen, gone are the elaborate sets, extreme scenarios and costly productions. Still an important part of the fashion calendar, the McQueen shows continue to reflect trends, style and desire but have taken a much less visible, much less subversive approach.

For those who witnessed the shows prior to his death, these spectacles of conspicuous consumption only exist in memory and so too do the dresses on display, which were never produced or sold. Evans states that 'only the photographs of the showpiece remain', when she refers to the 'indexical power' of the fashion image (Evans 2008: 22). For McQueen the symbolic production of fashion has taken an almost mystical role, outside temporal or physical dimensions. His catwalk shows that incorporate film or digital images offer an emblem of representation and both the still and the moving fashion image is rooted within a far more virtual culture of commodification.

The digital image has no natural end, but instead offers 'permanent presence' (Manovich 2001). Fashion's relationship with time has been altered through digital media and the transition from iconic images of particular catwalk shows have shifted to symbolic representation through online feeds or live streaming, (Khan 2012). The transition from live event to permanent image flow was not a sudden but a gradual shift. McQueen himself had moved away from simply relying on live performance until he incorporated digital technology into his shows, such as *Plato's Atlantis* (2010). Andrew Bolton (2011: 15), quotes Alex Fury, fashion director at SHOWstudio: 'Before our very eyes . . . garments became image rather than object, pixelated and broadcast worldwide within seconds' (Fury in Bolton 2011: 15).

McQueen's posthumous collection was very much informed by images: not staged performance but digital reproduction of classical painting. McQueen's assistant Sarah Burton has commented on the design process and the link between digital technology and craftsmanship, when she refers to the Flemish paintings, fabrics and making process that informed the work:

> There was still a Modernity in the way that the fabrics were developed. So, for instance, there's a dress with a Hieronymus Bosch jacquard on it, Heaven and Hell. And what we did is we scanned the painting and digitally wove the jacquard. So in a way you've still got this juxtaposition of the old and the new, that I think is always important in his work.
>
> (Burton in Bolton 2010: 135)

Recent literature has described 'Angels and Demons' as having a 'baroque aesthetic', influenced by medieval art (Knox 2010: 123). Over the course of his career, allegories of death and mortality have been formed an intrinsic part of McQueen's oeuvre. The art works, which were digitally recreated and printed on layers of fabric, used works by Jean Fouquet, Sandro Botticelli, Stephan Lochner, Grinling Gibbons and most importantly Hieronymus Bosch's conception of hell. By referencing scenes of violence, trauma and suffering the focus goes beyond the paradigm of fashion.

Many of the books written after McQueen's death have focused on the figure of the designer as 'genius' or 'artist'.[3] This way of elevating the craftsman or designer to a somewhat superior status poses questions in terms of the role of fashion and inherent value. Richard Sennett (2008) discusses the function and status of the craftsman within a historical and social context, when he examines the shift from medieval craftsman to renaissance artist. According to Sennett (2006), what elevated artists to the status of genius were 'self-destructive subjectivity' (Sennett 2008: 65), subsequent suicide or the embodiment of 'melancholy' in the work. Central to this shift in status is the notion of originality and authenticity, something that is seen as significant in the field of fashion and fashion design. As much as we can say that McQueen's 'Angels and Demons' collection embodied modes of subjectivity through the expression of melancholia, his work is both original and closely connected to his own subjectivity. McQueen is quoted to refer to the impact of the autobiographical in his work: 'My collections have always been autobiographical, a lot to do with my sexuality and coming to terms with the person I am – it was like exorcising my ghosts in the collections' (McQueen in Bolton 2011: 16).

As discussed in Khan (2000), the catwalk show becomes a stage, which embodies believable, if not 'true' emotional context. Teunissen (2006: 212) argues that 'in today's visual culture we have come to regard personal identity in aesthetic terms. And central to this is what Sennett (1976) refers to when he speaks of the 'intrusion of personality into the public realm'; in his account of the 'stage' he refers to the idea of personality in public as a reflection of emotion:

> The theatre was doing for them that which in the modern capital they could not do easily for themselves. The division between mystery, illusion, and depiction on the one hand and truth on the other were in the mid-nineteenth century drawn into a peculiar form: authentic life, which requires no effort of decoding, appeared only under the aegis of the stage.
>
> (Sennett 1976: 176)

McQueen offers a version of what Sennett calls 'authentic life': the catwalk show is a stage on which identity is lived out through spectacle and personal experience made public.

The catwalk show and permanent presence

Although the fashion calendar continues to rely on the traditional format of the fashion show, long gone are the elaborate displays and costly production that characterised the McQueen brand. Image culture and fashion media have changed since McQueen's March 2010 show. A shift from the catwalk as live event to the permanent flow of images online has altered the way audiences engage with images of fashion. Central to the catwalk show is, of course, the dressed body. The impact of technology and mass media has been profound on the fashion system, but it has also impacted on the way we perceive fashion in relation to the body and the garment. Duggen speaks of 'the problem' of virtual presentation and the idea of physicality when he refers to 'a conceptual rather than physical phenomenon'; in regard to the fashion show he 'relates to the physical body in terms of the spiritual rather than the functional' (Duggen 2006: 233). This is relevant if we consider wider impact of 'Angels and Demons'.

The ornate designs in McQueen's posthumous collection served as mirrors. The show did not rely on elaborate spectacle, as the garments themselves fulfilled this purpose. The impact of 'Angels and Demons' was defined by the absence of spectacle. Each tableau presented a moment of stillness. No spotlights, no gestures, no choreographed displays or swishing technology – just simply clothed bodies facing the audience. Models were arranged in what can be described as a *tableau vivant*: an image that created the semblance of a moment frozen in time through stillness and stagnation. As a consequence, the show was filled with what Samuel Weber (1996) describes as 'posthumous aftershock' in his discussion of Benjamin's notion of aura, art and media culture. Each moment is then filled with the immediacy of the experience, while the focus itself is turned away from the audience and solely focuses on the emotional content implicit within the design. Christina Binkley wrote in the *Wall Street Journal*: 'Perhaps the eeriest insight into the designer's final weeks was a dress imprinted with a scene from Bosch's triptych "The Garden of Earthly Delights", which shows the artist's hellish conception of the afterlife' (Binkley 2010: 7).

The garment expresses emotion, and each dress serves as a means of personal expression. Duggen has argued that 'since the 1990s, designers like Alexander McQueen have earned reputations for fashion shows that read like sequences of dream images or fantastical visions' (Duggen 2006: 223). But in 'Angels and Demons' such phantasmagorias were not part of the scenarios created on the catwalk; they were no longer staged, but digitally transferred onto the dress. The fashion critic, Binkley, was no longer able to differentiate between Bosch's vision of the afterlife and McQueen's own ordeal.

The recurring emblem of the skull and its allegorical reference to the vanitas tradition and renaissance still-life painting are important aspects of McQueen's designs. The extensive use of feathers and images of angel's wings, as discussed earlier in the final high-collared jacket, reference religious iconography. In addition many of the sixteen pieces referenced previous collections (Knox 2010: 122). Such an approach supports the idea that McQueen's posthumous collection had a momentous quality as it was staged as a memorial to the designer's career and his work. A moment in time stands for the whole and implies what Benjamin describes as a 'time filled by the presence of the now' (Benjamin 1970: 46). In this sense it can be seen as momentous, but at the same time it relies on the mechanisms of montage.

Fredric Jameson speaks of consciousness and realism within a modernist and postmodern context when he refers to cultural production and mental space (Jameson 2009: 25). McQueen's show created a form of pastiche as it references previous collections and individual iconic pieces. Time and temporality are important aspects of the way we perceive history in a postmodern context, and the final collection refers to its own history at one particular moment in time. Repeatedly referencing well-known silhouettes, or stylistic detail, it draws the spectator to the designer's past. Jameson (2006) argues that such an approach makes it impossible 'to unify the past, present and future' but instead we witness 'a series of pure and unrelated presents in time' (Jameson 2009: 27). In addition one might add that the collection is not simply a means of referencing the past, it also alludes to renaissance art and a montage of human suffering and mental images of death and resurrection.

The stage and the technological void

'Widows of Culloden' in 2006/07 was the first fashion show to employ virtual technology through the use of a hologram. The technique of holography is an optical process, which yields a virtual image of a visual field in three dimensions. Susanna Frankel commented in *The Independent* that 'Kate Moss loomed large over the designer Alexander McQueen': 'Rather than stalking the floorboards alongside her contemporaries, she had been filmed prior to the show and away from the crowds and her image was projected via an optical device, widely known as Pepper's ghost' (Frankel 2006: 7).

The 'Pepper's ghost' Frankel is referring to created the effect of a virtual body spontaneously floating in mid-air. A flickering light twisted and spun, within a large pyramid glass structure, expanded into floating fabric, then a dress and finally gave way to an image of McQueen's muse Kate Moss. McQueen's collaboration with the filmmaker Baillie Walsh is of course more than the creation of an optical illusion, as virtual representation creates epistemological doubt. Frankel (2006) comments on time and place and with it refers to aspects of the 'real'. As Moss's body is suspended in space, she is not represented through an image projection but her presence is replicated – which draws our attention to her own manufactured status. At the time of 'Widows of Culloden', Moss had been surrounded by scandal, and the dichotomy between the private and public persona had become increasingly important. One could argue that her virtual image responded to Barthes's (1972) notion of mythology. Myth relies on fame, controversy and public interest. At McQueen's show the audience was confronted with a virtual projection of aura, which solely depended on the process and techniques of an optical illusion.

The hologram breaks with notions of matter and time as Moss's image played with themes of presence and absence: at the end her appearance faded and turned back into small flickering lights. The virtual force of this projection reminded viewers that they were unable to capture or hold on to the image and with it the moment in time. The experience itself gained currency, as the show created not a moving body but virtual flow from the present to the future. More like a momentum, time itself is fetishised and the hologram inhabited the moment while we were reminded that the image does not belong to a lived or living body.

There is no 'through' the screen the way there is a 'through' the looking glass or mirror. The dimensions of time itself merge there in 'real time' (Baudrillard, 2002: 178).

Both Jean Baudrillard (1994; 2002) and Katherine Hayles (1999) are useful here as they discuss matter and time in relation to virtual reality. Kate Moss's physical presence in time and space becomes immediate as it is turned into a pure image. For Baudrillard, the hologram stands for a diffusion and sublimation of reality, when he speaks of a dream 'of being able to go through ourselves and find ourselves on the other side' (Baudrillard 1994: 105). Reality is simulated through a computer-generated image. But the virtual image serves not as a version but as a duplication of the real. The body becomes pure image, no longer material matter but virtual projection. Virtuality has been defined by Katherine Hayles as 'the cultural perception that material objects are interpenetrated by information patterns' (Hayles 1999: 13–14). When looking more closely at the nature of the projection it becomes clear that we do not deal with representation as we might through filmic projection. The hologram does not have the purpose of making things visible, but rather conveys the opposite. Kate Moss floated and disappeared from view; to begin with she was merely invisible until her floating movements turned her into a phantom. Automatic movement, as Hayles (1999) argues is mere interpretation of information patterns and of course very different from autonomous movement of the living body.

Kate Moss is no longer a mortal subject but perception made invisible. Her hologram image projection is as much a statement on the nature of public persona as it is on the desire to disappear, to be invisible or beyond grasp. Baudrillard (2002) speaks of the relationship between body and machine: 'So, the attraction of all these virtual machines no doubt derives not so much from the thirst for information and knowledge as from the desire to disappear, and the possibility of dissolving oneself into a phantom conviviality' (Baudrillard 2002: 180).

We may speak of a digital revolution, which has entered the catwalk and has changed the way we see and perceive fashion. Digital media had a profound impact on the catwalk and McQueen's shows utilised technology and mass media in order to develop a more precise and, in many ways, more progressive relationship between fashion, the body, technology and subjectivity. 'Widows of Culloden' went beyond the realm of conventional image production and some of the McQueen shows, which followed, such as 'Plato's Atlantis' (2010) transcended any notion of the catwalk show as an event in fixed time and place. Most powerful of all are those events in which perceptual technologies also serve as technologies of representation. When 'Kate Moss loomed large' (Frankel 2006: 6) above the audience, fashion broke with conventional ideas of matter and time. Images of fashion, which are formed by and through digital media, indirectly transform structures of fashion.

The impact of new technologies materialises in the way representation is constituted. Frederic Jameson (1991) speaks of historical moments marked by technological revolution. His analysis of cultural logic focuses on moments of major technological change, which revolutionised capitalism. The photographic, the cinematic and the electronic were each aesthetic means that informed realism, modernism and postmodern modes of representation. The cultural logic of digital technology implies a further break with realism and modernist understanding of time and place. As discussed earlier, McQueen's refusal of conventional modes of advertising can be seen as an attempt to facilitate myth. His reliance on the catwalk and digital media radically informed the brand's aesthetic. Kate Moss's digital immaterial version inhabits myth. Baudrillard (2005) argues that myth plays an important part in the production of aura.

Aura and fashion in a museum context

Just over a year after McQueen's show 'Angel and Demons', the Metropolitan Museum of Art in New York (MoMA), staged 'Alexander McQueen: Savage Beauty (2011)', a retrospective of McQueen's work as a designer. Since the Yves Saint

Laurent exhibition in 1983, curated by Diana Vreeland, the Met has not shown monographic exhibitions of living fashion designers. But as McQueen was no longer at the core of the brand the museum exhibited clothes, which could be seen in the context of social history rather than current or up-to-date collections.

'Savage Beauty' took a thematic approach, breaking down McQueen's design history into various sections, such as Romantic Gothic, Romantic Nationalism, Romantic Exoticism and Romantic Primitivism, each of which referred not only to the dresses on display but served a much grander theme. *Savage Beauty* aimed to establish myth and mythology around McQueen and his work. In the context of the museum the objects on display gain a different kind of aura. Without the live moment of the catwalk show, or permanent image projection within the digital frame, the dresses gain the longevity of a historic object. The numerous visitors at MoMA were able to bask in the aura of something that was no longer of the present. The impact of an object's longevity could be found in the way some of the pieces were displayed.

The first room (entitled 'Cabinet of Curiosities') included a casket that spotlighted McQueen's posthumous collection. Andrew Bolton (2011), the exhibition's curator explained that 'Cabinet of Curiosities' refers to 'the eighteenth-century and nineteenth-century practice of collecting objects from natural history as a way of viewing the world'.[4] Visitors were able to view the dresses, frozen in time, not unlike a corpse behind glass. Fashion within the museum context is no longer a commercial product. We are reminded that we cannot acquire or possess it, but instead have access to its aura. McQueen's designs had the ability to establish symbolic presence. The theme of presence and absence was mirrored again in the final room, which showed the Kate Moss hologram. But this time the model did not loom larger than life, but was shown in miniature. Visitors could view a tiny version of 'Pepper's ghost', through a small opening at the side of the box. The scale of the display reminded the viewer of the distant mystique of an event, which only existed through its visual projection.

Conclusion

'Angels and Demons' came at a particular moment in time, unique in the fact that it marked a shift from fashion to mythology. This essay has shown that the underlying response of fashion journalists, curators and writers to McQueen's show was not simply concerned with the level of showpieces or spectacles, but demonstrated how such an event represented the embodiment of subjectivity and emotion. After his death, McQueen's designs increasingly became associated with nostalgia for something greater than their original truth. The relationship between 'reality' and perception is central to forms of representation and an important part in establishing an idea of myth. With the last model leaving the room on 9 March 2010, the audience did not simply witness an exit, but something new made itself felt. Not a display of fashioned bodies but an inscription of a moment in time. Not just an image, but an already distant impression – Benjamin describes aura as 'a looking – back'. An image that is absorbed in the immediacy of the present and a moment – however momentous – that marks the end of an era.

Notes

1   Some of the articles which commented on McQueen's final show include Jess Carter Morley (2010) 'Alexander McQueen's last Collection', in *The Guardian*, 9 March 2010; Christina Binkley (2010) 'McQueen's Angels and Demons', in *The Wall Street Journal*, 9 March 2010; and Armand Limnander (2010) 'Alexander McQueen's Final Show', in *The New York Times*, 9 March 2010.

2   McQueen's 'Widows of Culloden' show famously referenced the battle of 1745.

3   (Gleason 2012; Watt 2012; Bolton 2011; Knox 2010).

4   Andrew Bolton, 'Alexander McQueen: Savage Beauty', The Metropolitan Museum of Art, accessed 28 February 2013, http://blog.metmuseum.org/alexandermcqueen/.

References

Barry, James Jr (1991) 'The Technical Body: Incorporating Technology and Flesh', *Philosophy Today* (Winter, 1991): 390–92.

Barthes, Roland (1983) *The Fashion System*. Berkeley: University of California Press.

——— (1972) *Mythologies*. Trans. Annette Lavers. New York: Noonday Press.

Baudrillard, Jean (2006) *Simulacra and Simulation*. Michigan: University of Michigan Press.

——— (2005) *The Conspiracy of Art*. New York: Semiotexte.

——— (2001) *Screened Out*. London: Verso Books.

——— (1991) *Seduction*. London: St Martin's Press.

Benjamin, Walter (1987) 'On the Mimetic Faculty', in *Reflections: Essays, Aphorisms, Autobiographical Writings*, New York: Schocken.

——— (2000) 'The Work of Art in the Age of Mechanical Reproduction', in *Illumination*, ed. Hannah Arendt. London: MIT Press.

Bolton, Andrew (2012) *Alexander McQueen: Savage Beauty*, New York: Metropolitan Museum of Art.

——— (2010) 'Alexander McQueen: Savage Beauty,' The Metropolitan Museum of Art, online at www.blog.metmuseum.org/alexandermcqueen (accessed 18 March 2013).

Crary, Jonathan (1990) *Techniques of the Observer: On Vision and Modernity in the Nineteenth Century*. Cambridge, MA: MIT Press.

Debord, Guy (1983) *Society of the Spectacle*. Detroit: Black and Red.

Duggen, G.G. (2006) 'The Greatest Show on Earth: A Look at the Contemporary Fashion Shows and their Relationship to Performance Art', in *The Power of Fashion: About Design and Meaning*, eds J. Brand and J. Teunissen. Arnhem: Terra and ArtEZ Press, pp. 222–48.

Entwistle, Joanne (2011) 'Dress, Social Structures and Bodily Order', in *The Fashion Reader, 2nd edn*, eds Linda Welters and Abby Lillethun. London: Berg, pp. 146–9.

——— (2001) 'The Dressed Body', in *Body Dressing*. Oxford: Berg, pp. 33–58.

Evans, Caroline (2006) *Fashion on the Edge*. London: Yale University Press.

——— (2001) 'Desire and Dread: Alexander McQueen and the Contemporary Femme Fatale', in *Body Dressing*. Oxford: Berg, pp. 201–14.

Frankel, Susanna (2006) 'Kate Moss Loomed Large', in *The Independent*. London.

Gleason, K. (2012) *Alexander McQueen: Evolution*, New York: Race Point Publishing.

Hayles, Katherine, N. (1999) *How We Became Posthuman. Virtual Bodies in Cybernetics, Literature and Informatics.* Chicago: University of Chicago Press.

—— (2002) *Writing Machines*. London: The MIT Press.

Jameson, Frederic (1991) *Postmodernism, or The Cultural Logic of Late Capitalism,* Durham, NC: Duke University Press.

Khan, N. (2000) 'Catwalk Politics', in *Fashion Cultures: Theories, Explorations and Analysis*, eds Stella Bruzzi and Pamela Church Gibson. pp. 114–27.

Khan, N. (2012) 'Cutting the Fashion Body: Why the Fashion Image is no longer still' in *Fashion Theory*, vol. 16, no. 2, June 2012, London: Bloomsbury Journals, pp. 235–50.

Khan, N. (2012) 'Stealing the Moment – the non-narrative films of Ruth Hogben and Gareth Pugh', in *Film, Fashion and Consumption* vol. 1 no. 3, 261–2.

Knox, K. (2010) *Alexander McQueen: Genius of a Generation*, London: A&C Black Publishing.

Lock, Isaac (2010) 'Which Celebrities are Wearing It, What Reviews Say . . . None of it Matters – Alexander McQueen', in *Love Magazine* S/S 2010, 324.

Manovich, Lev (2001) *The Language of New Media*. London: MIT Press.

—— (2005) *Soft Cinema*, Cambridge, MA: MIT Press.

Rio, Elena del (1996) 'The Body as Foundation of the Screen: Allegories of Technology in Atom Egoyan's *Speaking Parts*', in *Camera Obscura*, nos. 37/38 (summer 1996): 103–4.

Rocamora, Agnès (2009) 'Media Fashion Discourse', in *Fashioning the City – Paris, Fashion and the Media*. London: I.B. Tauris, pp. 54–64.

Scarry, Elaine (1994) 'The Merging of Bodies and Artifacts in the Social Contract,' in *Culture on the Brink: Ideologies of Technology*, eds Gretchen Bender and Timothy Druckery. Seattle, Bay Press, pp. 97–105.

Sennett, Richard (2008) *The Craftsman*. London: Allen Lane, Penguin Group.

—— (1977) *The Fall of the Public Man*. London: Faber and Faber.

—— (2006) *The Culture of New Capitalism*. New Haven: Yale University Press.

Silverman, Kaja (1986) 'Fragments of Fashionable Discourse', in *Studies in Entertainment – Critical Approaches to Mass Culture*, ed. Tania Modleski. London: John Wiley & Sons.

Steele, Valerie (2001) 'Style in Revolt', in *Radical Fashion*, ed. Claire Wilcox London: V&A Publishing, pp. 47–53.

Teunissen, J. (2006) 'Eternity: A Frill on the Dress', in *The Power of Fashion – About Design and Meaning*, eds Brand, J. and Teunissen, J. Arnhem: ArtEZPress.

Vilaseca, Estel (2009) *Runway Uncovered: The Making of a Fashion Show*. Barcelona: Prompopress.

Wall Street Journal (2010) McQueen's Angels and Demons. Christina Binkley. www.online.wsj.com/article/SB100014240527487047849045751119111307877710.html, accessed 20 January 2013.

Watt, J. (2012) *Alexander McQueen: Fashion Visionary*, London: Goodman Books.

Weber, Samuel (1996) *Mass Mediauras*. Stanford: Stanford University Press.

Wilcox, Claire (2001) 'I Try Not to Fear Radical Things', in *Radical Fashion*, ed. Claire Wilcox. London: V&A Publishing, pp. 1–6.

PART 5

Contestation, compliance, feminisms

Chapter 20

Hilary Radner and Natalie Smith

FASHION, FEMINISM AND THE
NEO-FEMINIST IDEAL
From Coco Chanel to Jennifer Lopez

FASHION HAS PLAYED A PIVOTAL ROLE in the development of feminist thought, from the moment, at the very least, when Susan B. Anthony successfully challenged Elizabeth Oakes Smith for the leadership of the Women's Convention in 1852, on the grounds that no woman who dressed as fashionably as Smith 'could represent the earnest, solid, hardworking women of the country' (Scott 2005: 23). Tensions between ideas about how dress might promote social equality as a utopian project, on the one hand, and, on the other, how an individual woman's engagement with consumerism might afford her a fuller economic and social life, continued to mark the history of feminism over the next century and a half. First wave feminists such as Elizabeth Cady Stanton and Amelia Bloomer believed that by freeing the body through wearing garments such as 'bloomers', they were liberating the mind (Purdy 2004: 111). Others sought 'improvements' in terms of comfort that were designed to be 'evolutionary, not revolutionary' (Cunningham 2003: 75–82). For yet another less privileged cohort, fashion, in its more conventional sense, offered a path to economic independence (Finnegan 1999: 18–19).

In the late 1960s, the conversation was further complicated by the development of yet another perspective, that of neo-feminism, voiced by women such as Helen Gurley Brown, who promoted the new ideal of the Single Girl – who would give way to the Yummy Mummy in the twenty-first century (Radner 2011: 6–25). For such women, dressing well proclaimed her financial success, enabling her further advancement, if coupled with a certain financial conservatism, by mobilising her sexual charms and exploiting her assets, both tangible and intangible. Tracing the history of this conversation illuminates the complex and often contradictory relations between fashion and feminism – between consumerism and economic agency – that characterise women's culture as its moves from the twentieth century into the twenty-first.

Designing women

In the aftermath of the First World War, as women gained more independence and, in many cases, the vote, fashion increasingly represented a means toward achieving full participation and economic independence within contemporary society. Thus, fashion historians Caroline Evans and Minna Thornton emphasise how

> fashion has offered opportunities of expression denied to them [women] historically by the male dominated world of fine art . . . *Couture* enabled women to be both creative designers and businesswomen. In the early twentieth century, the only comparable area of opportunity was show business.
>
> (Evans and Thornton 1991)

If austerity remained the norm among feminism's more idealistic proponents, women intellectuals, artists and entrepreneurs harnessed the opportunities afforded by the fashion industry to develop their social and economic positions. If, for the most part, male designers surpassed women in terms of numbers, female designers, nonetheless, had a significant impact on the field throughout the century (Steele 1991).

Coco Chanel, 'associated with the liberation of women's fashion' (Evans and Thornton 1989: 132) and certainly one of the most influential designers of the twentieth century, was a case in point (Picardie 2011: 138–9). While Chanel's prominence coincided with a period in fashion history in which women designers dominated the field, if briefly, her design strategies would have a lasting impact on the decades that followed (Steele 1991: 11). According to Evans and Thornton,

> Chanel's contribution to women's fashion was the adaptation of the form and details, but above all the meanings, of a certain type of masculine dress to that of women. In so doing, she developed a style that seemed, particularly at the height of her influence in the 1920s, to express the aspirations of early twentieth-century women towards independence and mobility.
>
> (Evans and Thornton 1989: 123).

While Chanel's influence was felt most strongly in the 1920s, reaching across the Atlantic (*Vogue*, October 1926), with the 1930s seeing a return to a more traditional femininity, including longer skirts and more elaborate hairstyles, these changes were largely cosmetic with women continuing to favour less elaborate and constricting fashions. These were fashions that facilitated the continued promotion of a more populist vision of style that could be adopted by everyone from the lowly shop girl to the high society debutante, with film stars vying with socialites as sartorial icons. Typically, hair care was one of the few sectors that remained unaffected by the depression (Scott 2005: 198).

Temporary setbacks

During the Second World War, women assumed responsibilities on the home front, even working in factories, with their clothing reflecting the greater degree of agency and autonomy that accompanied these activities. The emphasis on practicality in women's dress during the war years, exacerbated by fabric shortages and other restrictions placed on non-essential industries such as civilian clothing, gave way to a postwar conservatism exemplified by the work of French couturier Christian Dior. On 12 February 1947 Christian Dior revealed his 'New Look', drawing on a silhouette first reintroduced by French-American designer Mainbocher 'with his 1939 Victorian cinch-waist' (Palmer 2009: 25–7; Magidson 2010: 492). Post-Liberation France, where shortages in many areas were still the norm, was outraged by the new style with its longer, fuller skirts, girdled waists, sloping, narrow shoulders, delicate-heeled shoes, picture-book hats and general impression of decorative, fragile affluence (Quant 2012: 6–7; Palmer 2009: 25–7). In the United States, women gathered to protest against the New Look during Dior's first American trip (Palmer 2009: 29). In spite of these outbursts, the New Look was the single most important international fashion trend during the decade that followed, its excesses and impracticality suggesting that a woman's role was essentially passive: to exhibit her husband's wealth and status.

Not coincidentally, Simone de Beauvoir's *The Second Sex*, a crucial publication in the development of second wave feminism, appeared in 1949 in France and in English in 1953, pointing to the ways in which women's culture of the period was fragmented and ambivalent. For Beauvoir, '[d]ressing . . . expresses woman's social situation' particularly as it is tied to her marital status, but also to her sexual identity as feminine (De Beauvoir 2011: 588). She, however, also claims that – unlike most professional women who seek to overcome their status as dependent by denying the importance of appearance, and hence their identity as feminine – actresses, dancers and singers may achieve a certain coherence as subjects, 'as independent women', because in these professions the emphasis on the cultivation of physical presentation resolves the conundrum of woman as caught between the desire for autonomy and fulfilling herself as 'a sexed human being'. Because their 'professional successes contribute to . . . their sexual worth', she explains that 'realising themselves as human beings, they accomplish themselves as women; they are not torn between contradictory aspirations' (De Beauvoir 2011: 757). In essence, these women's looks operate in the service of their own self-advancement and fulfilment as independent. The same might be said of the women who turned to the fashion industry on the model of Chanel as a means of realising themselves professionally and economically without undermining their identity as feminine. These women, involved in the pursuit of uniquely feminine activities, like the actress highlighted by Beauvoir, dress to express their own activities and position in society rather than that of their husbands, an idea that would gain in significance, both among academic feminists as well as women consumers more generally, as the century progressed.

The youthquake and the single girl

The development of American sportswear in the 1950s and subsequent rise of youth culture afforded American designers, such as Claire McCardell, Clare Potter and Bonnie Cashin – many of whom began their careers in the 1930s, but did not receive popular attention until the postwar years – the opportunity of challenging the dominance of the male (and frequently European) couturier (Scheips 2007: 118, 41). These developments allowed more women to emerge as significant figures in the fashion world, such as the youth-oriented Betsey Johnson, followed by designer celebrities such as Diane von Furstenberg, or Norma Kamali in the 1970s, who 'had the task of creating a new strong image' (Steele 1991: 123, 142, 145). By the 1960s, with the explosion of clothing directed at the younger generation, like the miniskirt in the hands of young designers such as Mary Quant and Barbara Hulanicki (Biba), both media stars in their own right, the fashion world rejected the New Look and, by extension, the wealthy married woman as its primary exemplar. The designs of Quant and her contemporaries, such as Sally Tuffin of the design team Foale and Tuffin, emphasised girlishness, in contrast to the New Look connotations of wife, capturing the postwar baby boomer's desire to escape the staid style and way of life that they associated with their mothers (Lobenthal 1990: 10, 15–16; Scott 2005: 252–3).

American ready-to-wear manufacturers seized upon the work of these new designers, the simplicity of which suited the demands of mass manufacturing. Indeed, both Quant and her youthquake contemporaries, the Foale and Tuffin team, would spend time designing for the American chain J. C. Penney's (Quant 1966: 114–17; Victoria and Albert Museum, 2006). The dominance of the ready-to-wear market created its own designers, such as Sonia Rykiel in Paris, or, later, Norma Kamali in the New York, moving increasingly towards a populist vision of style that would reach full fruition in the twenty-first century. While fashion remained the terrain of the economically privileged, it had, nonetheless, significantly expanded its territory to include the middle classes, particularly young single women whose income was largely devoted to supporting themselves, rather than a family. Fashion historians Valerie Mendes and Amy de la Haye date the demise of haute couture as the late 1960s, with the closing of Balenciaga's 'Paris house' in 1968. In 1971, 'the death of Chanel marked yet another stage in couture's decline'. Subsequently, 'the couture shows were used to herald the big business of the prêt-à-porter collections'(Mendes and Haye 1999: 194).

If these ready-to-wear fashions were adopted by enthusiasts and promoters of the new Single Girl culture such as Helen Gurley Brown, editor of *Cosmopolitan* magazine and author of *Sex and the Single Girl* (1962), the 1960s also marked the beginning of second wave feminism. Popular media images of the period portray advocates for women's rights as representing the plurality of dress styles available to them, reflecting the times rather than feminism itself (Miss America Collections). While subsequent developments in feminist thought sought to provide a more unified vision of how the feminist ought to look, with resulting stereotypes often mobilised as a means of ridiculing women's concerns (Mendes and Haye 1999: 192; Groeneveld 2009), the 1960s also saw the rise of another version of the emancipated woman who may have proven more influential. These women, usually

Figure 20.1   Second wave feminists wore the fashions of their time, including miniskirts. Source: 'Freedom Trash Can', Miss America protest, Atlantic City, 1968, Courtesy of Duke University Libraries, Digital Collections.

associated with the media industries, such as Helen Gurley Brown, embraced the consumerism and the fashions that the feminists reviled. Recently reclaimed by feminist scholars such as Jennifer Scanlon, as giving voice to a form of popular feminism (2009; Ouellette 1999), Brown advocated that a woman exploit fashion and consumerism in order to maximise her sexual appeal while also honing her professional skills. She shared with Beauvoir a negative view of motherhood (Scanlon 2009: 180; Radner 2011: 94), while encouraging women to develop financial skills and preserve their attractiveness. While Chanel, for example, did not marry, and remained an outsider in terms of polite society, Helen Gurley Brown and the women of her generation dismantled the social structure that posited single women as limited to the roles of derogated and frustrated spinster or lusty and disreputable mistress, barely distinguishable from prostitutes. The Single Girl represented a new and glamorous ideal, who had the right to invest her time and money in herself and her own advancement, and was free to marry, or not, or, even, re-marry, according to her needs and priorities at a particular moment in her life.

Neo-feminism

Described as 'neo-feminism', this new ideal or, more accurately, set of discourses governing a particular group of behaviours, with an emphasis on individual accomplishment and self-realisation, sat easily with the prevailing neoliberalist policies that coincided with its evolution historically (Radner 2011: 6–25). In many ways, neo-feminism has proven more resilient and effective in speaking to women than has second wave feminism with its focus on social reform, to the degree that the two have become intertwined in the mind of many – such that figures like the pop singer Madonna have been routinely characterised as feminist heroines (Miller 2011: 58; Lewis 1990: 2–15). Even among feminist scholars, there is an increasing willingness, as evidenced in Scanlon's reappraisal of Brown, to assess any perspective that seems to advocate for the economic advancement of individual women as evidence of feminism. Indeed, the imagery associated with this ideal – or more accurately, set of behaviours – emphasises agency and mobility, fashion photography itself leaving the studio and taking to the streets, highlighting the emancipatory qualities of these new fashions that encourage women to stride confidently towards a new future (Radner 2000: 128–42; Harrison 1991).

Such images contributed to the concept that fashion was not a set of garments, but a lifestyle that was widely available, associated with a sense of autonomy, independence and self-actualisation, an idea promulgated by cross-media promotions for products such as scent and cosmetics, including 'Jean Naté ("Take charge of your life"), Rive Gauche (a woman "having too much fun to marry") . . . and, the L'Oréal color campaign theme' that 'touted individual self-fulfilment. "Because I am worth it"' (Sivulka 2010: 315). These campaigns illustrate how mainstream feminine culture, through the lure of the new woman, embraced fashion as a legitimate path toward feminine empowerment, conflating individual ambitions with certain sentiments (and even slogans) that appeared to have been borrowed from second wave feminism. American fashion, which was almost exclusively grounded in ready-to-wear, became the emblem of this new woman. In contrast, European fashion was increasingly influenced by a movement known as conceptual fashion, intermittently supported by feminist scholars and intellectuals (see for example Cixous 1994). Within the American context, what came to be thought of as fashionable was grounded in on what started as the tradition of American sportswear for day and Hollywood glamour for evening, including plunging necklines that would have seemed out of place in the more staid settings of a traditional or avant-garde fashionable elite that continued to characterise Europe. The fashionable ideal, then, was the professional woman who wore these clothes, with singleness, or the appearance of singleness, as one of her attributes – the supermodel with her various franchises, such as exercise programmes, scents, or fashion lines, leading the pack.

By the 1990s, intensifying in the twenty-first century, however, a number of significant shifts had occurred. Displaced by the media celebrity, the model no longer commanded the same attention. Fashion became another dimension of the broader domain of celebrity culture (Church Gibson 2011). Magazine covers featured movie stars and singers who were happy to forego the fees required by the supermodel in return for the publicity such a position afforded them (Coddington 2012: 249). Motherhood was increasingly associated with the new feminine ideal, so much so that a *New York Times* article written by Francine du Plessix Gray (2010), on the occasion of the re-translation of Beauvoir's *The Second Sex*, chastised the writer for her pessimistic view of maternity, reasserting emphatically the importance of motherhood to feminine identity. Twenty-first century fashion icons, almost inevitably mothers, both in their statements to the press and in the iconography deployed to create their media image, add weight to Gray's position as one that is held by many in the twenty-first century, highlighting how the Yummy Mummy has supplanted the Single Girl as the dominant ideal within popular discourses about style.

Jennifer Lopez: Twenty-first century neo-feminist fashion icon

Jennifer Lopez as a style icon represents this further evolution in the neo-feminist ideal that first emerged with Helen Gurley Brown and her contemporaries, and that was initially associated with the Single Girl. This new neo-feminist ideal continues to use fashion as a vehicle and expression of feminine empowerment, while incorporating motherhood as a sign of her fulfilment. The cross-media celebrity Jennifer Lopez offers a striking example of the viability of this new idea, exemplified in her remarkable comeback: in 2011, she was ranked number fifty on *Forbes* 'annual Celebrity 100 List'; by May 2012, she had climbed to top celebrity of the year according to the same magazine, testifying to the potency of her image (Elliott and Goudreau 2012; Goudreau 2012). Drawing on her cross-media reputation and her cross-over audience appeal as a star with a strong ethnic identity who had a mainstream fan-base, Lopez carved a niche for herself within high fashion, appearing on the covers of magazines such as *Harper's* and *Vogue*, notwithstanding her reputation for outrageous outfits and 'nip slips' (Radner 2011: 82–97; Robertson 2012). In 2012 she appeared on 46 major magazine covers, many of them Spanish-language publications (Goudreau 2012). Lopez's current prominence within the fashion system, including her own line of modestly priced clothing with Kohl's, categorised among 'low-end retailers . . . aiming to get cozy with the growing Latino consumer market' (Casserly 2012), suggests a shift away from a youthful vision of fashion in which adolescent-oriented disposable styles predominate to one that posits the mature, glamorous and financially savvy woman as the goal, in which a sexualised reinvented mother has supplanted the Single Girl in the public's imagination. Lopez's prominence highlights the dominance of the neo-feminist ideal that combines a rhetoric borrowed from feminism with an agenda that emphasises individual self-advancement and an Americanised vision of the fashionable woman, whose 'looks' confirm her position and identity, and

Figure 20.2   Jennifer Lopez promoted a warm and supportive persona in her role as judge on *American Idol*. Source: *American Idol* (Fox), Season 10, 2011, courtesy of Photofest.

whose status as mother both signals her maturity (she is no longer a girl) and her ties to a legitimate feminine genealogy. In the twenty-first century, Lopez as an icon calls into question what Caroline Evans sees as one of the fundamental tenets of twentieth-century fashion, which she claims 'has typically defined itself against the maternal body'. Evans specifies that 'early 1960s' fashion was hysterical in this respect' (Evans and Thornton 1989: 2). That Lopez (along with other women in the media eye, from the Kardashian sisters to Victoria Beckham) emphasises motherhood as a dimension of her glamour, exploited by Gucci, for example, in their campaign for their new children's line, is indicative of a sea change within the fashion world.

Lopez is not an isolated example: Diane Von Furstenberg – named by *Forbes* as the most powerful woman in fashion in 2012 – is a grandmother and of modest origins, the daughter of a Holocaust survivor (Karmali 2012; Leon 2007). Her reputation, like that of Lopez, depends upon a populist vision of fashion – one that extends into the home through such outlets as QVC, functioning as a brand that includes housewares as well as items of clothing that are widely available. Similarly, Michelle Obama was lauded by *Forbes* for 'her high-style low-budget strategy . . . [T]he first lady has . . . taken the stigma out of inexpensive clothes – regularly appearing in J. Crew and Zara separates' (Casserly 2012). All three offer a vision of the feminine body that is fuller, markedly adult (as opposed to girlish) and tied to motherhood as a positive attribute.

The ascendency of women such as Lopez and Von Furstenberg highlights not only what we might call a shift in values, but also the attributes of the twenty-first century clothing industry, what Deyan Sudjic calls 'the fashion system', which functions in terms of what he calls 'brand recognition', extending the earlier concept of promoting a lifestyle (2008: 150). The fashion system depends on the notion of branding, in which a particular line of clothing is articulated around a set of values that distinguishes it from other similar lines. Contemporary production and marketing techniques ensure that 'shops' are supplied 'with fresh product in a matter of days' and can 'restock with successful lines on a just-in-time basis, rather than relying on the old system and risking everything on a production run for a whole season'. Instead of promoting superior construction and rare fabrics, the twenty-first century fashion system 'turns shirts sewn together for pennies in Indonesia into high-margin goods' (Sudjic 2008: 149–50). In consequence, the notion of 'being fashionable' has permeated every stratum of society, with designers moving easily between haute couture, high street stores and even discount venues. The brand with which an item is associated makes an object desirable, rather than any specific attributes intrinsic to the item itself. Thus, *Time* reported that in 2013 as a result of an agreement with luxury department store Neiman Marcus, the discount store Target offered 'brand new pieces from 24 American designers, including Marc Jacobs and Oscar de la Renta' (Lukerson 2012). As a consequence, then, of its cost structure, and the industrial nature of its production and distribution, the fashionable object is ubiquitous and no longer the preserve of the wealthy.

Conclusion

This diversification of the fashion system, in particular its populist dimension, of which the emphasis on motherhood is an important facet (all women, even mothers, can be fashionable today), has presented significant challenges to feminist analysis. Certain scholars have viewed this pervasiveness of a more populist vision, touching women's lives across a wide range of social strata, as enabling a certain form of feminism to reach a wider audience (Budgeon and Currie 1995) – one, however, that seems closer to neo-feminism as described above, but also one that might appeal to Elizabeth Oakes Smith, condemned out of hand by Susan B. Anthony for dressing 'in the latest fashion of the day, low-cut and sleeveless' (Scott 2005: 23). Others, such as Linda Scott, call for women to move beyond appearance, echoing another sentiment that anti-feminists have repeatedly espoused – that feminine culture, such as fashion and style, is in and of itself trivial (Scott 2005). In contrast, feminists such as Angela McRobbie argue that it is not clothing as such that is the issue, but rather the fashion system itself – as an industry dependent upon production and distribution – should be called into question (McRobbie 1997; 1998, 2002). Notwithstanding, for Caroline Evans, the salient feature of contemporary high fashion, or what she calls 'experimental fashion', is its role as a symptomology that 'acts out repressed desires or fears' as an expression of 'historical rather than personal trauma' (Evans 2003: 6). Similarly, Rebecca Arnold deems that the creations of postmodern designers such as Miuccia Prada seek to document and display the consistent inconsistency of contemporary life and, in particular, femininity, inciting 'simultaneous feelings of pleasure and desire, alienation and anxiety' – again taking fashion as a social symptom (Arnold 2001: 207–20). In many ways, however, the diversity of these perspectives, all of which enlighten us about particular dimensions of fashion today, reflects the complexities and contraction of the system itself. The power of the twenty-first century fashion system derives from the fluidity of meanings that fashion and style in its various forms may hold for those who participate in this system, from the designer to the machinist to the consumer – in which style seems to hold out the promise of a terrain that remains, during a time of uncertainty and lack of clear expectations about the future, solely and uniquely under the control of the individual, whereby she (and increasingly also he) may carve out a sense of ownership and identity that is an expression of her or his self. In an era in which the earlier dream of owning a plot of land, a house, or even a home, recedes increasingly out of reach for much of the world's population, with promises of reform and revolution having less and less credibility, personal style remains her only recourse whereby she may assert her belief in self-improvement and self-transformation.

Indeed, contemporary politics have largely discredited the idea that the grand narratives of philosophy and social theory, the legacies of the Enlightenment, will provide a key that will unlock a happier future (Lyotard 1984). Nonetheless, most feminist attitudes towards fashion remain caught in nostalgia for these lost certainties. Fashion today includes the dark esoteric and sexually ambiguous visions of designers such as Rick Owens as well as the populist pleasures offered by Jennifer Lopez's line for Kohl's, in which 'Every look in this collection . . . is something that people know that I would wear' (kohls.com 2013). To be a feminist in the twenty-first century requires that we explore what people wear and why – that we wrestle with the reasons why neo-feminism has come to be so much more appealing to so many more women than feminism itself, with its emphasis on social reform. For the desires that drive women to participate in the fashion system, to strive for self-improvement for themselves and their children, may also be those that may potentially fuel the cultural, economic and ethical developments of the next century.

References

Arnold, R. (2001) 'Fashion', in Carson F. and Pajaczkowska C. (eds) *Feminist Visual Culture*. New York, Routledge, pp. 207–20.
Beauvoir, S. D. (1949) *Le Deuxième Sexe*. Paris: Gallimard.
—— (1953) *The Second Sex*. Translated by Parshley, H. M, New York: Knopf.
—— (2011) *The Second Sex*. Translated by Borde, C. and Malovany-Chevallier, S. New York: Vintage.
Brown, H. (1962) *Sex and the Single Girl*. New York: B. Geis Associates.
Budgeon, S. and Currie, D. (1995) 'From feminism to postfeminism: women's liberation in fashion magazines', *Women's Studies International Forum*, 18(2): 173–86.

Casserly, M. (2012) 'Michelle Obama, Anna Wintour – the most fashionable women of 2012', forbes.com, 9 December 2012. Available at: www.forbes.com/sites/meghancasserly/2012/09/12/michelle-obama-anna-wintour-and-the-most-fashionable-power-women-of-2012. Retrieved 20 September 2013.

Church Gibson, P. (2011) *Fashion and Celebrity Culture*. Oxford/New York: Berg.

Cixous, H. (1994) 'Sonia Rykiel in translation', in Benstock S. and Ferriss S. (eds) *On Fashion*. New Brunswick, NJ: Rutgers University Press, pp. 95–9.

Coddington, G. (2012) *Grace: A Memoir*. North Sydney, N.S.W. Australia: Knopf.

Cunningham, P. (2003) 'The invisibles: hygienic underwear, "dress systems," and making fashion rational', in *Reforming Women's Fashion, 1850–1920: Politics, Health, and Art*. Kent, Ohio: Kent State University Press.

Elliott, H. and Goudreau, J. (2012) 'The real American Idol: How J. Lo got her mojo back'. forbes.com, 16 May 2012. Available at: www.forbes.com/sites/hannahelliott/2012/05/16/the-real-american-idol-how-j-lo-got-her-mojo-back. Retrieved 20 September 2013.

Evans, C. (2003) *Fashion at the Edge: Spectacle, Modernity and Deathliness*. New Haven/London: Yale University Press.

Evans, C. and Thornton, M. (1991) 'Fashion, representation and femininity', *Feminist Review* 38: 48–66.

Evans, C. and Thornton, M. (1989) *Women and Fashion: A New Look*. London/New York: Quartet.

Finnegan, M. (1999) *Selling Suffrage: Consumer Culture and Votes for Women*. New York and Chichester: Columbia University Press.

Goudreau, J. (2012) 'How Jennifer Lopez climbed to no. 1 on the Forbes Celebrity', forbes.com, 5 May 2012. Available at: www.forbes.com/sites/jennagoudreau/2012/05/16/how-jennifer-lopez-climbed-to-no-1-on-the-forbes-celebrity-100-list/. Retrieved 20 September 2013.

Gray, F. (2010) 'Dispatches from the other', *New York Times*, 27 May 2010. Available at: www.nytimes.com/2010/05/30/books/review/Gray-t.html?pagewanted=all&_r=0. Retrieved 20 September 2013.

Groeneveld, E. (2009) '"Be a feminist or just dress like one": BUST, fashion and feminism as lifestyle', *Journal of Gender Studies* 18(2): 179–90.

Harrison, M. (1991) *Appearances: Fashion Photography Since 1945*. New York: Rizzoli.

just jared (2010) Jennifer Lopez's twins: Gucci ad campaign! justjared.com, 21 October 2010. Available at: www.justjared.com/2010/10/21/jennifer-lopez-twins-gucci-ads/. Retrieved 20 September 2013.

Karmali, S. (2012) 100 Most Powerful. vogue.co.uk, 23 August 2012. Available at: www.vogue.co.uk/news/2012/08/23/forbes-100-most-powerful-women---diane-von-furstenberg-tops-fashion-list. Retrieved 20 September 2013.

kohls.com. Available at: www.kohls.com/kohlsStore/ourbrands/jenniferlopez.jsp. Retrieved 20 September 2013.

Leon, M. (2007) 'A Yiddish word for all occasions: on the go', *The Jewish Daily Forward*, 27 December 2007 (published 28 December 2008). Available at: www.forward.com/articles/12357/a-yiddish-word-for-all-occasions-/. Retrieved 20 September 2013.

Lewis, L. (1990) 'Female Address on Music Video: Being Discovered', *Jump Cut*, 35: 2–15.

Lobenthal, J. (1990) *Radical Rags: Fashion of the Sixties*. New York: Abbeville Press.

Lukerson, V. (2012) 'Neiman Marcus and Target team up to go after the big middle', *Time*, 11 July 2012. Available at: www.business.time.com/2012/07/11/neiman-marcus-and-target-team-up-to-go-after-the-big-middle/. Retrieved 20 September 2013.

Lyotard, J-F (1984) *The Postmodern Condition: A Report on Knowledge*. Minneapolis, MN: University of Minnesota Press.

Magidson, P. (2010) 'Mainbocher', in Steele, V. (ed.) *The Berg Companion to Fashion*. Oxford/New York: Berg, pp. 491–3.

McRobbie, A. (1997) 'Bridging the gap: feminism, fashion and consumerism', *Feminist Review* 55: 73–89.

—— (1998) *British Fashion Design: Rag Trade or Image Industry?* London/New York: Routledge.

—— (2002) 'Fashion culture: creative work, female individualization', *Feminist Review* 71: 52–62.

Mendes, V. and Haye, A. D. L. (1999) *20th Century Fashion*. London/New York: Thames & Hudson.

Miller, J. (2011) *Fashion and Music*. Oxford/New York: Berg.

Miss America Collections. Available at: www.library.duke.edu/digitalcollections/missamerica. Retrieved 20 September 2013.

Ouellette, L. (1999) 'Inventing the Cosmo girl: class identity and girl style American dreams', *Media, Culture and Society*, 21(3): 359–83.

Palmer, A. (2009) *Dior: A New Look, A New Enterprise (1947–57)*. London: V&A Publishing.

Picardie, J. (2011) *Coco Chanel: The Legend and the Life*. London: HarperCollins.

Quant, M. (2012) *Mary Quant: Autobiography*. London: Headline Publishing Group.

—— (1974) *Quant by Quant*. Bath: Cedric Chivers.

Radner, H. (2011) *Neo-Feminist Cinema: Chickflicks, Girls Films, and Consumer Culture*. New York: Routledge.

—— (2000) 'On the Move: Fashion Photography and the Single Girl in the 1960s', in Bruzzi, S. and Church Gibson, P. (eds) *Fashion Cultures: Theories, Explorations and Analysis*. London: Routledge, pp. 128–42.

Robertson, J. (2012) 'Jennifer Lopez suffers embarrassing nipple slip in front of thousands of people during live show', *Mirror*, 14 October 2012. Available at: www.mirror.co.uk/3am/weird-celeb-news/jennifer-lopez-nipple-slip-wardrobe-1378929. Retrieved 20 September 2013.

Scanlon, J. (2009) *Bad Girls Go Everywhere: The Life of Helen Gurley Brown*. New York: Oxford University Press.

Scheips, C. (2007) *American Fashion*. New York: Assouline Publishing.

Scott, L. (2005) *Fresh Lipstick: Redressing Fashion and Feminism*. New York: Palgrave MacMillan.

Sivulka, J. (2010) *Soap, Sex and Cigarettes: A Cultural History of American Advertising*. Belmont, CA: Wadsworth.

Spring, A. (2013) 'Woman on fire', *Vogue* (Australian edition). January, pp. 92–3.

Steele, V. (1991) *Women of Fashion: Twentieth-Century Designers*. New York: Rizzoli.

Sudjic, D. (2008) *The Language of Things*. London: Penguin.

Victoria and Albert Museum (2006) Interview with Sally Tuffin and Marion Foale. vam.ac.uk, April 2006. Available at: www.vam.ac.uk/content/articles/i/marion-foale-and-sally-tuffin/. Retrieved 20 September 2013.

Vogue (American edition) (1926) 1 October, p. 69.

Chapter 21

Meredith Jones

NEW CLOTHES, NEW FACES, NEW BODIES
Cosmetic surgery and fashion

Introduction

IN THE LAST DECADE, the way in which we think about cosmetic surgery has undergone a dramatic change. What cosmetic surgery consists of, who has it, its costs and its aesthetic effects are markedly different than ten years ago. Feminist researchers, in diverse disciplines from film theory to anthropology, have led the way in showing that cosmetic surgery is more than surgical technology, more than medical discipline, and far more than something based in vanity or narcissism. While most scholarly feminists agree that cosmetic surgery reflects and perpetuates repressive views of the normative female body as well as creating its own new norms, it is also feminist scholarship that has shown how cosmetic surgery has deep symbolic meanings and rich cultural connotations (for an overview see Heyes and Jones 2009). Like fashion, cosmetic surgery is often dismissed as a superficial practice unworthy of scholarly attention but, like fashion, it is an important component of social, cultural and even moral life.

Perhaps the most significant change in cosmetic surgery over the past decade has been its incorporation into, or merging with, the fashion system. Cosmetic surgery now shares some of fashion's imperatives and raisons d'être, and deeper analyses of it in these contexts are needed. The cosmetic surgery industry is in a seemingly never-ending state of flux as it adjusts to this and many other changes, particularly those to do with consumerism, status, the idea of what 'natural' looks like, globalisation, celebrity culture, and ubiquitous pornography. In this chapter I outline the state of contemporary cosmetic surgery and trace its growing links with fashion from a feminist perspective. I conclude that stronger links between cosmetic surgery and fashion may allow the practice to become more ethical and its aesthetic effects to become more varied and interesting.

In the last decade we have seen recipients of cosmetic surgery move from being patients to clients. Patients were subject to the aesthetic judgement and medical expertise of the surgeons who were often their only point of contact with the industry (Spitzack 1988). In some countries patients had to be deemed *in need of* cosmetic surgery, either physically or psychologically, in order to undergo procedures (Davis 1995), and were labelled as under-confident, lacking in self esteem (Haiken 1997) or simply vain (Fraser 2003). Now, as clients, cosmetic surgery recipients are more able to pick and choose surgeons, research their procedures online, and talk to others who have had surgery via Facebook and YouTube. Contemporary cosmetic surgery is seen as a purchase rather than as a treatment for physical or mental deficiency. For some it is part of a regular beauty, fitness, or grooming routine, for others it is a treat or a reward, for example the 'mommy makeover' given to the self after childbirth and breastfeeding (Abate 2010). It can be fitted into a holiday (Bell *et al.* 2011; Jones 2011) or, because of a whole range of new technologies, into a lunch hour. It is no longer necessary to take weeks off work, recovering like a mummy or a burns victim. It is discussed far more openly and is no longer necessarily something to be ashamed of or embarrassed about. This is not to minimise the fact that cosmetic surgery is still often major surgery, consisting of anaesthesia, cutting into skin and flesh and the risk of all manner of complications including internal bleeding and deadly infections. Also, despite it becoming more ubiquitous, cosmetic surgery remains for many a deeply meaningful and life-changing experience.

Like fashion, cosmetic surgery is linked to the rise of cultures of consumption in the twentieth century and the parallel growth of middle classes in the overdeveloped world (Gilman 1999; Haiken 1997; Jones 2008). Its development over the past century has been intertwined with new practices of self-management, particularly makeover culture (Jones 2008) and new levels of grooming and beauty that are themselves closely aligned with cultures of media and celebrity (Blum 2003:145–87; 2008). In mainstream media, cosmetic surgery and fashion are interwoven to the extent that the most fashionable faces and bodies are now those that are also the most likely to have been surgically altered. A common reason given for having body-based cosmetic surgery such as breast implants or liposuction is 'so that clothes will fit me better'. As Efrat Tseëlon notes (2011), most fashion houses still refuse to accommodate a realistic range of body shapes and sizes, and it is ironic that cosmetic surgery as a complementary set of cultural processes is used to address this lack.

Just as new techniques of production (of labour and materials) helped fashion to become a part of mainstream culture through the twentieth century, there are now new technologies of cosmetic surgery that are making it less exclusive and more affordable. Products and procedures like botox, hyaluronic acid, laser hair removal, microdermabrasion and chemical peels now comprise the majority of cosmetic surgery procedures. Hyaluronic acid, known as 'filler', is injected to 'plump' or 'lift' sagging or wrinkled skin; botox is a toxin that paralyses muscles, thereby making wrinkles appear less obvious; chemical or mechanical peels polish the skin; laser beams promise to remove unwanted hair, broken veins and pigmentation spots. More controversial procedures include the use of ultrasound technology to 'disrupt' fat cells, the use of 'own-fat' where fat from one part of the body is extracted before being injected into another and 'own-blood' where blood is removed, 'purified', and re-injected as 'filler'. The rise of these so-called non-invasive treatments is important in the linking of cosmetic surgery and mainstream fashion. These treatments are generally cheaper than scalpel surgery, are faster to undergo and are widely available. Some can be administered by non-doctors and are available in high streets and malls. This makes them more accessible, less exclusive, more everyday.

Crucially, the results of these new technologies are largely *temporary*. This is the change that, I argue, has definitely located cosmetic surgery as part of the fashion system. We know that, if fashion has an imperative, then it is to always be 'new' (even if that new is retro or vintage). With scalpel surgery the 'new' could only happen once, but unlike their more permanent counterparts, fillers and other temporary modes of cosmetic surgery can be changed or altered from year to year, even from season to season (most last three to six months). In line with this, a cultural notion of new- versus old-fashioned cosmetic surgery is developing (Jones 2012), and it is the exact same new-versus-old dichotomy that is central to the fashion system. Like shoe shapes and heel heights, lips may now change size according to the season; like hemlines, the height of the brow may vary; cheeks may be plumper or more slender according to the season's silhouette. In contrast to scalpel surgery temporary procedures are relatively flexible. For example, skin was once stretched over the cheekbones and the excess cut away to get rid of wrinkles, and there was no turning back once surgery had been done. Now, cheek shapes may literally be changed from season to season by deploying different fillers in different amounts; the contours around the eye can be transformed according to fashion; even nose and chin shape can be temporarily altered with fillers. It is the new affordable and impermanent nature of much contemporary cosmetic surgery that brings it into alignment, symbolically and practically, with fashion.

Before returning to discuss possible future links between cosmetic surgery and fashion, I will outline some other recent changes to how cosmetic surgery comes about: globalisation, social media, the roles of the surgeon, and cosmetic surgery tourism.

Globalisation

Products and representations of cosmetic surgery are intricately tied to processes of globalisation. It is common knowledge that cosmetic surgery images, like most images in the contemporary world, are created by international conglomerates and that they circulate via global mass media (Kress and Van Leeuwen 2006; Croteau *et al.* 2011). However, it is less understood that the logistics of cosmetic surgery are also global. For example, a set of breast implants might be manufactured in a favela in Brazil (Edmonds 2009) or a factory in China, then branded by a French company before being inserted into a client from Australia who is having her surgery in Thailand performed by a surgeon who has trained in the USA.[1] These flows of products, processes and bodies, and their connections with labour, inequality and oppression, are still to be properly addressed by cosmetic surgery scholars.[2]

We know that globalisation is not a one-way process. In line with this, despite ongoing myths that globalisation equals Americanisation, there is no singular or universal fashion for cosmetic surgery (see Holliday and Elfving-Huang 2012). Rather, global flows of power and influence intersect with local histories, values and physical environments, creating all sorts of cosmetic surgery hybrids. For example, many young women in South Korea have their jaws made smaller to create a heart-shaped face, and also have a crease added to their upper eyelids to make their eyes appear bigger. They are perhaps influenced by Manga aesthetics and the looks of fashionable Korean pop stars. Older South Koreans are more likely to choose to have hand-sized flat implants put between the back of the skull and the skin to give their heads a more 'noble' or 'authoritative' shape. Leg lengthening, a painful, incredibly time-consuming and invasive set of procedures, is most popular in China and India and is deployed as a means to better career and marriage prospects. In Brazil, buttock implants are common whereas large breasts are seen as matronly and less desirable (Gilman 1999). In the USA, UK, Canada and Australia breast augmentation and liposuction are the most widespread scalpel surgeries, in line with those cultures' privileging of childishly thin bodies with prominent secondary sexual organs.

There is little to show in current research that people seeking so-called 'westernising' surgeries such as upper blepharoplasty (creating an eyelid crease) actually want to pass as Western, although this may well be complicated by ingrained race-based notions of what constitutes beauty (see Kaw 1993). South-east Asians who have this sort of eye surgery strongly deny a desire to look more Western, saying instead they want to look more awake or more fashionable. Often the reason given for having double eyelid surgery is to be able to wear eye shadow. If Westerners are to insist that there are so-called 'westernising' cosmetic surgeries then they must look at their own cosmetic surgery practices with a similar critical eye. In which case there is no doubt that Caucasians would deny that their body modifications are intended to make them look more African, despite the fact that they often seek larger lips and browner skins. It is clear that, like other global fashionable practices, most cosmetic surgery images are general and globalised while many of its practices and outcomes are specific and local, and that the global/local intersection varies from place to place. Cosmetic surgery is always hybrid.

Social media

The internet has, for several years, allowed people to gather information and knowledge about cosmetic surgery procedures, risks, places and prices, and consumers have consequently become more aware and even empowered. In turn, the rise of social media tools has added a new layer to online cosmetic surgery knowledge-gathering and meaning-making. Tools like Facebook and YouTube are being used to build communities of people interested in cosmetic surgery in which advice is given, support provided, information exchanged and friendships made. These communities are, for many, the primary way into the cosmetic surgery world and participation in them is often more important, and has more influence, than talking to a surgeon or reading hospital pamphlets.

Social media are often used performatively – in these online environments we choose personas, share personal details, and 'perform' ourselves in ways that both complement and contrast with our modes of being in the offline world (Miller 2011). Social media sites have changed boundaries between public and private spaces and these altered margins apply to cosmetic surgery as much as to any practice. Many cosmetic surgery recipients now candidly record, show, and in a sense perform themselves online, uploading videos of before and after moments, talking through their pain and recovery, showing their outcomes and generally making no secret of having had surgery (a search for 'my boob job' on YouTube gives hundreds of results). For these communities cosmetic surgery is something to be proud of, to discuss openly, even to wear as a badge of honour. Cosmetic surgery becomes something one displays openly, a status symbol and a profoundly important fashion accessory.

Surgeons

Medical practitioners obviously play a crucial part in the cosmetic surgery matrix. The internet and social media have also changed how they must work. Cosmetic surgeons have always occupied a contradictory space between promoter of health and seller of goods (Jones 2008). As health care providers they are bound to do no harm, yet they operate on healthy bodies, subjecting them to surgical trauma, anaesthetics and potential infection. Medical doctors and especially surgeons have traditionally held positions of social authority because of the respect gained through their professions. However, as specialist entrepreneurs cosmetic surgeons engage in less noble activities to do primarily with profit: they identify gaps in the market, and work to convince people (mainly women) via advertising and marketing that they need cosmetic surgery. For several decades cosmetic surgeons enjoyed the benefits of these contradictory modes of being: they were able to market their skills and their purported aesthetic sensibilities alongside their medical prowess, positioning themselves as the ultimate holders of expertise in the cosmetic surgery network. That authority is now being questioned and subsequently diminished by increasingly knowledgeable and information-rich clients who, sometimes defiantly, no longer see themselves as patients. Many surgeons find this challenging. Much of their knowledge about procedures and medical processes is now readily available on the internet, and they are seen no longer as aesthetic experts but rather as highly skilled technicians. Ironically, while surgeons are unhappy with their expertise being questioned, they have themselves, through greed, played a crucial role in the turning of cosmetic surgery from a medical procedure to a consumable item. They are now part of a buyers' market in which if someone is unhappy she will go elsewhere, even overseas.

Cosmetic surgery tourism

Providing opportunities for people from abroad to have cosmetic surgery – generally at prices lower than in their home countries – is a worldwide trend, with countries from Tunisia to Thailand becoming actively involved. Cosmetic surgery tourism is a growing and lucrative business that is often supported at government level (Jones 2011). In cosmetic surgery, tourism operations are often combined with glamorous holidays. Australians, for example, travel to Thailand or Malaysia to have surgery at much lower prices than at home, and to recuperate in tropical luxury that most could not normally afford, while Britons travel to Spain, the Czech Republic, Turkey and many other European countries.[3] In these scenarios cosmetic surgery can be linked to the status of an international holiday and the fashionable lifestyles associated with the rich and famous. Many of the agents in Australia who organise cosmetic surgery tourism emphasise bargain designer shopping in global cities such as Bangkok and Kuala Lumpur in their advertising and write shopping in as part of their clients' itineraries: thus a transformed body or face and a newly fashionable wardrobe go hand in hand.

Designer vaginas

There is one more dramatic change to cosmetic surgery in the last decade that must be mentioned here. With the rise of the 'designer vagina', cosmetic surgery has spread from faces and the more on-display parts of the body to women's genitals (Braun 2010). For some observers this has been the final straw in cementing cosmetic surgery as a practice that degrades women, deeming even the most intimate parts of our bodies unsatisfactory, finding and naming 'ugliness' in areas that were previously very private and not comparable with each other (Braun and Tiefer 2010). Capitalist logic dictates that new markets need to be continually identified. In the cosmetic surgery world this results in not just the promotion of new products and techniques, but also the identification of new body parts that require 'fixing'. Again there are important connections to fashion here. As many Western cultures have become 'pornografied' (see Attwood 2009), women's bodies, clothed or unclothed, hairless (pubic hair used to hide most details of the vulva) and splayed open, are on display more than ever before (ABC TV 2010). This, along with connected imperatives to look youthfully sexual even after pregnancy and childbirth, has led to labiaplasty becoming increasingly common.

Labiaplasty takes many forms but is most often the reduction of the labia minora. It can also include 'plumping up' the labia majora, tightening the vagina and even rebuilding hymens. Dystopic as this may seem, it should be noted that feminist analyses make interesting observations. For example, many cultures have been practising labial modification for centuries for symbolic and religious reasons. At its most terrible this results in permanent damage and mutilation but it is often less invasive and physically damaging than we might think (Weir 2000). The hypocrisy of Western condemnations of such practices as repressive and anti-woman – in the context of our penchants for inserting silicon sacs into our own chests and having our own vulvas cut into 'prettier' shapes – still needs careful feminist analysis (Greer 2012). There are several important 'fightback' projects around the 'designer vagina', including artist Jamie McCartney's *Great Wall of Vagina* (www.greatwallofvagina.co.uk) and the *101 Vagina Project* (www.101vagina.com/). These are part of a growing cultural awareness of cosmetic surgery and its powers.

Sophisticated cultural reactions such as these do not involve judging those who choose to have it but rather emphasise and celebrate beauty in difference.

Fashion, ethics and cosmetic surgery

While feminists have always been concerned about ethics and cosmetic surgery, cosmetic surgery's move into mainstream lifestyles and fashion poses new ethical dilemmas. Once, general feminist concerns about cosmetic surgery were about it representing a lack of authenticity, a loss of the 'real' self and a loss of the 'natural' (although scholarly feminists have always posed far more nuanced arguments; for example see the essays in Heyes and Jones 2009). Further, it was accepted that this loss was facilitated through violence done by men (surgeons) to women (patients) in the form of cutting into the flesh. And as part of a patriarchal regime, cosmetic surgery can still be seen as literally cutting women down to size, or inflating them to Barbie doll proportions in order to fit narrowly defined heterosexual male fantasies (see Jeffreys 2005). Overall, cosmetic surgery was seen, until the last decade, as undeniably repressive, and many feminists' responses were in the order of 'just don't do it' and 'I will never do it'. How times have changed. As shown above, cosmetic surgery is now ubiquitous. It is seen by many as being no more damaging or repressive than a lifetime of wearing high heels. Feminist politicians and celebrities display signs of cosmetic surgery (albeit while usually denying it) and most women in the public eye wear faces that have been altered in some way. Further, there is an increasingly persistent feminist understanding that nothing is 'natural' and that every body is created by a mix of cultural techniques and biological mechanisms. The notion of cosmetic surgery somehow hiding an 'authentic' face is old hat.

There are two broad ways to think about ethics and cosmetic surgery. The first is to do with its products and processes: how it is produced. Who, in the favelas and the factories, makes the implants or the pharmaceuticals? Who suffers in the global system of production, and who profits? This concern is a broad one that can be applied to all fashion products, from finest quality fur, silk and leather that involve great animal suffering to cheapest quality clothing made in sweatshops where humans work cruel hours for little pay. The second way to think about ethics and cosmetic surgery is to consider the recipients of cosmetic surgery (who are sometimes ourselves) in ethical ways. Questions to ask here are about coercion, about women and the workforce, about individual suffering weighed against individual gain, about the pressure for ideal bodies and endless reinvents of the self, and about systems of influence that radiate from media and celebrity bodies. Whichever way these questions are asked, it is clear that the greatest profits from cosmetic surgery go to those who are providers (surgeons, hospitals, clinics and pharmaceutical conglomerates) rather than those who are receivers or clients. Of course this dynamic is par for the course in a capitalist society, and is no different to that inherent in any supply-demand chain. However, cosmetic surgery's move to the fashion system makes it more available to these kinds of economic–ethical analyses, and this sort of work will, I hope, be done by feminist scholars in the next phase of critical cosmetic surgery examination.

Conclusion

Cosmetic surgery is a powerful expression of a culture of surveillance, a makeover culture in which bodies are scrutinised, assessed, measured and judged (and where every body always falls short of the ideal). And it is, too, part of an infinitely complex paradigm that increasingly sees the body as a mere envelope, a casing to be altered at will, that believes beauty can be purchased – and can't it? There is no turning away from cosmetic surgery now; it is embedded in many world cultures. Rather than mourn its ubiquity feminists need to accept it as a given, and rigorously examine the multifarious ways it is brought into being and deployed. If cosmetic surgery continues to grow and change in line with fashion then we will see it being scrutinised more closely in terms of ethics. I hope that we will also see far more variety in terms of its developing aesthetics. Perhaps one day the arched brows, big lips, wide-open eyes, large breasts and slim body of the West's ideal woman's body will be just one of many fashionable alternatives. I like to imagine a world where we might just as easily choose to adopt low brows, large foreheads, elongated eyes, tiny pointed breasts, large calves or sculptural shoulders. Perhaps if we embrace and explore all of cosmetic surgery's fashionable possibilities we can help to make it into a mode of expression rather than repression.

Notes

1   Many of these global flows are currently being researched as part of the *Sun Sea Sand Silicone: Aesthetic Surgery Tourism* project, a multidisciplinary, multisite project funded by the UK Economic and Social Research Council. www.gender-studies.leeds.ac.uk/research/cosmetic-cultures/aesthetic-surgery-tourism.php.
2   Ibid.
3   Ibid.

References

Abate, M. A. (2010) '"Plastic Makes Perfect": *My Beautiful Mommy*, Cosmetic Surgery, and the Medicalization of Motherhood', *Women's Studies: An inter-disciplinary journal*, Volume 39, Issue 7, 715–46.

ABC TV (2010) 'Labiaplasty', *Hungry Beast*, video available at www.abc.net.au/tv/hungrybeast/stories/labiaplasty.

Attwood, F. (2009) (ed.) *Mainstreaming Sex: The Sexualization of Western Culture*, I.B. Tauris, Michigan.

Bell, D., Holliday, R., Jones, M., Probyn, E. and Sanchez Taylor, J. (2011) 'Bikinis and Bandages: An Itinerary for Cosmetic Surgery Tourism', *Tourist Studies*, Volume 11, Issue 2, 137–53.

Blum, V. (2003) *Flesh Wounds: The Culture of Cosmetic Surgery*, University of California Press, California.

—— (2008) 'Objects of Love: I Want a Famous Face and the Illusions of Star Culture', *Configurations*, Volume 15, 33–53.

Braun, V. (2010) 'Female Genital Cosmetic Surgery: A Critical Review of Current Knowledge and Contemporary Debates', *Journal of Women's Health*, Volume 19, Issue 7, 1393–1407.

Braun, V. and Tiefer, L. (2010) 'The "Designer Vagina" and the Pathologisation of Female Genital Diversity: Interventions for Change', *Radical Psychology*, Volume 18, Number 1, online at www.radicalpsychology.org/vol8–1/brauntiefer.html.

Croteau, D., Hoynes, W. and Milan, S. (2011) *Media/society: Industries, Images, and Audiences*, Sage, London.

Davis, K. (1995) *Reshaping the Female Body*, Routledge, New York.

Edmonds, A. (2009) 'Learning to Love Yourself: Esthetics, Health, and Therapeutics in Brazilian Plastic Surgery', *Ethnos: Journal of Anthropology*, Volume 74, Issue 4, 465–89.

Fraser, S. (2003) *Cosmetic Surgery, Gender and Culture*, Palgrave Macmillan, New York.

Gilman, S. L. (1999) *Making the Body Beautiful: A Cultural History of Aesthetic Surgery*, Princeton University Press, Princeton, New Jersey.

Greer, G. (2012) 'Genital Cutting is Normal' (speech), *Festival of Dangerous Ideas*, Sydney Opera House, video available at www.play.sydneyoperahouse.com/index.php/media/1658-Genital-Cutting-Normal.html.

Haiken, E. (1997) *Venus Envy: A History of Cosmetic Surgery*, The Johns Hopkins University Press, Baltimore, Maryland.

Heyes, C. and Jones, M. (2009) *Cosmetic Surgery: A Feminist Primer*, Ashgate, London and New York.

Holliday, R. and Elfving-Hwang, J. (2012) 'Gender, Globalization and Aesthetic Surgery in South Korea', *Body & Society*, Volume 18, Issue 2, 58–81.

Jeffreys, S. (2005) *Beauty and Misogyny: Harmful Cultural Practices in the West*, Routledge, London.

Jones, M. (2012) 'Cosmetic Surgery and the Fashionable Face', *Fashion Theory*, Volume 16, Issue 2, 193–210.

—— (2011) *'Clinics of Oblivion: Makeover Culture and Cosmetic Surgery Tourism' Portal: Journal of Multidisciplinary International Studies*, online at www.epress.lib.uts.edu.au/ojs/index.php/portal/article/view/1843.

—— (2008) *Skintight: An Anatomy of Cosmetic Surgery*, Berg Publishers, Oxford and New York.

Kaw, Eugenia (1993) 'Medicalization of Racial Features: Asian American Women and Cosmetic Surgery', *Medical Anthropology Quarterly*, Volume 7, Issue 1, 74–89.

Kress, G. and Van Leeuwen, T. (2006) *Reading Images: The Grammar of Visual Design*, 2nd edn, Routledge, London.

Miller, D. (2011) *Tales from Facebook*, Polity, Cambridge UK.

Spitzack, C. (1988) 'The Confession Mirror: Plastic Images for Surgery', *Canadian Journal of Political and Social Theory*, Volume 12, Issues 1–2, 38–50.

Tseëlon, E. (2011) 'A critique of the Ethical Fashion Paradigm', *Critical Studies in Fashion & Beauty*, Volume 2, 3–68.

Weir, E. (2000) 'Female Genital Mutilation', *Canadian Medical Association Journal*, Volume 162, Number 9, 1344.

Chapter 22

Lorraine Gamman

FEMALE SLENDERNESS AND THE CASE OF PERVERSE COMPLIANT DECEPTION – OR WHY SIZE MATTERS . . .

IN DECEMBER 2012, THE *NEW SCIENTIST*, responding to the 'most comprehensive assessment of human health in the history of medicine' noted that 'excess weight is today a bigger health problem than malnutrition'. When I originally wrote about the culture of plenty and the fashion for super slenderness in *Female Fetishism* (1994) as being a perverse manifestation of the former, which led women to feast and vomit – either ensuring compliance to the slim feminine ideal through bulimia or, more typically, yo-yo dieting – I had no idea that obesity was to become such a pressing issue or that the fetishism of slenderness would reach new proportions. This was almost twenty years ago and when suggesting women might eroticise food I had no idea that the 'gastro porn industry' would escalate in the way it has, promoting the idea that you are what you aspire to eat – even if cordon bleu aspirations, via books or programmes, are read or watched while eating beans on diet toast. Today so many food programmes and celebrity chefs covered in the media regularly emphasise the need to eat more even while these programmes and articles are juxtaposed between diet advertisements and news bulletins about obesity; in retrospect, my previous account of the meaning of 'gastro porn' (Bruzzi and Church Gibson, 2000) seems rather understated.

The fashion for unrealistic slender images of women has increased despite all the current emphasis on cooking or consuming gourmet food. No wonder the fashion industry's attempts to promote normal sized models have been doomed (the April 2010 'plus' size issue of French *Elle* and Karl Lagerfeld's response comes to mind); all of them seem either to have led nowhere or to have ended nastily. Even the singer Adele has been singled out for abuse linked to her size, and her appearance on the cover of British *Vogue*. When documenting women's difficult relationship with food and making the case for female fetishism of food ('food is

Figure 22.1   Adele. Copyright Lucie Russell.

often far more erotic and dangerous to women than sex') I did not anticipate that UK size 16 pop singers would still be the subject of fashion criticism twenty years on or that the latest 'must have' fashion accessory would be the gastric band. This chapter aims to offer a new spin on ideas about women and slenderness. It will discuss the idea of perverse compliant deception in terms of changing fashions about how to lose weight and, second, how the use of health information may be linked to new forms of fetishist denial and possible self-oppression regarding the decision to resort to bariatric surgery.

Is fat still a feminist issue?

I was made aware of why 'fat is a feminist issue' thanks to Susie Orbach's efforts in 1978. The fact that most UK size 14 women today are considered 'overweight', not just by the fashion industry but also by the medical profession, is troubling too. I have just had a medical and am outraged to be termed 'very overweight' when I have worked hard to get myself down to a size 16 (it was the word 'very' that I objected to). Worse today, there is little agreement about what is unhealthy 'fat' and what is a 'normal' healthy average body size or weight. For instance, average UK size 14 and 16 women still have no hope of positive representation in the mainstream because UK sizes 8, 6 and even 4 are now the norm regarding those images of women we see most often. So I shouldn't be surprised to find that my 16-year-old daughter and her friends refuse to be more than a UK size 8–10, or that more middle-aged women than ever before are suffering from eating disorders – treatment centres have seen an increase in the number of middle-aged women seeking help for eating disorders such as anorexia and bulimia (Sheridan 2012). Nor to find that young women are regularly targeted for plastic surgery and that a medical journal devoted to obesity surgery has existed since 1991.

What I have been surprised about is discovering that two of the women I have celebrated in the past – Vanessa Feltz and Dawn French – have been alleged by newspapers in 2011 to have had bariatric surgery to deal with their weight problems. Perhaps I wasn't surprised as much as troubled by what seemed to me the perverse nature of their denials about such surgery.

Feltz eventually confirmed that she has indeed had a gastric band fitted. In the press her image continues, for all the wrong reasons, to be associated with the grotesque. Despite the band as a restraint, Feltz does not appear to have stopped eating too much, as can be observed from the regularly published unflattering pictures of her. She is damned if she does diet, and also if she doesn't, by sneering newspapers that feature close-ups of her irregular fleshy body and seem to use every opportunity to emphasise Feltz's failure to conform to the slim feminine ideal (Shaw 2011). Conversely Dawn French, who in 2011 said she had lost 6.5 stone but whose weight continued to fluctuate, denied she had had bariatric surgery (McQueeney 2011) and consequently the allegations stopped – she was shown as a 'successful' dieter in newspaper coverage.

My earlier discussion of these women's performativity had focused on the *eye* and the *mouth* – about how they are seen rather than what could be accommodated by their *stomachs* – and the connection in mainstream representation of fat as a form that cannot be easily consumed. Fat remains the repressed of fashionable femininity, despite the failed attempts to get plus-sized models onto the catwalk, so why then the backlash against celebrity surgery?

At first sight it would be easy to imagine that bariatric surgery equates with self-oppression rather than enhancement. Fern Britton and Anne Diamond talk about having kept their own gastric band surgery secret and the 'shame' of feeling out of control. In Anne Diamond's case she wrote a book on the subject (Diamond 2009) and argues that the 'freedom' of not having to make as much effort to self regulate, because of 'help' from her band, was of value to her. The bad news was that she had to have more than one band operation to get it to work. Also, Diamond appears to have found it helpful to understand her own situation in the wider context of what had led to an obesity epidemic across the world. To make the decision to have one's stomach made smaller by gastric bypass surgery or gastric band surgery seems a drastic and violent solution to a personal diet problem – or even the world's issues with food production. Certainly, obesity is what Rittel and Webber (1984) describe as a 'wicked' problem, a phrase originally used in social planning to describe an issue that is difficult or impossible to solve because one solution could never work, given incomplete, contradictory and changing requirements that are often difficult to recognise and virtually impossible to address.

Yet many public figures see surgery as that ultimate solution, but initially deny having undergone it, including Diamond (*Mail Online* 2008), Fern Britton (Thomas 2008), plus Vanessa Feltz and a host of American celebrities, including Roseanne Barr. Their denials are perhaps linked to their desire for privacy – but perhaps also embarrassment at being 'outed' as unable to self-regulate. Or at being privileged and vain enough to be able to afford surgery to design out their tendency to over-eat when so many ordinary people can't afford such medical restraint.

Growing numbers of ordinary men and women, including some teenagers who do not feel as beautiful as the 'plus' model Tara Lynn, have become so desperate about being overweight that many have allowed surgeons to reduce their healthy vital stomach organs (yes, some surgeons make the case for operating on teenagers)[1]. The fact that even moderately overweight people have had surgery, as well as the catastrophically overweight, means we need to understand this situation in a world context without a knee-jerk dismissal of such surgery as simply the dark side of the dominance of anorexic models, or as more 'fat oppression'. Fat may still be a feminist issue but 'fat liberation' cannot be an easy goal for obvious health-related reasons and effects. No wonder there are so many individuals on record who speak positively about the effects of bariatric surgery, who say they feel better through having reduced their physical size and thus, too, the related health problems. But it is hard to be easily reassured by this account given that in some cases – linked to gastric bypass surgery – the physical ability of the body to easily absorb some nutrients is compromised; we may also find that the surgery has led to other medical complications, or has not addressed the original psychological imbalance that may have been linked to a possible compulsive eating disorder. Ultimately, bariatric surgery seems such a perverse, if nevertheless effective, response to over-eating. It is clearly more significant as a cultural form than liposuction or operations to remove fat from specific areas of the body. But the idea that surgery can offset the worst consequences of world obesity, particularly when understood alongside the failure of representation to normalise the average woman who is fleshier than a supermodel, seems unlikely. So one can't help be suspicious of the medical profession's recommendations for still more future bariatric surgery. As one critic has already pointed out: 'the scientific evidence for obesity-associated mortality is at best ambiguous, and . . . some of the contemporary medical preoccupation with obesity has moral origins in that it seeks to correct unwanted or immoral behaviour' (De Vries 2007).

So why are an increasing number of medical doctors and surgeons suggesting that bariatric surgery is an ethical operation and a pragmatic alternative to spiralling health and medical costs? Many argue that such surgery is likely to be a sensible and successful pro-health option in addressing the problem that an overweight population brings – linked to epidemic numbers of related heart issues, diabetes, poor physical and mental health and so on. Some medical practitioners go further and make the argument that obesity is rarely 'self inflicted' – it should itself be regarded as a 'disease'. This is because food management in the West has spiralled out of control and produced unsustainable sugar-driven appetites (Lustig 2013), and possibly even gut bacteria that operates to keep us fat (*Science Daily* 2012). Here the fact that surgery can be used as a preventative measure to help reduce the spiralling economic burden on the state, regarding the impact of obesity on health care costs, as well as a way to improve individual health is seen as positive in a context where methods of food production and the promotion of food is out of synch with what is best for those of us who need to eat it. Could, then, the efforts of the bariatric surgeons be understood as helpful?

Certainly the benefits and harm of both obesity and bariatric surgery are too numerous and complex for me to assess adequately here, but what I am writing about is the message underlying medical and journalistic discourse. I am concerned that ideologies which reinforce the culture of slenderness may have combined to over-determine the obesity problem and so create a moral panic that connects the slightly overweight with the obese, and thus legitimises the surgery option. Are we really reading good sense about obesity management from the surgeons, or indirectly their response to the government's need for more social control regarding our fatter population, and the likely impact on the UK National Health Service? Countries such as Denmark have already trialled social policy measure such as putting a 'fat tax' on certain foods to discourage the over-eating of fat, but have recently abandoned it, some argue, in connection with pressure from the food industry (Nestle 2012). What is interesting is that in bariatric discourse, issues about willpower and self-regulation are no longer discussed because they are not seen as being likely to produce the result that will make a difference to health. Consequently, bariatric surgery may intend to deliver long-term 'disease management' of fat, and members of the medical profession argue that obesity surgery should be available or rationed like other treatments on the National Health Service; and arguments are made about its cost effectiveness to make their case.

Comparisons of the ethical discussions about bariatric surgery with those regarding reconstructive and cosmetic plastic surgery are perhaps apt. No one argues that those damaged by fire need plastic surgery, but cosmetic surgery when connected to vanity is not given such an easy hearing. With weight control issues there is a binary opposition between 'real needs' and 'vanity', so the subject doesn't get out of the starting block. Fat is always a crime, despite critics such as Shelley Bovey (1994) arguing that 'being fat is not a sin' because willpower rather than food production and promotion of the taste for sugar is rarely cited as the culprit.

In twenty years it has not been possible to get representations of plus-sized models into the mainstream and it may be impossible for weight problems to be properly discussed or for the state, faced with the burden of spiralling and related health care costs, not to take action. Preventing financial interests implicitly coming forward to join such a discussion, again, is probably impossible given that obesity is a wicked problem of consumer culture. Perhaps this is why it is easy to imagine, at first sight, that body fascism is at work regarding those who are persuaded to have surgery, including even those who advocate such options on 'health grounds'.

Certainly, the difference between what being overweight *looks like* and what it *feels like* and *means* needs to be understood better by those who wish to have such a debate. My sister had gastric bypass surgery in 2010 and believes it has massively improved her life. To a great extent I can see from my own observations that it has, even if I do worry about her ability to absorb nutrients such as vitamin D and iron. She tells me my concerns on this score are unfounded because her health is well managed, her operation has been successful and she is now less at risk from other serious diseases linked to previous high cholesterol and other issues than she was when she was overweight. She also tells me she no longer obsessively thinks about her weight in the way that she used to and has no embarrassment whatsoever about having opted for surgery, unlike the celebrities who hide this choice, or try to suggest self-regulation is more appropriate.

This access to a personal life experience, which I can verify, made me wonder what is happening that so many of the medical profession are advocating bariatric surgery or why averagely fat middle-aged celebrities such as Fern Britton and Vanessa Feltz are going for it too. As mentioned earlier, both these women tried to hide their decision to have bariatric surgery. Both their surgery and their denials seem to me to be deeply significant – a manifestation of perverse compliance to the oppression that the culture of slenderness and fat oppression delivers. In the wider context such denial can be understood linked to the fact that ideas about vanity or how the body should *be* are clearly not 'natural' but culturally formed. Such cultural definitions about fat are so powerful that they appear to make some men and women, who can't easily be thin, feel 'unnatural' – even about the way they choose to help themselves lose weight! Here, in the celebrity scenarios described, transference of shame about gastric surgery appears to me to move from shame about the deviance of 'fat' to the shame about the 'deviance' of having had bariatric surgery. The original perverse deceptive compliance to the social norm of slenderness, secretly delivered by the band while pretending that it is natural, keeps an unjust system in place. Ultimately, the need to hide what is happening is significant as it suggests something is 'wrong'. Shame and stigma are strong signs and signifiers of social regulation and even self-oppression and so it is no surprise when 'outed' by the press that such celebrities often speak in clichéd terms about the terrible 'before' and the positive 'after' fat script as an explanation of their actions.

Vanessa Feltz appears to be an exception. Despite the surgery she has not been perversely compliant with ideal female slenderness in order to deceive herself and the rest of us that her eating problem has resolved. But unlike Fay Weldon's *The She Devil*, who used surgery to get her own back and has evil fun transforming herself from a dumpy betrayed wife into a replica of the female writer for whom her husband betrayed her (so causing havoc in their world) I am not sure Feltz or those who have gastric band surgery appear to enjoy themselves as much as Weldon's anti-heroine. Vanity and self-oppression come in many forms – botox, face fillers and other forms of cosmetic surgery including bypass surgery are often located as signifiers of desperation, linked to a fashion culture obsessed with youth and slenderness. While an outward show of a fashionable body shape or a youthful face may produce conformity, perhaps we should ask not whether such conformity is less fun but whether or not it is any less liberating or oppressive than various forms of transgression that are celebrated? Whatever we decide, the increasing numbers of individuals engaging with bariatric surgery is worrying. It suggests our society is sliding closer to being out of control around food production and consumption, that it needs medical help – resorting to surgery – to manage and maintain an acceptable body size.

Surveys show that 99 percent of those who opt for the bypass or the band find it easier to lose weight and be physically healthier, although surgery doesn't work for everyone – as Vanessa Feltz's case indicates. What is happening in the heads of those who have surgery may tell a different story if it could be scrutinised and provide different data to that which we find in the medical 'success' bariatric case studies. Is the surgery always 'positive' if it connects the individual who loses weight this way to a discourse of 'discipline and punishment' or of fat hatred? The future will reveal more about this, no doubt.

Clearly, surgery to 'design out' obesity reflects all the contradictions of our consumer culture and perhaps indicates a tipping point, given that obesity has perversely co-existed with starvation, and now appears to be overtaking even malnutrition as a world health problem. As Susie Orbach (2009) points out, 'diet companies rely on a 95 per cent recidivism rate, a figure that should be etched into every dieter's consciousness'. This industry is worth $100 billion a year in the USA alone, compared to the American education budget that is estimated at $127 billion (Leith 2009). Ultimately diets make you fat – they don't work and encourage bodies to get better at surviving on less, so those who stop dieting and eat normally constantly expand and inflate and are forced back on the diet. No wonder bariatric surgery appears as a reasonable option given the consumer culture investment in encouraging individuals to 'remake' their bodies at every opportunity. Indeed, in this context, the gastric band or bypass could be seen as a 'hi tech' quick fix design solution to the problems of late modernity in the West, where exercise is no longer part of everyday working life, and where sedentary work and TV lifestyles are more commonplace in a high demand consumer culture. Bariatric surgery can deliver a solution to the diet problem. A corset placed inside the stomach seems to work a lot more effectively than one fitted outside of it, better even than the ideological corset for the brain that the diet and fashion industry try to deliver via the culture of slenderness that it produces.

For all these reasons, the gastric band or bypass operation as a bite-sized commodified chunk of artificial willpower is what many who are overweight wish for. How else are they to manage both the excess and lack that consumer culture accentuates – the idea that one can't be too rich or too thin? Or find ways to live within the culture of slenderness alongside contradictory 'success' messages that abundantly promote the need to consume. Surgery may help deliver a way out of this contradictory and fetishistic consumer dilemma, providing a magic product that makes a perverse compliant solution possible. Regarding the fat problem at an individual level as well as at the social level, it could be a way of ensuring that some in society can have their cake and not eat all of it too. It is a worrying thought that such medical procedures are now becoming routine without really challenging the consumer system, in particular the sugar-soaked food production system that created the supersized – as well as the over-determined ideological diet messages about slenderness. It is the ideological responses to the culture of plenty that in my view created the need for bariatric surgery in the first place. Less really may be more, and perhaps we need to move away not just from dieting but also from consuming the plentiful products from industrial farming throughout the world that produced such an unsustainable way of life for individuals and for the planet. So I certainly feel it will take more than surgery to respond to the obesity epidemic – perhaps a widespread *change* in food production, distribution, promotion and consumption – to really make a difference. Bon appetit.

Afterword

When editing the proof of this article I read about the 'fat tap' (the AspireAssist) which allows those who have the device fitted to their stomachs to insert a tube after eating to enable them to empty the contents of their stomach into the toilet. A horror movie sketch this is not! Given this body 'product' may actually be visible outside the body, I wonder if having one would be seen as shameful? Apparently, it is a potentially cheaper option than the band or bypass, but its very visibility may make it more shameful for the user, and less popular to those who prefer the perverse compliant deception of the band as an invisible corset . . . Who knows what comes next for the would-be fashionably thin domestic goddesses who want to make and eat cupcakes and not get too fat to wear vintage dresses . . . yuck.

Note

1   Angrisani *et al.* (2005) make an ethical case for giving gastric bands to teenagers: 'Ethical issues have presented obstacles to the development of pediatric bariatric surgery, and very few articles have been published on this topic . . . Operating on this young population is a great responsibility, but, at the same time, subjecting these young people to a multitude of ineffective nonsurgical weight loss modalities is not indicated and may even be unacceptable ethically. Obesity in teenagers should be treated aggressively to avoid progression to super obesity and/or complications. Early surgical intervention should be offered to adolescents to minimize the emotional and physical consequences of morbid obesity.'

References

Angrisani, L., Alkilani, M., Basso, N., Belvederesi, N., Campanile, F. and Capazzi, F. D. (2005) 'Obese teenagers treated by Lap-Band System: The Italian experience', *Surgery* (impact factor: 3.1) 138 (5): 877–81.

Bovey, S. (1994) *The Forbidden Body: Why Being Fat Is Not a Sin*, London: Pandora.

Bruzzi, S. and Church Gibson, P. (2000) *Fashion Cultures: Theories, Explorations and Analysis*, Routledge.

De Vries, J. (2007) 'The Obesity Epidemic: Medical and Ethical Considerations', *Sci Eng Ethics* 13 (1): 55–67.

Diamond, A. (2009) *Winning The Fat War*, Capstone and Wiley.

Fox, I. (2012) 'Karl Lagerfeld says Adele is "a little too fat"', *Guardian Fashion Blog*, 8 February, available at www.guardian.co.uk/fashion/fashion-blog/2012/feb/08/karl-lagerfeld-adele. (Accessed 16 September 2013.)

Gamman, L. and Makinen, F. (1994) *Female Fetishism: A New Look*, Lawrence Wishart.

Leith, W. (2009) 'Lessons on the body politic', *The Observer*, 1 February.

Lustig, R. (2013) *Fat Chance: The Bitter Truth About Sugar*, HarperCollins.

Mail Online (2008) '"Dear Fern, you look fantastic, but . . ." Anne Diamond warns of the physical and emotional trials of having a gastric band op', *Daily Mail*, 14 October, available at www.dailymail.co.uk/femail/article-1077696/Dear-Fern-look-fantastic–Anne-Diamond-warns-physical-emotional-trials-having-gastric-band-op.html. (Accessed 16 September 2013.)

McQueeney, K. (2011) 'Shut Up Anne Diamond: Comedienne Dawn French hits back at gastric band speculation', *Daily Mail*, 24 December, available at www.dailymail.co.uk/tvshowbiz/article-2078302/Comedienne-Dawn-French-hits-Anne-Diamonds-gastric-band-speculation.html. (Accessed 16 September 2013.)

Nestle, M. (2012) 'Fighting the flab means fighting makers of fatty foods', *New Scientist*, 26 November.

Orbach, S. (2009) *Bodies*, New York: Picador.

——(1978) *Fat Is a Feminist Issue: The Anti-Diet Guide to Permanent Weight Loss*, New York: Paddington Press.

Rittel, H. W. J. and Webber, M. M. (1984) 'Planning problems are wicked problems', in N. Cross (ed.) *Developments in Design Methodology*, New York: John Wiley & Sons, 135–44.

Science Daily (2012) 'Manipulating the Microbiome Could Help Manage Weight', *Science Daily*, 26 August, available at www.sciencedaily.com/releases/2012/08/12082 6142843.htm. (Accessed 16 September 2013.)

Sheridan, M. (2012) 'Eating Disorders Affecting More Midlife Women', *Huffington Post*, 8 August, available at www.huffingtonpost.com/2012/03/02/eating-disorders-middle-age_n_1313791.html. (Accessed 16 September 2013.)

Shaw, K. (2011) 'Battle of the gastric bands: it worked for Fern but not Vanessa – but one expert argues for more of the controversial ops to save the NHS billions', *Daily Mail*, 23 April.

Thomas, D. (2008) 'Fern Britton admits cheating at weight loss', *The Telegraph*, 1 June.

Chapter 23

Reina Lewis

HIJAB STORIES
Choice, politics, fashion

FOR MANY MUSLIMS UNDER THIRTY (and quite probably now under forty, and under fifty) living in Muslim minority contexts in Western Europe and North America (WENA) the practices they engage in as Muslims are increasingly understood as a matter of choice rather than diktat. Nowhere is this seen more clearly than in the adoption of the headscarf, or hijab, by young women. Depicted by many adherents as both a divine requirement and a personal choice, the wearing of the hijab (and other less common forms of covering or veiling) has become the most politicised sartorial decision of the early twenty-first century. Individual Muslim women in hijab are often regarded as emblematic of all of Islam and of all Muslims by observers within the faith and without. That their use of high street apparel and of 'ethnic' clothing is creating new fusion fashions in both sectors is rarely acknowledged. This chapter puts contemporary debates about the hijab in the context of previous instances of politicised de-veiling and re-veiling, in order to evaluate present veiling fashions in the context of neoliberal consumer culture, changing definitions of religious belonging, mainstream and diaspora fashion industries, and the development of transnational Muslim revivalist youth subcultures.

Choosing hijab: neoliberal consumer culture and agency in everyday religion

Contemporary forms of Muslim habitus, such as those grouped under the umbrella of 'European' or 'global' Islam are suffused with notions of choice (Roy 2004). This is often characterised as the rejection by a younger generation of parental norms, especially those norms underwritten by ethnic convention. But this 'de-ethnicisation' of religion (Goole 2011) is most often a process of negotiation between, rather than a rejection of, existing and localised practices. This syncretism, characteristic of contemporary 'everyday' religion in other faiths (McGuire 2008; Ammerman 2007), is also the grounds on which new practices may be validated or invalidated by both conventional Muslim religious authorities and by majoritarian social and political authorities. This is true for generations of Muslim migrants to non-Muslim majority countries and can also be true for religious Muslims in some Muslim majority contexts, such as in secularised Turkey where choice factors prominently in relation to the articulation of religious choice as a human right subject to protection under international law.

The prominent discourse of choice that is deployed in relation especially to women's veiling can be seen as part of a religious habitus formed through the expansion and diversification of Protestant ideas of religious voluntarism in the context of globalised neoliberal consumer culture. Religions are often divided into those that define faith as achieved through conscious individual choice and those that define faith as ascribed through being born into religious or 'tribal' communities. Muslims cross this divide. As a faith that welcomes converts (unlike Judaism) and that privileges the individual declaration of faith, Islam accords with the Protestant-inflected model of achieved religious individuated identity. But being Muslim can also be transmitted by birth (like Judaism) as an ascribed and collectivist identity that is in itself sufficient for membership.[1] Like Judaism, Islam has also been historically a faith that privileges forms of observance concerned with the clothing and feeding of the body. While the Protestant confessional approach is undeniably a factor in the formulation of faith as a matter of personal spiritual quest among younger Muslims, young Muslims are at the same time creating new practices through re-engagement with longstanding Muslim forms of embodied faith behaviour that include dress. The demonisation of Islam and Muslims within a securitising discourse since 11 September 2001 has also brought disproportionate attention to how Muslims look: dress has come to be one of the key forms through which Muslim identities are performed and contested, and women in identifiably Muslim clothing are aware that they are likely to be read as emblems of an entire community rather than as individuals.

Fashion often presents itself as all about choice – a binary opposition to the presumed impositions of religious dress. But in reality everyone's decisions about how to dress are formed by a mixture of choice and constraint, determined by personal and social circumstances or the cycles of the fashion system. Emphasising (*qua* Bourdieu 1984) that these dispositions and the tastes that they codify are embodied knowledges (learned from birth or acquired in the attempt to enter a different social group or class), Entwistle argues that by regarding subjectivity as embodied and as 'active in its adaptation to the habitus' a middle way can be discerned between determinism and agency:

> The notion of the habitus as a durable and transposable set of dispositions
> . . . enables us to talk about dress as a personal attempt to orientate
> ourselves to particular circumstances and thus recognises the structuring
> influences of the social world on the one hand, and the agency of
> individuals who make choices as to what to wear on the other.
>
> (Entwistle 2000: 37)

Thus it is not, *qua* Polhemus, that postmodern young people can choose freely from the 'supermarket of style', so much as it is that their range of choices and ability to pursue their desires are limited by social factors such as age, gender, class and ethnicity. Faith is obviously the additional social factor that is key to my study. First, because being Muslim often functions as a minoritising social factor in WENA territories, determining how young people are regarded by external observers; second, because the development of new Muslim youth cultural dispositions marks an intervention into existing Muslim habituses, often developed through negotiation with and selective adaptation rather than direct repudiation of parental codes.

Decisions about (forms of) veiling, re-veiling, and de-veiling are socially and historically contingent and are variably perceived by differently positioned contemporaneous and historical observers. Thus when (mostly elite) women in Egypt and the Ottoman empire engaged in public campaigns of de-veiling it was not simply a rejection of religion but was, as Leila Ahmed (2011) argues, also a response to the Western and colonial equation of veiling as a sign of Muslim and regional civilisational inferiority. Veiling was also dispensed with by women from Druze and Jewish communities as part of a wider regional assertion of modernity and (selective) Westernisation. However, uncommented by Ahmed, many of these very public 'de-veiling' acts involved only the removal of the face veil, not the garment covering women's hair. Prominent Muslim feminists and nationalists such as Huda Sha'rawi in Egypt and Halide Edib in the Ottoman empire retained a head covering for years to follow, a point lost on most Western observers (see Lewis 2004; el Guindi 1999). By the 1980s, Ahmed argues, the veil had been successfully recalibrated as both intrinsically Muslim and as the key indicator of female piety, reclassifying women who do not cover as less pious and as 'secular' – not an identification that would have been adopted by or applied to the unveiled Egyptian women of the 1940s and 1950s. The discursive impact of the global spread of Islamic revivalism thus impacts on Muslim women regardless of their personal preferences or understanding of their practices.

This is equally true today. In a landmark case in 2002 British teenager Shabina Begum took her school to court because she wanted to wear a jilbab rather than the salvar kameez uniform option that the school had agreed with the local South Asian community. In a context where the majority of the British Muslim population is of immigrant South Asian (and largely Pakistani) heritage, her argument about what constituted appropriate dress for a devout Muslim impacted on girls in her own school and around the country. Her case rested both on her right to express her faith as she chose and her need to distinguish herself through dress from other Muslims and from other Asians of other faiths (Tarlo 2010) without giving up her choice of school (Malik 2010).

It is undeniably a conundrum that some proponents of women's veiling present it as simultaneously a religious (divine) requirement and as a choice. The political ramifications of this dual rationale are pressing, and have come to preoccupy many commentators who often see the 'stock' responses of hijabis as evidence that they are the mere dupes of powerful male leaders (Begum indeed was known to have been 'advised' by the puritanical Islamist organisation Hizb ut Tahrir with which her older brother was associated). In the context of the veil's oversignification within neo-Orientalist stereotypes and especially the clash of civilisations rhetoric of the neocons since the first Gulf War, a challenge must be mounted to the idea that Islam is uniquely and overwhelmingly oppressive to women, while also supporting Muslim women in their challenges to forms of patriarchy that seek to legitimate themselves in Islamic terms (Malik 2010). Conversely, challenges must be mounted to Occidentalist stereotypes that construct 'Western' women as immoral (whether as victims or agents of a uniquely sexualised society) while also pointing out that women in the secular West are subject to constant surveillance and regulation of their dress and body management. Thus, as Elizabeth Wilson notes in her revised edition of *Adorned in Dreams*, 'to argue about or seek to legislate or criticise the veil is a displacement, and at the same time an expression, of the pressing issue of how different belief systems are to coexist in the contemporary world and of the unresolved status of women' (2003: 257). One of the first to incorporate hijab debates into the wider frame of fashion studies, Wilson repudiates as 'disingenuous' the attempt to defend veiling in terms of choice on two counts:

> for choice is surely not the point for religiously committed individuals. Rather it is obedience to a higher law. Moreover, choice, the mantra of western consumer society, cannot be the highest moral principle at the end of the day, and testifies rather to an emptiness at the heart of capitalist culture.
>
> (Wilson 2003: 262)

For these reasons, she argues, secularists and feminists (Muslim and non-Muslim) should 'defend women's right to wear what they like, not in terms of individual "choice", but as a mark of female autonomy and emancipation from patriarchal control'. Although I dispute the 'disingenuous' – Muslims are no more able to step outside prevailing discourses than anyone else – I agree with Wilson's argument that the veil should be de-exceptionalised and placed squarely within other contemporary discussions of fashion, gender and agency. Further, I propose that the inconsistencies predominant in discussions of and practices in veiling fashion can be regarded as the generic inconsistencies characteristic of everyday religion:

> At the level of the individual religion is not fixed, unitary, or even necessarily coherent. Rather, each person's religious practices and the stories they use to make sense of their lives are continuously adapting, expanding or receding, and ever changing.
>
> (McGuire 2008: 210)

The fact that some advocates of Islam present veiling as a requirement in contradiction to the choice discourse does not mean that those who conceptualise their veiling as a choice are wrong or are suffering from false consciousness. All lived religions are necessarily messy, contradictory, and changeable. Choice becomes one of the predominant modes through which religious activity is presented and experienced, and though this can be seen as contingent it does not minimise its effectiveness for different individuals and groups of women. Neither does it (nor should it) serve to present Islam as homogenous. Reflecting on responses from

Muslim women in North America, Jane Smith concludes that while 'many feel that the choice is *when* rather than *whether* to adopt the hijab' others resent the pressure to veil in order to prove their piety, arguing that 'the mark of a good Muslim should be her behaviour and not her appearance' (Smith 1999: 109–10, original emphasis). To continue to pose a binary opposition between freedom of choice and religious subjection (*qua* Mahmood 2005) makes it hard for Western-influenced feminists to recognise women's agency in choosing to veil as a particular form of subjection to faith, and to inscribe as natural the historically produced ethic of 'freedom' that is, as Nikolas Rose demonstrates, part of the mode of governmentality of Western liberal political statehood. Whatever the actual constraints, he argues, liberal governmentality requires us to understand ourselves as a choosing subject, so that each 'must render his or her life meaningful as if it were the outcome of individual choices made in furtherance of a biographical project of self realisation' (Rose 1999: ix). Central to this process is the narration of lives in psychological terms. The hijabi narratives that I discuss in this chapter and that are a mainstay of the blogosphere, magazines and social media (Lewis 2010; 2013b), fit this general trend towards self-realisation narrated as, and achieved through the narration of, a history of choice. This locates young Muslim women in WENA as typical of their wider social moment. In expressing their self-actualisation as pious Muslim subjects as a tale of conscious individuated choice, they depart from the narratives of inherited religious identity based in collective community and kinship ties characteristic of their first- and second-generation migrant parents or grandparents. In using clothing from the mainstream fashion industry as a mode for the expression of their spiritual selves they operate as the choosing subject of neoliberalism, becoming 'as it were, entrepreneurs of themselves', selecting from 'a variety of market options that extends from products to social goods to political affiliations' (Rose 1999: 230, see also Secor 2007).

Thus, women who experience and represent their religious dress as a form of subjection that is simultaneously required and willingly chosen are not invalidating their own arguments: they are engaging in practices of daily religion that are (and that they themselves often understand to be) produced in conditions of social, spatial and historical specificity. This is why many young women, when asserting their rights to choose to veil, will argue that it is just as wrong to compel women to veil as to force them to uncover against their will. Their willingness to present their acceptance of religious prescripts as part of a personal and autonomous journey to spiritual fulfilment is entirely in keeping with other narratives of religious and personal quest favoured by their generation and marks them as entirely typical of rather than distant from the preoccupations and modes of self-development of their peers. That many young hijabis (never mind niqabis) are going against parental wishes and family conventions is emblematic of the development of contemporary and multiple versions of Islam and marks participation in rather than rejection of 'Western' neoliberal consumer culture. That state agencies and majoritarian observers often fail to recognise this, locked into the need to protect Muslim girls and women from Muslim men (see also Scott 2007), belies the real challenges that impede Muslim women's autonomous expression of social and religious subjectivities.

Restrictive community norms are still a factor, and may continue to be so, despite the determination of young hijabis. Writing about young women in Britain, Werbner points out that though they intend to signal their rejection of 'village' Islam with their new styles of doctrinally informed hijab, 'they are unable to escape its self-evident connection – at least for the older generation of immigrants – to traditional ideas about what constitutes *dishonour*' (Werbner 2007: 165). Muslim women may make tactical use of choice-based rights arguments in their struggles against local Muslim patriarchies, using revivalist study of the holy texts to argue that local ethnic conventions contravene the inherent equality that Islam offers to women. But, as Brown points out, while this approach requires Muslim women to target both local male elders and state/municipal representatives (accustomed to male-dominated modes of community representation) it also depends on women 'being seen and known as "Muslim" in order to legitimate their claims' (Brown 2006: 425). While the external world might increasingly be anxious about (the still very small numbers of) women wearing niqabs, within the Muslim community it is the hijab that is a testing ground: wearing hijab and dressing 'appropriately' is often the price of admission for Muslim women who want to intervene in mosque activities or take part in theological discussions with senior men and the ulema who will otherwise refuse to meet with them (Kariapper 2009).

Hijab narratives: observing and being observed, da'wa and distinction

The first time I used the term 'coming out story' to some young women who were recounting to me their hijab narratives we all laughed in recognition. It made perfect sense (to these metropolitan, educated, British, young Muslims) to transpose a concept developed in relation to a sexual minority to their experiences as a religious minority. Indeed many hijab narratives follow the 'classic' coming out formula of first coming out to yourself, then to your family, then to the wider community; a process of personal liberation that is intended also to be part of a larger project of social development. Since then it has become commonplace to 'come out' about many elements of identity from disability and illness to ethnicity. To come out is to embrace that which was stigmatised, to make visible that which was hidden, to render political that which is relegated to the personal or private, to celebrate with 'pride' that which could be shaming (see also Sandıkçı and Ger 2011).

The decision to cover certainly brings Muslim women into new relations with other Muslims, which can be both a support and an unwelcome form of uninvited regulation. Women are subject to increased scrutiny by majoritarian observers who they know compare them to other Muslim women and most especially to other hijabis. Even those who are committed to a voluntaristic rationale for hijab find themselves evaluating Muslim women whose dress and behaviour provide cautionary tales and style inspiration. In seeking to present their choice of hijab as authentic, within a genre of narrative that is invariably relational, women often struggle to avoid appearing to judge or criticise the choices of others. All of these elements are present in Razia's story given below.

Razia describes her first day wearing hijab as challenging.[2] Presenting herself as not under any family pressure – 'my mum's never pushed me . . . they weren't very religious, they weren't that strict at all' – she arrived suddenly at her decision to wear hijab:

> [I hadn't] actually had a practice [at tying the hijab], so I just woke up that morning, spent like an hour in the mirror trying to fix it and I just thought, that's it, I'm going to walk out with it, if I don't walk out with it today I'll never wear it in my life. [It's] now or never.

The momentousness of Razia's decision meant that she was not able to get advice on styling from her older hijab-wearing sister, her mixed feelings prompting an almost adolescent display of show but not tell towards her (at the time) non-hijab-wearing mother:

> I quickly said to my mum, 'Mum, bye, I'm going to work' . . . She looked at me and I sort of just slammed the door and just went out before anybody else saw me . . . I felt embarrassed and I felt like I looked hideous in it . . . you know that image thing just kicks in . . . the person in the mirror isn't me any more, is this really me, and I felt like, did I do the right thing. And so I'm quite strong with my word, so I'm like, if I put this thing on I won't take it off again, I'll wear it properly like a 'good girl'. [laughs]

Presenting her decision as impetuous, Razia not only went out untutored in hijab wrapping, but did so on a day when she was due at work in her part-time shop job in London's West End rather than a day to spent at home or college. Having worked at a branch of fashion jewellers Swarovski in Oxford Street for two months, Razia found that it was not only to herself that her appearance was rendered unrecognisable:

> I just came into work and [said to my manager], 'Oh hi Chrissie', and she was like, 'Oh hello darling', she didn't look at me, she just said, hello because she thought someone just said hello to her. . . . and then she goes, 'Oh my God, what happened?' . . . She didn't recognise me at first . . . that day, I remember, was one of the worst days of my life because I went to the toilet about fifty times because I had about fifty different pins on me and I found it really difficult [and] and I couldn't put it on properly, . . .
> It was very uncomfortable, it was like really, really difficult and I thought no, . . . I've got to keep up, you know, I've got pride . . . I made a vow to myself, if I ever wear one, I'll wear it properly or I won't wear one.

Wearing it 'properly' also meant wearing it consistently and for the right reasons. Not necessarily apparent from Razia's account so far is that although she presents her Bangladeshi family as not very religious, and her decision to wear hijab as uninfluenced by others, she was in fact immersed in a Muslim habitus of modesty, experienced as understated and unproblematic:

> my family wasn't really bothered either because I mean modesty is something that I've always been bred and brought up with . . ., so like obviously I wouldn't wear a top with like my boobs hanging down or something that my mum would kill me [for, but] a skirt up to my knees wouldn't be such a big issue.

Razia's decision to wear a hijab was thus an adaption of an existing Muslim disposition in which women understood and expected their dress and body management to be subject to internal scrutiny and regulation. What changed when she decided to wear hijab was that she knew her Muslim embodiment would now be scrutinised by majoritarian viewers, bringing a new set of subjects in relation to whom she would need to self-regulate her dress decisions.

In this light Razia's determination to tough it out even after her first terrible day with a 'head full of pins' was determined not only by a personal commitment to faith but also by an acute awareness of the political damage done by women who start and stop, a form of hijab wearing that she regards as inauthentic because it signifies covering that has been imposed rather than freely chosen.

> The reason why I always said if I put it on I want to put it on properly, it's because I used to see girls at school, they used to come out the house wearing it properly, soon as they get on the bus, slowly, slowly the convertible scarf used to come off – so I call it the convertible headscarf.
>   *What, like a car?*
>   Yeah, it eases back, so when they used to go back home, before they got off the bus, it used to slowly come back on again and they used to walk into the house and I hated that. And I like really hate the parents for forcing the child to wear it. [They are] teaching the child bad principles and the wrong way to put it on because it shows a bad sort of reputation to the community . . . You're automatically [seen as] a Muslim because I've got a scarf and I portray my religion to show people that I am Muslim and this is who I am. But then if I'm going out now and I wear a scarf and I go out clubbing, people are like, I thought you're not supposed to be clubbing, you're Muslim, it's not in your religion to do that. . . . So I always thought if I do it, I should wear it, give it respect, to the religion, give respect to myself, give respect to my parents. . . .

Onjali Bodrum and Nathasha Ali, both interns working on the fashion pages at British Muslim lifestyle magazine *emel* (see Lewis 2010) tell very similar stories: about the 'freedom' of choice to wear the hijab,[3] and about wearing it well:

> I wore it trendily [until] twenty and then I started wearing it properly . . . I've had friends [who] as soon as their dad was round the corner

they'd take off the *hijab*, shorten their skirt, everything . . . it represented oppression to them, they hated it.

Wearing hijab only as far as the gates of the school may be a common practice
(Morey and Yaqin 2011), but the obverse is also true, with some students at
Muslim girls' schools only wearing the hijab at school where it is part of the
uniform but not at home or when socialising (Kariappur 2009). Razia and many
other women who spoke to me were at pains to avoid criticising other women's
hijab choices. By defining 'free choice' as the key indicator of authenticity, rather
than a particular style or degree of covering, they are able to project blame onto
the parents who wrongly impose the hijab. This rescues from criticism the girls
who wear it so casually and absolves them of appearing to judge other women.

In a non-Muslim majority context wearing hijab produces complex new
relationships with other Muslims, both positive and negative. Many women spoke
with pleasure of being greeted by other Muslims once their clothing makes them
visible:

> **NA**: I get more acknowledgement, you know, you do get a lot more
> smiles. That's one thing that I noticed when I started wearing *hijab*, it
> was like, wow, people know I'm Muslim all of a sudden, it's like I'm
> part of a bigger community . . . I remember the first time I walked
> on a bus and a lady turned round to me and said, '*Assalamu Alaikum*'.
> I was like, oh, you know I am Muslim. . .

According to many hijabis' accounts, these positive interactions with other Muslims
through which 'the hijab acts as a collective affirmation device' (Tarlo 2010: 55)
are often counterweighted by negative attention:

> **NA**: They will look twice at you, more so than maybe if you weren't
> wearing a *hijab* because they feel like they have the right almost to
> judge you . . . You do get more surveillance . . . I don't really enjoy
> that when people kind of like give you that second look.

Rendering oneself recognisable as Muslim by wearing hijab brings welcome inter-
pellation into community with the salaam, but also subjects one to detailed
evaluation and comment from diverse groups and individuals that is necessarily
inconsistent and contradictory. Noting that even 'people with the complete kit get
criticised' Nathasha concludes with a laugh, 'You can't win. You really can't.'

The sort of competitive piety they describe (common also in other religions)
is seen by some to be legitimated by the Islamic injunction of *da'wa*. *Da'wa* (literally,
the call or invitation) can focus outwards on encouraging conversion into the
faith, but also has an intra-Muslim mission, in the shared obligation to 'urge fellow
Muslims to greater piety' and to 'teach one another correct Islamic conduct'
(Mahmood 2005: 57). Previously the preserve of the ulema, *da'wa* was increasingly
preached in the early twentieth century as an obligation on all Muslims (Mahmood
2005: 57–60). Although women's *da'wa* was understood to be limited to other
women, when women come to participate in new veiling practices they also enter

a worldview that legitimates forms of female intervention in spheres not restricted to the private: enjoining a woman at work, or on the bus, to cover/cover more strictly is a validated behaviour. Within the 'democratisation' of *da'wa* in Europe since the 1980s, individuals might see the acquisition of religious knowledge as part of their cultivation of a pious self and as contributing to the wider project of building a 'virtuous community' in a non-Muslim majority context where Islamic values were not communicated by the state (Jouili and Amir-Moazami 2006).

In contemporary WENA, the creation of hijab fashion has been a key mode through which women communicate alternative interpretations of respectable or pious Muslim femininity. Their dressed practices and activities can be directed simultaneously at other Muslim women who can be guided to virtue, the collective Muslim community via the family, and the non-Muslim majority. The impact of *da'wa* on the majority observer is not necessarily conceptualised in terms of conversion. Rather, women hope that, through their exemplary behaviour and presentation as 'modern' and educated, they will counteract negative stereotypes about Muslim society as intrinsically primitive and patriarchal. Many women used similar terms when they explained to me the rationale behind their personal style: looking 'nice' as a way to demonstrate that Muslims are not 'dirty' or 'primitive' or old-fashioned, and the reason why they agreed to be interviewed: to contribute positive information to studies of Muslims.

Like the rapid fashion trends through which hijab wearers create their Muslim style, hijabi fashion is diversified by class and micro-generational changes. While the first tranche of second-generation South Asian Muslim young women in Britain may have established hijabi fashions as a way to emblematise their 'correct' revivalist understanding of Islam against the restrictions of their parents' 'ethnic' Islam, this is not always the case for younger second- and contemporary third-generation young women who have not faced similar restrictions from their parents and who come from families where mothers are uncovered (Kariapper 2009). In these instances, wearing hijab may often be more about challenging negative external presumptions and creating dress cultures of religious pride as an antidote to Islamophobia.

However, while some young Muslims, especially those with sufficient cultural and economic capital, might take up hijab as a conscious act of resistance to majoritarian stereotypes, others find themselves adopting forms of Muslim dress to avoid censure from local co-religionists, such as the Bengali migrants to London's Somerstown who started to wear abayas (not something they wore in Bangladesh) to avoid accusations of impropriety on the local gossip circuit (Tarlo 2010). Distinction may be based not on 'belonging to a certain social class, but rather in the sense of belonging to the group of "good" vs "less good" Muslims' (Amir-Moazami and Salvatore 2003: 63).

Razia has been made uncomfortable by other Muslim women's judgements. Presenting herself as unaware of the 'correct' terminology for 'Islamic' garments like the jilbab or abaya – 'because those words are quite new to me, I've only learnt those two words in the last two and a half years maybe, so even I was a bit like, you know, I didn't know what it meant properly' – Razia was aware of other staff (she was by then working for Swarovski in Debenhams) 'who were already wearing the whole thing'.

> I met a few girls [in the store's prayer room] who cover more than me, they'd actually wear the full thing and they were a bit more practising . . . So you'd see them in there and . . . they'd sort of try and give you some advice and say, oh you should try and wear the full thing . . .
>
> I felt a bit uncomfortable because I listened to them but I just felt like I was being in denial, if you like, because I didn't feel comfortable. I couldn't . . . even yet now I couldn't, I don't feel comfortable wearing the full thing. It's probably something to do with the person I was before. I love my jeans, I love my Western clothing, I wear dresses sometimes, I have like a mixture, I like the variety in my life.

This 'encouragement' to 'do it the proper way, if you like', was clearly somewhat uncomfortable, but Razia found a way through:

> But then I just sort of got used to them telling me these things and I said yes, thank you for the information, I really appreciate it . . . So it didn't sort of like overdo my power of what I wanted to do.

In the no doubt carefully neutral physical environment of the non-denominational prayer space provided by the store as part of its staff diversity policy, Razia faces the sort of Islamist progessivist narrative (first hijab, then jilbab, then niqab, then gloves) that young people more often report encountering in college and university Islam societies (Atasoy 2006). In the workplace staff facility, Razia uses a pluralist conception of religious practice to find a way through an intra-Muslim border dispute about what constitutes correct, authentic, hijab. Her apparent deference to the other women who are presented as having more religious capital ('more practising', 'more knowledge') allows her to demonstrate respect while rejecting their attempt to define Islam and lets her quietly continue with her 'mixture' of everyday religion. It is 'variety in my life', blending 'Western' clothing, rather than a progessivist narrative towards more clearly defined Islamic dress, 'the full thing', that supports her in 'my power of what I wanted to do'.

Finding clothes for hijabi fashion: overlapping fashion systems

While new companies aimed specifically at hijabi and modest fashion are making inroads (Lewis 2013a), it is clear that hijabi fashionistas continue to source garments from a mixture of high street and diaspora fashion. None of these systems entirely meet the needs of this particular style cohort, whose developing interpretation of appropriate dressing is pushing against both secular notions of public presentation and existing Muslim dress practice. It is not just that hijabis pounce on long-sleeved shirts when they are available on the high street; it is also that they are bulk buying items of ethnic and diaspora fashion when those clothing systems feature trends that are hijab friendly.

In Britain, the distinctive and varied needs of Muslim women were historically well understood within the thriving cross-faith Asian diaspora fashion scene. Very often dress for Muslim women, as with migrants of other faiths, was felt to express ethnic and regional identities rather than securing religious distinction. Among the majority South Asian Muslim population in Britain, Asian dress remains a popular choice and a sometimes required wardrobe feature for revivalist women – worn at home, the mosque and for family events and wedding.

A significant factor that traverses minority and mainstream fashion cultures has been the widespread take up of 'Asian' style through the 1990s. Building on the recurrent aesthetic for Asian and 'Oriental' styling, 'Asian Cool' became a global fashion story, integral to the longstanding boho trend of the mid-1990s and 2000s. The transformation of Asian garments and styles into fashion relied on their consecration by Western celebrities and fashion authorities, reinforcing the universality of the white body as the unmarked ground on which an Asian item could signify fashion rather than tradition (Bacchu 2003). However, diaspora Asian women themselves might recuperate pleasures in 'images and items outside of the Orientalist matrix in which they have been marketed' (Puwar 2002: 64). Thus while the 'trickle up' of Asian style into the mainstream can reinforce social divisions between those who wear 'Asian chic' as fashion or as habit, it can also signal both the influence of diaspora street style and the vitality of diaspora fashion entrepreneurship (Puwar and Raghuran 2003; Dwyer and Jackson 2003). The 1990s also saw a blossoming in Britain of what Werbner calls 'Asian fun': a mix of South Asian popular culture imports and British Asian writing, food, television, comedy and film that was embraced by many young British Muslims as being simultaneously 'Islamic and culturally open', while also enjoyed by other South Asians and white Britons (Werbner 2004: 192).

At the same time as the new assertive Asian cultural identity was celebrating ethnic affinities across religious divides, new revivalist hijab trends were being developed in order to assert specifically Muslim identities. In Britain young adherents adapted conventional Asian clothing systems so that they could express their particular forms of Muslim religious distinction to non-Muslims and to other Muslims. Clare Dywer interviewed British Muslim schoolgirls in 1993–4, at the end of 'the Rushdie Affair'.[4] The school students were combining items of 'Asian' and 'English' dress, together reworking 'the meanings attached to different styles to produce alternative identities' (Dwyer 1999: 5). Pilloried by classmates who mistrusted the commitment of hijabis, they also faced criticism from parents who equated respectable Muslim body management with Asian dress – one mother refusing to be seen in public in the local community with her daughter in a hijab.

Twenty years later and the hijab is now replacing the dupatta across the generations, with many young women reporting that their mothers have altered their habitual Asian clothing to accommodate what is now regarded as a more Islamically registered form of veiling. This applies to all forms of South Asian dress: Onjali's mother adds a hijab to her salvar kameez and Razia's now augments her sari, having started to cover her head in keeping with 'tradition' for married women, 'but now she wears it [the hijab] properly and puts a proper separate scarf on'.

The Muslim family habitus that led Razia's mother to encourage her towards slightly increased modesty in her later teens, has now been transformed by the developing religious consciousness of her daughter that renders the mother's habitual body management (the adjustable sari) insufficient and in need of reform. The impact of this new religiosity is seen (if not acknowledged) both on the high street where Razia shops for her modest wardrobe combinations and in the Asian fashion industry where her mother's saris are acquired. The upward movement of hijab wearing from daughters to mothers is well documented, but also has fashion implications that traverse the presumed boundaries between mainstream and ethnic fashion. Asian clothing that previously was integrally suited to the achievement of modest body management, such as the sari and salvar kameez, is now being worn with an additional scarf (and bonnet) to form a hijab. These significant alterations to the use of South Asian garments have not so far impacted on production: the traditional three-piece salvar kameez, or Punjabi suits, has not yet appeared with a fourth piece for hijab. Hijabi blogger and stylist, Adviha[5] explained the challenges of creating a functional hijab from the conventional items of salvar, kameez, and dupatta:

> girls are using their dupatta and tying it as a headscarf, but of course there's so much material and it's so long and wide that it can often prove quite difficult. [Some women will] find a colour in the suit which is the colour of the embroidery and [match that to] a normal scarf they've got and then just wear the dupatta round their neck . . .

This means that salvar kameez consumers are treating the suit like any other clothing from the high street. The add-on scarf disrupts the coherence of the suit to the extent that it no longer feels authentic:

> you just feel so disconnected and it doesn't feel right in a way because you've had to layer it in so many ways that doesn't suit what you're wearing . . . It loses its integrity and I just say I'd rather put on a pair of jeans.

Layering might be a good way to 'hijabify' mainstream trends, but it does not automatically translate into Asian fashion; however, the ever more rapid trend cycles in Asian fashions can similarly provide a culturally attuned window of style opportunity when, for example, kameez with long sleeves are in vogue.

Hypervisible and illegible: The paradox of hijabi subcultures

That the Muslimness of women's outfits swamps the fashionability of their carefully styled hijabi ensemble is frustrating and problematic. Contemporary hijabi fashions of all varieties nearly always suffer from a relative and located illegibility, faced with audiences unable to decode nuances of style and/or spirituality. Just as Asian women's finely tuned decisions about when and where to wear what forms of Asian dress in the era of Asian chic went largely unnoticed under the lumpen orientalising gaze of majority observers, so too with religious dress does legibility depend on 'who is performing, with what intentions, under what circumstances, and before what audience' (Jones and Leshkowich 2003: 8). Reliant on minority and subcultural competencies, the finessing of Asian or other ethnic or religious clothing is rarely discernible to people outside that particular community.

In her essay on subcultures, Caroline Evans summarises the political issues at stake in the ability or not of observers to recognise in-group distinctions. Early academic studies conceptualised (often working-class, mainly male) youth subcultures as forms of resistance to dominant and parental culture, heroicising forms of cultural activity that were presented as resistant to mere consumerism. While this might have made sense for the spectacular visibility of subcultures from the 1960s and 1970s such as mods and punks, by the end of the century it no longer adequately described youth cultures that, like the rave cultures of the 1990s (Thornton 1995), were determinedly 'opaque' in their styling and seemed to be more 'about finding a sense of community than about rebellion' (Evans 1997: 171). Evans advocates that rather than seeing subcultural identities as fixed, and as set points in a dichotomous opposition between youth/adult, subculture/mass culture, they should be understood as 'mobile, fluid, as a "becoming" rather than a "being"' (Evans 1997: 179). People move through subcultures (women often more than men it seems) and subcultures themselves 'mutate constantly'.

In terms of youth verses parents, much hijabi styling is indeed resistant to parental cultures as per the classic subcultural paradigm. But it differs in two keys ways. First, for hijabis in WENA the 'parental' Muslim culture is also itself structurally minoritised. Second, hijabi youth culture, while resistant to parental norms, is also characterised by a trickle-up from younger to older women, seen at a family level in some of the narratives in this chapter. More broadly, revivalist dress forms and related practices are being transposed and adapted by older women around the world (on Cairo see Serageldin 2005).

This is a youth cultural formation that is both defined against and working in conjunction with parental cultures, characterised like other revivalist practices of global or European Islam by negotiation and accommodation with existing religious authorities and community practices. If young women are using religious knowledge to assert themselves against conventional gender roles they are also committed to spreading those practices to others, including their family. They do want to distinguish themselves from the 'olds', but unlike other youth cultures that depend for their cool on keeping the olds out, this one also wants to bring them in, to help them 'do' Islam their way. This gives fresh impetus to the idea of subcultural participation as part of a life project, less a passing phase than linked sequences in which personal presentation is formed in dynamic relation with prevailing cultures, also themselves in flux.

Yet, while cool young hijabis may indeed be assembling their wardrobe from a melange of sources, hijabifying the high street and the ethnic brands alike, the ability of ethnic or religious minority cool to be recognised in its own terms is entirely dependent on the localised circumstances of both majority and minority viewership.

For Muslim women in WENA whose forms of dress render them hypervisible within the prevalent post 9/11 securitising discourse, there may be some mileage in being understood through a subcultural frame that recognises the support and community hijabi practices can provide without regarding their current incarnation as an essentialised unchanging version of self. Hypervisible they may be, but the very fact of their style decisions remain opaque to out-group observers who are formed by a fashion discourse that continues to regard Muslim dress as outside the domain of fashion.

Notes

1   In addition, some Muslims hold that all humans are born Muslim: thus some prefer the term 'revert' to 'convert', to signify a conscious return to an originary Muslim faith identity.
2   Personal interview, 29 September 2009, London. 'Razia' is a pseudonym.
3   Personal interview, Onjali Bodrul and Nathasha Ali, London 23 October 2009.
4   In Britain, responses to Ayatollah Khomeini's fatwa against Salman Rushdie over *The Satanic Verses* was pivotal to the development of identifications as Muslim rather than previous ethnic affiliations.
5   www.hijabilicious.com.

References

Ahmed, L. (2011) *A Quiet Revolution: The Veil's Resurgence from the Middle East to America*, New Haven, CT: Yale.

Amir-Moazami, S. and Salvatore, A. (2003) 'Gender, Generation, and the Reform of Tradition: From Muslim Majority Sources to Western Europe', in S. Allievi and J. S. Niessen (eds) *Muslim Networks and Transnational Communities in and Across Europe*, Leiden: Brill.

Ammerman, N. T. (2007) 'Introduction: Everyday Religion: Observing Modern Religious Lives', in N. Ammerman (ed.) *Everyday Religion: Observing Modern Religious Lives*, Oxford, New York: Oxford University Press.

Atasoy, Y. (2006) 'Governing Women's Morality', *European Journal of Cultural Studies*, 9:2: 203–21.

Bacchu, P. (2003) 'Designing Diasporic Markets: Asian Fashion Entrepreneurs in London', in S. A. Niessen, A. M. Leshkowich and C. Jones (eds) *Re-orienting Fashion: The Globalization of Asian Dress*, Oxford: Berg.

Bourdieu, P. (1984) *Distinction: A Social Critique of the Judgement of Taste*, London: Routledge.

Brown, K. (2006) 'Realising Muslim Women's Rights: The Role of Islamic Identity Among British Muslim Women', *Women's Studies International Forum* 29:4: 417–30.

Dwyer, C. (1999) 'Veiled Meanings: Young British Muslim Women and the Negotiation of Differences', *Gender, Place and Culture*, 6:1: 5–26.

Dwyer, C and Jackson, P. (2003) 'Commodifying Difference: Selling EASTern Fashion', *Environment and Planning. D, Society & Space*, 21:3: 269–92.

El Guindi, F. (1999) 'Veiling Resistance', *Fashion Theory*, 3:1: 51–80.

Entwistle, J. (2000) *The Fashioned Body: Fashion, Dress and Modern Social Theory*, Cambridge: Polity Press.

Evans, C. (1997) 'Dreams That Only Money Can Buy . . . Or, The Shy Tribe In Flight from Discourse', *Fashion Theory: The Journal of Dress, Body & Culture*, 1:2: 169–88.

Goole, N. (2011) *Islam in Europe: The Lure of Fundamentalism and the Allure of Cosmopolitanism*, Princeton, NJ: Markus Wiener.

Jouili, J. S. and Amir-Moazami, S. (2006) 'Knowledge, Empowerment and Religious Authority Among Pious Muslim Women in France and Germany', *The Muslim World*, 96:4: 617–42.

Kariapper, A. S. (2009) *Walking a Tightrope: Women and Veiling in the United Kingdom*, London: Women Living Under Muslim Laws.

Leshkowich, A. M. and Jones, C. (2003) 'Introduction: The Globalization of Asian Dress: Re-Orienting Fashion or Re-Orientalizing Asia?', in S. Neissen, A. M. Leshkowich and C. Jones (eds) *Re-Orienting Fashion: The Globalization of Asian Dress*, Oxford: Berg.

Lewis, R. (2004) *Rethinking Orientalism: Women, Travel, and the Ottoman Harem*, London: I.B. Tauris.

—— (2010) 'Marketing Muslim Lifestyle: A New Media Genre', *Journal of Middle East Women's Studies*, Fall 6:3: 58–90.

—— (2013a) *Modest Fashion: Styling Bodies, Mediating Faith*, London: I.B. Tauris.

—— (2013b) 'Fashion Forward and Faith-tastic! Online Modest Fashion and the Development of Women as Religious Interpreters and Intermediaries', in R. Lewis (ed.) *Modest Fashion: Styling Bodies, Mediating Faith*, London: I.B. Tauris.

Mahmood, S. (2005) *Politics of Piety: The Islamic Revival and the Feminist Subject*, Princeton, NJ: Princeton University Press.

McGuire, M. B. (2008) *Lived Religion: Faith and Practice in Everyday Life*, Oxford, New York: Oxford University Press.

Malik, M. (2010) '"Progressive Multiculturalism": Minority Women and Cultural Diversity', *International Journal of Minority and Group Rights*, 17: 447–67.

Morey, P. and Yaqin, A. (2011) *Framing Muslims: Stereotyping and Representation after 9/11*, Cambridge, MA: Harvard University Press.

Puwar, N. (2002) 'Multicultural Fashion . . . Stirrings of Another Sense of Aesthetics and Memory', *Feminist Review* 71: 63–87.

Puwar, N. and Raghuram, P. (2003) 'South Asian Women in the Diaspora', in P. Raghuram (ed.) *Fashioning the South Asian Diaspora: Production and Consumption Tales*, Oxford: Berg.

Rose, N. (1989) *Governing the Soul: The Shaping of the Private Self*, London: Free Association Books.

Roy, O. (2004) *Globalised Islam: The Search for a New Ummah*, London: C. Hurst & Co.

Sandıkçı, O. and Ger, G. (2010) 'Veiling in Style: How Does a Stigmatized Practice Become Fashionable?', *Journal of Consumer Research* 37:1: 15–36.

Scott, J. W. (2007) *The Politics of the Veil*. Princeton, NJ: Princeton University Press.

Secor, A. (2007) 'Afterword', in K. M. Morin and J. K. Guelke (eds) *Women, Religion, & Space: Global Perspectives on Gender and Faith*, 148–58. Syracuse, NY: Syracuse University Press.

Serageldin, S. (2005) 'The Islamic Salon: Elite Women's Religious Networks in Egypt', in m. cooke and B. M. Lawrence (eds) *Muslim Networks from Hajj to Hip Hop*, Chapel Hill, NC: University of North Carolina Press.

Smith, J. I. (1999) *Islam in America*, New York: Columbia University Press.

Tarlo, E. (1996) *Clothing Matters: Dress and Identity in India*, Chicago, IL: University of Chicago Press.

——— (2010) *Visibly Muslim: Fashion, Politics, Faith*, Bloomsbury Academic.

Thornton, S. (1995) *Club Cultures: Music, Media and Subcultural Capital*. Cambridge: Polity.

Werbner, P. (2004) 'Theorising Complex Diasporas: Purity and Hybridity in the South Asian Public Sphere in Britain', *Journal of Ethnic and Migration Studies* 30:5: 895–911.

——— (2007) 'Veiled Interventions in Pure Space', *Theory, Culture & Society* 24:2: 161–86.

Wilson, E. (1985; new edn 2003) *Adorned in Dreams: Fashion and Modernity*, London: I.B. Tauris.

Chapter 24

Pamela Church Gibson

FASHIONS, FEARS AND AGEING
Contradictions and complexity across the media

Shame . . . is typically expressed in acts of concealment – it is a reaction to the threat of demeaning treatment one would invite in appearing to be a person of lesser worth . . . Shame is the distressed apprehension of the self as inadequate or diminished . . . Further, shame requires the recognition that I am in some important sense as I am seen to be.

(Bartky 1990: 47/86)

In the old person that we must become, we refuse to recognize ourselves.

(de Beauvoir 1975: 11)

IN OUR FIRST ANTHOLOGY, I PUBLISHED A SHORT PIECE on the relationship between our ageing population and the fashion industry. Embedded in the essay, or so I hoped, was the notion that there were other factors to be considered, of more importance than fashion, as the demographics of the 'baby boom' changed both the conditions and the perception of ageing. The women whom I interviewed spoke of feeling the impact of what Susan Sontag had identified so long ago as the 'double jeopardy of ageing' (Sontag 1972). Problems, rather than solutions, seemed imminent, given the boomers' fear of ageing. As Kathleen Woodward said, they were already 'in hiding', disguising the ageing process by whatever means were within their income (Woodward 1991). Today, the model of the 'mask of ageing' (Featherstone and Hepworth 1991) might need to be modified; the continually increasing activities intended to alter the appearance of the selfsame 'mask', to halt or delay change through strategies of physical intervention, suggest that the model itself is in need of modification (see Tulle 2012: 6). However, the notion of 'the *masquerade* of ageing' provided by Woodward's reworking of Rivière

(1991: see also Biggs 1997) is still, perhaps, the most appropriate way 'to articulate the disjuncture people experience between their ageless selves, their ageing bodies and the resulting social undesirability' (Tulle, op. cit.).

Sadly, Sontag's model of 'double jeopardy' has not been superseded; if anything the feeling that age disadvantages women rather than heterosexual men has been exacerbated in the age of celebrity culture (see Feasey in Swinnen and Stotesbury 2012 and Church Gibson 2011). There is a significant body of work around the ageing of gay men which we should note (see for example Hughes 2006; Drummond 2006; Jones and Pugh 2005). However, the Sontag model has surely become for debates around ageing what Mulvey's theory of 'the male gaze' is to debates within film scholarship and elsewhere; it can be challenged, but it has never been refuted and is a constant reference point (Mulvey 1975).

I had hoped that those who read my original essay would identify the underlying problem: that of an increasingly confused and ambivalent attitude to ageing. But re-reading my own words, it almost seems as if I were encouraging fashion retailers simply to address the fact of an ageing population and thus maximise their own profit margins. This was hardly my intention. So from the start, I should like to make it clear that what follows is not simply about 'fashion'. Although the former thicket of literature around ageing has become a veritable forest in the intervening decade, it is not my plan here to guide the reader through the trees. There has been a good deal of activity within the academy; thankfully, debates around issues of ageing are no longer confined to the pages of journals on gerontology or social science. Forthcoming books on ageing and the media figure prominently within publishers' lists. There is even a small body of work on ageing and dress (see Twigg 2007 and 2013). Issues related to ageing are now being addressed by a growing number of cultural theorists from other disciplines; within the study of popular culture, studies of older women on screen (see Wearing 2007; Radner 2011; Whelehan 2010 and Kaplan 2012) have reflected onscreen activity. For cinema is increasingly using stars and storylines designed to tempt older viewers back into the multiplexes.

Outside the academy, within different strands of the media and in the retail sector, there has been, if not a frenzy, then certainly a flurry of activity, as the potential of this new consumer group has been assessed and realised. This is of course simply a second address to those consumers identified sixty years ago, in all their youth and spending power, as 'teenagers'. Many of them are now 'in hiding' not only from the population (Woodward, op. cit.) but also from *themselves*.

Despite the articles, the films, the conferences and the books there are, nevertheless, noticeable omissions. I am worried by the seeming inability of many, whether journalists or scholars, to make what I see as vital links across the entire spectrum of activity – both academic and commercial – and so fit together the various pieces of what turns out to be a disturbing jigsaw puzzle. The three things that particularly concern me are the lionising in both popular culture and the academy of a very selective mode of *stylish* ageing, the parallel and unacknowledged growth in recent years of new fears around ageing related specifically to appearance, and the silence of most feminist scholars.

Feminist scholars, of course, cannot solve the extraordinary *practical* difficulties created for so many women by the ageing of those around them. But they could

Figure 24.1
Advancing years have seen his
spending power increase – and,
despite the trainers-with-suit look
here, his interest in fashion seems
undiminished. Mick Jagger at a
Tommy Hilfiger show. Photograph
by Anne-Marie Michel, Catchlight-
Media.com.

perhaps address these problems in the debates surrounding 'postfeminism' and its
challenges. McRobbie and Negra, principal protagonists here, have chosen instead
to focus mainly on younger women (McRobbie 2008; Negra 2009), possibly
because the conflicts that they address are in part generational. Certainly Negra
ends her book with an acknowledgement of these difficulties: 'In tracking the
characteristic preoccupations of postfeminism, what is perhaps most striking is the
diversity of identities and social experiences it neglects' (Negra 2009: 153).

Within what little remains of feminism as a practical project, rather than
academic activity, Cynthia Rich's attempt to form a caucus group specifically
designed to address the numerous difficulties faced by ageing women was, as
she says in interview, spectacularly unsuccessful (see Barnes Lipscomb 2006).

Woodward, interestingly, sees feminism itself as having 'internalised cultural prejudices against ageing' (2009: xi).

New, growing fears of getting – or of looking – older have somehow escaped the gaze of journalists now seeking to glamourise ageing. But during the past decade, for those willing to scrutinise the lower depths of popular culture and the excesses of the internet, this new fear could easily be charted. It is at odds with the recent championing of stylish modes of ageing and new moves in the film industry to court the so-called and hopefully lucrative 'grey market' (Radio 4 website/programme, January 2013, see Blaikie 1999: 213). Furthermore, we should note that if manufacturers and retailers have been very active lately, it is not necessarily in an 'age-affirming' way. The marketing of 'anti-ageing' products is burgeoning, while dermatologists and plastic surgeons are busy as never before. But their clients span the entire age range; botox and fillers are now seen as necessary to ward off the advance of the third *decade*, rather than the Third Age. Advertisements show the disturbing reality of 'preventative Botox', a recent and widely advertised procedure where the substance is now injected in advance, into those spaces or places where wrinkles might later choose to appear. Magazines like *Grazia* – now syndicated across the world – *Heat* and *Allure*, targeted at women in their twenties and thirties, invariably discuss anti-ageing tactics within their beauty pages. 'Want to Look Younger?' is the bold – or bald – question emblazoned across the décolleté of the thirty-four-year-old actress Katie Holmes on the cover of *Allure* for April 2013. Older celebrities are frequently vilified both in print and online if they are not seen as actively striving to prevent the effects of ageing (see Church Gibson 2011).

If we look at the 'mature glossies', of course (*Vogue*, *Bazaar*, *Good Housekeeping* and others) we find the mantra 'Look Younger' invariably woven onto the covers, the return of the imperfectly repressed. The widespread availability of cosmetic intervention and its dedicated advertising, coupled with the ubiquity of photo-shopped images and digital manipulation in commercial photography, mean that young women in their teens and twenties are so used to the practice of airbrushing in fashion, publicity and advertising that they have actually forgotten what the human face looks like; in the same way, the combination of Barbie dolls, porno-graphic images and high fashion has practically banished pubic hair from public memory.

Two sharply contrasting pieces of journalistic evidence in recent months appeared, almost as if designed to validate my arguments. The January 2013 issue of *Harper's Bazaar* raised the very issue of the 'New Ageing' of high fashion and consumer culture (*pace* Katz and Marshall 2003) in its *Talking Points* pages. It had a special mini-feature, 'Ageless Beauty', which charted this new phenomenon with a breathless enthusiasm.

'It started in earnest last year', the journalist began, describing those advertising campaigns by leading fashion houses where older models had been used and the appearance of eighty-year-old actress Angela Lansbury on the cover of *The Gentlewoman*, one of the most stylish international magazines, in August 2012. The article listed a number of new British films either on release or in preparation that starred well-known British actors in their sixties as middle-class senior citizens. It noted the publication of Grace Coddington's autobiography and the fact that the blog *Advanced Style* was to be filmed. Announcing that 'the older consumer is a force – and a stylish one – to be reckoned with', the article closed by mentioning a forthcoming American documentary on supermodels of the past, and with a quote from possibly the best-known, Carmen dell'Orifice, on surgical intervention: 'If you had the ceiling falling down in your living room, would you not go and get it repaired?' (*Bazaar*, January 2013: 90)

The ideas of Carmen and the anonymous writer for *Bazaar* should be set against those of a fifty-eight-year-old woman who also featured prominently in print that same month. The media interest in Cambridge professor Mary Beard began with her BBC documentary series, *Meet the Romans*, in 2012, when she was taken to task – not for her programme but for her looks, for her long grey hair and overly casual dress. In response, Beard criticised, if only by implication, older women who could not accept the realities of ageing. She had exposed something very troubling – the seeming horror of many when confronted so publicly with age unadorned. It must be stressed that this is not simple misogyny, for a younger version of Beard would not invite such violent antagonism. Now, however, she seems to remind some viewers vividly and violently of Bakhtin's crones (1984) and Russo's 'female grotesques' (1994), the epitome of the abject.

In the era of 'Ageless Beauty', older women who make no attempt to disguise the ageing process are worrying for many – certainly there seems to be a feeling that they do not deserve a high media profile. Beard has a casual, even alternative, style of dressing and were she thirty, this mode of self-presentation would not have provoked such an acrimonious response. But an ageing woman, apparently, must disguise herself very carefully when in public; her critics felt that a woman who is chosen to present a television series should try hard to please. After watching her first programme, *Sunday Times* television critic A. A. Gill attacked her violently not for the material she had chosen to present, but for her physical attributes: 'From behind she is 16, from the front sixty . . . if you're going to invite yourself into the front rooms of the living, you have to make an effort' (*Sunday Times* 18 April 2012).

Beard was offered a chance to reply straightaway in the *Daily Mail*, a newspaper that addresses the very demographic affected by the subject, fifty-plus women. Here, she resurrected the old dichotomies of second wave feminism with her headline: Too ugly for TV? No, too brainy for men' (23 April 2012).

Beard attacked what she called 'the blokeish culture that loves to decry clever women, especially ones who don't succumb to the masochism of Botox and have no interest in dyeing their hair'. Finally, in a paragraph that included a description of her own 'uncompromising double chin', she announced:

> Sure, I don't wear makeup. I have nothing against those who do if it gives them pleasure, but actually I feel happy enough in my own skin not to feel I want to bother with it. I don't dye my hair for the same reason . . . if I did, what would I be covering up? And how do you stop doing it once you've started? I am fifty-seven and this is what I look like – this is what most normal women of fifty-seven look like (Ibid).

The questions Beard poses here, and the notion of interfering with what is 'normal', might have alarmed some Third Agers now adopting strategies of disguise or 'covering up'. She seems to suggest the possibility of their perhaps being discovered; of the worrying, concealed realities somehow coming to light. It might not be too fanciful to mention the fate of Ayesha, anti-heroine of the popular Victorian novel *She* (Rider Haggard 1899). In the closing chapters, the 'Fire of Life' that had given her permanent youth, beauty, and eternal life now reverses its strategies; before the horrified eyes of the infatuated explorer-narrator: the woman who has captured his senses ages a full 2,000 years in the course of a few minutes. He watches, appalled, as her face and body collapse spectacularly inwards, her hair falls out and she shrivels up completely, leaving, dead at their feet, 'a hideous little monkey frame, covered with crinkled yellow parchment' (Rider Haggard 1899/2008: 258).

The *Daily Mail* is more prosaic, but not prepared to stop mining a very rich seam, that of vilifying the older woman who does not follow the anti-ageing advice that is the staple fodder of its women's pages. A week later, it allowed the journalist Samantha Brick to write a reply headlined: 'Sorry, some women ARE too ugly for TV' (*Daily Mail*, 30 April 2012). Telling us that she wasn't at all surprised, she concluded:

> If I were Ms. Beard's executive producer, I would congratulate her on the rumpus and the publicity it generated. Then I would do what her bosses should have done when she signed her BBC contract – sit her down and discuss a makeover.

This makeover would involve 'wardrobe, makeup and grooming', plus some advice about weight loss and discreet 'procedures'. Beard took no such advice, but accepted further invitations to appear on high-profile television programmes. But it was her appearance on the BBC's *Question Time* in January 2013 that reignited the attacks on her mode of self-presentation. Here she attempted to counter fears around increasing immigration, as any liberal might; however, the storm of internet activity was focused on her appearance, not her views. A website had to be closed because of abuse posted there; Beard's Tweets in her own defence seemed to intensify the anger.

The *Daily Mail* again joined in, accusing Beard of not understanding the effect on an audience that long grey hair might have (22 January 2013). Columnist Rod Liddle went even further: 'It's not misogyny, Professor Beard, it's you'. Citing past attacks on 'his own person and penis', he claimed that all within the public arena are open to attack. But with Beard, he argued, that danger is intensified: 'because she looks like a loony, which is precisely why she along with Grayson Perry gets to be on television' (*The Spectator* 26 January 2013).

The linking of Beard with cross-dressing artist Perry shows just how transgressive her 'performance' of female ageing seems to be. Beard was interviewed in *The Observer* the following day. She reiterated her claims of the previous year, that her appearance was a reflection of reality and not a bizarre aberration: 'There clearly is a view of female normative beauty but more women of 58 do look like me than like Victoria Beckham' (*Observer* 27 January 2013).

Here Beard's refusal to feel what the public see as appropriate shame might even be seen as a kind of pride. If, as Sedgwick argued, 'shame and pride, shame and dignity . . . are different interlinings of the same glove' (2003: 38), then Beard is displaying that mode of pride that could be seen as 'an interface between abjection and defiance' (Edwards 2008: 99). Beard made one other observation here that seems pertinent. Asked about 'women in antiquity', she answered:

> Classical antiquity is always much more complicated than you think. But the basic position is that elderly men are admirable and that elderly women are awful – what is the point of a post-menopausal woman? Old women get laughed at. I thought we had moved on.
>
> (*Observer* interview, Ibid)

In the second half of this chapter, I will move to examine recent cinematic portrayals of older women who do not 'get laughed at' to discover and examine what, within those fictional constructions, ensures freedom from mockery, and what is presented to attract and reassure older audiences. I will finish by looking, in contrast, at a bleak and disturbingly honest film, Michael Haneke's *Amour* (2012).

Before we move onto the fictional recreation of ageing, we should mention a non-fictional woman who, like the actress Emmanuelle Riva in *Amour*, also found late onscreen stardom. Here it was through playing *herself*, filmed for a documentary about the fashion industry. It is important because her mode of self-presentation is atypical for this industry, and yet is acceptable, even singled out for praise. The woman is Grace Coddington, Creative Director at US *Vogue*, who was born in 1941; her new 'celebrity' status followed her appearance in R. J. Cutler's *The September Issue* (2010). Before the film appeared, Editor-in-Chief Anna Wintour was the only known 'face' of the magazine. But as it unfolded, Coddington's role within it – the creative stylist constantly foxed by commercial imperatives, the sage counsellor of bewildered younger employees – meant that she became its star. She was subsequently recognised on the subway, given an award for services to fashion, praised by bloggers and encouraged to publish her autobiography.

It is important to mention Coddington since she might at first seem to be 'transgressive' herself within that high-fashion context. Where Wintour glides, slender, polished and buffed, through the film and along the corridors, hair blow-dried to perfection, Coddington wears loose clothes and flat shoes; her long red hair falls around and below her shoulders while her face is that of a woman in her late sixties who has eschewed surgical intervention. Yet if readers are already thinking of Beard's 'anti-fashion' look, they are quite mistaken – and the reasons for this are central to this essay. First, Coddington's clothes, though loose and unrevealing, are the work of leading designers. Second, her hair is startlingly red; she speaks idly in her autobiography of perhaps allowing it to go grey, but also stresses the importance of always getting regular attention from a top hairdresser – here, her own partner (see Coddington 2012). Third – and of most significance – she began her career as a model in the 1960s by winning a *Vogue* competition. Her friends, lovers and husbands were key figures in the mythology of that decade and when it ended, Grace moved behind the cameras, as stylist, after a car crash. She went on to create seminal fashion imagery for three decades. Transgression of a kind is, it seems, permitted to certain older women, if they are known to carry such invisible baggage.

It is also permitted to unusual women such as Iris Apfel, heroine of all who appear on *Advanced Style* and of that blog's founder. She is in her nineties and has featured frequently in fashion magazines and colour supplements. She is both extremely rich and possessed of excellent, idiosyncratic taste. Consequently, she has amassed a collection not only of extraordinary, colourful garments from across the world but also of innumerable arresting accessories and jewellery. She can thus present herself as an objet d'art – another acceptable fashion option for the older woman, if sufficient aesthetic sense is deployed in the daily recreation of the artwork. Wardrobes full of clothes are not enough; the 'right' kind of fashionable eye is needed for the selection, combination, assembly and presentation of the contents. Consequently, Apfel has been the subject of a curated exhibition in 2005 and an accompanying coffee-table book; she created a makeup range for MAC in 2011, and appeared on the cover of *Dazed and Confused* in November 2012, modelling that season's Comme des Garçons collection for its fashion pages. She is the only nonagenarian to be so honoured; fashion can even look at the *Fourth Age*, if it is suitably tasteful.

It goes without saying that poverty does not figure in the fashion address to and depiction of old age, though to study any work on gerontology within the social sciences and indeed the current coverage of government plans, we find poverty central within the debates. It is among those problems for which social policy worldwide has yet to find an answer; other considerations cited are loneliness, bereavement, lack of mobility and confinement, illness and dementia. None of these figure in the selective 'New Ageing' of the fashion world and of consumer culture (Katz and Marshall 2003).

They are significantly absent, too, from most cinematic depictions of the Third Age. E. Ann Kaplan has rightly stressed the difference between the Hollywood treatment of the ageing woman and that found in European cinema (Kaplan 2011). She herself writes about the sympathetic portrayal and costuming of the sixty-something Ann Devlin in *The Mother* (Roger Michell 2003), a film interrogated elsewhere by Imelda Whelehan, and of the eighty-year-old Jeanne Moreau, who played the ageing Marguerite Duras in a French art-house film that chronicles her affair with a much younger man (*Cet Amour-là*, Josée Dayan 2001). Sadly, although these films are of great interest to feminist film scholars, they don't seem to have provoked a slew of imitations. Nor have they garnered significant returns at the box office.

That is the provenance of Hollywood films depicting and targeting an ageing population – particularly the female viewer, seen apparently as in most need of cinematic comfort. Nancy Meyers's film *Something's Got to Give* (2003) has been discussed at length elsewhere (by Wearing and Radner among others) and I want here only to make observations around the presentation, styling and cultural capital of its heroine. For those unfamiliar with the film, Diane Keaton plays a successful playwright and divorcée in her late fifties, slim, attractive and unattached. Jack Nicholson is Harry, music industry executive who only 'dates' women under thirty, and her own daughter's boyfriend at the start of the film. Keaton and Nicholson have an unexpected, brief affair; he then continues to philander. But Keaton's public pillorying of him in her next play precipitates a Damascene conversion; seeking forgiveness from all the women he has wronged, he finds Keaton and offers himself up, penitent. He discovers her, elegantly dressed, dining à deux in Paris with the much younger Julian (Keanu Reeves) who has been consoling her and who now cedes ground as she wishes. The film ends with Nicholson and Keaton lunching at one of the many expensive restaurants that feature in this film, together with her daughter, happily paired with a man of her own age, and granddaughter.

To call this film fantasy is perhaps unkind, but it seems accurate. It is also a very fashionable fantasy. For a start, Erica is extremely rich; as Nicholson first approaches her home in the Hamptons, he calculates aloud as to the value of the 'real estate' around him. She also has her acclaimed status within the highly competitive world of Broadway theatre; this provides her with the opportunity to humiliate the man who has awakened her dormant sexuality only to desert her. Finally, her lifestyle is one that reflects through its restrained elegance her cultural capital. Her house in the Hamptons is so extraordinarily tasteful as to have subsequently featured in *Architectural Digest*, where a photospread showed off the white-painted rooms with their pale wooden floors and furniture, cream linen curtains and sofas, white flowers and white porcelain bowls of beautifully arranged pale stones. Her own clothes reflect the chic neutrality of the house – beige cashmere sweaters, white linen trousers and white turtleneck T-shirts. And, provoking desire in both Reeves and Nicholson, for dinners and lunches she dons black designer dresses and expensive but discreet jewellery.

As with the *Daily Mail* and the Beard saga, Meyers realised that here was a profitable seam to mine. She created a second fictional heroine whose successful career, affluence and visible good taste would appeal to older women. In both

Figure 24.2   Diane Keaton's lady playwright dresses both herself and her home in chic neutral linens and cottons – cultural capital meets financial wherewithal.

films the heroine has the chance not only of love in later life but of a choice between *two* men, one of whom has previously behaved very badly to her. Meyers cast Meryl Streep in *It's Complicated* (2009) as a divorced mother of three who runs a successful bakery and restaurant. She too owns a large and enviable house, on the West Coast this time, with a kitchen as large as that of most restaurants. Although the film begins with the last of her children leaving home, she decides to enlarge and remodel her home, so that architect Adam (Steve Martin) comes to call. The 'complicated' nature of her life is provided by her rekindling of sexual relations with ex-husband and successful lawyer Jake (Alec Baldwin). He is now married to a much younger woman, who we see at an anniversary party for mutual friends in crop top and harem pants baring both midriff and impressively tattooed back.

The plot shows us Jane and Jake's affair, his plea to return home and her refusal, signalling an eventual partnering with divorced Adam. Dalliances take place in five-star hotels or in Streep's beautifully appointed bedroom. She herself is depicted as casually chic and sexually desirable. We watch her casting aside a white bathrobe under Jake's gaze, after a deep intake of breath; she is worthy of display. Earlier in the film she was considering surgery for a saggy eyelid, but she understands that this is unnecessary, with two men in thrall. It is Jake who is teased in dialogue for being overweight, he who has the transgressive, unruly body. In the sole moment of real humour, this body is inadvertently shown off to Adam as Jake unknowingly interrupts an intimate Skype session in Jane's bedroom. Just as in the first film, conspicuous consumption is on display – even Jane's children drive brand-new cars. Her house may be more relaxed than Erica's, but it is still spacious and tasteful. She has her own organic vegetable garden near the swimming pool, and a very pleasing selection of 'age-appropriate' clothes. She entertains her girlfriends in an oriental silk robe worn over wide trousers and for a 'date' with Adam wears yet another silk trousered outfit. She buys an expensive wrap dress for an intimate appointment with Jake; for the denouément, by contrast, she wears well-cut jeans and a blue denim shirt, matching the huge bunch of stocks she has picked from her garden.

The more modest success of this second film possibly prompted a move to shift the cinematic depiction of ageing further down the socio-economic scale. Streep was again cast in the film *Hope Springs* (David Frankel, 2012), seemingly designed to court Middle America. Here she is fifty-something wife, Kay, deglamourised though still attractive. Her cinematic life is far more modest, though enviable to many in a double-dip recession. The marital home in Omaha is much smaller and conventional in its decor. Her husband of thirty-one years, Arnold (Tommy Lee Jones) is a partner in an accountancy firm; she has what seems to be a part-time job in a dress shop. Their children, too, have left home; Arnold spends his evenings in a vast recliner, watching golf on cable television.

In the opening sequence, we see Streep checking her appearance in the glass. Although made up and carefully coiffed, she is wearing a nightdress – turquoise, Empire-line, perhaps her best. She enters the spare bedroom where her pyjama-clad husband is trying to sleep and suggests nervously that she might join him there. He says no, he has a busy day tomorrow – and she returns, rejected, to the marital bed.

This is the problem at the centre of the film; their sex life seems to be over. Kay may be modest in income and outlook, but she has saved carefully. Now she removes all her money and arranges a week of 'Couples Therapy' with a Dr Benny (Steve Farrell) in Hope Springs, Maine. Arnold is bewildered and even angry – but he joins her on the trip and they find themselves on a sofa together in front of the therapist. The sessions don't start well; Arnold is antagonistic and defensive. At one point he describes the therapist as a 'little prick' – and we can see his point; Farrell/Benny is often patronising, particularly in his assumptions about Arnold's conservative sexual tastes. The film lurches unevenly forward, through heavy-handed humour as Streep attempts to teach herself the technique of fellatio with a few small vegetables as props, and tears when the therapy seems to have failed. But the film has the obligatory Hollywood ending; Kay and Arnold renew their wedding vows in a ceremony on the beach, with the 'little prick' as a kind of unofficial best man, their children and grandchild in attendance.

What is interesting about this film is the fact that it was made at all, that Streep and Jones were happy to participate and that it met with some success. Even the critics seemed happy and Streep was nominated for a Golden Globe. The dress and styling is surely central to the film's box-office performance. Jones wears shirts and ill-fitting jeans that emphasise his paunch; while Streep is slim, her outfits could be seen on any woman of her age in high streets across America – floral printed frocks, pastel tunics and trousers seemingly made from synthetic fabrics, inexpensive necklaces and earrings. For dinner at an expensive hotel – implied as unusual – she wears a lilac wrap dress, a modestly priced copy of the Diane Von Furstenberg version she purchased as 'Jane'.

Obviously the Hollywood studios have decided that they should court the new demographic, and that this might be a better way forward. There are less stylish recent English films made about and for this age group – *Best Exotic Marigold Hotel* (John Madden, 2011) and *Quartet* (Dustin Hoffman, 2012) – that feature valued thespians, 'heritage' stars and thus, implicitly, heritage values. But here, however, Dames Dench and Smith are not witness to young love, as in the 1980s. Now they themselves can ignite passion; the dowager onlookers of those original 'heritage' films have become active participants in the romantic storylines. And the heritage elements are assumed to dignify these films, to give them a cultural cachet that Hollywood films can never possess. The characters do not have their own homes to feature in *Architectural Digest*, nor are they expensively styled; what is important, it is implied, is not for them to look younger than their years but to embody the ageless taste and abilities valued by the English middle classes.

Hollywood's presentation of the ageing *male* protagonist might best be done through a scrutiny of Clint Eastwood's recent films; he still wields enormous, unprecedented power there as actor, director, and producer in his eighties. In 1999, he directed *True Crime*, in which he played a reprehensible journalist with a taste for his colleagues' wives and where, at sixty-nine, he appeared semi-naked in a bedroom scene. Since then, he has foregone sexual liaisons or romantic encounters, now playing widower or bachelor. His body is hidden from sight; but his face, which grows ever more ravaged and bleak, is presented, lit, displayed as such. 'Men act and women appear' as Berger explained so long ago (1972: 47).

However, Eastwood brings onto the screen the whole history of the Eastwood persona, the Man with No Name and a cigarillo, Dirty Harry brandishing his massive handgun, the Outlaw Josey Wales taking on impossible odds, and the talented, deraciné photographer of Madison County who gave an Iowa farmer's wife a love she refused but never forgot.

Eastwood previously played charismatic outsiders; now, in his own films, he casts himself as isolated. In *Million Dollar Baby* (2004) he has somehow alienated his daughter; as Frank in *Gran Torino* (2008) he has two ungrateful sons. In this second film, he shows us every flaw in the character of the curmudgeonly and bigoted Korean War veteran he plays. Frank becomes involved with and protective towards the Hmong teenagers who move in next door. But he has to adopt a new way of resolving the film's difficulties; we see that the traditional Eastwood use of physical violence only creates further suffering. Frank/Eastwood solves the narrative problems and the plight of his young neighbours by offering himself up as sacrificial victim; he can still, despite his age, defend the vulnerable and so triumph. As the baseball scout of *Trouble with the Curve* (Robert Lorenz, 2012) he is able to spot a player's flaws despite his rapidly advancing glaucoma. This last film begins with Eastwood in his bathroom, attempting to pee; his member – so active in his earlier films – is unresponsive even to this simple demand. Here, again a widower, he has allowed his house to grow untidy; the protagonist of *Gran Torino* who maintained his property so carefully, flying the flag and mowing his lawn daily, has given up, and lives in mild semi-squalor, eating takeaway pizza for breakfast. No cinematic heroine could be shown in such a state of domestic abjection, whatever her age. His dysfunctional relationship with his daughter is miraculously restored, within the period covered by the narrative, through the magical powers of baseball, which for both is a quasi-religion. As she finds peace with her father, years of therapy finally behind her, and romance with Justin Timberlake, a gruff Clint leaves them embracing in the final frames.

Amour (Michael Haneke, 2012) is the antithesis to such anodyne moments. It is graphic and unflinching in its portrayal of the physical realities of old age. Haneke shows us pain, suffering and indignity where the only 'resolution' possible is the release of death. Other directors have suggested that they might portray the realities of ageing, but if we compare *Amour* with, say, *Away from Her* (Sarah Polley, 2007) the contrast is sharp. In the American film, Julie Christie takes herself to an expensive care home to spare her husband and herself the difficulties of her dementia. Even when it is acute and advanced, she still looks glamorous; her husband can point her out among the other patients as 'that woman – over there – with the glorious mane of hair'. The infrastructure of his life – and hers – remains intact.

Amour by contrast shows clearly and ruthlessly the terrible effects of a traumatic stroke for both victim and carer. The film is comfortless; even the 'love' of the title is problematic. Haneke began by casting two actors who cinéphiles might remember as both young and beautiful. Jean-Louis Tritignant first came to public notice in 1956 playing opposite Brigitte Bardot in her first success, *Et Dieu Crée La Femme*. Ten years later he starred with Anouk Aimée in a sentimental but very popular film *Un Homme et Une Femme*.

Emmanuelle Riva was the heroine of Duras' film *Hiroshima Mon Amour* 1959, the young woman recounting her affair with her Japanese lover. Since then she has been seen by few outside her native country. Consequently she is etched on the cinematic consciousness as the nubile, often naked, heroine of a seminal New Wave film.

Now in her eighties, she plays Ann, a retired pianist and teacher, living comfortably with her musician husband in a sizeable flat – the kind of flat inhabited by those with cultural rather than economic capital. It is comfortably bohemian, walls lined with bookshelves and oil paintings. Haneke insisted that he wanted his characters to have funds, so that audiences couldn't protest 'But if they'd had some money, things would have been different' (Haneke in interview, 2012).

The film opens with their return from a concert, Anne smartly dressed in black with pearls; her husband compliments her on her looks. When she suffers a mild stroke, and before a second stroke leaves her incontinent, virtually mute and semi-paralysed, she makes her husband promise that he will not put her in a home, whatever happens. He keeps his promise, managing with the help of hired 'carers'. However, he dismisses the last of these, having noted her callousness. In one particularly distressing scene we see her roughly brushing Ann's hair, and then holding up a hand mirror. Ostensibly, it is to show Ann her now tidy hair, but it forces her to confront her own face, lopsided and paralysed. Ann cries out and flinches in pain.

We see throughout the difficulties of caring for a paralysed, confused partner. It is presented as an endless, tiring task with no respite. The couple do have a daughter, but she is not the happy helpmeet of Hollywood cinema. Married to an irksome Englishman, her visits to Paris are sporadic, and her first question when she arrives after her mother's stroke is the wisdom of her parents remaining in their own home. Should they not sell the large flat and thus release some capital? She is quickly barred – and there is no reconciliation.

We see Anne spitting out baby food, tied into diapers, hosed down in the shower. Her husband retains his mobility but his increasing frailty is stressed; we see that he begins to wear trainers, to contain his increasingly swollen feet. However, as Haneke's film began to garner awards, with Riva finally nominated for an Oscar, only the traditionally acceptable face of female ageing was presented in the press and online. Riva's appearance within the diegesis was totally at variance with the images the media selected; reportage of the ceremonies showcased and valorised an elegant eighty-five-year-old actress. Notably, the only screen clip from the film used showed us Riva *before* the onset of her degeneration into mute semi-paralysis. There was instead global coverage celebrating the fact that an eighty-six-year-old woman could look so elegant at the Oscars; the images displayed her chic coiffure, scarlet lipstick, Lanvin gown and diamond necklace.

In her performance, however, there was honesty and disclosure; David Bowie has recently made his own radical intervention within music. The video he released after ten years' semi-retirement, to accompany the song *Where Are We Now?* was an interesting move for a performer whose career has been constructed around a series of extravagantly stylish constructs. In this video Bowie's face is seen throughout as part of a fairground exhibit; he peers through a billboard depicting a conjoined puppet, in what seems to be a lumber-room. There is no attempt to soften or disguise the face of a sixty-six-year-old man. Finally he walks away, simply dressed, quite happy to be seen without artifice or manipulation; like

Prospero, he bids farewell to his magic and its accoutrements. However, an exhibition at the Victoria and Albert Museum to showcase the costumes of his previous personae – his magical box of tricks – sold out before the doors were even opened. Now, he shows off himself in reality; as I have argued, this is still problematic for women in the public eye.

What this essay has suggested is that, although there is a growth of writing and media activity on and around age, fashion and popular culture, there are still difficulties to overcome. The new visibility is, it seems, possible for women who seem to have resisted the ageing process or who demonstrate a sense of style, a fashionability. The 'double jeopardy', then, remains. But, even for men, ageing is at its most acceptable if there is a story of some sort to remember, past images of virility as with Eastwood or of style for Bowie. Their pre-existing personae have made their honest presentation of ageing more palatable. For women, history can by contrast work against them. Rolling Stones' founder-member Keith Richards can be displayed as he is now, ravaged by time and excess, because of his past exploits on stage and off; his exact contemporary and fellow-performer Marianne Faithfull, also working in her sixties, is by contrast photographed and lit to minimise the damage caused by time. Fashion and style may appear to have come to terms with ageing, and even to have adopted a more enlightened attitude towards it. However, it seems that, more widely across the media, attitudes are still shaped by differences in gender – and, certainly with women, rooted in a suppressed yearning for youth.

Coda

In one single year, two Hollywood filmmakers chose to recreate the story of Snow White and her beautiful, ageing, stepmother. Both films starred, as the jealous older woman, Hollywood actresses who had not only won an Oscar but, in a world of approbation through advertising, had been chosen as the 'face' of a major cosmetic campaign. Julia Roberts, star of *Pretty Woman* (Gary Marshall, 1991) *Erin Brockovich* (Steven Soderbergh, 2001) and the Lancôme campaign, played the Queen in Tarsem Singh's *Mirror Mirror* (2012). In that very same year, the woman who was currently the 'face' of Dior, Charlize Theron, turned on her young stepdaughter in a much darker film, *Snow White and the Huntsman* (Rupert Sanders, 2012): the young actress Kristen Stewart, indelibly associated with the *Twilight* franchise, was cast as Snow White.

Meredith Jones, in her radical analysis of cosmetic surgery (2008), refers throughout to the potency of this particular fairytale. She suggests, in fact, that it might eventually be rewritten and all generational enmity resolved, since 'body technologies and lifestyle practices are working to create a swelled period of middle age'; she sees surgery as bedevilled by 'outdated and repressive paradigms that undermine the potentially innovative possibilities . . . it offers' (Jones 2008: 105). It is, she argues, a possible way to create 'infinite opportunities for ageism to diminish and for more lateral relationships to develop' (Ibid). Some might certainly reject this provocative idea outright, if only because of possible future inequality where smooth-faced plutocrats confront wizened paupers; others might speculate as to the plausibility of the schema she presents.

However, no 'intervention' nor rewriting will ever be needed for the fairytale's hero; in the current climate, with its still-gendered differences around ageing, his good looks will secure for him a safe autumnal afterlife as a 'silver fox'.

Acknowledgements

Pamela Church Gibson would like to thank Niall Richardson and Janice Miller for their suggestions during the writing of this chapter.

References

Bakhtin, M. (1984) *Rabelais and his World*, Bloomington, Indiana: Indiana University Press.

Bartky, S. L. (1990) *Femininity and Domination: Studies in the Phenomenology of Oppression*, New York: Routledge.

Barnes Lipscomb, Valerie (2006) '"We Need a Theoretical Base": Cynthia Rich, Women's Studies and Ageism', interview in *NWSA Journal*, Vol. 18. No. 1, Spring 2006.

Berger, J. (1972) *Ways of Seeing*, London: Penguin.

Biggs, S. (1997) 'Choosing Not to be Old? Masks, Bodies and identity management in later life', *Ageing and Society*, Vol. 17, No. 5, 553–70.

Blaikie, A. (1999) *Ageing and Popular Culture*, Cambridge: Cambridge University Press.

de Beauvoir, S. (1975), *The Coming of Age*, London: WW Norton & Co.

Church Gibson, Pamela (2011) *Fashion and Celebrity Culture*, London: Berg.

Coddington, Grace (2012) *Grace: A Memoir*, London: Chatto and Windus.

Drummond, Murray (2006) 'Ageing Gay Men's Bodies', *Gay & Lesbian Issues and Psychology Review*, Vol. 2, No. 2.

Edwards, J. (2008) *Eve Kosofsky Sedgwick*, Oxford: Routledge.

Feasey, Rebecca (2012) 'The Ageing Femme Fatale: Sex, Stardom and Sharon Stone', in *Ageing Studies in Europe: Performance Ageing and Stardom; Doing Age on the Stage of Consumerist Culture* 2, 109–30.

Featherstone, M. and Hepworth, M. (1991) 'The Mask of Ageing and The Postmodern Life Course', in Featherstone, M., Hepworth M. and Turner B. S. (eds) *The Body: Social Process and Cultural Theory* Sage: London, pp. 371–89.

Hughes, Mark (2006) 'Queer Ageing', *Gay and Lesbian Issues and Psychology Review*, Vol. 2, No. 2.

Jones, Julie and Pugh, Steve (2005) 'Ageing Gay Men – Lessons from the Society of Embodiment', *Men & Masculinities*, Vol. 7, No. 3, January 2005, 248–60.

Jones, Meredith (2008) *Skintight: An Anatomy of Cosmetic Surgery*, Oxford: Berg.

Kaplan, E. Ann (2011) 'Un-Fashionable Age: Clothing and Unclothing the Older Woman's Body on Screen', in Adrienne Munch (ed.) *Fashion in Film*, Bloomington, IN: Indiana University Press, pp. 322–45.

Katz, S. and Marshall, B. (2003) 'New Sex for Old: Lifestyle, Consumerism, and the Ethics of Aging Well', *Journal of Aging Studies*, Vol. 17, No. 1, 3–16.

McRobbie, Angela (2008) *The Aftermath of Feminism: Gender, Culture and Social Change*, London: Sage.

Mottram, James (2012) *The Curzon Interview*, in *Curzon Magazine*, Issue 35, Nov–Dec 2012, 26–30.

Mulvey, Laura (1975) 'Visual Pleasure and Narrative Cinema', *Screen*, Vol. 16, No. 3, 6–18.

Negra, Diane (2009) *What a Girl Wants? Fantasizing the Reclamation of Self in Postfeminism*, London: Routledge.

Radner, Hilary (2011) *Neo-Feminist Cinema: Girly Films, Chick Flicks and Consumer Culture*, London: Routledge.

Rider Haggard, H. (1899/2008) *She*, Oxford: Oxford University Press.

Russo, M. (1994) *The Female Grotesque: Risk, Excess, Modernity,* Oxford: Routledge.

Sedgwick, E. K. (2003) *Touching Feeling: Affect, Pedagogy, Performativity*, Durham, NC: Duke University Press.

Sontag, Susan (1972) 'The Double Standard of Ageing', *The Saturday Review*, September 23, New York.

Stock, Francine (2013) Presenter – BBC Radio 4 *The Film Programme*, 3 January 2013.

Swinnen, Agje and Stotesbury, John A. (2012) *Ageing Performance and Stardom: Doing Age on the Stage of Consumerist Culture*, Imbh Verlag, Germany.

Tulle, Emmanuelle (2008) *Ageing, the Body and Social Change: Running in Later Life*, London: Palgrave Macmillan.

Twigg, Julia (2007) 'Clothing, Age and the Body: A Critical Review', *Ageing and Society*, Vol. 27, 285–305.

—— (2013) *Fashion and Age*, London: Bloomsbury.

Wearing, Sadie (2007) 'Subjects of Rejuvenation: Ageing in Postfeminist Culture', in Tasker and Negra (eds) *Interrogating Postfeminism: Gender and the Politics of Popular Culture*, Duke University Press: Durham, NC and London, pp. 277–309.

Whelehan, Imelda (2010) 'Not To Be Looked At: Older Women in Recent British Cinema', in Melanie Bell and Melanie Williams (eds) *British Women's Cinema*, London: Routledge.

Wilson, Gail (2000) *Understanding Old Age: Critical and Global Perspectives*, London: Sage Publications.

Woodward, Kathleen (2009) *Statistical Panic: Cultural Politics and Poetics of the Emotions*, Durham, NC: Duke University Press.

—— (1999) (ed.) *Figuring Age: Women, Bodies, Generations,* Bloomington, IN: Indiana University Press.

—— 1991 *Ageing and its Discontents; Freud and Other Fictions*, Durham, NC: Duke University Press.

PART SIX

Making masculinities

Chapter 25

Janice Miller

HEROES AND VILLAINS
When men wear makeup

PERHAPS IT IS THE GENERAL REQUIREMENT that makeup *seem* imperceptible in its application to a woman's face that has in turn rendered it relatively invisible within the ever-increasing critical work on fashion and adornment. Richard Corson's (2003) historical study clearly demonstrates how makeup has a complex relationship to both social status and gender identity. While it has not always been the exclusive preserve of women, in contemporary terms makeup use has of course become synonymous with femininity (see for example Craik 1994).

Kathy Peiss (1999) gives us some of the most significant work on the subject, focusing on the beauty culture of America, where she demonstrates how makeup has been a contested site for both the possible expression and oppression of female identity. Alongside, the work of writers such as Jennifer Craik (1994) and Catherine Constable (2000) has made a clear case for makeup use to be seen as possessing deep cultural meanings in relation to feminine identity and gender politics (see also Biddle-Perry and Miller 2009). Still, there is much for us to learn about the role of makeup in social and cultural life. For example, in contemporary Western culture where makeup remains a largely feminine practice, music performance has been one space where many male performers have experimented with makeup. It is beyond the scope of this chapter to fully explain why. Instead it aims to give some possible explanation of how gender identity is at issue when they do so.

Thus, this chapter uses some familiar examples as case studies to make some suggestions of how male made-up faces could be understood in relation to selfhood and gender identity in music performance. In doing so, the main aim is to go beyond the usual and overly simplistic understanding of makeup use by men as 'drag', so often succumbed to by the popular media. The chapter employs concepts of masking and masquerade alongside the notion of the 'hero' as an enduring, hegemonic, masculine ideal to argue that the way the men in these examples use and wear makeup might be more masculine than it at first seems. Ultimately the chapter argues that such use of makeup is certainly transgressive, but not because it seeks to feminise men. Instead its power lies in its ability to make visible the oft-hidden possibility that all masculinity might be – at odds with most conventional representations – constructed, multiple and fluid, with spectacular potential.

It seems to be most often surmised, in the popular imagination at least, that when men wear makeup they adopt femininity and that such 'gender-bending' practices must in turn signal something about sexual identity. Such positions certainly seem to underpin the attitudes that compelled Adam Lambert, *American Idol* runner-up in 2009 to say on Twitter:

> I read a comment recently: 'eww men aren't supposed to wear makeup!' is there some rulebook somewhere I didn't get a copy of? Ha! I say do whatever the [fuck] makes u happy and expresses who you are! I make my own rules.
>
> (see Viscount 2010)

Whenever Lambert is interviewed about his music, discussion of his made-up face and his sexuality are never far behind – suggesting that for the popular media there is some conflation of the two. Described as just 'a 27-year-old white gay guy in makeup and heels on American Idol' in an article in *The Guardian* (Hann 2012), Lambert came out at the end of the series and has since become the first openly gay performer ever to top the US Billboard charts. It is no great stretch of the imagination to conclude that it is not the makeup itself but what it *seems* to symbolise in terms of his sexual identity that troubles more conservative audiences. As British newspaper the *Daily Mail* observed, 'The flamboyant 28-year-old's love of makeup, leather and lace and his flaunting of his sexuality has raised the ire of conservative and religious groups' (Anon 2010a).

While such technologies of the body might be an expression of sexual and/or gender identity for Lambert, at least in part, the first contention of this chapter is that this may not be the only message that we should read here. For example, the smoky eyeliner often worn by Lambert is a fairly conventional stylistic statement within the broad genre of rock music. As such his makeup might be argued to evoke nothing more in the face of postmodernity than a descent into pastiche. However, it might also be argued that rather than a meaningless image or a grandiose, controversial or individual, style statement, this makeup that is worn by many male (from Keith Richards of The Rolling Stones to My Chemical Romance) *and* female musicians (like Chrissie Hynde, Avril Lavigne and Pink) signals a by now quite familiar, music-specific identity not bound to any gender. Along familiar lines and through eye makeup Lambert applies symbols to his face that resonate with the historical trajectory of rock music to which any pre-existing transgressive symbolism arguably comes a poor second. Instead this would seem to be makeup as myth in the Barthesian sense: an encoded set of inscriptions that operate as an archetype – a 'prestigious imitation' to use Jennifer Craik's term (Craik 2009: 136). Thus the formulaic nature of this makeup might on the one hand legitimate a face to inhabit a particular cultural space, while on the other hand identifying it with a music genre or style.

As such, it might be argued that this makeup acts as a mask that when adopted for performance becomes both a signal of belonging and a moment of trans-formation. As Roland Barthes writes, the full mask 'implies . . . an archetype of the human face' (Barthes 2000: 56), and since makeup is a substance that is applied to, which covers and that is also, importantly, removed from, the face, it is unsurprising that shared meanings are created between it and the mask (see for example Constable 2000; Biddle-Perry and Miller 2009).

Mikhail Bakhtin argues for a dual understanding of the mask's ability to both reveal and conceal the identity of the person wearing it. For Bakhtin it is post Renaissance that 'the mask hides something, keeps a secret, deceives' (Bakhtin 1994: 40), while never entirely losing its associations with 'a peculiar atmosphere (where it is) seen as a particle of some other world' (Ibid). Thus, the mask must always be somewhat associated with 'transition, metamorphoses, the violation of the natural, to mockery' (Bakhtin 1994: 40), but what may differ in varied cultural and historical contexts are the positive or negative associations that such transformations carry.

These judgements are often shaped by an inherent concern with truthfulness. For most classicists clear equations were made between bodily artifices and false-ness, and between natural, 'healthy' bodies and virtue (see Craik 1994; Constable 2000). On such terms, to make up the face is to create a façade that must in turn carry the possibility of deceit. These concepts seem to be at play in the makeup worn by Freddie Mercury in the video for Queen's 'I'm going slightly mad' (1991). The song was written by Mercury after his diagnosis with HIV and expressed the anxieties of living and dying with this illness. Such concerns are mirrored in his made-up face. Here the familiar lines of the coherent face of rock music become a 'death mask'; the thickness of the makeup makes visible the unnaturalness of this face and thus acknowledges its construction.

We might also see here a clear resonance with the face of the tragic protagonist von Aschenbach in the latter scenes of the film *Death in Venice* (1971). In an emphatically painted mask-like makeup we see the face of the Fool. This might be comedic in some contexts but for both the character of von Aschenbach and for Mercury it is also suggestive of a desperate fight to maintain the social self, carefully crafted in life and at threat in the face of death. Thus we see traces of 'the intricate, multiform symbolism of the mask . . . parodies, caricatures, grimaces, eccentric postures and comic gestures' (Bakhtin 1984: 40), but here they are tinged with tragedy.

Von Aschenbach is persuaded to make up his face in an endeavour to reclaim his youth in the hope of attracting the teenaged boy Tadzio, with whom he is obsessed. The idea that lurking behind the constructed veneer of this made-up face might be his true self is made all the more clear when Von Aschenbach's makeup melts away as he dies. Thus both these mask-like faces seem to metaphorically represent commonly held ideas in the West since the Middle Ages that separated bodies, minds and spirits and understood the human body as 'a persona – a mask that its wearer only escaped at death' (David Napier 1986: 12).

Figure 25.1   Freddie Mercury's thick, visible makeup becomes a death mask in the video for 'I'm going slightly mad', 1991.

Neither the character von Aschenbach nor Mercury use makeup to be feminine. Instead, as men nearing the end of their lives, their makeup seems to mark out their passage into 'otherness'. Such gestures take us into the realm of the abject, since here we could argue that Mercury acknowledges himself as a dying man with all of the connotations of transformation that this carries. This face thus inhabits the liminal space between selfhood and otherness, and for Julia Kristeva this is the crux of abjection; it is that which inhabits

> an uncertain, transitory state between the subject and the object, appearing to consciousness as both fascinating and repulsive, a state of insecurity with respect to the identity of self and other. The abject must be radically excluded from conscious identity boundaries for it threatens the boundary between self and not-self, it disturbs identity, system and order: abjection is caused by the in-between, the ambiguous, the composite.
>
> (Van der Spek 2000: 122)

A general suspicion about the trustworthiness of the social identities fashioned by makeup are not specific to men or to abject faces. Questions of authenticity abound in much of the significant work on gender and identity. This work grapples with the interplay between long-held essentialist notions of gender identity as inherent and more contemporary contentions that gender identity should be seen as nothing more than a construction formed by social expectation (see for example Butler 1990). Such thinking led psychoanalyst Joan Riviere to argue that femininity itself can be likened to a mask 'behind which man suspects some hidden danger' (Riviere 2011: 101). In the case of Riviere's female clients it becomes not only a social expectation but also a psychological defence mechanism; a reaction formation that in its adoption 'guards' women from possible social 'reprisals expected' if they were found to be in 'possession' of attributes of masculinity (Riviere, 2011: 94). Thus Riviere, like many other writers, understands gender to be a social construction, a 'masquerade', and femininity–thus a set of practices expected of women, designed to shore up gender positions. Importantly, masquerade demands invisibility, requiring an adherence to hegemonic ideals of appropriate gender identity that come to seem natural over time. While masquerade has been most often discussed in relation to feminine identity, as Lisa Downing notes Lacan used the term 'parade virile' as a masculine equivalent; but beyond that 'little has been written . . . on the possibility of a male version' (Downing 2004: 55).

The masculine masquerade 'should' involve the kind of hyper-masculinity identified by Chris Holmlund in her work on Sylvester Stallone. This is man as hero, possessing masculinity that echoes with the 'industrial strength associated with the ideal hypermuscular superhero body: the look of power, virility and prowess' (Karaminas 2009: 179). But as Brown (2001) has demonstrated, many more contemporary representations of the superhero present masculinity as less resolved than this narrow ideal: the superhero must embody both the before and after of a masculine identity transported from ordinary to extraordinary. As Vicki Karaminas notes, adornment is key to the superhero's identity since it 'transforms and transports [him] from normality to super-ness' (Karaminas 2009: 134). In particular, the mask in this context functions on Karaminas's terms to manifest and manage 'paranormal energies' (Ibid: 180). The kind of transformative power attributed to masks in this context invokes a variety of cultural associations, some of which have already been discussed here. In some this transformation summons otherworldly power. In Bali for example 'masks are the medium . . . through which Gods manifest themselves' (David Napier 1986: 206).

In using makeup to paint a blue stripe across his eyes in the mid-2000s, then, REM's Michael Stipe might be seen to be experimenting with such notions. Here Stipe's skinny, wiry frame juxtaposed with this painted face seems to embody what Brown (2001) acknowledges is the superhero's contradictory masculinity. He evokes both the 'warrior-hero', a figure whom writers like Woodward and Winter (2007) argue has been one of the most historically pervasive forms of hegemonic masculinity that persists despite more recent pluralistic models alongside 'a softer, feminized other' to uphold the 'reader's fantasy of self-transformation' (Brown 2001: 175). Through this makeup, we could argue Stipe, has both made visible the generally held contention that masculinity might be heroic alongside a more challenging one: that it might also be a masquerade because in this use of makeup he acknowledges his identity as a 'construction . . . a performance . . . rather than a universal and unchanging essence' (Cohan and Hark 1993: 7).

In many ways then, Stipe presents the audience with a double identity. In one sense he proposes an entirely masculine made-up face, but not one without some ambiguity. This stripe of blue paint across the eyes seems to fulfil an ambiguous and paradoxical function that situates Stipe in the liminal space between 'secrecy and spectacle' (Cohan 1996: 33). In considering Stipe's sexuality for a moment it might be useful to contemplate how this might signify when, as the work of writers like Will Brooker (2005) and Joanna Di Mattia (2007) have argued, there is always a queer subtext to double identity.

Importantly, the form of facial decoration adopted by Stipe is at odds with the conventional ideals of feminine makeup which, as Jennifer Craik notes, carries the general expectation that it 'should not be visible in its component parts, only its transformative impression' (1994: 158). While this might be something of a generalisation, it still rings true that women's makeup functions largely to enhance, rather than to be at any way at odds with, idealised feminine features in a variety of ways. Thus if gender is a binary then perhaps it is visibility that might render makeup masculine. Here the language of face painting may play its part since it is a practice that, while sharing a clear relationship to Westernised makeup, is less universally bound to any one side of the gender binary. For example, as Sherrow writes, 'In the Congo, male Kota paint their faces a blue colour to show they have become men' (2001: 49). Thus, while it is beyond the scope of this chapter to fully navigate the complex semantic similarities and differences between face paint and makeup or to make a clear decision about where the boundary between should be, it is certainly true that in this example we see the possibility that men's use of makeup utilises contrasting methods and inscriptions from those of women.

Figure 25.2   David Bowie's largely feminine makeup is offset by blanked out eyebrows, which prevent the look from being too feminine.

Nonetheless, since makeup has come to be so strongly associated with femininity in Western culture at least, any visible act of painting on a male face must always result in at least a sense of ambivalence on the part of the wider audience. There is a temptation to read David Bowie's various 1970s makeup looks as knowingly ambivalent: an often largely feminine makeup is offset by blanked out eyebrows, or some detail that goes beyond makeup towards face painting: a gold disc on the forehead or a thunderbolt across the face that creates a gender-ambiguous tension, preventing an otherwise delicate makeup from being pretty or conventional. This ambiguity seems to place Bowie, like Stipe, somewhere between masculine subjectivity and feminine other – albeit via different methods. Just like Stipe, notions of heroism might be seen to be written into the makeup looks designed for Bowie (with Pierre La Roche from Elizabeth Arden) but with different cultural reference points.

Bowie's early makeup looks famously took inspiration from traditional Kabuki theatre makeup styles where a face 'rinsed of meaning' (see Roland Barthes 1982: 91) is created by painting a white base on to which marks are made to provide 'specific statements and signify certain emotions' (Craik 1994: 156). Like all forms of face painting, theatrical and otherwise, this 'stylized and conventionalized' [makeup denoted] 'character and social status' (Cavaye 1993: 84) for actors playing archetypal roles. Colour was significant to characterisation with social class denoted by skin colour and painted veins (red for heroes and blue for villains) and bright eyes for men to represent vigour and health. As with all representations, these marks are revealing not only of character but also of cultural idioms in relation to gender identity and masculine power: be it heroic or villainous.

As Roderick McGillis (2009) argues, heroes and villains are not so different, but what situates a villain on the wrong side of good is his 'Otherness', often constituted in the B movies of which he writes by his ethnicity. But otherness can be constituted through gender too. Both Bowie and Stipe propose through the use of makeup and how they use it 'visible examples of otherness' (McGillis 2009: 127) that challenge not because they necessarily become feminine but because they deviate subtly from the boundaries of conventional masculinity within their historical contexts, arguably representing an even greater threat. After all, as Rebecca Arnold notes, 'since masculinity is held up as a signal of the "norm" in western culture, any derivation from conventional male attire is viewed with great unease' (2001: 111). Thus, Stipe and Bowie challenge masculine norms so they are both cultural 'hero' and 'villain'. As the work of many writers including Michel Foucault (2003), Mary Douglas (2002) and Lynda Nead (1992) has shown, the boundaries between right and wrong, good and bad, normal and abnormal in any social context are thin and precarious and it is whatever wavers on the boundaries between these polarised binaries that is the greatest test.

Through this makeup, then, we are offered transgressive male faces but not, I would argue, feminine ones. These ambiguities carry through into Bowie's general attitude to the activity of acquiring and using makeup. 'You're just a girl, what do you know about makeup?' he says to then wife Angie in the opening scenes of the *Ziggy Stardust* Motion Picture. In this joke and perhaps more so in a 1973 article for the magazine *Music Scene* (Anon. 1973), Bowie reveals what might be argued to be a particularly masculine attitude. In something akin to a Grand Tour of makeup consumption he recounts his use of colours from a shop in Rome that imports from India, rice powder for his face from a general store in Tokyo and a gold paint made in Germany, but bought from a store in New York that also sells the best Japanese brushes for application. Here Bowie is connoisseur: a man who aims to 'legitimize his consumption through knowledge' (Rudy 2005: 65).

The notion of connoisseurship developed, as Bermingham and Brewer (1995) demonstrate, as a reaction to the positioning of consumption and culture alongside the feminine Other. This more technical approach to consumption shored up masculine subjectivity in the eighteenth century and continues here to be played out, as Bowie as connoisseur of makeup does it better than the girls. In his technical knowledge he could be seen as the archetypal connoisseur who 'derives pleasure from exerting male discipline over a fearsomely unruly feminine realm' (Schaffer 2000: 85). Bowie imprints this connoisseurship and in doing so makes a 'demonstration of sexual difference' (Bermingham 1995: 502) that could be understood to be much more conventionally masculine than it might at first seem.

Thus this chapter has, in calling for makeup to receive greater attention within the cultural analysis of adornment, aimed to make some suggestions of how the male use of makeup might be problematised to go beyond a simple reading of made-up male faces as 'drag'. In the examples discussed here the kinds of gender identity being expressed and navigated via makeup are far from straightforward or feminine. However, in focusing on the male side of the binary there is much that can be concluded about the other side and I think it might be worth returning after this discussion of men in makeup to women for a moment.

The controversy about Adam Lambert that began this chapter would seem in part to come from his position firmly in the mainstream. After all he is in the public eye thanks to the most mainstream of music shows: *American Idol*. However, I would argue that equally if not far more controversial was an image of Katy Perry with a face clean of make-up, which created considerable furore when it was posted on Twitter by her now ex-husband Russell Brand. Much of the new media chatter suggests that very many women felt divorce was the appropriate response after this. But many other users both male and female decided that without makeup Perry was ugly (see for example valemigente.com) as did Perry herself, at least in her younger days, admitting in an article in *Seventeen* magazine that she had sometimes gone to sleep with her makeup on (see Anon. 2010b).

This clearly demonstrates that gender masquerade remains fraught for men and for women in different and complex ways. Perry's feelings on the subject seem to reflect how makeup use for women on Joan Riviere's (2011) terms must be understood as one of a number of technologies of femininity that could be understood as an 'anxiety ridden compensatory gesture' (Doane 1991: 38). Thus, while any mainstream male musician who puts on makeup will find that this remains worthy of popular comment, the idea of a female music performer not wearing makeup remains, it seems, far more controversial.

Though studies of masculinity call for an understanding of it as multiple, fluid and complex (see for example Edwards 2006), the media often fail to represent it as such. Of course several of the men discussed in this chapter are openly gay and while the fact of their sexuality might play some part in the representations discussed here it has not been the central emphasis. Instead the chapter has aimed first and foremost to focus on masculinity, to eschew the crass connections made between makeup on men, queer identity and effeminacy, instead arguing that makeup in these examples functions to signify the complex nature of masculine identity. Here sexuality may or may not play some part. Since makeup most strongly connotes femininity in Western culture, then on any male face and however painterly its application, it will arguably continue to have more transgressive potential than on a woman's. Since Riviere (2003), later writers have also been keen to argue that adopting the masquerade knowingly and vehemently, might be a form of resistance for women, one which 'destabilizes the male gaze' (Craft-Fairchild 1993: 60; see also Doane 1991). As Fereday's (2007) work on burlesque describes, such forms of hyper-feminine embodiment make visible the hard work required of women by hegemonic ideals of femininity, and employs them for political effect. Thus it seems possible that the transgressive potential of makeup on both male and female faces is located in its visibility as a declaration of identity in which some invest that is transgressive because it makes conspicuous in differing ways the possibility that gender is masquerade.

References

Anon. (1973) 'David Bowie's makeup dos and don'ts', *Music Scene*, November 1973.

Anon. (2010a) 'Undercover idol: Adam Lambert ditches the glam rock to go incognito in Miami Beach', *Daily Mail* [online], 17 September, available at www.dailymail.co.uk/tvshowbiz/article-1312979/Adam-Lambert-ditches-glam-incognito-Miami-Beach.html.

Anon. (2010b) Katy Perry: cover, *Seventeen*, September 2010.

Arnold, R. (2001), *Fashion, Desire and Anxiety: image and morality in the twentieth century*, London: I.B. Tauris.

Bakhtin, M. (1984) *Rabelais and his World*, Bloomington, IN: Indiana University Press.

Barthes, R. (1982) *The Empire of Signs*, London: Jonathan Cape.

——— (2000), *Mythologies*, London: Vintage.

Bermingham, A. (1995) 'Elegant females and gentleman connoisseurs: the commerce in culture and self-image in Eighteenth-Century England', in Bermingham, A. and Brewer, J. (eds) *The Consumption of Culture 1600–1800*, London: Routledge.

Bermingham, A. and Brewer, J. (eds) (1995) *The Consumption of Culture 1600–1800*, London: Routledge.

Biddle-Perry, G. and Miller, J. (2009) '. . .and if looks could kill: making up the face of evil', in C. Balmain and L. Drawmer (eds), *Something Wicked This Way Comes: Essays on Evil and Human Wickedness*, New York: Rodopi.

Brooker, W. (2005) *Batman Unmasked: Analysing a Cultural Icon*, New York: Continuum.

Brown, J. A. (2001) *Black Superheroes, Milestone Comics, and their Fans*, Jackson. MS: University Press of Mississippi.

Butler, J. (1999) *Gender Trouble: Feminism and the Subversion of Identity*, London: Routledge.

Cavaye, R. (1993) *Kabuki: A Pocket Guide*, Singapore: Charles E. Tuttle.

Cohan, S. (1996) 'So functional for its purposes: The bachelor apartment in Pillow Talk' in Sanders, J. *Stud: Architectures of Masculinity*, New York: Princeton Architectural Press.

Cohan, S. and Hark, I. R. (eds) (1993) *Screening the Male: Exploring Masculinities in Hollywood Cinema*, Oxford: Routledge.

Constable, C. (2000) 'Making up the truth: on lies, lipstick and Friedrich Nietzsche', in S. Bruzzi and P. Church Gibson (eds), *Fashion Cultures: Theories, Explanations and Analysis*, London: Routledge.

Corson, R. (2003) *Fashions in Makeup: From Ancient to Modern Times*, London: P. Owen, 3rd rev. edn.

Craft-Fairchild, C. (1993) *Masquerade and Gender: Disguise and Female Identity in Eighteenth Century Fictions by Women*, Pennsylvania, PA: Pennsylvania State University Press.

Craik, J. (1994) *The Face of Fashion: Cultural Studies in Fashion*, London: Routledge.

——— (2009) *Fashion: The Key Concepts*, Oxford: Berg.

David Napier, A. (1986) *Masks, Transformation and Paradox*, Berkeley and Los Angeles, CA: University of California Press.

Di Mattia, J. (2007) 'No apologies, no regrets: making the margins heroic on Queer as Folk', in W. Haslem, A. Ndalianis and C. Mackie (eds), *Super/Heroes: from Hercules to Superman*, Washington: New Academic Publishing.

Doane, M. A. (1991) *Femme Fatales: Feminism, Film Theory, Psychoanalysis*, New York: Routledge.

Douglas, M. (2002) *Purity and Danger*, London: Routledge.

Downing, L. (2004) *Patrice Leconte*, Manchester: Manchester University Press.

Edwards, T. (2006) *Cultures of Masculinity*, London: Routledge.

Fereday, D. (2007) 'Adapting femininities: the new burlesque', *M/C: A Journal of Media Culture*, [online] 10 (2), www.journal.media-culture.org.au/0705/12-ferreday.php, accessed 13 December 2012.

Foucault, M. (2003) *The Birth of the Clinic*, London: Routledge.

Hann, M. (2012) 'Adam Lambert interview: I wasn't being controlled', *Guardian*, [online], 4 June, www.guardian.co.uk/music/2012/jun/04/adam-lambert-american-idol-interview, accessed 2 July 2012.

Holmlund, C. (1993) 'Masculinity as multiple masquerade: the 'mature' Stallone and the Stallone clone', in C. Cohan and I. R. Hark (eds) *Screening the Male: Exploring Masculinities in Hollywood Cinema*, Oxford: Routledge.

Karaminas, V (2009) 'Über men: masculinity, costume and meaning in comic book superheroes', in P. McNeil and V. Karaminas (eds), *The Men's Fashion Reader*, Oxford: Berg.

Nead, L. (1992) *The Female Nude: Art, Obscenity and Sexuality*, London: Routledge.

Peiss, K. (1999) *Hope in a Jar: The Making of America's Beauty Culture*, New York: Henry Holt.

Riviere, J. (2011) 'Womanliness as masquerade', in A. Hughes (ed.) *The Inner World and Joan Riviere: Collected Papers, 1929–1958*, London: Karnac.

Rudy, J. (2005) *The Freedom to Smoke: Tobacco, Consumption and Identity*, Quebec: McQueen-Gills University Press.

Schaffer, T. (2000) *The Forgotten Female Aesthetes: Literary Culture in Late-Victorian England*, Virginia, VA: University of Virginia Press.

Sherrow, V. (2001) *For Appearance' Sake: The Historical Encyclopedia of Good Looks, Beauty and Grooming*, Westport, CT: Oryx.

valemigente.com (n.d.) Katy Perry, www.valemigente.com/node/662, accessed 2 February 2012.

Van der Spek, I. (2000) *Alien Plots: Female Subjectivity and the Divine in the Light of James Tiptree's A Momentary Taste of Being*, Liverpool: Liverpool University Press.

Viscount, M. (2010) 'Adam Lambert outraged over "rule" that men can't wear makeup', examiner.com [online], 12 September 2010, www.examiner.com/article/adam-lambert-outraged-over-rule-that-men-can-t-wear-makeup, accessed 3 July 2012.

Woodward, R. and Winter, T. (2007) *Sexing the Soldier: The Politics and Gender of the Contemporary British Army*, Oxford: Routledge.

Chapter 26

Stella Bruzzi

THE ITALIAN JOB
Football, fashion and that sarong

Foreword
By Stella Bruzzi and Pamela Church Gibson

SHORTLY BEFORE THIS VOLUME WENT TO PRESS, Paul Smith provided multi-coloured suits for the Manchester United team. The pictures in that week's *Observer* magazine only served to underline that English footballers are uncomfortable with high fashion. Thirteen years ago, David Beckham was still etched on the public memory as the footballer who dared to wear a skirt. Today, that crown has been usurped by possibly the most flamboyant dresser in international football: Djibril Cissé. His sartorial experimentation seems to have no boundaries, whether referencing Blaxploitation films of the 1970s or donning a Gaultier skirt to receive an award. All footballers experiment with their hair, but none so extravagantly or often as Cissé – the cobweb, the red Mohican, the Dynel extensions, the canary yellow bunches (Church Gibson 2008).

When this essay first appeared, Beckham was not usually associated with high fashion. However, he, like Victoria, has proved us wrong and, as a result, is now an international fashion icon, frequently appearing on the Best-Dressed Man lists. The Italian national team has been inconsistent on the pitch since 2000 – as indeed it has been on the fashion pages. In 2012, Dolce & Gabbana hosted a football viewing during Milan's Men's Fashion Week; on the pages of *The Telegraph* Leonardo Bonucci shows off his six-pack next to Antonio Nocerino in a velvet smoking jacket and big trendy horn-rimmed spectacles. Of course, there is also the *Top Gun* locker room-esque Spring 2010 campaign for D&G: five sweaty players, muscles tautened, standing against a background of grimy tiles clad in tight 'calcio' briefs. The flip side of the Italian story is Antonio Balotelli's vast, knitted, five-fingered hat, both tribal and toddler-like in inspiration.

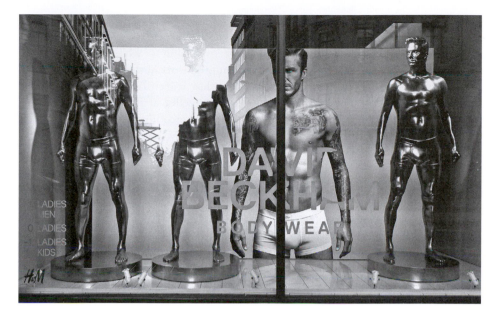

Figure 26.1   Designer and model, David Beckham. Photographer Shaun Cole.

'The Italian Job' makes reference to Barry Venison, now rarely a football pundit, who has in more recent times been replaced by Robbie Savage, whose blond locks (layered or lanky) distract us from serious matters on *Match of the Day* – and the sub-Gabicci shirts so beloved of Alan Hansen, Alan Shearer and Mark Lawrenson. However, one English footballer and his wife have acquired such fashionable gravitas that their names recur frequently throughout the pages of this anthology. We are, of course, referring to David and Victoria Beckham again and thinking of David's comparable H&M underwear ads. But whereas 'The Italian Job' argued for the supremacy of Italian style over English aspiration, the roles seem temporarily to have been reversed, for David Beckham not only modelled the underpants but, it seems, designed them.

Reference

Church Gibson, Pamela (2008) 'Concerning Blondeness: Gender, Ethnicity, Spectacle and Footballer's Waves', in *Hair: Styling Culture and Fashion*, London: Berg, pp. 141–9.

The Italian Job: Football, fashion and that sarong

IN 1990 ITALY HOSTED THEIR FIRST WORLD CUP since 1938, then under the shadow of Mussolini and the Fascist statues around the Stadio Olimpico in Rome. Italia 90 would be different, a chance to cut a fine figure and, more importantly to Italian football fans, win a third World Cup (*Mondiale*), thus going ahead of Brazil. Expectations were high; Italian club teams had just won all the European trophies, they had in Roberto Baggio – whose recent sale by Fiorentina to Juventus for $20 million had prompted riots in the streets of Florence – the new Paolo Rossi, their hero of 1982, and they were playing at home. Things started well – to a superstitious Italian maybe too well – as Italy, thanks ironically to their new Sicilian striker Toto Schillaci, arrived unproblematically at a 1–0 lead in their semi-final against an inferior Argentina. Then Argentina scored and the home team choked, losing eventually 4–3 on penalties, ensuring Germany an improbable number of *tifosi* (fans) for the Final. Like the Victorian gentleman who shouted out to Othello before the end of Shakespeare's tragedy that Iago was not to be trusted, this disaster wasn't part of the script. Italy weren't supposed to end their World Cup campaign slugging it out in a lacklustre, also-rans, third-place play-off in Bari (albeit in a sumptuous, new Renzo Piano-designed San Nicola stadium) against an England team bereft of Gazza, tears and flair; they were destined for the reinvigorated Stadio Olimpico. It was not for this that Italy had designed, redesigned and renovated twelve stadiums, held a national poll to decide the official mascot's name ('Ciao' beating off the challenge of 'Dribbly' and 'Bimbo') and commissioned its filmmakers to direct short films about their home towns and cities. As the despairing headline in *La Gazzetta dello Sport* declared the day after the calamitous defeat in the semis: 'Italia Noooo'.

Despite the resulting anticlimax for the host nation and the choice of Giorgio Moroder's 'Un Estate Italiana' as the championship's accompanying pop song, Italia 90 was a turning point for how football was perceived, particularly in the UK where, in its wake, it became synonymous with style, desire, melodrama and spectacle. 'Football' had a new aura; the Pavlovian response to the word was no longer to think of bobble hats and beery, leery men in smelly sheepskin and scarves swaying on the terraces like tinless sardines between other 'white males of little education and even less wit' (Ian Taylor in Williams 1995: 243) on wet, wasted afternoons. Although the pre-Hillsborough and Heysel image of the fan is as much a cliché as the new man with muscles and Italian-cut suits who has replaced him, the shift is monumental and irreversible. Significantly, it wasn't all footballers whose images altered and the newfound football chic was firmly rooted in Italianness – or rather the British reconfiguration of Italianness. There is a marked difference in British attitudes to, for instance, David Ginola's 'Eurotrash' look of jacket, T-shirt, jeans, loafers and no socks than to Gianluca Vialli, player and ex-manager of Chelsea. Ginola is coded as sexy but available: he advertises hair products, he appears with monotonous regularity in the pages of *Hello!* The Premiership reincarnation of Vialli, though, is another matter. On the eve of Chelsea's FA Cup Final against Aston Villa in May 2000, the *Guardian*'s Jim White remarks upon the club's final press day. Unexpectedly for a sports pages feature, perhaps, White begins by dwelling upon the 'Giorgio Armani' press pack that was handed out, in which the squad were pictured donning natty 'three-button, single-breasted suits in charcoal-grey wool worn, according to the blurb, "with light grey tone on tone shirt and tie combination"' (White 2000: 1). White here seems proud of his ability to describe, with admirable accuracy, the Armani garb, while simultaneously sneaking in that the journalists themselves were dressed 'in the standard fashion-free manner'. He reserves his greatest admiration, however, for the manager, commenting 'no one wears the ensemble as well as Gianluca Vialli'. This is a curious thing – prior to Vialli's departure from Juventus to Chelsea as a player under his managerial predecessor, Ruud Gullit, Vialli was a favourite target of the Italian sports press, not for his style but his lack of it. As Vialli started to thin on top, so he began tinkering with his mane and his facial hair: from wild curls to crew cut, from clean-shaven chin to designer stubble goatee (ostensibly illustrating the old truism that if you want to change something about your appearance that you'd rather went unnoticed, divert attention to some other feature at the same time). In England, Vialli's very Italianness ensures his fashion status.

Vialli took over at Chelsea from another Serie A export, Dutchman Ruud Gullit. Gullit's arrival at Stamford Bridge under Glenn Hoddle was another key post-Italia 90 moment of transition, although he was nearing the end of his career and had got a bit stocky, slow and ungainly on the pitch. Gullit, however, descended in his Milanese suits (and his own clothes line) and transformed the image of the team of Dennis Wise, London's Gazza. Several factors united to make Gullit such a key icon: his legendary status as a player, particularly at AC Milan; his sartorial panache; his intelligence both as a player and a TV pundit. The English reverence of Gullit (I distinctly recall several minutes of *Match of the Day* being given over to a discussion of the correct pronunciation of his name, as if Alan Hansen *et al.* just liked saying it) was relatively short-lived as he left Chelsea under a cloud and had little managerial success subsequently with Newcastle United. Alongside his 'culturedness', the other significant facet of Gullit's appeal was that he was black, and like English football has sought a patina of Italian finesse, so it has often been a place for acknowledging black stylishness. Storm, the London model agency, started signing up footballers in 1995 and those on its books by 1998 included Ruud Gullit, Les Ferdinand and Ian Wright. The common factor, of course, is that all three are black, more effortlessly cool and inherently stylish than their pasty-skinned colleagues. Another high-profile footballer-cum-model is David James, the Liverpool then Aston Villa goalie who has done Armani catwalk shows and, in 1996, appeared on a 50ft-high poster wearing only Armani underpants. Chelsea's transformation from a parochial, technically crude squad pre-Hoddle to one that starts the 2000 FA Cup Final with only one native player is Gullit's lasting legacy. As if to render himself more stylish, Chelsea's only Englishman, Dennis Wise, went up to receive the cup clutching the new century's latest male fashion accessory – his baby.

It was thus more than Gazza's iconic tears of Italia 90 that have cemented the notion of fashionable football in the UK. At the time of the championships, the choice of Pavarotti's rendition of Puccini's 'Nessun Dorma' as the BBC's official Italia 90 anthem was extremely influential in reconstructing football spectatorship as a couch activity worthy of the chattering classes. Although Pavarotti was the masses' opera star, and, alongside Placido Domingo and José Carreras, has become a fixture of British World Cup coverage since, 'Nessun Dorma' was a far cry from Chelsea in 1971 grunting 'Blue is the Colour' or Glenn Hoddle and Chris Waddle appearing on *Top of the Pops* sporting spangly 1980s jackets, feathercuts and quiffs. During the BBC's 1990 coverage there was also the unusual side-tracking commentary by its pundits on the gorgeousness of the Italian stadiums, asides that inevitably contextualised football within society and culture at large. Italy and football were perhaps the significant if unconscious catalysts for the attitude change elsewhere; perhaps it was evident simply from how even designer-clad, middle-class Italians treated football as a significant part of their cultural lives that the sport could be sexy. Certainly in the aftermath of Italia 90 in Britain more women started to watch and be interested in football, Channel 4 began broadcasting live Serie A action and the accompanying *Gazzetta Football Italia* and footballers became fashion icons. To become fashionable, British football has had to become less parochial and less male, for this was the rite of passage that enabled footballers in general to become objects of pulchritude and aspiration.

There are other less frivolous factors that may have contributed to the need to find the chic in football, the most socially significant being the immediate call for all-seated stadiums after ninety-six fans – the majority from Liverpool – died at Hillsborough, Sheffield on 15 April 1989. The need for such measures had already been signalled by the violence that erupted between Liverpool and Juventus fans at the 1985 European Cup Final at Heysel Stadium where thirty-nine, mainly Italian, fans died. These ugly scenes (which led to English clubs being banned from Europe for five years) have been interpreted as the result of English fans' xenophobia, which is ironic considering their subsequent obsession with the European game. Lord Justice Taylor's official inquiry after Hillsborough stipulated that all stadiums in England, Scotland and Wales would need to become all-seated by the start of the 1994–5 season. The drop in attendances that this entailed meant in turn that ticket prices had to rise (Manchester United's average receipts per spectator, for example, rose by almost 223 percent between 1988–9 and 1992–3) and 'raised the spectre, for some, of the sport increasingly becoming distanced, socially and spatially, from its "traditional" audience and being played in soul-less "production-line" concrete bowls in front of passive and affluent consumers (not supporters)' (Williams 1995: 225).[1] This, ironically, is more akin to the dominant European model for viewing football already in place by 1989–90, and it is significant that many commentators on the continental game cite as an important difference between the game in England (or Germany) and France or Italy the fact that in the latter countries it has traditionally been a cross-class activity, for spectators and players alike (Mignon 1999: 82; Lanfranchi 1994: 152–3). The changing image of football chic in the UK coincided, therefore, with the general poshening of the national game. An accurate gauge of this is the changing responses to Graham Le Saux's *Guardian*-reading middle-classness: whereas now he is deemed to fit in, earlier in his career he was ridiculed for being a boffin.

What then happened in the UK during and immediately after Italia 90 that was so radical? First, there was 'Gazza', the contradictory, loaded icon of 1990s English football: a Geordie genius whose famous tears at being issued with another yellow card in England's semi against Germany (that would mean, if England got there, that he wouldn't play in the Final) made him into a national institution, epitomising the British fixation upon the 'if only' brand of glorious sporting failure. Gazza's image, though, was a complex one; he was likewise renowned for his stupidity, bigotry and bad behaviour, and it was Gazza who declared to Terry Wogan 'I'm norra poof, like', who beat up his wife and got legless on the eve of Glenn Hoddle's selection of England's France 1998 squad. Gazza never lost his

Englishness but it was also he who transferred to Lazio in the aftermath of Italia 90 and who, much more than David Platt who went to Serie A at the same time, exemplified the continuation of the British love affair with *calcio*.

Symptomatic of the essential ambiguity of Gazza's image, the dream combination of Gazza and Italy never took off: at Lazio he was plagued by injury and bad press, he never made efforts to learn Italian and he was swiftly marginalised from his 'news round-up' slot on *Gazzetta Football Italia*. Gazza was as much a symbol of the old image of football as the new; like Maradona and Schillaci, two of the other stars of Italia 90, he was the epitome of the working-class boy made good. There were also parallels to be drawn between Gazza and George Best (with his line of boutiques in the 1970s, one of the few footballers of the pre-1990s era to cash in on the football/fashion intersection): both were resonant icons for their respective generations, both squandered their talents by boozing, womanising and generally going off the rails. Herein lies the first of many contradictions pertaining to the renaissance of football in the 1990s: that the stylish, fashionable and image-obsessed game is in part a re-fashioning or reclamation of the old drab one. When *Hello!* magazine featured Gazza's wedding to Sheryl in July 1996 (white morning suits and stretch limos), it did so because there was a voracious audience for its kitsch appeal, not because Gazza had suddenly been immortalised into the incarnation of good taste. It was Gazza, the cheeky chappy who farted and belched at the Italian press, who was canonised by the intelligentsia in the UK, and to whom Ian Hamilton dedicated over half an edition of *Granta* in 1993 ('Gazza Agonistes').

As with Gazza's image, the whole issue of football's relationship to style is fraught with anomalies. First, in the fashion pages of men's 1990s style magazines it is often the old image of football that is evoked, obviously out of nostalgia for 1966 and all that but also out of an understanding that 'football chic' will remain a complex and equivocal term to do, for instance, with the inherently ambivalent ways in which designer leisurewear labels have been reappropriated and universalised. The rise of leisurewear as chic is very different from the smartening up of football by an association with more formal designer wear. As Robert Elms writes in *Arena*, the 'genesis of the footballer as style god' is the sartorially challenged footballer of the 1970s with his collar-length hair and floral shirts, but the 'real style icons' of the mid-1990s football fashion scene are 'the lads on the terraces'; these rather than the Ginolas or the Jameses on the catwalks are what football chic is about (Elms 1996: 142–4). However much Armani Gazza has worn – and for a 1991 cover article for *GQ* he reputedly wanted a £5,000 fee plus £3,000-worth of Armani clothes – there's still something of the shellsuit brigade about him.[2] This is still where British football chic and its Italian equivalent diverge. In the run-up to USA 94, British *Esquire* ran a fashion article in which several Italian players modelled exclusive ready-to-wear Italian designs by Gucci, Cerruti, Zegna, Armani, Dolce & Gabbana, Valentino and Versace. It's not that all the players selected (who include the hardly stunning – though brilliant – AC Milan defender and national captain, Franco Baresi) are beautiful, nor that they are all super-successful. Indeed, one of the intriguing features of the article, which in June 1994 was prepared reasonably close to team selection time, was that it chose as its models several players – such as Roberto Mancini and Marco Simone – whom few Italians would have tipped to feature in the World Cup squad. The significant 'it' factor seems to be that the footballers are Italian. It's hard to imagine a comparable Italian style monthly running a feature in which David Beckham, Nicky Butt and David Seaman model Paul Smith, Katharine Hamnett and Nicole Farhi.

In Italy there is a clear history of football being seamlessly integrated into the nation's style and culture, and this became one of the lasting legacies of Italia 90 in Britain. Again in June 1994, as their prelude to that year's World Cup, *GQ* studies the form of the countries involved (which didn't include England) in terms of what it calls 'elements of style'. For many of these countries their 'element of style' is related to their footballing chances, so the Cameroon are labelled 'uncontrollable' and the Irish 'optimistic' (although it was Ireland who beat the fancied Italy in their group's opening match). When it comes to the Italians, under 'Style' *GQ* identifies 'Michelangelo, Da Vinci, Verdi, the lot', under 'Strength' it singles out 'gorgeousness' and under 'Weakness' it mentions 'insane media'. Obviously, very little of this has to do with football and much of it has to do with style. This automatic assimilation of leisure and social activities such as football into what's generally held to be attractive about Italy (its art, architecture, people, food, cars) is a recurrent theme in *GQ*. In October 1994, the magazine ran a piece 'Gran Turismo' on Italian cars and clothes featuring the juxtaposition, sensually photographed, of details of the fabric and cut of loose Italian tailoring with close-ups of Alfa Romeo dashboards: the cars are vintage; the clothes soon will be. Then, in December 1998, *GQ* ran a short article again in praise of Italian design in which it yokes together by a sometimes unseemly violence, such eclectic manifestations of this as Leonardo, the Lira notes, the Alfa Romeo badge, the Fiat 500, the Beretta, the Romans, the Cosa Nostra and the Juventus kit. This arbitrary list, which ranks Sicilian organised crime alongside a Renaissance artist, crudely illustrates the point that Italy is innately fashionable and that we in England want to emulate it. Intriguingly, of the Juventus kit *GQ* says it is as 'Subbuteo as shirts come, which would seem appropriate given that their inspiration came from a visit by Notts County' (*GQ* December 1998: 262). Although the same 'inspiration' on the similarly clad Newcastle United would, perhaps, have been treated ironically, the contradiction of retro English league non-fashion having influenced Agnelli's slick winning machine is what creates the strip's aura of chic. It is hard to imagine that same British men's style magazine praising the very similar Newcastle monochrome strip, which makes the reverence towards Italian style seem totally uncritical.

In 1982 Mick Jagger, while performing with The Rolling Stones at the Stadio Comunale in Torino after Italy's World Cup victory that summer, donned a Paolo Rossi Number 20 shirt. There is a sense of Italian football having always been cool and evoking effortlessly a whole aura and lifestyle – despite many a naff haircut (Roberto 'the divine ponytail' Baggio's of USA 94 being the most obscene) or the potentially emasculating shots of an entire team in baby blue vests during the shirt-swapping ritual with Brazil after the 1978 third-place play-off. A distinction can be made between the 'full' and the 'empty' footballer as fashion icon image. Whereas a picture of David Beckham in Gucci, for example, is 'empty' because it is just a picture of David Beckham in Gucci, a picture of Gianni Rivera at the height of his fame and powers in the late 1960s/early 1970s, nonchalantly propped up against a bookcase perusing a hefty tome in slim-line black suit and patent Gucci brogues, is 'full' because it evokes not just Rivera and football but an aspirational lifestyle. Beckham's clothes too often wear him, he doesn't look natural in his designer casuals, his 'intellectual' spectacles or indeed posing shirtless on the golf course; he's always self-conscious, always performing and demanding to be looked at. That Italian golden boy Rivera is reading and ignoring us is significant, and the way in which we are invited to view that image (used, for instance, in an *Homme Plus* feature on the fifty most stylish sportsmen of the twentieth century [*Homme Plus* 1996: 89–99]) is as evocative of an unmeasurable cool, a certain lifestyle. The Rivera image is symptomatic of Britain having also caught the Italian need to take football itself so seriously. *Calcio*, one writer suggests, is automatically placed alongside Fellini, Ferrari and wine as something quintessentially Italian, but it is given disproportionate sobriety by, for example, programmes such as RAI 3's weekly post-mortem football analysis programme *Processo del Lunedì* ('Trial on Monday') in which experts adopt absurdly 'lofty tones and flowery language' in their discussion of the matches held the day before (Lanfranchi 1994: 155). The treatment in Britain of football by mainstream culture (as opposed to legitimately interested sports academics) is too frequently ironic or knowing, Nick Hornby being a notably sincere exception. So men's magazines, alongside articles genuinely praising the pervasiveness of Italian style, run features on awful 1970s football haircuts (Kevin Keegan 'the Permed Prince of the Park' [Webb 1998]) and the gaudiness of goalkeepers' strips (see *GQ* June 1994). It is this equivocal response to the pairing of football and style that informs the distressed, trendified Parka image of Fat Les, the trio of Damien Hirst, Keith Allen and Alex James, who had a 1998 World Cup hit with 'Vindaloo' and brought out a version of 'Jerusalem' for Euro 2000.

The emergence of football chic in Britain, therefore, has continued to be double-edged. Sartorially speaking, even the more recent history of English football's relationship with fashion is characterised by disasters rather than successes. There was, for instance, the scorn poured on the Liverpool team's emergence for the FA Cup Final of 1996 wearing (ironically) pale beige Giorgio Armani suits. One journalist likened the team to ice-cream salesmen (Greenberg 1998) while a fan commented, 'I held my face in my hands in shame. From the moment they stepped out in those suits, I knew we were going to lose' (Blanchard 1998). Then there was the scrutiny of Glenn Hoddle's managerial decision to put the England squad for France 98 in darker beige (or taupe) suits designed by Paul Smith. Smith had suggested navy for the suits but Hoddle wanted something more 'summery'. Not often has what the England squad elected to wear off the pitch been front-page news, but in this instance the matter was treated with earnest interest, one journalist making the preparation for the big day when the suits would finally be unveiled sound like an important nuptial:

> Final fittings will take place shortly. Because of their training programme, players change shape in a matter of weeks and can only be certain of their final sizes just before the tournament starts.
>
> (Kennedy 1998)

Here the England squad are described in more feminine terms than normal; more common were references to Paul Ince's thighs bursting out of the flimsy linen-viscose mix trousers or comments such as, 'If the players had their way, they'd arrive [in France] looking like the bad guys in a Tarantino heist movie' (Greenberg 1998). Just as Glenn Hoddle was nicknamed 'Glenda' during his days at Tottenham Hotspur for his silky skills and dainty, leggy appearance, so the unmentionable implication of 'those suits' was that the England team's collective machismo and potential coolness were under threat. In October 1999, David Beckham was stung with a £50,000 fine (later revoked) by the Manchester United coach Alex Ferguson for breaking the club curfew before a Champions League game and turning up at a London Fashion Week show. Although Beckham assured Sir Alex that he and his wife Victoria Adams were in bed by midnight, a taste for fashion has become, like sex before crucial encounters, a factor that can detract from a player's footballing skills. As *The Mirror* put it, 'pictures of him [Beckham] wearing a trendy headscarf put him and United on the spot' (Nixon and Harris 1999).

Apparently most of the squad of France 98 had favoured blue, the colour of the suits Paul Smith had designed for England's Euro 96 team, and although the players were given both the beige and the blue versions of the 1998 suit, this wasn't sufficient – except for the ever-diplomatic and dull Alan Shearer, who thought the beige looked fine against his lads' tanned skin. Although many a critical journalist who attended the taupe extravaganza recalled the Armani/Liverpool embarrassment, none of them seemed to remember Glenn Hoddle's last notable fashion decision as a manager – to put his Chelsea squad for their doomed 1994 FA Cup Final against Manchester United in pale purple because it was, as Hoddle commented at the time, a little bit 'different'. Indeed Paul Smith, who two years previously had simply been given the go-ahead by then England manager Terry Venables, was surprised at Hoddle's interference, remarking, 'I don't think he's well known for his dress sense' (Lee 1998). Several points of emphasis emerge from the coverage in June 1998 of the unveiling of the England's off-pitch uniforms: that beige reflected Glenn Hoddle's taste (after all, Hoddle on the touchline was often to be seen in tracksuit bottoms hitched up just a tad high, which made him look like a relaxed version of Reeves and Mortimer's King's Singers); that the suits did not reflect the players' keener fashion sense and masculinity; that this choice suggested the team would fail. Journalists vied with each other to heap the most withering insults on the beige creations: they were not as sharp as the 1966 World Cup winners in 'slim, dark razor-cut' suits – although better than the off-the-peg Burton's numbers of 1970 or the sporty blazers of 1990 (Mouland 1998); they looked like a 'convention of double-glazing salesmen' or a 'pack of Scout leaders at the annual jamboree' (Spencer 1998); they weren't a patch on the French team dressed by Daniel Hechter or the FIFA officials in their Yves Saint Laurent. Even the dubious 'Gallic flair' of the 'former French internationals Eric Cantona and David Ginola' (Webb 1998) was dragged in for comparison. The realm of football and fashion overflows with such exquisite ironies: for Euro 2000 England reverted to suits by Burtons Tailoring, so that they were seen to be wearing clothes that the average fan could afford to emulate.

Paul Smith himself was never blamed for the France 98 sartorial faux pas, perhaps because he was Britain's favourite designer and because football coverage is, above all, patriotic (some journalists and fans, for instance, had taken umbrage at both Arsenal and Newcastle walking on to the Wembley turf the day before their FA Cup Final clash just a month before wearing unpatriotic Hugo Boss suits rather than designs by 'local' designer Katharine Hamnett [Blanchard 1998]).

As proof of Smith's worth, it's significant that several of the June 1998 articles estimated the cost and exclusivity of the beige ensemble (£600 suits, £95 dark blue shirts, £55 pound cufflinks, a £50 tie and blue suede shoes from Cheaney of Northamptonshire) as if to deflect criticism. The England team could – for once – have been stylish, but 'Glenda' had thwarted their ambitions. The real problem with the men in beige was that they raised the ugly spectre of the pre-Italia 90 football fashion dark ages, a stigma that the English game has never quite been able to shake off. For while the England 98 squad would dearly have liked to resemble their Italian and French counterparts, the images most often evoked throughout the discussions of the beige suits were fellow disasters: John Barnes's shiny suits and unconventional tailoring, Barry Venison's debut as a TV pundit in a silver waistcoat and sporting a 'mop of straggly bleached hair' (Webb 1998) – since dispensed with and replaced with a sombre crop and yet another pair of unshowy 'intellectual' glasses – and Gazza's hair extensions. These were painful reminders of old football and the ridiculously tight shorts of the 1980s, summoning up from the murky depths of fan memory those images of Keegan missing a sitter against Spain in the 1982 World Cup. The *Sun* had asked of David Beckham after the Manchester United midfielder had been spotted in the South of France wearing a sarong, 'Is he trendy, or a twit?' Those suits precipitated a crisis precisely because the English press didn't know what was good fashion and what was Venison fashion and they needed to be told. The maligned Barry Venison himself self-effacingly admitted to being in the dark about this; when questioned about why he'd chosen to look so awful for his television debut, he admitted 'I was not trying to look silly on purpose, it was purely down to my bad taste' (Webb 1998).

Two approaches to the fashion and football intersection have dominated British responses: that footballers are the new Hollywood stars – free, over-exposed and influential clothes horses – and that English football is still 'a style disaster waiting to happen' (Webb 1998). As always, it's a fine line between clever and stupid. Fashion, as the Ferguson–Beckham conflict illustrated, is perceived as a threat to football as well as the salvation of its image, despite the suggestion that the feminisation of the male is an essential component of the macho footballer image: Gazza crying, David Beckham wearing a sarong or the Italian Euro 2000 defence keeping their fringes out of their eyes with dainty hair bands. Real men accessorise. However, as Ginola modelled for Cerruti and David James for Armani, or as Marilyn Gauthier Models (MGM; the leading model agency in France), sent scouts to France 98 with the specific brief to get fresh footballing talent on their books, a definite sense emerges of the image being more important than the game. MGM signings include Thierry Henri, Patrick Viera, Emanuel Petit, Ibrahim Ba and Zvonimir Boban, but as a spokesperson for the agency comments, 'Footballers are sexy when they're doing well on the field because they exude confidence and the camera picks that up' (Grey and Lang 1998). No matter how much fashion has radically altered football's public face, or how differently a wider audience has perceived it since Italia 90, the relationship with the players' real performances on the pitch is still paramount – the bad kits, tight shorts and vests won't go away.

The most prevalent English example of fashion dominating the image of football and concomitantly of it being hard to erase the negative connotations of football and football chic is David Beckham. He is the archetypal football-fashion icon: successful on the pitch, with a famous and even wealthier wife – Victoria Adams (aka Posh Spice) – a penchant for shopping and bland, malleable good looks. There is, however, the ominous suspicion that, just as his wife is more Essex than posh, Beckham might be more John Barnes than Paolo Maldini: mutton dressed up as lamb. Gianni Rivera later became an MP (for the Christian Democrats); this is probably a fate not awaiting David Beckham, despite the recent lowering, it seems, of his falsetto voice. So, is he trendy or a twit? The Beckham's wedding on 4 July 1999 at Luttrellstown Castle, near Dublin, would imply the latter (although the ostentatious glamour of the event was not without its fans). Posh went down the aisle in a champagne-coloured Vera Wang satin gown (made of Clerici Duchess satin, 'the finest Italian satin in the world', as *OK!*'s 'David and Victoria: their complete story' Special breathlessly informs us). David wore a complementary three-piece designed by English designer Timothy Everest and shoes by Manolo Blahnik. For the Robin Hood theme reception, the couple changed into matching head to toe purple Antonio Berardi outfits: he wore a double-breasted jacket with quite wide leg trousers over a splayed (shades of George Best) collar shirt, while she wore a slim-line, strapless gown of stretch satin with a thigh-high slit that revealed a red lining (to match the swathe of red and purple roses tumbling off her right shoulder) and silver Blahnik strappy sandals. Their uncomprehending baby Brooklyn had matching baby get-ups (two copies of each – in case he was sick down the first); particularly memorable is the purple sheriff's hat he was forced to wear for the reception. Victoria Adams maintained that many of the touches were 'tongue in cheek' (*OK!* 1999: 24), but she omitted to mention walking to the reception marquee to the theme tune from Disney's *Beauty and the Beast* or intertwining 'VD' on their specially designed coat of arms.

The entire voracious relationship between the press and the Beckhams exemplifies the current state of the relationship between football and fashion that seems to dictate that we forget the Italian, tasteful aspirations and accept football chic's ambiguity and innate tackiness. Apart from feeding us a limitless supply of photos of Posh, Becks and Brooklyn, the contract with *OK!* is characterised by twin revelations: the extent of the couple's designer shopping and how much their respective outfits cost. In the 31 March 2000 edition, under the headline 'David and Victoria's style sensation', the family step out to reveal their radical new haircuts: Beckham and Brooklyn's crew cuts and Victoria's blonde spikey look. In a typically insipid accompanying article, Victoria reveals that she doesn't expect her husband's £300 shave to jeopardise his contract with Brylcreem (*OK!* 2000: 10) and hairdresser Nicky Clarke is quoted as stating the very obvious – that Beckham's style 'looks like a number one or a number two' (*OK!* 2000: 9). Posh and Becks have made themselves into consumable fashion icons; what's really on sale in this *OK!* feature is thus a composite image and its concomitant price tags: his Timberlands cost £130, his Hilfiger jacket £100, his Diesel jeans £80, her Gucci leather jacket over £1,800 and her Maharishi orange trousers (or are they Gap

Kids as one caption says?) £100. Itemising and costing their clothes in this way is symptomatically tacky; as Chanel once remarked, good fashion doesn't draw attention to itself, if clothes are truly well designed what they do is subtly and unobtrusively compliment their wearer. The delicious perversity of Chanel has always been that its real signs of class (the braid concealing the join between lining and outer fabric) often remain concealed. This clearly couldn't be further from the point in the case of the Posh 'n' Becks phenomenon; their designer labels give them an identity rather than vice versa. They are contemporary signifiers of power and success, not of taste. Their combined image is an ambivalent one; on the one hand, we know that Beckham and Adams have courted *OK!* and the kind of paparazzi fame it offers, on the other they're rather sweetly gooey, particularly about each other and Brooklyn. One would like to simply hate them for their scowling, posturing expressions when caught on camera, their affluence and their exhibitionism. There is, though, something endearing – if, again, terribly current – about Beckham's tattooed homages to Brooklyn: the boy's name across his lower back, the guardian angel across his shoulder blades watching over him and the promise that 'Et Animus Liber' (Free Spirit) is to follow. As with so many football and fashion fusions, however, there is the hint of a design hiccup here: having told the *Sun* (10 May 2000) and *Esquire* (June 2000) that he intends to have the names of any other offspring likewise tattooed under the angel (presumably between 'Brooklyn' and it) where is 'Et Animus Liber' going to go unless it consciously spoils the symmetry of the design? The Latin could, writ small, go above the angel, but this might look messy peeking out from underneath Beckham's football shirt.

The Beckhams, for all their appropriation of Gucci, are the style descendants not of the Italian aristocracy but of the floral shirts and fast cars of Rodney Marsh and the gold-laden 'Big' Ron Atkinson. The marriage of Gucci in particular and football has a certain resonance. In an interview since his retirement in March 1999, Vinnie Jones the ex-Wimbledon player mentions that he used to have his clothes made for him at Mr Ed in Berwick Street, London (one of the notable 'flash Harry' Soho tailors), and that the Gucci-Versace style of young football celebrities leaves him cold as he's not a label but an 'if I see something I like I buy it' person (Alexander 1999). He since became the 'unofficial ambassador' for Yves Saint Laurent in the UK ('I just go in and tell them what I want and they make it'). Vinnie Jones has classically been pigeon-holed the hard man of British football, an image immortalised by the snap of him squeezing Gazza's scrotum during a match and refined through many adverts and his acting debut in *Lock, Stock and Two Smoking Barrels*. His conscious distancing of himself from Gucci is especially significant because Gucci in particular epitomised the anomalous affiliation of a certain type of Italianate stylish dress and violence – British football hooligans in pristine Sergio Tacchini, Louis Vuitton and Gucci.

This is all a far cry from the veneration of Rivera, Verdi and Valentino Couture. What has happened as we start the new millennium is that football's fashion-conscious image has once again either dumbed down or got confused. With speculation about a forthcoming David Beckham module at the University of Staffordshire or the domination of the British Premiership by foreign players (in 2000 they numbered approximately 200), the identity of British football chic – whether it's related to the gentrification of the game through an association with

Serie A and the rest of Europe or to the continued supremacy of home-grown football wide-boy fashions – is ambiguous. But then, with Vinnie Jones as YSL's unofficial ambassador and jockey Frankie Dettori as its official one, perhaps the relationship between football and fashion in this country was doomed never to be taken too seriously.

Acknowledgements

I would like to thank Mick Conefrey, Stephen Gundle, Barry Langford and Zara Bruzzi for their assistance in the researching of this chapter.

Notes

1   The Italian model would refute British Premiership claims that lower attendance figures coupled with soaring player salaries has forced ticket prices up: you can still get into a Serie A game for £10.
2   Ironically, Jim White maintains that Armani himself in the Chelsea FA Cup Final press pack 'appears to be wearing a shellsuit' (White 2000: 1).
3   Hamnett, at the time this comment was made, lived in Highbury.

References

Alexander, Hilary (1999) 'Fashion: Mr Jones strikes again', *Daily Telegraph*, 10 May.
Blanchard, Tamsin (1998) 'The fashion victims of football', *Independent*, 16 May.
Davies, Pete (1990) *All Played Out: The Full Story of Italia 90*, London: Heinemann.
Elms, Robert (1996) 'Saturday best', *Arena*, June: 142–4.
Fulton, Tamara (1996) '*Arena*'s essential guide to style and fashion', *Arena*, June.
Greenberg, Simon (1998) 'Three lions, the pitch and the wardrobe', *Evening Standard*, 8 June.
Grey, Toby and Lang, Kirsty (1998) 'Model footballers kick into fashion', *The Sunday Times*, 31 May.
Hamilton, Ian (1993) 'Gazza agonistes', *Granta*, 45, Autumn.
Homme Plus (1996) '50 most stylish sportsmen of this century', *Homme Plus*, Spring/ Summer: 89–99.
Kennedy, Dominic (1998) 'Team in red, white and blue wears Paul Smith', *The Times*, 15 May.
Lanfranchi, P. (1992) (ed.) *Il Calcio e il Suo Popolo*, Naples, Rome and Milan: Edizioni Scientifiche Italiane.
—— (1994) 'Italy and the World Cup: the impact of football in Italy and the example of Italia 90', in John Sugden and Alan Tomlinson (eds) *Hosts and Champions: Soccer Cultures, National Identities and the USA World Cup*, Aldershot: Arena.
Lee, Adrian (1998) 'Players get the blues over Hoddle's beige', *The Times*, 9 June.
Mignon, Patrick (1999) 'Fans and heroes', in Hugh Dauncey and Geoff Hare (eds) *France and the 1998 World Cup: The National Impact of a World Sporting Event*, London and Portland, OR: Frank Cass.

Mouland, Bill (1998) 'The men in beige', *Daily Mail*, 9 June.

Nixon, Alan and Harris, Harry (1999) 'Football: fashion victim', *Daily Mirror*, 1 October.

OK! (1999) 'David and Victoria: their complete story', *OK!: The Premium Millennium Edition*.

—— (2000) 'David and Victoria Beckham', *OK!*, 21 March, 206: 4–11.

Pennaccia, Mario (2000) *Il Calcio in Italia*, Torino: UTET, 2 vols.

Redhead, Steve (1991) *Football with Attitude*, Manchester: Wordsmith.

—— (ed.) (1993) *The Passion and the Fashion: Football Fandom in New Europe*, Aldershot: Avebury.

—— (1997) *Subculture to Clubcultures: An Introduction to Popular Cultural Studies*, Oxford: Blackwell.

Spencer, Mimi (1998) 'How can England score in beige?', *Evening Standard*, 8 June.

Walker, Howard (1999) 'In boots and boutiques George was always the best', *The Journal*, 3 August.

Ward, William (1990) 'Letter from Rome', *The Face*, May: 50–51.

Webb, Ben (1998) 'You'll never score in that kit, boys', *The Times*, 6 June.

White, Jim (2000) 'FA Cup Final', *Guardian*, 20 May, Sport Section: 1–2.

Williams, John (1995) 'English football stadiums after Hillsborough', in John Bale and Olof Moen (eds) *The Stadium and the City*, Stoke-on-Trent: Keele University Press.

Williams, John and Wagg, Stephen (eds) (1991) *British Football and Social Change: Getting Into Europe*, Leicester: Leicester University Press.

Chapter 27

Vicki Karaminas

VAMPIRE DANDIES
Fashionable masculine identities and style in popular culture

Introduction

MEN'S FASHION PHOTOGRAPHY and allied industries such as clothing production and consumption, retail branding and advertising, participate and construct an all-viewing subject; a subject that 'desires to be desired' by both men and women. These eroticised images, often found in magazines that target women and male consumers, present their male models as sexually appealing subjects and invite viewers to consume the 'products' by either (over) identifying with the image as in the case of a heterosexual male gaze, or as an object of desire for appreciation and consumption by a spectatorial heterosexual female and/or homosexual male spectator. These representations of men, often in sexually provocative poses, produce a space that encourages women, and men, to *desire* and *consume* the male image. This space allows heterosexual men to indulge and participate in homosocial/homoerotic behaviour in culturally acceptable ways. At the same time, these images reveal something about the way that representations of masculinities are being constructed and circulated.

Since the emergence of the 'new man' and the rise of style magazines for men, such as *GQ* and *Arena* in the 1980s, the study of men's fashion and male buying power has taken a new turn as cultural conceptions of masculinity continue to shift. Sean Nixon (1996) points to key areas for the 'circulation' of the 'new man': television and press advertising, menswear retail shops and the magazine press. Male subjectivity is now constructed through advertising and marketing discourses, which combined with the consumption of imagery, fashion and cosmetic products, produce a range of idealised and eroticised masculine identities.

Wider social movements of the 1970s such as feminism, movements for sexual liberation and a range of identity-based political movements, such as gay and civil rights, have also influenced images of contemporary masculinity. These social movements have disrupted traditionally held views of race, sexuality, class and identity and have promoted a model of democratic gender equality. The outcomes of these movements challenged hegemonic models of masculinity, articulated as a 'crisis in masculinity' (see Mort 1986; Chapman and Rutherford 1988; Simpson 1994 and Edwards 1997) and created new ways of conceptualising and articulating masculine identity. Since the emergence of the 'new man', a proliferation of masculinities has challenged conventional categories of male subjectivity, including the 'emotionally sensitive new lad' of the 1990s and the narcissistic twenty-first century gender-bending metrosexual who is in constant flux with his 'feminine side'.

As members of the 'cult of the self', the metrosexual has much in common with the Victorian dandy. While dandyism existed in the realm of the 'elite' and 'aristocratic' and metrosexuality is a 'mainstream, mass-consumer phenomenon' (Simpson 2004), both subjectivities embody the 'spirit of the times', namely decadence, excess, artifice, beauty and aestheticism and both, most importantly, problematise and blur the gender binaries of homo/hetero and masculine/feminine opting for a more hybrid or queer identity.

The recent resurgence of the vampire narrative in popular culture, from cinema to the fashion catwalk and male fashion photography, signals a fundamental shift that is occurring in the deployment of concepts of masculinity. Male models with powdered hair and pallid maquillage, for example, strut candidly down the catwalk styled as vampires to emulate the romantic dandies of nineteenth-century Vienna for Robert Geller's Fall 2009 collection (New York). Male vampires were again used in the short film for Fendi: *The Golden Mirror* (Luca Guadagnino, 2009). Like the dandy and the metrosexual, vampires are hybrid identities existing on the borders between life and death, human and animal, masculinity and femininity and heterosexuality and homosexuality both transgressing and disturbing boundaries. Similarly, the vampire is a consuming body; 'insatiable' in its own appetites and desires. A romantic dandy par excellence.

The description of a vampire who attacks people and sucks their life-blood easily lends itself to various metaphorical extensions and appears in popular literature at times of political and economic turmoil. Karl Marx in *Capital* used the vampire as a metaphor to depict the way that human life is turned into dead labour to feed the insatiable machine of capitalist production. Marx borrowed the image from Frederick Engels, who had made a passing reference to the 'vampire property-holding' class in *The Condition of the Working Class in England* (1845), and spoke of British industry as vampire-like, living by sucking blood, or the French middle class stealing the life of the peasant. In France the system had 'become a vampire that sucks out its the peasant's blood and brains and throws them to the alchemist's cauldron of capital' (Marx 1889: 816). In chapter ten of *Capital* Marx stated, 'Capital is dead labour that, vampire-like, lives only by sucking living labour, and lives the more, the more labour it sucks' (Ibid: 819).

This essay will explore the representation of the vampire via cinematic and literary case studies as well as men's fashion editorial images. It will argue that the blurring of gender and sexuality inherent to the depiction of the vampire can be seen in the appeal of the twenty-first century modern dandy. By examining the work of Charles Baudelaire and other key cultural theorists this article proposes that the vampire represents a polymorphic identity that emerges at times of political crises and economic excess.

Vampire narratives of queer desire

> he sensed with an infallible instinct what was happening . . . the powerful instinct of a vampire to whom even the slightest change in a human's facial expression is as apparent as a gesture. Lestat had preternatural timing . . . I refused to look at him, to be spellbound by the sheer beauty of his appearance . . . he lay down beside me now on the steps, his movement so graceful and so personal that at once it made me think of a lover.
>
> (Rice 1976: 463–65)

The description of the character Lestat by Louis in Anne Rice's *Interview with the Vampire* (1994) exemplifies the seductive sovereignty of the vampire. Louis describes Lestat's supernatural instinct, which enables him to exude charisma, love and sex at once. As Richard Dyer states, 'Only the vampire could produce such an intensely erotic panegyric: certainly, it is the most seductive of all the fictionalised monsters. Its proximity always, at some level at least, involves a sexual charge. . .' (1986: 62). Similarly, Ursini and Silver state that

> the character of the vampire itself, whether described as a vortex of malevolence, lust, and savagery or, alternately, as the unwilling victim who becomes a tormented, driven, even tragic figure. . . [is] seductive, erotic, possessing a hypnotic power that makes its questionable charms seem irresistible to its victims. . .
>
> (Ursini and Silver 1975: 54)

Vampires are a construct of many binary definitions, and represent a polymorphic and mobile sexuality that eludes the restrictions encoded in traditional gendered roles. Dracula, for example, appears in both the novel and the cinema adaptation as a bat, a wolf and floating dust. So powerfully decadent is Dracula's energy that it cannot be contained in any solid form and is depicted as a shape shifter that eludes definition. The vampire as 'queer' is strongly implied throughout Bram Stoker's *Dracula*, by Dracula's homoerotic desire for Jonathan Harker, and queer desire likewise appears in Rice's *The Vampire Chronicles, Interview with the Vampire* (1976). Set in 1791 New Orleans, the novel tells the story of queer vampires Louis, Lestat and Armand and invites the reader to share Louis' experience:

> Never had I felt this, never had I experienced it, this yielding of a conscious mortal. But before I could push him away for his own sake, I saw the bluish bruise on his tender neck. He was offering it to me. He was pressing the length of his body against me now, and I felt the hard strength of his sex beneath his clothes pressing against my leg. A wretched grasp escaped my lips, but he bent close, his lips on what

must have been so cold, so lifeless for him; and I sank my teeth into
his skin, my body rigid, that hard sex driving against me, and I lifted
him in passion off the floor.

(Rice 1976: 248)

Finally Louis is 'converted' into vampirism and 'queerness' as the two become
immortal companions.

The erotic perversity of Rice's tale is comparable to Poppy Z. Brite's *Lost Souls*
(1992) in that queer interactions between vampires and 'mortals' are celebrated
sexually:

Christian nipped the boy's throat gently, not breaking the skin this time
. . . The boy's back arched; he made a low gasping sound. Christian's
tongue found the tender spot under the jaw, and he sank his teeth in.
. . . He clasped the boy more tightly, and their bodies locked together
in a final wash of ecstasy.

(Brite 1992: 67)

The mixed nature of the vampire genre that causes it to blur defined categories
relates to the concept of the queer that characterises the postmodern age. Sue
Ellen Case notes that the term 'queer' 'challenges the very notion of being-in-the-
world' and is the 'taboo-breaker, the monstrous, the uncanny' (Case 1991: 61–2).
Blurring conventional notions of biological reproduction, the vampire likewise
disrupts gender roles. Take for instance, Louis, Lestat and Claudia in *Interview With
The Vampire*, who represent a queer family. Louis and Lestat are simultaneously
Claudia's queer male parents and her lovers, 'the queerness of their relationship
lies partly in the folding together of gay love with heterosexual incest/paedophilia'
(Gelder 1994: 113). In *Twilight* (Catherine Hardwicke, 2008) a film based on the
novel by Stephenie Meyer, the Cullens are a queer family where siblings are also
lovers. Similarly, in *Let the Right One In* (2008) a Swedish vampire film directed
by Thomas Alfredson and based on the highly successful novel by John Ajvide
Lindqvist, Håkan and Eli are also queer. The film is set in Blackeberg, a suburb
of Stockholm. Eli is a 200-year-old vampire in the body of a twelve-year-old girl,
Håkan is in his mid-thirties and together they share a pederastic relationship, but
to outsiders they pass as father and daughter. Yet again, traditional family roles
are replaced by non-heteronormative relationships such as paedophilia and incest.
Placing the vampire within a family invests the character with vulnerability and
pathos. Here, the syntax of the lone vampire has been replaced with one belonging
to a group or family. This contributes to 'the humanization of these characters and
their adoption of 'feminine' traits such as nurturing and empathy . . . suggesting
that traditional gender roles may be transcended, that certain characteristics are
not intrinsic to one sex alone' (Short 2005: 104).

The vampire dandy

In *The Painter of Modern Life* (1863) Charles Baudelaire writes of the 'modern'
phenomenon of the dandy in nineteenth-century Paris. He describes the dandy as

an aesthete, who is 'wealthy', 'blasé' and 'elegant' and is defined by luxury and 'the perpetual pursuit of elegance' (Baudelaire 1981: 26–7). He writes 'these beings have no other calling but to cultivate the idea of beauty in their person, to satisfy their passions, to feel and to think' (Ibid: 27). For Baudelaire, dandyism contains a discrete set of rules that requires self discipline: 'Dandyism, an institution beyond the laws, itself has rigorous laws that all its subjects must obey, whatever their natural impetuosity and independence of character' (1981: 26–7) Such laws go beyond the excessive delight in clothes and material elegance and are more about cultivating 'distinction, aristocratic superiority and simplicity in the habit of command' (Ibid).

When Baudelaire penned his seminal paper in 1863, the spirit of dandyism was flourishing not only in Paris but also in London, where dandyism originated in the form of the aristocratic socialite Beau Brummell (George Bryan Brummell, 1778–1840). By the time dandyism reached French shores in 1830, the aristocratic elite had lost its political dominance to the newly emerging middle class. 'In a society where bourgeois loudly proclaimed the virtues of thrift, utility and work', writes Rosalind H. Williams, 'the dandy rejected all these values as vulgar and sordid, and increasingly as irrelevant (1982: 117). Many worthy successors followed in the footsteps of Beau Brummell; the Comte d'Orsay (1801–52) with his extravagant love of perfumed gloves, furs, velvets and silks and Jules Barbey d'Aurevilly (1808–89), who elevated dandyism to a spiritual level, a holy man who 'carries within himself something superior to the visible world' (d'Aurevilly, cited by Williams 1982: 116). Likewise, Lord Byron, who Baudelaire hails (along with Sheridan and Brummell) as a dandy, became synonymous with the bohemian. He was a figure who was ambivalent, flouting social conventions and vacillating between political radicalism and aristocratic elitism. Byron lived the role of an outcast, but despite his social alienation the bourgeois public remained fascinated with him. 'Byron's image', writes Williamson, 'was fused with an aura and doom and this too is merged with vampirism' (2005: 36). This was partly due to John Polidori's novel, *The Vampyre*, whose vampire, Lord Ruthven, was based on Byron, and Byron's already 'soiled' reputation in London social circles as a homosexual and sexual deviant. Despite this, 'the bourgeois public', writes Williamson 'remained fascinated by Byron, for he seemed to live the role of glamorous outcast and the romantic bohemian'.

Dandy-like in their glamorous rebellion, vampires refuse to conform to societal conventions. Ostracised outsiders and refined hedonists governed only by their own manifesto of decadent aestheticism, Rice's vampires are very much the image of the dandy and carry over the bohemian themes of intellectual, artistic and creative superiority. According to Rob Latham, Rice's novels 'are disturbingly ideological in their celebration of the headless arrogance of the new consumption classes . . . their affirmative portrayal of a self confident urban subculture organised around alternative form of erotic bonding converged with the assertive consolidation of gay rights/pride movement' (2002: 98). Adopting a cultured and rebellious pose, writes Williamson, 'Lestat and Louis express this in the two modes common to modernity: Lestat's conspicuous consumption and addiction to luxury and Louis' bookish asceticism (2005: 38). Both vampires spend much of their time in philosophical contemplation (of the meaning of their existence), hold an appreciation of the arts, travel and adventure and display a preference for collecting objets d'art. In fact, writes Ken Gelder in *Reading the Vampire*, 'Rice's fiction flaunts its high cultural orientations, drawing in particular on Italian Renaissance and Baroque iconography – where high culture is at its most sensual' (1994: 119). 'To be a vampire' he continues, 'is to *be* "cultured" – that is to have "aristocratic" tastes – and also to be idle. Louis, Lestat and other vampires do not work. . . their job is, instead, to find out who they are and were they come from' (119). David Punter writes of *The Vampire Chronicles*: 'here Paris is certainly the capital of the nineteenth century, and the vampires who stroll its night-time, gas-lit streets are nothing but the very image of the flâneur' (cited by Williamson 2005: 38).

Interestingly, *Interview with the Vampire* and Brite's *Lost Souls* are both set in New Orleans, the setting for much of Brite's[1] and Rice's horror fiction. Set in the America south on the Bayou St John, a short distance from the Mississippi River, New Orleans was an important French and Spanish colonial trading port from 1718 and acted as 'gateway' to the 'exotic' New World. Because much of the population in the early days of settlement consisted of deported galley-slaves, fur trappers, gold hunters and wealthy plantation owners, the city has come to be represented in travel journals and literature as more decadent and aristocratic than Europe; 'simultaneously "primitive" and sophisticated', with a 'mixture of all kinds of people', what Ken Gelder terms the 'global exotic' (1994: 110). Vampire fiction overrides class, gender, age, sexual and ethnic differences emphasising mobility and movement. 'The vampire', writes Gelder, 'was consciously constructed as a "citizen of the world", a figure to whom boundaries (national boundaries in particular) meant very little' (1994: 111).

It is not surprising then, that *The Tale of the Body Thief* (1992),[2] Rice's fourth volume in *The Vampire Chronicles*, is not set in New Orleans, but in another decadent Southern American metropolis, Miami, where Lestat is a vigilante pursuing serial killers. His solitary dandy-like posture and sense of style sets him apart from the other characters in the novel, 'Lestat is essentially *different*', writes Gelder, 'he has style; he breaks the rules . . . with his Parisian background and his refined sensibilities, he might in fact be viewed as a kind of flâneur . . . a Parisian dandy [who] puts his idleness to good use' (1994: 120).

Baudrillard's vision of the dandy is of a figure who retreats from social and cultural life into the twin cults of beauty and aestheticism and away from the harsh realities of politics and history. 'Dandyism', writes Baudrillard, 'appears above all in periods of transition, when democracy is not yet all-powerful, and aristocracy is only just beginning to totter and fall' (1981: 28). Like the dandy, the vampire is characteristic of unhappy periods of social and political change;[3] according to Rob Latham, the vampire acts as a privileged metaphor that evokes the psychological and social experience – the relationships of desire and power – that are characteristic of postmodernist culture.[4] The vampire is literally an insatiable consumer driven by a hunger for perpetual youth (2002: 11).

Consuming the dandy vampire

During the 1970s and 1980s, advertisers and marketers began to actively solicit affluent young gay male consumers via strategies that mobilised homoerotic imagery and latent homosexual messages. 'The basic approach of these ads', says Latham, involved appealing to consumerist narcissism by fetishizing images of sleek young bodies living a dream of glamorous affluence and perpetual adolescence' (2002: 99). In the process, argues Latham, the advertisements blurred the distinction between heterosexual and queer consumers, 'since all were linked in their common narcissism: the consumers' desire to *be* young and beautiful was conflated with the desire to possess youth and beauty as incarnated in the beguiling models' (2002: 99). It was in the 1980s that new discourses about masculinity began circulating in Britain, with one motif occurring repeatedly: the image of the 'new man'. 'A hybrid character, the new man . . . was . . . the condensation of multiple concerns that were temporarily run together' (Mort 2009: 454). For the advertising industries, the emergence of the new man signalled a growing cultural and commercial confusion around gender privilege and masculinity. In its Spring 1988 issue, *Arena* magazine posed the question 'How *new* is our New Man?' and, according to author Jon Savage, his image was initially circulated through style magazines such as *ID* and *The Face*: 'The image is up to date yet aspirant . . . recognisably male yet admitting a certain vulnerability, still able to be interested, obsessed even, with clothes, male toiletries and new gadgets' (1988: 34). The 'Style Culture', he argues, 'has effectively helped to fuel a new type of consumption and has codified a fresh marketplace: the 19–45 year old male' (1988: 34).

The influence of gay pornography in the 1990s, through the work of photographers such as Bruce Weber and Herb Ritts, also attributed to key developments in the representation of masculinities in fashion iconography. This homoerotic style of photography also found expression in the work of fashion stylists including Nick Knight and Ray Petri. Men were depicted before the camera as actively masculine or passive, inviting men not only to consume the products, but also to look at themselves and other men as objects of desire to be purchased and consumed, which Latham calls 'consumer vampirism'. 'The capitalist market, in its ceaseless hunger for profit . . . infects the consumer with its own vampiric appetites, in the process of conflating relations based on voyeurism, narcissism, and homoeroticism with specifically consumerist desires and pleasures' (Latham 2002: 100). This raises a very important issue concerning the representation and spectatorship of masculinities as a site for scopophilic pleasure. To whose spectatorial delight is the male body offered, for instance? Heterosexual or queer men or heterosexual women, or both heterosexual men *and* women?

Since the emergence of the narcissist 'metrosexual', a term coined by Mark Simpson in 1994, heterosexual men have been encouraged to be a little more feminine. They are taught to be active consumers and purchase high-end luxury goods and styling products, live in a hip urban area and aspire to drive a sports car, or a Vespa. The metrosexual spends time shaping his body at the gym and looking at magazines such as *GQ*, *Arena* and *Men's Health*. In short, whether straight or queer, the metrosexual's *sexuality* is irrelevant. As a category, the metrosexual effectively queries/queeries the normative binaries and establishes fluid notions of sexuality. Today's men *look at* men and today's men like *to be looked at*. Not only do these representations of men appear in men's magazines, they also appear on fashion catwalks and in magazines targeting women as consumers. It is too simple to say that heterosexual women are 'enticed' by these representations in order to purchase goods for 'their' men, though this is partly so. To accept this as the sole reason for these images circulating would be to ignore the key political and social shifts that have occurred and influenced the codification of masculinity in the last thirty years, namely identity-based political movements such as feminism and gay and civil rights.

In 2007, issue two of the British biannual men's fashion magazine, *Fashion Inc*, subheaded 'The Thinking Man's Bible', was dedicated to the 'Dark Side' and featured a fashion editorial on Alexander McQueen entitled 'Prince of Darkness' photographed by Kyoko Homma, and another on Hedi Slimane appropriately titled 'L'Homme Fatal' and photographed by Carlotta Manaigo.

Both editorials make explicit reference to the vampire, McQueen to the Prince of Darkness and Slimane to darkness and fatality via black leather blousons, satin trenches and dramatic capes. Editor Adrian Clark describes Slimane's Autumn/ Winter collection as 'darker and more eerie' than his previous shows. 'Models were thinner and paler than before . . . From out of the shadows they sauntered: gaunt, haunted and partially illuminated by a column of fire at the end of the runway' (2007: 139). The magazine cover's subheading states '276 pages of fearless fashion for men . . . take a bite from Autumn's forbidden pleasures' and contains a dark and gloomy edge, with the cover model dressed in black leather pants and an unbuttoned black velvet shirt revealing a pale and hairless chest. He is seated on a black leather sofa gazing at the viewer and inviting them to join him 'on the dark side' and 'take a bite'.

In April 2008, *Fashion Trend Australia* ran a fashion editorial titled 'The Lost Boys', photographed by Cameron Grayson and styled by Mike Adler. The editorial's

Figure 27.1
Photography by Kyoko Homma. Black organza kimono with gold embroidery. Alexander McQueen. Copyright Fashion Inc.

title made reference to the 1987 Joel Shumacher film of the same name, starring Kiefer Sutherland. The film's tagline, 'Sleep all day. Party all night. Never grow old. Never die. It's fun to be a vampire', follows the lives of two young Arizonans who move to California and encounter a gang of teenage vampires.

The central setting for *The Lost Boys* is the fictitious Santa Carla boardwalk, a combination open-air shopping mall, gaming arcade and amusement park, where teenagers are seen shopping and browsing (adolescent flâneurs) playing videogames and riding the roller coaster. The intertextual device of linking the fashion images with the film via the film's title serves to create a consumer relationship based on an already existing utopian narrative of youth, freedom and consumption. The fashion editorial, along with the film, highlights young men as lost souls, vampires wondering along the fringe of mainstream society; but a very clear connection via styling and lighting techniques is also made between the male models featured in the editorial, the vampire and the dandy, with explicit visual referencing to Tom Cruise from the film *Interview with the Vampire* (1994). The model, dressed in blue silk shirt unbuttoned to reveal a muscular chest in the style of the romantic dandy, lies passively on a bed of plastic sheeting setting a subversive tone to the image and producing a series of oppositions between hard and soft masculinities and straight and gay sexualities. The image disrupts conventional notions of masculinity and constructs an all-viewing subject that posits pleasure and power.

Conclusion

The emergence of the figure of the vampire dandy in cinema and male fashion photography in recent times indicates, on the one hand, a relationship between

Figure 27.2
Pants and cravat by Bally, shirt and vest by Bowi, jacket by Comme des Garçons. Photography: Cameron Grayson. FASHIONTREND Australia, www.fashiontrend. co.au.

consumption, desire (and spectatorship) as well as power, whereas on the other, it raises questions about the relationship between masculine identity, as a social subject, and the types of identities that are being constructed via visual codes. The vampire and the dandy are seen as metaphorically or conceptually connected. Both figures are men of leisure, who pride themselves on aesthetic superiority, seeking distinction through exquisite taste. Yet the vampire and the dandy are also historically connected, first appearing at the turn of the nineteenth century amid social and political turmoil and reappearing in the last few years amid the current global economic crises of the twenty-first century. But what is most interesting is that the vampire and the dandy also share a genealogy that transcends their historical convergence: blurring gender binaries of homo/hetero and masculine/feminine and encompassing a more hybrid and queer identity – especially as it relates to masculine identities as a means for analysing and critiquing postmodern subjectivities. Indeed, the appearance of the vampire dandy indicates that masculinities are once again on the move.

A version of this essay appeared in the Sweish journal *Lamda Nordica* (special issue on fashion, No. 3–4, Vol. 14, 124–156, 2009).

Notes

1   Brite's trademarks have included using gay men as main characters, graphic sexual descriptions in the works, and an often-wry treatment of gruesome events. Some of her better-known novels include *Lost Souls* (1992), *Drawing Blood* (1993), and *Exquisite Corpse* (1996).

2   *The Tale of the Body Thief* (1992) is Anne Rice's fourth novel in The Vampire Chronicles following *The Queen of the Damned* (1988). Rice's first novel in the trilogy was *Interview with the Vampire* (1976) followed by *The Vampire Lestat* (1988).

3   See Gordon and Hollinger (1997) who explore the vampire's transformation in contemporary culture and focuses on the metaphorical roles played by vampires in contemporary fiction and film, and how these images manifest in times of political unrest.

4   Throughout the twentieth century, the vampire has become a stock image utilised internationally by political cartoonists and commentators to describe the objects of their hostile political commentary. In recent decades, war, fascism and economic depression has been labelled as vampiric entities. The vampire metaphor appeared in the wake of the fall of Communism in Russia and Eastern Europe at the end of the 1980s and the proclamation by then US President George Bush of a 'New World Order'. (See also Baldick (1987), Arata (1990), Engles (1953), Marx (1889), Wilson (1985), Reinmer (1939) and McCabe (1939) for a comprehensive analysis of the vampire as metaphor for political economy.)

References

Arata, S. D. (1990) 'The Occidental Tourist: Dracula and the Anxiety of Reverse Colonization', *Victorian Studies* 33, 4 (Summer 1990): 621–45.

Baldick, C. (1987) *In Frankenstein's Shadow*, Oxford: Clarendon.

Baudelaire, C. (1987) 'The Painter in Modern Life', in *The Painter in Modern Life and Other Essays*. Trans. By Jonathan Mayne. London: Phaidon, pp. 1–41.

Brite, P. Z. (1992) *Lost Souls*, London and New York: Penguin.

Case, S. E. (1991) 'Tracking The Vampire', in Gelder, K. (ed.) (1994) *Reading the Vampire*, London: Routledge, pp. 61–2.

Craft, C. (1990) 'Kiss Me With Those Red Lips: Gender and Inversion in Bram Stoker's Dracula', in Showalter, E. (ed.) *Speaking of Gender*, New York and London: Routledge.

Dyer, R. (1986) 'Children of the Night: Vampirism as Homosexuality, Homosexuality as Vampirism', in Radstone, S. (ed.) *Sweet Dreams: Sexuality, Gender and Popular Fiction*, London: Lawrence & Wishart.

Edwards, T. (2009) 'Consuming Masculinities: Style, Content and Men's Magazines', in McNeil, P. and Karaminas, V. (eds) *The Men's Fashion Reader*, Oxford: Berg.

Engels, F. (1953) 'The Conditions of the Working Class in England', 1845. Rept. in: *Karl Marx and Frederick Engels on Britain*. Moscow: Foreign Languages Publishing House.

Gelder, K. (1994) *Reading the Vampire*, London and New York: Routledge.

Gordon, J. and Hollinger, V. (1997) *Blood Read: The Vampire As Metaphor in Contemporary Culture*, Philadelphia, PA: University of Pennsylvania Press.

Latham, R. (2002) *Consuming Youth: Vampires, Cyborgs and the Culture of Consumption*, Chicago, IL: University of Chicago Press.

Lindquist, A. J. (2007) *Let the Right One In*, Ebba Sergerber (trans), Thomas Doon; New York: St Martins Press.

Marx, K. (1889). *Capital*, New York: Appleton.

McCabe, J. (1938) *What War and Militarism Cost: A Realistic Survey of the Vampire of the Human Race and the Supreme Enemy of Human Progress*, London: Girard, KS: Haldeman-Julius.

Mort, F. (2009) 'New Men and New Markets', in McNeil, P and Karaminas, V. *The Men's Fashion Reader*, Oxford: Berg.

Rice, A. (1976) 'Interview With The Vampire', in Haining, P. (ed) *The Vampire Omnibus*, London: Orion Books.

Reiman, G. (1939) *The Vampire Economy: Doing Business Under Fascism*. New York: Vanguard Press.

Rutherford, J. and Chapman, R. (1987) (eds) *Male Order: Unwrapping Masculinity*, London: Lawrence & Wishart.

Savage, J. (1988) 'What's So New About the New Man?', *Arena*, March/April, No. 8, Spring, pp. 33–5.

Simpson, M. *Meet the Metrosexual*. *Salon.com*. available at www.salon.com/ent/feature/2002/07/22/metrosexual/ (accessed 22 July 2002).

Stoker, B. (1995) *Dracula*, New York: Running Press.

Ursini, J. and Silver, A. (1975) *The Vampire Film*, London: The Tantivy Press.

Williams, R. H. (1982) *Dream Worlds: Mass Consumption in Late Nineteenth-Century France*, Berkeley, Los Angeles, CA: University of California Press.

Williamson, M. (2005) *The Lure of the Vampire: Gender Fiction and Fandom from Bram Stoker to Buffy*, London: Wallflower Press.

Wilson, K. M. (1985) 'The History of the Word "Vampire"', *Journal of the History of Ideas* 44, 4 (October-December): 577–83.

Films

Interview with the Vampire (1994) director Neil Jordan, Warner Bros. Pictures International.
Twilight (2008) director Catherine Hardwicke, Goldcrest Pictures, Washington.

Chapter 28

Claire Jenkins

'I'M SAVING THE WORLD, I NEED A DECENT SHIRT'

Masculinity and sexuality in the new
Doctor Who

T HE REVAMP OF *DOCTOR WHO* in 2005 saw the Doctor (played by
Christopher Eccleston) emerge as a more modern man than his predecessors,
in both outward appearance and temperament. When subsequently in 2010, Matt
Smith became the youngest actor to take on the mantle of the Doctor, the transition
became even more pronounced. This was coupled with a keen interest in his
costuming by the media: the BBC website employed a number of fashion experts
to give their opinions on Smith's 'look' (Geoghegan 2009), and more recently the
first publicity images for series seven were accompanied by headlines interested in
the 'first photo of Matt Smith's new costume' (Wace Peck 2012). While Smith's
attire references his predecessors,[1] there remains a significant emphasis on
contemporary fashion. Furthermore, whereas David Tennant's tenth Doctor chose
affordable high street footwear in the form of Converse trainers, Smith's eleventh
Doctor wears Prada boots (Geoghegan 2009), emphasising the high-end fashionability of the show's protagonist. However, the responses to Smith's costuming
speak volumes about attitudes to contemporary masculinity. Although the outfit
has been easily appropriated by fans, through cosplay,[2] fashion critics have been
less accepting of its style. Hadley Freeman, deputy fashion editor of *The Guardian*,
and some of the other fashionistas polled by the BBC, were vehemently unim-
pressed. It seems unusual that the fashion choices of a lead character in what is,
ostensibly, a family television show, should attract so much discussion, but what
is most telling in Freeman's assertion that the Doctor looks too trendy because
a 'Time Lord should not read *Grazia*' (Freeman 2009), is that her dislike of
the outfit is tied to what it says about the Doctor's masculinity; for Freeman, the
'Time Lord's' interest in fashion is too feminised. For Andrew Groves, one of
the BBC's chosen fashion critics, Smith is apparently made to look less attractive
by his sartorial choices (Geoghegan 2009). In both instances costume is linked to

masculine virility and the geek chic look sported by Smith/the Doctor poses a threat to this.

This chapter argues against such claims, suggesting, instead, that the appropriation of geek chic by Smith/the Doctor evokes metrosexuality. Indeed, the fashion choices of the Doctor can be read in tandem with Smith's off-screen persona as well-dressed tabloid 'hottie'. Both Smith's persona and performance depict a shift towards a postfeminist masculinity that re-asserts the traits of hegemonic masculinity in the face of the 'threat' posed by shifting gender boundaries. *Doctor Who* is an ideal programme to utilise in a discussion of masculinity (although few scholars have approached it from this perspective) as the very nature of a regenerating hero speaks to masculinity as fluid. The Doctor is, furthermore, an interesting character precisely because he has not, historically, evoked the traits of traditional, heroic masculinity, having been introduced, initially, as a grand-fatherly figure. Since the series' return in 2005[3], however, increasingly younger men have been cast in the lead role: Christopher Eccleston; David Tennant and Matt Smith, demonstrating a move towards a more mainstream male hero. Britton notes this, as he asks if, resultantly, Smith is the most heterosexualized of the Doctors (2011: 102). While he finds the answer to be that Smith is in fact more 'queer' than his predecessors in the newer series, I will suggest that Smith's costuming and related masculinity is more complex, depicting a refiguring of heterosexual masculinity in line with challenges to hegemonic masculinity, through notions of a crisis, manifest in metrosexuality and geek chic.

While there is some literature discussing the representation of metrosexuality on television and in the media more generally (see Cohan (2007), Shugart (2008) and Hall and Gough (2011)) and indeed the study of geeks/geek chic has extended to television representations, this chapter argues that contemporary geek chic has been appropriated into a post-metrosexual expression of masculinity (if we are to agree with Shugart that metrosexuality inhabited a discreet moment in time rather than an ongoing trend (Shugart 2008: 295)), that links geek chic to a pointedly heterosexual masculinity. This offers up a definition, or understanding of, geek chic, an ambiguous phrase that within scholarly work remains largely tied to technology[4] through the 'technosexual' (Quail 2011: 465).

Geek chic is a phrase that fits neatly with the sartorial choices of the Doctor, who has always dressed in unusual ways that play up his eccentricity and non-normative heroism. Britton voices this opinion of Smith's eleventh Doctor arguing that 'His elbow patched tweed jacket and bow tie hyperbolically evoke the "boffin" or "nutty professor"' (2011: 104). However, by appropriating nerdiness through fashion choices, rather than actually *being* a boffin, Smith/the Doctor depicts a playful heterosexual masculinity. The 'geeky' look of the eleventh Doctor does reference his predecessors; Nicholas Cull suggests that successive Doctors have evoked various different 'British types' who all embody what he deems to be a national preoccupation with 'brains over brawn' (Quoted in Britton 2011: 42). Throughout the years the figure of the Doctor has taken on numerous 'different' guises, all linked to a more thoughtful, and less active, masculinity. The original Doctor was a cantankerous old man – a wizened figure of authority though not an entirely likeable chap. The 'older' authoritative model of masculinity dominated arguably until the 1980s, and Chapman describes the Doctor as possessing masculine 'authority', particularly as played by Jon Pertwee and Tom Baker (Chapman 2006:142). Although his age varied, the Doctor in his earlier incarnations was a mature man. Peter Davison (the fifth Doctor) became the youngest, taking on the role at the age of 30. Although Davison was potentially the first dishy Doctor, Tulloch notes in his research on *Doctor Who*'s audiences that the Doctor was thought of as a paternalistic hero rather than a romantic one (1995: 111).[5]

The Doctor's sense of masculine authority was never related to physical strength, rather his respectful and intelligent nature invoked images of the classic English gentleman, visually evident in his costumes that depict various elements of English Heritage. For example over the years we have seen the grandfather, the dandy and the gentleman cricketer. His other worldliness is then linked into an image of British, if not English, eccentricity, seen beyond *Doctor Who* in shows such as the BBC's *Sherlock* (2010 –). The new Doctors' appropriating of fashion trends is not necessarily unique in the programme's cannon. As Britton notes 'Hinchcliffe [a former producer of the show] has said that he thought of Baker's as the 'Woodstock' Doctor' (2011: 46). Baker's Doctor, who made a nod to counter-culture through his costuming, was tied to contemporary fashions, much as Pertwee's sartorial choices were in keeping with the other heroes of the decade such as John Steed of *The Avengers* (1961–9) (Britton 2011: 43). Costuming here also echoes Luckett's discussion of a resurgence of dandyish fashion in the 1960s and 1970s as evidenced in popular British films of the period (2000). Both Luckett (2000: 320) and Britton relate such fashions to a discourse/playfulness around national identity and class:

> [N]early all the Doctor's first eight incarnations have worn outfits that were not merely redolent of the past but more specifically past modes of *finery*. . .until the advent of the ascetically clad Christopher Eccleston in the new series, silks, velvets, plaids and embroidery have been very much in evidence (all markers of the 'foppery' from which Eccleston was expressly keen to distance himself)
>
> (Britton 2011: 35).

Although the Doctor was often well dressed, this was not linked to his sexuality. It is a point of note that, while the Doctor's companions, such as Leela (Louise Jamieson), were famed for their attractiveness, this was in the eyes of the audience, not the Doctor, who remained steadfastly asexual in his relationships with women (with the exception of his kiss with Grace in the 1996 television movie), that is until the 2005 re-boot. The overriding character of the Doctor, historically, was as a man who is heroic and knowing but not physically masculine, and not led by, or really affected by (hetero)sexual desire.

When the Doctor returned to our screens in 2005, his outward appearance and renewed back-story – as a veteran of the Time War – gave the character a harder edge. The incarnation of the Doctor as a three dimensional character and an emotionally scarred man is in keeping with popular representations of masculinity across contemporary Western film and television. The new man is thoughtful, soulful and damaged. This harshness is echoed in the Doctor's costuming: gone is the Edwardian dress of the previous Doctor replaced with a leather jacket, plain sweater and buzz cut, stepping away from historic English or British-ness and making the character immediately more contemporary. Jones suggests this is not the first time 'ancestral authority' is overthrown in the series. He argues that the individualism of Tom Baker's fourth Doctor threw off British heritage (and his own heritage as a Time Lord) (Jones 2010: 90). Baker's nod to counter culture or rebellion is repeated in the new series, but here it is a harder notion of anti-establishment, signalled by the leather jacket and the Doctor's persona as a maverick warrior, being the sole survivor of the Time War. Not only does the ninth Doctor's costuming give him a harder edge, but it is also unremarkable allowing him to blend in and to be 'one of us'. Jones suggests his image is one of a 'pared back modern hero, free from the trappings of his past that was appropriate considering that the last time we saw him his planet had burned and his people perished' (Jones 2010: 97).

Although Jones argues that the Doctor, in the post-2005 series, is free from his past, he seems to carry more emotional baggage rather than less. This marks a distinct difference to previous Doctors, for as Tulloch notes, audiences were used to seeing the Doctor as emotionless and detached (1995: 118). The emotionally troubled Doctor has continued through the contemporary incarnations with both Tennant and Smith portraying a lonely character in need of companionship. The re-vamped Doctor is representative of contemporary notions of masculinity that see it as 'in crisis'.

The contemporary crisis in masculinity is more widely recognised as a response to female advancement and resultant shifts in gender roles. Shugart argues that metrosexuality functions as an outlet for precisely this concern, although she posits that masculinity has long been unstable. That said, Shugart demonstrates that although metrosexuality can be seen as a response to masculinity in 'crisis' critics of this trend felt that it *was* the crisis as 'commercial masculinity' and the commodification of men threatened normative masculinity (Shugart 2008:281).

Although not necessarily espousing 'commercial' masculinity in its truest sense, *Doctor Who* demonstrates the commodification of masculinity and male sexuality as a way of reinforcing normative masculinity. In the opening episode of Series Five ('The Eleventh Hour'), in which the audience is introduced to Smith's Doctor, an interesting exchange occurs between him and his new companion Amy Pond (Karen Gillan). The Doctor, fresh from regeneration and therefore still sporting the, now tattered, clothing of his previous incarnation, decides that before he has a final showdown with alien invaders of Earth he must find a suitable outfit; in his words: 'I'm saving the world, I need a decent shirt'. While trying to find such a shirt he strips off in front of Amy and her geeky boyfriend, Rory (Arthur Darvill).

Rory seems dismayed that the Doctor is undressing and the following exchange occurs:

The Doctor:	Turn your back if it embarrasses you.
Rory:	Are you stealing clothes now . . . those clothes belong to people, you know.
(To Amy)	Are you not going to turn your back?
Amy:	No.

Figure 28.1   The Doctor's new outfit is carefully chosen, as he asserts himself before invading aliens, *Doctor Who*.

Amy's response is delivered with a slight raise of the eyebrow, as she crosses her arms and gently purses her lips, intently watching the Doctor undress, allowing him to become the object of her active, (hetero)sexualised gaze. Furthermore, Amy is working as a kiss-o-gram and, at the time, is dressed as a 'sexy' police officer. The Doctor becomes sexualised in this sequence, not only as object of Amy's gaze, but also in his own masculinity. He is cocky when he tells Rory to turn away if embarrassed, and having announced that he needs a shirt, the Doctor adds it is 'time to put on a show'. There is a self-assured masculinity being performed here. This continues throughout the new series, in particular through exchanges with River Song (Alex Kingston), who, it is hinted, is the Doctor's future wife (in Series Six a makeshift wedding ceremony does take place, although it is for practical rather than romantic reasons). In the opening episode of the sixth series ('The Impossible Astronaut') the Doctor's flirtatious nature is again evident in his banter with River:

The Doctor:	Doctor Song, you've got that face on again.
River:	What face?
The Doctor:	The 'he's hot when he's clever face'.
River:	This is my normal face.
The Doctor:	I know.

The conversation ends with the Doctor shrugging the front of his jacket, aligning his self-assured sexuality with his costuming. Previously in the same episode the Doctor has mentioned America's founding fathers (Jefferson, Adams and Hamilton) telling his companions 'lovely fellas, two of them fancied me'. This initially queers the Doctor, but coupled with his continued heterosexual flirting, the result is a notion of masculinity that is so potently sexualised it is irresistible. This is in stark contrast to earlier incarnations of the Doctor. As Tulloch notes of his audience research, viewers discussing the show agreed the Doctor was 'not a stud' (Tulloch 1995: 116): a feature they all felt was positive.

Although still not a muscular hero, the new Doctor is a stud. Smith's onscreen sexualisation is underpinned by his offscreen persona, which similarly evokes the idea that he is a stud. His on/off relationship with model Daisy Lowe has taken a prime spot in gossip pages over the past few years. Both the on again/off again nature of the relationship and the choice of headlines build an image of Smith as either a sexualised character or, at times, a playboy, evident in stories that detail public displays of affection and comment on the intricacies of their romantic relationship.[6] Smith is seen as part of an over-sexed celebrity couple, and at the same time a bachelor playboy. This is upheld by other news stories that have hinted at a relationship between Smith and his co-star Karen Gillan, such as: 'Who's your favourite leading lady? Matt Smith arrives at Pam Hogg fashion show with Karen Gillan . . . but leaves with Daisy Lowe' (Magrath 2011a). This tabloid version of Matt Smith, frequently linked to *Doctor Who* in the wording of headlines, all aids the way in which the newest Doctor's character can be read: this Doctor certainly is a stud.

Smith's tabloid persona is not just built around his heterosexuality, but also around his sartorial choices. The copy-light stories of internet news sites such as *The Daily Mail* frequently rely on paparazzi photographs as the bulk of their celebrity news and as such images of Smith's fashion choices become the basis of an article. The 2012 *Daily Mail* headline 'Rolled-up jeans, Disney jumper and dark glasses: Doctor Who's Matt Smith and Karen Gillan are too trendy for their own good' (Littlejohn and Dadds 2012) precedes little more than a series of images of Smith and Gillan wearing fashionable clothes while walking through a town in Spain. Smith's Disney-character sweatshirt and rolled up trousers evoke a relaxed version of his character's style, still reminiscent of geek chic. While offbeat, Smith's style is clearly recognised by the tabloids as 'on-trend'. These personal fashion statements are inherent in Smith's costuming as the Doctor. As Britton explains, Smith had to persuade producer Steven Moffat to allow him to wear the bow tie (2011: 104). The Doctor's sartorial decisions have, as noted above, been a point of criticisms that imply that these choices, representative of 'commercial' masculinity or metrosexuality, pose a threat to hegemonic masculinity.

The metrosexual male, although in touch with his feminine side, according to Shugart (2008) and Tuncay (2004) is, in fact, pointedly heterosexual, with the emphasis on style seen as a way to promote virility: a concern with the body, grooming and heterosexual coupling. Although the sexuality of Smith's Doctor may appear ambiguous throughout the first part of the series (in particular in the opening episode where he refers to Amy's friend Jeff as 'the good looking one'), his masculine prowess is seen on the football field in 'The Lodger', an episode where he becomes flatmates with Craig (James Corden). As Collins notes, although Craig seems initially unsure of the Doctor's sexuality, he soon becomes a threat to Craig's masculinity as he excels both at work (taking on a temp job with Craig) and at sports (Collins 2010). The Doctor has never played football before but he naturally takes to the game as if an expert.[7]

Collins suggests this episode speaks about a crisis in masculinity that is explored through Craig and his relationship with the Doctor. This crisis is evident throughout the show, not only in the pairing of laddish Craig and the 'weird' (in Craig's words) Doctor, and in particular the lad's pale comparison to the initially less normative masculinity, but also through the show more broadly in its representation of masculinity as fluid. The very nature of the Doctor's regeneration allows masculinity to be constantly in flux. While Tom Baker's Doctor of the 1970s embodied counter-cultural concerns through his anti-establishment behaviour and his distinct way of dressing, Eccleston's character – both in his more hard-edged appearance, and through narratives – indicates a tougher yet more emotional man, and Smith's Doctor comes to represent another facet of masculinity as the trendy young hipster.

The eleventh Doctor's fashionable appearance might not initially seem to be part of a metrosexual look. Although it is now a term that is frequently thrown about to describe men who take pride in their appearance, in its truest form, as 'commercial masculinity' (Shugart 2008: 281), metrosexuality seems a far cry from the masculinity performed by Smith's rendition of the Doctor. Indeed as Shugart opines, the metrosexual male has roots in the 1980s, a period that

> [W]itnessed the start of a dramatic shift toward the general object-ification of the male body, specifically due to the convergence of the proliferation of men's fashions; new aesthetic codes for the representation of men in advertising, film, and television; and the advent of style (or 'lifestyle') magazines for male audiences.
>
> (Shugart 2008: 282)

Cohan discusses non-conformist masculinity in the 1980s – relating this more closely to a 'crisis', or at the very least a refiguring of masculinity in the wake of radical political discourses, including the gay rights movement and feminism (Cohan 2007: 182).

The metrosexual male is linked to the 1980s figure of the yuppie, who commodified masculinity with clothing such as sharp suits, flashy sports cars and grooming products (Edwards cited in Shugart 2008: 282). The yuppie male is representative of a 'traditional' notion of masculinity in that he represents the middle-class, professional, heterosexual man. Although similarities exist between the metrosexual and the yuppie, the roots of metrosexuality stretch back further than the 1980s. The nineteenth-century dandy, with his interest in luxury fashion, who came out of a desire to display upwards mobility at a time when conspicuous consumption rose alongside the birth of the department store,[8] is a predecessor to the metrosexual. The emphasis here, though, was on ostentatious clothing that depicted luxury and wealth such as silks and frills.

The Doctor's metrosexuality can more readily be traced back to a pre-metrosexual male described by Tuncay; she recognises the metrosexual's predecessor in the 1920s and 1930s, where she suggests:

> [T]here was an undercurrent of an alternative type of man. This new man was embodied by the Peter Pan ethos and represented the seeds

of a new type of masculinity where men wanted to engage in a never-ending childhood of play, games, thrills and personal satisfaction.
(Tuncay 2004: 315)

While Tuncay links this to consumerism, playful and childish masculinity is certainly demonstrated by the Doctor. Tuncay suggests this man developed in the 1950s and 1960s to be the 'playboy', a distinct contrast to the stable breadwinner. The Doctor is certainly the antithesis of the breadwinner in his role as wandering hero and his refusal to settle down, demonstrated neatly in 'The Power of Three' as he struggles with domestic life, finding it dull and tedious.

Furthermore, Smith's Doctor evokes the playfulness of the Peter Pan-like male, both through his performance and costuming. His is a childish masculinity that finds delight in adventure, and in dressing-up; for example, he takes to wearing a fez in Series Five, because 'Fezzes are cool', and a Stetson in Series Six for the same reason. This echoes his assertion that bow ties are cool. The bow tie is an object of ridicule within the show, as is all the Doctor's eclectic costuming. Amy, his companion, cements the view that his penchant for idiosyncratic attire is childish by arguing, in 'Vampires of Venice', that he could not possibly pass as her father as he 'looks about nine'. The quirkiness of the Doctor's playful clothing is certainly reminiscent of previous incarnations, in particular the whimsical question marks that adorned the collar of Colin Baker's sixth Doctor. The boyishness of the eleventh Doctor, however, does set him apart, and is undoubtedly linked to his suit, echoing the style of designer Thom Browne who has put the just-a-little-too-short trouser on the fashion map. The very nature of the Browne style hints at boyishness in its 'shrunken'-ness; as if a man has outgrown his childish clothes, reminding us both of playful youth, but also the manliness of the figure now too masculine for this suit. The suit is a sartorial choice indicative of a specific sort of masculinity; as Browne himself says, it is effortless but smart dressing for men, that is 'polished and powerful' (Blasberg 2012). It is heavily associated with heteronormative masculinity.[9]

Smith's suit is, of course, not indicative of the power-hungry yuppie, but is more relaxed in its style. Britton, as noted above, suggests the elbow patches of his tweedy jacket make the Doctor fusty, professor-ish and almost uncanny in highlighting his youth and age simultaneously (2011: 104). The Doctor's suit in series Five and Six is less 'sharp' and more thrown together out of un-matching garments (although promotional images for the latter part of Series Seven suggest he will return in a more natty, matching, three-piece suit that still maintains a similar cut), in this respect the Doctor has styled the suit, and bow tie, to provide a version of metrosexuality that plays into geek chic. It is worth noting that although the Doctor's style looks thrown together, it is carefully chosen just as he asserts himself before an invading alien force, closely aligning within the text the importance of attire to personality.

Smith's appropriation of metrosexuality through geek chic, as noted by Freeman, references a number of different trends. One in particular is the quirky bow tie of American hip-hop producer and artist Pharrell Williams. In *Time* magazine, Tyrangiel (2003) and Gregory (2012) both discuss geek chic, relating the style to an expression of African-American masculinity, with references to both

Williams and NBA player Kevin Durant. The styling as 'geek', including accessories such as bow ties, is seen as playful by NBA players who, when not on the bench, are required to wear 'smart-casual' clothing (Gregory 2012). This style becomes a mode of personal expression. In both articles geek chic is depicted as 'softening' black masculinity: Durant says it helps him to come across 'nicer' than if he is clad in baggy, dark clothing (Gregory 2012), and Pharrell's styling is linked to his middle-class upbringing, his lack of success with women and the nerdy persona, which he consciously performs (Tyrangiel 2003). Neither, then, are actual 'geeks' but the look is chosen to promote a specific sort of masculinity.

As Quail notes, the appropriation of 'geek chic' provides an opportunity to 'try on a different type of masculinity or identity' (2011: 466). She also demonstrates a difference between geek/nerd and geek chic; whereas the true nerd 'has been constructed as an awkward math-savvy social and sexual failure' (2011: 460), the parodic nature of geek chic relies on an understanding that there is always a true geek/nerd who is 'less cool' as there remains a 'tension between "geek chic" and more caustic versions of nerddom' (Quail 2011: 467). Quail's notion of the hip – square dialectic, whereby square is depicted in opposition to hip in popular culture, reinforcing the stereotypes of the two (geek/nerd as non-masculine and sexually awkward, hip as physically masculine and pointedly heterosexual) (2011: 460), is illustrated in *Doctor Who* with Amy Pond, the spunky and fashionable companion providing the 'hip' to the latest Doctor's 'square'. Amy is certainly pointedly heterosexual – emphasised through her first appearance as a kiss-o-gram and her active gaze watching the Doctor change. However, rather than reinforcing the Doctor as square and sexually awkward, her desire for him (evidenced as she kisses him in 'Flesh and Stone') heterosexualises the Doctor. This is not the only example of the Doctor as heterosexualised: in the opening episode of Series Six he is seen posing nude for an unnamed royal and hiding under her full skirts from her angry father. This reiterates the playboy image of the metrosexual, and the parodic appropriation of geek chic. Indeed, the Doctor's chic-ness is heightened by his comparison to Rory, arguably the real geek of series Five and Six. If, as Quail suggests, real masculinity is linked to technological and practical devices and gadgets (lawnmowers, barbecues), and geek masculinity to scientific technologies (computers, calculators) (2011: 463), then the Doctor and his TARDIS are surely part of geek masculinity.[10] But Rory, the nurse, is even further separated from technology and masculinity in his feminised, caring role.

The Doctor's fashion choices, and heteorsexualisation, evoke the metrosexual man; a heterosexual male dealing successfully with shifts in genderered images and roles. The move towards a postfeminist masculinity is evident in the regenerations of the Doctors since 2005 as continually younger men. The youthful regeneration speaks to concerns about masculinity and ageing, allowing the Doctor to become a figure embodying the fantasy of youthfulness. The attempt to deny ageing suggests masculinity faces comparable pressures to femininity. Ageing women are often figures of derision and have become the subject of frequent discussion in popular and academic discourse. Wearing suggests that the denial of female ageing is often demonstrated in the 'girl-ing' of the older woman (2007): this is certainly applicable to the Doctor who exudes childish whimsy, and looks boyish in his costuming. While masculinity is fluid, it is noteworthy that the transformations the Doctor

Figure 28.2   Amy is 'hip', the Doctor is 'square' and Rory is squarer yet.

undergoes also allow him to embody a hegemonic masculine ideal, he is now youthful, attractive, virile and heroic. *Doctor Who* promises, and often delivers, non-traditional gender roles, yet its hero and central character remains tied to a dominant model of masculinity that is white, English, heterosexual and middle class. Indeed, although the Doctor's outward appearance evokes a trendy, youthful masculinity, the leather elbow pads and bow tie also point towards the middle-class English gent; as Freeman suggests, the floppy fringe evokes images of Hugh Grant and other public schoolboys (Freeman 2009). While *Doctor Who* seems consciously aware that masculinity is in flux, the heroic male still conforms to a refigured, but essentially traditional, set of gender structures.

Notes

1   The bow tie, in particular, evokes the outfit of Jon Pertwee's Doctor but the suit, and eccentric styling, recalls the costuming of the majority of previous Doctors including Patrick Troughton, Sylvester McCoy and more recently David Tennant.
2   Blogs such as www.eleventhdoctorcostume.blogspot.co.uk among others, demonstrate the interest in recreating Smith's costuming, and online tailors Magnoli clothiers sell a high-end version of Smith's jacket: www.magnoliclothiers.com/smith-tweed-jacket-blazers-p-325.html.
3   The show had been off-air for sixteen years, excluding the one-off television movie in 1996, starring Paul McGann as the eighth Doctor.
4   See Waters (2008), Gilligan (2009) and Quail (2011).
5   The shift from paternal hero to a romantic one can also be linked to the shift in the show from an educational programme aimed at children, to an entertainment show for a more broad 'family' audience.

6   See Thompson (2011), Moodie (2011), Magrath (2011b), among others.
7   This relies on extra-textual knowledge that Smith was himself a good youth player, whose professional career was halted as a result of injury. It is also reminiscent of 'The Black Orchid' (19:05) in which Peter Davison's Doctor excelled on the cricket pitch, in this instance a reference to the actor's own cricketing prowess.
8   See Breward (2000), Lucket (2000), and Shannon (2004).
9   Suits have been worn by both the tenth and eleventh Doctors. They are not 'sharp' suited, but rather appropriate the garment into fashion trends, with David Tennant sporting his with Converse trainers, hinting at Britpop styling, and Smith playing up geek chic. Both of these suited Doctors express a specific sort of attractive, heterosexual masculinity which has been coupled with romantic entanglements for their characters: Tennant/the tenth Doctor's almost-relationship with Rose, and desirability in the eyes of his next companion Martha, and Smith/the eleventh Doctor's implied romance with River Song.
10   This is a recognisable facet of contemporary masculinity that is becoming increasingly more visible in popular culture, as evidenced by Ben Whishaw's Q in *Skyfall* (2012); a further example of the tech-savvy, chic geek.

References

Blasberg, Derek (2012) 'The interview: Mr Thom Browne', in *Mr Porter* [online] 31 July www.mrporter.com/journal/journal_issue75/4#1 (accessed 14 November 2012).

Breward, Christopher (2000) 'The Dandy Laid Bare: Embodying practices and fashion for men', in Bruzzi, S. and Church Gibson, P. (eds) *Fashion Cultures: Theories, Explorations and Analysis*, London; New York: Routledge, pp. 221–38.

Britton, Piers D. (2011) *TARDISbound: Navigating the Universes of Doctor Who*, London; New York: I.B. Tauris.

Chapman, James (2006) *Inside the TARDIS: The Worlds of Doctor Who*, London; New York: I.B. Tauris.

Cohan, Steven (2007) 'Queer Eye for the Straight Guise: Camp, postfeminism, and the Fab Five's makeovers of masculinity', in Tasker, Y. and Negra, D. (eds) *Interrogating Postfeminism: Gender and the Politics of Popular Culture*, Durham; London: Duke University Press, pp. 176–200.

Collins, Frank (2010) 'Ooh monkeys, monkeys', Behindthesofa.org.uk: www.behind thesofa.org.uk/2010/06/oooh-monkeys-monkeys.html (accessed 14 November 2012).

Freeman, Hadley (2009) 'Matt Smith's Doctor Who proves a fashion flop', in *The Guardian* [online] 22 July www.guardian.co.uk/media/2009/jul/22/dr-who-matt-smith-fashion (accessed 14 November 2012).

Geoghegan, Tom (2009) 'The fashion police on Doctor Who's new outfit', in *BBC News Magazine* [online] 21 July www.news.bbc.co.uk/1/hi/magazine/8160710. stm (accessed 14 November 2012).

Gilligan, Sarah (2009) 'Becoming Neo: Costume and transforming masculinity in the Matrix films', in McNeil, P., Karaminas, V. and Cole, C. (eds) *Fashion in Fiction: Text and Clothing in Literature, Film and Television*, Oxford: Berg, pp. 149–59.

Gregory, Sean (2012) 'NBA nerd alert', in *Time Magazine* [online] 14 May www.time.com/time/magazine/article/0,9171,2113816,00.html (accessed 14 November 2012).

Jones, Matthew (2010) 'Aliens of London: (Re)reading national identity in *Doctor Who*', in Hansen, C. J. (ed.) *Ruminations, Peregrinations and Regenerations: A Critical Approach to Doctor Who*, Newcastle Upon Tyne: Cambridge Scholars Publishing, pp. 85–99.

Littlejohn, Georgina and Dadds, Kimberley (2012) 'Rolled-up jeans, Disney jumper and dark glasses: Doctor Who's Matt Smith and Karen Gillan are too trendy for their own good', in *The Daily Mail* [online] 13 March www.dailymail.co.uk/tvshowbiz/article-2114040/Doctor-Whos-Matt-Smith-Karen-Gillan-trendy-good.html (accessed 14 November 2012).

Luckett, Moya (2000) 'Performing Masculinities: Dandyism and male fashion in 1960s–70s British Cinema', in Bruzzi, S. and Church Gibson, P. (eds) *Fashion Cultures: Theories, Explorations and Analysis*, London and New York: Routledge, pp. 315–28.

Magrath, Andrea (2011a) 'Who's your favourite leading lady? Matt Smith arrives at Pam Hogg fashion show with Karen Gillan . . . but leaves with Daisy Lowe', in *The Daily Mail* [online] 21 February www.dailymail.co.uk/tvshowbiz/article-1359021/London-Fashion-Week-2011-Dr-Who-star-Matt-Smith-arrives-Pam-Hogg-Karen-Gillan-leaves-Daisy-Lowe.html (accessed 14 November 2012).

—— (2011b) 'Doctor Endless Love: Matt Smith and Daisy Lowe take their never-ending PDA Stateside', in *The Daily Mail* [online] 30 June www.dailymail.co.uk/tvshowbiz/article-2009724/Doctor-Who-star-Matt-Smith-Daisy-Lowe-ending-PDA-Stateside.html (accessed 14 November 2012).

'Making my eleventh Doctor costume' www.eleventhdoctorcostume.blogspot.co.uk/ (accessed 14 November 2012).

Moodie, Clemmie (2011) 'How I keep the romance with Doctor Who star Matt Smith', in *The Mirror* [online] 2 April www.mirror.co.uk/3am/celebrity-news/how-i-keep-the-romance-with-doctor-who-120004 (accessed 14 November 2012).

Quail, Christine (2011) 'Nerds, Geeks and the Hip/Square Dialectic in Contemporary Television', *Television and New Media*, 12:5, 460–82.

Shannon, Brent (2004) 'ReFashioning Men: Fashion, masculinity, and the cultivation of the male consumer in Britain, 1860–1914', *Victorian Studies*, 46:4, 597–630.

Shugart, Helene (2008) 'Managing Masculinities: The metrosexual moment', *Communication and Critical/Cultural Studies*, 5:3, September, 280–300.

'Smith Tweed Jacket' www.magnoliclothiers.com/smith-tweed-jacket-blazers-p-325.html (accessed 14 November 2012).

Thompson, Jody (2011) 'Doctor ooh la la! Matt Smith and Daisy Lowe a fashionable pair as they cuddle up on the front row at Paris Couture Week', in *The Daily Mail* [online] 7 July www.dailymail.co.uk/tvshowbiz/article-2012168/Paris-Couture-Week-2011-Doctor-Who-star-Matt-Smith-Daisy-Lowe-cuddle-up.html (accessed 14 November 2012).

Tulloch, John (1995) '"But Why is the Doctor so Attractive?": Negotiating ideology and pleasure', in Jenkins, H. and Tulloch, J. (eds) *Science Fiction Audiences: Watching Doctor Who and Star Trek*, London; New York: Routledge, pp. 108–24.

Tuncay, Linda (2004) 'Conceptualizations of Masculinity among a "New" Breed of Male Consumers', *Gender and Consumer Behaviour*, 8, 312–27.

Tyrangiel, Josh (2003) 'Hip-hop's chic geek', in *Time Magazine* [online] 25 August www.time.com/time/magazine/article/0,9171,1005509,00.html (accessed 14 November 2012).

Wace Peck, Matthew (2012) 'Dr Who: First photo of Matt Smith's new costume, new companion', in *Digital Journal* [online] 8 June www.digitaljournal.com/article/326283 (accessed 14 November 2012).

Waters, John K. (2008) 'How geek became chic', in *T.H.E. Journal* [online] 2 January www.thejournal.com/Articles/2008/02/01/How-Geek-Became-Chic.aspx?Page=6 (accessed 14 November 2012).

Wearing, Sadie (2007) 'Subjects of Rejuvenation: Aging in postfeminist culture', in Tasker, Y. and Negra, D. (eds) *Interrogating Postfeminism: Gender and the Politics of Popular Culture*, Durham; London: Duke University Press, pp. 277–310.

Chapter 29

Lauren Jade Thompson

SUITING UP AND STRIPPING OFF
The male makeover

S INCE THE FIRST EDITION OF *Fashion Cultures* was published in 2000, there has been a significant expansion in the number of makeover programmes on television, and the trope has become increasingly visible in wider culture. With shows such as *What Not To Wear* (BBC, 2002–7), *How To Look Good Naked* (Maverick Television for C4, 2006–) and *10 Years Younger* (Maverick Television for C4, 2004–), pedagogic discussion of fashion has become a regular feature of primetime television schedules, and now almost always takes place within a makeover format. This chapter is concerned with exploring one specific facet of the debates about makeover television, gender, and fashion, namely the male makeover and the importance of the suit to the re-constructions of masculinity as represented within the genre. My aim here is to open up lines of enquiry around the idea of male makeover itself, as part of the 'ungendering' (as Rachel Moseley has termed it) of a previously feminine paradigm (Moseley 2000). I am interested here in what the implications, complications and tensions produced by such a process might be, and how they are textually negotiated. The emblematic garment of the suit emerges within these texts as a key motif that embodies the self-improvement ethos of the makeover and ensures continuity with older formations of masculinity in order to re-secure gender norms in the aftermath of the potentially disruptive and feminising process of makeover.

Makeover shows are usually conceived of as being concerned with the feminine, focused on domains such as the home and seen as emerging from a long history of literature for women on how to present oneself as appropriately feminine and desirable. While acknowledging that the vast majority of makeover shows do feature female participants and operate on a mode of address that invokes 'feminine cultural competencies' and concerns (Brunsdon 1981: 36), my focus here will be on the ways in which, 'men are being brought into the makeover game as never before', a 'normalized if secondary concern of many TV makeover shows' (Ouellette and Hay 2008: 120, 121). Increasingly, within these shows and in other media forms such as Hollywood film, advertising and magazines, men are, as Moseley suggests, 'on display as shoppers and make-over subjects . . . as consumers of fashion and grooming products . . . as citizen-consumers engaged in care of the self' (in Brunsdon *et al.* 2001: 35). Such new formations of masculine subjectivity require complex textual negotiations between dominant, residual and emergent features of masculine identity and role (as we might think of them after Raymond Williams's work on cultural process [1977]).

The explicit aim of many makeover texts is to produce men who are suitable as romantic partners for postfeminist women for whom 'choice' in their 'life paths' is key. Often, the shows discussed here will take a 'failing' singleton, divorcee or widower, and seek to prepare him for (re)entry into the contemporary dating market. This impetus towards coupling is also often linked to issues around employment, and in particular with a concern for men's economic roles in a post-industrial, service sector workforce.

Makeover television takes on a narrative form, with transformation ritualised through the strict repetition of a 'before and after' structure. In most personal makeover shows, the (sometimes unsuspecting) subject is visited by the show's expert or experts who identify and explicate the problems that need to be fixed, guide him through a series of small lessons and transformations that are designed to target the areas identified as deficient and finally 'reveal' him to himself, his partner, his friends and his family. As the title of this piece might indicate, my analysis will look in detail at two particular 'before' and 'after' stages of the process: the investigation of the subject and his being stripped – literally and figuratively – of his existing, deficient, unreformed masculinity; and the recon-struction of his identity via the garment of the suit and its symbolic potential. The suit, as will be explored in more detail later in this chapter, holds important continuities with older forms of masculine identity, and is invoked within a potentially destabilising, feminising process in order to 'shore up' masculinity. In the male makeover, the suit acts as a residual technology of masculine identity alongside newer, emergent technologies of the self, such as botox and waxing, that the masculine subject is also encouraged to consume.

The opening scenes of makeover television shows present the audience with the individual to be transformed: highlighting and identifying his problems. Many existing analyses of lifestyle television have focused on the legitimation and naturalisation of surveillance technologies, gazes and discourses within such scenes. As Gareth Palmer has argued, lifestyle television uses the 'myth of effectivity' of surveillance technology in order to welcome surveillance into the home (Palmer 2008: 7). Here, however, I am interested in analysing these same scenes with a slightly different (though closely related) inflection; one that focuses on the pre-sentation of the surveyed subject through a process of stripping and exposure. This repeated motif of makeover amounts not just to a literal 'stripping off' of cloth-ing, although this is frequently a prominent feature of such scenes, but also to other elements of the participant's lifestyle, appearance and personality that are 'exposed'. This process, which not only involves a visual investigation of a subject, but also a physical and metaphorical breaking down of their selfhood for the purposes of the camera, provides an interesting framework through which to view the work of the male makeover. The 'fragmentation' of appearance, in the most literal sense, holds significant interest if we are to view male makeover shows as part of a wider discourse in contemporary culture that is concerned with the reformation and production of emergent heterosexual masculine identities against a changed socio-cultural backdrop.

The most visible way in which 'exposure' is invoked in the opening sections of makeover shows is through the filming of participants without clothes. Despite an ostensible pedagogy of 'fashion' within makeover shows such as *What Not To Wear*, the concerns of the personal makeover show almost always begin with the naked body. Thus, while the participant's existing wardrobes might be paraded and 'shamed' at the beginning of such shows, as in Trinny and Susannah's police line up of loud Hawaiian shirts and cheap tracksuits, scenes in which the participants are stripped are never far behind. Corporeality is king, and the process of stripping is one way in which the agency of the clothed experts, with their 'correct' fashion choices, is cemented. In one episode of *What Not To Wear*, participants Tommy and Steve each stare at themselves in Trinny and Susannah's mirror booth and attempt to 'learn' to self-survey, identifying a long list of 'problems' that they hope the makeover will fix. The experts then enter the booth, and strip the men down to their underwear before continuing to outline all the faults that have been missed. Here, the power dynamic of expert and subject is made visible, not only through the fact of the subject's nakedness, but through the act of exposure itself, which is performed by the female experts in a tactile, aggressive process of stripping.

In other shows, such as *Extreme Male Beauty*, both camerawork and staging are used to reinforce the effects of exposure on unclothed subjects. In early 'investigative' sequences, the participant in each episode is filmed entirely naked against a white studio background. The *mise-en-scène* of the blank proscenium further enhances exposure, making the subject's naked body the only visual point of interest for the camera and viewer. Extreme close-ups of the men's bodies are shown in a series of rapidly intercut and constantly moving shots that display wrinkled stomach skin, sagging 'man-boobs' and flaccid penises. The brevity with which each image is displayed to the audience contrasts with the extreme and indecent detail within the frame, and the cumulative effect of this is an overwhelming display of problematic (according to the aesthetic standards of the makeover) bodies that one is both encouraged to look at and to be repelled by, as demonstrated by the speed with which the editor cuts away from the flesh. Problematic areas of the body are fragmented by the use of extreme close-up framing: the camera itself becomes a tool of exposure that fetishistically disrupts and disassembles the bodily 'self' of the participant. Furthermore, the unmoving, passive male body under the roving gaze of the camera is a disruptive image in another sense, inverting traditional visual representations of male corporeality as 'hard', 'taut' and active. As Richard Dyer notes, even in male pin-up imagery, 'images of men are often images of men doing something', and 'promise . . . activity in the way the body is posed' (Dyer 1982: 66). The soft, sagging physicality and prone passivity of the male bodies in *Extreme Male Beauty* disrupts the scheme of representation of dominant masculinity, subjecting the men to the 'controlling and curious' scopophilic gaze of the camera.

The process of male makeover involves, at this stage, a deliberate feminisation of its subjects, the removal of power and agency by insertion into a structure of looking previously associated with the display of femininity (Mulvey 1975: 8).

Indeed, *Extreme Male Beauty* actually enacts the reversal in the cinematic structures of looking described by Laura Mulvey, in sequences when men are lined up for examination by a roomful of women (Mulvey 1975). These scenes also take the abstraction of body parts described above to an even greater degree, with each episode focusing on analysis of a particular area, the men standing behind a white wall with holes cut out to expose the relevant section of their bodies (penises in Episode 2, abs in Episode 3 and faces in Episode 4). The extended exposure of male bodies in this way is in opposition to the conventions of gender representation in visual culture, even within the makeover format. As many theorists of masculinity have noted, part of the way in which male power is maintained is through its resistance to representation that makes corporeality visible. Art historian Mira Schor suggests that to subject the penis to representation is to strip the phallus of its empowering veil (Schor 1997: 14). Thus, because they are used to a gendered visual schema in which '[w]oman is the *site* of representation' (Ibid), the images of male exposure within the makeover show are experienced as disruptive by audiences, and serve to place the male makeover subject in a feminised position. The added presence in *Extreme Male Beauty* of a diegetic audience of women (as well as the presumed extra-textual feminine audience of this and other makeover shows) also makes explicit the process by which women 'come to look quizzically and critically at men's bodies' in a way that 'demystifies' masculinity (Morgan 2006: 111). In order, therefore, for 'bad' masculinity to be reformed, the makeover show seems to suggest that the subject must be placed in a feminised position: one that makes him passive and amenable to the intervention of the show's experts. Furthermore, this exposure both erases the subject's 'bad choices' and acts as disciplinary retribution for his socially deviant behaviours.

Although participants in *Queer Eye for the Straight Guy* are not physically stripped naked, a similarly thorough and aggressive sequence of exposure forms the basis of the set-up of each episode of the show. Once again, scrutiny goes well beyond a subject's wardrobe, and each episode's 'straight guy' is subject to a tactile and aggressive invasion of his own private space. While the blank proscenium of the television studio draws attention to the failing male bodies in *Extreme Male Beauty*, in *Queer Eye* the subject's entire lifestyle, as represented through his home, is not only laid bare for the camera, but again has its layers stripped back and its secrets exposed.

Almost without exception, the first thing that the Fab 5 do when entering the home of a subject is to touch the straight guy, often all at once. The removal of the subject's clothes by the experts is once again a feature of the makeover and is pushed urgently to the foreground: in one episode, fashion expert Carson is shown taking off Rob's jumper after only thirteen seconds of screen time within his apartment, and, in another, Darin has his lab coat and goggles pulled off. The subjects' hair is manipulated by the experts, who remove hats (John Bargeman), stroke bald heads (Vincent, John Verde) and tease curls (Josh, Tom Kaden). These processes of stripping and touching, however, are not restricted to the straight guy, but are applied to his entire domestic space and everything in it.

Fridges, freezers and cupboards are thrown open and the contents pawed and removed. Wardrobes are emptied and clothes thrown onto the floor in disgust. Boundaries of privacy that would be adhered to on most makeover shows are transgressed by *Queer Eye*, as the Fab 5 read and watch the straight guy's porn, pull condoms out from under their beds, strip off their bed sheets and empty out the dirty underwear from their laundry baskets. The stripping of domestic space in order to reveal the extent of a dysfunctional lifestyle is taken to extremes, never more so than in the Tom Minogue episode, in which the Fab 5 break and pile all of his furniture into the centre of his living room and ask 'anybody got a match?', effectively destroying the apartment. As with the investigation of bodies in *Extreme Male Beauty*, editing and camerawork play a crucial role here, emphasising the cumulative effects of failure through the use of rapid intercutting, moving cameras and up-tempo non-diegetic music. Once again, the opening of the male makeover show enacts a symbolic violence against the order of the straight male, the disintegration of the subject's domestic space a way of literalising the breaking apart of masculine identity.

The lessons that the makeover experts teach their subjects cover a wide variety of 'lifestyle' arenas: shopping, grooming, cooking, etiquette and domestic skills. In this section of this discussion, however, I would like to focus on one specific transformative gesture of the male makeover that is so widely applied as to be almost ubiquitous: the use of a suit as a signifier of improved and achieved masculinity. The suit is used across male makeover programmes as a motif that symbolises the completion of a reformed image of masculinity, the creation of a 'new' whole achieved identity tied up with images of success and strength. The centrality of the suit to male transformations brings with it a whole raft of external meanings and implications that the experts draw upon in order to produce the 'after' image of the male makeover.

Part of the suit's power lies in the persistence and consistency of both the sartorial scheme itself and the values associated with it. As David Kuchta argues: 'If the three-piece suit is still with us, it is because the values of masculinity that it embodies today are more or less the same as those that ushered it in' (Kuchta 2002: 2). In the makeover show, the suit is used as elegant and self-evident shorthand for secure heterosexual masculinity, thus providing a coherent aesthetic for the reconstructed masculine subject that insures against any suggestion of feminisation that might have occurred during the process of the makeover. However, the suit's inclusion in an explicit narrative of masculine reconstruction also makes visible what Kuchta calls the 'conspicuous construction' of Modern English masculinity (Ibid: 3). The next section of this essay will examine the meanings of the suit and how these are invoked, directly or indirectly, by male makeover narratives.

'The black broadcloth suit' is a cultural image so pervasive that Richard Sennet, borrowing from Karl Marx, termed it a 'social hieroglyphic' (Sennet 1986: 164). Although the suit has, of course, its own 'mutating' history, it is a relatively fixed and evocative dress scheme, in contrast to the rapidly changing and varied styles, fabrics and designs of women's fashion (Edwards 1997: 21). In contemporary culture, as it has for 200 years, the suit acts as a symbol of the achievement of successful and professional masculinity, both through its aesthetic emphasising of the shape of the masculine form (broadening shoulders, slimming waists) and through its connotations of financial and managerial status in employment.

Tim Edwards gives a fascinating account of the cultural connotations of the suit, which include 'success', 'virility', 'maturity', and 'strength' (Edwards 1997: 9–22). All of these ideals and more are clearly at play in the suit's role as the 'final piece' of the male makeover. Most importantly, however, the suit is inextricably linked to masculinity itself. It is perhaps unsurprising, then, that in many of the British makeover shows, the destabilisation to hegemonic masculinity threatened by the processes of makeover is contained by a persistent emphasis on the suit. Although the male subject's attitude to grooming, domesticity and aesthetic detail may have had to be corrected (and feminised), the final image that programmes such as *What Not To Wear* and *10 Years Younger* seek to create is one of apparently effortless and stalwart professional masculinity. The suit as a garment is used within the makeover to link traditional masculinity and the transformative process at stake through the role of the breadwinner. Even in postfeminist, post-industrial culture, the figure of the 'self-made man', the individual who strives for his own financial success independently of the support of others, is still promoted by the television makeover show as an essential aspect of contemporary masculinity, and the suit is the emblematic uniform of that character (see Kuchta 2002: 2). The 'look' of the self-made man is largely achieved in these shows through instructing the subjects on how to purchase and wear a suit.

Scenes in which the participant is dressed by the presenter in a suit in front of a mirror in a dressing room are frequent components of the male makeover show. In *10 Years Younger*, Nicky Hambleton-Jones coaches her subjects on the way the suit affects the look of their bodies: 'can you see how that gives you a body shape like that and makes you look like you've got big shoulders? And a big chest?', she asks a less than enthusiastic Richard Power. 'The single breasted jacket is very slimming . . . there's no sign of a pot belly' she reassures Tony Goodwin, thus offering the suit as the very antidote to the exposure that the male subject has suffered during the makeover process, a garment that will hide and disguise the body and its problems. In the makeover, the suit acts as a garment of recovery, hiding and masking masculine embodiment both physically and symbolically.

Furthermore, such shows also relentlessly stress the suit's association with what we might call, after Tim Edwards, 'intense masculinity' (Edwards 1997: 20). *What Not To Wear*'s Susannah Constantine enthusiastically conveys her impression of the benefits of the suit to Steve's aesthetics and presence: 'Steve, look at you. You're standing tall, you look more masculine, more male, more in control.' The suit is linked to masculinity within these shows both in terms of the garment's actual aesthetic effect on body shape, and its economic and status-related conno-tations. The presenters and narrators of shows frequently stress the importance of 'business' as a crucial element of the desired aesthetic for the subject. In *10 Years Younger*, the voice-over hails Tony Goodwin as 'looking like he means business' and Simon Dehany as 'starting to look the business'. Most revealing, perhaps, is the desire expressed by presenter Nicky Hambleton-Jones to give Richard Power 'a look of someone who's running a business rather than someone who's got their finger down the toilet bowl'. This is, of course, achieved by dressing him in a suit. Hambleton-Jones's comment upon the links between employment and

Figure 29.1   Presenter Nicky Hambleton-Jones talks Tony Goodwin through the benefits of the suit in *10 Years Younger*.

clothing highlights the desired identity constructed by the male makeover through the suit. It is not just that the aesthetics of the suit here represent employment of a higher social status, the accumulation of money, and a position further up the class scale. The transition here is clearly framed as a shift from an activity that is not only low-status but also traditionally *feminising* – cleaning toilets. The wish expressed by the lifestyle presenter here is for a shift in the subject's aesthetics from those that represent low-paid, low-status, feminine domestic labour to the look of the 'self-made man'. According to the fashion logic espoused by the make-over show, a man who does not wear a suit not only appears to lack status and wealth, but also power and masculinity itself.

This is particularly true in the case of the 'Steve' episode of *What Not To Wear*, where the unemployed subject is transformed from a failing 'couch potato' into a 'businessman'. Throughout the episode, Trinny and Susannah repeatedly draw attention to Steve's failure in the breadwinner role and his inferior status in relation to his successful wife Carol, who, as they stress, dresses smartly and professionally, in suits. Steve's wardrobe overhaul, including, of course, the addition of several suits, is represented by the show as a complete transformation of his life and self-perception into that of a 'breadwinner'. As they watch Steve's reveal to the camera that he has a new job and a new home, the presenters gush over the positive and masculinising effects of their transformation: 'he's in control of his life', exclaims Susannah, 'he feels in charge'. 'He's *got back his masculinity*' asserts Trinny. The climax of Steve's makeover is a scene in which he goes to meet Carol for dinner in a restaurant, and the attempt to restabilise masculinity in the face of postfeminism could not be more clear, as Trinny self-congratulates: 'you know what they are, they're equals. They're both in their suits, they look smart, she's got back the man she thought she'd lost.'

As Trinny's comments highlight, the suit is employed in the makeover show not just as a uniform for work, but as a costume for heteronormative romance, too. Episodes of *Queer Eye for the Straight Guy* that feature weddings and proposals emphasise the suit as an integral part of heterosexual dating ritual, and, as 'fashion expert' Carson comments, the way to 'get a yes'. In one episode, the Fab 5 make over John Bargeman in preparation for his proposal to his girlfriend Tina. During a scene in which John is instructed in the buying of a suit in the dressing room of a luxury tailor, the experts make reference to the Hollywood glamour of film stars such as Gary Cooper, Humphrey Bogart and, most repeatedly, Cary Grant. Carson even furnishes John with the book *Dressing in the Dark*, open at a page of Grant posing intently in a tuxedo, citing this as their inspiration. The experts draw specifically on the iconography of a Hollywood studio era film star in order to create the desired look for John's proposal, and celebrate jubilantly when they deem themselves to have achieved 'the movie star look'. The invocation of Cary Grant as the intended final image of masculinity is particularly interesting. As Steve Cohan has noted, Grant's star image is bound up in a celebration of tailoring, fashion and fastidiousness in dress. Cohan points to contemporary press releases that describe in great detail Grant's exacting standards of dress:

Figure 29.2   John Bargeman is dressed by the 'Fab 5' in *Queer Eye for the Straight Guy*.

His shirts, also always tailor made, have fly fronts concealing the
buttons. He never folds his jacket pocket handkerchief in points,
always folds it square and just tucks it in carelessly. His ties are never
pointed, always have rounded edges. . .

(quoted in Cohan 1997: 17)

Such an image, Cohan argues, makes Grant 'instantly recognizable' as 'the original
representative of his kind, the middle class professional, whose values had come
to dominate the entire culture during the post-war era' (Ibid: 19). Grant's carefully
suited body, then, comes to represent not just an iconographic masculinity, but
one that is hegemonic and tied to a 'stable' yet historically specific set of values,
ones from an era in which the lines between masculinity and femininity were being
re-drawn. It is also, of course, an image constructed through the star system of
Hollywood, and thus the identity displayed is at once accessible and yet unachievable
and distant enough to represent 'glamour'. Cary Grant, and the connotations of
era and place that are bound up in his image, seem to suggest the residual nature
of the 'after' image of masculinity that is the desired aesthetic goal of the makeover.
Such an image reaches back to older formations of masculine identity, to such an
extent that the masquerade and performativity of the look is fully acknowledged.
In donning the suit for his proposal, John becomes *costumed*, having the 'look' of
a movie star without ever being expected to *be* a movie star.

This point applies more widely to the 'after' image of the makeover across
the genre. As Hollander has described, 'in a general social atmosphere inflexibly
ruled "informal" . . . [d]ressing up is more risky than dressing down, too much
respect for the occasion is considered worse than too little' (Hollander 1994: 176).
The makeover show's insistence upon the suit therefore seems excessive, out of
step perhaps, with the 'sartorial consciousness' (Ibid: 175) of the time. While the
suit is clearly a persistent feature of the construction of a hegemonic masculine
identity through dress, it also represents the past-ness of such constructions.
Conflictingly, then, the suit might be read as a marker of both the fragility and
the stability of hegemonic masculinity. In the male makeover show, hegemonic
masculinity has a uniform, a costume that must be donned in order to perform
the gender role. It is a costume with significant ties to older, more traditional
(and, arguably, more stable) forms of masculine identity, a generational inheritance,
perhaps, of masculinity, but one that is now seen as outdated.

Furthermore, the male makeover's insistence upon the suit as integral to the
formation of the masculinity that it produces threatens to expose, and therefore
remove, the symbolic power of the garment itself. If, as Kuchta argues, much
of the power in the image of the suit comes from its silent, 'obvious' and
'unquestioned' embodiment of values of modern masculinity (Kuchta 2002: 2),
then the makeover is a disruption to this order. Indeed, Kuchta's mission in his
book, to 'repoliticize, denaturalize and destabilize these values of masculinity'
(Ibid), is, whether intentionally or not, enacted by the male makeover. As Trinny
and Susannah or Nicky Hambleton-Jones provide a commentary on precisely *why*
they are dressing their subjects in suits, some of the meaning of the garment itself
is exposed, 'returning anxiety and instability to that invention' (Kuchta 2002: 3)

by making visible the suit's role as a crucial element in the construction of contemporary masculine identity. There is an obvious contradiction here in the way that the suit's role in male makeover is supposed to remove these anxieties. It is employed precisely because its meaning is seemingly so fixed and unchanging, but the effect of its inclusion in an explicit narrative of masculine reconstruction makes visible what Kuchta calls the 'conspicuous construction' of modern English masculinity (Kuchta 2002: 3).

As in other contemporary media texts in which attention is drawn to the meanings and purpose of the suit, such as its fetishisation by the womanising yet camp figure of Barney Stinson (played by openly gay actor Neil Patrick Harris) in US sitcom *How I Met Your Mother*, the male makeover unwittingly frames the garment as costume. As its meanings are revealed, the suit itself is exposed as an element of the performance of gender identity. The purposes of the suit outlined within – its connections to a high-status employment, romance, and assured masculinity – are only possible because of its longevity and hidden, unchallenged meanings. But the very process of the makeover, and the suit's inclusion in this paradigm, unmasks the values and ideologies within and makes visible its role and construction, thus removing some of the garment's power. The male makeover anchors its articulations of desirable masculinity in a motif that is clearly residual, and in doing so seems to indicate the instability of the very images that it strives to construct.

References

Brunsdon, C. (1981) '"Crossroads": Notes on Soap Opera', *Screen*, Vol. 22, No. 4, 32–7.

Brunsdon, C., C. Johnson, R. Moseley and H. Wheatley (2001) 'Factual Entertainment on British Television: The Midlands TV Research Group's 8–9 Project', *European Journal of Cultural Studies*. Vol. 4. No. 1, 29–62.

Cohan, S. (1997) *Masked Men: Masculinity and Movies in the Fifties*. Bloomington, IN: Indiana University Press.

Dyer, R. (1982) 'Don't Look Now', *Screen*, Vol. 23, No. 3–4, 61–73.

Edwards, T. (1997) *Men In The Mirror: Men's Fashion, Masculinity and Consumer Society*. London: Cassell.

Hollander, A. (1994) *Sex and Suits*. New York: Random House.

Kuchta, D. (2002) *The Three-Piece Suit and Modern Masculinity: England, 1550–1850*. Berkeley, CA: University of California Press.

Morgan, D. (2006) 'You Too Can Have A Body Like Mine: Reflections of the male body and masculinities', in Whitehead, S. M. (ed.) *Men and Masculinities: Critical Concepts in Sociology. Volume III: Identity, Association and Embodiment*. Oxford, New York: Routledge, pp. 105–27.

Moseley, R. (2000) 'Makeover Takeover on British Television', *Screen*, Vol. 41, No. 3, 299–314.

Mulvey, L. (1975) 'Visual Pleasure and Narrative Cinema', *Screen*, Vol. 16, No. 3, 6–18.

Ouellette, L. and J. Hay (2008) *Better Living Through Reality TV: Television and Post-welfare Citizenship*. Malden; Oxford; Victoria: Blackwell.

Palmer, G. (ed.) (2008) *Exposing Lifestyle Television: The Big Reveal*. Aldershot; Burlington, VT: Ashgate.

Schor, M. (1997) *Wet: On Painting, Feminism, and Art Culture*. Durham: Duke University Press.

Sennet, R. (1986) *The Fall of Public Man*. London: Faber.

Williams, R. (1977) *Marxism and Literature*. Oxford: Oxford University Press.

Index

Note: page numbers in italic type refer to Figures; those followed by 'n' and another number refer to Notes.